THE CAMBRIDGE
ARISTOTL
ETHICS

MW01156084

Aristotle's *Nicomachean Ethics* is the first and arguably most important treatise on ethics in Western philosophy. It remains to this day a compelling reflection on the best sort of human life and continues to inspire contemporary thought and debate. This *Cambridge Companion* includes twenty essays by leading scholars of Aristotle and ancient philosophy that cover the major issues of this foundational text. The essays in this volume shed light on Aristotle's rigorous and challenging thinking on questions such as: Can there be a practical science of ethics? What is happiness? Can we arrive at convincing accounts of virtues? Are we responsible for our character? How does moral virtue relate to good thinking? Can we act against our reasoned choice? What is friendship? Is the contemplative life the highest kind of life?

Ronald Polansky is Professor of Philosophy and Chair of the Department of Philosophy at Duquesne University. He has been editor of the journal *Ancient Philosophy* since its beginning in 1980. Polansky is the author of *Aristotle's* De anima: *A Critical Commentary* (Cambridge University Press, 2007) and *Philosophy and Knowledge: A Commentary on Plato's* Theaetetus (1992), and co-editor of *Bioethics: Ancient Themes in Contemporary Issues* (2002).

CAMBRIDGE COMPANIONS TO PHILOSOPHY

OTHER RECENT VOLUMES IN THIS SERIES OF CAMBRIDGE
COMPANIONS

The Cambridge Companion to

ARISTOTLE'S NICOMACHEAN ETHICS

Edited by Ronald Polansky
Duquesne University, Pittsburgh

CAMBRIDGE
UNIVERSITY PRESS

CAMBRIDGE
UNIVERSITY PRESS

32 Avenue of the Americas, New York NY 10013-2473, USA

Cambridge University Press is part of the University of Cambridge.

It furthers the University's mission by disseminating knowledge in the pursuit of education, learning and research at the highest international levels of excellence.

www.cambridge.org
Information on this title: www.cambridge.org/9780521122733

© Ronald Polansky 2014

First published 2014

A catalogue record for this publication is available from the British Library

Library of Congress Cataloguing in Publication data
The Cambridge companion to Aristotle's Nicomachean
ethics / edited by Ronald Polansky,
Duquesne University, Pittsburgh.
    pages   cm. – (Cambridge companions to philosophy)
Includes bibliographical references and index.
ISBN 978-0-521-19276-7 (hardback : alk. paper) – ISBN 978-0-521-12273-3 (pbk.)
1. Aristotle Nicomachean ethics.   2. Ethics.   I. Polansky, Ronald M., 1948–
editor of compilation.
B430.C36   2014
171'.3–dc23   2014009858

ISBN 978-0-521-19276-7 Hardback
ISBN 978-0-521-12273-3 Paperback

Contents

Contributors

SUSANNE BOBZIEN is Professor of Philosophy at the University of Oxford and Senior Research Fellow at All Souls College, Oxford. Previously, she was Professor of Philosophy at Yale. She is the author of several books, including *Determinism and Freedom in Stoic Philosophy*, and of numerous articles on ancient as well as contemporary philosophy. Her work focuses on determinism, freedom, and moral responsibility (Aristotle, Epicurus, Stoics, Kant); contemporary philosophy of logic and language; and the history of logic (from Aristotle to Boethius).

LESLEY BROWN is Fellow Emeritus in Philosophy at Somerville College, Oxford, and member of the Philosophy Faculty at the University of Oxford. She is responsible for the Introduction and Notes to the Oxford World's Classics translation of Aristotle's *Nicomachean Ethics* (2009) and has published extensively on Plato's *Sophist*.

HELEN CULLYER is currently Associate Program Officer at the Andrew W. Mellon Foundation in New York and was formerly Assistant Professor of Classics and director of the Classics, Philosophy, and Ancient Science graduate program at the University of Pittsburgh. Her primary research interests are in the ethical philosophies of Aristotle and the Stoics, and she has published articles and essays on Socratic and Stoic conceptions of courage, the virtues and vices associated with humor in Aristotle, and Stoic interpretations of Homer. She has also published critical assessments of Ayn Rand's interpretation of Aristotle's ethics.

VERITY HARTE is Professor of Philosophy and Classics at Yale University. She is the author of *Plato on Parts and Wholes: The Metaphysics of Structure* (2002) and of various articles on ancient philosophy. She is co-editor (with M. M. McCabe, R. W. Sharples, and Anne Sheppard) of *Aristotle and the Stoics Reading Plato* (2010) and (with Melissa Lane) of *Politeia in Greek and Roman Philosophy* (2013).

D. S. HUTCHINSON is Professor of Philosophy and Fellow of Trinity College at the University of Toronto. He is the author of *The Virtues of Aristotle* (1986) and the chapter on "Ethics" in *The Cambridge Companion to Aristotle* (edited by J. Barnes, 1995). He is the co-editor (with John Cooper) of *Plato: Complete Works* (1997). His current research is reconstructing Aristotle's lost dialogue *Protrepticus*, with Monte Ransome Johnson, on the basis of the results of their 2005 *Oxford Studies in Ancient Philosophy* article, "Authenticating Aristotle's *Protrepticus*."

KRISTEN INGLIS is an Assistant Professor in the Philosophy Department at the University of Pittsburgh. Her research focuses on Aristotle's ethics and moral psychology.

MONTE RANSOME JOHNSON is an Associate Professor of Philosophy at the University of California, San Diego, where he teaches courses on Greek and Roman philosophy and researches the influence of ancient thought on modern philosophy and science. He is the author of *Aristotle on Teleology* (2005) and essays on Democritus, Plato, Aristotle, Epicurus, and Lucretius. He is currently working with D. S. Hutchinson on a reconstruction of Aristotle's lost dialogue *Protrepticus*.

LAWRENCE JOST is Professor of Philosophy at the University of Cincinnati. His publications have centered on Aristotle's ethical writings. He co-edited Eudaimonia *and Well-Being* (2003) and *Perfecting Virtue: New Essays on Kantian Ethics and Virtue Ethics* (2011). He is especially concerned with the intersection between ancient ethical theory and contemporary theories of well-being and virtue. He is working on a monograph dealing with the central argument of the *Eudemian Ethics*, which, when treated as a coherent whole containing the common books, may place more emphasis on individually tailored, yet objective, conceptions of *eudaimonia* than the *Nicomachean Ethics*.

RACHANA KAMTEKAR is Associate Professor of Philosophy at the University of Arizona, where she mainly teaches ancient Greek and Roman philosophy. She writes on ancient political philosophy, ethics, and moral psychology and is currently working on a book on Plato's moral psychology.

THORNTON LOCKWOOD is Assistant Professor of Philosophy at Quinnipiac University. He has published articles on Aristotle's *Nicomachean Ethics* and *Politics* in *Phronesis, Journal of the History of Philosophy, History of Political Thought, Ancient Philosophy,* and *Oxford*

Bibliographies On-line. He is the associate editor (book reviews) at *POLIS: The Journal of Ancient Greek Political Thought.*

HENDRIK LORENZ is Associate Professor of Philosophy at Princeton University. He is author of *The Brute Within: Appetitive Desire in Plato and Aristotle* (2006) and articles about Plato, Aristotle, and Stoicism.

PATRICK LEE MILLER is Associate Professor of Philosophy at Duquesne University, where he specializes in ancient philosophy, existentialism, and psychoanalysis. His first book (*Becoming God*, 2011) traced the connections between reason, selfhood, and divinity in early Greek philosophy (Heraclitus through Plato). He is now working on a sequel that extends his argument into a later period (Aristotle through Plotinus). He has published articles on Sophocles, Augustine, Nietzsche, Freud, and the films of David Lynch.

JESSICA MOSS is Professor of Philosophy at New York University. She is the author of *Aristotle on the Apparent Good* (2012), as well as of articles on Aristotle's and Plato's psychology and ethics that have appeared in publications such as *Oxford Studies in Ancient Philosophy*, *Phronesis*, and *The Cambridge Companion to Plato's* Republic.

CARLO NATALI is Professor of History of Ancient Philosophy at Università Ca Foscari Venezia. In English he has published *The Wisdom of Aristotle* (2001) and the chapter "Schools and Sites of Learning" in *The Greek Pursuit of Knowledge* (2003); his volume *Aristotle: His Life and School* was originally published in Italian in 1991 and updated in an English version edited by D. S. Hutchinson (2013). In French he has published *L'action efficace. Etudes sur la philosophie de l'action d'Aristote* (2004). In Italian he has translated and annotated Aristotle's *Nicomachean Ethics,* Xenophon's *Oeconomicus,* and Alexander of Aphrodisias's *On Destiny.*

GILES PEARSON is Senior Lecturer in Philosophy at the University of Bristol. He is author of *Aristotle on Desire* (2012) and a number of articles on Aristotle's ethics and philosophical psychology, and he is co-editor (with Michael Pakaluk) of *Moral Psychology and Human Action in Aristotle* (2011).

RONALD POLANSKY is Chair of the Department of Philosophy at Duquesne University. He has been fortunate to learn from good teachers, including Joseph P. Maguire, Hans-Georg Gadamer, and Gregory Vlastos. He edits the journal *Ancient Philosophy* and has published *Philosophy and*

Knowledge: A Commentary on Plato's Theaetetus (1992) and *Aristotle's De anima: A Critical Commentary* (2007).

C.D.C. REEVE is Delta Kappa Epsilon Distinguished Professor of Philosophy at the University of North Carolina at Chapel Hill. He works primarily on Plato and Aristotle, but is interested in philosophy generally and has published on film and on the philosophy of sex and love. His books include *Philosopher-Kings* (1988, reissued 2006); *Socrates in the* Apology (1989); *Practices of Reason* (1995); *Substantial Knowledge: Aristotle's* Metaphysics (2003); *Love's Confusions* (2005); *Action, Contemplation, and Happiness: An Essay on Aristotle* (2012); *Blindness and Reorientation: Problems in Plato's* Republic (2012); and *Aristotle on Practical Wisdom* (2013). He has translated Plato's *Euthyphro, Apology, Crito, Meno, Cratylus,* and *Republic* (2005), as well as Aristotle's *Politics* (1998) and *Nicomachean Ethics* (2014).

T.D. ROCHE is Associate Professor of Philosophy at the University of Memphis. He is the author of articles on moral theory and Greek philosophy. His essays have appeared in such journals as *Phronesis, Journal of the History of Philosophy, Philosophical Review, Mind,* and *Ancient Philosophy.* He is currently working on a book on Aristotle's conception of happiness in the *Nicomachean Ethics.*

DANIEL C. RUSSELL is Professor of Philosophy in the Center for the Philosophy of Freedom at the University of Arizona and the Seymour Reader in Ancient History and Philosophy at Ormond College, University of Melbourne. He is the author of *Plato on Pleasure and the Good Life* (2005), *Practical Intelligence and the Virtues* (2009), and *Happiness for Humans* (2012) and the editor of *The Cambridge Companion to Virtue Ethics* (2013).

1 Introduction
Ethics as Practical Science

Aristotle's *Nicomachean Ethics* is among the first systematic treatments of ethics, and it is arguably the most important and influential philosophical work ever devoted to its field.[1] With glorious preparation in the thought of Socrates and Plato, and equipped with a rigorous depth in all the principal areas of inquiry, Aristotle aimed for a comprehensive presentation of ethics that could stand the test of time. He deals in a compelling and authoritative way with most of the issues that confront anyone considering the best sort of life to lead. His topics of investigation include: happiness, the role of chance or fortune in life, the place of character and intellect, deliberation and choice, the contrast of making and doing, desire overriding our better judgment, and the importance of friendship and pleasure.

Subsequent authors borrow heavily from him or make his positions their target. The appeal of his work has reasserted itself in recent decades as the hold of Kantian and utilitarian approaches has somewhat lessened and applied ethics and virtue ethics have gained urgency. The sense of breakdown in modern ethical thought, the turn to applied and virtue ethics, the reassertion of the importance of literature and narrative for ethics, and the longing for a thorough guide to life have fastened attention upon Aristotle. Focus on this fundamental work in ethics is not, however,

---

I have enjoyed working with all of the authors and expect that you will profit as well from their contributions. Besides the contributors, I wish to thank the Cambridge University Press editors and my graduate students, especially Jacob Greenstine, Kamal Shlbei, Justin Habash, and Stephen Krogh, for their challenging comments on the essays. Also, I thank Susanne Bobzien and Thornton Lockwood for their assistance with this Introduction.

[1] Its field is ethics as practical knowledge or science. Plato's Academy may have divided philosophy into physics, logic, and ethics, but none of the early Academicians before Aristotle is reported to have written a treatise called "ethics," and in fact the term ἠθική (*ēthikē*) does not appear prior to Aristotle's time. The *Nicomachean Ethics* may be only among the first systematic works in ethics, however, since also attributed to Aristotle are the *Eudemian Ethics* and the *Magna Moralia*, which cover much of the same terrain as the *Nicomachean* version. The *Protrepticus* also touches on themes of ethics, but it is primarily devoted to a genre of literature turning its readers to the philosophical life.

the result of its being easy to read, immediately engrossing, or obviously soul stirring.[2]

In antiquity Aristotle's treatises received careful commentary, and they continue to require these efforts since his thought needs unpacking. Argument follows argument with only limited explanation of their aim. Some of the argumentation resembles Socratic dialogue with opposing positions confronting each other. Key phrases and terms are often ambiguous, as in ordinary speech. Each sentence, paragraph, chapter, and book warrants elucidation. Though Aristotle's ethical inquiry aims to be practical, and serious reflection on ethics should explore this treatise, guidance helps with reaping the reward of his succinct and profound work.[3]

I. THE EUDAEMONIST APPROACH

Though people have probably always given some consideration to what they should do and how to live, a systematic philosophical approach originates around Socrates. In the late fifth and early fourth century BCE, the framework or paradigm for ethical thought becomes the search for the ultimate goal or end for human life. There was agreement to name the goal happiness (*eudaimonia*), but disagreement prevailed about what happiness is, some proposing pleasure and others other ends. This approach of looking toward the highest end, called eudaemonism, generally dominated ethical reflection until at least the sixteenth century CE.[4] Evidently, one hardly has to accept eudaemonism. Before Socrates

[2] Burnyeat 1980, 81, comments: "He [Aristotle] is not attempting the task so many moralists have undertaken of recommending virtue even to those who despise it: his lectures are not sermons, nor even protreptic argument, urging the wicked to mend their ways.... Rather, he is giving a course in practical thinking to enable someone who already wants to be virtuous to understand better what he should do and why."

[3] Though Aristotle has written a treatise rather than a dialogue, his mode of writing forces the reader to the sort of effort needed to read Platonic dialogues well. Salem 2010, 9, comments that "the task he [Aristotle] imposes upon his readers is not that different from the task he imposes upon himself: We, too, are forced, again and again, to return to, reflect upon, and think through our ordinary experience of the world, a task made more rather than less difficult by the 'history of philosophy.' Like Plato, his friend and fellow lover of wisdom, Aristotle the inquirer writes his books for inquiring – and patient – minds." Probably the comprehensive and detailed treatise was intended for careful discussion rather than lecture.

[4] Vlastos 1991, ch. 8, observes that eudaemonism develops around Socrates. With the loss in modern times of the view that we can reasonably speak of or agree about human nature, rejection of purpose in nature, and with the modern quest to eliminate uncertainty and chance (see esp. Machiavelli's *Prince* xv), the eudaemonistic pattern of ethical reflection became less prominent. Schneewind 1990, 42–63, argues that weaknesses in applicability of virtue theory led to the decline of eudaemonism with its emphasis upon virtue. Modern ethics tends to seek a criterion or rule for a good or right act rather than to concentrate upon the best sort of life to lead.

there was no such systematic scheme, and persons offered the eudaemonist framework can dismiss the possibility of a best life for humans, doubt
any need for a life organized toward a single goal, or deny any limit to
human desires.

Plato's dialogues show Socrates pushing interlocutors toward
eudaemonism, to acknowledging that they seek happiness and do
not wish to be miserable (see, e.g., *Euthydemus* 278e and *Meno* 78a).
This is an effective argumentative strategy, because once Socrates
gets the interlocutor to accede to desiring happiness, virtue becomes
crucial. Any likely definite end that the interlocutor embraces, even
pleasure, makes virtue an important means for achieving this end, or
even an intrinsic part of the end aimed at.[5] Eudaemonism forces the
interlocutor to take virtue seriously and therefore to care for the soul.
Whereas the sophists might seem to have been irresponsible intellec-
tuals inasmuch as they did not emphasize the good for the sake of
which one should seek the powerful means of rhetorical persuasion,
Plato's Socrates responsibly championed eudaemonism, the concern
for the end, the good, and the soul. If human goods can be roughly
distinguished into external goods (such as honor and money), bodily
goods (such as strength and beauty), and goods of the soul (such as
intelligence and justice), then external goods may be most necessary
for life, but goods of the soul are most essential for the good life, since
they enable us to utilize all the other goods well. Without effective
order in our soul, external and bodily goods may prove destructive
rather than be contributors to happiness.[6]

Aristotle elaborates the Socratic heritage of eudaemonism in composing treatises devoted to ethics. While Plato's dialogues and other
Socratic writings foster ethical reflection, Aristotle develops this so
systematically that it deserves to be called "practical science." He
divides the sciences into theoretical, practical, and productive sciences
(see *Topics* 145a13–18 and *Metaphysics* vi 1). This division can be based
on such factors as the subject matter of the science, the science's aim,
the methods used, and the precision of the science. For Aristotle a

---

[5] Moderate hedonism or pleasure seeking, such as Socrates proposes for Protagoras in
Plato's *Protagoras* or Epicureanism, conforms to eudaemonism. But extreme hedonism,
such as Callicles perhaps comes to embrace in Plato's *Gorgias*, does not. The eudaemonist position assumes that there are limits to human desires. Extreme hedonism
denies this, as does the view that humans are endlessly trying to outdo each other, as
defended by Thrasymachus in *Republic* i and Glaucon in *Republic* ii.
[6] Since for Aristotle external goods are necessary and vital for the happy life, this life is
somewhat dependent upon good fortune. Already in antiquity the Stoics fought against
this, and modern political and ethical thinkers have tried to limit the role of chance in
political and ethical life, if not always in economic affairs.

science provides knowledge, and knowing requires apprehending principles or causes that explain what follows from them. Theoretical
sciences, which for him are first philosophy (metaphysics), natural
science (physics), and mathematics, have their principles in the very
subject matters under study so that these sciences pursue the truth for
its own sake. In contrast, the practical sciences – ethics, politics, and
household management (*oikonomia*) – have their principles in us inasmuch as we engage in action and choose what to do; and these sciences
have the practical aim of good choices and appropriate passions for a
happy life.[7] The productive sciences, which include all the productive
arts, such as medicine, rhetoric, carpentry, gymnastics, weaving, and
painting, also have their principles in us insofar as we make the specific
product of the art, the end being the product we make.[8] In making and
productive science, the producer applies form to some already provided
material, the materials perhaps being supplied by a different art, as the
builder arranges bricks and boards into a house. But in action and
practical science, the doing deals with both form and matter. The
statesman molds the population and sets up its political arrangement,
thus engaging with both the matter of the community and the form
developed for it. Analogously, ethics has passions and actions as the
matter to which it gives form by the shaping of character and development of practical wisdom.

The division of the sciences has great significance for Aristotle.
Respecting the division, he scrupulously avoids using theoretical principles in practical science. The best evidence for this may be his rejection of
appeal to the Platonic idea of the good, an appeal that he views as going
outside practical science (see *NE* i 6). Were theoretical principles
employed in practical contexts, all knowledge would perhaps derive

---

[7]   If Aristotle in fact holds that ethics belongs within political science (see *Nicomachean
      Ethics* i 2), then the *Nicomachean Ethics* joins with the *Politics* as the first part of a
      two-part treatment of political science, and so practical science – the philosophy
      concerning human things (1181b15) – is political science.
[8]   The distinction of making and doing that demarcates productive and practical sciences
      relates to Aristotle's further distinction of motion (*kinesis*) and activity (*energeia*).
      A motion takes time as it proceeds toward its end, e.g., walking toward a place, and
      the motion is over when it arrives at its end. Motion can be faster or slower. An activity
      is complete at every moment from its onset, e.g., smelling an odor, but it can continue
      indefinitely. So typically motion has an end beyond itself, whereas activity is an end in
      itself, though activity may also have a further end. Hence, doing or action (*praxis*) is
      activity that contributes to the ultimate activity, happiness. Making (*poiēsis*) is motion
      that originates from choice to make the product, choosing being an activity.
      Consequently, motions and activities will often be interwoven. For example, choosing
      a brave action is activity, but such action typically involves motions, such as advancing
      in formation, thrusting a spear, and so on.

from the same principles, resulting in total unity in science rather than a division of the sciences.[9] Opposing our modern tendency to expect any science to resemble mathematical physics, this approach of Aristotle should be refreshing and exciting. He recognizes disagreement about theoretical science, for he views his predecessors as a philosophical tradition in conflict over ultimate principles (see *Metaphysics* i 3–7). If practical science depends upon theoretical principles, this might jeopardize its genuine scientific status. Ethics should be able to stand on its own and be convincing even to those not engaged in theoretical sciences. As a consequence of his well-considered approach, if he succeeds in elaborating a practical *science* independent of his possibly discredited theoretical works, his ethics can still hold for us.[10]

Yet interpreters of Aristotle, aware of his division of the sciences and that ethics and politics are for him practical sciences, nonetheless frequently saddle him with appeals in his ethics to theoretical positions. This leads to the major modern criticism that his central arguments have premises that we can no longer take seriously (see, e.g., MacIntyre 2007, 58, 148, 162, 196–197; and Williams 1993, 161, and 1985, 52). This is an unfortunate misunderstanding of the project and how Aristotle argues in the *Ethics*. The other major complementary objection to his practical works, the claim that in their assumptions they apply merely to the ancient Greek world, is also a misunderstanding.

Aristotle is, of course, most familiar with his own time, but ancient Greeks were everywhere in the Mediterranean region, including Egypt and Persia. Their exposure to various cultures was much wider than we might suppose. Beyond this, Aristotle aims for a scientific treatment. He appreciates that cultures differ; after all, the sophists were emphasizing the contrast of nature and convention (*physis* and *nomos*), so philosophers must consider diversity seriously. Can the eudaemonist approach,

---

[9] It may look as if Plato aspires to have all the sciences united in derivation from the idea of the good (see *Republic* 511b–c). For Aristotle the sciences must be divided because being is not a single genus (see *Metaphysics* 998b17–28), which prevents there being a single science of all that is, and he insists in *Posterior Analytics* i 7 that sciences of different genera of things cannot share principles (cf. *Rhetoric* 1358a1–26).

[10] This is hardly to deny that the practical works are generally compatible with the theoretical works, and it is not to assert that Aristotle could have written them without also writing his theoretical works. Practical philosophy or science presupposes that there is philosophy, and practical thinking may even be an application to action of theoretical notions. Aristotle does not, however, make explicit appeal anywhere in the *Ethics* or *Politics* to theoretical principles. Ethics and politics are too important to rest upon principles that others may simply disregard. Practical thought as science requires its own principles. Should this not apply to ethics always, or do we expect results in biological science, psychology, neuroscience, and such fields to change the framework of ethics?

or any ethical reflection, escape cultural narrowness and attain to practical scientific status?

II. PRACTICAL SCIENCE AND CULTURAL NARROWNESS

Eudaemonism along Aristotle's lines, while avoiding theoretical premises, aspires to cover all of human life. Humans typically act for a purpose, such as walking to get to some location or for exercise. Other animals also do things for purposes – for example, birds build nests, and spiders spin webs. It does not seem, however, that the other animals reflect upon what they are doing and deliberate about choices: they merely do what is natural for them. Humans are capable of much more planning and deliberation than the beasts, or we routinely engage in these while the beasts do not or cannot (cf. Frede 2011, 15–16). Thus, living an examined life appears to be peculiar to humans and even their function.[11] Ability to speak and think is natural for humans, but using this ability well requires special effort and not merely naturally instinctive behavior. Reflection about what we do enters into and encompasses everything humans do in their human way. While only humans may tell jokes, pray, farm, and play sports, reflection enters into each of these and to all specifically human activities. When Aristotle develops his "function argument" in *Nicomachean Ethics* i 7 and singles out acting according to reason as the human function, he most obviously means human reason in its widest capacity enabling us to reflect, deliberate, and choose. He is himself of course engaged in reflection throughout the opening of the *Ethics* and subsequently, and so part of what he discloses is what permits his own setting out of this practical science.

If the human function consists in acting purposively reflectively, then doing so well requires virtue, both moral and intellectual virtue. Whatever has a function, for example, a knife to cut, must have the requisite virtue to do the function well, which for the knife is to be sharp and of appropriate size and strength. So a *good* knife has the relevant virtue for its function. Analogously, humans need appropriate virtue or excellence to act well reflectively. Intellectual virtue pertains to our having reason and being able to initiate thinking, whereas moral virtue concerns desire's capacity

---

[11]   It is often supposed that because Aristotle speaks in *NE* i 7 of the human function (*ergon*) that he is engaged in theoretical reflection since we may suppose that all natural beings have functions. Examination of the corpus reveals, however, that though Aristotle speaks of the functions of artifacts that are instruments, e.g., the function of a hammer, and the function of the bodily parts or organs of plants and animals, he does not generally speak in theoretical contexts of the function of an entire natural being, animal or plant. This way of speaking must rather be especially appropriate for a practical context.

to follow the guidance of reason.[12] One sort of intellectual virtue, theoretical wisdom (sophia), enters into theoretical science; another kind of intellectual virtue, practical wisdom (phronēsis), enters into practical action. Fully good human action demands both practical wisdom and moral virtue since we must deliberate well and desire appropriately. A very strong point in his ethics is the way Aristotle brings together in the good life the formation of character and development of intellectual insight. Moral virtue is the shaping of our desire and character, which makes us tend to choose appropriate actions and to have appropriate emotional responses. As practicing sports develops bodily skill to perform well at them, from choosing appropriate sorts of actions we get the skill to act well and the dispositional desire to do so. Becoming accustomed to enjoy what we should and to be pained by what we should avoid, we gain the sort of disposition that is the virtue of character, the proper orientation of our desires. Aristotle thinks this shaping of our desires comes along only with the maturing of our practical intelligence that enables us to discern what is appropriate. The fullest completion of our practical intellect has us practically wise – that is, possessing practical science.

Most of the *Ethics* works out accounts of the virtues, both those of character and intellect, to equip us to live a happy life, to engage in activity in accordance with virtue in a complete life.[13] Modern ethics subsequent to the Renaissance typically renounces the project of locating the best life and describing virtues essential for it and instead seeks a test or criterion for good or right actions. This is often called normative ethics, with metaethics considering the presuppositions of "moral" thought and how "moral" terms are to be understood. For such modern approaches, only some subset of actions and the motivations guiding them are "moral" and have "moral worth or value." Much of our life would not enter, then, into ethical reflection but exclusively what has to do with "morality."[14]

---

[12] From the eudaemonistic perspective, desire is following reason's guidance toward the ultimate human good, but from the standpoint of practical deliberation and choice, well-developed desire, i.e., our character and virtue, directs us toward the end that our practical, deliberative reason calculates the way to achieve.

[13] Along with moral virtue and vice, Aristotle lines up at least six *named* character dispositions: heroic (divine) nature, virtue, continence, incontinence, vice, and brutishness (see *NE* vii 1). He might also add to this scheme endurance and softness between continence and incontinence, with most people being between endurance and softness.

[14] This modern term "morality" derives indirectly from Aristotle since for him virtue of character is due to habituation, which connects with Latin *mos* and *mores*. But our understanding of "morality" comes, according to Anscombe 1958, more directly from the Christian tradition of divine law. Regarding the term "morally wrong," she says, "it has no reasonable sense outside a law conception of ethics ... you can do ethics without it, as is shown by the example of Aristotle. It would be a great improvement if, instead of 'morally wrong,' one always named a genus such as 'untruthful,' 'unchaste,' 'unjust.'"

Aristotle offers a fuller or more encompassing account of human life than does this concentration on morality. Because humans can reflect and aim their lives at various ends, these ends and everything having connection with them is of concern to ethics, at least as pertaining to the good and happy life. Practical science differs from theoretical and productive science, and yet practical science has to consider even the place of these other sciences in a good human life. For all human activities, what they seek as their ends and what motivates them are relevant concerns. When Aristotle treats the virtues of character and intellect, he aims to be comprehensive. The eleven or so virtues of character intend to cover all that contributes to making actions and emotions appropriate. Virtues having to do with fear and confidence, bodily pleasures, money, honor, anger, social interactions, and fairness hardly seem antiquated, and they may deal with all the vital areas of practical life. Aristotle has virtues relating to sense of humor and expenditure on parties, not because the ancient Greeks had a culture so different from ours, different though it might be, but because these have a role in any culture, and they pertain to how we assess human lives. Aristotle tries to include all the crucial areas of human action and emotional response in his accounts of the virtues of character rather than narrowing his attention to what we might label "morality."

We often suppose that "morality" requires caring most for others. While Aristotle understands the emphasis on being good to others – we see him suggesting in *Rhetoric* i 9 that speakers emphasize it to be persuasive, and in *NE* 1120a22–24 he acknowledges that liberality is the most popular virtue and justice is virtue with respect to others – the eudaemonist approach does not focus on helping others. The concern has to be with living well or happiness, which includes doing what is appropriate. Doing what is appropriate for the right reason requires virtues.

Commentators sometimes protest against Aristotle's seeming to limit a virtue such as courage to battle. Or his taking seriously, as when he comments upon greatness of soul, matters that look to be indifferent, such as how someone walks or talks. Again this misunderstands his project and approach. If he can present the features most characteristic of those in possession of the virtue, he helps us to identify them. And to

See more recently Kraut 2006, esp. 163 and 190–191. Kraut pertinently argues that Aristotle does not, like those influenced by Kant, have *two* sorts of justifications for action, the good and the right, where moral rightness must always have precedence (see pp. 195–199). Aristotle employs only the good to justify action, where the good can be narrow, as the good in cooking, or broad, as the human good and the political good. Yet contemporary loss of confidence in a basis for determination of the good beyond personal preferences, along with fear that pursuit of the good may lead to trampling upon rights, explains the attraction to distinguishing right from good.

get to what is most essential in the account of a moral virtue, he seeks the sphere in which the virtue best manifests itself. According to an ancient saying, "Fine things are hard"; so to act according to virtue and to act finely or nobly is difficult, and virtue best displays itself in certain difficult settings. Aristotle is not denying, say, that courage appears in terminal illness or elsewhere besides battle, but he supposes that if someone can do well in the difficult special sphere or theater of the virtue, then the person will also do well everywhere else (see esp. 1127a33–b7, and *Rhet.* 1367a33–b7). He thus offers practical accounts of the virtues through focusing upon the special theaters for action according to virtue and what most deserves praise and blame.[15] If his ten or eleven moral virtues cover as intended all the relevant areas of human action and passion, then the special theaters are the main challenges.[16] He looks to poetry, observation, praise and blame, argument, and such matters for a practical and compelling account of the moral virtues. When he describes what we may suppose irrelevant to "morality," he is still dealing with something he considers important for character. He well recognizes that faults in fairly small matters of character do not amount to wickedness, though they may be vices. To be wicked we have to harm others or seek to (see, e.g., 1123a31–33 and 1125a16–19). Perfection of character leads consistently to appropriate action and passion, and good character is what he endeavors to clarify. Accusations that his accounts of the virtues present us merely his own or his culture's prejudices are thus very open to challenge.

We confuse ourselves and are unfair to Aristotle, therefore, through supposing he comments upon a special sphere of "morality" and comments in odd ways pertinent only to his time. The ancients have no terminology paralleling our usage of "moral" and "morality" when they

[15] The focus is thus upon the fine or noble rather than exclusively assisting others. He probably always has in view the depiction of Socrates in Plato's dialogues. So the virtue having to do with sense of humor may in fact resemble Socrates' awareness of his and other persons' limitations.

[16] When we depict the whole realm of human action and passion as a large circle with the special theaters of the moral virtues as much smaller circles scattered within the encompassing circle, the special theaters resemble chocolate chips in a cookie. Thus envisioning our lives helps clarify the way character training through habituation or practice occurs. To develop courage, for example, a young child need not go frequently into battle. Nibbling on the rest of the cookie, i.e., engaging in less difficult efforts, as in participating in sports, crossing the street, or playing at being a soldier, prepares for the chip, i.e., the more demanding special theater for brave action and passion.

are put in sharp contrast with "immoral" and "immorality." This lack of terminology may well be strength, however, rather than weakness. We get along better by speaking of actions as appropriate, noble, useful, just, or the opposite of these rather than moral or immoral, and limiting "moral" merely to the phrase "moral virtue" that means character virtue. Aristotle's way of speaking does not neglect a large part of human action and passion to focus upon a realm of choices deemed "moral" or "immoral," and neither does he favor action and passion foreign to our understanding. He can reject egregious behavior as we do, while reflecting broadly upon the appropriate and inappropriate in action and passion and praiseworthy or blameworthy character. Action can be inappropriate and indicate bad character, that is, vice, well before it causes harm to others and crosses over into being wicked and unjust. His appreciation of the depth of feeling about appropriate action and emotional response is seen in the emphasis upon virtue of character and the comment that we do not forget practical wisdom (see 1140b28–30).

III. INTELLECTUAL VIRTUE AND PHILOSOPHICAL PREFERENCE

The prominent intellectual virtues for Aristotle are philosophic wisdom (*sophia*) and practical wisdom (*phronēsis*). That he considers both fits with the comprehensiveness of practical science. But it may surprise or disappoint us that he seems to give the preference for the happy life to the activity stemming from philosophic wisdom or theoretical science.[17] Is this a mere prejudice of the philosopher?

The intellectual virtue relating to practical life is practical wisdom. Practical wisdom enables us both to deliberate generally about what is happiness and what contributes to it, that is, to develop practical science as Aristotle does, and to deliberate about what to do in particular situations. Moral virtue gives us our practical end, for example, we aim to act bravely or justly, and for the calculation or deliberation of what contributes to brave or just action, Aristotle appeals to practical wisdom.[18] Now not all calculation or deliberation has a good end because those with vice

[17] This becomes clear in *NE* x 7–8, though it is hinted before this (see 1096a4–5). Commentators have debated the "inclusivist" and the "dominantist" interpretations of Aristotle's ethics. The inclusivist view holds that all the sorts of virtue, moral virtue and both prominent types of intellectual virtues, have to belong to the happy person, whereas the dominantist position reads the work as favoring the theoretical life for the most complete happiness (these terms were introduced in Hardie 1967).

[18] Though practical wisdom mainly calculates the means to a given end, it has cognizance of the end and, by its deliberation and determination of the means to the end, endorses and in a way chooses the end, i.e., has the end as its purpose, along with the means toward the end.

have bad ends. There is a faculty that Aristotle calls cleverness (deinotēs) that is sharp at calculation of means, whether for good or bad ends. When it calculates consistently to attain the good end toward which moral virtue aspires, cleverness becomes practical wisdom. Aristotle thus seems basically to hold: cleverness + moral virtue ≡ practical wisdom. One cannot then be practically wise without also having moral virtue, and hence all the moral virtues come together with practical wisdom rather than apart from each other. Moreover, one cannot have fully developed moral virtue without practical wisdom since Aristotle suggests that moral virtue derives from natural virtue – that is, an innate tendency to have good desire or proclivity for virtue – when in the course of our development of character our practical insight matures and turns natural virtue into full moral virtue. So he also has this view: natural virtue + practical wisdom ≡ moral virtue. He therefore makes moral virtue and practical wisdom mutually entailing. Becoming a good person and being insightful about this requires both practice (i.e., habituation to develop suitable dispositions of character) and matured intellectual sensitivity.

The person who is practically wise and has moral virtue, if we assume that the circumstances of life cooperate (i.e., the person is not starving, in chains, suffering overwhelming losses, and so on), will be doing good actions and therefore be leading a happy life. Action in accordance with virtue is noble and an end in itself. This contrasts with the arts or productive sciences that have narrower ends that go beyond the arts themselves while still only being means to a happy life.[19] Though good action for its own sake is constitutive of a happy life, and much of the *Nicomachean Ethics* (books 2–9) has been largely devoted to the political life of good action, Aristotle seems even from the first book to prepare to have the theoretical life of contemplation – *theōria* (contemplation) is the exercise of *sophia* – emerge as the best and most complete happiness. Contemplation is mentioned in book 1, and it is made clear that happiness is sought as the most complete and self-sufficient end. How plausible is it that theoretical activity should best satisfy these criteria and that it should fulfill the political life?

Aristotle elevates *theōria* as he does because the theoretical life can be seen most to possess the essential features of the happy life. We expect the happy life to be most continuous, most pleasant, most self-sufficient,

[19] The Marxist tradition does not maintain Aristotle's distinction of *praxis* (doing or action) and *poiēsis* (production or making). Consequently, for Marxists ethics and politics lose any proper domain and can seem merely ideology or domination. They may then suppose that the state will wither away following the elimination of social classes. Similarly, noncognitivists and those endorsing a sharp fact-value distinction seem to make ethics a matter of ideology or whim.

most loved for itself, and most leisurely (*NE* x 7). Theoretical activity based on philosophic wisdom best fulfills each of these and hence best satisfies the requirements for happiness. In accord with our previous urging that practical science should have no theoretical assumptions, Aristotle supports the priority of theorizing with *practical* arguments. And he may have a further practical reason for supposing that, even though activity in accordance with moral virtue (i.e., the life of good action and the political life) is an end in itself, it generally needs to contribute to some higher end to keep itself well in line. Here Aristotle may join Plato in having some doubt about the reliability of human virtue and political action. In *NE* x 7 (esp. 1177b1–26) he brings up conquest and tyranny in speaking of the political life because political practice without an end beyond itself in philosophizing can tend to lose its way (cf. *Politics* vii 2–3). Whereas most arts have something definite to show for their efforts (e.g., a builder produces a house), political action does not have such clear results. Those in a position of power may tend to seek more than honor and praise for their efforts – namely, conquest and tyrannical control – if the rewards of good action seem inadequate. Moral virtue and practical wisdom perfected should be reliable, but how many persons achieve these, and how likely is it that such complete virtue will be in charge? The most practical solution is to have political life in service to a higher life, pursuit of theoretical understanding. Hence, in both the *Ethics* and *Politics*, practical wisdom and practical science contribute to an even higher end, the theoretical life (see *NE* vi 13 and *Pol.* vii 2 and 14). So possible difficulties with the practical life, besides the splendor of theoretical activity itself, suggest that the practical life should support this as a further end.

Need the theoretician be also practically wise? This is desirable, of course, but not assured. There seems an instance of this in Aristotle himself. But will all mathematicians, natural scientists, or first philosophers also have practical or political science? They may lack the time and concern. It may be enough to ensure a very happy life, however, if their great desire for theorizing keeps them from unjust action. The effort they put into their primary activity prevents them from engaging in actions that might derive from vice, even if they are not also endowed with real practical insight or much engaged in practical life.

This introduction should hopefully have challenged the reader to benefit from Aristotle's seminal text on the happy life and to appreciate many of the issues interpreters raise. The essays contained in this volume seek fruitful engagement with Aristotle's thought on ethics. Since his provocative text leads to scholarly controversy, it should not be expected that all the authors included agree regarding issues large or small. Some contributors register disagreements with my suggestions. This is part of the delight of thinking about Aristotle: his writings are rich and sustain many lines of interpretation. Thus the *Nicomachean Ethics*, along with Aristotle's other ethical treatises, are vital and living texts. So long as humans seriously concern themselves with how they should live, Aristotle's reflections will be important and influential.

WORKS CITED

Anscombe, G. E. M. 1958. "Modern Moral Philosophy." *Philosophy* 33: 1–19.

Burnyeat, Myles. 1980. "Aristotle on Learning to Be Good." 69–92 in A. O. Rorty ed. *Essays on Aristotle's Ethics*. Berkeley: University of California Press.

Frede, Michael. 2011. *A Free Will: Origins of the Notion in Ancient Thought*. Berkeley: University of California Press.

Hardie, W. F. R. 1967. "The Final Good in Aristotle's Ethics." 297–322 in J. M. E. Moravcsik ed. *Aristotle: A Collection of Critical Essays*. Garden City, NY: Anchor.

Kraut, Richard. 2006. "Doing without Morality: Reflections on the Meaning of *Dein* in Aristotle's *Nicomachean Ethics*." *Oxford Studies in Ancient Philosophy* 30: 159–200.

MacIntyre, Alasdair. 2007. *After Virtue*. 3rd ed. Notre Dame, IN: University of Notre Dame Press.

Salem, Eric. 2010. *In Pursuit of the Good: Intellect and Action in Aristotle's Ethics*. Philadelphia: Paul Dry Books.

Schneewind, J. B. 1990. "The Misfortunes of Virtue." *Ethics* 101: 42–63.

Vlastos, Gregory. 1991. *Socrates: Ironist and Moral Philosopher*. Ithaca, NY: Cornell University Press.

Williams, Bernard. 1985. *Ethics and the Limits of Philosophy*. Cambridge, MA: Harvard University Press.

1993. *Shame and Necessity*. Berkeley: University of California Press.

2   Beginning and Ending with *Eudaimonia*

Aristotle claims that almost everyone agrees that the highest of all practical goods is called *eudaimonia* (adjective: *eudaimōn*) and that living well (*to eu zēn*) and doing well (*eu prattein*) are the same as being *eudaimōn*, but that people disagree about what *eudaimonia* is (1095a15–20).[1] The majority think it is pleasure and so consider the life of enjoyment to be the best one (1095b16–17). "Sophisticated people, men of action, see *eudaimonia* as honor" (1095b22–23), so they think the political life is best, since honor is pretty much its end or goal (1095b23). Finally, there is "the life of contemplation" (1095b19), of which Aristotle says that it is the one "we shall examine in what follows" (1096a4–5). The other lives are then quickly set aside (1096a10) by appeal to a few fairly simple considerations. The life of enjoyment is "fit only for cattle" and merits inclusion on the list of putatively *eudaimōn* lives because pleasure is at least liked for itself. Money, which does not share this feature, is thus a nonstarter for consideration (1096a5–7). Similarly, honor is "too shallow" (1096b24) to be *eudaimonia* or the good, since it depends on what other people think of us, whereas the good is "something of one's own that cannot easily be taken away" (1096b25–26). Even when virtue rather than honor is regarded as our end, a political life is still rejected, because virtue too "seems to be lacking something, since apparently one can possess virtue even when one is asleep, or inactive throughout one's life, and also when one is suffering terribly or experiencing the greatest misfortunes" (1095b31–1096a1).

This chapter was commissioned for and especially written for the present volume. However, I subsequently included much of it in my 2012 book, which for various reasons having to do with publication schedules, appeared first. There it is incorporated into a much fuller discussion of action and contemplation in Aristotle. I am grateful to Pierre Destrée and Gerd Van Riel for inviting me to present an earlier version at KU Leuven, to members of the audience, especially Roger Crisp, for their comments and questions, and to Richard Kraut, Patrick Miller – and especially Ron Polansky – for written comments.

[1] Unless otherwise indicated, references are to the Greek text of the *Nicomachean Ethics* (Bywater, 1894). I use square brackets to number individual clauses for ease of reference.

The fact that people generally agree that the term *eudaimonia* applies to the best good shows that the term has an uncontroversial meaning (or, equivalently, that *eudaimonia* itself has an uncontroversial nominal definition). A plausible candidate is "what all by itself makes a life worthy of choice and lacking in nothing" (1097b14–16), since this explains why the three candidate *eudaimōn* lives have different goals or ends: each takes a different thing to be what makes a life entirely worthy of choice. It also explains why advocates of the different lives disagree, since "people seem, not unreasonably, to base their conception of the good – *eudaimonia*, that is – on their own lives" (1095b14–15). For it is by living in a certain way that we acquire the habits of being pained and pleased that shape our conception of what makes something – a life included – worthy of choice. That is why only someone "brought up in noble habits" has access to the correct starting points or first principles of ethics and political science (1095b4–8; also 1098b3–4) – starting points of which *eudaimonia* properly conceived is prominently one (1102a2–3).

To work out what *eudaimonia* is when properly conceived, Aristotle draws on its nominal definition, as well as on other commonly accepted beliefs (*endoxa*) about it, which is his standard procedure for dealing with a science's first principles (1145b2–7).[2] In this chapter, we investigate the connection between political science and *eudaimonia*; the completeness, self-sufficiency, and worthiness of choice of *eudaimonia* as an end; and, finally, the connections between *eudaimonia*, virtue, and the human function or characteristic activity (*ergon*).

I. EUDAIMONIA AND POLITICAL SCIENCE

The discussion that leads to the identification of *eudaimonia* (as yet referred to simply as "the good") with the end or target aimed at by political science begins with a commonly accepted belief (signaled by *dokein*):

[1] Every skill and every inquiry (*methodos*) and similarly every action and rational choice is thought (*dokei*) to aim at (*ephiesthai*) some good; and so [2] the good has been aptly described as that at which everything aims (*ephietai*). (1094a1–3)

According to [1], four different endeavors seek a good, just as medicine, for example, seeks health (1094a8). [2] concludes that the good is what everything – that is, all such endeavors – seeks.

[3] But it is clear that there is some difference between ends: some ends are activities (*energeiai*), while some are products that are additional to the activities.

---

2 See Reeve 2012b.

[4] In cases where there are ends additional to the actions, the products are by their nature better than the activities. (1094a3–6)

Since for one end to be *better* than another it must be a better *good*, [4] entails that the ends mentioned in [1] are goods; [3], that the good mentioned in [2] is either an activity or the additional end of one. On the assumption that this good is better than any other good, and so the best one (confirmed at 1094a22), [4] entails that it must be a *terminal* activity (one with no additional end that is worthy of choice), or the additional end of a *nonterminal* activity. But if that additional end were itself a nonterminal activity, it could not be the best good, since its own additional end would be better than it is. Either it must be a terminal activity, therefore, or it must not be an activity of any sort.

A possible objection to [1–2] is that it does not follow from the fact that every endeavor of a certain sort pursues a good that there is a good every such endeavor pursues. (One must always sneeze into a handkerchief, but there is not a handkerchief into which one must always sneeze.) The next sentences – as well as doing other important things – seem to begin an implicit response:

[5] Since there are many actions, skills, and sciences, it happens that there are many ends as well: the end of medicine is health, that of shipbuilding, a ship, that of military science, victory, and that of domestic economy, wealth. [6] But when any of these actions, skills, or sciences comes under some single faculty (*dunamis*) – as bridle making and other sciences concerned with equine equipment come under the science of horsemanship, and horsemanship itself and every action in warfare come under military science, and others similarly come under others – then [7] in all these cases the end of the master science is [the ends of the architectonic (*architektonikōn*) sciences are] more worthy of choice than the ends of the subordinate sciences, since [8] these latter ends are pursued also for the sake of the former. (1094a6–16; also *Ph.* 194a33–b8)

The existence of hierarchies among ends or *telic hierarchies* holds out the possibility, then, that [1–2] could be true even in face of the fact, acknowledged in [5], that different endeavors have different ends (compare 1097a15–24).

When [1–2] is reprised a little later, it is stated more simply: "Every sort of knowledge (*gnōsis*) and rational choice pursues some good" (1095a14–15). This suggests that the skills, lines of inquiry, sciences, and capacities mentioned in [1–8] can all be bundled together as sorts of knowledge, whereas rational choice merits separate mention. The association of rational choice with action in particular suggests that action is its primary sphere of operation, so that what we rationally choose, in the first instance, is to act in some way. Since rational choice (*prohairesis*) is literally the choosing (*hairein*) of one thing before (*pro*) another, the idea of assessing relative goodness through some sort of process of rational deliberation seems integral to it (1112b15–17). Moreover, the sort of knowledge that constitutes skills, inquiries, sciences, and capacities is [2] the sort that, like action and rational choice, aims at the good – that is, the human good (1094b7). Since a skill (bridle making) is a science (1094a11, a18), and a science is both an inquiry (1094a1, a7) and a faculty or capacity (1094a10, a18), all the good-seeking sorts of knowledge mentioned in [1–8] may be referred to as "choice-relevant sciences" – meaning no more by "science" than Aristotle does by *epistēmē*.[3] Apparently, then, the actions referred to in [1] belong to *rational* agents (1112a19–21), whose behavior is governed by rational choice, and so by the norms and principles of these sciences.

Choice-relevant sciences, like sciences generally, can be conceived in two ways: as bodies of knowledge (theories) or – on the model of a skill or craft – as faculties or capacities someone has. Aristotle's use of the term *dunamis* in [6] suggests that he is thinking of them in the latter way, so that a science is a faculty or capacity a scientist possesses (1139b15–17). Since such a capacity can be dormant (as it is in someone who is not currently exercising his knowledge) or active (as it is in someone now using the knowledge), and since the term Aristotle usually employs to refer to an active capacity is *energeia* (as at 1098a5–8), the contrast drawn in [3–4] is almost certainly that between the case where the action – considered as the activity resulting from the activation of a capacity – is the end (terminal activity), and the case where that action, though perhaps also an end, has some additional end (nonterminal activity).

If [8] implies that whenever X is pursued for the sake of Y, Y is more worthy of choice than X, it provides no support for [7]: we can listen to Bach's French Suites for the sheer enjoyment of it and for the sake of the relaxation it causes, although (as we may also believe) the enjoyment is more worthy of choice than the relaxation. Apparently, then, [8] is more restrictive in meaning, applying only to cases in which the Y for whose sake we pursue X is above X in a telic hierarchy. The sort of hierarchy envisaged in [6–7] is not generated, then, whenever X is pursued for the sake of Y, which can be a chance or circumstantial matter, but is rather

---

[3] Aristotle usually works with a tripartite division of sciences (*epistēmai*) into theoretical, practical, and productive (skills) (*Top.* vi 6, *Meta.* 1064a16–19), but he sometimes distinguishes sciences, such as physics, which he usually classes as theoretical (*Meta.* 1025b25–28), from a narrower group, including astronomy and theology, calling the first natural and only the second theoretical (*PA* 639b21–640a8). Moreover, he sometimes uses *epistēmē* somewhat strictly to apply only to knowledge of "what cannot be otherwise" (*NE* 1139b18–24), while at others he applies it also to "what holds for the most part (*hōs epi to polu*)" (*Meta.* 1027a19–21), a class into which the truths of ethics apparently fall (*NE* 1094b21).

something objective, which is fixed by the concepts or natures of the things in the hierarchy. It is because bridle making is the very craft it is that it is subordinate to horsemanship, with the result that its end (good bridles) is less worthy of choice than the latter's (well-trained horses). This helps explain why [4] speaks of a higher end in such a hierarchy as "by nature" better than any below it.

Although [8] might seem to apply only to cases in which X has an additional end, the next sentence extends its scope beyond them:

[9] And it makes no difference whether the ends of the actions are the activities themselves, or [10] something else additional to them, as in the sciences just mentioned. (1094a16–18)

[9–10] reprises [3] "some ends are activities, while some are products that are additional to the activities." It distinguishes between cases [9] in which the action, considered as the result of activating a choice-relevant capacity or science, is the end (terminal activity) and [10] cases in which the action or activity has some additional end (nonterminal activity). But because a terminal activity has no further end, it must be the topmost good in any hierarchy in which it occurs and so must be better and more worthy of choice than anything below it. Since [3] some ends are terminal activities, it follows that some hierarchies must have them as their topmost and best goods. But if there is to be a unique good, which is better or more worthy of choice than absolutely any other, it is not enough that choice-relevant sciences and the rest form telic hierarchies. In addition, all of them must form a single such hierarchy at the apex of which there is a unique science whose end or goal is – as [7] asserts – better or more worthy of choice than any of those below it. Since this hierarchy must contain terminal activities, the end or goal in question must be a terminal activity.

A new chapter begins at this juncture,[4] but the argument itself seems to make more sense, as we shall see, if it is treated as continuing:

[11] If, then, there is some end of things done in action that we wish for because of itself, but the others because of it, and [12] we do not choose everything because of something else – for [13] if that is the case, it will go on without limit, so that the desire will be empty (kenēn) and vain (mataian) – [14] it is clear that this will be the good, that is to say, the best one. (1094a18–23)

A *nonterminating* desire – which is a desire for X because of Y, for Y because of Z, and so on – will, [13] says, be *kenon* and *mataion*. Like their English counterparts "empty" and "vain," these terms are somewhat vague, but the primary meaning of the former is that of being like an

---

4   Chapter divisions do not go back to antiquity, let alone to Aristotle, and so reflect the views of editors and interpreters.

empty cup or vessel. In Plato's *Republic*, as elsewhere, it is thus readily applied to desires: "Hunger, thirst, and the like are some sort of emptiness (*kenōseis*) related to the state of the body," "lack of knowledge (*agnoia*) and lack of wisdom (*aphrosunē*)" are "some sort of emptiness (*kenotēs*) related to the state of the soul" (585a8–b4). Presumably, then, a *kenon* desire is one that, as (always) empty, cannot be satisfied, which is just what a nonterminating desire seems to be like. None of this implies, of course, that a desire cannot be *kenon* but only that one that is *kenon* comes at a high enough cost to raise a question about the rationality of acting on it. It is this fact that lays the ground for *mataion*, the primary connotation of which is foolish or without reason – vain. Thus, it is *mataion* for a young person to study a practical science like ethics or political science, since he tends to follow his feelings, not what he will learn by studying it (1095a5).

While a nonterminating desire may be one that it cannot be rational to act on, it seems that a desire for anything desired because of itself does not suffer from this defect. If that is how we are to understand [13], however, it seems obvious that all it entails is – as [12] seems to say – that there must be some end (though not necessarily only one) that we do not desire because of something else, but (implicitly) because of itself. So if [11–14] is supposed to be an independent argument for the existence of the good, it is not a compelling one. The question is, is it any more compelling if we see it as continuing the argument of [1–10]?

Suppose that the sphere mentioned in [11] of things done in action is the one within which the various choice-relevant sciences operate. The end we wish for or choose or desire *because of itself*, and not – lest our desire be nonterminating – because of anything else, will be a terminal activity or an end of a nonterminal one that is not itself an activity. Suppose that [11] this end is also such that we choose all the others we wish for or desire because of it, then [14] will follow at once. That is what the discussion of telic hierarchies [1–10] adds to discussion of empty and vain desires [11–14]. What the discussion of empty and vain desires adds to that of telic hierarchies is a solution to the problem of how to fit terminal activities into such hierarchies – a solution that, in turn, gives us a tighter grip on the good. If a terminal activity is worthy of choice at all – and some may not be (*Pol.* 1332a9–21) – it must be solely because of itself, since, unlike a nonterminal activity, it is not worthy of choice because of any additional end. That means that while things coming under it in a hierarchy may be worthy of choice because of it, it cannot be worthy of choice because of anything above it. Consequently, as we saw, it must be the apex of any hierarchy in which it occurs. Put the other way around, if anything is the apex of such a hierarchy, it must be a terminal activity. It follows that if the good is such an apex, it must be a terminal activity (1098a16–17).

While this is no doubt a significant result, it still presupposes rather than proves that there is such a thing as *the* good, and not rather a variety of goods, each a terminal activity, and each the topmost end of a distinct telic hierarchy. The next sentences seem to share that presupposition:

[15] Surely, then, knowledge of the good must be very important for our lives? And if, like archers, we have a target, are we not more likely to hit the right mark? If so, we must try at least roughly to comprehend what it is and which science or faculty [capacity] is concerned with it. [16] Knowledge of the good would seem to be the concern of the most authoritative science, the highest master [the most architectonic] science. (1094a23–27)

It is also possible, however, that [15] remains under the umbrella of the "if" in [11]: *if* there is something worthy of choice in the way [11] specifies, it will be the good and will be important to know about (compare 1097a22–24). The good's status, therefore, may still be hypothetical. Nonetheless *if* it exists, it belongs to – or is the proper end of – a choice-relevant science, and so is subject to the conclusions reached in the discussion of telic hierarchies in [1–10].

By identifying the most architectonic choice-relevant science as the one with the most control, [16] paves the way for the good's further specification:

And [17] this is obviously the science of politics, because [18] it lays down which of the sciences there should be in cities, and which each class of person should learn and up to what point. And we see that even the most honorable of faculties [capacities], such as military science, domestic economy, and rhetoric, come under it. Since [19] political science employs the other [practical (*praktikais*)][5] sciences, and also lays down laws about what [actions] we should do and refrain from, [20] its end will include (*periechoi*) the ends of the others, and [21] will therefore be the human good. (1094a28–b7)

The primary connotation of the verb *periechein*, which is a compound of the preposition *peri* (around) and the verb *echein* (have, possess), is that of containing by surrounding.[6] But it is difficult to see how that can be its meaning here. For what entails that the end of a science S_1 *periechein* the end of a science S_2 is simply that S_2 falls under S_1 in a telic hierarchy – or, equivalently, that S_1 is more architectonic than S_2. Thus, while political science may be the *most* architectonic science, generalship is also architectonic, since it is higher in a telic hierarchy than horsemanship, which is itself higher than bridle making. Yet generalship's end – victory – does not seem to contain either trained horses or their bridles, any more than

---

[5]   Some editors bracket or omit *praktikais*.
[6]   Ackrill 1974 interprets *periechein* in this way.

health, which is medicine's end and a certain bodily condition, contains medical instruments, medical treatment, or drugs.

Just as "contain" can also mean "circumscribe" or "limit," however, as in the doctrine of containment familiar from the Cold War, so too can *periechein*.[7] [20] could mean, then, that political science's end *limits* or *circumscribes* the ends of all the choice-relevant sciences, including those of the other practical sciences and of actions. This idea seems to fit nicely with the account given in [18–19] of what political science does. By looking to its own end, it sets limits to which sciences should be in cities, to which groups should practice them and to what degree, and to what actions should be done and which avoided. It is when we try to give [7] the purchase on [20] necessary for [21] to follow from it that we run into a problem, since it is unclear why a limiting end of this sort would have to be [14] the best or [21] human good. Other people's rights, for example, may set absolute limits to our pursuit of *eudaimonia*, and so be limiting ends, but it is not obvious that respecting their rights is the *best* good. A third meaning of *periechein* is "to be superior to" or "surpass." It is in this sense, apparently, that Aristotle uses it to describe God or the unmoved mover (*Meta.* 1074b3). If this is its meaning here, [20–21] simply recapitulates what has already been stated by [14] and implied by [7]. Since a maximally architectonic good can also serve as a limit in an obvious way, the benefits of understanding it as such a limit carry over even when *periechein* is not taken to mean "limit."

When [20–21] is understood in this deflationary fashion, the evidence [17–19] provides for the existence of the good, and so for the antecedent of the conditional [11–14], is somewhat weak, since it presupposes the existence of a unique maximally architectonic science. The existence of the good, however, seems to be something Aristotle took to be uncontroversial:

Let us say what we claim the aim of political science, that is, of all the good things to be done, what is the highest. Most people, I should think, agree about what it is called, since both the masses and sophisticated people call it *eudaimonia*, understanding being *eudaimōn* as equivalent to living well and acting well. They disagree about substantive conceptions of *eudaimonia*, the masses giving an account that differs from that of the philosophers. (1095a14–22)

[1–21] may be intended less to establish the existence of the good, therefore, than to establish its relationship to political science. The sequel confirms this:

---

[7] An interpretation proposed in Kraut 1989, 220–227, which remains one of the best discussions of Aristotle on the good.

[22] For even if the good is the same for an individual as for a city, [23] that of the city is obviously a greater and more complete thing to obtain and preserve. For while the good of an individual is a desirable thing, what is good for a people or for cities is a nobler and more god-like thing. [24] Our inquiry (*methodos*), then, is a kind of political science, since these are the ends it is aiming at (*ephietai*). (1094b9–11)

The noun *methodos* and the verb *ephienai* in [24], both used in [1–2], indicate that the argument has come full circle, suggesting that its goal has been to characterize the inquiry the *Nicomachean Ethics* will pursue, and to identify ethics as a choice-relevant science, which, as a sort of political science, is maximally architectonic. Nonetheless, the argument also helps us better understand what the good or *eudaimonia* is. It is a terminal activity that, as the end of the maximally architectonic science of politics, is the apex of the unique telic hierarchy, H, which includes all other ends or goods that are worthy of choice.

II. COMPLETENESS, SELF-SUFFICIENCY, AND WORTHINESS OF CHOICE

The notion of the completeness of an end or good is explained as follows:

[25] We speak of that which is worth pursuing for its own sake as more complete than that which is worth pursuing only for the sake of something else and [26] that which is never worth choosing for the sake of something else as more complete than things that are worth choosing both in themselves and for the sake of this end. And so [27] that which is always worth choosing in itself and never for the sake of something else, we call complete without qualification. (1097a30–4)

[25] explains the notion of completeness in terms of worthiness of pursuit, and so of goodness. If end E_1 is worthy of choice for its own sake, while end E_2 is so solely because of some other end, E_1 must be higher in the hierarchy H than E_2. Hence, achieving E_2 must be the best means of achieving E_1. Achieving E_1, then, involves already having achieved E_2, whereas the converse does not hold. In an obvious sense, then, E_2 must be less complete than E_1, since it is a *part* of achieving E_1.[8] That is why the very existence of incomplete ends is made clear by the fact that some ends are the means to others: "Since there appear to be several ends, and some of these, such as wealth, flutes, and implements generally, we choose as means to other ends, it is clear that not all ends are complete" (1097a25–27).

The case described in [26] involves an end E_1 that – while worthy of choice – is never worth choosing for the sake of something else, and an end E_2 that is worthy of choice both for its own sake and for

---

[8] This would explain why the good of a city is greater and more complete than the good of one of its individual citizens (1094b7–9).

the sake of E_1. Here E_2 is less complete than E_1 since again E_1 must be higher in H than E_2, so that achieving E_1 has achieving E_2 as a part. The end described in [27], since it is always worth choosing for its own sake, but never for the sake of something else, must be the topmost good in H, and so, for parallel reasons, must be the most complete one. Since this topmost good is *eudaimonia*, it follows that *eudaimonia* must be the most complete of goods: "The chief good manifestly is something complete. So that if there is only one end that is complete, this will be what we are looking for, and if there are several of them, the most complete" (1097a28–30).

As completeness is allied with the telic structure H, introduced by the identification of *eudaimonia* with the end of political science, so self-sufficiency is allied with completeness:

The same conclusion [that *eudaimonia* is the best good] seems to follow from considering self-sufficiency, since the complete good is thought to be self-sufficient. ... For now, we take what is self-sufficient to be that which on its own makes life (*bion*) worthy of choice and lacking in nothing. We think *eudaimonia* to be such. (1097b6–16)

What sort of human life is it that a self-sufficient end or good makes worthy of choice and lacking in nothing? Is it some particular sort of human life or any sort of human life at all? That it must be a human life of a particular sort becomes clear later on when complete *eudaimonia* is identified with contemplation in accordance with (theoretical) wisdom (*sophia*) (Section 4). For once that identification is made, Aristotle goes on to say that because "the *eudaimōn* person is human, he will also need external prosperity; for human nature is not self-sufficient for contemplation, but the body must be healthy and provided with food and other care" (1178b33–35).

The implicit contrast is with some other beings whose nature is self-sufficient for contemplation, and so for complete *eudaimonia*. These beings, not surprisingly, are the gods:

That complete *eudaimonia* consists in some contemplative activity is apparent also from the following. We assume the gods to be supremely blessed and *eudaimōn*; but what sorts of actions should we ascribe to them? Just actions? But will they not obviously be ridiculous if they make contracts, return deposits, and so on? Courageous acts, then, enduring what is fearful and facing dangers because it is noble to do so? Or generous acts? To whom will they give? And it will be absurd if they have money or anything like it. And what would their temperate acts consist in? Is such praise not cheap, since they have no bad appetites? If we were to run through them all, anything to do with actions would appear petty and unworthy of the gods. Nevertheless, everyone assumes that they are at least alive and therefore engage in activity, since we do not take them to sleep like

Endymion. So if we remove from a living being the possibility of action, and furthermore the very possibility of producing anything, what is left apart from contemplation? So the god's activity, which is superior in blessedness, will be contemplative; and therefore the human activity most akin to this is the most conducive to *eudaimonia*. (1178b8–23)

Since the life of the gods consists in contemplation alone, their nature, which that life actualizes and expresses, must be self-sufficient for it (*Meta.* 1072b26–28; also 1074b34–35). In order for *eudaimonia* on its own to make a *human* life worthy of choice and lacking in nothing, however, the life itself, since it is not naturally self-sufficient for *eudaimonia*, needs some other things:

Eudaimonia obviously also needs the presence of external goods as well, since it is impossible, or at least no easy matter, to perform noble actions without resources. For in many actions, we employ, as if they were instruments at our disposal, friends, wealth, and political power. Again, being deprived of some things – such as high birth, noble children, beauty – spoils our blessedness. For the person terribly ugly, of low birth, or solitary and childless is not really the sort to be *eudaimōn*, still less, perhaps, if he has children or friends who are thoroughly bad, or good but dead. (1099a31–b6)

Moreover, a human life must last long enough to count as complete, since "one swallow does not make a summer, nor one day. Neither does one day or a short time make someone blessed and *eudaimōn*" (1098a18–20).

When the *eudaimonia* in question is the sort constituted by activity in accordance with practical wisdom and the virtues of character, then, its dependence on external goods is quite substantial. When it is of the sort constituted by contemplation in accordance with (theoretical) wisdom, its dependence on them is much less (1177a9–1178b7). But where lifespan is concerned, both sorts of *eudaimonia* are in the same situation. That is why contemplation will only be "complete *eudaimonia* for a human being – if it consumes a complete span of life, because there is nothing incomplete in matters of *eudaimonia*" (1177b24–26; compare 1098a18).

Worthiness of choice is so related to self-sufficiency that each illuminates the other:

We think *eudaimonia* to be ... the thing most of all worth choosing, not counted as just one thing among others. Counted as just one thing among others it would clearly be more worthy of choice with even the least good added to it. For the good added would cause an increase in goodness, and the greater good is always more worthy of choice. (1097b16–20; also 1172b28–32)

Because contemplation that receives a complete life is self-sufficient, it can make a human life worthy of choice and lacking in nothing on its own, without the aid of even the least additional good. Contemplation can make the life of the gods that way, after all, and their life consists entirely in it. To be sure, a human *life* needs to be augmented with external goods if it is to be apt for such *eudaimonia*, but the *eudaimonia itself* needs nothing. If the addition to it of even the least good increased its worthiness of choice, and so that of the life to which it was added, this would not be so. Hence it must already be the end or good that is most worthy of choice.

III. EUDAIMONIA AND THE CHARACTERISTIC ACTIVITY OF HUMAN BEINGS

The fact that *eudaimonia* is complete and self-sufficient, and so maximally worthy of choice, argues for its being the best human good, but it does not yet tell us clearly enough what *eudaimonia* is. It is with the aim of providing the requisite clarity that the human *function* or characteristic activity (*ergon*) is introduced (1097b22–25). Yet Aristotle does not tell us explicitly what such an activity is. Presumably we are supposed to understand that already. He treats it as an uncontroversial fact, in any case, that craftsmen have such activities, as do bodily parts, such as eyes, hands, and feet (1097b28–33). Then, instead of arguing directly that human beings also have a characteristic activity, he treats the uncontroversial fact as making it absurd to think that they do not have one.

[28] Well, do the carpenter and the tanner have characteristic activities and actions, and a human being none? Has nature left him without a characteristic activity to perform? [29] Or, as there seem to be characteristic activities of the eye, the hand, the foot, and generally of each part of the body, should one assume that a human being has some characteristic activity over and above all these? (1097b28–33)

The thought in [28] seems to be that if in his roles as craftsman of various sorts a human being has characteristic activities, then he must also have a characteristic activity of a more general type that suits him to play those roles, and so to adapt himself to the rational principles and norms of the various choice-relevant sciences. [29] seems to reach the same conclusion by something like the reverse route. Here the thought seems to be that if each part of the human body has a characteristic activity, the whole of which they are the parts must also have one, to which each of theirs contributes, so that its characteristic activity explains theirs.

Whatever the human characteristic activity turns out to be, then, it must be something that we can intelligibly think of as explaining the characteristic activities of the parts of the human body and as explaining how it is that human beings can be craftsmen who are subject to rational norms. It is these two requirements that shape Aristotle's search:

[30] What sort of thing, might it [the human characteristic activity] be, then? For living (zēn) is evidently shared even by plants, while what we are looking for is something special (idion) to a human being. We should therefore rule out the life (zōēn) of nutrition and growth. Next would be some sort of sentient life, but this again is clearly shared by the horse, the ox, indeed by every animal. [31] What remains is a life, concerned in some way with action, of the element that possesses reason. [32] (Of this element one part has reason in being obedient to reason, the other in possessing it and engaging in thought.) [33] As this kind of life can be spoken of in two ways, let us assume that we are talking about the life concerned with action in the sense of activity, since it seems to be the more proper use of the phrase. (1097b33–1098a7)

Two Greek words correspond to the English word "life" – zōē (zēn) and bios. Zōē refers to the sorts of life processes that biologists, zoologists, and other scientists (including psychologists and theologians) study: growth and reproduction are such processes, as are perceiving and thinking. Bios refers to the sort of life a natural historian or biographer might investigate: the life of the otter, the life of Pericles. Both terms are ambiguous.

The ambiguity in zōē is diagnosed in [33] as that between a potentiality and an actuality or activity: the potential to grow, reproduce, perceive, on the one hand, actually growing, reproducing, perceiving, and thinking, on the other. The ambiguity in bios is of a different sort. In the first instance, bios refers to a biographical life, to a span of time throughout which someone possesses potential zōē: "The good and bad person [are thought] to be hardest to distinguish when they are asleep (hence the saying that the eudaimōn are no different from the wretched for half their lives (bios)" (1102b5–7). Practical or action-related zōē will not be eudaimonia for a human being, therefore, unless it occurs "over a complete bios" (1098a18–20). In the second instance, bios refers to a mode of biographical life, distinguished from others by its aim or goal, such as "the life (bios) of politics" (1095b23). It is because their modes of life are different, as we saw (Section I), that people's conceptions of eudaimonia are also different.

What is characterized in [33] as "concerned in some way with action" is the zōē of the element that possesses reason. This might quite naturally lead us to think that the life activity being referred to is peculiarly practical as opposed to theoretical or contemplative. What is praktikē, however, often includes what is theoretical or contemplative, rather than excluding it:

It is not necessary, as some suppose, for a praktikos life to involve relations with other people, nor are those thoughts alone praktikos that we engage in for the sake of the consequences that come from actions (praxeis), on the contrary, much more so are the theoretical or contemplative (theōrētikos) activities and thoughts that are their own ends and are engaged in for their own sake. For doing well in action (*eupraxia*) is the end, so that a sort of action (*praxis*) is too. (*Pol.* 1325b16–21)

[32] seems intended, indeed, to remind us of just this. Rational activity, it tells us, is twofold – that of the part that obeys reason and that of the part that autonomously thinks and understands. The part that obeys reason is the desiring part (1102b30–31), but when we consider it as actively obeying reason, it involves the activity of the calculative subpart of the part that possesses reason autonomously (1139a3–15). The twofold activity of what possesses reason, therefore, is not [a] nonrational active desiring and [b] practical or theoretical active thinking, but rather [c] active desiring in accordance with practical thinking and [d] theoretical thinking. That is why it is immediately recharacterized as "activity of the soul in accordance with reason or at least not entirely lacking it" (1098a7–8). It is the distinction between [c] and [d], too, that paves the way for the disjunctive conclusion of the argument as a whole: "The human good turns out to be activity of soul in accordance with virtue and, if there are several virtues, in accordance with the best and most complete" (1098a16–18). For the most complete virtue turns out to be (theoretical) wisdom, which is the virtue of the soul's scientific part, and is responsible for active theoretical thinking or contemplating, while the less complete one is the amalgam of practical wisdom and the virtues of character, which is the virtue of the calculative and desiring parts, and is responsible for active practical thinking (1177a12–1178a22).

When Aristotle elsewhere employs the notion of a characteristic activity for more general philosophical or scientific purposes, he identifies a thing's characteristic activity with its essence, substance, or what defines it (*Mete.* 390a10–12, *PA* 648a15–16, *GA* 731a25–26), its virtues or excellences with what enables it to carry out that activity well (1098a15), and its end with the activity carried out in accordance with those virtues (1168a6–9). In assuming [30] that the human characteristic activity must be *special* to human beings, he might be relying on this nexus of doctrines, then, some elements of which, such as the connection between characteristic activity and virtue, appear elsewhere in the argument itself (1098a8–15).[9] For the essence of a kind of thing must be special to it, since it is definitive of the kind. But if this were his reason for thinking that the characteristic activity of a thing must be special to it, it is surprising that he does not say so. The supposedly uncontroversial examples he gives of things that have characteristic activities suggest that he has something somewhat different in mind. Having the capacity to become a practitioner of a craft or skill does seem

---

9 When a thing is complex, however, and – like a human being – has an essence that involves many functions (648a16), "the best one is always its proper function" (*Protr.* B65).

to be something special to human beings: "It is special (*idion*) to a human being to be capable of learning grammar, since if something is a human being, it is capable of learning grammar, and if it is capable of learning grammar, it is a human being" (*Top.* 102a18–22). Hence, the human characteristic activity might be special to human beings because it is presupposed, in the way we explored, by capacities that are special to them.

The implicit argument by elimination that Aristotle uses in [30–33] to identify the human characteristic activity presupposes that there are just three life activities: nutritional, perceptual, and rational. It thus seems to presuppose his own account of the soul (1102a26–1103a10), since he thinks ethics must presuppose some such account (1102a18–19). Nonetheless, whichever account we appeal to, it will surely be rational activities that emerge as best fitted for the double explanatory duty the human characteristic activity must perform. For the crafts and choice-relevant sciences are rational endeavors, and the parts of the human body, since they can be moved in accordance with these sciences, must be naturally suited to subserve and further their ends or goals: "The hand is not to be looked at as one tool, but as many, since it is just like a tool for using tools" (*PA* 687a19–21). Presumably, that is why [29] the human characteristic activity, as a rational activity of the soul, is "over and above" all their characteristic activities.

Once the human characteristic activity is identified with rational activity, the conceptual or analytic connection between a thing's characteristic activity and its virtues or excellences (1139a16–17) is used to legitimate the latter's introduction:

If the characteristic activity of a human being is an activity of the soul in accordance with reason or at least not entirely lacking it; and if we say that the characteristic activity of anything is the same in kind as that of a good thing of the same type, as in the case of a lyre-player and a good lyre-player, and so on, without qualification, in the same way in every case, the superiority of the good one in virtue being an addition to the characteristic activity (for characteristic activity of the lyre-player is to play the lyre, that of the good lyre-player to play it well); then if this is so and we take the characteristic activity of a human being to be a certain kind of life (*zōēn tina*); and if we take this life to be activity of the soul and actions in accordance with reason, and the characteristic activity of a good person to be to carry this out well and nobly, and a characteristic activity to be accomplished well when it is accomplished in accordance with the appropriate virtue; then if this is so, the human good turns out to be activity of the soul in accordance with virtue, and if there are several virtues, in accordance with the best and most complete. Again, this must be over a complete life (*biō(i)*). For one swallow does not make a summer, nor one day. Neither does one day or a short time make someone blessed and *eudaimōn*. (1098a7–20)

Much of the remainder of the *Nicomachean Ethics*'s investigation of *eudaimonia* now focuses on the various candidate virtues governing rational activity, with the aim, finally, of identifying which of them is most complete.

IV. TWO SORTS OF EUDAIMONIA

So much for *eudaimonia* at the beginning of the *Ethics*; now for *eudaimonia* at the end. When Aristotle explicitly reengages with the question of the definition of *eudaimonia* in the final chapters of the work (x 7–8), he compares the intellectual virtues of (theoretical) wisdom to practical wisdom – which involves such virtues of character as courage, temperance, and generosity (1144b15–17) – to see which is best and most complete. The criteria of completeness, self-sufficiency, and so on used to isolate *eudaimonia* are now redeployed for this new purpose, as are other similar criteria that have emerged in the subsequent discussion. (Theoretical) wisdom is the virtue of intellect (*nous*), which is the best and most divine element in us (1177a12–18) and the one with which we are most of all to be identified (1178a2–8). Activity in accordance with it is the most continuous activity of which we are capable (1177a21–22), the most pleasant (1177a22–27, b20–21), the most self-sufficient (1177a27–b1, 1178a23–b7), the most leisurely (1177b4–15), and the only one worthy of choice for itself alone (1177b2–4). Practical wisdom is the virtue of the merely human compound of body and soul (or rational part and desiring part) (1177b26–29, 1178a14–23) and the one with which it would be absurd to identify (1177b31–1178a4). Activity in accordance with it is not the most continuous activity of which we are capable, or the most pleasant; or, since it needs many external goods, the most self-sufficient; or the most leisured, since the politics and wars within which it occurs are trouble zones; or worthy of choice for itself alone, since we engage in it also for the sake of a further end. Thus (theoretical) wisdom emerges as the best virtue (1177a13) and activity in accordance with it as complete *eudaimonia* (1178b8–9).

Because contemplation is complete *eudaimonia*, practical wisdom, in prescribing with the aim of furthering *eudaimonia*, must prescribe for its sake (1145a6–9). It seems, indeed, that it must prescribe with its maximization in view, since "the more contemplation there is in one's life, the happier one is, not incidentally but in virtue of the contemplation" (1178b29–30). Since contemplation requires leisure time, free from practical responsibilities and importuning wants and needs, practical wisdom must thus serve as "a sort of steward of theoretical wisdom, procuring leisure for it and its function by restraining and moderating the feelings" (*MM* 1198b17–19).

Unlike a god, however, a human being needs friends and other external goods if he is to have a *eudaimōn* life; he cannot survive on a diet of contemplation alone (1178b33–35). Hence, "insofar as he is a human being and lives together with a number of others, he chooses to do actions in accordance with virtue [of character]" (1178b5–7). For these actions are prescribed by the most architectonic practical science (political science) and so are the ones that best further his contemplative goal. Moreover, they themselves constitute *eudaimonia* of a secondary sort: "The life in accordance with the other kind of virtue [practical wisdom and virtue of character] is *eudaimōn* in a secondary way, since the activities in accordance with it are human" (1178a9–10).

V. EUDAIMONIA, HAPPINESS, AND CREDIBILITY

Even though our own conception of happiness is unsettled and disputed, being happy seems to be a favorable emotional state of some sort. If someone endorses his life, so that he is cheerful or joyful rather than sad, is engaged in it, so that he is absorbed by it rather than bored or alienated, and is attuned to it, so that he is relaxed rather than anxious or stressed – or are these things more than their contraries – he is happy.[10] It may be, then, those who think that *eudaimonia* is pleasure (1095a22–23) come close to thinking of it as we think of happiness. Yet pleasure does not seem to be happiness, even if it is somehow involved in it: one can be unhappy even though one is regularly experiencing pleasures, and an intense pleasure need not make one very happy; being in constant pain is not the same as being unhappy, although it can, of course, be a source of unhappiness. Those who think the *eudaimōn* life is the political life or the contemplative one seem yet further away from thinking of them as *happy* lives. For nothing about these lives seems to ensure that those who live them or live them well or excellently will necessarily be in a favorable emotional state – an excellent politician or philosopher can be sad, alienated, or anxious. Worthwhile lives, they may be, but a life can be worthwhile without being happy.

Aristotle's own account avoids some of these problems of fit with happiness, in part because it intentionally incorporates elements of the other conceptions (1098b22–29). It is thus an important point in favor of treating *eudaimonia* as activity in accord with the best and most complete virtue that it makes pleasure intrinsic to the *eudaimōn* life (1099a11–16). Aristotle is not equally explicit that his account also incorporates such truth as there is in the view of those who make *eudaimonia* reside in honor or in contemplation. But he is explicit that any adequate

---

[10] I draw here on Haybron 2008, 79–81.

account would have to do so (1098b22–1099a31). In any case, his own two-tiered conception – consisting of the second-best sort of *eudaimonia* (activity in accord with full virtue of character) that is for the sake of the very best sort (activity in accord with theoretical wisdom) – does seem designed to meet this adequacy condition.

Since the Aristotelian *eudaimōn* life is intrinsically pleasant or enjoyable, it is plausibly seen as cheerful or joyful, especially since, as in accord with correct reason, whether deliberative or architectonic, it would seem to be reflectively endorsed by the agent in a way that these emotions evidence. For the same reason, the *eudaimōn* person seems unlikely to be bored, alienated, or anxious about living the life he has been trained and habituated to live and has chosen as best. Although *eudaimonia* is an activity, not a favorable emotional state, it would not be *eudaimonia* if it did not involve such a state by being the actualization of it. In this regard, *eudaimonia* is like the simple pleasures it may at times involve – pleasant and valuable in part because evoking desire. Nonetheless, the activity itself in which *eudaimonia* consists is relatively more important than the enjoyment of it, since it is better to do the noble things that the virtuous person would do, even if it makes one sad, bored, and anxious (as might be true of the continent person), than to do something else that inspires the contrary feelings (as might be true of the incontinent one). For Aristotelian *eudaimonia*, the noble activity counts for more than the emotional state it evokes in the agent. That is why Aristotle cites with approval the words of Hesiod:

> The person who understands everything for himself is best of all,
> And noble is that one who heeds good advice. (1095b10–11)

Because happiness does consist in a favorable emotional state, moreover, what evokes it can vary from person to person, and – arguably – the person himself or herself is the final authority on its existence: if X feels happy, he is happy. These, too, are important points of difference with Aristotelian *eudaimonia*. A further difference seems more important still. When we say that someone is happy, we describe his life in psychological terms. We do not, in the relevant sense, evaluate it. A happy life need not be successful or accomplished or admirable. It need not, as we say, amount to much. The very modest can be very happy, while the driven, the brilliant, the heroic, the creative, and even the saintly may have a much harder time of it. Children can be happy, dogs too, it seems, but neither can be *eudaimōn*. Aristotelian *eudaimonia* has a large perfectionist element, in other words, that happiness seems to lack.

When we see what Aristotle thinks *eudaimonia* actually consists in, however, we are bound to wonder how seriously we can take that recommendation, once the details are filled out in the way he argues they should be. Could contemplation really be happiness of the best kind? At the end of the *Ethics*, Aristotle tells us how to go about answering this question. The somewhat abstract considerations he has provided in favor of the contemplative life, he says, do carry some conviction, but only go so far:

> The truth in practical issues is judged from the facts of our lives, these being what really matter. We must therefore examine what has been said in the light of the facts of our life, and if it agrees with the facts, then we should accept it, while if it conflicts, we must assume it to be no more than theory. (1179a17–22; also 1105b10–18, 1172a34–b1)

That, though, seems to make matters worse. For who among us lives the contemplative life or can claim on the basis of experience that it is indeed the happiest of all? At the same time, few will want to consider the *Ethics* no more than theory – no more than mere words (*logous*) – on these grounds. They will be more inclined to turn toward the second-best kind of *eudaimonia* that consists in activity in accord with practical wisdom and the virtues of character. For them, and that includes almost every reader, *Nicomachean Ethics* vi and not x will be more like the true culmination of the work – the place where the account of the virtues of character is completed by the account of the correct reason with which they must be in accord. Practical wisdom and the virtues of character it involves will then emerge not just as a central topic of the *Ethics* but as its most valuable legacy.

WORKS CITED

Ackrill, J. L. 1974. "Aristotle on *Eudaimonia*." *Proceedings of the British Academy* 60: 3–23. Reprinted 179–200 in his *Essays on Plato and Aristotle*. Oxford, 1997.

Barney, R. 2008. "Aristotle's Argument for a Human Function." *Oxford Studies in Ancient Philosophy* 34: 293–322.

Bush, S. 2008. "Divine and Human Happiness in the *Nicomachean Ethics*." *Philosophical Review* 117: 49–76.

Bywater, I. 1894. *Aristotelis Ethica Nicomachea*. Oxford: Clarendon Press.

Charles, D. 1999. "Aristotle on Well-Being and Intellectual Contemplation." *Proceedings of the Aristotelian Society*, suppl. 73: 205–223.

Cooper, J. M. 1998. "Contemplation and Happiness: A Reconsideration." 212–236 in his *Reason and Emotion: Essays on Ancient Moral Psychology and Moral Theory*. Princeton: Princeton University Press.

Crisp, R. trans. 2000. *Aristotle: Nicomachean Ethics*. Cambridge: Cambridge University Press.

Haybron, Daniel M. 2008. *The Pursuit of Unhappiness: The Elusive Psychology of Well-Being*. Oxford: Oxford University Press.

Irwin, T. H. 1980. "The Metaphysical and Psychological Basis of Aristotle's Ethics." 35–53 in A. Rorty, ed. *Essays on Aristotle's Ethics*. Berkeley: University of California Press.

Kraut, R. 1989. *Aristotle on the Human Good*. Princeton: Princeton University Press.

Lawrence, G. 2006. "Human Good and Human Function." 37–75 in R. Kraut ed. *The Blackwell Guide to Aristotle's Nicomachean Ethics*. Malden, MA: Blackwell.

Lear, G. R. 2004. *Happy Lives and the Highest Good*. Princeton: Princeton University Press.

Reeve, C. D. C. 1992. *Practices of Reason*. Oxford: Oxford University Press.

2006. "Aristotle on the Virtues of Thought." 198–217 in R. Kraut ed. *The Blackwell Guide to Aristotle's Nicomachean Ethics*. Malden, MA: Blackwell.

2012a. *Action, Contemplation, and Happiness: An Essay on Aristotle*. Cambridge, MA: Harvard University Press.

2012b. "Aristotle's Philosophical Method." 150–170 in C. Shields ed. *The Oxford Handbook of Aristotle*. Oxford: Oxford University Press.

Roche, T. 1988. "On the Alleged Metaphysical Foundation of Aristotle's Ethics." *Ancient Philosophy* 8: 49–62.

Scott, D. 1999. "Aristotle on Well-Being and Intellectual Contemplation: Primary and Secondary *Eudaimonia*." *Proceedings of the Aristotelian Society*, suppl. 73: 225–242.

Wilkes, K. 1978. "The Good Man and the Good for Man in Aristotle's Ethics." *Mind* 87: 553–571. Reprinted 341–357 in A. Rorty ed. *Essays on Aristotle's Ethics*. Berkeley: University of California Press, 1980.

3   Happiness and the External Goods

At the end of the function argument of *NE* i 7, Aristotle offers an initial description of his view of the human good or happiness (*eudaimonia*). He tells us that

> the human good turns out to be activity of the soul in accordance with virtue, and if there are several virtues, in accordance with the best and most complete. Again, this must be over a complete life. For one swallow does not make a summer, nor does one day. Neither does one day or a short time make someone blessed and happy.[1] (1098a16–20)

Immediately after presenting these statements, Aristotle says: "So let this serve as an outline of the good, since perhaps we have first to make a rough sketch, and then fill it in later" (1098a20–22). The main points of this rough sketch are that *eudaimonia* involves activity in accordance with virtue, and it involves a complete life.[2] With respect to the first point, Aristotle will later distinguish between virtues of character and

---

[1] I mostly follow the translation in Crisp 2000. When I occasionally depart from this translation, I call attention to the modification in the notes.

[2] There is a long-standing debate about the meaning of the final phrase of the sentence at 1098a16–18, "and if there are several virtues, in accordance with the best and most complete." Some interpreters hold that Aristotle introduces the phrase "the best and most complete virtue" in order to offer a description that is only later (in book 10) revealed to be uniquely satisfied by theoretical wisdom (σοφία); some also argue that in book 10 Aristotle identifies the complete or perfect happiness with activity in accordance with σοφία alone (e.g., Kraut 1989, 239–242; Kenny 1992, 18). Other interpreters deny the first claim (e.g., Ackrill 1974, 352), and some deny the second (e.g., Whiting 1986; Roche 1988 and 2013). However, it is clear that in *NE* i 8–13, the chapters immediately following the initial account of happiness and including those with which we are primarily concerned, Aristotle works with a conception of happiness that does not exclude activities in accordance with the virtues of character but takes activity in accordance with those virtues to be a component of happiness, or even its primary component. Moreover, since I am concerned with the role of external goods in Aristotle's account of happiness, and since both the perfect and the secondary forms of happiness require those goods (cf. x 8.1178a23–1179a13 and i 8.1099a31–b8), there is no need to enter into the debate about the implication of the final phrase of the sentence at a16–18. I will therefore suppose Aristotle to have said simply that the human good is activity in accordance with virtue.

virtues of thought (*NE* i 13). Virtues of character include such dispositions as temperance, courage, generosity, and justice, which are studied
in some detail in books 2–5. Virtues of thought, demarcated in *NE* vi,
include, especially, wisdom (σοφία) and practical wisdom (φρόνησις).[3] It is
also argued, in *NE* x 7–8, that the activities flowing from these virtues are
primary components of *eudaimonia*. Thus, many of the inquiries that
follow *NE* i 7 carry out the project of "filling in" its rough sketch of
eudaimonia.

The investigations of the different virtues and their activities, however, are not the only investigations relevant for working out the details
of the account of *eudaimonia*. *NE* i 8–12 clearly also assign a role in the
happy life to goods other than the virtues. Thus, at the end of i 10,
Aristotle appears to arrive at a revised statement of his earlier sketch of
eudaimonia:

What is to prevent us, then, from concluding that the happy person is the one who,
adequately furnished with external goods, engages in activities in accordance
with complete virtue, not for just any period of time but over a complete life?[4]
(1101a14–16)

It is important, then, to examine the discussions in the *NE* that have
some bearing on the issue of how these "external goods" contribute to
human happiness. Aristotle also considers in i 10 the question of whether
it is ever appropriate to call someone happy while he is still living. For a
person who seems now to be happy may subsequently suffer the deprivation of many important external goods. One may then wonder whether
the term "happy" ever really did apply to him. An examination of this
question may help us understand Aristotle's view of the manner of, and
extent to which, the external goods contribute to a person's *eudaimonia*.
It may also help us understand what Aristotle means by saying that
eudaimonia involves a complete life. We begin with Aristotle's method
of argument in *NE* i 8–12, the sorts of goods he classifies as external goods,
and the main disagreements of interpreters of his view of the relation
between the external goods and happiness.

---

[3] Crisp 2000 translates σοφία as "wisdom," but one should note that Aristotle's account
and use of the expression in the *NE* reveals that he employs it to refer to a type of
wisdom concerned exclusively with theoretical, as opposed to practical, matters
(cf. *NE* vi and *NE* x 7–8).

[4] Cooper 1985, 173–174, takes this passage to indicate that Aristotle revised his i 7
account of *eudaimonia* in such a way that "adequately furnished with external
goods" has become a requirement embedded within that account, that is, a requirement
in addition to "activity of soul in accordance with virtue over a complete life." The
external goods thus turn out to be "actual constituents of *eudaimonia*" (174). See, too,
Nussbaum 1986, 330. Brown 2005, 58, 61–62, denies that external goods are constituents of *eudaimonia*. See Section III for an objection to Brown's interpretation.

I

At the beginning of i 8, Aristotle checks his outline account of *eudaimonia* against the received views on the subject. His methodology here, and throughout many of his works, begins with a consideration of the reputable beliefs (ἔνδοξα) about a particular philosophical question. The reputable beliefs include those "accepted by everyone or by the majority or by the wise" (*Top.* 100b21–22). An example of the procedure deployed with respect to the beliefs of the "wise" is evident in Aristotle's frequent practice of beginning a discussion with a review of the opinions of his philosophical predecessors.[5] Examples of the procedure in which the beliefs of everyone or the majority of people are invoked are scattered throughout the corpus.[6] Aristotle sometimes simply relies on these beliefs as further support for his position on a particular issue. But often he argues that some or all of these opinions need to be revised in some way because, as expressed, they are clearly false, or they create philosophical puzzles (ἀπορίαι) that must be solved if we are to avoid embracing absurd positions. However, although Aristotle frequently takes received views to be mistaken, he believes they are probably not utterly mistaken. They typically represent some portion of the truth regarding the issue at hand. Consequently, he also thinks it is valuable to compare the results of his arguments with the reputable beliefs – presumably because we can then be assured of the fact that we have not strayed too far from the mass of opinions that, taken together, likely depict some part of the truth.[7]

Thus, at the beginning of i 8 (1098b12–20) Aristotle tells us that the first principle he has formulated (i.e., the sketch of *eudaimonia* given at i 7.1098a16–20) must now be considered in the light of the things that people say about happiness. He begins with the received view that all goods belong to one of three classes: goods of the soul, goods of the body, and the external goods (τὰ ἐκτὸς ἀγαθά). Goods of the soul include excellent states of intellect or character, such as the virtues, and positive feelings or affections, such as pleasure. External goods comprise things that are "good" but that lie outside of a person's mind, feelings, character, and

---

5 See *Phys.* i; *Meta.* i 3–10, ii 1; *De An.* i; *Pol.* i 1–8; *NE* i 4–6, 8, vii 1–3 (esp. 1145b2–7).
6 In the *NE*, see, e.g., 1095a18–25 and b19–23 (for beliefs of the many) and 1129a6–9, 1146a6–7, and 1155a5–6 (for what everyone believes).
7 See *Meta.* ii 1. Still, Aristotle rejects both opinions of the many and opinions of the wise whenever he takes them to conflict with views that can be supported by sound arguments (see, e.g., *NE* i 4–6, vii 2–3, x 2–3). It will be important to keep this point in mind when we consider the question of whether Aristotle accepts the common view that dead people may be happy (or unhappy). See Section V.

body.[8] Goods of this sort include such things as wealth, friends, political power, noble birth, good children, and honor (cf. 1099a31–b8, 1100a18–21, 1123b17–22, and *Rh.* i 5–6). Goods of the body are those desirable qualities that pertain to one's physical condition (health, strength) and appearance (good looks). While Aristotle here divides goods into these three types, he is not especially interested in the distinction between goods of the body and external goods, for his main point is that his account of *eudaimonia* is consistent with the received view that goods of the soul are superior to any other type of good.[9] It is not surprising, then, that when he later discusses how the deprivation of external goods diminishes or destroys our happiness, he mentions the lack of good looks – a good elsewhere classified as a good of the body (*Rh.* i 5.1360b22) – along with other goods more strictly "external" (1099a31–b8).[10] It therefore seems appropriate henceforth to take both goods of the body and Aristotle's narrow class of strictly external goods together as one group of goods distinct from the goods of the soul. I will use the expression "external goods" here to refer to this group of goods.

Most interpreters agree that Aristotle holds that a human life can be regarded as happy only if it has an adequate supply of external goods. It is useful to compare a Stoic conception of happiness with Aristotle's in this regard. The Stoics notoriously claimed that living in accordance with virtue was sufficient for *eudaimonia*. As long as an agent retains virtue, she cannot be dislodged from happiness. Even were the person to encounter what most people regard as great misfortune, such as poverty, dishonor, intense physical pain, and even the deaths of all of a person's children and friends, the person's virtue ensures that the term "happy" continues to apply to her. The Stoics go so far as to deny that the things Aristotle calls "external goods" are really *ever* goods at all, reserving that expression for what they take to be the conditions that constitute *eudaimonia*, namely, the virtues. Wealth, honor, political power, friends, and children all belong in their category of "preferred indifferents." Although the two interpretations of Aristotle I am about to discuss seem to be in agreement in distinguishing Aristotle from the Stoics, one

---

[8] My use of scare quotes here is intended to alert the reader to the fact that Aristotle believes that the external "goods" are not, in fact, good in every circumstance or for every individual. See Section II.

[9] The distinction between types of goods drawn in the *Eudemian Ethics* is more in line with Aristotle's interest here in highlighting goods of the soul over all other types of goods. There he offers a bipartite distinction between goods in the soul and goods outside of the soul, using ἐκτός to refer to a broad class of goods, including any lying outside of the soul (*EE* 1218b32–36). For a more detailed discussion of Aristotle's use of the expression τὰ ἐκτὸς ἀγαθά throughout the corpus, see Cooper 1985, 176–178.

[10] See also *NE* x 8.1178a34–35 where health of the body is mentioned in connection with our need for "external prosperity" (a33) and with "external goods" (1179a2).

interpretation (the "E" interpretation) understands Aristotle's position in a way that brings it considerably closer to the Stoic position than the other one (the "I" interpretation).[11] Let us review the main lines of these interpretations.

Some scholars hold that Aristotle takes the relation between happiness and the external goods to be one of *inclusion* – the external goods, or at least some of them, are components of happiness along with activities in accordance with virtue.[12] Let us call this the "I" interpretation, and its proponents, "I-interpreters." Other scholars deny that Aristotle takes any external good to be included in happiness; they claim that happiness is constituted *solely* by activity in accordance with virtue.[13] Since this interpretation *excludes* external goods from the constituents of happiness, let us refer to it as the "E" interpretation, and its proponents as "E-interpreters." I-interpreters hold that external goods, for Aristotle, make a direct, as well as indirect, contribution to *eudaimonia*.[14] External goods, according to this view, not only supply means to, or conditions for, the exercise of the virtues, but their possession may help one to realize or increase *eudaimonia* in its own right. Moreover, their

[11] Annas 1999, 43–46, refers to a "proto-Stoic" interpretation and a "Peripatetic" interpretation of the relation between external goods and *eudaimonia*. These views correspond roughly to what I am calling the E interpretation and the I interpretation. However, later I wonder whether the E interpretation is better understood as a flat-out Stoic interpretation instead of a proto-Stoic one.

[12] Ackrill 1974; Irwin 1985 and 2007; Nussbaum 1986; Annas 1993 and 1999; and Broadie and Rowe 2002 seem to prefer the I interpretation over the E interpretation (though Annas believes that Aristotle's position, so interpreted, turns out to be incoherent). Cooper 1985 seems to accept the I interpretation insofar as he takes Aristotle to hold that external goods are constituents of *eudaimonia*. However, unlike other I interpreters, he holds that the external goods promote *eudaimonia* only *indirectly* by contributing to its main element, activity in accordance with virtue. See note 14 for additional comments on this position.

[13] Kraut 1989; Kenny 1992; Brown 2005; and Cooper 2004 accept the E interpretation; Cooper 2004, esp. 286 thus appears to have reformulated the earlier position advanced in Cooper 1985.

[14] Cooper 1985 holds that although external goods are included "as actual constituents of *eudaimonia*" (174), they promote *eudaimonia* not in their own right but only insofar as they provide means, contexts, or opportunities for activities in accordance with virtue (cf. 180 ff.). This view distinguishes Cooper from E-interpreters (or most of them) insofar as it accepts the idea that for Aristotle external goods are *constituents* of *eudaimonia*; it aligns him with E-interpreters insofar as it takes Aristotle to hold that external goods make only an *indirect* contribution to *eudaimonia*. I suspect that Cooper 1985 thinks that the manner in which external goods enter into *eudaimonia* explains why they make only an indirect contribution to it. I surmise that he believes that insofar as virtuous activities always involve the use or pursuit of external goods, they may be regarded as constituents of *eudaimonia*. Nonetheless, the contribution of these goods to happiness lies entirely in the role they play in supporting virtuous activities. Hence, they do not make a direct contribution to *eudaimonia*. Only virtuous activities do that.

absence may diminish a person's *eudaimonia* or entirely deprive him of it, and this is so even apart from any role such goods may play in promoting or realizing activities in accordance with virtue. E-interpreters universally deny these claims and assert that the presence of external goods in a person's life makes only an *indirect* contribution to that person's *eudaimonia*, through either (i) providing the agent with means toward, or objects for, activities in accordance with virtue (e.g., as wealth may be used for acts of generosity or as friends serve as objects or recipients of generosity), or (ii) providing the agent with opportunities to expand the range of excellent activities (e.g., as good looks may afford a person extensive opportunities to exercise temperance, or as good children may contribute to one's social prestige, which, in turn, leads to political office where virtues are exercised on a grand scale), or (iii) providing the agent with resources to maintain attitudes needed for (a) the acquisition of the virtues or (b) the steady exercise of virtues one possesses.[15]

Why have scholars reached such different conclusions about Aristotle's view of the relation between the external goods and *eudaimonia*? One reason is that in his sketch of the human good at the end of the function argument (1098a16–20, quoted earlier) Aristotle seems to *equate* happiness with just one type of good, namely, activity in accordance with virtue. E-interpreters have inferred that Aristotle cannot then believe that external goods are components of happiness. Another reason E-interpreters give is the passage i 8.1098b12–20 in which Aristotle seems to say that *eudaimonia* includes only goods of the soul and not external goods or goods of the body.

I-interpreters have not been persuaded by such arguments. They reject the claim that Aristotle in i 7 strictly equates happiness with activity in accordance with virtue. They contend that this text is meant to specify only the primary, central, or most authoritative, component of happiness, not to equate happiness with activity in accordance with virtue alone.[16] In favor of this reading, recall that Aristotle describes his initial

---

[15] Despite some differences in their accounts, Cooper 1985, 179–184, and Kenny 1992, 38–42, seem to think that i and ii adequately explain the contribution external goods make to *eudaimonia*. Kraut 1989, 253–260, and Brown 2005, 68–75, argue that iii b is an additional way in which external goods contribute to *eudaimonia*. Cashen 2012, 12–16, maintains that Aristotle also takes external goods to contribute to *eudaimonia* in the manner described in iii a.

[16] Thus, Broadie argues that Aristotle's frequent descriptions of happiness in terms of activity in accordance with virtue are to be explained by his use of synecdoche, the figure of speech in which an expression for a part of something is used to refer to the whole of it (Broadie and Rowe 2002, 278 at 1098a18 and 292 at 1102a3–4). I argue shortly that Broadie's suggestion is confirmed by remarks Aristotle makes in the *NE* and elsewhere.

account of *eudaimonia* as an "outline" or "rough sketch" and promises to present further details as the argument proceeds. Later, in i 10 he arrives at a more fully worked-out description of the happy person (quoted earlier), and it is one in which that person is said to be "adequately furnished with external goods" (1101a14–16).

In response to the second argument that Aristotle equates *eudaimonia* exclusively with goods of the soul, an I-interpreter insists again that we must take Aristotle to mean only that goods of the soul are what *eudaimonia* consists in primarily, or in the strict sense, not that the supreme good for human beings consists in nothing but the exercise of good psychic states. Such a view of happiness seems at odds with Aristotle's suggestion that human nature is complex and includes desires for a variety of things, such as friends, honor, a good family, and the avoidance of great physical pain (cf. 1154b21–22, 1169b16–20, 1095b30–1096a2, 1096b16–19, 1097b2–11, 1123b17–1124a15, 1153b1–25).

While I believe I-interpreters are correct in thinking that at least some external goods make an intrinsic contribution to a person's happiness, I believe that a crucial qualification to this position is required. The qualification is this: an external good, for Aristotle, can directly promote a person's happiness only if that person is a virtuous person and therefore pursues and uses external goods in an excellent manner. The condition for the possibility of an external good's contributing directly to happiness is that it is possessed by an agent who reliably acts in accordance with virtue.[17] E-interpreters might think that this claim makes my view coincide with theirs, but I do not think that it does. For I do not think that, for Aristotle, activity in accordance with virtue (over a complete life) is the only thing that makes a *direct* contribution to a person's *eudaimonia*. But it appears that a consistent E interpretation is committed to ascribing this position to Aristotle.

II

I now present some evidence for thinking that Aristotle does not equate *eudaimonia* with virtuous activity alone but believes that external goods also directly promote human happiness. Moreover, I defend the view that an external good may promote a person's happiness only if that person is a virtuous person.

---

[17]   I allow that in this circumstance possession of an external good may *directly* promote, sustain, or increase a person's happiness, but such a good may *also* provide means to, or enhanced opportunities for, virtuous activity. However, those are ways in which the good contributes *indirectly* to the agent's *eudaimonia*. I-interpreters may agree with me on this, but since they do not all seem to take a clear stand on this issue, it is important to state and defend the point in an entirely explicit way.

When Aristotle subsequently alludes to his *NE* i 7 account of happiness, he does not always merely repeat the claim that happiness is activity of the soul in accordance with virtue. Sometimes he uses language that indicates that his conception of happiness is more complex than his first "rough sketch" of it. In *NE* i 10, Aristotle rejects the idea that a person's happiness or unhappiness is determined, *merely*, by his good or bad fortune.

(A) They are not what doing well or badly depend on, though, as we said, human life must have them in addition. What really *controls* (κύριαι) happiness are activities in accordance with virtue, and what controls its contrary, are the contrary activities.[18] (1100b8–11)

To say that activity in accordance with virtue *controls* happiness falls short of saying that happiness consists in nothing but virtuous activity.[19] This point is supported by Aristotle's use of comparative forms of the term κύριος (e.g., at 1094a26, 1098b14–15, 1168b30, b31–32, 1178a34–b3; *GC* 335b34, and *PA* 640b28). Control is often a matter of degree: x may control y, or *be* y in a certain sense, but not fully or absolutely. If Aristotle really believes that virtuous activity and happiness are the same, his use of the expression κύριος to express this idea has to be singularly inept. Continuous repetition of the claim that happiness is identical to virtuous activity might be somewhat tedious, but under the present assumption it would at least express Aristotle's actual position. On the E interpretation, it is hard to see how Aristotle's insertion of "controls" between virtuous activity and happiness should not be looked on as an egregious muddying of the water. Moreover, if Aristotle believes, as E-interpreters allege, that happiness consists in activity in accordance with virtue alone, then it is difficult to understand why he never says explicitly that virtuous activity is sufficient (αὐτάρκης) for happiness.[20]

---

[18] Here and elsewhere I insert letters and sometimes numbers to make it easier to refer to passages. In A, I depart slightly from the Crisp 2000 translation of κύριαι. Crisp translates the term as "really matters" while I prefer "controls."

[19] Alternative translations might be "activity in accordance with virtue is what happiness is *in the strict sense*," or "virtuous activity is the *authoritative* element in happiness." But even if we prefer one of these translations, to say that x is y in the *strict sense*, or is the *authoritative* element in y clearly indicates that x is not the *only* component of y (see, e.g., 1168b28–34 where Aristotle maintains that intellect is the most authoritative element in a person without implying that a person is nothing but his intellect). The ruling body in a city is the most authoritative (or controlling) element in it without being the only constituent of a city. When he says in 1157a30–31, "Friendship in the primary (πρώτως) and strict sense (κυρίως) will be the friendship of good people in so far as they are good," he does not mean that this is the *only* form of friendship.

[20] It might be thought that I attribute an odd view to the E-interpreter here since it is obvious that external goods are needed for happiness and are presupposed by virtuous activities. But the fact of the matter is that E-interpreters do say that for Aristotle virtuous activity is sufficient for happiness. See, e.g., Kenny 1992, 14, 28–29, 35, 39,

Evidence of what Aristotle does mean by saying that virtuous activity is the controlling element in happiness may be found in *NE* i 2. Here he points out that knowledge of the highest good is the concern of the most controlling (κυριωτάτης) science, the highest master (ἀρχιτεκτονικῆς) science, political science (1094a26–28). Political science *uses* (χρωμένης) the other sciences in order to achieve its aim of attaining and preserving the highest good for the city (cf. *Pol.* 1252a1–7). Therefore, one way for something to be controlling or authoritative over other things is to *use* those other things to achieve its aims. In *NE* iv 1 Aristotle writes:

> Things that have a use can be used both well and badly. Riches are among the things that can be used; and each thing is used best by the person with the relevant virtue. Riches, therefore, will be used best by the person who has the virtue concerned with them, and this is the generous person. (1120a4–8)

Not just wealth but external goods generally admit of being used either well or badly (1099a31–b2). If virtue and virtuous activity control the use of the external goods, the ends pursued are guaranteed to be noble ones. Aristotle's position is clarified in the *Politics*:

> We say, and we have given this definition in our ethical works ... that happiness is a complete activation or use of virtue, and not a conditional use but an unqualified one. ... Just actions that aim at honors and prosperity are unqualifiedly noblest ... [for] ... they are preparatory to, and productive of, goods. To be sure, a virtuous man will deal with poverty, disease, and other sorts of bad luck in a noble way. *But blessedness requires their opposites. For according to the definition established in our ethical works, a virtuous man is the sort whose virtue makes unqualifiedly good things good for him.* Clearly, then, his *use* of them must also be unqualifiedly good and noble. That is why people think *the external goods* are the causes of happiness. Yet we might as well hold that a lyre is the cause of fine and brilliant lyre playing, and not the performer's craft. (*Pol.* 1332a7–27; emphases added)

The unqualifiedly good things to which Aristotle refers in line 23 are, or include, the external goods (cf. *EE* 1249a7–17, 1248b26–37, 1238a17–18, *NE* 1148a23–b4, 1124a26–31, 1129b1–6). When these are possessed and used by the virtuous person, they really are *good* for that person and *contribute to his happiness*. Their being good for a person depends upon their being controlled by virtue. *Merely possessing* external goods cannot cause a person to be happy any more than the mere possession of a lyre is

---

40–41; Cooper 2004, 286, 296, 304, 306; Kraut 1989, 9, 198, 259, 265; Brown 2005, 57. However, as far as I can tell, *Aristotle* never says that virtuous activity is sufficient for happiness. E-interpreters appear unmoved by this fact. They insist that, for Aristotle, when the necessary conditions or objects for virtuous activity are supplied, then that activity alone suffices for happiness. But I find Aristotle's failure to affirm this position explicitly to be further evidence that he does not hold it.

all that is required for fine and brilliant lyre playing. The following passage adds further support to this interpretation.

What is just is found among people who have a share of things that are good without qualification, and whose share can be excessive or deficient. No share can be excessive for some – for example, I suppose, the gods – *and for others – those who are incurably vicious* (τοῖς ἀνιάτως κακοῖς) – *none of them is beneficial, but they are all harmful*; there are yet others for whom they are beneficial up to a point. (*NE* 1137a26–30, emphasis added; Cf. *MM* 1183b27–1184a4)

Vicious people are actually harmed by their possession and use of external goods because they employ those goods in the performance of vicious acts. But for virtuous persons, the external goods are "beneficial up to a point." They are "beneficial up to a point" because while living well requires external goods, there is a limit to their enhancing a person's life and being put to good use (cf. *NE* x 8.1178b33–1179a5, ix 10; *Pol.* i 9, vii 1.1323a40–b6). Tremendous wealth, for example, may require spending more time in actions aimed at protecting and employing it than is consistent with being optimally engaged in a range of virtuous activities. Moreover, as Aristotle indicates in the following passage, nonvirtuous (but perhaps not yet entirely vicious) persons are drawn toward vice when they acquire an excess of the external goods.

People who have the advantages of fortune, but lack virtue (ἄνευ ἀρετῆς), cannot justly claim to be worthy of great things, nor are they rightly called great-souled; these are impossible without total virtue. But when they possess the advantages of fortune they become supercilious and wantonly violent, since in the absence of virtue it is not easy to carry such goods gracefully.[21] (1124a26–31)

A nonvirtuous person may incorrectly judge that the possession of external goods, all on its own, can produce happiness. However, the virtuous person judges correctly and reliably what is and is not good for him. Since the nonvirtuous person lacks practical wisdom, he may not use the external goods in a consistently correct manner; his possession of those goods may even lead him to become haughty and hubristic.[22]

---

[21] Note that the goods of fortune are identical to, or at least overlap with, the external goods. This is confirmed by several passages in the *NE* (e.g., 1099a31–b7, 1124a12–31, 1153b17–25) and is explained by a remark made in the *Politics*: "The goods external to the soul come by chance and by luck, whereas no one is just or temperate from or on account of luck" (1323b27–29). One might complain that Aristotle counts friends as external goods, but friends – at least those who enjoy the complete form of friendship – do not come and go merely by chance. This is true, but it is also true that whether a person's friends continue to live is *never* entirely under her control or her friends' control. Even here, one cannot escape the reach of fortune.

[22] Does Aristotle think that a nonvirtuous, but not yet vicious, person derives no benefit at all from good fortune, or does he merely think that good fortune cannot help to

And separated from virtue, no quantity of external goods can help an agent realize happiness.[23]

Aristotle's doctrine that the good person is the standard (κανών) and measure (μέτρον) of what is good and what is bad can be related to his view that the external goods are genuinely valuable only when possessed by the good person (see, e.g., 1113a22–33, 1166a12–16, 1176a15–24). He frequently defends the measure doctrine with an analogy to healthy and sick bodies. He tells us that

things that are truly healthy are healthy for bodies that are in good condition, while for those that are diseased other things are healthy; and the same goes for things that are bitter, sweet, hot, heavy, and so on. The good person judges each case rightly, and in each case the truth is manifest to him. (1113a26–31; cf. Plato, *Gorgias* 504e–505b)

External goods are good for a good person, and the good person rightly judges them to be so. However, while the external goods "are always good without qualification," they are not always good "for a particular person" (1129b2–4). Aristotle claims that "people pray for and pursue these things, but they should not; rather, they should pray that those goods that are good without qualification may also be good for them, and they should choose things that are good for them" (1129b4–6). People should pray that they become good persons, for only then can the external goods contribute to their happiness.

We have now seen some evidence that virtuous activity, for Aristotle, is not the sole component of happiness. It is, rather, the element that controls happiness by ensuring the proper use of external goods, goods that contribute directly to happiness only when so used. A passage in *NE* i 10, reveals additional information about Aristotle's

realize *happiness* for such a person? The passage just quoted speaks of those who "lack virtue," and if we suppose that this expression does not refer again to the "incurably vicious" for whom the external goods were said to be positively harmful, then Aristotle's position is striking. He would seem to believe that even merely incontinent and self-controlled persons will be tempted to engage in bad actions if they possess an abundance of external goods.

23 Aristotle appears to have been influenced by Plato's discussions of how the value (or disvalue) of external goods is dependent upon their use. See, e.g., *Euthydemus* 279a–281e; *Gorgias* 504e–505b; *Laws* 660e–661d. Those discussions, however, do not present a consistent position. In the *Euthydemus*, Socrates ends up saying that the only true good is wisdom and denies that the external "goods" are, in themselves, any good at all (281d2–e5). But this is not the position defended in the other dialogues. In the *Laws*, for example, the Athenian says in reference to external goods and evils: "Although 'evils' are in fact evil for the just, they are good for the unjust; and 'goods,' while genuinely good for the good, are evils for the wicked" (661d1–3). On my interpretation, Aristotle accepts the view expressed in the *Laws* but rejects the one expressed in the *Euthydemus*.

view of the relation between virtuous activities and happiness, and his view of the relation between happiness and the external goods:

(B) (1) If activities control life (κύριαι τῆς ζωῆς), as we have said no one blessed (τῶν μακαρίων) could become wretched (ἄθλιος) since (2) he will never do hateful and petty actions. For (3) the truly good and wise person, we believe, bears all the fortunes of life with dignity and always does the noblest thing in the circumstances, as a good general does the most strategically appropriate thing with the army at his disposal, and a shoemaker makes the noblest shoe out of the leather he is given, and so on with the other practitioners of skills. (4) If this is so, (a) the happy person (ὁ εὐδαίμον) could never become wretched, though (b) he will not be blessed (μακάριος) if he meets with luck like that of Priam. (5) Nor indeed will he be unstable and changeable. He will not be shifted easily from happiness (εὐδαιμονίας), and not by ordinary misfortunes, but by many grave ones. (6) He would not recover from these to become happy again in a short space of time. (7) If he does recover, it will be after a long and complete period of great and noble accomplishments.[24] (1100b33–1101a13)

In B1 Aristotle asserts that no one who is blessed can ever become wretched. There is ample evidence that by "wretched" Aristotle means the contrary of "happiness" (e.g., 1100a29, b6, 1101a7, 1102b7). This claim, together with B2–4, indicates two things. First, it suggests that Aristotle is using "the blessed person" (τὸ μακάριον) interchangeably with "the happy person" (ὁ εὐδαίμον). For Aristotle supports B1 with B2, B2 with B3, and then reasserts his initial claim in B4a but now uses "happy person" in place of "blessed person" (only to switch back to "blessed person" again in B4b!). The argument makes sense only if the terms are being used synonymously.[25] Second, B1–4 implies that Aristotle believes that no happy person who continues to engage in activities in accordance with virtue will become unhappy, though he may well lose his happiness (as B4–7 clearly imply).[26] Hence, Aristotle recognizes a middle position between happiness and unhappiness. One might cease to be happy, but that does not imply that one has descended into unhappiness. One may be neither happy nor unhappy. Presumably, this is the condition of the person who continues to live engaged in activities in accordance with virtue despite having suffered great

---

[24] Crisp 2000 translates the first part of B1 as follows: "If activities are, as we have said, what *really matter* in life ..."

[25] The main significance of my remarks about Aristotle's use of these expressions will become clear when we consider his discussion of Solon's view of happiness in Section IV.

[26] This is certainly at odds with a modern and common understanding of the relation between virtue and happiness for we do not suppose that persons living in accordance with virtue are incapable of unhappiness. It is also at odds with many of the received views with which Aristotle was familiar.

misfortune. Certainly, B2, B4a, and B4b together seem to imply that this is Aristotle's position.[27]

The reason given in B2–3 for why the happy person will not fall into unhappiness is that such a person will not engage in "hateful and petty actions," that is, vicious actions. This is so because the happy person has put activity in accordance with virtue in "control" of his life. As Aristotle reveals in B5, the fixed disposition to engage in such activity is the stable element in a life that, in other respects, is subject to changes arising from good or bad fortune. While grave misfortunes can indeed dislodge the happy person from his happiness, such a person cannot be shifted so far from happiness that he comes to possess its contrary, unhappiness. And perhaps this is a further implication of what Aristotle means by saying that activities in accordance with virtue control happiness: any change away from happiness is so constrained by noble activities that it can never proceed as far as the extreme limit of such change, namely, the *contrary* of happiness – wretchedness.

Perhaps an E-interpreter might object that it has not been conclusively demonstrated that Aristotle holds that external goods make a *direct* contribution to happiness. She might continue to insist that such goods contribute to the happiness of the virtuous agent only indirectly, for example, because their possession helps to eliminate psychological impediments to a robust engagement in virtuous activity. For such an interpreter might argue that even if it is granted that external goods cannot contribute to any happiness of a vicious person (since the vicious are incapable of happiness), it has not been shown that for Aristotle happiness *consists in* anything more than virtuous activity. In response, I consider several passages in *NE* i 8–10 that along with claims made in passage B show that for Aristotle external goods do indeed make a direct, as well as an indirect, contribution to a person's happiness.[28]

III

At the conclusion of i 8, Aristotle writes:

(C) (1) It [happiness] obviously needs the presence of external goods in addition (προσδεομένη), since (2) it is (a) impossible, or (b) at least no easy matter, to perform noble actions without resources. For (3) in many actions we employ, as if they

---

[27] Aspasius interprets Aristotle precisely in this way (see *in Ethica Nicomachea, CAG* xix 30.5–12). So too Arius Didymus (see Stobaeus, *Eclogae* II, 133.6–11, 133.19–134.1).

[28] Here I adopt a strategy employed by Irwin 1985, 95ff. Irwin argues, convincingly, that when we carefully compare these passages, each of them appears to make the same distinction between two different ways in which external goods contribute to our happiness. External goods promote human happiness indirectly by providing support for virtuous activity, but they also contribute to our happiness in a direct way.

were instruments at our disposal (καθάπερ δι᾿ ὀργάνων), friends, wealth, and political power. Again, (4) being deprived of some things – such as high birth, noble children, beauty – spoils our blessedness (τὸ μακάριον). For (5) the person who is terribly ugly, of low birth, or solitary and childless is not really the sort to be happy (εὐδαιμονικός), (6) still less perhaps if he has children or friends who are thoroughly bad, or good but dead. As we have said, then, (7) there seems to be an additional need for some sort of prosperity like this. (8) For this reason, some identify happiness (τῇ εὐδαιμονίᾳ) with good fortune (εὐτυχίᾳ), while others identify it with virtue.[29] (1099a31–b8)

Again, Aristotle clearly uses the term εὐδαιμονία (happiness) interchangeably with the term τὸ μακάριον (blessedness).[30] Εὐδαιμονία must be understood in C1 since it is the only term used in the immediately preceding line that could possibly be understood there. In C4 Aristotle continues his argument for the claim in C1 that happiness needs external goods. But if blessedness is not here synonymous with happiness, then it is unclear how C4 might be used to support C1. In C5 and C8 Aristotle continues to talk about happiness without any hint that he has strayed from that subject with his reference to blessedness in C4. So it seems quite unlikely that Aristotle here takes the meaning of εὐδαιμονία to differ from that of τὸ μακάριον.

What does passage C imply about the relation between happiness and the external goods? In C1 Aristotle tells us that happiness requires external goods "in addition," and this surely means that happiness cannot exist for someone unless that person possesses external goods in addition to being disposed to engage in activities in accordance with virtue. In C2 Aristotle offers reasons for C1, namely that (a) it is not possible to engage in such activities without external goods. or (b) it is difficult to engage in such activities without external goods.[31] In C3 Aristotle offers a reason for C2, or perhaps just C2a: we require means for the performance of

[29] In C, I depart from Crisp's translation only for lines 1099a31–32. Here and elsewhere I prefer the translation of προσδέομαι as "need in addition" to Crisp's "need as well."

[30] The term τὸ μακάριον can convey the idea of a supreme happiness, a thoroughgoing blissfulness akin to what the gods enjoy. However, the occurrences of εὐδαιμονία and τὸ μακάριον in NE i 8–12 must be used similarly. If not, many of Aristotle's arguments become impossible to understand. Brown 2005, esp. 63–75, argues that τὸ μακάριον in C4 does not have the same meaning as εὐδαιμονία and that the line is meant to support an inference to C2, not C1. (See, too, Cashen 2012, 14–16.) I believe this interpretation is indefensible. See further Sections III and IV for reasons in favor of my reading of Aristotle's use of these terms.

[31] Aristotle says that "noble actions" (τὰ καλὰ πράττειν) are impossible or not easy "without resources" (ἀχορήγητον). But his notion of the noble is intimately connected with his notion of virtuous or correct action (see, e.g., 1115b12, 1116a28, 1117b9, 1119a18, 1120a12, 1122b6; cf. Rh. i 9.1366a33–36). Moreover, Aristotle uses the expression "resources" (χορηγία), as a way of referring to some external goods (see, e.g., 1178a23–b9, 1178b33–1179a3, 1179a9–13).

activities in accordance with virtue, and external goods often provide us with such means. Why Aristotle accepts C2b as a reason for C1 is not immediately clear. Why would one be deprived of happiness if one could engage in activities in accordance with virtue but only with difficulty? Perhaps Aristotle's close association of pleasure with happiness helps to explain this idea. He agrees with the received view that a happy life is a pleasant one (1154a1–2; cf. 1098b22–25, 1099a7–25).

What is more, for Aristotle, pleasure is an unimpeded activity of a natural state (1153a12–15), or that which supervenes upon, or completes, the unimpeded activity of a state in good condition (1174b31–1175a1). He connects pleasure and happiness with the possession of external goods in the following passage:

And this is why everyone thinks that the happy life is pleasant and weaves pleasure into happiness – reasonably enough, since no activity is complete when it is impeded (ἐμποδιζομένη), and happiness is something complete. The happy person therefore needs bodily goods, external goods, and good fortune, so that he will not be impeded in these respects. (1153b14–19)

The argument seems to be this: since a happy life must be a pleasant one, and since impeded activities are unpleasant, the virtuous person, if he is to be happy, must have sufficient external goods to ensure that his activities, or most of them, and the most important of them, are not impeded. The passage does not imply that the *only* reason external goods are needed for happiness is that their possession prevents impediments to our activities (or our taking pleasure in those activities).[32] But it appears to be one reason supporting Aristotle's view.

But what of C4? Is Aristotle also suggesting that the happy person needs the external goods mentioned in it (and in C6) because they *indirectly* contribute to his happiness by supporting the performance of unimpeded acts in accordance with virtue? The grammatical structure of the passage might be taken to support this reading.[33] For if both C3 and C4 are offered as reasons for C2, which, in turn, is presented as a reason for C1, then Aristotle is arguing that external goods contribute to happiness solely by providing instruments for, or necessary conditions for, engaging in activities in accordance with virtue. But a more plausible reading is that

[32] Contra Cooper 1985. See my further discussion in note 34.

[33] Brown 2005, 64–65, argues that the μὲν ... δέ (on the one hand ... on the other hand) construction appearing in C3–4 (but not apparent in Crisp's translation) suggests that both C3 and C4 are offered in support of C2. I agree that this is a plausible reading of the text if we consider only the grammatical point. But the other considerations I present suggest a different view of the passage. Moreover, Aristotle might have both C1 and C2 in mind as one complex claim and then offers to support that claim with C3 "on the one hand" and C4 "on the other." This reading would make the grammar of the passage cohere with the interpretation I defend.

C3 and C4 are offering different accounts of how external goods contribute to happiness, and not merely providing lists of different goods, all of which contribute to happiness in exactly the same way, namely, by enabling virtuous activity. It appears that both C5 and C6 are asserted in order to support C4, but C6 contains another reference to friends; since we have already been told in C3 that friends may be used as instruments for the performance of acts in accord with virtue, Aristotle would simply be repeating himself if C4 is reaffirming that friends (along with the other external goods mentioned) are instrumentally useful. Of course, even if this point is accepted, the passage does not show that the goods mentioned in C4–6 – high birth, good children, good friends, and good looks – make a direct contribution to happiness. Recall that on the E interpretation, external goods provide *either* (i) instrumental means (or objects) for the performance of virtuous acts *or* (ii) advantageous conditions for the performance of such acts *or* (iii) freedom from the psychological pain that might interfere with our ability to engage in such acts. So, even if an E-interpreter would agree that in C4–6 Aristotle is not merely repeating his claim that external goods provide us with instruments or objects for virtuous activities, she might say that he could suppose that possession of such goods will contribute to our happiness in the ways described in ii or iii. In that case, the possession of external goods still would not make any direct or intrinsic contribution to our happiness.

It is not clear, however, that ii provides a credible interpretation of Aristotle's reasoning. Option ii does not have any direct support from *NE* i 8–12: Aristotle does not say that besides supplying us with means (or objects) for virtuous activity, external goods provide us with normal contexts or expanded opportunities for activity in accord with virtue.[34] Moreover, it is arguable that reading him in such a way saddles him with an "outrageous" and "ludicrously contrived" position.[35]

[34] Cooper 1985 bases his interpretation on a passage from *NE* vii 13.1153b14–19, some passages of the *Politics*, and evidence drawn from Aristotle's ancient commentators (see esp. 181–196). These passages are insufficient to show that Aristotle's *only* reason for believing that external goods are needed for happiness is that they promote, or prevent impediments to, our activities in accordance with virtue. Aristotle's aim in *NE* vii 13 is to rebut the argument that pleasure is not a good, not to give a general theory of how the possession of external goods contributes to human happiness. Note that immediately following the passage at 1153b14–19 he adds: "People who claim that the person being tortured, or the person who has fallen on very bad times, is happy if he is good are, whether voluntarily or involuntarily, talking nonsense" (1153b19–21). The example of being tortured goes beyond the point that lack of external goods is an *impediment to virtuous activity*. Clearly his point here is that the pain we endure while being broken on the wheel is *itself* incompatible with living happily.

[35] Annas 1993, 380, thinks the interpretation is outrageous because "we feel that sterility is in itself frustrating, if one wants children; and we especially feel that losing children is a terrible thing in itself, and not just because it deprives us of the chance to help our

Option iii fares no better. On this interpretation, lacking or losing external goods such as children, honor, or friends will cause psychological distress that interferes with our ability to engage in, or even develop the capacity for, virtuous activity (see Kraut 1989, 256–260; Brown 2005, 72–73, 77, and 79; and Cashen 2012, 12–16). Neither the distress itself nor the deprivation of these goods is supposed to be a direct cause of the loss or diminishment of happiness; rather, the idea is that the person feels the loss of such goods deeply and this resulting psychological condition interferes with his ability to engage in noble activities.

But this does not seem to be the best way to interpret Aristotle. Proponents of the view never show Aristotle claiming that although no external good is a constituent of a person's happiness, the morally virtuous and practically wise person would be so disturbed by the loss of his children or friends, his shocking disfigurement, or his deprivation of honor that his will to engage in his most cherished activities would be significantly impeded. Aristotle tells us that his virtuous agent has his feelings "at the right time, about the right things, towards the right people, for the right end, and in the right way" (1106b21–22). If the virtuous agent feels anguish at the loss of external goods, it seems plausible to think this is because he believes that the loss has caused a diminishment of his happiness; distress at the loss of objects that are not parts of his happiness suggests that the agent's feelings are *not* "about the right things."[36] Moreover, as we have seen, Aristotle in B3 maintains that the good or virtuous person "always does the noblest thing in the

children on their careers and to look after grandchildren." Botros 1987, 113, thinks the view is ludicrously contrived because it implies that Aristotle believes "good looks are necessary to virtue because if we are ugly we shall lack lovers and so won't have the opportunity of virtuously resisting temptation!" The goods in question pertain to our social nature, and therefore, are not desirable only because they are means to the exercise of the virtues. Human happiness depends upon feeling and acting in ways that are expressive of human nature. Lack of honor, friends, good appearance, and the like have a direct impact on a person's well-being.

36 Brown 2005, 72–76, maintains that the loss of such external goods causes psychological pain, which, in turn, impedes virtuous activity. But he does not explain the source of this pain or how its intensity is compatible with his view that these goods are not regarded by the virtuous person as parts of her happiness. Kraut 1989, 257, maintains that what grounds the pain we feel at the deaths of our children and friends is that "we have an interest in their well-being compatible in depth to our self-love." But Kraut takes this interest to be somehow separate from our interest in our own happiness. When we consider our own happiness, he says, we view our children and friends as "resources for the achievement of fine acts; but since we are also concerned with their happiness, we do not view them merely as resources." But I do not think this position is consistent with the evidence. Aristotle frequently discusses our desire for friends and children, and when he does so in contexts where our own happiness is at issue, he often offers reasons for our interest other than the one cited by Kraut. These include, for example, the fact that life is not worth living without friends (1155a5–6),

circumstances," yet ill fortune deprives him of happiness. A passage we consider in a moment reinforces the point here – the loss of happiness does not necessarily entail the cessation or reduction of virtuous activity.

Although Cashen is also a proponent of option iii, he argues that Aristotle here also takes the external goods to be important because they are needed to prevent the psychological pain that would interfere with the cultivation and development of the virtues. His idea is that the loss or absence of important external goods, such as adequate financial resources, loved ones, and freedom, will have a devastating effect upon a person's moral development. But while I do not think Aristotle would disagree with this point, there is no evidence to support the view that he is thinking along these lines in passage C, or in other parts of NE i 8–12. In fact, I believe that he is probably not thinking along these lines in C and positively cannot be thinking along these lines in B or in another crucially important text that we will consider shortly.[37] First, it is not in the least clear that Aristotle has moral development in mind in C. On the contrary, he discusses the need for resources for performing noble actions (C2b), such as wealth and political power (C3). But his point is best understood if we take him to be referring to a mature person who already has a virtuous character and is eligible for political office, not a child or young man who has yet to acquire the virtues. His references to a person being deprived of children (C4–5) reinforces this point. Passage B simply cannot be understood in the manner proposed by Cashen. For there Aristotle is considering a person who is already blessed or happy (B1, B4a, B6), is a "truly good and wise person" (B3), and is "shifted from" happiness through suffering grave misfortunes (B5). So, again, Aristotle is not considering persons endeavoring to acquire virtue and happiness, as Cashen must have it, but already virtuous persons who suffer the loss of happiness. So much then for option iii. Passage C can, and I think should, be read in a way that provides support for the I interpretation.

Let us now compare C with other passages in NE i. Aristotle indicates that his discussion preceding NE i 9 provokes a question about how happiness is acquired. If virtue is the central component of happiness,

solitude suits the blessed least of all (1157b20–22), and we assign all good things to the happy person (1169b8–10); the reason Aristotle gives most frequently to explain our desire for family and friends is that we are by nature social animals (1097b6–11, 1161b12–1162a29, 1169b16–20). See, too, Irwin 2007, 150, who argues that Kraut's interpretation conflicts with Aristotle's view of happiness as a self-sufficient end and an end for the sake of which we do all that we do.

[37] This is the passage I label "E." In E Aristotle is clearly thinking of persons who attain happiness but then lose it through suffering great misfortune. He tells us that even in the midst of disaster, "what is noble shines through," indicating that the example he is using is of a person who has already attained nobility (i.e., virtue), not a person whose psychological condition prevents him from cultivating virtue in the first place.

one might think that the acquisition of happiness requires our own efforts in some sort of practice or training; if happiness consists entirely in good fortune (εὐτυχία), then it is something beyond our control. Aristotle first seems to concede that since happiness is the best thing for human beings, it *is* reasonable to think that it is somehow transmitted to us by the gods. But although he agrees that happiness is one of the most divine things (1099b16), he believes it is plausible to suppose that it arises mainly through the exercise of virtue and, therefore, is due to our own individual efforts. He contends that it would be better if happiness is attained through our efforts since then it would be more widely shared than if it arose entirely through chance; it is quite inappropriate for luck to explain why any human being is in possession of the greatest good (1099b21–25).

Aristotle next appeals to his outline account of happiness in order to flesh out his answer to the question of how happiness is acquired.

(D) (1) We said it [happiness] was a certain kind of activity of the soul in accordance with virtue; and (2) of the other goods, some are (a) necessary (ἀναγκαῖον) [to happiness][38] and others are (b) naturally helpful and serve as useful means to it (συνεργὰ καὶ χρήσιμα πέφυκεν ὀργανικῶς). (1099b26–28)

D1 refers us back to Aristotle's account of happiness in i 7: happiness, or its primary component, is activity in accordance with virtue. Since virtue, according to Aristotle, arises either through some kind of teaching and learning (1099b9, 1103a14–16) or through habituation (1103a17), the acquisition of happiness involves our own voluntary efforts. However, Aristotle in D2 refers to "the other goods," and these seem to be the external goods that come to us largely through chance. Whether or not a person is well supplied with external goods is beyond her control. But the principal component of happiness does not depend on chance, and therefore it is the stable component of human happiness (1100b2–17).

What does Aristotle mean by distinguishing D2a, goods necessary for happiness, from D2b, goods that are helpful and useful as means to happiness? Since much of his discussion has pointed out that happiness involves both activities in accordance with virtue and external goods, it seems likely that the goods mentioned in both D2a and D2b are the external goods. He seems to intend no definite distinction between those goods that are helpful and those that are means to happiness in D2b. What of the other category of external goods mentioned in D2a, those that are necessary to happiness? E-interpreters generally suppose that Aristotle is referring to goods that are necessary conditions of

[38]   Crisp 2000 translates the Greek in D2a as "necessary conditions of happiness." For reasons that will become clear, I think this is a questionable translation. I prefer the translation in Broadie and Rowe 2002, 105.

happiness, where happiness is construed narrowly as activity in accordance with virtue; moreover, these interpreters point out that such goods obviously are not included in happiness so understood (e.g., Kraut 1989, 253–255). But on this interpretation, what could be included in this class of goods that is not already included in the class of goods that are means to virtuous activity? Wealth, political power, and so on may be necessary conditions, but they are also *means* to virtuous acts. Moreover, an examination of the uses of the expression ἀναγκαῖον and its variants in the *NE* reveals that none appear to require the translation "necessary condition," while most clearly do demand a translation of "necessary [to]" or "must."[39]

An E-interpreter could alternatively suggest that the goods necessary to happiness in D2a are not a certain group of external goods, but the virtues themselves. This is a possible reading, but not, I think, the most plausible one. The discussion in i 9 leading up to passage D is about how happiness is acquired. In passage C concluding i 8, Aristotle says that in addition to virtuous activity, happiness requires the presence of external goods. So it seems natural to suppose that the "goods" distinguished from virtuous activity and said to be necessary to happiness in D2a are external goods. Aristotle could not suppose that a reader would straightaway understand that the reference to "goods" in D2 is to the individual virtues, for he has not so far committed himself to a plurality of virtues.[40]

If we read passage D in the way that I am suggesting, it makes the same distinction found in C between two contributions that external goods make to happiness, "necessary" components of happiness and instrumental means to happiness. For if D2a refers to external goods as *necessary* constituents of happiness, then the deprivation of these things would eliminate one's happiness. Another passage, from *NE* i 10, seems to express the very same distinction between the ways in which external goods contribute to happiness.

(E) Many things, however, both large and small, happen by chance. Small pieces of good fortune or its contrary clearly do not affect the balance of life. But (1) many great events, if they are good, will make a life more blessed (μακαριώτερον) since (a) they will themselves naturally embellish it (συνεπικοσμεῖν) and (b) the way a person

---

[39] See, e.g., 1103b29, 1105a5, 1109b33, 1120b1, 1122b10, 1124b26, 1128b4, 1144a1, 1153b9, 1155a28–30, 1164b9, 1180a18–20. In *EE* i 2 Aristotle does make the point that it is important to distinguish between the necessary conditions of happiness and its parts. But the expression Aristotle uses for "necessary conditions" is *not* ἀναγκαῖα. It is ὧν ἄνευ οὐχ οἷόν, literally, "things without which it is not possible [for happiness] to be" (see esp. 1214b26–27).

[40] In i 7.1098a17–18 he tells us that *if there are several virtues*, then happiness will involve activity of soul in accordance with the best and most complete of these. The other use of "virtues" occurs at i 6.1096a25 in Aristotle's criticism of Plato.

uses them (χρῆσις αὐτῶν) can be noble and good. But (2) if they turn out the other way, they will oppress and spoil what is blessed since they (a) bring distress (λύπας) with them and (b) hinder (ἐμποδίζει) many activities. Nevertheless, even in their midst what is noble shines through, when a person calmly bears many great misfortunes, not through insensibility, but by being well-bred and great-souled. (1100b22–33)

Aristotle maintains that happiness may be increased or diminished by major incidents of good or bad fortune. As I understand him, great good fortune may increase one's happiness in two different ways (as described in E1a and E1b). It may "embellish" or "add ornament to" one's life (as stated in E1a), making it happier not (or not merely) by supplying one with instruments, opportunities, or conditions that help in the perform-ance of noble activities (which is the import of E1b), but by making life better, more attractive, more pleasant, as befits a person of excellent character (cf. 1099b20–25, iv 2, 1127a2, 1128a19, 1178a13).[41] When Aristotle turns in E2 to explain the effect of great ill fortune on a person's life, he mentions again two distinct ways in which such bad luck may diminish or destroy one's happiness. E2a and E2b roughly parallel E1a and E1b, except that the opposite effects of ill fortune are being described. Major unfortunate events bring distress or pain, which itself degrades or spoils happiness; or such events, by depriving us of external goods, hinder activities in accordance with virtue, which again diminishes or erases happiness.

E-interpreters resist this sort of interpretation and claim that Aristotle is giving us not two ways in which good or bad fortune affects happiness but only one. Kraut (1989, 258–260) argues that E1a is not describing a way in which happiness is increased independently of E1b; rather, E1a is only a *cause* of E1b. The suggestion is that good fortune makes a person shine in the eyes of others, and this increased social prominence provides that person with enhanced opportunities for engaging in activities in accordance with virtue. Against this interpretation, Aristotle does not mention the alleged causal connections between E1a and E1b. And Aristotle suggests that even in the midst of extreme bad fortune, the virtuous agent's nobility and goodness continue to shine. Immediately prior to passage E, he indicates that despite reversals of fortune, the

[41] Cf. 1098b22–26, 1099a7–b8; vii 13–14; *Pol.* viii 5.1339b17–19. At 1124a1–2 Aristotle says: "Greatness of soul, then, seems to be a sort of *embellishment* (κόσμος) of the virtues, because it makes them greater and does not occur in isolation from them." (Crisp translates κόσμος as "crown.") This is an important passage because Aristotle explains his use of the metaphor of "embellishment," and this is relevant to the interpretation of E1a. If an embellishment of X makes X greater, and if great good fortune embellishes a happy life, then the goods of fortune must themselves make a happy life happier.

virtuous person "will spend all, or most, of his time *engaged in action* and contemplation in accordance with virtue" (1100b19–20, emphasis added). This contradicts the claim that the pain caused by ill fortune must cause an extensive diminishment of virtuous activity.

Thus, it appears that C3, D2b, and E1b refer to external goods as means to actions in accord with virtue, while C4–6, D2a, and E1a refer to external goods as direct contributors to happiness, as components of it. If this is so, there is reason to favor the I interpretation over the E interpretation.[42]

IV

In *NE* i 9 Aristotle also points out that his account of happiness explains why we do not call any of the nonhuman animals or children happy. Since activity in accordance with virtue is the primary component of happiness, incapacity for this activity precludes happiness. Happiness requires complete virtue and a complete life (1100a4–5). The discussion of children suggests what Aristotle means by "complete virtue." Happiness requires habituation, reflection, and experience culminating in the acquisition of practical wisdom and all of the moral virtues (cf. *NE* vi 13). "Complete virtue" is this full realization of virtue. That happiness requires a "complete life" presumably does not mean that happiness must be possessed continuously up to a ripe old age. We have already seen (in B5–7) that such a view is inconsistent with Aristotle's belief that a person can possess happiness during some but not all stages of her life. Happiness can be ascribed to persons who have attained maturity and have lived for some significant (but not precisely determinable) period of time engaged in activities that express practical wisdom and moral virtue.

---

[42] Another line of argument against the E interpretation is that it abolishes any fundamental distinction between Stoic and Aristotelian conceptions of happiness. However, we know that the Stoics and Peripatetics carried on a vigorous debate about the nature of happiness, so if the E interpretation were correct, it would be very difficult to make much sense out of that debate. It is not possible to go further into the details of this issue here, but a passage in Alexander may illuminate the point. Recall that the "preferred indifferents" include those things that the Peripatetics refer to as "external goods"; Alexander refers to the Stoics with the expression, "the later philosophers."

> Thus it would be shown that each of the things called preferred indifferents by the later philosophers is choiceworthy and good. For each of them being added to virtue makes the whole more choiceworthy for the good person. For life in accordance with virtue is more choiceworthy if it is conjoined with health, and abundance, and good reputation; for choiceworthy things and things to be shunned are judged by the choice and avoidance of the good person. (Alexander of Aphrodisias, *in Aristotelis Topica, CAG* ii 2.211.9–14)

But while complete virtue and a complete life are necessary for happiness, Aristotle reminds us, again, that more is required:

For there are many vicissitudes in life, all sorts of chance things happen, and even the most successful can meet with great misfortunes in old age, as the story goes of Priam in Trojan times. No one calls someone happy who meets with misfortunes like these and comes to a wretched end (τὸν δὲ τοιαύταις χρησάμενον τύχαις καὶ τελευτήσαντα ἄθλιος οὐδεὶς εὐδαιμονίζει). (1100a5–9)

Homer depicts Priam as having been a pious and virtuous monarch, loved by the gods. Yet his final days are terrible. He sees his many sons killed in battle, his city sacked and burned, the women of his family led into captivity, and then he is killed. Priam's fate brings home the point that happiness for any human, even a mighty king, is vulnerable to chance and ill fortune.[43]

NE i 10, in light of Priam's fate, asks whether we should call anyone happy while still alive, or should we wait to see how the life turns out, as Solon advises (see the account of Solon's meeting with Croesus in Herodotus, *Histories* i 29–33). Even if we agree with Solon, a further question arises, namely, whether we thereby commit ourselves to saying that a person is happy (or unhappy) when he is dead. Aristotle immediately asks whether an affirmative answer to this question would be "ridiculous, especially for us, claiming as we do that happiness is some kind of activity?" (1100a13–14). Aristotle proposes that we understand Solon's advice to mean only that once a person dies, we can now look at her life from its beginning to its end, and then decide whether the person, *during that earlier stretch of time*, can rightly be called happy.

But the discussion is made more complicated by the point that both evil and good are "thought to happen to a dead person, since they can happen to a person who is alive but not aware of them" (1100a18–20). Such unrecognized good and evil things include the good and bad fortunes of descendants. So the happiness or unhappiness of the dead might be thought to change along with the changing fortunes of their descendants.

(F) It would indeed be odd if (1) the dead person also were to share in these vicissitudes and be sometimes happy, sometimes wretched. But it would also be odd if (2) the fortunes of descendants had no effect on their ancestors for any time at all. (1100a27–30)

---

[43] Suppose that Priam survived the sack of Troy and that Aristotle regarded him as a virtuous person. Suppose too that Priam lived on for a short while in another city where he continued to engage in virtuous activity. On the interpretation defended here, Aristotle would claim that Priam was deprived of happiness through the loss of important external goods and not because he was no longer capable of exercising the virtues.

Aristotle takes F2 to be odd because it conflicts with the received view that a person's life may be evaluated in terms of the destinies of her descendants. He also believes that Solon's advice to wait to see how a person's life turns out before declaring it happy implies that (α) we are unable to assert that a person is happy during the (only) periods of time in which she actually does appear to be happy. However, he maintains that (β) we believe that happiness is something (relatively) permanent and not easily changeable (1100b2–3). β can be seen to explain why Aristotle takes F1 to be odd. If a person's changing fortunes determine, at every moment, whether or not she is happy, "we should often call the same person happy and then wretched, representing the happy person as a kind of chameleon, or as having an unsound foundation" (1100b5–7). This is inconsistent with our conception of happiness as a relatively permanent condition.

(G) (1) What prevents us, then, from concluding that the happy person (εὐδαίμονα) is the one who, adequately furnished with external goods, engages in activities in accordance with complete virtue, not for just any period of time but over a complete life? Or (2) should we add that he will live like this in the future and die accordingly? (3) The future is obscure to us, and we say that happiness (εὐδαιμονίαν) is an end and altogether quite complete. This being so (4) we shall call blessed (μακαρίους) those of the living who have and will continue to have the things mentioned, but blessed only in human terms. (1101a14–21)

I noted earlier that in G1 Aristotle may be filling out his i 7 sketch of *eudaimonia* by including external goods within it (see text with note 4). As we have seen, this claim is very much in dispute. The rest of the passage (G2–4) is also in dispute. G2 seems to ask, again, whether Solon's dictum is correct: must we consider the whole of a person's life in order to judge whether it can be called "happy"? One might think that it would be strange if Aristotle now agreed with Solon's position. For his emphasis on the relative permanence of happiness, because happiness is primarily virtuous activity, tells against a Solonian view of happiness. Moreover, Aristotle denies that ill fortune on its own can make a person unhappy, but this seems to be a position he ascribes to Solon. And passage B makes it clear that Aristotle thinks one might lose and then regain happiness, but this view may conflict with Solon's position, for Solon might require a consistently happy life.[44] But G3–4

---

[44] In Herodotus the examples Solon gives of happy lives, those of Tellus, Cleobis, and Biton, involve no major misfortunes and all end gloriously. Moreover, when Solon wraps up his view of the happy person, he describes him as "he who continues (διατελέῃ) in the possession of the greatest advantages and at last makes a gracious end of his life" (*Histories* i 32).

seems to concede that given the requirement that happiness is something complete, a person can be called happy only if she has that property continuously up until the time of her death.

Some scholars have despaired of finding any plausible interpretation of G that frees Aristotle of the charge of inconsistency and have therefore suggested that the passage is an interpolation (e.g., Gauthier 1970, ad 1101a16–21). But others suggest that Aristotle is proposing in G4 that we should now reserve the expression "blessed" for those who were happy throughout their mature lives, had lived out their days, and died in happiness. We should also continue to employ the term "happy," but only for living persons who continue to be vulnerable to misfortune (Broadie 1991, 287, and Kenny 1992, 34–36, defend this interpretation). This has Aristotle compromising with Solon. He refuses to agree with Solon that we should never call a person happy while alive, but he agrees we should "call no one *blessed* while alive." However, as I have pointed out, Aristotle uses the expressions "happiness" and "blessedness" interchangeably in i 10, so it is difficult to believe that at the conclusion of i 10 he would suddenly rely on a distinction in meaning between these terms. Moreover, if we are to believe that in G4 Aristotle has decided to assign different meanings to the expressions μακαρία and εὐδαιμονία, then we should not expect him to continue using the terms interchangeably. However, he does continue to use them interchangeably and does so quite frequently.[45] What is more, his later uses of the expression μακάριος are not confined to persons who have died, but such a use is prohibited by his putative decision to employ the term only of persons who are beyond the reach of ill fortune.[46]

I think we must defend an interpretation of the phrase "continue to have the things mentioned" (in G4) that does not require certainty of the person's continued good fortune for calling the person "blessed." Aristotle emphasizes the fact that happiness is not liable to change because of the stability and permanency of its primary component, virtuous activity. We should, therefore, be justified in applying the term "happy" to a person engaged in virtuous activity over a substantial portion of his life and not presently suffering, or clearly headed for, grave misfortune. Aristotle claims that although a child is not strictly capable of happiness, we still call him happy or blessed "on account of the potential he has" (1100a3–4). He does not insist that we abandon this way of speaking. Our reasonable expectation of the child's future

[45]   See, e.g., 1101b4–5, b24–25, b26–27; 1169b3–5, b17, b19, b22, b24, b29, b31; 1170a2, a4, a8; 1176a27, a31; 1177b14, b23, b24, b26; 1178b7, b9, b22–24, b26, b28; 1179a1–3.
[46]   See, e.g., 1169b3–5 and 1177b24.

justifies our continued application of the term "happy," and this should apply in G4 even more to adults. Unless it is clear that a virtuous person is, or will be, suffering grave misfortune, there is no reason to cease calling him happy. Finally, in G4 Aristotle says, "we shall call blessed those *of the living* (τῶν ζώντων) who have and will continue to have the things mentioned" (1101a19–20, emphasis added). His resolve to refer to the *living* as blessed surely indicates that here he has not compromised with Solon.[47]

V

In *NE* i 11, Aristotle returns to the common opinion that the fortunes of descendants and friends have some effect upon the dead. Lack of awareness may not be decisive for good and bad things also happen to living persons unaware of those events. So he upholds his conviction that the dead should not be regarded as happy or unhappy while salvaging as much of the common view as he can. Clearly some misfortunes have a greater, others a lesser, influence, and whether they occur while the person is alive or not seems to matter.

(H) (1) If anything good or bad does actually affect [the dead], it will be pretty unimportant and insignificant, either in itself or in relation to them; or (2) if not, it must at least be of such an extent and kind as not to make happy those who are not happy already nor deprive those who are happy of their being blessed. So (3) when friends do well, and likewise when they do badly, it does seem to have some effect on the dead. But (4) it is of such a nature and degree as neither to make not happy those who are happy, nor anything like that.

H1 is supported by the contrast between the impact on a theatrical audience of actions that happened before the beginning of the play and those performed during the play. In H2, Aristotle suggests that even if we allow that significantly good or bad things affect the dead, the effect should not alter our judgments about their happiness or unhappiness. His use of the present tense in H2 and H4 ("neither to make not happy those who *are* happy") might suggest that he accepts that some of the

---

[47] In the *EE*, Aristotle agrees with Solon that one ought not call a person happy while he is still living (1219b6–8). I believe that in the *NE*, Aristotle's deeper reflection on the issue causes him to provide a more nuanced response to Solon. In particular, the paradoxical implication that arises when we combine Aristotle's account of happiness with Solon's prohibition against calling anyone happy while he is alive (namely, that we must not call a person happy at the only time at which he actually is happy), moves Aristotle to the more complex position. *Contra* Kenny 1992, here at least we find that the *NE* exhibits more rather than less philosophical sophistication than the *EE*.

dead *are* happy and some are not.[48] But Aristotle nowhere suggests that persons survive the destruction of their bodies, have postmortem feelings or desires, or engage in postmortem incorporeal activities.

The best way to understand H is as follows. In H2 he should be taken to mean that a deceased person who was rightly judged to have been happy during his life cannot now be rightly judged not to have been happy given what we now know about the misfortunes of his descendants. Aristotle is not conceding that the dead are happy or unhappy; he is denying that the fortunes or misfortunes of descendants might require us to alter our judgments about whether the dead person was happy or unhappy *while he was alive*. But Aristotle grants that such fortunes or misfortunes have some effect upon the *person* now deceased. Perhaps he simply holds that some posthumous events affect our evaluation of the person without having a bearing on their happiness (cf. Scott 2000, 219). If all his children die (of plague, say) almost immediately after a happy person's death, we are likely to feel that something bad has happened to the person despite being deceased. The project of raising a family that consumed a good portion of his life is utterly ruined by ill fortune. Yet that cannot imply that the person was not happy. So Aristotle rejects both F1 (the happiness or unhappiness of living persons alters along with good or bad posthumous events) and F2 (the fortunes of descendants have no effect at all on their ancestors). The effects that the good or ill fortune of descendants have upon their ancestors do not cause any change in their happiness or unhappiness.

VI

In *NE* i 12 Aristotle concludes his book 1 examination of happiness by considering whether happiness is a thing to be praised or honored. The question appears trivial but Aristotle seems to think that answering it will reveal some truths about happiness and its relation to other goods. He begins by arguing that things praised stand in a certain relation to (πρός τι) something else (1101b12–14). He illustrates: "The just person, the brave person, and the good person and virtue in general we praise for their actions and what they bring about" (1101b14–16). Praise properly applies to things productive of other good things, and those good things are even better than the things praised (cf. 1094a1–16, 1097a25–b6, ii 5–6). While justice, courage, practical wisdom, and such

---

[48] See Pritzl 1983, 108–111, whose argument for thinking that Aristotle allows for the happiness or unhappiness of the dead rests on giving too much weight to common opinion. See also Gooch 1983 and Scott 2000.

excellent states of the soul are great goods, the *activities* of these states are even greater goods. So "it is not praise that applies to the best things, but something greater and better" (1101b22–23). This is clear because we do not praise the gods and the most godlike people but call them blessed and happy (1101b23–25). The same point applies to goods: we do not praise the best goods, happiness and blessedness. Praise and censure are tools for encouraging persons to perform acts in accordance with virtue (and to acquire the virtues), and to commend those who have acquired virtue, but activity in accordance with virtue is the core constituent of happiness, and "happiness is something honorable and complete" (1101b35–1102a1).[49] Since happiness is a cause of goods, we take it to be something honorable and divine (1102a3–4). What does Aristotle mean by saying that happiness is "the cause of goods" (τὸ αἴτιον τῶν ἀγαθῶν)? He cannot mean that happiness *produces* all good things. His point rather is that if we consider *eudaimonia* in terms of its primary component, activity in accordance with virtue, then external goods, those things that are good without qualification (i.e., ideally, but not necessarily, good for a person) really do become goods for the happy person. Activity in accordance with virtue ensures the actual goodness of those "goods." For the virtuous person is the standard and measure of what is good (1113a22–33, 1166a12–13), has the proper attitude toward the external goods (1124a1–20), and always uses them rightly.[50]

WORKS CITED

Ackrill, John. 1974. "Aristotle on *Eudaimonia*." *Proceedings of the British Academy* 60: 339–359.
Alexander of Aphrodisias. 1891. *in Aristotelis Topica. Commentaria in Aristotelem Graeca* ii 2. M. Wallies ed. Berlin: Reimer.
Annas, Julia. 1993. *The Morality of Happiness.* Oxford: Oxford University Press.
    1999. "Aristotle on Virtue and Happiness." 35–55 in Nancy Sherman ed. *Aristotle's Ethics: Critical Essays.* Lanham, MD: Rowman and Littlefield.
Aspasius. 1889. *Aspasii in Ethica Nicomachea. Commentaria in Aristotelem Graeca* xix 1. G. Heylbut ed. Berlin: Reimer.

[49] The idea that virtue is the object of praise whereas honor is accorded to happiness appears to contradict Aristotle's later claim that honor is the prize of virtue (iv 3.1123b35). Perhaps we can explain the apparent inconsistency by the fact that in i 12 Aristotle is considering virtue abstractly and as a state that may or may not be exercised (as 1101b31–32 may suggest). However, in iv 3 he has in mind the great-souled and happy person's virtue, or virtue *as* exercised or active and accompanied by an ample supply of the goods of fortune. Since that sort of virtue is essentially identical to happiness itself, Aristotle may have been led to claim that it is honorable.

[50] See in addition to the passages of the *NE* cited in support of this interpretation, *EE* 1248b31–34, 1237a4–5, *Pol.* 1332a7–24, and esp. *MM* 1183b27–35 and 1183b39–1184a4.

Barnes, Jonathan ed. 1984. *The Complete Works of Aristotle*. The Revised Oxford Translation. Princeton: Princeton University Press.

Botros, Sophie. 1987. "Precarious Virtue." *Phronesis* 32: 101–131.

Broadie, Sarah. 1991. *Ethics with Aristotle*. Oxford: Oxford University Press.

Broadie, Sarah, and Christopher Rowe. 2002. *Aristotle. Nicomachean Ethics. Translation, Introduction, and Commentary*. Oxford: Oxford University Press.

Brown, Eric. 2005. "Wishing for Fortune, Choosing Activity: Aristotle on External Goods and Happiness." 57–81 in John J. Cleary and G. Gurtler, S. J. eds. *Proceedings of the Boston Area Colloquium in Ancient Philosophy*, vol. 21. Leiden: Brill.

Cashen, Matthew. 2012. "The Ugly, the Lonely, and the Lowly: Aristotle on Happiness and the External Goods." *History of Philosophy Quarterly* 29: 1–19.

Cooper, John M. 1975. *Reason and Human Good in Aristotle*. Cambridge, MA: Harvard University Press.

  1985. "Aristotle on the Goods of Fortune." *Philosophical Review* 94: 173–196.

  2004. "Plato and Aristotle on 'Finality' and '(Self-)Sufficiency.'" 270–308 in John M. Cooper ed. *Knowledge, Nature, and the Good: Essays on Ancient Philosophy*. Princeton: Princeton University Press.

Crisp, Roger trans. 2000. *Aristotle: Nicomachean Ethics*. Cambridge: Cambridge University Press.

Gauthier, R. A., and J. Y. Jolif. 1970. *Aristote, L'Éthique à Nicomaque – II,1*. 2nd ed. Louvain: Publications Universitaires.

Gooch, Paul W. 1983. "Aristotle and the Happy Dead." *Classical Philology* 78: 112–116.

Irwin, Terence. 1985. "Permanent Happiness: Aristotle and Solon." *Oxford Studies in Ancient Philosophy* 3: 89–124.

  1999. *Aristotle. Nicomachean Ethics*. 2nd ed. Indianapolis: Hackett.

  2007. *The Development of Ethics*. Oxford: Oxford University Press.

Kenny, Anthony. 1992. *Aristotle on the Perfect Life*. Oxford: Oxford University Press.

Kraut, Richard. 1989. *Aristotle on the Human Good*. Princeton: Princeton University Press.

Nussbaum, Martha. 1986. *The Fragility of Goodness: Luck and Ethics in Greek Tragedy and Philosophy*. Cambridge: Cambridge University Press.

Pritzl, Kurt. 1983. "Aristotle and Happiness after Death: *Nicomachean Ethics* 1.10–11." *Classical Philology* 78: 101–111.

Rassow, Hermann. 1874. *Forschungen über die Nikomachische Ethik des Aristoteles*. Weimar: Hermann Böhlau.

Roche, T. D. 1988. "The Perfect Happiness." 103–125 in T. D. Roche ed. *Southern Journal of Philosophy*. Supplementary Volume 27. *Aristotle's Ethics*.

  2009. "Commentary on Russell." 112–125 in John J. Cleary and Gary M. Gurtler, S. J. eds. *Proceedings of the Boston Area Colloquium in Ancient Philosophy*. Vol. 24. Leiden: Brill.

  2013. "The Private Moral Life of Aristotle's Philosopher: A Defense of a Non-intellectualist Interpretation of *Nicomachean Ethics* 10.7–8." Forthcoming in P. Destrée and M. Zingano eds. *Theoria: Studies in the Status and Meaning of Contemplation in Aristotle's Ethics*, a volume of the series Aristote. Traductions et Études. Leuven: Peeters.

Scott, Dominic. 2000. "Aristotle on Posthumous Fortune." *Oxford Studies in Ancient Philosophy* 18: 211–229.

Stewart, J. A. 1973. *Notes on the Nicomachean Ethics of Aristotle*. 2 vols. New York: Arno Press.

Stobaeus. 1884. *Eclogae* II. C. Wachsmuth ed. Berlin: Wiedmann.

Taylor, C. C. W. 2006. *Aristotle: Nicomachean Ethics Books II–IV*. Oxford: Clarendon Press.

Whiting, Jennifer. 1986. "Human Nature and Intellectualism in Aristotle." *Archiv für Geschichte der Philosophie* 68: 70–95.

4   Why Is Aristotle's Virtue of Character a Mean?

Taking Aristotle at His Word (*NE* ii 6)

Why, for Aristotle, is a virtue of character a mean, a *mesotēs* (or "between-state")? The usual answer is: because each virtue is *between* two vices, one an excess and one a deficiency. But this, while true, is not Aristotle's own most definitive answer – or so I shall argue here. Rather, a virtue is labeled a "between-state" because to possess a virtue is to be disposed to aim at and achieve what is *meson* or "in between" (in other words, just right) in one's actions and feelings. This is what Aristotle insists in the passage I scrutinize in Section I. A person's actions and feelings – or, in short, a person's responses – are "in between" when they avoid "too much" or "too little," that is, excess and defect, and so are just right for the given circumstances. The between-ness of a given virtue derives from the between-ness of the responses typical of a person possessing that virtue, not (primarily) from its lying between two vices, one of excess and one of deficiency (Section II). In Sections III–V, I examine (and reject) the reasons some critics have given for refusing to take Aristotle at his word, and for insisting that it is the between-ness of the virtuous disposition that is primary, rather than that of the responses typical of the possessor of virtue. Since to be "between" in the relevant sense is to be good or right (as Section I shows), the goodness or rightness of a virtue, the state or disposition, derives from that of the responses typical of that virtue – that is, from the right or appropriate feelings and actions typically manifested by, say, a brave or a temperate person. This has important implications for the question whether Aristotle agrees with some modern proponents of virtue ethics, in holding the thesis of the primacy of character. In Section VI, I argue that he does not.

To show all this, I take a close look at *NE* ii 6, the chapter in which Aristotle fulfills his promise to show *what sort of* state a virtue is. Earlier in *NE* ii he has shown that a virtue of character is a state or disposition (*hexis*), not a feeling or a capacity. And he has argued that to acquire a

Thanks to Ron Polansky for his helpful comments.

character virtue one must practice doing the corresponding acts, that it involves correct feelings as well as actions, and that it is intimately connected with pleasure and pain. But now, at the start of ii 6, he promises to show not just the genus – virtue is a state – but what kind of state it is (*poia hexis*). And by a few paragraphs later, two-thirds of the way through our chapter, he has established the key point, which I label K (or Key thesis):

(K) Virtue, then, is a *mesotēs*, insofar as it aims at and achieves[1] what is *meson*. (*NE* ii 6.1106b27–8)

Literally, a *mesotēs* is a "between-state"; and what is *meson* is what is "in between" in a sense I shall explain shortly. (As it will transpire, it is actions and feelings that are here labeled *meson*.) How should we translate these terms? Here are some English published versions.

(1) Virtue, then, is a kind of mean, at least in the sense that it is able to hit the mean. (Crisp)
(2) Virtue, then, is a mean, insofar as it aims at what is intermediate. (Irwin)
(3) Excellence, then, is a kind of intermediacy, insofar as it is effective at hitting upon what is intermediate. (Rowe)

The most commonly found version, (1), is unsatisfactory because it uses the same translation – "mean" – for the two different terms: *mesotēs*, what a virtue *is*, and *meson*, that which a virtue (or, rather, a person possessing a virtue) *aims at and achieves*. Critics have different views on how important the distinction is, and on whether Aristotle observes it consistently. But we should try to avoid using the same translation for the two terms.[2] Version (2) is an improvement in this respect, and it keeps the familiar term "mean" for the state that a virtue is. But it suffers from two drawbacks: by using the unrelated words "mean" and "intermediate," it hides the relationship that the Key thesis asserts; and the translation "intermediate" cannot convey the essentially evaluative force that belongs, as Aristotle makes clear, to the relevant kind of

---

[1] I follow Taylor in translating *stochastikē* in this way: the translation needs to capture both aspects.

[2] That is a fault I was guilty of in Brown 1997 where I used "mean" to translate both *meson* and *mesotēs*, though at some points I used "mean state" for *mesotēs*. I now regret not distinguishing them more consistently in that article. But I remain convinced that my 1997 explanation of what Aristotle does and does not intend by the two expressions "*meson* relative to us" and "*mesotēs* relative to us" is correct. In Section I of this chapter, I briefly resume my 1997 defense of the view that, in speaking of aiming at a *meson* "relative to us," Aristotle means by "us" human beings generally. Müller's (2004, n11) endorsement of this reading offers as explication "with regard to the kind of creature we are."

meson.[3] To be *meson*, as we shall see, is to be good or right, or more precisely: just right – neither too much nor too little. Version (3) is the most scrupulous, maintaining both the difference between *mesotēs* and *meson* and the link between them. But, like (2), its use of "intermediate" gives no hint of the positive evaluative force of *meson* and *mesotēs*, and it uses the unfamiliar – and rather ugly – term "intermediacy" to render *mesotēs*. I have come to the conclusion that, in English at any rate, it is not possible to find fully suitable translations of the two terms.[4]

What K conveys – as I shall argue – is that a character virtue is an in-between-and-so-just-right state (a *mesotēs*), insofar as it aims at and achieves what is in-between-and-just-right (what is *meson*) in feelings and actions. From now on I will leave the key terms untranslated. As well as giving a careful reading of the argument, I aim to show that we should take Aristotle at his word when he asserts the Key thesis.

I. THE PROOF THAT VIRTUE IS A MESOTĒS (NE II 6)

I first set out the opening two-thirds of the chapter, numbering the sentences or groups of sentences for ease of reference in my subsequent discussion.

(1) But we must say not just that virtue is a state, but what kind of state. We should mention, then, that every virtue causes that of which it is a virtue to be in a good state, and to perform its characteristic activity well. [Some examples are omitted.] If this is so in all cases, then, the virtue of a human being too will be the state that makes a human being good and makes him perform his characteristic activity well. (2) We've already said how this will happen, and it will be clear also from what follows, if we consider what the nature of virtue is like. (3) In everything continuous and divisible one can take more or less or an equal amount, and each either in respect of the thing itself or relative to us; and the equal is a sort of *meson* between excess and deficiency. (4) By the *meson* in respect of the thing itself I mean that which is equidistant from each of the extremes, this being one single thing and the same for all, and by the *meson* relative to us I mean that which is neither excessive nor deficient – and this is not one single thing, nor is it the same for all. (5) If, for example, ten are many and two are few, six is the *meson* if one takes it in respect of the thing, because it is by the same amount that it exceeds the one number and is exceeded by the other. This is the *meson* according to arithmetic proportion. (6) The *meson* relative to us, however, is not to be obtained in this way. For if ten pounds of food is a lot for someone to eat, and two pounds a little, the trainer will not necessarily prescribe six, for this may

---

[3] The French translation by Gauthier and Jolif captures the evaluative force with "le juste milieu," which does duty both for *meson* and, at many points, for *mesotēs*. However, in translating K, they use "une sorte de moyenne" for *mesotēs tis*.

[4] Another possibility would be to use "mean" only for *meson*, and "mean state" for *mesotēs*, despite the more usual use of "mean" for the state, *mesotēs*.

be a lot or a little for the person to eat – for Milo a little, for the beginner at gymnastics a lot. The same goes for running and wrestling. (7) In this way every expert in a science avoids excess and deficiency, and aims for the *meson* and chooses it – the *meson* not in the thing itself but relative to us. (8) If then every science does its job well in this way, with its eye on the *meson* and judging its products by this criterion (which explains both why people are inclined to say of successful products that nothing can be added to or taken away from them, implying that excess and deficiency ruin what is good in them while the *mesotēs* preserves it, and why those who are good at the skills have their eye on this, as we say, in turning out their products), and if virtue, like nature, is more precise and superior to any skill, it will also be the sort of thing that is able to hit the *meson*. (9) I'm talking here about virtue of character, since it is this that is concerned with feelings and actions, and it's in these we find excess, deficiency and the *meson*. (10) For example fear, confidence, appetite, anger, pity and in general pleasure and pain can be experienced too much or too little, and in both ways not well. (11) But to have them at the right time, about the right things, towards the right people, for the right end and in the right way is the *meson* and the best, and this is the business of virtue. (12) Similarly there is an excess, a deficiency and a *meson* in actions. (13) Virtue is concerned with feelings and actions, in which excess and deficiency constitute missing the mark, while the *meson* is praised and on target, both of which are characteristics of virtue. (14) Virtue then is a kind of *mesotēs*, at least in the sense that it is able to hit a *meson*. (1106a14–b28, Crisp trans., adapted)

So the proof starts by reminding us that virtue is a good state, and concludes that it is a *mesotēs*, since it is able to hit a *meson*. How are we to understand the argument for (14)?[5] And how does Aristotle explain the key terms, including that of a *meson* relative-to-us? On my reading, this part of the chapter rolls together in a somewhat confusing way a Chief Argument (from the nature of goodness in continua), a Subsidiary Argument (from skills), and an explanation of the key notion of a "*meson* relative to us."

What I label the Chief Argument comes mainly at (9)–(14), but important groundwork is laid in (2)–(6), with the distinction between two ways in which a continuum may have a more, a less, and an equal/*meson*. Aristotle sets aside one way (the arithmetic equal or "between") and focuses on the other, that which is between excess and deficiency, and so is neither *too* much nor *too* little (but, as we may add, just right). Aristotle explains this notion, which he labels "the *meson* relative to us" (6), and states that it is what skills achieve (7)–(8): this is the Subsidiary Argument. Though he has not yet said so explicitly, it is clear that what avoids too much and too little is *good* or *right*, and that in this second use *meson* carries essentially evaluative force. Aristotle

---

[5] Rapp 2006 has an excellent account; a key point is made at 114–115. My analysis owes a lot to his, though I differ in identifying a subsidiary argument as well as the chief one.

adds the qualification "relative to us" to show that he is invoking an evaluative way of being *meson* or "in-between," that is, the "just right" rather than the middle. As I argue in this chapter, the measure of "just-rightness" is human concerns generally.

The evaluative force, and the application to virtue, will be made clear in (9)–(14), but before completing the main argument he offers a subsidiary one, from expertise or skills (7–8). It comes immediately after Aristotle's contested and confusing explanation of his invented label "the *meson* relative to us." As we saw, this evaluative notion is distinguished from the irrelevant arithmetic *meson* or midpoint. It is what is neither excessive nor deficient – and this is not one single thing, nor is it the same for all. The verb used in (4) for "to be excessive" – *pleonazein* – makes it clear that to be excessive is bad, and to avoid it is good or just right.[6] To illustrate it, Aristotle chooses a trainer who is responsible for prescribing athletes' diets; he knows that ten pounds of food is too much and two too little for any athlete. Ignoring the arithmetic midpoint of six, the trainer selects what is neither too much nor too little but just right for each of the athletes in his charge, prescribing a hefty diet for Milo, the champion wrestler, and a modest one for a beginner. So the "*meson* relative to us" is what's best or right or appropriate in each set of circumstances and obviously will differ according to the circumstances; hence, it is not one and the same in all cases. And, claims Aristotle at (7), it is what every expert aims at. Continuing what I dubbed the argument from skill or expertise, he recalls the familiar terms of praise for a work of art or craft: "It's just right – anything more or less would ruin it" (8). And since virtue is superior to skill, it too must be *tou mesou stochastikē* – able to hit the *meson*.

What are we to make of this subsidiary argument? I think Aristotle would readily admit that it is an overstatement to claim that *every* expert aims at the "*meson* relative to us" (the "just right"). I believe he has in mind, in addition to craftsmen, chiefly those with the skills he mentioned before (*NE* ii 2.1104a7–10), such as medicine and navigation, where *judgment* is essential, and where no formula can be given to deliver an excellent result, and no rulebook consulted to get the "right" answer (Brown 1997, 88–89). Architecture and gymnastics are added to medicine and navigation in the equivalent passage in *Eudemian Ethics* (*EE* 1220b21–29). And why is virtue more precise and superior to any skill (8)? With Aquinas, I suggest that virtue is superior because it does

---

[6] The terminology of excess and defect (*huperbolē* and *elleipsis*) can be used both in a merely descriptive way and evaluatively, as (3) indicates. (Compare: "Mary's weight exceeds her sister's" with "Mary's weight is excessive.") Usually the context indicates which use is involved, but to make the evaluative use clear Aristotle changes to *pleonazein* at this point. Henceforth in ii 6 the terms *huperbolē* and *elleipsis* always have an evaluative force.

not matter what motivation a *skilled* person has in producing his excellent product, while someone manifesting *virtue* must have the right motivation as well as the relevant knowledge (*NE* ii 4).

Even if not meant to be conclusive, the subsidiary argument is helpful for two reasons. First, we note that *outcomes* (in his example, works of art) are described as produced by keeping an eye on the relative-to-us-*meson*; they are said to be just right. Likewise, at (11) human responses (actions and episodes of feeling) will be described as *meson* and best. Second, the remark that every skilled person aims at the "*meson* relative to us" confirms the interpretation of this phrase that I argued for in Brown 1997. By "us" Aristotle means human beings and human nature generally, not different individuals.[7] Like virtues, the skills he has in mind have a human dimension, and – this is the point – success in all of them is (at least in part) a matter of finding what is "just right" in a given set of circumstances. This, I think, is how we should understand the remarks about the trainer. In comparing the exercise of virtue to the trainer's skill by saying each of them aims at a *meson* relative to us, Aristotle is *not* suggesting that different possessors of virtue of character, just by being different persons, will find a different *meson* when responding with virtue. Clearly the trainer does not aim at a *meson* relative to himself; all trainers aim at the "*meson* relative to us," that is, the just right, where human concerns settle what is just right.[8] In exercising their skill, they will adjust their action to all aspects of the situation, including the recipients. Likewise, the responses of a possessor of virtue will be correct provided they are just right and appropriate, and neither too much nor too little, for the circumstances.[9]

---

[7]   ii 8.1109a12–16 could be cited in further support, as R. Polansky has pointed out in correspondence with me, since "we" there refers to human beings generally. Contrast ii 9 where Aristotle speaks of different tendencies of different individuals.

[8]   A clarification to avoid misunderstanding: when I argue that by "us" in the expression "relative to us," Aristotle means human beings generally, I do not mean to suggest that he regards ethics as a matter of universal principles, rather than as a matter of finding a response appropriate to the circumstances. My view is this: in the expression "relative to us," here as elsewhere, "we" are human beings generally. What it is for an ethical response or a work of art to be *meson* in the "relative to us" way is for it to avoid defect and excess and to be just right in the particular circumstances, where human concerns set the standard of "just-right"ness.

[9]   Gottlieb 2009, 25–30, countering Brown 1997, argues that a number of factors about the agent are relevant to what counts as a *meson* response and infers that in those respects the corresponding virtue is "agent-relative." She instances truthfulness (*NE* iv 7), which requires giving an accurate account of one's own abilities: "The virtue of truthfulness … will be relative to the abilities of the agent" (19). This is a somewhat attenuated sense of agent-relativity. And it does not counter the chief thesis I argued for in Brown 1997: in calling virtue a "*mesotēs* relative to us," Aristotle is not claiming that it is relative to the agent who possesses the virtue, as his explanation of the *meson* relative to us shows.

Now back to the Chief Argument, which he resumes at (9), putting to use the notion of the evaluative *meson* (the *meson*-relative-to-us), which he explained at (3)–(6). He now reveals why he began with a claim about what is continuous and divisible. Why? Because feelings and actions – which are the province of virtue of character – are continua. "For example fear, confidence, appetite, anger, pity and in general pleasure and pain can be experienced too much or too little, and in both ways not well." In such continua, the good or right or well is neither too much nor too little but what is *meson* in the "relative to us" way – that is, just right. In feelings and actions you can miss the mark by excess and defect, or hit the target and be praised for your responses, which are deemed *meson*. Now he infers (14) that virtue is a *mesotēs*, insofar as it is able to hit the *meson*.

This completes the Chief Argument. I set it out here, referring to the key points in the stretch of *NE* ii 6, with numbered sentences.

(i)   Virtue is a good state. (1)
(ii) Virtue of character concerns feelings and actions. (9)
(iii) Feelings and actions are continua. (9)
(iv) In continua, what is good or right or well done or praiseworthy is what is neither too much nor too little but *meson*relative-to us. (4–6) and (10)

Conclusion: Virtue, as a good state, achieves the *meson*relative-to-us in feelings and actions and hence is a *mesotēs*. (14)

After an important remark about how one can go wrong in many ways but get things right in only one, Aristotle continues with his famous definition of virtue of character as

(15) a state involving rational choice, consisting in a *mesotēs* relative to us, and determined by reason – the reason, that is, by reference to which the practically wise person would determine it. (16) It is a *mesotēs* between two vices, one of excess, the other of deficiency. (17) It is a *mesotēs* also in that some vices fall short of what is right in feelings and actions, and others exceed it, while virtue both attains and chooses the *meson*. (1106b36–1107a6)

In the next section I discuss the apparently rival reasons given, in (16) and (17), for the claim that virtue is a *mesotēs*. First, a few words about (15). I will not pursue the reference to the *mesotēs* being determined by reason, that is, as the practically wise person, the *phronimos*, would determine it. It is a crucial part of his account of virtue that such determination is the role of reason, specifically of the *phronimos*. But that is not my concern here. This is the first time he has used the phrase "*mesotēs* relative to us," and we must interpret it with the help of the notion he has just carefully defined: the *meson* relative to us: what is neither excessive nor deficient, but in between, that is, just right, for the specifics of the situation. So Aristotle has given us no reason to interpret him as saying that my virtue is relative to me, yours is relative to you, and so on. The Milo illustration, read in its context, should not (mis)lead us to such an interpretation. A virtue is a *mesotēs* relative to us precisely because it attains a *meson* relative to us, in just the way the trainer and other experts such as craftsmen do. That is all the argument from (1) to (14) allows us to infer.[10]

II. TWO COMPETING REASONS WHY VIRTUE IS A MESOTĒS?

Two apparently different reasons for calling virtue a *mesotēs* follow hard on the definition in (15). The second, at (17), is a fuller statement of what I have called the Key thesis (K): virtue is a *mesotēs* because it attains and chooses the *meson*. But just before that we get a different reason, which I will call the Usual thesis or (U), since it is the reason usually given (by commentators) for why virtue is a *mesotēs*:

(Usual) Virtue is a *mesotēs* because it is between two vices, one of excess and one of deficiency.[11]

On my reading, the Usual thesis is true and is not in competition with the Key claim (K), but K is the more fundamental thesis. When a virtue is said to be a *mesotēs*, that *is derivative* from it being a state in which one chooses and hits the *meson* in actions and feelings. Likewise, a given vice of excess, say self-indulgence (*akolasia*), is an excessive state derivatively from the fact that it is related to excessive actions and feelings, and similarly for a vice of deficiency.[12] In *NE* iii and iv Aristotle puts flesh on the bones of the theory he sketches in ii 6 by listing and discussing triads consisting of vice-of-excess/virtue/vice-of-deficiency. These are of great interest, not least because, with the help of his conceptual framework, he identifies some virtues or *mesotētes* that previously had no

---

[10] The treatment in *Eudemian Ethics* confirms my reading. There too (1220b21) Aristotle first introduces the *meson* relative to us, calling it what is best and what knowledge and reason (*logos*) command. Only after that does he introduce virtue as a *mesotēs*. The confusing Milo illustration is absent from *EE*.

[11] Sentence (17) does not contain a Greek word corresponding to "between"; literally it says that virtue is a *mesotēs* of two vices. Only at vi 1 in *NE* (i.e., in one of the "common books") is the expression "between excess and defect" used (1138b24). But frequently in *NE* ii–iv, Aristotle writes "x is the *mesotēs* of y and z," where we have to translate this "is the *mesotēs* between y and z."

[12] Aristotle uses the same pair of terms, *huperbolē* and *elleipsis*, for both the vice (the defective or excessive state) and the associated excessive or defective responses, whereas he distinguishes the virtue as a *mesotēs* from the good response, which is *meson*.

name, but it is not my task here to discuss them at any length. To explain the sense in which each triad contains one vice labeled excess, a virtue labeled *mesotēs*, and another vice labeled defect, we must invoke the character of the responses that each state typically prompts.

I offer two grounds for insisting that the fundamental thesis is K. The first is the now familiar point that the proof he gives in ii 6 that virtue is a *mesotēs* insists on K. And the point is repeated twice, first at (16), and again when Aristotle summarizes his results at the beginning of ii 9: note the last clause. "Enough has been said then to show that virtue of character is a *mesotēs*, and in what sense it is so, and that it is a *mesotēs* between two vices, and that it is such because it is the sort of thing able to hit the *meson* in feelings and actions."

My second ground is this. Aristotle introduces the relative-to-us *meson* as what is good or best in continua, because it avoids both being excessive and being defective. Feelings, he has told us, are continua, such that one can feel them too much, or just right, or too little. But, if we turn to the triads, there is no continuum linking vice of defect–*mesotēs*–vice of excess, and it would be quite wrong to think that way (Rapp 2006, 114–115). A triad of vice-virtue-vice does *not* form a continuum. The sense in which a virtue is "between" a vice of defect and one of excess is derivative from each of them being related to responses – whether actions or passions or both – which are, in the primary application, either too little or just right or too much. The relevant scales or continua are scales of feelings or actions, not of states or dispositions.[13]

III. WHY HAVE CRITICS BEEN EAGER TO DENY OR PLAY DOWN THE KEY CLAIM: THAT VIRTUE IS A MESOTĒS INSOFAR AS IT ACHIEVES WHAT IS MESON?

Many critics refuse to take Aristotle at his word – Urmson (1980, 161), for example: "It is perfectly plain, in fact, that what is primarily in a mean is a settled state of character. . . . thus an emotion or action is in a mean if it exhibits a settled state that is in a mean." Later on the same page, with my letters inserted, he continues: "Aristotle holds excellence of character to be [i] a mean or intermediate disposition regarding emotions and actions, not [ii] that it is a disposition towards mean or intermediate actions." In reply, I urge that Aristotle plainly asserts [ii], and that Urmson is wrong to find it absurd. He argues that [ii] would commit Aristotle to the view that virtue is a disposition to *moderate* emotions

---

[13]   That is, vices do not shade into virtues. Of course, there are states that are in some sense *between* a vice and a virtue, in that a person could count neither as mean nor as generous, while "verging on" meanness. In ii 6 Aristotle makes clear that the continua he has in mind are actions and feelings.

and actions. But this is wrong, as we know. *Meson* emotions and actions are ones that avoid too much and too little; they are not (necessarily) moderate. So we *can* safely ascribe to him the view Urmson denies.[14]

Bostock (2000, 42–43) notes: "The best suggestion seems to be that it is not the virtuous action, on each occasion, that has something middling about it, but rather the general disposition from which it flows." Now this plainly contradicts what Aristotle tells us in ii 6, but Bostock notes here a different passage, in ii 2. "The man who flees from everything, fears everything, and withstands nothing becomes a coward; the man who fears nothing at all but goes to meet everything, becomes rash." He comments: "Undoubtedly Aristotle is thinking here not of the intensity of the emotion on a given occasion, but of the way it may be displayed on too many, or too few, occasions (or types of occasion)." Now this is a fair reading of that earlier passage, in ii 2. There, where Aristotle is describing how we *come to be* brave, rash, or cowardly, he focuses not on the appropriate intensity of fear (if any) on a given occasion, but on the frequency with which a person feels the emotion. Bostock suggests that Aristotle may not have clearly distinguished the two lines of interpretation and acknowledges the clear statements of the other view. "But, to be charitable, we may suggest that what is uppermost in his thought is that virtue is a middling disposition." Well, I do not think that it is uppermost in Aristotle's view, nor that we are charitable to Aristotle to ignore his Central Argument in ii 6.

Broadie (1991, 98–101) also appeals to the ii 2 passage to draw a similar conclusion to that of Bostock. Of the key discussion in our chapter, ii 6, when at (11) Aristotle speaks of responses as *meson* and best, she writes that "'intermediate' seems virtually a synonym for 'right' and it includes every category of rightness, with no special emphasis on the intermediate." So why, she wonders, does Aristotle cling to the term "intermediate" (i.e., *meson*)? "The explanation must lie not in the presumed intermediacy in any substantial sense (for none applies) of the right response itself, but rather in some sort of intermediacy belonging to the disposition that gives rise to the right responses" (Broadie 101).

Once again I reply that that this directly contradicts Aristotle's own explanation, which quite clearly goes the other way. But would it be an improvement if Aristotle had seen things the way Broadie argues for? Here is how she argues the point. "Encouraging a prospective agent to aim at the intermediate is not appropriate even as a metaphor." But, she continues, encouraging someone to aim at a *balanced temperament*, on the other hand, might be of practical value, and advice to a learner neither to avoid all bodily pleasure nor to indulge whenever possible would be

[14] Hursthouse 1981 and Welton and Polansky 1995, 90, criticize Urmson on this point.

sensible advice. So in a nutshell Broadie's argument is this: calling the right response *meson* is of no practical value, whereas calling the good disposition a *mesotēs* (i.e., a balanced one) is. To reply fully to this argument, we must finally turn to consider a familiar difficulty for Aristotle's theory (Section IV), one that bears on the practical value of the *mesotēs* theory (Section V).

IV. THE PROBLEM OF THE PARAMETERS

At a key point in what I called the Chief Argument, Aristotle introduced what have come to be called the parameters for responding in the best way. *(11) But to have them [that is, feelings of fear, anger or whatever] at the right time, about the right things, toward the right people, for the right end and in the right way is meson and the best, and this is the business of virtue.*[15] Here he no longer talks simply of avoiding too much and too little; rather, the agent must get *a number of features* right to respond in the best way. Now this is a welcome refinement, as Broadie and other critics note. But they object that, in effect, it makes redundant the notion that the best response is *intermediate between excess and defect*. Ridding the theory of its quantitative aspect is, they argue, a distinct improvement, since the wrong-making features of a response cannot be captured simply by talk of too much or too little.

A modest reply to this objection runs as follows. Even if it is correct, Aristotle himself is clearly not aware of the problem, since he is happy to *elucidate* the notion of a *meson* response in terms of the different parameters (at the right time, about the right things, and so on). He does so not only in this passage but also throughout his discussion of the specific virtues of character in iii 6–12 and iv. He clearly would not accept Broadie's claim that the right response is not intermediate in any substantial sense.

A more ambitious reply tries to vindicate Aristotle, by finding a way or ways in which one can properly combine the quantitative language of the *meson*, the right degree or amount of something, with the recognition of the parameters (Welton and Polansky 1995; Curzer 1996; Rapp 2006). One favored way to do so is to say that for Aristotle "the question whether we feel an emotion too much or too little can only be assessed by checking whether our responses are right in the sense of the different parameters" (Rapp 2006, 124). Thus, if I get only a tiny bit angry for no good reason, then that counts as an excess, while if I do not feel at all

---

[15]   Some translations avoid "right" and instead use "should"; thus Taylor "but to feel such things when one should, and about the things one should, and in relation to the people one should (etc.)."

angry at – say – an unprovoked attack on a defenseless relative, that counts as a defective response.

Now the ambitious reply succeeds in vindicating Aristotle's approach for many cases, but I am inclined to agree with the skeptics (such as Hursthouse 2006, 108; Taylor 2006, 110–111) that it is not always successful.[16] I do not think Aristotle can "have it both ways," by retaining the language of excess, defect, and *meson*, and at the same time recognizing that a response may be inappropriate for any of a number of reasons. Indeed, he himself uses the image of hitting a target to emphasize that "one can miss the mark in many ways, but one can get things right in only one" – with which we may compare Plato (*Republic* 444c): vice has many forms but virtue only one. But, as I noted earlier in the more modest reply, Aristotle himself evidently saw no tension between the two accounts: the insistence that going wrong is always a matter of excess or of deficiency, and the recognition of a whole array of reasons why a response may be wrong. So we should not go along with Urmson, Bostock, and Broadie and ascribe to Aristotle the view that while virtue really is some kind of "in-between" state or disposition, the right response is not in any substantial sense "in-between." Aristotle never wavers from labeling the right response *meson*, or from the view that right responses are indeed "in-between," that is, just right.

V. OF WHAT PRACTICAL VALUE IS THE THEORY?

As we saw, Broadie argued that describing a *state* as an intermediate or balanced one is of some educational value, while calling the correct *response* on a given occasion "intermediate and best" is of no practical value at all. That is why she disregards what I called the Key claim K. I first consider her negative claim.

I readily agree that, in calling the best response *meson*, Aristotle did *not* see himself as offering a decision procedure for finding the right action. He emphasizes this in two ways: first, by distinguishing the relative-to-us *meson* from one which *can* be calculated and does not vary from occasion to occasion and, second, by comparing the possessor of virtue with a skill that enables its possessor to get things just right. As

---

[16] The ambitious line of defense will argue that, say, getting angry with a blameless person is displaying too much anger. But suppose through bias I get angry with blameless X instead of with the real culprit Y. This line would have to call my anger both excessive and defective: an unfortunate result. In truth the fault is (neither excess nor defect but) that I got angry *with the wrong person*. I owe the example to Lindsay Judson.

argued earlier, he seems to have in mind a kind of knowledge or expertise that cannot be spelled out in a way that would enable an unskilled person to follow instructions and achieve the same success. In many passages, Aristotle denies that there are universal truths in ethics, by which he seems to mean that there are none that do not also require ethical judgment to apply them successfully. As Aristotle makes clear throughout the work, the best way to put yourself in a position to have the right responses to a given set of circumstances is by keeping good company in your youth, developing the right ethical sensitivity, and cultivating the virtues. Far from offering a decision procedure, his account of what makes a response "*meson* and best" shows, and is intended to show, that *no such decision procedure can be offered.* So we can agree with Broadie that in calling the correct response *meson* Aristotle does not thereby offer a novice a decision procedure for identifying the correct response.

But, for all that, Aristotle *does* think it helpful to give some advice on aligning one's responses with the best, that is, the *meson* ones, in ii 9. Most of us have an idea in which direction we tend to err – no doubt from the advice and admonition of others, as well as from our own reflections. So we should examine our own natural tendencies and "drag ourselves in the opposite direction (as people do in straightening wood)" so as to hit the *meson*. Despite what Broadie argues, Aristotle *does* seem to be offering this as advice on how to find the right response, and not just as advice on how to acquire a balanced state, *hexis*. But, of course, he does not think that the mere label *meson* will help someone, regardless of their stage of ethical development, to identify the correct response.

What about Broadie's positive claim, that there *is* a substantial sense in which the good state, the virtue, is intermediate, and that here it *is* of practical value to advise someone to acquire an intermediate disposition? One might expect the sense of "intermediate" to be the one Aristotle himself suggests, that the state is between two vices, one of excess and one of deficiency. Now I argued earlier for the following way of interpreting those labels. Each member of the triad, vice of deficiency–*mesotēs*–vice of excess, is so-called derivatively from the nature of the responses they typically prompt. But the view I am opposing denies this and holds that it is the between-ness or middling-ness of the virtue state that is primary. And in any case, the substantial sense in which, for Broadie, a virtue is a *mesotēs*, is that it is a *balanced* state.[17] And this cannot mean that it is a balanced mixture of two vices!

<hr />

[17]   Similarly Gottlieb 2009, 22–25, argues that we should understand *mesotēs* as equilibrium. But, if so, it loses the connection with the *meson* response.

VI. MESOTĒS AS DEVELOPING VIRTUE: AN EMPIRICAL APPROACH?

Broadie and Bostock support their position by pointing to Aristotle's discussion, in ii 2, in which he introduces the term *mesotēs*. Here, in what Rapp (2006, 106–107) calls the empirical version of the theory, Aristotle compares becoming virtuous with becoming strong or healthy, where both deficiency and excess (of food or of exercise) are harmful. He advises that *to acquire* temperance one should pursue some pleasures but not all, and *to become* courageous one should face some dangers but not all, concluding that "temperance and courage are ruined by excess and deficiency and preserved by *mesotēs*." As often noted, the passage has echoes of Hippocrates' *On Ancient Medicine*, chapter 9, with its injunction to avoid excess and deficiency in diet. Here a correct diet may well be a balanced one, so Broadie's position may seem vindicated, at least regarding the appeal to *mesotēs* in ii 2.[18]

But I do not think that this low-level advice ("pursue some pleasures but not all; face some dangers but not all") qualifies as giving a substantive sense in which a virtue is an intermediate (i.e., balanced) state and hence as being of some practical use, as Broadie argues. Indeed, Aristotle follows that bit of advice with a much more weighty thesis, one that is of huge importance in his account of character virtue: doing actions of a certain good kind develops a good state, which in turn makes us better able to do those actions. This is evident, he says, both in weight training to acquire strength and in the acquisition of the virtues. The claim that to acquire virtue V a young person must be encouraged to do V acts is sensible and practical, while the claim that to acquire virtue V he should take a balanced approach and take some but not all opportunities to display a given feeling or do a given action is hardly practical unless the learner has some advice on which opportunities to take and which to pass up.

So none of the reasons these critics give for denying the Key claim is strong enough to license us in refusing to take Aristotle at his word. Even though he also has a somewhat different way of talking about *mesotēs* in ii 2, perhaps invoking a medical theory that Hursthouse (2006, 99) has dismissed as "simply whacky," his official account of why virtue is a *mesotēs* relative to us is precisely that it is a tendency to

---

[18] Broadie and Bostock might defend their line by pointing out that the ii 6 discussion (as quoted above at (2)) recalls the earlier (ii 2) introduction of a *mesotēs*. While this is a problem for the view I defend (cf. Rapp) by which the analytic account of *meson/mesotēs* in the ii 6 discussion is the key one, it is also a problem for those critics who stress the importance of the "empirical" account of ii 2 but have to downplay or deny the Key claim in ii 6.

aim at and achieve responses that are *meson* (in the relative-to-us sense) and thereby best.

VII. IMPACT ON A CURRENT DEBATE IN VIRTUE ETHICS

The thesis I have defended has an important bearing on an ongoing debate. A central tenet of modern virtue ethics is that of the primacy of character: the claim that "the concept of virtue is explanatorily prior to that of right conduct, prior indeed more generally to the concepts that fall under the heading 'morally good conduct'" (Watson 1997, 58; see also Statman 1997, 7–11). Should Aristotle be included in those who subscribe to the view that virtue, that is, goodness of character, is explanatorily prior to right or good conduct? The answer is no, if what I have argued here is correct.

But, critics urge, surely Aristotle has already asserted the priority thesis in *NE* ii 4.1105b5–7: "Actions, then, are called just and temperate when they are such as the just and the temperate person would do."[19]

My response is this. Though that *can* be read as asserting definitional or explanatory priority to the just or temperate person over just or temperate acts, it *does not have* to be read that way, and indeed the context of ii 4 shows – I believe – that Aristotle is there making a different point. He is reasserting, against an objector, his important claim that to acquire a virtue V, one must do V acts. He has explained what further conditions, over and above merely doing V acts, are needed for the agent to be acting V-ly (justly, or temperately). Then, to hammer home his point, he emphasizes that though (1) actions are called just and temperate when they are such as the just and the temperate person would do – that is, *all* just acts are such as a just person *would do*, (2) some just acts are done by persons who are not yet just. And (2) allows him to restate his claim that "it is by doing just actions that one becomes just, and by doing temperate actions temperate; without doing them no-one would have even a chance of becoming good" (1105b9–12). Given the thrust of his argument, there is no need to read (1) as an assertion of definitional priority, in my view.

And a different priority suggests itself, if what I have argued is correct – that is, if Aristotle makes the status of a virtue as a *mesotēs* derivative from the *meson* nature of the responses it prompts.[20] We already saw that Aristotle spells out what it is for a response (whether a feeling or an

---

[19] Taylor 2006, 94, commenting on 1105b5–9, writes, "Aristotle here assigns definitional priority to the agent over the act." See also his introduction, xvi and xvii n9. Reviewing Taylor, Morison 2007, 244–245, contests this interpretation of the passage.

[20] Santas 1997, 273, concurs. Commenting on 1106b27–8, what I have labeled herein the Key claim, he writes, "Once more first actualities (states of character) are explicated in

action) to be *meson* in terms of its being "at the right time, about the right things, toward the right people," and so on. A *meson* response is one that is done or felt *hōs dei*, as one should. And, when Aristotle comes to substantiate his claim that virtues of character are *mesotētes* by examining them one by one, he characterizes the *mesotēs*, or rather the person possessing a virtue, in terms of what he typically does or feels in a variety of circumstances.[21] His way of putting flesh on the bones of the *mesotēs* theory is to spell out the kinds of consideration that make a given response *meson*, and he does so by a variety of means, typically invoking evaluative terms such as how one should (*dei*) feel or act, what is *kalon*, and what someone deserves. The possessor of a given virtue has learned how to recognize these considerations and responds accordingly.

To restate my main thesis and conclude: A virtue of character is labeled a "*mesotēs* relative to us" precisely because it is a state that aims at and achieves what is *meson* relative to us – a term Aristotle has carefully explained in ii 6 before making his Key claim. Given this prominent claim, it seems clear that Aristotle does *not* subscribe to the thesis of the explanatory or definitional priority of virtue (good character) over good or right action. So, *if* that is a central tenet of modern virtue ethics, Aristotle's view cannot be claimed as an ancestor. I see no conclusive reason from elsewhere in the *NE* (and in particular not from ii 4) to think that it was an aberration on Aristotle's part to derive the "between"-ness of a character virtue from the "between" or "just right" nature of the responses it prompts, as he clearly does in ii 6. The more Usual claim, that a virtue is a *mesotēs* because it is *between two vices*, one of excess and one of defect, is also correct, but it is not the fundamental one. It is *derived from* the Key claim in the way I have explained (Section II). Those who try to rewrite the theory (Section III) do Aristotle no favors, and I see no reason not to take him at his word.[22]

WORKS CITED

Bosley, R., R. Shiner, and J. D. Sisson eds. 1995. *Aristotle, Virtue and the Mean. Apeiron* 25, no. 4.
Bostock, D. 2000. *Aristotle's Ethics*. Oxford: Clarendon Press.

part at least by second actualities (the actions), and, because the actions constitute well-functioning, the states of character are said to be virtues."
[21] 1127a15–17: we will become more confident that the virtues are *mesotētes* by going through them one by one.
[22] Young 1997, 94, agrees in reading Aristotle as giving priority to what Young labels Intermediacy, and I label the Key thesis. However, his worry that "Aristotle simply doesn't tell us how to understand Intermediacy [i.e., the key thesis]" is misplaced in my view. I thank M. Pakaluk for drawing my attention to Young's fine article.

Broadie, S. 1991. *Ethics with Aristotle*. New York: Oxford University Press.

Brown, L. 1997. "What Is the 'Mean Relative to Us' in Aristotle's Ethics?" *Phronesis* 42: 77–93.

Crisp, R. trans. 2000. *Aristotle, Nicomachean Ethics*. Cambridge: Cambridge University Press.

Curzer, H. J. 1996. "A Defense of Aristotle's Doctrine That Virtue Is a Mean." *Ancient Philosophy* 16: 129–138.

Gauthier, R. A., and J. Y. Jolif. 1958. *L'Éthique à Nicomaque*. Louvain: Publications Universitaires.

Gottlieb, P. 2009. *The Virtue of Aristotle's Ethics*. Cambridge: Cambridge University Press.

Hursthouse, R. 1981. "A False Doctrine of the Mean." *Proceedings of the Aristotelian Society* 81: 57–92.

    2006. "The Central Doctrine of the Mean." 96–136 in R. Kraut, ed. *The Blackwell Guide to Aristotle's Nicomachean Ethics*. Oxford: Blackwell.

Irwin, T. H. 1999. *Aristotle, Nicomachean Ethics*. 2nd ed. Indianapolis: Hackett.

Morison, B. 2007. "Aristotle, Almost Entirely." *Phronesis* 52: 239–249.

Müller, A. W. 2004. "Aristotle's Conception of Ethical and Natural Virtue: How the Unity Thesis Sheds Light on the Doctrine of the Mean." 18–53 in J. Szaif and M. Lutz-Bachmann eds. *Was ist das für den Menschen Güte?/What Is Good for a Human Being?* Berlin: De Gruyter.

Rapp, C. 2006. "What Use Is Aristotle's Doctrine of the Mean?" 99–126 in B. Reis ed. *The Virtuous Life in Greek Ethics*. Cambridge: Cambridge University Press.

Rowe, C. 2002. *Aristotle, Nicomachean Ethics*. Oxford: Oxford University Press.

Santas, G. X. 1997. "Does Aristotle Have a Virtue Ethics?" 183–194 in Statman ed. 1997.

Statman, D. ed. 1997. *Virtue Ethics: A Critical Reader*. Edinburgh: Edinburgh University Press.

Taylor, C. C. W. 2006. *Aristotle: Nicomachean Ethics Books II–IV*. Oxford: Clarendon Press.

Urmson, J. O. 1980. "Aristotle's Doctrine of the Mean." 157–170 in A. O. Rorty ed. *Essays in Aristotle's Ethics*. Berkeley: University of California Press.

Watson, G. 1997. "On the Primacy of Character." 56–81 in Statman ed. 1997.

Welton, W., and R. Polansky. 1995. "The Viability of Virtue in the Mean." 79–102 in Bosley et al eds. 1995.

Young, C. M. 1997. "The Doctrine of the Mean." *Topoi* 15: 89–99.

5 Choice and Moral Responsibility (*NE* iii 1–5)

I. INTRODUCTION

The passage *NE* iii 1–5 is located at the end of Aristotle's account of the character virtues and their acquisition in general in book 2 and before his main discussion of the particular virtues in books iii 6–v 11. In the passage, Aristotle considers – in traditional translations – praise and blame, voluntariness, choice, deliberation, wanting and the things in our power.[1]

Aristotle never explicitly states the purpose of *NE* iii 1–5. It is a matter of debate what his intention in this passage was. According to some of the major views of Aristotle scholars, Aristotle intends

1. to provide the notions required for the discussion of the individual virtues and vices;
2. to show that praise and blame are justified for our being noble or base in our actions or our virtuous or vicious dispositions, because these are voluntary;
3. to capture the causal conditions of praise and blame;
4. to discuss intentional action;

I would like to thank Susan Sauvé Meyer, Carlo Natali, and Ronald Polansky for their most helpful comments on a draft version of this contribution.

[1] *NE* iii 1–5 is one of the parts of the *NE* that is not shared with Aristotle's *Eudemian Ethics* (*EE*) and where there is a long parallel treatment of mostly the same issues (*EE* ii 6–11). Although one should always allow for the possibility that Aristotle changed his mind or refined his theory in the interval between writing (and revising) one and the other, the close similarities make *EE* ii 6–11 an invaluable source for better understanding *NE* iii 1–5. Any reader with a serious desire to master *NE* iii 1–5 is advised to study *EE* ii 6–11. (See the commentary in Woods 1992 and Meyer 2006 for helpful notes on the *EE* passage.) It is also worth keeping in mind that *NE* iii 1–5 is bound into the whole treatise of the *NE* and involves many philosophical notions and distinctions that Aristotle introduces elsewhere in the *NE* (especially in books 1, 2, 6, and 7, as well as in other writings, and that these passages, too, help in understanding *NE* iii 1–5. Furthermore, *NE* v 8 overlaps in content with *NE* iii 1.

5. to discuss the efficient cause of action;
6. to discuss Socrates' view that no one is willingly bad.[2]

De facto, Aristotle does all of 1–6. We prefer a version of 2, for reasons expounded below. There is no dispute that, if anywhere in the NE Aristotle considers what renders people responsible for their actions and character and justifies praise and blame, he does this in NE iii 1–5. The chapters are also central for Aristotle's theory of action. In addition, many scholars have espoused the views that NE iii 1–5 is pivotal in Aristotle's works for his treatment of freedom of choice, free will, and freedom-to-do-otherwise.[3] For all these reasons, NE iii 1–5 remains one of the most-discussed passages of Aristotle's oeuvre.

In the following, we focus on Aristotle's theory of what makes us responsible for our actions and character. After some preliminary observations about praise, blame, and responsibility (Section II), we set out in detail how all the key notions of NE iii 1–5 are interrelated (Sections III–IX). The setting out of these interconnections makes it possible to provide an overall interpretation of the purpose of the passage. The primary purpose of NE iii 1–5 is to explain how agents are responsible for their actions not just insofar as they are actions of this or that kind, but also insofar as they are noble or base: agents are responsible for their actions qua noble or base, because, typically via choice, their character dispositions are a causal factor of those actions (Section X). We illustrate the different ways in which agents can be causes of their actions by means of Aristotle's four basic types of agents (Section XI). A secondary purpose of NE iii 1–5 is to explain how agents can be held responsible for consequences of their actions (Section XII) and, in particular, for their character dispositions insofar as these are noble or base, that is, virtues or vices (Section XIII). These two purposes are not the only ones Aristotle pursues in the passage. But they are the ones Aristotle himself indicates in its first sentence and summarizes in its last paragraph; and the ones that give the passage a systematic unity.[4] We briefly consider the issues of freedom-to-do-otherwise, free choice, and free will in the contexts in which they occur (in the final paragraphs of Sections VI, VII, XII, XIII).

[2] See, e.g., Grant, 1874, vol. 2, iii; Taylor 2006, 125 for 1; Irwin 1985, 315, 319 for 2; Meyer 2006, 137–138, 139, 144, 152, 154 for 3; Charles 1984 for 4; Burnet 1900 and Joachim 1951 for 5; Gauthier and Jolif 1959, 168–169 for 6.
[3] This interpretative tradition starts already in antiquity and is still going strong today (Broadie 1991; Destrée 2011), but has little basis in the text; see Bobzien 1998, 2012; Frede 2007, 2011, ch. 2; also Grant, 1866, 316–318.
[4] These two purposes also tie in with Aristotle's claim at NE ii 4.1105a28–33 that for actions to be performed in a virtuous way, (i) the agent has to choose them insofar as they are good (just, temperate, etc.) and (ii) the choice has to be based in a firm and unchangeable character disposition (i.e., in the virtues of justice, temperance, etc.).

For the central terms of *NE* iii 1–5, we generally follow standard translations and add alternatives in footnotes – both for the benefit of Greek-less readers. We use the expression "virtuous agent" ("virtuous individual") for an agent, who has, as character dispositions, the charac- ter virtues. Aristotle sometimes uses the term *spoudaios* for such indi- viduals. We use the expression "vicious agent" for an agent who has some character vices as dispositions. For such individuals, Aristotle sometimes uses *phaulos*. We use "virtuous disposition" as short for "character dispositions that are identical with the character virtues"; and "vicious disposition" as short for "character dispositions that are identical with the character vices." We use the word "moral" exclusively as a generic term that covers the evaluative element, aspect, or dimen- sion of what Aristotle calls, on the side of positive value, noble (*kalos*), good (*agathos*), fine (*epieikēs*), or virtue (*aretē*); and, on the side of negative value, shameful (*aischros*), base (*phaulos*), wicked (*mochthēros*), bad (*kakos*), or vice (*kakia*) (when using these terms in the context of human agency and character respectively).[5] Accordingly, we also use the expression "moral disposition" as a generic term for virtuous and vicious disposition. Our use of "moral" should not be conflated with such modern notions as rule following, altruistic or utilitarian norms, and religion-based morality, as we find them only in post- Aristotelian thought.

II. FROM PRAISE AND BLAME TO MORAL RESPONSIBILITY

Aristotle considers it a fact that we praise and blame people with respect to their virtues and vices (e.g., *NE* 1106a1–2). In effect, for him virtues *are* the character dispositions that are praise*worthy* (1103a8–10; cf. 1101b13–15, b30–31). He argues that what makes these dispositions virtues is that they are directed toward the intermediate in action (1106b36–1107a1); and that this is also what makes them praiseworthy (1109b24).[6]

---

[5] We make no attempt at interpreting what it is that Aristotle considers to be of positive value in nobility, goodness, fineness, or virtue and what it is that Aristotle considers to be of negative value in shamefulness, baseness, wickedness, badness, or vice. We simply take it that his consistent use of the respective Greek terms is sufficient indication that he assumed there to be some relevant positive or negative value to these things.

[6] See Brown in this volume. Aristotle also uses the fact that we praise people who hit the intermediate in order to support his view that virtue is the mean; cf., e.g., 1106b25–28, 1108a14–16. But one must not confuse (i) Aristotle's use of people's actual praise and blame as evidence for his theory of the mean with (ii) Aristotle's own theory of what makes the character dispositions praise*worthy* or blame*worthy*.

At the beginning of *NE* iii 1, Aristotle draws the connection between virtue and vice, praise and blame, and voluntariness, if in a rather unspecific way: Praise and blame are bestowed only on actions and emotions[7] that are voluntary (1109b30–31), and virtue is concerned with actions and emotions. In his summary at the end of *NE* iii 5, Aristotle states that he has shown that the virtues are voluntary and that virtues and actions are voluntary in different ways (1114b26–31).

This suggests that Aristotle assumes that voluntariness is a necessary condition for justified praise and blame – a fact commonly used to support the assumption that *NE* iii 1 presents a discussion of *moral responsibility*. It is worth pointing out, though, that Aristotle does not have an expression for moral responsibility,[8] and that in *NE* iii 1 he talks mostly about people's *actual* practices of praising and blaming, not about praise*worthiness* and blame*worthiness*. Thus in *NE* iii 1 Aristotle may – as he often does – simply start out from empirical considerations: People bestow praise and blame for certain things; they do this only when they believe that these things have certain characteristics; these characteristics are those commonly collected under the heading of voluntariness.

Consider societies, like those in ancient Greece, which are simpler than ours in that they do not have the complex intellectual, religious, and ethical traditions instilled in us from childhood. Imagine typical cases of praising and blaming in such societies: a runner is praised for winning a sports contest ("We are proud of you!"); an adolescent for his or her beauty ("Your looks are those of a god(dess)."); a wife is blamed for poor cooking skills ("You dimwit, why can't you cook like our neighbor?"); a slave for having broken a vessel ("It's your fault I have to buy a new vessel!"). The expression "moral responsibility" does not come to mind readily to characterize such cases. It is far from clear whether morality, in any sense, is at issue. Praising and blaming are human activities that are reactive to certain kinds of – mostly – human behavior and habits that please or annoy. The purpose of praising and blaming may simply be that (i) of expressing one's appreciative or disapproving sentiments or (ii) of encouraging or discouraging repetition of the relevant behavior. There are certain conditions that have to be met for such activities to be appropriate – that is, conditions not for whether the appropriate reaction

---

[7] "Emotions" translates *pathē*. Alternative translations are "feelings," "passions," "undergoings," and with them come different interpretations. Accordingly, some have questioned whether for Aristotle *pathē* are voluntary. We disregard these difficulties and focus solely on actions.

[8] We use "moral responsibility" as a generic term that covers praiseworthiness and blameworthiness of someone for something with regard to the nobility, fineness, or goodness on the one hand, shamefulness, wickedness, baseness, or badness on the other of that someone or that something.

is praise *or* blame, but for whether *any* such reaction is appropriate. (For example, it is not appropriate to blame anyone for the weather, or to praise a stone for its weight.) No notions like noble (*kalos*), shameful (*aischros*), fine (*epieikēs*), or base (*phaulos*) need to be involved in this context. We can first sort things according to whether they are the kind of thing that can be praised or blamed and then correlate these things with acts of praising or blaming.

To get from the situations of blaming and praising considered by Aristotle in *NE* iii 1 to *moral* responsibility (i.e., responsibility related *in some sense yet-to-be-determined* to what is noble or shameful), the things that are praised or blamed must in addition be classified as noble or shameful, and the praise or blame must attach to them because of their being noble or shameful.[9] In the remainder, we show that in *NE* iii 2–5 Aristotle provides a theory of the conditions of moral appraisal that does precisely this.

Aristotle's move from generally accepted conditions of praise and blame to *moral* responsibility is in parallel with his move from common-sense-based and common-opinion-based discussion of the voluntary as a requirement for praise or blame in *NE* iii 1 to his explanation of the underlying psychological apparatus in *NE* iii 2–5 – an explanation that is based on his own view of the soul (as set out in *NE* i 13 and vi 1). Aristotle introduces choice as a psychological feature that characterizes the appropriate subjects and objects of praise and blame and that provides the channel by means of which both rationality and the moral dispositions of character can manifest themselves in adult human action. Choice turns out to be characteristic of any kind of moral responsibility. We begin with the manifestation of moral responsibility in action (Sections III–XI). We consider moral responsibility for character in Section XIII.

III. ACTION AND VOLUNTARINESS

According to Aristotle, action (*praxis*) is a specifically human activity.[10] An action is a change (*kinēsis*) that has its origin (*archē*) in the human

---

[9] Aristotle is aware of the difference between praising someone or something (i) for nobility or character-virtue-related goodness and (ii) for some other not character-virtue-related trait: "(i) we praise the just or brave person, and generally both the good person (*ton agathon*) and virtue itself, because of the actions and pursuits involved, and (ii) we praise the strong person, the runner, and so on, because they are of a certain kind and are related somehow to something good and excellent" (*NE* i 12.1101b14–18).

[10] *EE* 1222b18–20; *NE* 1139a19–20. The classic work on Aristotle's theory of action is Charles 1984.

being, who is also the efficient cause of the actions (*EE* 1222b28–31).[11] All action is goal-directed, that is, aims at an end (*telos*), though its end may lie in itself (*NE* i 1). Action requires the agent to have a reasoning capacity (*EE* 1224a29–30). This is why people do not say of toddlers or animals that they perform actions (*EE* 1224a28–30).

Although Aristotle defines action as change, when he discusses voluntariness he is concerned equally with situations in which individuals perform an action and in which they refrain from performing an action. (For something to be a refraining from an action, broadly, the action must be something the agent could have considered doing.) Praise and blame are bestowed on both action and refraining from action. Accordingly, Aristotle uses "action" (*praxis*) sometimes in the wider sense that covers both action and refraining. This is in line with Aristotle's theory of efficient causation, which allows for the case in which someone is an efficient cause of an absence of change, as opposed to an efficient cause of change (*Phys.* 194b29–30, 195a11–14). We, too, shall use "action" in places to cover actions and refrainings.

Aristotle holds that an action is voluntary (*hekousios*)[12] precisely if both the origin of the action is in the agent and the agent knows the relevant particular circumstances of the action.

The action's origin is in the agent, when the agent is the action's efficient cause and the action is not the result of external force. Aristotle is aware that there are cases in which it is doubtful whether the agent was externally forced, and that the boundary between the unforced and forced cases is difficult to draw. We will not dwell on the details.[13] What matters for us are the following – undisputed – points. (i) For an action to be unforced, the agent has to contribute something (*NE* 1110b2–3); that is, the agent has to be at least a causal co-contributor. (ii) The problematic cases are those in which the force seems to take the

---

[11]   Aristotle says or implies that actions are changes (*kinēseis*) both in the *EE* (e.g., 1222b29) and in the *NE* (e.g., 1139a31–32). This is in line with his assumption that actions have an efficient cause (ibid.). Here "efficient cause" is the standard translation for the kind of cause that Aristotle refers to as "that from which" (ibid.) or as "the origin of change" (*Phys.* 195a11), and that he defines as "that from which the alteration or absence of alteration has its origin" (*Phys.* 194b29–30). In the *NE* Aristotle refers to actions both as changes (*kinēseis*) and as activities (*energeiai*) (e.g., *NE* i 1; iii 5). We assume that, rather than contradicting himself, Aristotle does not use *energeia* in its narrow, technical sense when calling actions activities. This assumption is supported by the fact that Aristotle's practical sciences tend not to make direct appeal to his theoretical positions.

[12]   Alternative translations of *hekousios*: "willing," "intentional," "witting." For discussion of voluntariness in the *EE*, see *EE* ii 7–8.

[13]   For an excellent discussion, see Meyer 2006, 141–149. The classical treatment is Kenny 1979.

form of compulsion.[14] By and large, Aristotle maintains that compulsion, as long as it does not put the agent under duress that overstrains human nature (one may envision severe torture; *NE* 1110a24–26; *EE* 1225a21), does not render the act forced. (iii) Aristotle explicitly rejects the suggestion that an agent's action is forced when it is the result of a desire (for pleasure or avoiding pain) in the agent that conflicts with the agent's end. (Imagine someone following a desire for doughnuts despite having adopted eating healthy as an end.) The possibility of a conflict between nonrational desires (e.g., appetite and anger) and rational ones is characteristic of humans. Aristotle argues that the agents' appetites and emotions are no less human than their reason and originate no less from the agents than their reasoned ends.[15]

The second criterion for voluntariness, absence of ignorance, covers only ignorance regarding specific circumstances of the action. Aristotle provides many examples. Thus one may be unaware that one's fencing sword is missing its button, and subsequently involuntarily injure a friend. Again, there may be doubtful cases: it may be unclear whether in a particular case the ignorance at issue qualifies for removing voluntariness (see Section XII). Aristotle himself does not discuss such doubtful cases. But he explicitly excludes ignorance of general truths, including what the right end is (*NE* 1110b28–33), and ignorance that is itself the result of a voluntary action (see Section XII).[16]

With both criteria (agent-internal origin, absence of ignorance), Aristotle seems to capture commonsense opinion. From a contemporary perspective, it is remarkable how close Aristotle's criteria tally with those of present-day criminal law. Even with much advanced psychological and technological methods, the problems a judge or jury faces as to whether an agent can be held responsible are pretty much the same.

[14] By compulsion I mean a force that does not cause or prevent movement of the individual's body directly (like strong winds or shackles) but that instead makes the agent move (or refrain from moving) as a result of action-promoting (or refraining-promoting) activity in the individual's soul. Thus, if an agent utters "he is in the basement" in order to avoid further beatings, the compulsion works via the agent's soul and is *thus* psychological. The force would be solely physical, if it were to work directly on the agent's vocal cords, making her produce the phonetic sounds "he is in the basement."

[15] *NE* 1111a24–b3, cf. *EE* 1224b7–14, 1224a23–25. Aristotle also rejects the possibility that pleasant things (the doughnut over there) can externally force an agent to act. Rather, insofar as they are envisaged as good, such external things function as final cause or goal of the action (*NE* 1110b9–15).

[16] Aristotle never says or implies that responsibility is a matter of degree. Rather, either one is morally responsible for something (i.e., one deserves praise or blame) or one is not. Of course, if one *is* responsible, there is the independent question of what kind or amount of praise or blame, respectively, would be appropriate, and this will depend on the circumstances of the action and agent. Aristotle shows awareness of this second point where he mentions that the punishments for actions done while drunk are double (*NE* 1113a30–34).

IV. WHAT HAPPENS IN THE AGENT'S SOUL

The commonsense account of voluntary action in *NE* iii 1 explains only why actions like throwing cargo overboard or eating doughnuts are praised or blamed. A – positive – connection between the agent's praise-worthy and blameworthy dispositions (i.e., virtues and vices) and voluntary action is not drawn. Nor do we obtain any information about what happens in the agent's soul in cases of voluntary action. Yet Aristotle thinks virtues and vices are dispositions of the human soul. Thus, to draw the relevant connection, Aristotle needs to provide the psychological details of human agency. He does this in *NE* iii 2–5, where it becomes clear that, with the exception of spur-of-the-moment acts (for which see Section IX), human agency essentially involves choice, and that via choice the connection between voluntary action and virtues and vices is drawn.

Aristotle defines choice (*prohairesis*) as an agent's deliberated desire for things that are in the agent's power.[17] Every choice has two aspects: it is *for the sake of* something and *of* something (*EE* 1227b36–37). In the *NE*, Aristotle expresses these two aspects by saying that choice is with regard to an end and concerns the means to that end (*ta pros to telos, NE* 1111b27, 1113b3–4). Choice occurs in the agent's soul, more specifically in the ruling part in the agent's soul (iii 3.1113a6), and for each of the two aspects, a different subpart of this part of the soul is responsible, one rational-in-itself, one desiring and capable-of-listening-to-and-obeying reason.[18]

The desiring part of the human soul is one of its two nonrational parts.[19] It comprises all human desires (*orexeis*), including appetite, anger, wanting.[20] A person's character (*ēthē*) is manifested primarily in this desiring part of the soul. What type of character a person has is determined by what character dispositions (*ēthikai hexeis*) it comprises. For example, if the character is excellent, these character dispositions will be the character virtues (courage, generosity, etc.): the character virtues *are* the excellences of this part of the soul (*NE* ii and iii 6–v). The agent's character dispositions determine what ends the agent

---

[17]   Alternative translations: "decision," "intention," "purpose," "resolution." The reason for these alternatives will become clear in what follows.

[18]   The main passages about the parts (or aspects) of the human soul are *NE* i 13 and vi 2 and *DA* iii 9; cf. also *DA* ii 2.

[19]   The other is the vegetative part, responsible for digestion, sleep, breathing, growth; see *NE* i 13; *DA* ii 2.

[20]   The desiring element, though nonrational, shares in reason insofar as it "can listen to it and obey it" and thus differs from the desiring part in nonrational animals. The human desiring part can wholly or partly be in conflict with the rational part or "speak on all matters with the same voice" as it (*NE* 1102b13–31). Section XI provides details.

has – that is, what the agent's goal-directed desires are directed toward. The specific desire a person has for these ends is called wanting (*boulēsis*).[21] It is this wanting that is causally responsible for the "for-the-sake-of-which," or the end, of the choice. Without character dispositions that determine what a person wants, there can thus be no choice (1139a33–34). (In short: The desiring part, via the agent's character dispositions, including virtues or vices, determines the agent's ends and provides the agent with a certain kind of desire, a wanting, for that end.)

The relevant rational part of the soul is the one that deals with contingent or changing (as opposed to necessary, unchanging) things. This part is called calculative. Aristotle states that calculation and deliberation are the same (*NE* 1139a11–13). This explains why this part is responsible for deliberation. The excellence of this part of the soul is practical wisdom.[22] Via deliberation, the calculative part determines the means by which the wanted end can be realized.

Thus, the desiring part of the soul provides that *for-the-sake-of-which* a choice is; the calculative part provides that *of which* that choice is. Together, the two parts make up the efficient cause and origin of the choice (*NE* 1139a31–34). Every choice necessarily needs both. Without a wanted end, there is nothing that can function as a means, and hence no action to choose. Without the means, there is no way to reach the end. We consider each aspect separately.

V. CHOICE OF, DELIBERATION, AND THE THINGS WITHIN THE AGENT'S REACH

A choice is *of* the action-to-be-performed, where an action can also be a refraining (Section III). The calculative part of the soul is needed to figure out what action this is going to be. It does so by means of a certain activity: a process of deliberation (*bouleusis*).[23] For Aristotle, deliberation is practical inquiry (*NE* 1112b22–3) that regards the possible means that allow agents to reach their ends. In terms of Aristotelian syllogistic, deliberation is the search for the middle term (1142b24) or terms of a practical (i.e., action-related) syllogism. For Aristotle, practical reasoning seems to be a form of syllogistic reasoning that involves at least one universal term that expresses something the agent has adopted as an

---

[21]   Wanting is a desire that requires the listening and obeying ability of the desiring part of the soul to have been used. It presupposes, and depends on, the rational part of the agent's soul. (For a different interpretation of how wanting is related to the soul, see Lorenz 2009.)

[22]   *Phronēsis*; cf. *NE* 1103a3–6, and see Natali, in this volume, for details.

[23]   Also *boulē*, alternative translation: "reasoning." Aristotle discusses deliberation also in *NE* vi 9 and in *EE* ii 10.

end (e.g., eating healthy), and whose conclusion states the action-to-be-done as a case of the universal term.[24]

Our main interest regards the things that deliberation is about, that is, the objects of deliberation (*bouleuta*). Aristotle states that the objects of deliberation must belong to the class of things that are in the agent's power.[25] There are two features of the things in the agent's power that demarcate them as the proper objects of deliberation and choice: (i) that they are things that are within the agent's reach; and (ii) that they provide alternative options.

Deliberation is aimed at action that leads toward one of the agent's ends. Hence deliberation is about things that are within our reach and that allow us to obtain our ends. Deliberating about any other things would be pointless. Aristotle argues this point repeatedly (*NE* iii 3.1112a21–b16, vi 2.1139b5–11; *EE* ii 10.1226a21–32), listing all the things that are not within our reach, in order to arrive by elimination at those that are. He rules out:

- Eternal (i.e., unchanging) things, like mathematical truths or astronomical facts
- Changing things that always happen the same way, like the rising of the sun
- Changing things that follow unpredictable patterns, like the weather
- Chance events, like finding a treasure
- Human affairs that are out of our reach, like the political affairs of remote states
- Particular facts, like whether this is bread
- The past, like to have sacked Troy
- Our own ends, since we have them or set them, but do not deliberate about them
- Things that happen through us, but always in the same way[26]

---

[24] For more information on deliberation, see Segvic 2011, sections 1–3, and Natali, in this volume.

[25] *epi* with dative: Aristotle uses this mostly, but not exclusively, in the form *ta ēph'emin*, "the things in our power" and *eph ēmin* plus infinitive of verb of action, "in our power to do" something. Alternative translations are "up to us," "depending on us," "lie within us." Aristotle takes this phrase from ordinary language. Only in post-Aristotelian philosophy do we find *to eph ēmin* used as a philosophical term; see Bobzien 1998.

[26] Aristotle does not explain these last ones. He may have in mind things like sleeping, breathing, blinking. We don't deliberate whether we should sleep, breathe, blink, although we may deliberate whether we should sleep, breathe, blink, *now*. Alternatively he intends unreflective habits; e.g., we may always put our left sock on before our right. There is nothing to deliberate about in this (in ordinary circumstances); we may never have deliberated and chosen to do it this way round. We just do it.

By way of this elimination argument, Aristotle determines the possible objects of deliberation, that is, the things in our power. His narrowing of the scope is entirely common sense. As Aristotle himself says, he is concerned with what reasonable people would deliberate about; people who are mentally handicapped or unstable may deliberate about things not in their control (*NE* iii 3.1112a19–21). Aristotle is correct that reasonable people do not deliberate about the types of things excluded. They deliberate only about things that they consider to be, with a reasonable certainty,[27] within their control to achieve.[28]

Positively, Aristotle determines the possible objects of deliberation as those things that *can be brought about through us by action*.[29] As sufficient condition for this, he mentions that the origin of the action is in us (1112b27–28). As we know, this entails that we are the efficient causes of those actions. Presumably preempting a possible objection, Aristotle notes that things we ask our friends to do *for us* count among the things brought about through us by action. Thus, the possible objects of deliberation turn out to be what we consider possible actions of ours – in a suitably loose sense.

VI. THE NECESSITY OF ALTERNATIVE OPTIONS

Voluntariness was a necessary condition for praise and blame for actions. As such, it is a property of actions,[30] and that is of things that actually occur. But restriction to things that actually occur, and their properties, is insufficient to capture a vital aspect of human agency – namely, that the agent must have *alternative options*. These come in at the stage of deliberation: Agents will deliberate about a possible course of action only if they have more than one possible course of action. It does not suffice that the agent is the origin and efficient cause of some change. (For the agent is also, say, the origin and efficient cause of her digestion and her reflex actions, but does not deliberate about these.) Deliberation and choice both require that the agent has alternative options. It is an

---

[27] There is no guarantee ever: external circumstances can prevent the action. Aristotle indicates that the agent is aware of this, when he states that agents deliberate about things that happen for the most part (*hōs epi to polu*, 1112b8–9). They do not need certainty that they will bring about the action, just that, regarding comparable situations, for the most part this is so.

[28] Even reasonable people may err, of course, due to ignorance of circumstances: you may think that you can take the train, yet unbeknownst to you, it just derailed. Whether such deliberation would be apparent only, as opposed to actual, Aristotle does not say.

[29] *NE* 1112a31–32, 1111a33–34. It seems that Aristotle takes it for granted that all agree that the things he needs to demarcate are the things in our power. His question is *what classes of things satisfy this condition*.

[30] Or a relation between an action (or refraining) and the agent.

essential feature of the things we deliberate about, and that are in our power, that they come in pairs.[31] Following ordinary Greek language use, Aristotle uses the phrase "in our power" also to express this necessary feature of human agency. We articulate this by saying that he uses the expression as two-sided. That is, he assumes the following principle: if it is in the agent's power to do something, then it is also in the agent's power not to do it, and vice versa (see *NE* 1110a17–18, 1113b7–8 and Section IX). Aristotle also sometimes uses "being master of" (*kurios* + genitive) and expressions of possibility (*exēn*) in this two-sided way to express the same requirement for human agency (e.g., *NE* iii 5.1113b32–33, 1114a2–3, a16–17, a19–20).

For agents to act, it is not sufficient that they *have* alternative options. They also need to *be aware* that they have them. If agents do not believe that both doing and not doing something are in their power, they will not deliberate about whether to do it.[32] Possibly, when Aristotle says that it is unclear how the things we deliberate about will turn out (*NE* 1112b9), he wishes to draw attention to this fact.[33]

In any event, in *De Interpretatione* 9, where Aristotle draws out the consequences of the hypothesis that everything happens by unconditional necessity,[34] he states "there would be no need to deliberate or busy oneself with anything, thinking that if we do this, this will happen, but if we do not, it will not" (*DI* 9.18b31–32, Ackrill trans., modified). This shows that Aristotle assumes (i) that agents generally believe that they have alternative options and consider them part of their deliberation; moreover, (ii) that they (or at least the reflective agents) believe their deliberation is a determining factor for which option is going to be realized. (ii) is confirmed when Aristotle, in the same context, appeals to the facts, writing "we see that what will be has an origin both in deliberation and in action" (9.19a7–9, Ackrill trans.). Thus, Aristotle takes it for granted not just that agents have alternative options but also that they are aware both that they have these options ("if I do this, this will happen; if not, it won't") and that their deliberation process and its result are necessary causal factors that (co-)determine what action they will perform and whether they reach the goal the action was directed at.

[31] The pairs are related to each other as *F* and not-*F* are. Of course there may be many other options, *G*, *H*, *I*, etc. (with which there then also come not-*G*, not-*H*, not-*I*, etc.).

[32] Of course, in the course of a deliberation, there may be, e.g., dead ends, or discoveries that presumed options are actually not options. Aristotle is aware of this; cf. *NE* 1112b24–26.

[33] This is one of several possible interpretations of this sentence. Alternatively, Aristotle could refer to the fact that the type of actions deliberated about do not always reach their end (see Joachim 1951, 101; Taylor 2006, 150). But this would make either this or the "for the most part" clause (see note 28) redundant.

[34] Unconditional necessity: necessarily *p*, no matter what else is the case.

The required alternative options and the agents' awareness of these entail neither (i) that the agents are causally undetermined in their action nor (ii) that the agents *believe* they are causally undetermined in their action. That is, Aristotle's *NE* iii 1–5 and *DI* 9 are compatible with (i) that, the agent and the circumstances being what they are, they together are sufficient causal factors to bring about the action and (ii) that the agents do not hold beliefs that they are causally undetermined in their action. All that the text suggests is that (reflective) agents are aware that without their deliberation the action would not take place – that their deliberation is a necessary causal factor in the process that brings about the action (18b31–32, 19a7–9); and that Aristotle holds that through their deliberation (and choice) the agents themselves become a decisive causal factor of the action and its direct consequences (18b31–32 and 19a7–9 together with *NE* iii 2, 5, e.g., 1113b30–33).

VII. HOW DELIBERATION AND CHOICE ARE RELATED

Aristotle holds that the objects of choice (*prohaireta*) are taken from the same pool of things as the objects of deliberation: the things within our reach. Every object of choice was at some point an object of deliberation. However, being an object of choice is not the same as being an object of deliberation. An object of deliberation is something the agent deliberates about. An object of choice is something the agent has come to be choosing. There is a significant difference here. The object of deliberation has an element of indefiniteness to it. By contrast, the object of choice (i.e., the chosen course of action) is determinate (1112b9, 1113a3). An object of deliberation becomes an object of choice via the agent's judging or deciding (*krinein*, 1113a4, 1113a12). At the moment when the agent judges to pursue one of the courses of action about which they deliberated, the agent starts to have a deliberated desire – that is, a desire in accordance with the judgment (*krisis*) resulting from the deliberation (1113a11–12) – for pursuing the respective course of action. This desire *is* the agent's choice.[35] Hence, where there was an indeterminacy between at least two possible courses of action, there is only one course, once the choice has come into being. The object of choice is thus determined and rationally desired, whereas the object of deliberation was not (yet). Being a desire, choice essentially has a duration, which in the standard case continues from the moment of judgment to the completion

---

[35] In fact, Aristotle wavers about how to categorize choice. Since both elements of reason (via reasoning process) and of desire (via character disposition; see also Section VIII) are preserved in choice, Aristotle alternatively calls it reasoned desire and desiring reason (*NE* 1139b4–5, *EE* 1227a3–5, 1226b17).

of the action.[36] The English translation "choice" does not (clearly) capture this point; but it is important for a full understanding of Aristotle's theory of agency.

What is it that determines which course of action (of those under deliberation) becomes rationally desired or the object of choice? The answer is: the agents' deliberation and ends. The agents assemble the premises and go through a – potentially rather complex – course of reasoning, and it is their drawing the conclusion that is the judgment that brings into being their choice. What conclusion an agent arrives at likely depends on a variety of factors. These include what ends the agents started with as general premises (Section VIII), how well developed their reasoning ability is, how well their memory and perception function,[37] and probably what various external circumstances occur during the deliberation process, such as possible distractions, time pressure, and which people the deliberator may consult for help (NE 1112b10–11, b27–28).

Hence Aristotle's choice (prohairesis), as he uses it in NE iii 1–5, is nothing like an act of deciding or an act of choice between alternatives.[38] Nor is it (or is it issued from) a faculty for causally undetermined choice or decision, or of free will, as is sometimes assumed (e.g., Grant 1874, ii 14). The judgment (krisis) that co-causes this desire, too, is not a faculty for undetermined decision making, nor is there any decision-making faculty such as a will in the agent that determines which way the judgment will go.[39]

VIII. CHOICE FOR THE SAKE OF, WANTING AND THE TRANSFER OF THE MORAL ASPECT TO CHOICE

Aristotle's discussion of choice of in NE iii 2–3 elucidates the relation between the things in our power, deliberation and choice, but links the

[36] This becomes more intelligible, if we consider that for Aristotle the choice (prohairesis) of a particular action is the actuality (energeia) of a dispositional state of the soul, and as such is complete at any moment and can be continued (until the action is completed).

[37] Cf. the mention of intellect (nous) in NE 1139a33 and Aristotle's description of its role in deliberation in NE vi 11.

[38] When Aristotle says, at NE 1112a16–17, that the name prohairesis suggests that to prohaireton is something (to be) chosen before, or in preference to, other things, this does not imply that prohairesis is an act of choice between alternatives. Rather, one needs to read it in its context, where Aristotle emphasizes that reason and deliberation are necessary conditions for prohairesis. It is since prohairesis requires reason, that prohairesis is of what is preferable to other things.

[39] In the virtuous agent, the dispositional state of the soul of which a choice is the actuality, is the respective virtue (see Sections VIII and X). This is why Aristotle sometimes says that virtue is prohairesis (NE 1106a2–4), where he intends the dispositional state from which the desire issues.

voluntariness of actions neither with moral responsibility nor with virtue and vice. For this connection to become apparent, we need to examine *for-the-sake-of-what* a choice is. Aristotle tackles this issue in *NE* iii 4, and draws the connection explicitly in *NE* iii 5.[40]

We saw that the part of the soul causally responsible for the *for-the-sake-of-what* of choice is the desiring part – that is, the part where a person's desires, including his wants, as well as the person's character dispositions (e.g., the person's virtues and vices), are manifested (Section IV). Without character dispositions that determine a person's ends, there can be no choice (*NE* 1139a33–4, b3–4).

Virtuous agents have as an end that which is truly good, since they have the correct view of what is good. In *NE* ii, Aristotle established this end to be the intermediate in action. In the *Eudemian Ethics*, Aristotle explicitly considers the function of the desiring part of the soul for the case of virtuous and vicious agents (*EE* 1227b34–1228a5): since virtuous individuals have (hitting) the intermediate as their end, their choice is *for the sake of* (hitting) the intermediate. Thus a character virtue is the *cause* of the intermediate *qua* being intermediate (*EE* 1227b36–8). It causes the end of the choice to be correct. That is, the virtuous agent, when judging, brings about a choice with a view to (hitting) the intermediate *qua* intermediate. (An agent may choose to tip a certain amount because it is the intermediate between being stingy and being wasteful; or because this happens to be the amount of cash in the agent's pocket. In the latter case, tipping that amount is not chosen *qua* intermediate.)[41]

In *NE* iii 4, Aristotle explains by means of which element of the desiring part of the soul this causation works: it is via wanting.[42] Wanting is *of* the end (*NE* 1111b26–28, 1113a15, 1113b3), which in the case of action is (truly or apparently) good action and their (truly or apparently) good consequences. Virtuous agents both want what is truly good (1113a31–33, *eupraxia*, 1139a34) and have all their other desires aligned with their wanting. It is by this internally unchallenged want for the intermediate that a virtuous character disposition causes the intermediate. Vicious agents may not want what is truly good, but only what – since pleasant – *appears* good to them. Their vices make them want incorrect ends and thus cause their not realizing the intermediate.

---

[40] Commentators on *NE* iii 1–5 are often somewhat unclear about what the purpose of *NE* iii 4 and its location between *NE* iii 3 and *NE* iii 5 are. A reading of the passage like the one presented here that explains the purpose of *NE* iii 4 in its context thus has the edge over those.

[41] For this distinction, see also Aristotle *NE* v 8.

[42] Translators of the *NE* have also chosen "wish" or "will" (Rolfes 1921: "Wille") or "willing" instead of "wanting" for *boulēsis*.

Generally, the agents' character dispositions (in the case of the virtuous and the vicious, their virtues and vices) cause the agents to have a
certain type of goal-directed desire: wanting. This wanting provides the
deliberative part of the soul with the *starting point* for their deliberation,
by providing a universal term (e.g., healthy eating) for the major premise,
to which term is tied the agent's desire for its realization.

Since the virtuous and vicious agents' character disposition has essentially a moral aspect to it (it *is* virtue, or *is* vice), this moral aspect is, via
their wanting, transferred to their choice. For example, if the agent's end
was not the intermediate, their choice would – mostly – not be for actions
that are intermediate.[43]

IX. FROM CHOICE TO ACTION

Choice is caused by a cooperation of two causal factors, issued from two
different parts of the agent's soul. They both together make up the origin
and efficient cause of choice (*NE* 1139a31–34). It is in choice that a
person's reason and her desire (which is expressive of her character
disposition) are joined and preserved. This is a precondition for human
agency – as opposed to animal behavior.

Choice, in turn, is the efficient cause and origin of action
(*NE* 1139a31–32; see also Segvic 2011, sec. 4). We saw that choice is a
type of desire and, as such, has a duration. But not every choice ends in
the action chosen. Choice continues from its beginning until either
(i) the action has been completed, or (ii) something external interferes
with the realization of the action, or (iii) the agent reconsiders her
options and redeliberates, with a different choice as result, or (iv)
(if there is a time limit on its possible realization) the agent fails
internally to realize the action – a case taken up in Section XI.

There are two further reasons why there is no one-to-one correlation
between choice and adult human action. On the one hand, Aristotle
acknowledges spur-of-the-moment acts that are voluntary (*NE* 1111b9–
10; *EE* 1224a2–4, 1226b3–4). So we may incur praise or blame for them.
(We may shoo away a fly, thereby brushing a glass off the table; or
throw ourselves in front of a car to save a child.) But, Aristotle holds,
these spur-of-the-moment acts do not involve choice. No deliberation
precedes them. They may be reflex actions or caused directly by one's
dispositions (*NE* 1117a20–22). On the other hand, one choice can be
sufficient for repeated action. For example, you may resolve to floss
your teeth daily, and then, caused by this reasoned desire for daily

---

[43] *NE* 1113a18; 1113b1–2; 1139a33–36, a39; *EE* 1128a4–5; cf. *NE* 1144a20: the virtue
makes the choice right.

flossing, floss every day. It may be that Aristotle thought – correctly – that a large part of our actions are of this type.

X. TRANSFERENCE OF THE MORAL ASPECT FROM CHOICE TO ACTION

Via choice, the moral aspect, that is, the element of good or bad, is transferred from the agent's character disposition to the agent's action. It is this transference of the moral aspect to action, and consequently the voluntariness of this aspect in the action, which Aristotle explains in the first part of NE iii 5, taking up what he laid out in NE iii 4:[44]

(1) The end being the object of wanting (2) and the means to the end being the objects of deliberation and choice, (3) the actions with regard to these [means to the end] would be in accordance with choice and [that is] voluntary. (4) And the activities of the virtues are [activities] with regard to these [means to the end]. (NE 1113b3–6; emphasis added)

This is the first time, since the beginning of NE iii 1 (1109b30–31; cf. Section II), that Aristotle mentions virtue, action, and voluntariness together. Naturally, here, we should expect him to provide information about the connection between them that he hinted at there. If read carefully, the passage does just this: (1) and (2) introduce the two causal strands that together cause choice. (1) Wanting, the goal-directed desire whose end is determined by the agent's character dispositions, is responsible for *what the end of an action is*. (2) Deliberation, the process of reasoning determined by the calculative part of the agent's soul, is responsible for *what kind of action the action is*. (3) Since these two together cause choice, and the choice causes the action (Section IX), the action is expected to be in accordance with choice and hence voluntary.[45]

It is in (4) that Aristotle expressly draws the connection to virtue. We assume that by "activities of the virtues" Aristotle denotes the actions of the virtuous agent.[46] Thus the character virtues are active via actions in which the intermediate is realized. In fact, the *only way* in which character virtues can be realized in action is via realizing the intermediate in action. As (1)–(3) make clear, not just any action of the agent will do. For the moral aspect of virtue (or vice) to be transferred to action, it has to be the result of choice. Thus, we can make explicit an

44 Remember that the division into chapters is not Aristotle's, so the beginning of NE iii 5 would have followed without pause upon the end of NE iii 4.
45 Anything that occurs in accordance with choice is voluntary; cf., e.g., NE 1112a14–15, EE 1226b34–35.
46 Cf. NE 1094a4, a6, a16: actions are a kind of activity.

implicit conclusion of Aristotle's argument: the activities of virtues are actions that are in accordance with choice. The only way in which virtues can be realized in action is via *choice and* realization of the intermediate in action. For example, the only way the end of healthy living can be reached is (via wanting of that end) by *choices and* actions that realize that end, for example, *choosing and* eating a balanced meal rather than doughnuts galore.[47]

And since all action in accordance with choice is voluntary, we can make explicit a second implicit conclusion in Aristotle's argument: the activities of the virtues are voluntary. This squares with Aristotle's account of the voluntary. As the virtues (or vices, respectively) are one of the two causal factors of choice, and there is no external force, or ignorance of the relevant kind, involved in their co-causing choice, what they contribute to the action (i.e., its moral aspect) should be expected to be voluntary.

In the following lines, Aristotle provides an argument that has the function of explaining how it is that virtue and vice in action themselves are in our power (and thus voluntary). This argument is based on the point established in (1)–(4) that the activities of the virtues (and vices) concern the means to the end.[48] Here is, first, the passage:

(5) And virtue, too, is in our power, and equally vice. (6) For where it is in our power to act, it is [also in our power] to not act, and where [it is in our power] to not [act], also to [act]. (7) Hence, if acting, being noble, is in our power, not acting, being shameful, will also be in our power, and if not acting, being noble, is in our power, acting, being shameful, [will] also [be] in our power. (8) But if doing noble things and doing shameful things are in our power, and equally, too, not doing [noble things and not doing shameful things], (9) and this was [as we said earlier] being good and being bad, (10) then being fine and being base will be in our power. (*NE* 1113b6–14)

Aristotle's use of the singular terms "virtue" and "vice" suggests that he is talking about virtue and vice as characteristics manifested in an action, and about the agent *qua* agent of the action, rather than about the character dispositions.[49] (In (4) he made the move from (i) virtue as

---

47   This fact, that the moral aspect can be expressed (or failed to be expressed) only if there is choice explains why toddlers and dogs, though they may be de facto praised and blamed, are not held *morally* responsible for what they do.

48   Aristotle never states the purpose of these lines; moreover, they contain some textual issues. We here provide what we consider the most plausible reading and mention and assess alternative suggestions in footnotes.

49   We agree with Meyer 2006, 129–131, that Aristotle appears to use the expressions for virtue and vice, and for our being good and bad, noble and base, in two quite different ways. When he uses the expressions in the plural, he talks about the moral dispositions, and our having virtue or vice, in this context, means that we have those character dispositions. When he uses the expressions in the singular, he often simply means the

character disposition to (ii) the manifestation in action of the character disposition that is virtue. In (5)–(10), he is talking about (ii).)

We believe that Aristotle assumes an implicit conclusion (C), "the activities of the virtues are activities in accordance with choice and voluntary"; and parallel to (4), "the activities of the vices are [activities] with regard to these [means to the end]" and to (C), "the activities of the vices are activities in accordance with choice and voluntary." In other words, we believe that Aristotle takes it for granted that the same psychological structure-and-procedure by which virtues become active are in play when vices become active. The purpose of 1113b7–14 is then to set out how the moral aspects of the virtues and vices (that which makes them virtues or vices) are manifested in action in such a way that praise and blame can be attached to the agents for the resulting noble or base action (*qua* noble or base action).

The argument starts with a statement of the thesis to be proved, that is, (5). This is standard procedure from Aristotle's dialectic. Next, Aristotle introduces a two-part premise, (6), stating the two-sidedness of things being in our power. Its truth seems taken for granted. The points that human actions are goal-directed, and their end, which is an aspect of them, is determined by the agent's character dispositions (including their virtues or vices), are taken from (1)–(4) as additional premises. Thus, a full description of the actions at issue would not be "(not) doing x" but "(not) doing x, x being noble" or "(not) doing x, x being shameful" respectively. In (7), Aristotle combines (6) with (1)–(4) and draws an intermediate conclusion ("hence"): since between good and bad actions the relations hold that if by doing x one is hitting the intermediate, then by not doing x one is not; and if by not doing x one is hitting the intermediate, then by doing x one is not, we get the expanded statement of the two-sidedness of things being in our power. From (7), there follows the antecedent of (8)–(10), that is, (8), which rearranges the possible cases, putting the cases of acting before those of refraining. In (9), Aristotle restates as an additional premise an account of what it is to be good or bad in action that he used before. Finally, from (8) and (9) he concludes (10), assuming that if x is in our power and $x = y$, then y is in our power. The conclusion (10) is an alternative formulation of the thesis (5): being fine and being base are in our power.

Aristotle's argument (1113b3–14) is then in short: all action is goal-directed. The end is determined by the agent's character dispositions and wanted by the agent because of this character. An action with which the

goodness and badness manifested in an agent's action: "you were bad, you lied to me"; "you were good, you didn't have dessert." Here, when agents are called good or bad, etc., this is a "punctual" and "re-flective" (from the action back to the agent) use: the agents are called good or bad insofar as their action was good or bad.

agent aims at the intermediate is a good-and-noble action; an action with which the agent aims at an extreme is shameful-and-bad. The goodness or badness are transferred to the action from the character disposition virtue and vice, by means of a choice. (Character virtue is good; character vice is bad.) Actions that are the result of choice are in our power, and so are their opposites. But the actions at issue that result from a choice have a moral aspect, which is manifested in them because the moral disposition is a co-cause of the choice.[50] Thus it is correct to say of these actions that they are in our power, being good, and that they are in our power, being bad, respectively; and hence that the good actions and the bad actions are in our power, respectively.

And in the sense in which we are fine-and-good or base-and-bad, insofar as we performed a good or bad action, it is also correct to say that our being good, or our being bad, is in our power. Aristotle is here not talking about it being in our power that we are fine or base in the sense of *having virtuous or vicious dispositions*. Evidently, the argument proves no such thing.[51] Rather, the goodness or badness of the agent that is in the agent's power is derived from the good or bad actions. And this is all that is required to establish the *moral* responsibility of the agent for her actions. As her being good/bad (*qua* doing something good/bad) is in her power and thus voluntary, she can be praised/blamed as being fine/base (*qua* having done something good/bad).[52]

---

[50]   Aristotle considers only the character dispositions of vice and virtue here – not any in-betweens, for which see Section XI.

[51]   There are several alternative interpretations of *NE* 1113b3–14. These either (i) leave Aristotle arguing fallaciously, or (ii) needlessly change the text, or (iii) face some other interpretational difficulties. *Ad* (i): both the interpretations (a) that the passage is a self-contained proof that virtue and vice in action are in our power and (b) that the passage is a proof that virtuous and vicious dispositions are in our power make Aristotle reason incorrectly (cf. Meyer 1993, 129–131). *Ad* (ii): the interpretation that in this passage Aristotle shows that we have undetermined, free, choice (Broadie 1991; Destrée 2011) is based on an emendation, introducing a verb of saying into (6), and reading "no" (*ou*) instead of "not" (*mē*) (cf. Bobzien 2014). *Ad* (iii): the asymmetry interpretation of this passage (e.g., Broadie and Rowe 2002, 317; Pakaluk 2005, 145–146) assumes either (a) that it is assumed *ad hominem* that virtue is in our power or (b) that this has been shown in lines 1113b3–6; and argues from there that vice, too, is in our power. One problem with this interpretation is that it sits badly with Aristotle summarizing iii 1–5 by saying that virtue is voluntary and in our power: (a) makes his summary equal an *ad hominem* assumption of his; (b) makes his summary regard only four lines of *NE* iii 5 and leads to the philosophical oddity that while the voluntariness of virtue was justified by its being caused by our virtuous disposition, via choice, the voluntariness of vice is justified in an entirely different and needlessly complex argument, although an equivalent argument to that for virtue would have suggested itself and is assumed, e.g., in *EE* 1228a4–5.

[52]   Cf. also *NE* iii 5.1113b21–26, where private individuals and lawmakers are said to punish people who do wicked things and praise people who do noble things: it is only after the argument 1113b3–14 that the praise of noble actions is mentioned in *NE* iii 1–5. But

At this point, Aristotle has completed showing how virtue concerns actions (*NE* 1109b30) in such a way that its manifestation in action is voluntary and in our power, so that praise or blame can be attached to the agent for having performed a noble or shameful action: we can say "you are noble insofar as you did this," or "your doing this was bad." The blame or praise can be attached to the agent, since it was something in the agent, namely the agent's character disposition, which is causally responsible for the moral dimension of the action.[53]

XI. CHOICE AND ARISTOTLE'S FOUR TYPES OF AGENTS

It is instructive to consider the causal sequences from an agent's dispositions and intellect, via their wanting, deliberating, and choice, to action, as they occur in Aristotle's four main types of agents: the virtuous, vicious, strong-willed, and weak-willed.[54] We disregard all possible external interferences in the process from forming the choice to completing the action. These would include cases in which, unbeknownst to the agent, external factors cause something usually in the agent's power not to be so; and cases in which, unforeseeable for the agent, external factors thwart the realization of their choice. We consider only cases in which, in Aristotle's view, the agent is the origin of the action.

1. The Virtuous Agent

The virtuous agent is one in whom all factors of voluntary action are realized in an excellent way. (i) The agent's character dispositions are good; they are virtues. They cause the agent's ends, which are the intermediate relative to each dimension of virtue. Since the character dispositions are states of the desiring part of the soul, the virtuous agent desires – more precisely, wants – the intermediate with respect to each dimension of virtue. (ii) The agent's practical intellect works without flaws. The agent has practical wisdom. As a result, and given the

---

Aristotle noted the link between virtue and noble action already at *NE* i 12.1101b31–32: "As a result of [virtue] people tend to do noble things (*ta kala*)."

[53] Perhaps this transference might be expressed using Aristotle's model of efficient causation in *Meta.* vii: As the form of health in the doctor's soul is the efficient cause of any particular coming-to-be-healthy produced (1032b21–24), so the form of good action (its intermediateness) in the agent's soul is the efficient cause of the agent's particular good (i.e., intermediate) action. Either way, it is the person's desire (the doctor's desire to heal, the agent's *prohairesis*) *via* which the efficient cause realizes the effect.

[54] Of the remaining two named types, Aristotle mentions, at *NE* vii 1 and 5, that brutes may be beyond blame, godlike heroes beyond praise.

agent's wants, the agent reasons correctly about how to realize the intermediate in her action, using an accurate assessment regarding what is in her power. (iii) All other desires of the agent are fully aligned with what the agent wants. (Not only does the agent want health-promoting food, and deliberates that leafy greens are health promoting; she also loves leafy greens, that is, has an appetite for them, and has a heartfelt dislike for fast food.) The agent's wanting-of-the-end and deliberation-of-the-means together then cause a choice.[55] (iv) Since the agent's other desires are fully aligned with what the agent wants, at the appropriate time the agent's choice causes the action. Thus the action is voluntary. It is also (internally and externally)[56] noble (kalos), and that aspect of the action is also voluntary. The action, qua being noble, is thus praiseworthy.

One noteworthy aspect of the actions of completely virtuous agents is that, although nothing forces the agents to act, for psycho-logical reasons (i.e., for reasons to do with their soul), the agents cannot choose or act otherwise than they do. In the same circum-stances, the same virtuous agent will always choose and follow up the same noble course of action. There is nothing in the agent that could interfere with this. For Aristotle, this is no reason to question the voluntariness of the action or the agent. On the contrary, completely virtuous agents act with the minimal possible amount of force, since in addition to the absence of external force, there is also a total absence of psychological, internal factors that could be considered as compelling them to act.[57]

[55] What happens if there are two equally good actions toward reaching the end? In that case, we can assume, external circumstances or nonmoral elements of the agent's character (a preference for red over blue, say) will determine the agent's choice. If there are no such circumstantial elements, rather than not acting at all (like Buridan's Ass) the rational agent would do something comparable to tossing a coin.

[56] An internally good/bad action is one co-caused by the respective virtue/vice. An externally good/bad action is one that is indistinguishable from an internally good/bad one, except for the fact that it is not co-caused by the respective virtue/vice. The internal/external terminology is ours. But the distinction is Aristotle's: cf. NE 1105b5–9. (From the externally good actions one must distinguish the accidentally [kata sumbebēkos] good actions from NE v 8 that were illustrated by our tip example in Section VIII. They do not have the intermediate as end.)

[57] Cf. also NE 1111a29–31, where Aristotle mentions that it would be absurd to call involuntary the things that one ought to desire. The fact that for Aristotle the com-pletely virtuous person cannot choose other than he does provides no support for the assumption that Aristotle was a determinist. (After all, few of us, if any, are completely virtuous, and thus barred from the exhilarating experience of conflicting desires.) Rather, what the fact shows is that being able to choose otherwise was for Aristotle in no way a condition for being justifiably praised. (Cf. also Frede 2011, ch. 2.)

2. The Strong-Willed Agent

(i) The strong-willed and the virtuous agents have and want the same ends: the intermediate in actions.[58] The ends wanted are thus good (as opposed to just appearing good to the agent). What differentiates the strong-willed from the virtuous is that not all their desires are aligned with their wanted ends. (ii) The agents may or may not reason correctly about the means to their ends, and they may or may not accurately assess what is in their power. For simplicity, we assume they do both right. (iii) The agent's willing-of-the-end and deliberation-of-the-means together cause a choice for the action that promotes the intermediate. (iv) Despite the agent's desires that conflict with their wanted end, at the appropriate time the agent's choice causes the action (*NE* 1111b13–15). (The agent wants health-promoting food, chooses to eat, and eats, the leafy greens, although the agent's appetite is for the greasy sugary doughnuts.) Thus the action is voluntary. It is also (externally) noble,[59] and the result of a strong-willed disposition.

3. The Weak-Willed Agent

In points (i) to (iii), the weak-willed agent does not differ from the strong-willed. (iv) The element of weak-willedness (*akrasia*) comes to the surface in the relation between choice and action. It is at the point when one would expect the choice to cause the action that the agent's conflicting desires interfere (*NE* 1111b13–14). They cause a temporary state of ignorance about some property of some object involved in the action (e.g., that this thing is sugary; that doughnuts are sugary; that sugary food is unhealthy).[60] As a result, the persons' behavior is aligned with their conflicting desire, say their appetite for doughnuts. It is this desire that causes an alternative to the chosen action (not eating the leafy greens; eating the doughnuts instead). The action is thus neither externally nor internally noble.

Actions caused by weak-willedness are nonetheless voluntary. Aristotle is unequivocal on this point. First, he argues that actions that might be described as actions in which the agent was compelled to act the way he did by irrational desires like appetite or anger do not thereby

---

[58] Arguably, one could have an ignoble end and be strong-willed, or an ignoble end and be weak-willed, but we disregard these possibilities here, too. A full classification of actions based on the various factors involved would provide a much larger number of possible cases than four.

[59] If the deliberation process was flawed, there would be no guarantee that the action is noble.

[60] Different interpretations of Aristotle's theory of weak-willedness assume different objects of ignorance. For an in-depth discussion of the topic, see Lorenz, in this volume.

become involuntary. Rather, appetite and anger are no less manifestations of who the agent is than is his reason; hence actions that "come
from anger or appetite, too, are the actions of the person" (NE 1111b1–2).
Such actions satisfy the account of voluntariness, since external force is
absent and the action's origin is in the agent. Moreover, the temporary
forgetfulness or ignorance is also not of the kind that exempts actions
from voluntariness. For the cause of the forgetting is internal to the agent,
not external. Virtuous and strong-willed individuals would not have
forgotten. Thus, although for Aristotle choice is characteristic for actions
that are not "spur-of-the-moment," it does not follow that the choice is
always the *cause* of the action. In weak-willed actions, it is not.

4. The Vicious Agent

(i) The vicious agent's character dispositions are bad. They are character vices. They cause the agent's ends, which are bad, although they
appear good to the agent. The ends are extremes, rather than the intermediate, with respect to a dimension of virtue. The vicious agent wants
those extremes. (ii) Vicious agents may or may not deliberate correctly
or accurately assess what is in their power. For simplicity, we assume
they do both right. (iii) None of the other desires of the agent seem in
conflict with what the agent wants. (Not only does the agent *want* to
eat huge amounts of fast food; he also *loves* quadruple cheese-burgers
and grease-dripping doughnuts.) The agent's want for some extreme
together with his deliberation causes a choice. (iv) Since the agent's
other desires do not conflict with his wants, his choice causes the
action, which is thus voluntary. It is also (internally and externally)
bad, and that aspect of it is also voluntary. The action, *qua* being bad,
is thus blameworthy. (*Qua* being an action of burger eating, it may
be praiseworthy: no ketchup on the shirt, no pickles on the pants, no
choking on the bun.)

5. Agents with Not Yet Fully Developed Character

Thus the actions of all four agent types involve choice, but only in three
cases does their choice cause the action. Yet the conditions of voluntariness are satisfied each time. Each case involves choice and thus the
relevant rational psychological process. Each time, the origin of the
action is in the agent, and there is neither external force nor ignorance
of the kind that eradicates voluntariness. Of course, for Aristotle, adult
humans do not start out with a fully developed character. Hence we
consider how action is brought about in agents with not yet fully
developed character. (i) Such agents do not yet have moral dispositions.

Still, they have wanting (*NE* 1114a11–13), that is, goal-directed desire, in the desiring part of their soul. Depending on their *natural* dispositions, their ends may or may not coincide with the intermediate (*NE* vi 13). The agents also have other desires, which are likely in conflict with some of their wants. (ii) Such agents have an ability for practical reasoning, and for assessing what is within their reach. They may not be very accurate on either front. (iii) This notwithstanding, the agent's wants and deliberation together (and, thus, the agent) will cause a choice. (iv) Depending on the strength of the agent's conflicting desires, either the choice causes the corresponding action, or the conflicting desires prevail. Either way, the action is voluntary. The action may be externally noble or bad. If it is bad, whether by choice or weak-willedness, the agents may be blamed for it. If it is good as a result of choice, they may be praised.

XII. VOLUNTARY CONSEQUENCES OF ADULT VOLUNTARY ACTION

People are praised and blamed not just for things they do or do not do, but also for consequences of things they did or did not do. Since voluntariness is a prerequisite for praise and blame, Aristotle also discusses voluntariness as it attaches to consequences of things people did or did not do. We call this indirect voluntariness. The main case of indirect voluntariness that Aristotle explains in *NE* iii 5 is that of the moral dispositions. But he starts with a more straightforward kind of indirect voluntariness, using examples.

In his first example, a drunk person does something that she would not have done, had she had some relevant circumstantial information, and that is punishable by law (and thus assumed to be blameworthy). Since the person lacks some relevant circumstantial information, what she *did* would not count as directly voluntary. It is no voluntary action. How can blame be attached to it nonetheless? The answer is that it is a consequence of an action that *was* directly voluntary. The person desired to drink, deliberated, chose, and drank. (Whether the choice was to drink or the drinking resulted from weak-willedness is irrelevant.) Nothing external forced her to drink. Hence her drinking – at least of her first few drinks – was voluntary. It was a foreseeable consequence of her drinking that she became drunk. This consequence, being drunk, a temporary condition, is indirectly voluntary. It is a consequence of being drunk that the person did not have certain information, which, had she had it, would have prevented her from acting. Thus, her acting is also indirectly voluntary (twice removed from the action, as it were). Hence it can be blamed.

In a second example, a person breaks a law that he did not know existed, but whose existence would have been easy for him to discover, had he cared to find out. Such persons are punished by law (and Aristotle assumes they are blameworthy). Perhaps the person did not know that it is illegal to dump dioxin in the public garbage site. A quick online search would have revealed this to him. Common sense would have suggested he check. Here we have a refraining (i.e., from checking), which is directly voluntary. The refraining is an instance of not taking care. (Not taking care here is neither a temporary condition, nor a character disposition, of the agent.) The refraining caused the condition of ignorance, which is indirectly voluntary; it in turn led to an act of lawbreaking, which is indirectly voluntary (twice removed from the refraining).[61]

What Aristotle's examples have in common (what makes them blameworthy) is that they are foreseeable consequences of voluntary action.[62] In terms of causation, there is a foreseeable causal chain that has its origin in the agent (NE 1113b30, 33). To express this fact, Aristotle invokes the alternative options the agent had when performing the (directly voluntary) actions.

Here he uses the expression "master of" (kurios + genitive, 1113b32) in a two-sided way: at the time of their actions, the agents were masters both of doing and of not doing those actions. This kind of formulation has been used to argue that Aristotle was an indeterminist with respect to voluntary actions: if at a time t the agent was master of not doing what she did at t, then at t the agent must have been causally undetermined with respect to doing or not doing what she did. She had the – indeterminist – freedom to do otherwise. However, just as in the case of Aristotle's use of "in our power" (Section VI), this is not so. For Aristotle, it is the fact that the agents (including their ends, awareness of alternative options, deliberation and choice) are causally responsible for what they do that makes their actions and their foreseeable consequences voluntary – not that their actions or choices were causally undetermined.

[61] The action of breaking the law is indirectly voluntary. The action of dumping dioxin in the garbage site is directly voluntary.

[62] At this point we see how the criterion of absence of ignorance for direct voluntariness can produce borderline cases. The person who injured her friend when fencing since she did not know the button was off was assumed not to have injured her friend – directly – voluntarily (see Section III). But if it was a case in which she simply did not bother to check, she injured her friend voluntarily nonetheless, just indirectly so. And there may be no natural cut-off points for situations in which people are expected to check from those in which they are not. (In ordinary circumstances, we would not be expected to do a chemical analysis of a drink we offer a friend, to check for potential poisoning.)

XIII. THE VOLUNTARINESS OF VIRTUOUS
AND VICIOUS DISPOSITIONS

So far, we have seen that for Aristotle, praise and blame can be (and are) bestowed on people for their individual actions, for the moral aspects of those actions, and for the foreseeable consequences of individual actions, including temporary mental states of the agent.

Aristotle recognizes that people are also praised and blamed for who they are, in the sense of what moral dispositions they have.[63] People may be blamed for being bad, that is, not for any particular bad action, but for those character dispositions that make them perform bad actions with some regularity; likewise, they may be praised for being virtuous. People may also be blamed for being weak-willed, in the sense of continuously falling short of their choices owing to conflicting desires. In *NE* iii 1, Aristotle introduced voluntariness as a necessary condition for praise and blame. Accordingly, in *NE* iii 5, he provides a theory of the voluntariness (and being-in-our-power) of character dispositions (1114a3–b25). Whatever his primary purpose for the passage may be,[64] in it he explains that, how, and why virtuous and vicious dispositions are voluntary. At the end of the passage he believes he has shown that the virtues, *qua* character dispositions, are in our power and voluntary; and the text where he shows this is *NE* iii 5.1114a3–b25.[65]

In outline, Aristotle's theory of the voluntariness of moral dispositions is the following. Virtues and vices are character dispositions. They are produced by an agent by repeatedly performing the actions that the disposition, once developed, will be a disposition for. Any agent who is not entirely uneducated knows this. The disposition-producing actions are voluntary and usually the result of choice – which warrants their voluntariness. Thus, (i), the disposition can be regarded as a foreseeable consequence of accumulative voluntary action of certain types. Moreover, (ii), the origin of the disposition lies in the agent – since the agent is the originator of the repeated action. Factors (i) and (ii) together qualify the

---

[63] *NE* 1101b14–15, 1101b31–32, 1103a8–10, 1114a28–31. For an excellent discussion of Aristotle's theory of our responsibility for our character, see Meyer 1993.

[64] The purpose (in fact of all of 1113b14–1114b25) is debated. Some think it is to show that the character dispositions are voluntary. Others think that the passage presupposes that *virtuous* dispositions are voluntary and argues from this to the conclusion that *vicious* dispositions are voluntary, too (e.g., Meyer 2006). Still others think that the purpose of the passage is to show that we are morally responsible for our character since causally undetermined, free actions are a partial cause of our character formation (e.g., Destrée 2011). For a counter to this assumption of causally undetermined choice, see my subsequent discussion.

[65] *NE* 1114b20–25 uses "voluntary" for virtues and vices, in the plural; 1114a28–31 uses "in our power" for dispositions (of body and soul).

disposition itself as voluntary – even though the process of its coming into being is a long, complex one and is more vulnerable to external interferences than individual actions. Agents can work toward having certain character dispositions (e.g., certain virtues) similar to the way they can work toward achieving certain consequences of individual actions. The main differences are, first, that the kind of action needs repetition and, second, that the location of the consequence is the agent's own soul.

Aristotle brings to the reader's attention one fundamental difference between direct and indirect voluntariness. This is the fact that agents can end directly voluntary things (like actions) at any point, but not indirectly voluntary things, including character dispositions (NE 1114a13–21; 1114b30–1115a3). Take a voluntary action: in standard cases, it is possible for agents to "change their minds," that is, to reverse their choice, at any point during their performing the action, and consequently stop the action. For example, on your way to the store you can turn around and go home; or you can terminate your daily flossing any day. In the case of voluntary character dispositions, the equivalent does not hold. Here a change of mind would amount to a reversal of wanting (1114a13–14). But the reversal of wanting, say, from wanting extremes as the end to wanting the intermediate as the end, or the change from wanting a vicious disposition to wanting a virtuous one, does not enable the person, as a result, to cease to have the disposition they have – or, in any case, not instantaneously.

Thus it is not a prerequisite for something x to be voluntary that at any time during which x is present, x's originator can, upon reversing her desire for x, make x stop or cease to exist – even if at no point during that time x is externally forced or the originator is relevantly ignorant. This should not surprise. First, it is a common feature of many indirectly voluntary things that they are not, or not instantly, reversible upon the originator's desire for reversal: consider being drunk or serious self-mutilation. Second, voluntariness helps single out cases for justified praise or blame; and it would be absurd if it was a requirement for justified praise or blame that its object could be reversed or undone by its originator. Persons could then only be blamed for the death of someone they deliberately killed if they could bring them back to life upon accordingly reversing their desire.

It is sometimes claimed that Aristotle maintains that the reason why actions of a vicious agent are voluntary and hence blameworthy lies in the fact that at some point in the past the agent could have reversed her development toward a vicious disposition (and *mutatis mutandis* for virtuous agents). But Aristotle never suggests or implies anything like this. His view is that any action that satisfies the criterion for direct voluntariness is voluntary *for that reason*. The fact that at some past time it was in the agent's power to reverse her path toward a vicious disposition is as irrelevant to the action's blameworthiness or praiseworthiness as is the fact that for psychological reasons an agent may be unable to act otherwise than she does.

WORKS CITED

Bobzien, Susanne. 1998. "The Inadvertent Conception and Late Birth of the Free-Will Problem." *Phronesis* 43: 133–175.

2012. "Found in Translation: Aristotle's *Nicomachean Ethics* 3.5, 1113b7-8 and Its Reception." *Oxford Studies in Ancient Philosophy* 45: 103–148.

Broadie, Sarah. 1991. *Ethics with Aristotle*. New York: Oxford University Press.

Broadie, Sarah, and Christopher Rowe. 2002. *Aristotle: Nicomachean Ethics; Translation, Introduction, and Commentary*. Oxford: Oxford University Press.

Burnet, John. 1900. *The Ethics of Aristotle*. London: Methuen.

Charles, David. 1984. *Aristotle's Philosophy of Action*. London: Duckworth.

Destrée, Pierre. 2011. "Aristotle on Responsibility for One's Character." 285–318 in Pakaluk and Pearson eds. 2011.

Frede, Michael. 2007. "The ἐφ' ἡμῖν in Ancient Philosophy." ΦΙΛΟΣΟΦΙΑ 37: 110–123.

2011. *A Free Will: Origins of the Notion in Ancient Thought*. Sather Classical Lectures. Berkeley: University of California Press.

Gauthier, R. A., and J. Y. Jolif. 1958–1959. *Aristote: L'Éthique à Nicomaque*. 3 vols. Louvain: Publications Universitaires de Louvain.

Grant, Arthur. 1866. *The Ethics of Aristotle*. Vol. 1. London: Longmans, Green.

1874. *The Ethics of Aristotle*. Vol. 2. London: Longmans, Green.

Irwin, Terence. 1985. *Nicomachean Ethics. With Introduction, Notes, and Glossary*. Indianapolis: Hackett.

Joachim, H. H. 1951. *Aristotle, The Nicomachean Ethics. A Commentary*. Oxford: Clarendon Press.

Kenny, Anthony. 1979. *The Aristotelian Ethics*. Oxford: Oxford University Press.

Kraut, Richard ed. 2005. *The Blackwell Guide to Aristotle's Ethics*. Oxford: Blackwell.

Lorenz, Hendrik. 2009. "Virtue of Character in Aristotle's *Nicomachean Ethics*." *Oxford Studies in Ancient Philosophy* 37: 177–212.

Meyer, Susan Sauvé. 1993. *Aristotle on Moral Responsibility*. Oxford: Oxford University Press.

2006. "Aristotle on the Voluntary." 137–157 in Kraut ed. 2005.

Pakaluk, Michael. 2005. *Aristotle's Nicomachean Ethics: An Introduction*. Cambridge: Cambridge University Press.

Pakaluk, Michael, and Giles Pearson eds. 2011. *Moral Psychology and Human Action in Aristotle*. New York: Oxford University Press.

Rolfes, Eugen. 1921. *Aristoteles, Nikomachische Ethik*. Leipzig: Meiner.

Segvic, Heda. 2009. "Deliberation and Choice in Aristotle." 144–171 in her *From Protagoras to Aristotle: Essays in Ancient Moral Philosophy*. Princeton: Princeton University Press. Reprinted in Pakaluk and Pearson eds. 2011, 159–186.

Taylor, C. C. W. 2006. *Aristotle: Nicomachean Ethics Books II–IV*. Oxford: Oxford University Press.

Woods, Michael. 1992. *Aristotle's Eudemian Ethics: Books I, II, and VIII*. 2nd ed. Oxford: Clarendon Press.

6   Courage and Temperance

In *Nicomachean Ethics* iii 6, Aristotle turns from his general account of virtue and its preconditions (ii to iii 5) to consider the specific character virtues and their related vices in more detail. The first two virtues he discusses, of central importance to the Greeks in general and Aristotle in particular, are courage (*andreia*, iii 6–9) and temperance (*sōphrosunē*, iii 10–12). As we shall see, Aristotle's accounts of these virtues are interesting both in their own right and in a number of ways for his general ethical views.

I. COURAGE (NE III 6–9)

1. The Sphere of Courage

Aristotle claims that courage (*andreia*: lit. "manliness" or "manly spirit") is a mean with respect to fear (*phobos*) and confidence (*tharros*), but in *NE* iii 6 he delimits the sphere of courage specifically by reference to the kind of fear that it concerns. He notes that the things that we fear are, without qualification, evils (*kaka*: bad things), and that for this reason some even define fear as "expectation of evil" (1115a7–9). He does not here offer his own definition of fear, but elsewhere he defines it as follows:

Fear (*phobos*) may be defined as a pain or disturbance caused by envisaging some destructive or painful evil in the future. For there are some evils, e.g., injustice or stupidity, the prospect of which does not frighten us: only such as amount to great pains or losses do. (*Rhetoric* ii 5.1382a21–24)

On this account, fear is tied to the prospect of *great* pains or losses, to the anticipation of certain fairly major traumatic incidents. This notion of fear is narrower than the one that we standardly recognize, which seems tied to negative prospects more generally, not just the specific negative prospects that Aristotle mentions – we *can* fear appearing stupid or (suffering) some injustice. However, Aristotle's notion of fear is itself broader than he requires for his account of courage. This is because he thinks that courage is not properly concerned with all the objects we may, even by his lights, fear:

What sort of fearful things, then, do concern the courageous man? Surely the worst kind, since no one is more likely to stand his ground in the face of horrors? Death is the most fearful thing of all, since it is a limit, and when someone is dead nothing any longer seems good or bad for him. (*NE* iii 6.1115a24–27)

Courage, then, is first and foremost concerned with death. However, Aristotle immediately goes on to qualify even this restriction:

But not even death in all its forms, such as death at sea, or from illness, seems to be the concern of the courageous person. Which forms do concern him, then? Surely the most noble. These are deaths in battle, because they take place in the greatest and noblest danger; and this fits with the way honors are bestowed in cities and the courts of monarchs. So it is the person who is fearless with respect to a noble death, or the risks of immediate death, that should really be described as courageous; and risks in battle are most of all like this. (1115a28–35)

It is the noblest kind of death that is the concern of the courageous agent. Risking one's life in warfare, Aristotle claims, is most of all like this, but presumably other emergencies in which we risk our lives for a noble end would count as well, for example, attempting to save someone from a blazing fire.

One might naturally object that restricting courage to such contexts unduly restricts Aristotle's account. Could we not manifest courage by resisting other sorts of fear? In fact, Aristotle does think that courage can be exhibited in other circumstances; he maintains only that the cases he points to are the purest manifestations of this virtue. So, for example, he concedes that we think that people who stand up to their fear of poverty, disease, or friendlessness are courageous, but he maintains that we apply the notion in these cases *because of a similarity* they have to the most proper manifestations of courage, not because they are examples of acting courageously in the strictest sense themselves. But why are these other cases not just as "pure"? Aristotle thinks that two conditions for true courage are missing. First, there must be the possibility for displaying *alkē*, feats of strength or prowess; second, the death must be noble (1115b4–6). Consider manifesting courage in the face of a terminal disease. Although one may well have to withstand great physical pain, it is hard to see how dying of some terminal disease could help one show off one's prowess or display feats of strength. With the second condition, the thought seems to be that standing up to danger in life-threatening circumstances, when one ought to, is a noble goal to aim at, and the nobility of the goal is conferred on to the agent insofar as he aims at it. When someone is dying of a terminal disease, by contrast, although he may be able to bear the disease with dignity and nobility, dying from the disease can hardly be construed as a noble end he aims at: he can *die nobly* in the disease case, but the death is not *for the sake of a noble end*. Thus, if we understand Aristotle to be pointing to the purest cases of acting courageously, his focus on death seems reasonable. We surely do think that *what* we fear has a bearing on how courageous the agent could be in facing up to that thing. Standing up to fear of death in war surely manifests one as more courageous than standing up to, for example, one's fear of giving a speech at a wedding. Likewise his focus on a noble death seems understandable. Risking one's life for a noble or honorable end does seem to reveal one as more courageous than risking one's life for some base self-interested goal, such as, the financial gain one might achieve from armed robbery. Finally, it seems reasonable for Aristotle to pick out as the most pure manifestations of courage those cases in which agents *place themselves* into the danger *for the sake of* the noble end. This feature of such cases seems to make resistance more praiseworthy than resistance in cases in which the agent is simply thrown, without any alternative (as with the disease case).[1]

2. The Role of Fear in Courage

From the discussion in *NE* iii 6, in which Aristotle delimits the sphere of courage, one would naturally draw the conclusion that the courageous agent is fear*less* with respect to death: as we saw, Aristotle claims that it is "the person who is fearless with respect to a noble death, or the risks of immediate death, that should really be described as courageous" (1115a32–34 quoted in full in the preceding extract; see also especially 1115a16: "The courageous man is also a fearless person"). However, at the beginning of iii 7, Aristotle writes:

> Not everyone finds the same things fearful. But we do say that there are things beyond human endurance, which would be fearful to anyone – anyone sane that is. Things not beyond human endurance differ in scale and degree, and so do those that inspire confidence. The courageous person will be undaunted so far as humanly possible; so, though he will fear even the things not beyond human endurance, he will stand his ground for the sake of what is noble (since that is the end of virtue) in the right way and as reason requires. But one can fear these things to a greater or lesser degree, and even fear things that are not fearful as if they were. (1115b7–15)

Now, it seems, despite the references so far to the courageous agent being *fearless*, Aristotle crucially points out that even he does experience fear. With some things (perhaps, e.g., earthquakes or tsunamis: see

---

[1]   Further discussion of the narrowness of Aristotle's notion of courage can be found in, e.g., Ross 1995, 213–214; Urmson 1988, 63–64; Welton and Polansky 1995, 98; Pakaluk 2005, 160–164; and Taylor 2006, 178–179. Adair, Bagwell, and Polansky 2009 suggest that focusing on this specific sphere can serve helpful pedagogical and appraisal purposes.

1115b24–28), it is beyond a human being's power not to fear them (unless the human is mad), whereas with others it is possible to fear them or not fear them. And yet Aristotle here explicitly claims that the courageous agent will fear not only the things that it is beyond human capability not to fear but also the things that it is *not* beyond human capability not to fear ("will fear even the things not beyond human endurance").[2]

So we have a tension between the iii 6 characterization of the courageous agent as fearless and the iii 7 characterization of him as experiencing reasonable fear. The most plausible resolution to this difficulty is that Aristotle employs two different notions of "fear."[3] In the *NE* iii 7 passage just quoted (1115b7–15), Aristotle claimed that the courageous agent, though afraid, would nevertheless *stand up* to the things he fears when doing so would be for the sake of the noble and as reason directs (and so he would be "undaunted so far as humanly possible"). This naturally invites the idea that Aristotle has two different significations of "fear" in play; one in which the courageous agent will rationally feel it, and another in which he will be courageously fearless. The Greek for "fear," *phobos*, just like our "fear," can be used in two senses. (1) It can be used, as it is in the passage from *Rhetoric* ii 5 that we quoted earlier, to refer to an evaluative impression an agent has of some destructive or painful evil in the future. In this sense of "fear," the courageous agent experiences fear: he undergoes a distressful impression that is coordinate to the danger in question.[4] And (2) it can be used to refer to a motivation of the agent, a desire to escape the feared object. In this sense of "fear," the courageous agent is fearless "toward" (*pros*) the things in question and "stands his ground" (*hupomenein*) against them (*EE* iii 1.1228b26–27; *NE* iii 7.1115b12–13), that is, he is motivated to stand firm and face up to them. If this is right, the courageous agent can feel fear while being motivationally fearless; he can experience fear without that leading to a desire to flee.

---

[2] Or at least some of them: presumably he will not fear the squeak of mice, doors creaking, or anything else that he should not fear *at all*.

[3] Cf., e.g., Pears 1978, 281–282; 1980, 178–179; Broadie 1991, 91; Charles 1995, 143–144; and Heil 1996. See also *EE* iii 1.1228b24–29.

[4] It may seem that his fear cannot be *just* as the definition in *Rhet.* ii 5 states because Aristotle characterizes fear there as a "distress or *disturbance*" (*lupē ē tarachē*), but claims in the *NE* that the courageous agent is *undisturbed* (*atarachos*, iii 7.1117a19, 8.1117a31). However, if the disturbance component in the *Rhetoric* definition is optional (as suggested by the "or"), its presence there will obviously not be problematic. (And note that the definition of fear mentioned at *NE* iii 6.1115a9 ["expectation of evil"] does not mention disturbance.) Alternatively, we may think that just as Aristotle possesses two notions of fear, so he possesses two different notions of "disturbance," one as an evaluative impression, and the other as a motivation, and that he has these different notions in play in the passages referred to earlier.

It is worth emphasizing *why* Aristotle thinks that the courageous agent must feel fear. Aristotle holds that the courageous agent's emotions and actions must be appropriate for the circumstances in question. In *NE* iii 7, he writes:

The courageous person is the one who endures and fears – and likewise is confident about – the right things, for the right reason, in the right way, and at the right time; for the courageous person feels and acts in accordance with the merits of the case, and as reason requires. (1115b17–20)

Now, as we have seen, Aristotelian courage is manifested most purely in situations that require one to risk one's life in battle (1115a32–35). But it is not as if Aristotle thinks that the courageous person should have no concern for his death. On the contrary, in *NE* iii 9 he claims that the more virtuous and happy an agent is, the more he will be pained at the thought of his death, since life is best worth living for such a man, and he is thereby knowingly losing the greatest of goods (1117b10–13, quoted in section 6). Thus, in life-threatening situations at war, if the courageous agent is to feel (*paschein*) "in accordance with the merits of the case" (*kat' axian*), he will experience fear: he is confronted by an evil (knowingly losing his own life) that is close at hand, significantly great, and that causes him distress. Not to do so would make him excessively fear*less* in this sense of fear (see *NE* iii 7.1115b24–28).[5]

3. The Role of Confidence in Courage

Aristotle, we have noted, thinks that courage is concerned with fear *and* confidence. In what way is the courageous agent confident?[6] Aristotle provides the following characterization of confidence (*tharros*) in the *Rhetoric* (he does not offer an account in the *NE*):

[Confidence is] expectation (*elpis*) of safety accompanied by the impression (*meta phantasias*) of it as near, while fearful things either do not exist or are far away (*porrō*). Confidence is inspired by dreadful things (*ta deina*) being far off (*porrō*) and sources of safety being near at hand. (1383a17–20)

The basic idea is that confidence is connected to the impression that one will be safe from something one considers fearful. Also, although it is not explicitly stated here, just as fear is a distressful emotion, confidence would presumably be some kind of pleasurable emotion.

Now, given that Aristotle thinks that the emotion of confidence involves construing oneself as safe from something fearful, one might

[5] Cf. also Charles 1995, 146–147.
[6] In this section, I follow my argument in Pearson 2009.

think that the courageous agent would be confident in this sense only if he thought that he would survive the battle unscathed. However, as we noted in the preceding section, it is clear that Aristotle thinks that courageous agents will frequently realize that they will *not* survive the battle. The courageous person chooses the noble deeds of war even when he knows that in so doing he will lose his life. If, then, the courageous agent's confidence is connected to the impression that he will survive the battle, it would seem that he cannot be confident in these desperate cases.[7]

A passage in *NE* iii 8 suggests, however, that Aristotle thinks that the courageous person is confident even when he recognizes that he will die. In this chapter Aristotle distinguishes courageous agents from several other agents who might appear courageous but in fact fail to be so. Concerning those who are hopeful or optimistic (*hoi euelpides*), he writes:

Nor are hopeful people courageous, since they are confident in danger only because they have often been victorious over many enemies. They resemble the courageous, however, because both are confident; but courageous people are confident for the reasons given earlier, while the hopeful are so because they think that they are strongest and that no harm will come to them (drunks behave like this as well, because they become hopeful). And when things do not turn out as they expected, they run away; as we noticed, however, it is characteristic of the courageous person to endure what is – and appears – fearful for a human being, because it is noble to do so, and shameful not to. (1117a9–17)

It is not immediately obvious what the phrase "the reasons given earlier" is meant to refer to, as there does not seem to be an earlier passage that spells out why the courageous agent is confident in danger. But it seems likely that Aristotle is referring to the idea that the courageous agent faces terrible things for the sake of the noble. He mentions this at *NE* iii 7.1115b23–24: "It is for the sake of what is noble that the courageous person stands his ground and acts in accordance with courage"; and again at 1116a11–12: "[Courage] makes choices and stands its ground because it is noble to do so, or shameful not to." If Aristotle took it for granted that in these passages he was not simply explaining why the courageous agent acts as he does, but also pointing to the source of his confident behavior, this would explain the "given earlier" (see also Heil 1996, 70–71). The rest of the passage can be taken to provide support for this reading if it is paraphrased as follows:

---

[7] This is roughly the view in Pears 1980, 182–183. Pears maintains that Aristotle's courageous agent could not have a confident impression; although Pears does allow that Aristotle's courageous agent might be confident in a motivational or behavioral sense, i.e., be motivated to stand firm.

Hopeful people and courageous people resemble each other because both are confident, but in fact they are so for different reasons. Hopeful people are confident because they think that they are the strongest and so no harm will come to them. This is why, when things do not turn out as they expected, they run away (for then they finally realize that they are not the strongest, and so lose their confidence). Courageous people, by contrast, are confident because they believe that they are acting for a noble end, and so will endure what is fearful for a human being even when they realize that they will not succeed.

On this account, the courageous agent will endure what is fearful because of his confident emotional state, an emotion that involves him believing that he is fighting for a noble end. And since this emotion stems not from an assessment of his chances of survival or victory but from an assessment of the nobility of his action, it is consistent with the belief that he has a very slim chance of surviving the battle.

But how could such confidence, stemming from the agent's belief that he is fighting for a noble end (rather than the expectation that he is going to survive the battle), fall under the definition of confidence we found in the *Rhetoric*? That notion of confidence, recall, requires one to expect that one will be safe from something fearful; thus, hopeful people are confident because they think that they will be safe from physical harm. But, in desperate cases at least, the courageous person has no such impression and recognizes that he will die. However, there is one thing that he *does* think he is safe from, something that matters to him more than death, and that it is in fact right and noble to fear. This is the very opposite of the nobility that the courageous agent so resolutely seeks, namely, *ignobility*, *shame*, or *disgrace*. Given that disgrace is something that the courageous agent construes as fearful, perhaps Aristotle's courageous agent could possess a confident emotional state owing to the fact that he thinks that he is safe from it? For, since he believes that in his current situation he is acting for a noble end, he would indeed seem to construe himself in this way.

When seen from this perspective, some of Aristotle's other remarks take on a different light. For example, consider the way in *NE* iii 8 he distinguishes those with experience of particular facts from the truly courageous. Aristotle notes that professional soldiers can appear courageous because of their experience. They may remain undisturbed in some crisis, for example, because their experience in the techniques and weapons of warfare makes them most capable of "doing without being done to," and so (against the right opposition) they "fight like armed men against unarmed or like trained athletes against amateurs" (1116b9–12). However, if such experience is the sole basis for their courageous behavior, they will be the first to run away if they suddenly realize that in the case at hand they are inferior in numbers and equipment; for, like hopeful agents, they faced the danger on the assumption that they were stronger. (By contrast, citizens, or at least those for whom "flight is disgraceful and death is preferable to safety on those terms," will stand fast, and die if necessary, even if they realize that they are inferior in these ways (1116b6–19).) Significantly, Aristotle describes the professional soldiers he has in mind, that is, those who only appear courageous owing to their experience, as "fearing death more than disgrace," and asserts, by contrast, that the courageous agent "is not like this" (1116b22–23). The proposed analysis suggests that we could complete Aristotle's thought: "... for he fears disgrace more than death."[8]

4. The Vices

No account of an Aristotelian virtue would be complete without a sketch of the corresponding vices. Interestingly, with respect to courage, Aristotle distinguishes not two but three vices.

COWARDICE. Aristotle writes of the first vice:

The person who exceeds in fear is the coward, since he fears the wrong things, in the wrong way, and so on. He is also deficient in confidence, but he reveals himself more in his excessive distress (lupē). So, because he fears everything, he is a despondent sort. (NE iii 7.1115b33–1116a3)

The coward is excessive in fear and deficient in confidence. Note that Aristotle explicitly states that the coward exceeds in fear not just because he fears certain objects more than he should, but because he fears the wrong objects simpliciter.[9] So, although he fears, for example, pain more than he should (he, say, fears a sprained ankle, not just great physical pain), he also fears some things that he should not fear at all (perhaps, e.g., he has to sleep with a night light on, or jumps at creaking doors). Given that Aristotle employs two notions of fear (see Section II), the coward will presumably be prone to excessive fear in both senses, when that is possible. He will, that is, be distressed at dangers that are not real or more distressed by dangers that, though real, do not warrant being terrified at, and he will also be prone to motivational/behavioral

---

[8] See also iii 8.1116a27–29. The general idea is, I think, intended to be familiar; see, e.g., Plato Apology 28c–d, in turn alluding (at 28c3–4) to Homer's Iliad xviii 91ff. For more discussion, see Pearson 2009, 131–132.

[9] On the appropriateness of quantitative language in this context, see Hursthouse 1980–1981, 2006; Curzer 1996; and Pearson 2006a.

fear: he will run away from what he is afraid of or hide under his bed covers trembling.

RASHNESS. Aristotle's characterization of the rash agent is simply:

> The person who exceeds in confidence about fearful things is rash. (*NE* iii 7.1115b28–29)

Given the connection between confidence and nobility, the rash agent might appear problematic for Aristotle. For, insofar as confidence is tied to nobility, the courageous agent is maximally confident. However, an agent can manifest excessive confidence in other ways. Most straightforwardly he might be overly confident that he is going to survive the battle. Such an agent might be behaviorally indistinguishable from the courageous agent in certain circumstances, but the courageous agent would still be more praiseworthy because he would stand his ground even when fully aware that his actions will bring about his death. Again, just as the coward might fear things that he should not, the rash agent might be confident with respect to things he should not, for example, certain activities involving taking extreme physical risks, as occurs in certain extreme sports. The courageous agent, by contrast, would not think it worthwhile to risk his life "for the buzz."

If someone is overly confident that he is going to survive the battle, and this is the only reason he is motivated to fight, then if things start to go badly, he may well turn cowardly:

> The rash person also seems to be a boaster and a pretender to courage; at any rate, in relation to what is fearful, he wishes to appear like the courageous person is in reality, and so imitates him when he can. This is why most of them are rash cowards; for on these occasions they put on a show of confidence, but they do not stand their ground against what is really fearful. (1115b28–33)[10]

EXCESSIVE FEARLESSNESS. Aristotle also recognizes a third vice in contrast to courage. This state was first mentioned in his initial list of virtues and vices in *NE* ii:

> In fear and confidence, courage is a mean. Of those who go to excess, the person who exceeds in fearlessness has no name (many cases lack names), while the one who exceeds in confidence is rash. He who exceeds in being afraid and is deficient in confidence is a coward. (ii 7.1107a33–1107b4)

---

[10]   Cf. the drunks mentioned in iii 8.1117a14–15 who become excessively confident so long as things go their way, but sober up rather quickly, and turn cowardly, as soon as a few blows go in.

In *NE* iii 7, he returns to the no-named state of excessive fearlessness:

Among the excessive, the person who exceeds in fearlessness has no name (we said before that many do not have a name), but if he feared nothing – neither an earthquake nor the waves,[11] as people say of the Celts – he would be a sort of madman or insensible. (1115b24–28)

The question to ask is this: Why should Aristotle wish to distinguish this vice from rashness? Let us take the case of someone who is overly confident that he is going to survive the battle. Why might Aristotle want to distinguish such an agent from someone who is excessively fearless? Consider what might drive one to such fearlessness? Imagine an agent who had lived through some terrible natural catastrophe (e.g., an earthquake, volcano, flooding, or tsunami) even though all of his family, friends, and possessions had been wiped out. Such a person might feel that there is nothing more that life could throw at him that would make him suffer any further – least of all his own death, which would almost be a blessing – and might then manifest the inhuman fearlessness that Aristotle mentions.[12] Would this make him excessively confident as well? There seems to be no reason to think so: he may be well aware that the extremely destructive thing that approaches him will kill him and need not be delusional about his own prospects of safety. He could simply be excessively fearless because he does not care about his own life anymore, not because he is sure that he will survive. In fact, his excessive fearlessness would even be consistent with *deficient* confidence about his chances of success. Thus the two vices, excessive fearlessness and rashness, are distinct.[13]

[11] Crisp 2000 translates "not even an earthquake or rough seas," but there is reason to think that Aristotle is referring to an earthquake and the resulting tsunami waves, see Sedley 2005.
[12] Cf. *Rhet.* ii 5: "Nor [are those afraid] who think they have already suffered all dreadful things possible and have become coldly indifferent to the future, like those in the process of being executed (*hoi apotumpanizomenoi*). [For fear to continue] there must be some hope of being saved from the cause of agony" (1383a3–6, translation modified from Kennedy 1991) – although in fact the case that Aristotle appears to have in mind in the quoted *NE* passage is one in which a group of agents is systematically deluded into thinking that the earthquake and resulting tsunami waves are "enemies" against which they can sensibly fight.
[13] On the other hand, it *does* seem that excessive confidence of one's prospects of survival would generally imply excessive fearlessness of one's prospects of survival; for, if one is sure of one's survival, that would tend to make one unafraid of the prospect of not surviving. However, "would generally" and "tend to" are required because we also accept the possibility of phobics: people who are confident that they will survive but cannot stop themselves from irrationally feeling fear.

However, if Aristotle wants to distinguish the excessively fearless person from the rash agent in some such way, perhaps he also ought to recognize a *fourth* vice, this time a variation on cowardice, namely, the agent who is simply deficient in confidence. This is because it also seems plausible to think that there could be agents who are deficiently confident about their prospects of survival without that entailing that they are excessively fearful of that prospect. Some agents might be prone to underestimate their chances of survival – insisting that they have no chance when in fact they have a pretty decent one (cf. paranoid fans of a football team) – but that need not imply that they are excessively fearful of not surviving. It seems possible for some agents to hold that they have no chance of surviving while not caring about their chances of surviving in any event.[14]

Nevertheless, the fact that Aristotle mentions the excessively fearless agent is significant. Although he asserts several times in *NE* ii that virtue is a mean between two vices, one of excess and one of deficiency (e.g., ii 8.1108b11–13, ii 9.1109a20–22), in acknowledging this additional vice he shows that he does not feel constrained by his general theory to overlook subtleties in his particular accounts. The threefold structure (virtue, vice of deficiency, vice of excess) is not rigidly applied come what may. The theory is a guide, not something that dictates the form of the account to be developed in specific cases.[15]

5. Courage and Nobility

We have seen that the nobility of a course of action or goal is of crucial importance for courage:

The end of every activity is being in accordance with its state. To the courageous person, courage is noble; and so its end is also noble, since the character of everything is determined by its end. So it is for the sake of what is noble that the

---

[14] Whereas, again, excessive fear of not surviving *would* seem to demand deficiency in confidence: if one is terrified of not surviving, then that will generally imply that one would not be confident about surviving (the phobic again being the exception). Note that although Aristotle characterizes rashness just in terms of confidence (iii 7.1115b28–29), he explicitly characterizes the coward in terms of both fear and confidence (1115b33–1116a3).

[15] In line with this there appear to be other cases where the threefold structure is adapted or emended; see, e.g., the virtue concerned with temper in *NE* iv 5, where we get a variety of excessive states, e.g., the irascible, the irritable, and the sulky; and also the virtue concerned with private relations with others discussed in *NE* iv 6, where we get two types of excessive state: the "obsequious" person being distinguished from the "flatterer" depending on whether there is an ulterior motive in play.

courageous person stands his ground and acts in accordance with courage.
(*NE* iii.7 1115b20–24)

Exactly what Aristotle means in claiming that an action is noble is
beyond the scope of this chapter.[16] But the chapter so far has suggested
two ways in which an agent might *fail* to be courageous by failing to
aim for a noble end, even though the agent stands up to something
fearful. First, there may be cases in which, although the agent can die
nobly in the presence of something fearful, he cannot die *for the sake of*
a noble end. We saw this earlier with an agent who faces up to a
terminal illness. Second, there may be cases in which agents stand up
to something fearful fully aware of the fact that the act in question is
not for the sake of a noble end. This would be, for example, those
partaking unnecessarily in extremely dangerous activities, say, fighting to death over a trivial disagreement. In such cases, no matter how
fearless one is, and no matter how much "prowess" one shows facing
the fear, one's act will not manifest one as courageous since it is at the
service of a shameful or at least a nonnoble, end. A third way in which
an agent might fail to aim for a noble end would be if he stood up to
something fearful in the belief that he was acting for a noble end, when
in fact that end was ignoble. Suppose, for example, an agent stands up to
fear of death in war, but it turns out that unbeknown to him the war
itself is being waged for the wrong reasons (e.g., to steal resources out of
greed), then such an agent would aim (*de re*) at an ignoble end, even
though he might aim at it (*de dicto*) *as* noble. Would such an agent
count as courageous? There seem to be two ways we could go. We could
either say that manifestations of genuine courage are tied to the agent's
beliefs (cf. Plato, *Republic* i 340a–c), and hence maintain that, since the
agent believed that he was fighting for a noble end, his action can still
count as fully courageous (presumably just so long as the agent was not
himself culpable in forming the mistaken belief); or, alternatively,
we could insist that genuine courage requires the end aimed at (*de re*)
to be *actually* noble and so hold that an agent who stands up to his fear
for the sake of an ignoble end cannot count as truly courageous, even if
he (mistakenly) aims (*de dicto*) at it *as* noble. On this view, we would
then say that if such an agent is nonculpably ignorant of acting for the
sake of the ignoble end, then he nonculpably *fails* to perform a truly
courageous act, and his act *would have been* truly courageous had his
belief been true. There is reason to think that Aristotle would advocate
the second of these approaches. In a different context, he appears to
hold that for an action to count as an intentionally performed *just* act it

[16] For some discussion, see, e.g., Cooper 1999, 270–276; Lear 2004, ch. 6; and Pakaluk
2005, 153–154. See also Lear 2004, 148–162 on courage in particular.

must actually bring about a just outcome (cf. *NE* v 8.1135a15–23; and, for more discussion, see Pearson 2006b, §2).

6. *Courage and* Eudaimonia

Consider the following argument:

1. Action in accordance with virtue contributes toward one's *eudaimonia* (well-being, flourishing, or life happiness).
2. Acting courageously is an instance of acting in accordance with virtue.
3. Acting courageously might bring about one's death in battle.

So:

4. Dying in battle can contribute toward one's *eudaimonia*.

Does not the conclusion sound paradoxical? Suppose a soldier dies at a young age in battle. How can thus dying have contributed to making his life happy? Indeed, in *NE* i 7 Aristotle asserts that the activity of virtue would lead to *eudaimonia* only if it took place over a complete life: "One swallow does not make a summer, nor does one day; and so too one day, or a short time, does not make a man blessed and happy" (1098a18–20). But the preceding argument seems valid, so if we deny its conclusion, we must deny one of its premises. The natural premise to deny is (1). One could say that, although this is generally true, it need not always be the case, courage being the prime exception. However, I doubt that Aristotle would respond to the argument in quite this way. Instead, I think that he would insist that acting courageously does contribute to one's *eudaimonia*, and that if courage demands that one die at a young age, then the best one can get is imperfect *eudaimonia*, *eudaimonia* that fails to meet the complete life condition:

> The more [the courageous agent] is possessed of virtue as a whole and the happier he is, the more pain he will feel at the thought of death. For life is especially worth living for a person like this, and he knows that he is losing the greatest goods – and this is painful. But he is no less courageous for that, and perhaps even more so, because he chooses what is noble in war at the cost of these goods. So it is not true, then, except insofar as one achieves the end, that the exercise of every virtue is pleasant. (1117b10–16)

Subject to the limitation that one will thereby not live a full life, dying in battle could perhaps be said to contribute to one's *eudaimonia* insofar as, in making the ultimate sacrifice for a noble end, one's life flourishes as best it can. We can also turn the point around. It seems highly unlikely that Aristotle would allow that one could trade acting cowardly now for a greater number of virtuous actions later on. If courage (which is essentially noble) demands that one fight to the death, rather than, for example, live at the whim of some ignoble tyrant, then failure to do so could not properly be compensated for by a few good deeds at a later date. Virtue cannot aggregate: acting cowardly in this situation will *taint* one's whole subsequent life. Thus, although such an agent cannot achieve the fullest kind of flourishing, it is the best he can get.

II. TEMPERANCE (NE III 10–12)

7. *The Sphere of Temperance*

The sphere of temperance (*sōphrosunē*) is pleasure. However, just as courage in the strictest sense is concerned only with certain fearful things, so too, temperance in the strictest sense pertains only to certain pleasures. To begin with, mental pleasures are not relevant (iii 10.1117b28–1118a1): one is not, Aristotle suggests, called temperate or self-indulgent[17] owing to whether one takes appropriate or inappropriate pleasure in learning or reading, for example, and those who go to the excess with respect to telling stories and chatting are called "idle gossips," not self-indulgent. Rather, temperance and self-indulgence pertain to bodily pleasures. But in fact not all of these are relevant either. Aristotle first rules out pleasures connected to the distal senses of sight and hearing:

People who enjoy what they see, such as colors, shapes, a painting, are called neither temperate nor self-indulgent. ... The same goes for what we hear; nobody who describes people who enjoy music or acting to an inordinate degree as self-indulgent. (*NE* iii 10.1118a3–5, a6–9)

Nor, Aristotle continues, does temperance concern pleasurable odors (at least not in the strictest sense): we do not, he suggests, call those who delight in the smell of apples, roses, or incense "self-indulgent." Instead, it is the pleasures that nonrational animals also enjoy, and that therefore appear "slavish and brutish" (1118a24), that pick out the proper domain of temperance and self-indulgence, and these are pleasures connected to taste and touch. However, having announced this (1118a26), Aristotle immediately goes on to qualify his position with respect to taste:

---

[17] I translate *akolasia* with "self-indulgence" (after, e.g., Ross 1925) rather than Crisp 2000 "intemperance." The problem with the latter is (i) that it suggests a linguistic connection between *sōphrosunē* (temperance) and *akolasia* that is not there; and (ii) that insofar as "intemperance" suggests simply *lacking* temperance it fails to pick out the element of excess inherent in *akolasia*: one could be intemperate by *failing* to go after the pleasures one should, as with Aristotle's insensible person.

But even taste appears to have little or no role to play. For the job of taste is to discriminate flavors, as do wine tasters, or cooks preparing dishes; but people do not really enjoy these sorts of thing – or at least self-indulgent people do not – but rather the gratification itself, which arises entirely through touch in the cases of food, drink, and what people call sexual pleasures. This is why a certain gourmet prayed that his throat might become longer than a crane's, demonstrating that it was the touching which gave him pleasure.[18] (1118a26–1118b1)

What should we make of this restriction of temperance and self-indulgence to tactile pleasures? The first thing to note is that Aristotle is appealing to linguistic usage. He repeatedly insists that "no one calls" a person with such-and-such a type of defect self-indulgent or temperate (1117b32, 1117b35–1118a1, 1118a4–5, 1118a8–9, 1118a11). His restriction, then, appeals to how Greek speakers of his time would employ the words in question (at least on reflection).[19] Second, he is careful to note that he is not denying that there can be excess and defect with respect to the pleasures that he is excluding from the domain of temperance and self-indulgence (see, e.g., 1118a5–6), just that such defects do not pick out the domain under consideration. Third, he allows that pleasures stemming from other sense modalities besides touch can manifest temperance or self-indulgence in a secondary sense, that is, via touch. For example, he notes that we might label those who delight in certain odors, for example, perfumes and delicacies (opsoi), as "self-indulgent," but only because such smells "remind them of the objects of their appetites" (iii 10.1118a13), that is, (presumably) certain sexual conquests or debauched feasting.[20] Fourth, he does have a principled reason for distinguishing touch from the other senses. He claims that this sense is "the most widely shared" of all the senses and that it "seems justly subject to criticism, because it is something we do not possess insofar as we are human, but insofar as we are animals" (1118b1–3). Thus, he suggests, "to enjoy such things [sc. tactile pleasures] . . . and to love them most of all is brutish" (1118b3–4). Aristotle thinks that the defining characteristic of being an animal (in contrast to plant life) is sense perception, and that the most basic sense – which can exist alone, but which the other senses cannot exist without – is touch (see, e.g., De An. ii 3.415a3–6). Touch is,

---

[18] EE names and shames the culprit as Philoxenus, the son of Eryxis (iii 2.1231a15–17).
[19] Or at least to how those who are "properly brought up" would employ these words, for it is to such people that Aristotle is addressing his Ethics (see, e.g., NE i 4.1095b2–6).
[20] Crisp 2000 translates opsoi by "cooked dishes," but the Greek refers to delicacies (of which fish was a common example in ancient Athens; see LSJ s.v.), seasonings, or sauces. (If Aristotle had sauces in mind, it may be that he was thinking of a case in which the smell of some sauce reminds the agent of eating some delicacy.)

therefore, the sense that relates most of all to our animality.[21] Thus, just as the strictest notion of courage was manifested in the purest kind of case, so too temperance and self-indulgence pertain especially to pleasures of the sense modality that we share with even the most basic kind of animal. It is this, Aristotle claims, that makes going wrong with respect to such pleasures most subject to criticism.

The passage quoted earlier (*NE* iii 10.1118a26–1118b1) makes it clear that Aristotle's prime examples of such pleasures are those bound up with eating, drinking, and sex. And it is specifically the tactile element of the pleasure we get from doing these things that he has in mind. It is how cold water *feels* as one drinks it on a hot day after exercise, or the *actual sensation* of food sliding down one's throat if one is extremely hungry that are the kinds of pleasure he is referring to.

8. *Particular versus Common Appetites*

In *NE* iii 11, Aristotle further clarifies the domain of temperance by introducing a distinction between different types of appetite (*epithumia*):

Some appetites are thought to be common (*koinai*), others to be particular (*idioi*) and acquired (*epithetoi*). That for sustenance, for example, is natural (*phusikē*), since everyone who needs it has an appetite for food or drink, or sometimes both; and that for sex, when one is, as Homer puts it, young and blooming. But not everyone has an appetite for this or that kind of sustenance or sex, nor the same kinds; so it seems to be a matter of personal taste. (1118b8–13)

The distinction is between common and particular appetites. In general, common appetites are natural whereas particular appetites are acquired. When we are hungry, we desire food, but we do not all desire sausages. If we are thirsty, we desire to drink something, but not all of us desire orange juice. What makes a desire "common" appears to be that it operates at a level of description that picks out a core feature of our

---

[21] Cf. Young 1988, 537–538. Sisko 2003 suggests that touch may be singled out in this respect owing to a functional feature. If animals possessed only the sense of *taste*, they might do no more than taste their food, not consume it. But it is essential for their survival that they do in fact consume their food, and, on Aristotle's view, they do so out of a desire for the more fundamental tactile pleasure of food passing down the gullet and distending the esophagus. Therefore touch is more fundamental than taste since it plays the fundamental functional role in nutrition (and for this reason it is most closely connected to our animal nature). Aristotle does allow that certain tactile pleasures (e.g., getting hot in the sauna) may fall outside the domain of temperance and self-indulgence. He suggests a difference here might be that they concern the whole body, not a part of it (iii 10.1118b4–8). Perhaps he would also allow that tactile pleasures that are distinctively human and do not contribute functionally in the way that Sisko mentions would also fall outside the domain of temperance, e.g., the pleasure someone might get from touching silk.

animal nature, for example, we need to sustain ourselves and procreate. Particular appetites, by contrast, operate at a lower level of description and pick out particular types of food or drink, reflecting the tastes of the individual (or subgroup) in question. Although these appetites are acquired, it is notable that in the lines that immediately follow the preceding passage, Aristotle allows that there is "something natural" in them, "because one thing will please one kind of person, another another, and some things are more pleasant to everyone than certain others" (1118b13–15). What makes a desire a particular appetite is that it picks out some specific pleasure, rather than, for example, the pleasure of eating when hungry. But insofar as these particular pleasures might be shared by certain kinds of people (with certain natures), and perhaps by everyone, appetites for them will have something "natural" or "common" in them, to a varying degree. Aristotle next notes:

> In the case of the natural appetites, the number of people who miss the mark is low, and they do so in only one direction, that of excess. To eat whatever is at hand or to drink until one is full to bursting is to exceed the amount that accords with nature, since natural appetite is the replenishment of what one lacks. This is why these people are called "belly-crazy," since they fill their bellies beyond what is right; it is utterly slavish people who become like this. (1118b15–21)

This suggests that natural or common appetites have a physical basis and explanation – natural appetite is replenishment of one's deficiency: if one lacks food, this explains why one eats something, but it does not explain why, of several options, one chooses cheese and onion crisps. Aristotle thinks that going wrong at the level of natural appetites is rare and is possible only in the direction of excess. These are agents who simply desire food and drink – not some particular food or drink – beyond any bodily need. In the case of sex, they would presumably be sex addicts. We would, I think, hold that the deficiency can also exist: for example, agents who fail to desire to eat even when they are hungry, as with some anorexics.

With regard to pleasures peculiar to individuals, Aristotle thinks that many people go wrong and in many ways (1118b21–22). And it is appetites for these pleasures, rather than natural/common appetites, that fix the domain of temperance and self-indulgence.[22] Let us follow Aristotle

---

[22] It would seem that often the same desire could be described as either a common appetite or a particular appetite. Suppose a normal healthy individual is hungry and desires a salad. At one level of description, his desire is a desire for food in response to a lack and so is a general appetite. At another level, the agent has a desire to eat a salad, and this is a desire for a particular kind of nourishment and so a particular appetite. There is only one desire here, but it can be described from two perspectives. Nevertheless, it is *qua* particular appetites, on Aristotle's account, that we describe agents as temperate or self-indulgent.

in first characterizing the vices that correspond to temperance before turning to the virtue itself.

9. Vice of Self-Indulgence

Aristotle writes:

In the case of the particular pleasures, however, many people miss the mark, and in many ways: people are called lovers of such and such because they enjoy the wrong things, enjoy things more than most people do, or enjoy things in the wrong way. And self-indulgent people go to excess in all these ways; for they enjoy certain things they should not (because those things are detestable), and if they enjoy the sort of things that it is right to enjoy, they enjoy them more than is right or more than most people enjoy them. (1118a21–27)

Aristotle here introduces three ways in which an agent can go wrong in excess: he may enjoy the wrong things, enjoy things too much, or enjoy things in the wrong way. Given that Aristotle thinks that temperance and self-indulgence pertain to particular appetites for tactile pleasures connected to food, drink, and sex, one way of filling out his account of self-indulgence is to attempt to provide examples (as he himself does not) of appetites that are defective in the three ways he mentions for each of the three types of pleasure. Let us, then, try to find examples that fit the following table:

	Wrong Object	Too Much (but Right Object, and Right Way)	Wrong Way (but Right Object and Right Amount)
Food	(1)	(4)	(7)
Drink	(2)	(5)	(8)
Sex	(3)	(6)	(9)

WRONG OBJECT. Examples of (1), (2), and (3) seem to fall into two broad types. They are either (i) dishonorable or ignoble or (ii) bad for one's health (see NE iii 11.1119a16–18). For (1ii) we might cite items that we think it would be ignoble or ethically repugnant to eat, for example, human flesh, or perhaps foods that have been prepared in ethically dubious ways, as is now commonly believed of *foie gras*.[23] For (1ii) we might cite foods that are extremely bad for us; contemporary examples would be lard-drenched

[23] Aristotle might view cannibalism as moving beyond the domain of self-indulgence into "bestial" subvicious states. In NE vii 5, he writes: "By brutish states I mean, for example, the female human who people say rips open pregnant women and devours their babies; or the pleasures of some of the savages that live around the Black Sea, who

chips, extremely rich chocolate or sweets, or food from late-night kebab vans. The idea is that these are meant to be items no amount of which would be good for us to eat. Similarly with (2). Drinking another human's blood or products produced in ethically dubious ways might fit (2i), whereas drinking absinthe or very cheap supermarket wine might be examples of (2ii). With respect to (3i), examples might be bestiality, necrophilia, or "adultery" (*moicheia*; *NE* ii 6.1107a8–17). I suppose bestiality might also fall under (3ii), depending on the beast in question (!), as might sexual activity that involves inanimate objects if that puts one in physical danger. A good contemporary example of something that seems to fit the category of wrong object, but that does not concern food, drink, or sex, would be smoking.

TOO MUCH. With this category of error, the pleasure is not inherently wrong (unhealthy or ignoble), but becomes so when taken to excess. Examples of (4) would be to desire to eat sweets, desserts, chocolate, crisps, and chips more than one should. Examples for (5) would be people drinking more coffee than one should, or too much alcohol. For (6) it would have to be instances in which agents pursue sex more than is physically advisable, without giving their bodies any chance to recover physically from the activity. Each such excess might not only seem unhealthy but also somewhat ignoble or dishonorable if the excessive pursuit of such things involved devoting more time and energy to these tactile pleasures than would be consistent with decency. It also seems likely that if one were dominated by such desires, that would have a detrimental effect on other aspects of one's life; for example, if someone drinks too much coffee, he or she may not sleep very well; if someone drinks too much alcohol, he or she may constantly have a hangover; and if a couple is constantly having sex, there may be no time for other friends or family.

WRONG WAY. For this category, I doubt Aristotle is intending to pick out specific mistakes of etiquette, such as using the wrong fork in a restaurant, or passing the port the wrong way after dinner. Rather, it is more likely that the category concerns cases in which there is something peculiar about the way the agent wants to get pleasure from the thing in question that makes doing so socially unacceptable or unhealthy. An example for (7) might be someone who takes pleasure in eating *stolen* food. Or, for (8), consider someone who satisfies his desire for alcohol by drinking all the dregs from other people's drinks at the pub. An example for (9) might be cases in which agents violently abuse their partners for sexual gratification.

> are alleged to eat raw flesh, or human flesh, or to lend their children to one another to feast upon" (1148b19–24).

OTHER DIMENSIONS TO SELF-INDULGENCE. Besides the three categories of error Aristotle explicitly mentions, there would seem to be other
ways that one could manifest self-indulgence, corresponding to the
other Aristotelian categories.[24] One might, for example, delight in
something at the wrong time: for example, have a four-course meal at
four o'clock in the morning or have four or five pints of beer on one's
lunch break. Again, one might delight in something at the wrong place:
for example, satisfy one's sexual desire with one's partner during a
degree awards ceremony, or while driving; or one might eat a packet
of crisps noisily during a play.

Why does Aristotle insist (in the passage quoted at the beginning
of this section) that the self-indulgent person goes wrong in *all three* of
the ways he mentioned? It might seem that repeatedly going wrong
with respect to just one category should be sufficient to be characterized
as such. If someone is extremely overweight because he constantly
eats sweets, one might well think that would make him self-indulgent,
even if he did not go wrong in the other ways. There are two things to say
in response. First, in the passage quoted, Aristotle claims that if an agent
goes wrong only with respect to one of these categories, he may be
labeled "a lover of" the thing in question, not self-indulgent. This
again (see Section 7) seems to be a point about linguistic usage. An
agent counts as "a lover of," for example, sweets, rather than "self-
indulgent" (*akolastos*), Aristotle holds, if he like sweets too much,
whereas to call someone self-indulgent picks out a more general trait
involving a variety of patterns of behavior. Second, the characterization
fits Aristotle's general tendency, already witnessed, to focus on the
purest exemplars of the characters in question. Clearly, an agent is
more defective in this sphere if he goes wrong in each of the ways
Aristotle mentioned. It seems, then, that he would allow that agents
can go wrong with respect to just one category, but that he wishes to
reserve the title "self-indulgent" for the pure type.

10. Vice of Insensibility

Concerning the vice of deficiency, Aristotle writes:

People who are deficient in relation to pleasures and enjoy them less than they
ought are not generally found, since such insensibility is not a human characteristic. Even the other animals make discriminations between different kinds of food
and enjoy some but not others; and if there is anyone who finds nothing pleasant

---

[24] I suppose Aristotle might have considered all of these to fall under the "wrong way"
heading, and so have intended that third category to be a broad one, picking up all the
other ways in which an agent might go wrong.

and is indifferent about everything, he must be far from being human. And because he is found so rarely, this sort of person has not been given a name. (1119a5–11)

One might, in response to this, wonder why Aristotle does not think that there are lots of ways of manifesting the vice of deficiency with respect to particular appetites. Are there not people who are, for example, overly obsessed with dieting who do not enjoy certain types of food enough? Or people who will never have an alcoholic drink, even when they would enjoy it and it would do no other harm to them? Or people who lack a "healthy" sex drive? Perhaps not everyone will answer in the affirmative to all of these (e.g., about alcohol), but surely we think that the deficiency is possible in general for particular appetites. It seems that just as Aristotle thought that the deficiency did not exist in the case of general appetites – but certain kinds of anorexia seem to fit it – so too people could be deficient with respect to particular appetites in a way that contradicts Aristotle's account. However, the current flaw would be more fundamental: Aristotle may well not have encountered agents with certain eating disorders at the level of general appetites, but surely he would have encountered people who were deficient with respect to particular appetites?

However, we can reply to this objection on Aristotle's behalf. Just as he wanted to reserve "self-indulgent" for those who go wrong in lots of ways at the same time, so too he seems to envisage the deficient agent as someone who is not merely deficient in one respect but deficient in general (he "finds nothing pleasant and is indifferent about everything"). When this is taken into account, it is surely more plausible that such characters would be rare; for it is hard to find agents who do not have *any* particular appetites or specific activities that provide them with bodily pleasure. As Aristotle claims in the preceding passage, such an agent would seem "far from being human."

Again, this will mean that there will be a number of agents who are less than ideal (going wrong in some limited respect, to either excess or deficiency) but that do not fall under either of Aristotle's vices. Presumably, Aristotle is once again trying to emphasize the purest types of character.[25]

---

[25]   It is worth noting that with courage Aristotle was mainly concerned to characterize the purest type of virtuous character, whereas here he is more concerned to characterize the purest types of vicious character. I think that this emphasis accords with the fact that the vicious characters (especially self-indulgence) are more center stage for the virtue of temperance than with courage: Aristotle provides only a (brief) positive characterization of temperance at the very end of iii 11, as we shall now see. (Note also that in *EE* temperance is *only* characterized negatively, i.e., by contrast with the other vices, see iii 2.1231a34–1231b2.)

11. Temperance

Aristotle initially characterizes the temperate agent negatively, by contrast with the self-indulgent agent:

The temperate person occupies an intermediate position with regard to pleasures. For he does not enjoy the things that the self-indulgent enjoys most – rather he actually dislikes them – nor, in general, pleasures it would be wrong to enjoy; nor does he enjoy any pleasure to excess; nor does he feel pain or appetite at the absence of pleasures, except perhaps in moderation, and not more than is right, at the wrong time, and so on. (1119a11–15)

But, interestingly, he then also provides a positive characterization of this agent:

But things that are pleasant and conducive to health or good condition he desires in a moderate way (*metriōs*), as is right, and other pleasant things as well, as long as they are not incompatible with health or good condition, contrary to what is noble or beyond his means. For the person who fails to abide by these limitations enjoys such pleasures more than they deserve; the temperate person is not like this, but enjoys them as correct reason prescribes. (1119a16–20)

Aristotle claims that the temperate agent will enjoy (i) things that make for health (*hugieia*) and good condition (or fitness, the Greek is *euexia*), and (ii) other pleasant things if they are not hindrances to these ends, or ignoble, or beyond his means.

If (i) constituted the full specification of temperance, then Aristotle's temperate agent would desire only what directly contributes to his health or fitness. If eating a large salad for lunch is most healthy, he will desire to do this, and if it is best for one's health to drink isotonic sports drinks regularly (and I do say *if*), he will desire to drink these; and presumably his sexual activity will provide valuable aerobic exercise (besides facilitating procreation). But (ii) shows that Aristotle also allows the temperate agent to desire things that do not directly contribute to his health or fitness, so long as the pleasures in question are not (a) detrimental to health, (b) ignoble, or (c) beyond the agent's means (*ousia*: substance, property).[26] This moves Aristotle's account beyond a simple doctrine of

---

[26] With respect to (ii), Young 1988, 534–535, writes: "Apparently [Aristotle's] idea is that a temperate person will on occasion eat or drink something solely for the sake of the pleasure it brings." This contrasts, on Young's reading, with the "mere acceptance" that temperate agents will have with respect to the pleasures of eating or drinking healthful things. As I understand Aristotle, this is a misleading way to put the contrast. The temperate agent will in each case still desire the object in question *as* pleasant; it is just that the object he so desires will in fact be good for his health or good condition (for (i)), or in fact satisfy (a), (b), and (c) (for (ii)). I discuss this feature of Aristotle's account further in Pearson 2012, ch. 4, sec. 3.

moderation. Sometimes it may seem right to let one's hair down and make a really good night of it, for example, for birthdays or other celebrations. Aristotle can accommodate this. Whether or not the activity in question promotes one's bodily health, or is a positively noble thing to aim at, so long as it is not *detrimental* to one's health (as, e.g., smoking is), and so long as one does not behave *ignobly* (e.g., get so drunk that one strips off and runs around town) or attempt to do something beyond one's means (e.g., buy everyone at the concert a drink), then Aristotle will allow that the activity is compatible with temperance. If eating an ice cream every now and again or having a few alcoholic drinks is not detrimental to one's health (and Aristotle's other conditions are satisfied), then one will not manifest self-indulgence in enjoying these things. Indeed, more than this: it may well be better for one's overall well-being if one really lets oneself go and enjoys oneself when the occasion is right.

It is worth emphasizing as well that, insofar as temperance is determined in part by what is healthy, it will apply in the private sphere no less than in the public sphere. Thus one can fail to act in accordance with virtue even if one's own health is the only thing affected by one's action, and nothing besides. In this way, one is a potential subject of Aristotelian ethical appraisal even at home behind closed doors or even if one lives alone on a desert island.[27]

12. *The Importance of Temperance*

Even though temperance concerns the pleasures of eating, drinking, and sex, we should not get the idea that it is a trivial or unimportant virtue. For Aristotle, at least, it is very important indeed. In *NE* vi 5 he connects temperance (*sōphrosunē*) with the saving or preserving of one's practical wisdom (*sōzein tēn phronēsin*). On his view, pleasure and pain have the power to destroy our perception of the starting points (*archai*) of action:

If a person has been ruined by pleasure or pain, it follows that the starting point will not be evident to him, nor the fact that this ought to be the goal and cause of everything he chooses and does; for vice tends to destroy the starting point. (*NE* vi 5.1140b17–20)

Temperance, then, appears to be necessary for our practical wisdom to function properly. In another passage, Aristotle explains *how* pleasure can distort an agent's perspective:

---

[27]   One dimension of virtue that is essentially social (or at least interpersonal) is picked out by Aristotle's notion of general justice, which amounts to complete virtue (*aretē teleia*) insofar as that concerns our relations to another (*pros heteron, NE* v 1.1129b26–27).

Each state [of character] has its own conception of what is noble and pleasant, and one might say that the good person stands out a long way by seeing the truth in each case, being a sort of standard and measure of what is noble and pleasant. In the case of the masses, however, pleasure seems to deceive them, because it looks like a good when it is not; people therefore choose what is pleasant, thinking it to be a good, and avoid pain, thinking it to be an evil. (NE iii 4.1113a31–b2)

Pleasure can appear as a good thing even when it is not; so being properly orientated with respect to it is crucial in order for us to be correctly orientated with regard to what is really good (see also Young 1998, 535).

III. CONCLUSION

Aristotle's accounts of courage and temperance and their corresponding vices are doubly interesting. First, they are interesting in their own terms. For instance, Aristotle's account of courage encourages us to draw a distinction between emotions as distressful or pleasurable representative states and emotions as behavioral or motivational states. It also indicates a role for both fear and confidence in the virtue. Equally, Aristotle's account of temperance invokes a distinction between different types of appetite, general and particular, and prompts us to consider the wide variety of ways agents can go wrong with respect to a key dimension of human life that we share with nonrational animals, namely tactile bodily pleasure. Second, Aristotle's accounts of courage and temperance are also relevant to his broader ethical views. Courage is problematic for the relation between virtue and happiness and provides a counterexample to the notion that virtue is a mean between precisely two vices. And temperance is explicitly said to be fundamental for the proper functioning of our practical wisdom, and reveals that ethical appraisal is not restricted to public matters, but extends to the private activities of agents as well. Thus, in attempting to characterize these particular spheres of ethical life, Aristotle's discussions of courage and temperance invite reflection on more general features of his ethical thought.

WORKS CITED

Adair, S., G. Bagwell, and R. Polansky. 2009. "The Field for Virtue and Getting a Feel for It." Skepsis 20: 15–26.
Broadie, S. 1991. Ethics with Aristotle. Oxford: Oxford University Press.
Charles, D. 1995. "Aristotle and Modern Realism." 135–172 in R. Heinaman ed. Aristotle and Moral Realism. London: UCL Press.
Cooper, J. 1999. "Reason, Moral Virtue, and Moral Value." 253–280 in J. Cooper, Reason and Emotion. Princeton: Princeton University Press.
Crisp, R. trans. 2000. Aristotle: Nicomachean Ethics. Cambridge: Cambridge University Press.

Curzer, H. J. 1996. "A Defense of Aristotle's Doctrine That Virtue Is a Mean." *Ancient Philosophy* 16: 129–138.

1997. "Aristotle's Account of the Virtue of Temperance in *Nicomachean Ethics* III.10–11." *Journal of the History of Philosophy* 35: 5–25.

Duff, A. 1987. "Aristotelian Courage." *Ratio* 29: 2–15.

Heil, J. F. 1996. "Why Is Aristotle's Brave Man So Frightened? The Paradox of Courage in the *Eudemian Ethics*." *Apeiron* 29: 47–74.

Hursthouse, R. 1980–1981. "A False Doctrine of the Mean." *Proceedings of the Aristotelian Society* 81: 57–72.

2006. "The Central Doctrine of the Mean." 96–115 in R. Kraut ed. *The Blackwell Guide to Aristotle's Nicomachean Ethics*. Malden, MA: Blackwell.

Kennedy, G. A. 1991. *Aristotle On Rhetoric: A Theory of Civic Discourse*. Oxford: Oxford University Press.

Lear, G. R. 2004. *Happy Lives and the Highest Good: An Essay on Aristotle's Nicomachean Ethics*. Princeton: Princeton University Press.

Pakaluk, M. 2005. *Aristotle's Nicomachean Ethics: An Introduction*. Cambridge: Cambridge University Press.

Pears, D. F. 1978. "Aristotle's Analysis of Courage." *Midwest Studies in Philosophy* 3: 273–285.

1980. "Courage as a Mean." 171–187 in A. O. Rorty ed. *Essays on Aristotle's Ethics*. Berkeley: University of California Press.

Pearson, G. 2006a. "Does the Fearless Phobic Really Fear the Squeak of Mice 'Too Much'?" *Ancient Philosophy* 26: 81–91.

2006b. "Aristotle on Acting Unjustly without Being Unjust." *Oxford Studies in Ancient Philosophy* 30: 211–233.

2009. "Aristotle on the Role of Confidence in Courage." *Ancient Philosophy* 29: 123–137.

2012. *Aristotle on Desire*. Cambridge: Cambridge University Press.

Ross, D. 1925. *Aristotle: The Nicomachean Ethics*. Oxford: Oxford University Press.

1995. *Aristotle*. 6th ed. London: Routledge (first published 1923).

Sedley, D. 2005. "Plato's Tsunami." *Hyperboreus* 11: 205–214.

Sisko, J. 2003. "Taste, Touch, and Temperance in *Nicomachean Ethics* III.10." *Classical Quarterly* 53: 135–140.

Taylor, C. C. W. 2006. *Aristotle: Nicomachean Ethics Books II–IV*. Oxford: Clarendon Press.

Urmson, J. O. 1988. *Aristotle's Ethics*. Oxford: Blackwell.

Welton, W., and R. Polansky. 1995. "The Viability of Virtue in the Mean." 79–102 in *Aristotle, Virtue and the Mean*. Special issue, *Apeiron*. Vol. 28.

Young, C. M. 1988. "Aristotle on Temperance." *Philosophical Review* 97: 521–542.

7   The Social Virtues (*NE* iv)

In book 4 of his *Nicomachean Ethics*, Aristotle discusses in detail a number of virtues that fall outside the scope of those cardinal virtues with which we are familiar from Plato's *Republic* and other philosophical texts both ancient and modern. Some of these virtues, such as generosity, are reasonably familiar as virtues, but others, particularly magnificence, greatness of soul, and quick-wittedness, strike us as odd. Why should these be virtues at all? Part of the answer is that Aristotle strives to provide a comprehensive view of the flourishing life in accordance with virtue and tends to divide up the virtues of character into those different spheres of activity and types of emotion and goods that are most crucial for individual and communal flourishing. Thus there must be virtues dealing with wealth and expenditures, honor and reputation, humor and anger, since the ways in which we handle these activities, goods, and emotions either enhance or disrupt human life on the individual and communal levels. Further, the life in accordance with virtue is, according to Aristotle, a life in accordance with nature. Aristotle's account of the virtues is thus a totalizing and naturalizing account. The virtues that he is delineating should be applicable both to fourth-century Greece and to other times and places.

However, Aristotle's view is undoubtedly in some ways colored by the time and place at which he was living and philosophizing. His standard of virtue is the virtuous, free male citizen of the fourth century BCE. There will likely always be vigorous scholarly debate about the extent to which the ethical virtues that Aristotle discusses can be extended to contemporary societies and other cultures; and about the extent to which he is caught within the conventions of his own time, claiming erroneously, as some critics would argue, that the virtues of the fourth-century Greek male are applicable to all humans. My approach here will be to uncover some of the philosophical underpinning of the social virtues of *NE* iv and some of the historical contexts of those virtues. For even those virtues that are understandable to us and can be understood philosophically out of historical context are colored in Aristotle's text by examples of the fourth century. We should note that within book 4, we do find elements of cultural prejudice encoded, particularly in the vices of vulgarity (Greek, *banausia*) and boorishness (Greek, *agroikia*). The term *banausos* means a manual laborer, usually one who worked indoors, and *banausia* is the name of the vice (related to magnificence) that consists in a tasteless display and expenditure of wealth on a large scale. The term *agroikos* means a rustic, and *agroikia* is used to connote an insensitivity to humor, owing to the common opinion that farm workers were hard-working but somewhat asocial and uneducated.

It is a mistake, however, to conclude from the names and scope of the virtues and the clear allusions to fourth-century Greek life that the virtuous states discussed in book 4 are uncritically those values of a fourth-century Athenian male citizen. First, the definition of the virtues and what constitutes behavior in accordance with virtue were all vehemently debated not only in philosophical but also in rhetorical writings of the fourth century. Second, while Aristotle includes many virtues that would have been familiar to his audience, the definition and discussion of those virtues provide nuanced accounts of what types of behavior count as in accordance with each virtue, understood as an intermediate state between the extremes of two vices; and these accounts often show Aristotle in implicit dialogue with other philosophers and rhetoricians of the fourth century such as Plato, Isocrates, and Demosthenes. Finally, Aristotle discusses several virtues and vices that are nameless, indicating that not all the states of character that he is describing are commonly thought of as virtues and vices. Like most philosophers engaged in ethical discourse, Aristotle is both a critical thinker regarding the ethical issues and questions of his day and a thinker who is caught to some extent within the cultural norms and prejudices of his own era.

I. GENEROSITY AND MAGNIFICENCE

The first virtue discussed by Aristotle in book 4 is generosity. As we would expect of an Aristotelian virtue, the mean state and the activities in accordance with it concern what is of benefit both to the agent himself and to others. The virtue concerns both the giving and taking of wealth (1119b25).[1] The properly generous person will neither waste his wealth nor take wealth by unjust or other inappropriate means. However, the emphasis is clearly on the giving of wealth to others (1119b25–26). The generous man tends to be excessive in giving to others and does not look to his own interests. Yet, if they are to be in accordance with virtue, expenditures must be proportionate to the agent's property and not exhaust or exceed it. There is a careful balancing between what the agent can actually afford to give and a too-stingy calculation of what is

---

[1]   All references are to *NE* iv, unless otherwise stated.

prudent to expend. The prudential aspects of the virtue are shown by considering the excessive vice of wastefulness. Wastefulness could be exemplified in two different ways: wasting money on extravagant goods, thus depriving the agent and his family of necessary goods; or giving away wealth to the wrong people who do not deserve it. The latter would be a form of wastefulness, even if that wastefulness did not occur together with the former. These two forms of excess are crystallized in the phrases "giving and spending" (1120b26–27) and "give and spend" (1120b29), where giving means donating money to others, and spending could include both donations to others and expenditures that would procure goods for oneself. The generous person who acts with pleasure and for the sake of the noble (to kalon) in acting generously is thus not a pure altruist but rather acts appropriately insofar as he understands the limits of his own wealth, as well as the nobility of giving away wealth, sometimes spontaneously, without too careful a calculation of profit and loss, but yet prudently.[2] The balance between prudent and altruistic use of wealth is surely what makes this virtue difficult to attain and maintain.

The account of generosity is somewhat complicated by the following virtue of magnificence (megaloprepeia), a virtue primarily concerned with expenditures on a greater scale. What is at first sight confusing is that actions in accordance with magnificence seem to be included within the discussion of generosity. If there is a virtue concerning the taking and giving of wealth, then a further virtue of magnificence seems to be redundant. One possible interpretation is that a separate virtue is needed for very large-scale expenditures such as the public liturgies, because virtuous expenditures on smaller scales do not actually build and maintain the habits and reasoning necessary to act in accordance with virtue regarding large donations. To use a modern analogy, just because I am generous to my friends and family, that does not mean that I could act virtuously in, for example, personally disbursing millions of dollars to others. In fact, in contemporary society, we have developed large philanthropic organizations to do that work, rather than relying merely on the virtue of individuals. However, we may still think of magnificence as a relevant modern virtue that comes into play when the very wealthy or even, as I shall argue here, most of us spend our surplus wealth on charitable donations or make any expenditure beyond the usual household and domestic costs.

The paradigmatic examples of magnificence in book 4 are the civic liturgies – such as equipping a chorus, trireme, and leading delegations to

---

[2] For a helpful discussion of the emphasis on the prudential and more altruistic aspects of this virtue, see Taylor 2006, 204–206.

the Panhellenic Games. These liturgies constituted a combination of taxation and philanthropy in fourth-century Athens. Appointed by the Athenian magistrates each year, the liturgists were required to carry out their duties, but it was up to them how much money to spend and how they would spend it on their appointed task. Only a very small percentage of the Athenian population would have been wealthy enough to take on most liturgies, and attitudes to this form of civic munificence are complex in fourth-century literature. Clearly the liturgies gave the richest Athenians an opportunity to benefit the city while winning great honor for themselves. The outlay of expense was compensated by prestige, much as philanthropic donors are often honored today in the press and with physical monuments. In many fourth-century speeches, however, orators often complain that the liturgies are unfair and burdensome on the rich.[3] Thus Demosthenes complains that "no one ever blamed himself for squandering his wealth; on the contrary, he claims that the city has robbed him of his property" (Demosthenes, *Against Nausimachus* 26). Aristotle, therefore, by including a separate virtue of magnificence is emphasizing the responsibility of wealthy individuals to use their wealth for the benefit of the city-state, while also emphasizing, as he does in the account of generosity, that any expenditure must be proportionate to the wealth of the agent. Aristotle would not endorse as in accordance with virtue someone who spent all his money on equipping a trireme.

Is it the case, however, that magnificence is a virtue that can be exercised only by the very wealthy, such as those who were capable of performing liturgies? Aristotle states that the magnificent expenditures should be relative to the agent, circumstances, and object (1122a25–26). He also argues that while magnificent expenditure without qualification is great in quantity and for a great object (presumably a liturgy or something similar), "a noble ball or oil-flask is magnificent as a gift for a child although its cost is small and petty" (1124a14–15). It is, therefore, reasonable to interpret the scope of this virtue as one that covers all expenditures beyond those of normal household outlays, as Pakaluk 2002 has argued.[4] It is a way to spend surplus wealth, on presents to a child, parties, or liturgies in accordance with virtue, and as such it can be exercised by anyone with some surplus wealth to spend, not only the wealthiest.

As we have seen, both generosity and magnificence concern primarily the giving away of wealth to others. The actions in accordance with these virtues are done with pleasure, "for the sake of the noble," and of course

---

[3] For a helpful discussion of the evidence, see Christ 1990; and for a very detailed analysis of the institution of and attitudes toward the trierarchy, see Gabrielsen 1994.

[4] For differing interpretations, see Irwin 1988 and Gardiner 2001.

in the right time and in the right way. The "nobility" of these actions is thus a medial appropriateness – not born from pure altruism but rather from a sense that this action at this time is fully appropriate for a citizen with this amount of wealth in these circumstances. The generous and magnificent person will give gladly but not without any thought of how much wealth he and his family need to survive and, in the case of magnificence, not without furnishing and equipping a home that is worthy of him (1123a6). The "nobility" of the expenditure is a function of its appropriateness to occasion and to means with the result that "noble" or "fine" expenditures exhibit what we may call good taste.[5] There is certainly an aristocratic bent to the account of *megaloprepeia*, but it is to be understood in a fourth-century context in which many of the aristocratic class were shirking their civic responsibilities. Moreover, Aristotle, by relativizing great expenditures to objects and circumstances, seems to widen the class of those who could be called magnificent beyond what may have been commonly understood in fourth-century Athens.[6]

II. GREATNESS OF SOUL AND APPROPRIATE AMBITION

Since honor may be won by the virtues of generosity and magnificence, it is perhaps natural that Aristotle treats greatness of soul immediately after the large-scale virtue dealing with wealth. For Aristotle, greatness of soul (*megalopsuchia*) is a type of pride, defined as being worthy and deeming oneself worthy of great things. Specifically these "great things" are instances of honor, the esteem, and respect bestowed on the virtuous agent by others. The great-souled individual has a high opinion of himself that is entirely justified, a well-founded sense of pride. Yet what the English term "pride" as a translation of the Greek *megalopsuchia* does not really capture is the idea of greatness. Some philosophers in the modern era have made the connection between pride and greatness,

---

[5] Rogers 1993 stresses that the noble or fine (*to kalon*) is to be understood in Aristotle's *Ethics* as the fitting or appropriate (*to prepon*). Lear 2004, 129–130, emphasizes that, in addition to being appropriate, *to kalon* is visibly "showy." The combination of showiness and suitability in the sphere of magnificence results in expenditures that are aesthetically stunning but yet tasteful.

[6] It is uncontroversial that appropriate and noble expenditures are relative to the object of those expenditures and the wealth of the agent. However, that does not mean that virtue itself is relative to the agent in the sense that: (a) the virtuous mean varies according to our state of moral progress; (b) the mean varies according to our susceptibility to the passions; (c) the mean varies according to our station in life; or (d) the mean varies according to an individual's beliefs. While (c) may seem close to what I am arguing, I take the paradigm of virtue to be the free Greek male for Aristotle, and differences in wealth and circumstance do not affect that "station." For more on the "mean relative to us" (1106a28), see Brown 1997.

most notably Hume when he states that what we term heroic or great virtue is "nothing but a steady and well-established sense of pride and self-esteem, or partakes largely of that passion" (*A Treatise of Human Nature* iii.2). *Megalopsuchia* is related in Greek thought and literature prior to Aristotle to the concepts of great-heartedness and great-spiritedness, the qualities of the Homeric heroes. In the fourth century BCE, greatness of soul is most often attributed to generals, men of politics, and kings, including Philip of Macedon the empire builder and father of Alexander.[7] Plato, however, redefines greatness of soul as the quality of the philosopher when he describes the man with a great soul born in a small city who remains uncorrupted by political machinations (*Republic* iv 496b).

Given this contextual background to the concept of *megalopsuchia*, we are led to ask not only why pride should be a virtue for Aristotle but also in what this "greatness" of character consists. What exactly is great about the great-souled, proud individual? What is the connection between pride and greatness? And what is the relationship to the smaller-scale virtue of appropriate ambition? The interpretation of this virtue is highly contested and it has been argued that the account of greatness of soul is internally inconsistent, that the virtue constitutes an aristocratic ideal that we cannot endorse as virtuous, and that even by Aristotle's own standards the quality should not be a virtue. Later in this section I pursue a line of argument that shows how and why greatness of soul should be a virtue for Aristotle and how it coheres with the other virtues. Nevertheless, readers should be aware that there are other interpretations available.[8]

Two concepts are crucial to Aristotle's definition of the virtue: the activity of deeming oneself worthy; and honor, in the sense of the external honor bestowed by others. It is honor that the great-souled person deems himself worthy of. The connection between the virtue and honor is striking. It would be logically possible to define the virtue as "deeming oneself worthy of x" without x being honor. The great-souled individual could be defined as one who deems himself worthy of good things in general. Aristotle's reasoning, however, runs along the following lines: the great-souled person is worthy of and deems himself worthy of the greatest things: it is external goods that we are properly said to be "worthy of"; honor is the greatest of external goods; and in order to be worthy of honor, the great-souled person must be completely good, since honor is properly speaking the prize of virtue and assigned to the good. The logic of the argument should be unsurprising when we consider the importance

---

[7] See, e.g., Demosthenes, *De Corona* 68.

[8] In particular, see Curzer 1990 and 1991; Cooper 1989; and Held 1993.

that honor had for the Greeks from Homer onward, and the connotation of *megalopsuchia* in fourth-century literature as a high degree of pride and ambition.[9] However, Aristotle is clearly cognizant of the danger that excessive honor-loving can lead to destructive anger. In *Posterior Analytics* 97b15–25 he alludes to two apparently different types of greatness of soul: that of Achilles, Ajax, and Alcibiades, exemplified by an inability to endure dishonor; and that of Socrates and Lysander, which is manifest as an indifference to fortune, good and bad. The positive exemplum of Socrates and the negative exemplum of Achilles, whose angry withdrawal from battle in Homer's *Iliad* causes numerous Greek deaths, both lie behind Aristotle's account of the virtue. But rather than distinguishing two types of *megalopsuchia*, one honor-loving and the other honor-indifferent, Aristotle instead crafts an account of the virtue that is centered around having the right attitude to external honors and a justified sense of pride.

Since the great-souled agent is a virtuous man, he has the proper intellectual and emotional orientation to honor. As a virtuous person, who has all the other virtues, he deems himself worthy of honor on the grounds of virtue and realizes that honor itself as external good does not match the worth of action according to virtue. He is moderately pleased with honors bestowed by good people on the grounds of good action. But he totally discounts honors bestowed on trifling grounds (1124a10–11). We can imagine him disdaining honors that are offered because he is tall or good-looking. Indeed, Aristotle roundly condemns those who claim honors on the grounds of external goods such as beauty, wealth, or power (1124a29–30). The great-souled, proud individual certainly may not always appear to be a "nice" person, as judged by those who do not understand his character. He will appear haughty, disdainful, and even arrogant (1124b4–5). But those attitudes do not spring from a disdain for the lowly in the sense of those who do not have wealth or power, but rather a disdain for vice and the mistaken notion that external goods trump the worth of virtue. He thus appears arrogant in the way that Socrates appeared arrogant to the Sophists.

I sketch out three reasons why greatness of soul, defined as being justifiably worthy of honor, should be a virtue for Aristotle. In Plato's *Republic* ii, we are presented with the famous thought experiment in which we are asked to imagine a perfectly just and virtuous person with a reputation as bad and unjust. The point is to determine why virtue is in fact a good thing irrespective of the external rewards, the praise and

---

[9] E.g.: "For we will find that highly ambitious and proud men (*tous philotimous kai megalopsuchous*) ... not only choose to die gloriously instead of to live but are more eager for reputation than for life" (Isocrates, *Evagoras* 3).

honors, that virtue wins. Subsequently in the *Republic* we learn that virtue is its own reward in that a harmonious and perfect soul is exponentially more valuable than any honor or other good external to the soul. Thus, the specters of the Homeric heroes, such as Ajax and Achilles, who manifest aspects of virtue but are too tied to honor as reputation are banished from the virtuous life.[10]

In one way, of course, Aristotle agrees with the Platonic stance. The work of virtue and the soul from which virtuous action springs are for Aristotle more valuable than externals, and this is made very clear in the account of *megalopsuchia*. However, how are we to negotiate the perilous territory of honor, disrespect, praise, and blame? When is honor to be accepted and rejected? What sort of honors are valuable and which are not? Plato himself approaches answers to these questions in his discussion in the *Republic* of the just city, *Kallipolis*, where honor is the appropriate award for each citizen who assumes his or her proper role. Thus, for example, the auxiliaries are honored for their brave actions on the battlefield (*Republic* v 468b). Moreover, Plato recognizes, as does Aristotle, that the desire for honor is connected to feelings of self-respect and self-esteem.[11] The spirit (*thumos*), the honor-loving part of the soul, is also concerned with avoiding what the agent takes to be shameful. However, Plato does not provide a detailed discussion of an ethical virtue that includes both self-respect and the capacity to deal with honor and dishonor bestowed by others. Aristotle's *megalopsuchia* is the disposition of the virtuous agent that enables the practically wise negotiation of this territory.

We are to imagine that the great-souled individual (a) is completely virtuous; (b) has knowledge of his own worth; and (c) understands that honor is only valuable when bestowed on certain grounds by certain people. If we do not believe that (a) and (b) are possible, that is, if we take it that complete virtue is not possible, or that it is possible but that self-knowledge is impossible, then we will not find this concept compelling. We may be more attracted by a virtue according to which an agent acknowledges his or her limitations, and deems himself worthy of praise and honor when justified, but also of blame and shame when appropriate. Note that later in book 4, shame is defined merely as an emotion and not as a virtuous state (1128b10 ff.). It is appropriate for those learning to be good but not for those who are fully good. Yet given premises (a) and (b), *megalopsuchia* is an attractive virtue. For the bestowing and acceptance

---

[10]   On the relationship of the Homeric heroes to Plato's *Republic*, see Hobbs 2000, esp. 199–210.

[11]   See the anecdote about Leontius (*Republic* iv 440a). Moss 2005 provides a helpful analysis of spirit (*thumos*) in the context of the tripartite division of the soul in the *Republic*.

of honor is surely crucial to the maintenance of virtue within a community and contributes to the happiness of individuals. It would be an odd situation for a virtuous agent to reject honors when worthy of them. As a token of virtue, honor should be a good thing. Not only does it seem odd to reject a reward one is worthy of, but also such a rejection seems to be a denial that what one has done is good and that one is good, which has consequences that reach far beyond the individual. How is anyone to learn to be good, if honors are not regularly bestowed and accepted for virtuous conduct? Honor as a sign and reward of virtue has an important social function. Although honor is not the greatest thing – relative to goods of the soul – it certainly is a good thing for both the individual and community.

Nevertheless, even if honor is a good thing, what may seem objectionable about the great-souled man is that his decisions about the virtuous thing to do seem to run through thoughts of his own worth and honorableness. Should the great-souled man, qua virtuous individual, not be instead devoted to some impersonal ideal of the good and noble? Although there is no indication that Aristotle thinks the great-souled person is always actively thinking about his own worth, Aristotle's sketch of the great-souled does suggest that he has a great sense of ambition and dignity, based on his high sense of his own worth. He also suggests that this sense of self-worth is necessary in some contexts actually to act virtuously, and the small-souled are deficient in that they underestimate themselves: "Each sort of person aims at what is in accordance with his worth, and these people abstain from noble actions and projects and similarly from external goods, because they feel unworthy of them" (1125a25–27). Although earlier Aristotle has suggested that it is external goods that people are properly speaking "worthy of," in this passage the notion of being worthy of certain actions is introduced. What does it mean to think that one is "unworthy" of undertaking an action? An agent could think that he is unworthy because he lacks the necessary skill or physical ability that is requisite for that undertaking, or he could have a lack of confidence in his own character, perhaps shrinking from battle because he is concerned that he will be overcome by fear. A mismatch is perceived between the worth of the action and the worth of one's ethical character. It is this feeling of hesitancy, of feeling unworthy of undertaking certain virtuous actions when one is in fact worthy of them, that Aristotle attributes to the small-souled. These people have the capacity to be virtuous, but fail to actualize that potential because of a lack of self-worth.

In this way, *megalopsuchia* entails a kind of self-esteem. It is not only that the great-souled individual is proud of his achievements and character, taking them to be worthy of honor, an external good, but also that his self-esteem enables him to attempt certain virtuous actions in the first place: he sees himself as an honorable person, capable of and willing to undertake certain projects. Some instances of virtue are surely spontaneous and do not involve thoughts of self-worth. But where we face danger, or a difficult practical problem to solve, or pain, what is necessary is both the thought "x is a good and noble action" and "I am worthy of undertaking x." Although Aristotle does not devote that much attention to this aspect of the virtue, he clearly thinks that self-esteem is crucial to *megalopsuchia*. In fact, he notes that smallness of soul is more opposed to greatness of soul than vanity is opposed to the virtue: for smallness of soul occurs more frequently and is worse (1125a33–34). Self-esteem engenders a sense of ambitiousness, of seeking out opportunities for virtuous action and grabbing them when they are presented, because the great-souled person is able to imagine himself performing actions that the small-souled cannot imagine performing, although they may wish to undertake them.

Thus far I have argued that greatness of soul is a virtue because (1) honor really is a good thing; and (2) the self-worth of the great-souled man is actually necessary for certain virtuous undertakings. However, a third reason why pride should be a virtue for Aristotle is that it makes the other virtues stable and difficult to dislodge. A sense of self-worth is necessary in that it gives one the confidence to undertake certain actions; but it is also necessary in another way, namely insofar as it enables one both to withstand misfortune and to weather extreme good fortune virtuously. The great-souled man views his own character and actions as infinitely more valuable than any external goods, and thus he is able to bear good fortune becomingly and virtuously, a thing that is hard to do, as Aristotle states at 1124a31. His attitude to misfortune is alluded to at 1124a16 – he does not grieve excessively when unfortunate. Strikingly, this aspect of the virtue is alluded to in book 1: "Nevertheless … the noble shines through, when a person calmly bears many great misfortunes, not through insensibility but by being well-bred and great-souled" (1100b30–32). One may wonder why a sense of self-worth is necessary to engender this attitude. Is it not enough to judge in an impersonal way that the worth of virtue far outstrips the worth of external goods? I would argue that it is not; and that, in fact, there may be a disconnect between thinking that it is noble to continue to act virtuously and stick to one's core values in the face of misfortune, and maintaining virtue while facing the onslaughts of fortune. To use the metaphor of greatness, to withstand such onslaughts and maintain virtue is to believe that one's own soul – my soul, not a soul in the abstract – is in a very personal and immediate sense greater than those onslaughts.

I have then sketched three reasons why pride or greatness of soul should be a virtue for Aristotle: (a) honor is in fact a good thing; (b) a sense of self-worth is necessary for undertaking action in difficult circumstances; and (c) a sense of self-worth makes virtue more stable in the face of extreme swings of fortune. These reasons illuminate some important things about *megalopsuchia*. It is both a particular virtue whose sphere is external honor and self-assessment and a virtue, as Aristotle says, that makes the other virtues greater (1124a2).

The relationship between greatness of soul and the other virtues has always been a puzzle. It is especially vexing as Aristotle includes in *NE* a small-scale unnamed virtue of appropriate ambition concerned with honor, in much the same way as magnificence is juxtaposed with liberality. However, note that in the *EE*, no such small-scale virtue concerning honor appears. One possibility is that *megalopsuchia* is some kind of super virtue: that is, great-souled people are just more virtuous than ordinarily virtuous people. Indeed, as argued earlier, it is *megalopsuchia* that allows people to maintain virtue when faced with the extremes of good and bad fortune. However, it would be a mistake to conclude from that premise that *megalopsuchia* is a heroic degree of virtue, with appropriate ambition serving as the virtuous norm. As Pakaluk 2004 has argued, the language of Aristotle's account in *NE* implies that great-souled people are very good but not that they are superlatively so. To put it another way, the heroic response in the face of good and bad fortune is actually one exhibited by all fully virtuous agents and not just moral heroes. We see perhaps an implicit critique of the term *megalopsuchia* as used in fourth-century Greece. It is a virtue, according to Aristotle, that is part of the fully virtuous life and not the virtue of heroes alone.

Another interpretation is that appropriate ambition in *NE* is concerned with small honors (honors bestowed for one's wealth or looks or strength), while *megalopsuchia* is concerned with great honors, that is, those earned by virtuous activity (Pakaluk 2002). The unfortunate result of that interpretation, however, is that the great-souled person then seems to have to despise exactly those small honors that the person of appropriate ambition accepts and desires appropriately, and this violates the unity of the virtues. A solution is perhaps that the great-souled person despises "small" honors in the sense of those bestowed for nonvirtuous or vicious actions, but readily accepts "small" honors if they are bestowed on the grounds of external goods. Yet this interpretation relies on two separate senses of the "small," which seems awkward. To preserve a unified sense of "small," we could admit that ambition and greatness of soul are in fact something like degrees of virtue, with ambition a smaller-scale virtue that is most appropriate to those who are, and deem themselves, worthy of smaller honors, won deservedly as the result of virtuous actions, but who are not yet fully virtuous (Nieuwenberg 2010). However, if this is the case, then ambition does not seem to be a virtue but rather a state that occurs before full virtue and practical wisdom are developed, and thus it does not seem to deserve the status of a virtue. We should note that taking the *EE* and *NE* together, Aristotle himself seems uncertain whether there should be one virtue concerned with honor or two. My reading is that the virtue of appropriate ambition in the *NE* is inherently problematic and that the *EE*, in which no such virtue appears, is a corrective to the *NE*. For Aristotle, *megalopsuchia* is the primary virtue concerned with honor, and one cannot be fully practically wise and good without greatness of soul, and greatness of soul is the primary virtue concerned with honor.

In what does this greatness consist? It seems to consist in the ability to take virtuous action where others may lack the confidence to do so, and in the ability to withstand the swings of good and bad fortune. Greatness of soul makes us great both in making us more practically ambitious and less hesitant and in making us more able to withstand good and bad luck. That is not to say that the great-souled person is a hero, but rather that greatness of soul is exhibited when the good person has the opportunity to act in ways that are conspicuously heroic, that is, when circumstances make the acts of justice, courage, liberality, and all the other virtues incredibly difficult to perform because one may be either tempted by the prospect of great pleasures or discouraged by the prospect of excessive pains. Some scholars have argued that greatness of soul may be exhibited only when sufficient external goods are available as the "equipment" for the exercise of virtuous actions that may win honor. Instead, I contend that greatness of soul is exhibited in extreme circumstances, in the heights of good fortune and depths of misfortune, both of which make virtue particularly difficult to maintain and exercise. As noted earlier, Aristotle in the *Posterior Analytics* mentions two apparently different senses of greatness of soul, an inability to bear dishonor and an indifference to fortune. In the *NE*, rather than distinguishing between these two senses of *megalopsuchia*, Aristotle provides us with a unified virtue that combines aspects of the Socratic and Achillean paradigms. The great-souled individual is committed to doing what is truly honorable and to claiming the justified honors for that action in the face of whatever good or bad fortune may come his way. However, his attitude to external honor is far more Socratic than Achillean.

I have said nothing thus far about the goals of the great-souled person. Since greatness of soul is a second-order virtue concerned with self-worth and the honor that one wins from virtuous activity, it is reasonably easy to discuss the virtue while sidestepping the questions of what the great-souled individual is committed to as goals of action. Although *megalopsuchia* may seem like an egoistic virtue, in that its sphere is honor and self-worth, in fact it would be perfectly consistent for the great-souled person to have a sense of self-worth that is predicated on his ability to act in accordance with other virtues that are directed toward the common good. One can be proud of one's service to the common good. Moreover, although it is certainly pleasant to win honor, I suggested earlier that the distribution of honors is crucial to the political health of the community, and thus we are not to take the emphasis on honor as somehow a sign of egoism. As with generosity and magnificence, the goals of greatness of soul encompass what is good both for the agent and for others.

What activities Aristotle's agent can legitimately take pride in are circumscribed by the other virtues. Let us imagine an Aristotelian great-souled individual who takes pride in his magnificent expenditures: those expenditures may include both costs to furnish his family home and expenditures on behalf of the city. Also, as a liberal individual, he will spend virtuously on "normal" household expenditures and be generous with money to his friends. These are all actions in which the great-souled person can be proud. However, would he feel similar pride in taking care of aged parents when they need his care? There is no Aristotelian virtue that encompasses such activity. Perhaps it is encompassed in the discussion of (*philia*) friendship in books 8 and 9, which includes discussion of familial relationships. In fact, Aristotle does note at *NE* ix 2 that it is noble to provide both food and honor to one's parents, suggesting that parental care is not beneath the dignity of the great-souled man, although surely Aristotle would have thought that the menial tasks of elder care were best performed by women and slaves. Yet the virtue of *megalopsuchia* itself, combined with the accounts of friendship in books 8 and 9, can be read as suggesting that parental care counts as an honorable thing insofar as it is activity directed toward *philoi* (friends or dear ones): an activity that in fact involves a great-souled sense of self-worth and stability of other virtues, as it is certainly a difficult undertaking, fraught with pain, and in which nobility can "shine out." Aristotle in some ways portrays greatness of soul as a heroic virtue, but it is not heroic in the sense that it is a state that can be developed and exercised only by kings and heroes. Rather it is a virtue that can be developed by all, although certainly it is difficult to attain, and that can be exhibited in times of stress by all who have attained *megalopsuchia*, along with all the other moral virtues, and thereby have the strongest claim to honor.

III. THE OTHER VIRTUES

In many ways, the account of greatness of soul and the unnamed virtue of appropriate ambition are the centerpieces of book 4. The virtues

following them – even temper, the nameless qualities of general friendliness and truthfulness, and quick-wittedness – all seem to be consistent
with the virtue of greatness of soul and contextualize it within other
aspects of the social life in accordance with virtue. Even temper, the
virtue that prevents us from becoming too angry for too long, is quite
consistent with the great-souled man's judgment that honor is a small
thing. Even when deprived of the greatest good of which he is worthy, the
great-souled man's anger will not rise to levels that compromise the
activities of the other virtues. A general friendliness may seem antithet-
ical to the haughtiness of the great-souled man, but the disposition is
contrasted with a vice, obsequiousness, which is also banished from
greatness of soul. The great-souled man is no flatterer (1125a1–2).
Truthfulness with regard to one's own qualities and accomplishments
also seems entirely consistent with greatness of soul that includes the
quality of being open in likes and dislikes and speaking the truth
(1124b30). Aristotle does, however, allow the great-souled to play down
their merits to inferiors, which is echoed by the mention of Socrates in
the account of truthfulness: a man who disclaimed those qualities that
others hold in esteem (1127b25–26).

The virtue of quick-wittedness – or having an appropriate sense of
humor – is perhaps the virtue that seems most out of place in book 4.
However, in its place as the final virtue discussed in the book, it, along
with the preceding quality of friendliness, has the effect of dismissing
the impression that the virtuous agent, particularly insofar as he is
great-souled, takes himself too seriously. This virtue is an important
virtue in leisure time, and its sphere is the pleasure of social interaction. The witty individual makes playful and appropriate jokes in
the style of an educated and free person, and also appreciates the
humor of others. It is tempting to draw out an implicit connection
between this virtue and the urbane style of discourse in the *Rhetoric*
1410b1–1413b1, that relies on metaphor, antithesis, and "actuality"
(*energeia*) of language, best described by Halliwell (1993, 65) as "witty
and piquant." The pleasure taken in the urbane joke is not only that of a
clever putdown or an ingenious pun but is also the intellectual pleasure
of grasping an idea. The deficiency related to quick-wittedness is boorishness (*agroikia*), the disposition of those who are unable to make or
appreciate any kind of joke. This seems to be not only an intellectual
but also a social deficiency in that boors derive little or no pleasure
from shared laughter. The excess related to the virtue is buffoonery,
exemplified by the shameful speech characteristic of the "old com-
edies" and probably most famously manifest by the sausage-seller in
Aristophanes' *Knights*, a socially disruptive element. There may be
elements of prejudice here. While *agroikia* seems to be the vice of the

uneducated rustic, buffoonery appears, through its connection with Old Comedy, to pertain to the urban mass.[12]

It is significant that Aristotle does include a sense of humor within his discussion of ethical virtues and gives it a reasonably robust discussion. In addition to courage, justice, civic munificence, and greatness of soul, humor stands as essential to the good and happy life. If Aristotle engages in redefinition of the virtue of magnificence by relativizing it to the object and means of the agent, and of greatness of soul by finding a definition that encompasses both its connection to honor and steadfastness in the face of fortune, then he seems to invent a new virtue of quick-wittedness. Once again, Socrates appears, albeit implicitly, as an exemplum of the type of virtue and life that Aristotle is describing, as he does in the accounts of greatness of soul and truthfulness. For surely it is hard to think of a figure who wields the social and intellectual power of humor more effectively than the snub-nosed philosopher who is the gadfly of Athens with his wit and irony. In the same way, it is hard to think of a figure other than Socrates who, in the manner of Aristotle's great-souled man, both is proud of his accomplishments and yet takes honor itself to be a small thing relative to virtue. Although we do not tend to think of Socrates as generous and magnificent, in that he was not someone who conserved his wealth to give it away but rather emphasized his poverty, Socrates is a reasonably consistent, if often implicit, example throughout *NE* iv.

WORKS CITED

Bae, Eunshil. 2003. "An Ornament of the Virtues." *Ancient Philosophy* 23: 337–349.
Brown, Lesley. 1997. "What Is the 'Mean Relative to Us'?" *Phronesis* 42: 77–93.
Christ, Mathew R. 1990. "Liturgy Avoidance and Antidosis in Classical Athens." *Transactions of the American Philological Association* 120: 147–169.
Cooper, Neil. 1989. "Aristotle's Crowning Virtue." *Apeiron* 22: 191–205.
Cullyer, Helen. 2006. "*Agroikia* and Pleasure in Aristotle." 181–218 in I. I. Rosen and R. Sluiter eds. *City, Countryside and the Spatial Organization of Value in Classical Antiquity.* Leiden: Brill.
Curzer, Howard. 1990. "A Great Philosopher's Not So Great Account of a Great Virtue: Aristotle's Treatment of Greatness of Soul." *Canadian Journal of Philosophy* 20: 517–531.
1991. "Aristotle's Much Maligned *Megalopsuchos*." *Australasian Journal of Philosophy* 69: 131–151.
Gabrielsen, Vincent. 1994. *Financing the Athenian Fleet: Public Taxation and Social Relations.* Baltimore: Johns Hopkins University Press.
Gardiner, Stephen. 2001. "Aristotle's Basic and Non-basic Virtues." *Oxford Studies in Ancient Philosophy* 20: 261–295.

[12] For a more detailed discussion of *agroikia*, including an analysis of how this vice in the *Ethics* relates to the discussion of farmers in the *Politics*, see Cullyer 2006.

Gauthier, R. A. 1951. *Magnanimité: L'idéal de la grandeur dans la philosophie païenne et dans la théologie chrétienne.* Paris: J. Vrin.

Halliwell, Stephen. 1993. "Style and Sense in Aristotle's *Rhetoric* Bk. 3." *Revue Internationale de Philosophie* 184: 50–69.

Held, Dirk t. D. 1993. "*Megalopsychia* in *Nicomachean Ethics* iv." *Ancient Philosophy* 13: 95–110.

Hobbs, Angela. 2000. *Plato and the Hero: Courage, Manliness and the Impersonal Good.* Cambridge: Cambridge University Press.

Irwin, T. 1988. "Disunity in Aristotelian Virtues." *Oxford Studies in Ancient Philosophy* 7: 61–78.

Lear, G. R. 2004. *Happy Lives and the Highest Good.* Princeton: Princeton University Press.

Moss, Jessica. 2005. "Shame, Pleasure and the Divided Soul." *Oxford Studies in Ancient Philosophy* 29: 137–170.

Nieuwenberg, Paul. 2010. "Aristotle on Ambition." *History of Political Thought* 31: 535–555.

Pakaluk, Michael. 2002. "On an Alleged Contradiction in Aristotle's *Nicomachean Ethics*." *Oxford Studies in Ancient Philosophy* 22: 201–219.

   2004. "The Meaning of Aristotelian *Megalopsychia*." *Oxford Studies in Ancient Philosophy* 26: 241–275.

Rogers, K. 1993. "Aristotle's Conception of *To Kalon*." *Ancient Philosophy* 13: 355–371.

Stover, James, and Ronald Polansky. 2003. "Moral Virtue and *Megalopsychia*." *Ancient Philosophy* 23: 351–359.

Taylor, C. C. W. 2006. *Aristotle: Nicomachean Ethics Books II–IV.* Oxford: Oxford University Press.

8   Giving Justice Its Due

In *Nicomachean Ethics* iii–iv, Aristotle has discussed ten moral virtues and the passion of shame that can resemble a virtue of character. The remaining virtue of character to be considered, justice, requires an entire book of the *Ethics*. The length of investigation indicates the significance and difficulty of this virtue.[1] Justice pertains to political communities as well as the assessment of individuals and their actions. Unjust treatment or its appearance causes all political agitation and change (see *Politics* v 1–2), and we may detest those who are unjust or unfair. Plato's *Republic* is the major predecessor of Aristotle's work. Plato shows that what is lawful is just (see *Rep.* 338d–339b), and also that the proper or fair distribution of goods, such as tasks and property, is just (432d–433c). The *Republic* displays justice on different levels: the *polis* or city-state is just when individuals and classes of individuals, that is, artisans and farmers, soldiers and rulers, do their own task in the community; justice resides within the individual when each part of the soul – appetitive, spirited, and reasoning part – performs its own function; the entire universe exhibits justice since all its parts keep good order.[2] Here in his

---

I thank Patrick Miller, Jacob Greenstine, and Christopher Kurfess for their very helpful suggestions.

[1]   The book on justice is one of the three "common books" belonging to both the *Nicomachean* and *Eudemian Ethics*. It is book 5 of the *Nicomachean Ethics* and book 4 of the *Eudemian*. Whichever version was its origin, its appearance in both suggests Aristotle's satisfaction with his treatment of justice. Bostock 2000, 54 claims, however, "book V, taken as a whole, is an unsatisfying piece of composition, and here, more than anywhere else in the *Ethics*, one has to bear in mind that what we are dealing with is not a finished work, prepared by Aristotle himself for publication. It is rather a compilation of several different essays, written sometimes from rather different perspectives, and not always brought into harmony with one another" (cf. Gauthier and Jolif 1959, 328; and Hardie 1980, 184). I shall be challenging much of this.

[2]   The justice of the universe is seen in the argument about the gods (*Rep.* ii 382b–383c), the discussion of the forms (504a–519d), and the myth of Er (608c–621d). Already the first preserved Presocratic fragment, Anaximander DK 12B1, connects justice with the arrangement of the cosmos: "The things that are perish into the things out of which they come to be, according to necessity, for they pay penalty and retribution to each other for their injustice in accordance with the ordering of time."

work on ethics, with his predecessors' writings as background, Aristotle aims to give the crucial virtue justice fair treatment.

NE v concentrates upon justice and injustice as states of character or dispositions of persons, in line with the other moral virtues. In clarifying justice as a virtue, Aristotle reflects to some extent upon what is just and unjust since justice is a disposition to do just actions and injustice to do unjust actions. But the just and unjust are much wider notions than justice and injustice as dispositions. An action, law, or judicial verdict can be just without being justice of character or even presupposing it. Hence, in focusing upon justice and injustice of character, Aristotle deals only with part of what is just and unjust. This explains why the book does not extensively discuss crime and punishment and other such topics pertinent to what is just and unjust. Recognition of this limitation of treatment removes much of the interpreters' difficulties with Aristotle's account of justice and the just. We shall see that the book divides this way: the first half (*NE* v 1–5) provides the account of justice of character, and the second half (v 6–11) defends this account.

I. JUSTICE IN GENERAL

Setting off, Aristotle indicates three things he especially wishes to ascertain regarding justice and injustice and how the investigation will be conducted:

We must consider justice and injustice (περὶ δὲ δικαιοσύνης καὶ ἀδικίας) – what sort of actions they are concerned with, what kind of mean (ποία μεσότης) justice is, and what are the extremes between which the just is an intermediate (καὶ τὸ δίκαιον τίνων μέσον).[3] Let our inquiry be conducted in the same way as our preceding discussions. (1.1129a3–6)

He seeks the states of character, justice and injustice. He will locate these by finding the special field or fields for just and unjust actions, as other moral virtues have their special field, for example, courage pertains especially to battle. What sort of mean justice is will further disclose the virtue and its relation to the general scheme for the moral virtues. As a mean, justice should aim at the intermediate in action, and he should ascertain that between which the just in action is intermediate. The three

---

[3] I have modified the translation in Crisp 2000 since he, unfortunately, translates both *mesotēs* (μεσότης) and *meson* (μέσον) as "mean." The former might be translated as "mean" and the latter as "intermediate." Only good states of character are means between extremes, while actions, passions, and character states can be intermediate and so appropriate. The character state in a mean (*mesotēs*) aims for the intermediate or appropriate (*meson*) in action and passion (see Brown's contribution in this volume). Distinguishing the mean in a character state and the intermediate in action and passion is vital for understanding how justice can be a mean.

sorts of things he must consider regarding justice accord with what
he sought for the other moral virtues.[4] We shall find that this introduction to the treatment of justice and injustice covers the whole of *NE* v.[5]

For Aristotle, scientific investigations – whether in theoretical or
practical sciences – typically first establish that there is in fact a subject
matter for investigation prior to determining what precisely the subject
matter is (see *Posterior Analytics* ii 1). That there is something just
and unjust seems so obvious that it requires no argumentation and
can be assumed, but this is less the case for justice as a state of character.
All communities and all individuals in communities suppose some
things just and others unjust, though there is disagreement whether
these are merely conventionally considered just and unjust, or there is
something truly just and unjust by nature. Aristotle seeks in the book's
first half to establish that there is justice, what the virtue is, and how it is
a virtue, before tackling in the second half questions about naturalness or
conventionality and other such difficulties to secure his account.

All agree, Aristotle affirms, that justice is a disposition (ἕξις, *hexis*)
according to which people are capable of doing and do just actions and
wish for the just things, while injustice is a disposition leading to unjust
actions and the wish for unjust things (1129a6–11).[6] This outline account
of justice and injustice that all might readily accept involves circularity:
justice and injustice are defined in terms of the more obvious just
and unjust. Aristotle softens this circularity by noting that a moral virtue
as a disposition (*hexis*) is incapable of contraries, unlike knowledge
or a capacity (*dunamis*). Justice leads the just person to choose just
actions, while knowledge empowers its possessor to choose opposites,
as the skilled doctor may choose to produce health or its opposite. Hence
justice has a tight connection with the just, because it already involves

---

[4] When Aristotle declares that his inquiry into justice follows the lines of the previous
investigations of the virtues, he may mean those which he set out in 1115a4–5: what the
virtue is, what actions or passions the virtue pertains to, and how it pertains to them.
Unlike the other moral virtues, as we shall see, justice has more than one special field.

[5] Bostock 2000, 54, urges, "the overall structure of V.1–5 is reasonably clear and
coherent. ... But the remaining chapters are disjointed, and follow no clear overall
plan." Yet, since the rest of book 5 supports the result of chapters 1–5, the introduction
also applies to the remaining chapters 6–11.

[6] Aquinas 1993, §885, suggests that the treatment of justice concerns action whereas that
of the previous ten moral virtues concerns passion. If Aquinas means that there is no
definite passion involved in justice as with the other virtues, and many subsequent
interpreters have agreed with this point, perhaps we may counter that the wish to be
just is such a passion. Moreover, it is equally doubtful that every moral virtue, e.g.,
friendliness or truthfulness, relates to definite passions, and of course the other moral
virtues all have some relation to action rather than merely to passion. Aristotle's
emphasis on justice as *disposition* confirms that *NE* v is about justice as virtue of
character rather than the just more widely.

a commitment of desire for the just. And since a disposition is frequently known by what it pertains to or what underlies it, justice may be known through the just (1129a11–23).[7]

Yet if the just and the unjust, through which we learn the corresponding dispositions, are of more than one sort, we expect that the dispositions too will have more than one sense (1129a23–31). And justice indeed has more than one sense, Aristotle suggests, but because closely related these are hard to ascertain and keep separate. Probably the *unjust* person is at first more evident to us than the just, so he sets out the unjust persons to elucidate different ways to be just. Both the lawless person (ὁ παράνομος) and the person who is greedy (ὁ πλεονέκτης) and unfair (ἄνισος) are unjust. The unjust being the lawless and the unfair, the just person and the just generally, then, can be the lawful and the fair (1129a31–b1).

A person may be grasping and unfair about good things, but not all good things (1129b1–11). We cannot, for example, be grasping about virtue and wisdom as goods of the soul, though we can be grasping for the reputation of having these. Goods of the soul cannot be taken from others, and their acquisition requires effort on the part of the person gaining them. What can be grasped unfairly are what Aristotle calls goods of fortune and misfortune (εὐτυχία καὶ ἀτυχία), subsequently specified as honor, money, and security (see 1130b1–5).[8]

Whereas the just as the fair thus relates merely to certain goods, the just as the lawful, Aristotle announces, concerns all things (see 1129b14–15 and 1138a5–7). Law in traditional societies, written or unwritten, is understood to pronounce on nearly everything, and hence readiness to obey the law encompasses all virtue.[9] That law pertains to all things – all that concern relations to others – should be evident since law aims at

---

[7] Aristotle also indicates that a disposition can often be recognized by way of the contrary disposition and that to which it pertains (1129a17–23). He illustrates only that from the good disposition one may recognize the bad, however, rather than vice versa. Since, as 1106b28–35 has suggested, there is one way to be right and unlimitedly many ways to be wrong, we expect the good to help reveal the bad with much less assistance coming from the reverse direction.

[8] The inclusion of security or safety may seem an unusual "external good," but such goods save or help secure our lives. Security is probably intended as a catchall for goods besides money and honor, e.g., land. Humans generally pray for these goods of fortune, Aristotle observes (1129b4–6), though they should rather pray that such goods will be simply good for them, which they will be if the person is in good condition (cf. Plato's *Phaedrus* 279b–c and *Alcibiades II*).

[9] Modern, liberal societies, separating church and state and distinguishing law and morality, restrict written laws to property widely construed, which includes even intellectual property and in Locke's phrase, "life, liberty, and estate" (see *Second Treatise of Government* §§87 and 123), and hence still may go somewhat beyond mere goods of fortune and misfortune. Yet in line with this more limited view of law, we distinguish the moral and the legal unlike traditional communities. In fact, our modern uses of the terms

the advantage of the community and its happiness (eudaimonia), and happiness as the ultimate good embraces all other goods.[10]

The only traditional restriction on law, then, is that it does not concern passions, attitudes, and opinions that do not become manifest in impact upon others, though even these may pertain to moral virtue in its full extension. Aristotle illustrates that the law demands all the virtues: courage by forbidding leaving the military formation and throwing down weapons, temperance by rejecting adultery and insolence, even temper by renouncing striking and speaking evil of others, and the other virtues similarly (1129b19–25). All these examples are careful to show that each of the virtues as required by law involves actions related to others and not merely to oneself.

Justice that is adherence to law is then complete virtue (τελεία) – even if laws can be better or worse – yet not simply or absolutely (ἁπλῶς) complete virtue since justice is in relation to another person or group (πρὸς ἕτερον, 1129b25–30). Though law pertains to all things, it can regulate only my actions and passions as relating to others, not those relating exclusively to myself. Obeying laws relating to others impacts upon our self-relation, but law has sanctions only for the impact upon others. Hence, complete as the virtue that law ordains is in requiring the actions of all the moral virtues, nonetheless this virtue is not absolutely complete since law cannot regulate our passions and actions relating solely to ourselves and to some extent our family.[11] And many manage to exercise

"moral" and "morality" in opposition to what is "immoral" and "immorality" really have no closely related ancient notions (cf. Nussbaum 1986, 5n). Aristotle extends virtue of character to all that is appropriate in action and emotional response rather than limiting it to some region of special "moral worth" or "value." As we shall see, he distinguishes within virtue's contrary, vice, a narrower sort of wickedness (μοχθηρία), which is the vice that causes harm to others. Wickedness is injustice.

[10] The ultimate end for the individual, happiness, is also the end for the community, and this is the subject matter of the ultimate practical science, politics (see 1094a24–b11). Eudaemonism, ethics and politics directed toward the ultimate good, dominates the Socratic tradition carrying through much of traditional philosophy (see Vlastos 1991, ch. 8). For Aristotle, a community's laws tend to conform to its constitution: a democracy has democratic laws, an oligarchy oligarchic laws, etc. Law then should mandate all virtues in conformity with the sort of constitution, so some constitutions and laws are better than others, and the best constitution would most strictly seek human virtue, happiness, and the common good (1129b14–19).

[11] Having mentioned that law is slanted toward the kind of constitution (1129b14–19), Aristotle allows that legal justice is complete virtue toward another in relation to the sort of constitution. Hardie 1980, 185–186, says that what Aristotle means by having justice in relation to another is unclear, for: "Most virtues and vices [not merely justice] are manifested in actions which affect, and often are in their nature intended to affect, others." He suggests that an action unjust in this way is one that "can lead to prosecution in the courts." But stingy actions, being unfriendly, being ungrateful, and other such actions unjust in the widest sense of law need not land one in court. Still Aristotle

virtue in their own affairs but not with respect to others. He means that many act well enough within their families and their immediate concerns, but they function poorly in positions of political authority where they have to deal with the interests of fellow citizens. Thus Bias, one of the traditional seven wise men, said that rule will reveal the man (ἄνδρα, 1130a1–2). The appearance here of "man" as male may have Aristotle envisioning law as aiming for the complete virtue of the *citizen*, who is able to rule and be ruled, though this citizen virtue may fall short of the complete and absolute virtue of the human being (cf. 1130b26–29 and *Politics* iii 3).[12] Citizen-rulers as dealing with others, and assumed to be under law, cannot help but display how they stand with respect to general justice.

Justice as complete virtue concerning others, especially those outside one's own family sphere, looks to what is advantageous for others. Now it is characteristic of action according to virtue to be difficult (χαλεπόν, see 1105a7–10), for as the Greek saying has it: "Fine things are hard" (see, e.g., Plato's *Hippias Major* 304e8). Just action looking out for the interests of others should be difficult (1130a7–8). In Plato's *Republic* i 343b–c, Thrasymachus asserts that justice is another's good, and especially the advantage of the ruling group. Aristotle recalls Plato's discussion (see esp. 1130a3–5). But whereas Plato views justice in relation to the other as secondary to justice as doing what is one's own task and especially within the soul (see *Rep.* iv 441d–443b), Aristotle will keep justice primarily in relation to others, which accords better with our basic understanding of justice.[13]

Since justice connected with law embraces all the moral virtues, we might deny that it is a distinct virtue (see 1129b25–1130a1 and

says in 1138a19–20 that "the just and the unjust must always involve more than one person," and this will be crucial to his overall treatment and its divergence from Plato. Though fear, appetite, honor, money, anger, and so on may enter into our relations with others, they do not have to. Complete virtue applies to all our actions and passions, even when they are not at all manifest and impacting upon others so as to come under the law and justice. And even intense love of gain, which soon enters into particular injustice, only becomes a legal matter or unjust action through affecting others. Moreover, Aristotle goes on to indicate that "with relation to another" means fellow citizens rather than immediate family members, who can be considered particularly close parts of oneself (see 1097b6–11).

[12]   Kristen Inglis in this volume observes that in 1130b22–27 Aristotle distinguishes general justice, which the law prescribes for the citizen and is complete in setting out appropriate actions in relation to others, from the virtue of character of the good human, which demands more than the disposition to obey the law. It demands the full possession of *phronēsis*.

[13]   Law governs only relations to others (and hence might be another's good); thus justice as being lawful is in relation to another. Merely adhering to law has some degree of difficulty but less than the actions fully deriving from the particular virtues.

1130b20–24). There could then in effect be but the ten moral virtues already elaborated, with justice as the complete collection. But if there is also the narrower sort of justice having to do with the fair, then justice as the lawful and complete virtue must cover all the moral virtues including this narrower sort of justice. In calling the universal justice complete virtue in relation to others (1129b25–27), Aristotle takes the total set of moral virtues to be the virtues already treated along with the narrow sort of justice he will go on to consider. If universal justice pertaining to the lawful is complete virtue comprehending all the other virtues, the moral virtues should form a definite, limited set, and NE v, then, should confirm the completeness of Aristotle's account of the various virtues of character.

II. PARTICULAR JUSTICE

Aristotle insists that along with universal justice covering all the moral virtues there is more particular justice and injustice (2.1130a14–16). Those acting according to any of the vices of character may do what is unjust in the sense of unlawful, yet they need not be grasping. A distinctive blameworthy vice of injustice characterizes the grasping and unfair person. Actions due to seeking unjust gain (κέρδος) can resemble those from other vices, as adultery resulting from desire for gain rather than appetite resembles adultery due to intemperance, but only when motivated by gain are they unjust in the narrow sense. So the virtue concerned with gain differs from the other moral virtues, yet ranks with them as parts of general justice constituting all that is lawful (1130a16–33). Like the broader sense of justice, the narrower sort is with respect to other persons (1130a33–b2). Belonging in the same genus, *virtue in relation to others*, both the universal and the particular are kinds of justice. The narrower kind specifically concerns honor, money, and safety, from which comes the pleasure of gain (1130a32–b5).[14]

---

[14] Williams 1980 supposes Aristotle attributes all unjust acts to *pleonexia*, graspingness. He faults Aristotle for seeking such a single motivation for injustice when in fact, "Important among the motives to injustice (though they seem rarely to be mentioned) are such as laziness or frivolity. Someone can make an unfair decision because it is too much trouble, or too boring, to think about what would be fair" (197). Williams proposes against Aristotle that possible motives for injustice include anything that makes one indifferent to justice (198–199; cf. Hardie 1980, 188). But Williams here locates only possible sources of unjust *acts* rather than injustice as a *state of character*. Those who are lazy, e.g., may do unjust actions, but Aristotle hardly supposes that all unjust actions derive from unjust character or that everyone not perfectly just is an unjust person. Aristotle should link unjust character with a settled pleasure in gain over others rather than laziness or frivolity. Analogously to Williams's cases, someone may

Having established that there is some particular sort of justice, Aristotle seeks what it might be by looking toward particular spheres of just action, which recalls how he looked for courage, temperance, and the other moral virtues. Commentators, however, typically divide what he sets out into two sorts of justice, distributive justice and rectificatory (or corrective) justice. They arrive at this understanding from this passage:

> One type of particular justice, and of what is just in that same sense, is that found in distributions of honour or money or the other things that have to be shared among members of the political community (since here one person can have a share equal or unequal to another's). Another type is that which plays a rectifica-tory role in transactions. This type divides into two, since some transactions are voluntary, others involuntary.[15] (1130b30–1131a3)

Though it may look as if he refers to two types of particular justice, and commentators have embraced this interpretation, there should in fact be merely one virtue, particular justice of character, which displays itself especially in distribution or rectification. My basis is that nothing previous to this prepares us for dividing justice as a particular virtue. In 1130b6–8 Aristotle says there are more sorts of justice than one, but he speaks of particular justice in the singular, as if to emphasize that there is only it besides general justice, and he asks merely what particular justice is and what sort it is rather than how many kinds there are of it. In chapters 3–4 that speak of distribution and rectification, Aristotle refers only to the *just* (as in 1131b27–28 "the just in distribution") and never to *justice*. In 1131b23–27 that alludes to our quoted passage, he refers only to the just: "This, then, is the first species of what is just. The other kind is rectificatory, which is found in both voluntary and invol-untary transactions."[16] At the end of both the quoted passages, Aristotle distinguishes two sorts of transactions, voluntary and involuntary, which can only mean that he primarily is dividing classes of actions in which justice appears. So even where it looks as if he distinguishes two forms of particular *justice*, which has led the commentators to speak of distributive justice and rectificatory justice, he is really only distinguishing two spheres of *just action* in which the single virtue

---

throw down his spear from laziness without being cowardly; cowardice is faulty rela-tion to fear and confidence.

[15]   τῆς δὲ κατὰ μέρος δικαιοσύνης καὶ τοῦ κατ' αὐτὴν δικαίου ἓν μέν ἐστιν εἶδος τὸ ἐν ταῖς διανομαῖς τιμῆς ἢ χρημάτων ἢ τῶν ἄλλων ὅσα μεριστὰ τοῖς κοινωνοῦσι τῆς πολιτείας (ἐν τούτοις γὰρ ἔστι καὶ ἄνισον ἔχειν καὶ ἴσον ἕτερον ἑτέρου), ἓν δὲ τὸ ἐν τοῖς συναλλάγμασι διορθωτικόν. τούτου δὲ μέρη δύο· τῶν γὰρ συναλλαγμάτων τὰ μὲν ἑκούσιά ἐστι τὰ δ' ἀκούσια.

[16]   τὸ μὲν οὖν ἓν εἶδος τοῦ δικαίου τοῦτ' ἐστίν. τὸ δὲ λοιπὸν ἓν τὸ διορθωτικόν, ὃ γίνεται ἐν τοῖς συναλλάγμασι καὶ τοῖς ἑκουσίοις καὶ τοῖς ἀκουσίοις. I have removed "justice" from the Crisp translation since it is not in the text.

justice comes into play: justice in character should enter into both distributive and rectificatory actions.

Since in unjust, unfair (ἄνισον) action there is the more and the less, there will be some action that is appropriate or intermediate (μέσον), fair (ἴσον), and just (3.1131a10–15). What is intermediate between more and less is the fair (τὸ ἴσον), which is also the Greek word for "equal." Where things are equalized, there must be at least two terms brought into equality, but the just in distribution involves a division of goods between persons, and hence requires at least four terms put into proportion, two relating to the goods divided and two to the persons. Person A is to person B as the goods A receives to the goods B receives. Each person can receive more or less than deserved of the goods divided; each can also receive an intermediate, fair, and just amount. For the distribution to be fair, it should accord with some merit, value, or worth of the parties in relation to the goods divided (1131a24–26).

Aristotle insists that "everyone agrees that the just in distribution must be in accordance with some kind of merit (τὸ γὰρ δίκαιον ἐν ταῖς νομαῖς ὁμολογοῦσι πάντες κατ᾽ ἀξίαν τινά δεῖν εἶναι), but not everyone means the same by merit" (1131a25–27).[17] Will disputes be about what constitutes merit or even about this as the principle of fair distribution? Apparent alternatives to Aristotle's principle may really primarily dispute what constitutes merit, for example, the Pythagorean formula that everyone should get what they give (see v 5), the Marxist formula "from each according to his ability to each according to his needs" (Marx, *Critique of the Gotha Program*), or John Rawls's proposal that inequalities be permitted only so long as they acceptably work for the advantage of all parties involved (Rawls 1958). It looks as if Aristotle's principle has general agreement.

What can be distributed includes tasks, political offices, medals, land, tools, wages, and medical care.[18] These all fall under the goods of fortune and misfortune, honor, money, and security, referred to previously (see 1130b2). What constitutes "merit" varies with what is being divided. Wages might be divided by time worked or contribution to the productive process. Musical instruments could be distributed by ability to play them or to pay for them. Medical care might be extended more to those who are sicker, unless they are so sick it will do little good, or to those better able

---

[17] He need not suppose that everyone immediately accepts this principle of the just (cf. 1131a13–14 where he refers to what is accepted even without argument), but through discussion they should recognize that they agree (cf. the claim in Plato's *Theaetetus* 177b that if Socrates' interlocutors defending injustice stick around in conversation they will end up dissatisfied with their own arguments).

[18] Plato's *Republic* is more concerned to distribute tasks. See 1137a12–17 about distribution of medical care (πῶς δεῖ νεῖμαι πρὸς ὑγίειαν καὶ τίνι καὶ πότε, τοσοῦτον ἔργον ὅσον ἰατρὸν εἶναι).

to pay. Thus what "merit" means in any situation is a matter of dispute, but if it can be fairly established there may be just distribution.

Most significant for Aristotle is division of political offices. Here democrats, mainly free nonrich citizens, suppose they have merit because of their nonslave status; oligarchs, the wealthy, suppose this merits office for them; those of noble birth look toward family origin; aristocrats have merit due to virtue (1131a25–29). Political sagacity seeks just adjudication of these claims. Aristotle, following Plato (*Statesman* 302d–e), recognizes six basic types of political constitutions determined by one, few, or many ruling and divided into good regimes where the rulers rule in the interest of the ruled and deviant regimes where rulers rule in their own interest. In accord with the eudaemonist approach to ethics, each constitution has its own principal end or goal that impacts on all else within the community: democracy aims at freedom, oligarchy at wealth, and aristocracy at virtue.

There is fair and just distribution when a geometric proportion is established, A: B :: C: D, where A and B are persons and C and D their respective shares. The ratio of merit of the persons should be in relation to the goods to be divided. And since also A: C :: B: D, the ratio of merit of each to his or her share of goods will be proportional to the other person's.[19] Any division except what establishes such fair proportion is not just. The person doing what is unjust gets the greater share (or those to whom he is partial), and the person suffering what is unjust the lesser share (1131b17–24). Of course, in distribution of evils or misfortunes, things reverse since it is preferable to receive a lesser share of the evils.

The just in distribution is one form of the just, fundamental in political life. The other narrow form of the just is the just in voluntary or involuntary transactions (4.1131b25–27). How distribution (ἡ διανομή) differs from transaction (τὸ συνάλλαγμα) is that, where there is a *distribution*, something initially held in common or unassigned is distributed based on some principle applied to the parties receiving the distribution and what is distributed (1131b27–1132a2). For example, the law may determine what sorts of persons are eligible for political office or who has the right to a type of property. It is always as if there were an

---

[19] The Greek for proportion is *analogia* and for ratio *logos* (1131a29–b17). Proportion belongs not only to abstract mathematical number (μοναδικοῦ ἀριθμοῦ), but also to concrete numerical quantities generally so that persons or goods can be set into proportion. Since the geometric proportion is, as Aristotle says, "whole will bear the same ratio to whole," i.e., (A+C) : (B+D) :: A : B. Of course the addition of the person and the person's goods, which is the "whole," is hard to understand strictly quantitatively. In appealing to mathematics here in this practical context, Aristotle also offers much elucidation of the mathematics since theoretical principles or results are rather out of place. Note his offering the mathematicians' name for geometric proportion (1131b12–13).

external judge or agent making the distribution of what previously was unassigned to the parties. But *transactions*, whether voluntary or involuntary, have the parties initially having some share entering into an interaction changing their shares. Someone outside the transaction might witness or subsequently judge it, but is not at first part of the transaction itself, as some outside party may make a distribution. Clearly voluntary transactions are fundamental to political and economic life, while involuntary transactions, such as theft and murder, are those the community tries to eliminate or inhibit.

As observed previously regarding distribution, Aristotle does not really speak of "distributive *justice*" but the just in distribution, and neither does he speak as commentators often suppose of "rectificatory justice," but more prominently of "the just in transactions" (τὸ δ᾽ ἐν τοῖς συναλλάγμασι δίκαιον, 1131b32–33). He does, however, refer to τὸ διορθωτικόν, typically translated the corrective or the rectificatory (1131b25). This translation seems to have misled commentators. Aristotle's concern is with the just in transactions and not merely with correcting them when they go wrong, as usually supposed.[20] Of course there is the just correction that should be sought when a transaction is unjust, but distributions may also be unfair and in need of correction. The standard of fairness in distributions is geometric proportion regarding the merit of the parties in relation to the goods divided. In transactions the just sought is what avoids gain and loss, so that each party receives what is intermediate and fair. When in a transaction one party may get or gets more than its arithmetically proportionate fair share and the other party may get or gets less, the corrective is taking the gain or possible gain from one party and giving it to the party with the loss, thereby arriving at the intermediate. As the just in distribution assigns according to merit fairly, the just in transaction fairly evens out possible gain or loss, sometimes correcting after the transaction. *Diorthōtikon* should translate as that which sets things right rather than be restricted to correction *after* an unjust transaction, or if kept as "corrective," Aristotle should be understood to employ this available particular name for something wider. The term indicates that there is in fact the intermediate and fair in transactions. We might expect that

---

[20] I have found proper understanding in Burnet 1900, 213 (cf. Sachs 2002, 83n107): "Much confusion has been caused by the current translation 'Corrective Justice.' The *iustitia directiva* of the schoolmen is really more accurate; for διορθοῦν is a word of far wider meaning than ἐπανορθοῦν and signifies 'to adjust,' whether before or after the transaction." And Burnet adds, "we shall see that all the examples given refer to the preliminary adjustment of terms, and not to the rectification of wrong." In 1132a18 he does speak of τὸ ἐπανορθωτικὸν δίκαιον, which is strictly and narrowly "the corrective just" (and see 1137b12–13 on the equitable as a correction [ἐπανόρθωμα] of the legally just).

especially in voluntary transactions, the just person attempts to do the adjustment prior to the transaction, and the adjustment will frequently not give the just person a material advantage.[21]

Talk of gain (κέρδος) and loss (ζημία) may be used generally for transactions, Aristotle says, though it probably derives from voluntary transactions (1032a10–14 and b11–13). The just that concerns him in transactions is that which results in no gain or loss, the intermediate and fair, whether in the original transaction itself or in a subsequent correction. If a transaction will or has caused gain and loss, the needed adjustment or correction is to take the excess from the one and bestow it on the party with the deficiency. Calculation of gain and loss does not concern itself with the merit of the parties, as applies to distributions, but solely the gain and loss caused by the transaction, that is, how much more and less the parties have than would be fair.[22] Determination of what is fair in the transaction depends upon the situations of the parties prior to the transaction and the outcome of the transaction. If A seems ahead unfairly by an amount C, then taking C from A and adding it to B is fair.[23] When the parties to the transaction dispute how much the one has gained and the other lost, a judge is sought to make the determination (1132a18–24). Aristotle even derives the name just (δίκαιον) from what the judge does, that is, divides in two (δίχα), so that the just (δίκαιον) would seem to be etymologically δίχαιον, as the judge (δικαστής) is a divider (διχαστής).

We recall that the goods of fortune and misfortune, honor, money, and security, enter into the just (see 1129b1–11 and 1130b2–5). This applies for distributions and transactions. Transactions involving things readily measured monetarily make for easier determinations. Aristotle's primary

[21] Commentators supposing that the just in transactions concerns only correcting them, but bothered that there should be correction regarding *voluntary* transactions, suggest that such correction is required merely in the case when one party subsequently fails to meet its obligation, so there is breach of contract (see Finley 1977, 143). But a party to a voluntary transaction may appeal for correction when deficiency in the goods exchanged has been concealed (see interesting instances in Cicero, *De Officiis* iii 12–14), and the just person may make an adjustment for the sake of justice even prior to the voluntary transaction.

[22] Merit is not involved in adjusting involuntary transactions since the original condition is to be restored by removing the gain and returning it to the losing party, and in voluntary transactions the adjustment is to what the parties themselves may agree to or have agreed to.

[23] Aristotle emphasizes mathematically that C must be both removed from the one and added to the other to arrive at what is fair. Though Aristotle's mathematics in *NE* v 4 is correct, it has been criticized as "mathematically rather childish" (see Heath 1949, 274). We may account for this and the other mathematical sections in *NE* v by insisting that Aristotle should not seek a mathematically sophisticated presentation in the context of a practical science.

concern is that there be the intermediate and fair concerning transactions. Surely involuntary transactions such as theft and murder, and even some voluntary transactions, lead to punishments beyond reestablishing the fair in the transaction. But what goes beyond the fair and the just in the transaction need not occupy Aristotle insofar as he seeks the just in order to clarify justice of character.[24] Punishment going beyond merely removal of the gain may look to the motivation of the unfair party, which involves the merit of the persons.

Aristotle has so far located two ways or spheres in which the just can be particular and fair. The just in distribution is fair by being in geometric proportion according to merit intermediate between the more and the less, while the just in transaction is fair by being in arithmetic proportion intermediate between gain and loss. Regarding what he set out to consider about justice in 1129a3–5 – (a) what types of actions it concerns, (b) what sort of mean it is, and (c) between what things the just is – he has displayed (a) and (c) regarding each of the two areas of just action, but should say more about the third (b), what sort of mean justice will be leading to these two types of just action. Before entering upon this topic, he takes up a possible further conception of the just.

III. RECIPROCITY AND JUSTICE AS A MEAN

Aristotle has allowed but two sorts of the just in connection with justice as a particular virtue of character, the just in distribution and in transactions (see 1130b30–1131a1). But now he takes up the claim of some, such as the Pythagoreans, that the just simply is reciprocity with another (ἁπλῶς τὸ δίκαιον τὸ ἀντιπεπονθὸς ἄλλῳ, 5.1132b21–23). They suppose that it is unqualifiedly just if one gets in return what one gives, that is, one is treated as one treats others. In this square deal, each side treats the other the same as itself, represented by the Pythagoreans as a "square number" (n^2, where n is an integer; see *Meta.* 985b29). But Aristotle complains that such reciprocity quite fits the just neither in distribution nor in transaction, though its proponents clearly wish it to cover these (1132b23–25). The emphasis Aristotle puts upon "simply" or "unqualifiedly" (ἁπλῶς) in 1132b21–23 shows that he resists their claim that reciprocity absolutely covers all the just.

It does look, however, as if reciprocity approaches in some cases to the just in transactions, though not simply. The just of Zeus's son Rhadamanthus judging the dead in accord with "a person should suffer

Some who have overemphasized correction link it closely to Athenian legal practice and contend that Greek law did not distinguish criminal and civil procedures, so even a private suit can gain some vengeance for the victim (see Kussmaul 2008, 30–31, 41–42). Harrison 1957 argues against linking Aristotle's comments to Athenian law.

what he did" (1132b25–27) might seem the just in transaction and reciprocity. But when a ruler strikes someone or someone strikes a ruler, straightforward reciprocation is hardly absolutely just. Here the merit of the parties involved cannot be ignored as in the just of transaction, but the motivation of the participants and whether the interaction is voluntary or involuntary cannot be overlooked. Aristotle has shown in 1132b23–31 that reciprocity does not simply amount to the just in transactions, and as basic equality it can hardly be geometric proportionality and the just in distribution. Reciprocity thus fails neatly to correspond to or substitute for either of the two sorts of the just Aristotle has demarcated.[25]

Yet reciprocity might apply as just for certain transactions where motivation and merit only limitedly come into play. Bartering of goods and market transactions appear cases of reciprocity.[26] Of course, instead of simple equality, where someone gives exactly the same as he gets, gold for gold, usually there is proportionate reciprocity, for example, shoes for gold (1132b31–34). While such proportional reciprocity serves for the just in voluntary transactions in barter and market exchanges, it hardly introduces another kind of the just, changing our understanding of justice of character.[27] Bartering and market exchange as pervasive in communal life can achieve reciprocity and be fair without requiring the participants to have exceptional justice of character. Aristotle discusses the just and the fair or equal with regard to exchange, but because "in buying and selling, for example, and other transactions in which the law has left people free to decide their own terms" (1132b15–16), those entering the exchange accept its terms, generally the just does not much come into question (also see 1133a22–25).[28] Hence this section on reciprocity, showing that reciprocity does not much involve justice of character,

[25] Gauthier and Jolif 1959, 369, state that the relation of reciprocity to the just in distribution and correction is one of the major difficulties in interpreting *NE* v. It seems that reciprocity neither reduces to either of the other two nor is a third kind of the just. They suggest it is a type of natural right at the basis of human association and so prior to and the condition for the just in distribution and correction (371–372; cf. *Politics* 1261a30–b6). This will be seen to be questionable.

[26] Those entering into barter or market exchange seem to do so voluntarily, and the merit of the parties only matters under conditions such as that the exchange is of the services involving the skills of the parties.

[27] The treatment of reciprocity in *NE* v 5 (along with related sections of *Politics* i) interests historians of economics as one of the earliest accounts of the functioning of markets. Some have faulted Aristotle's analysis (Schumpeter 1954, 1, 21), others have lauded him for clarity about economic relationships (Polanyi 1968), but Finley 1977 seems correct that Aristotle is not engaged in a modern type of economic analysis if this means determining how prices are in fact set.

[28] The just might come into question, however, where the poor quality of the goods exchanged or other crucial circumstances of the exchange is concealed (see note 21).

tends to confirm the completeness of Aristotle's account of particular
justice as the state of character giving rise to just actions in the main
spheres, distribution and transaction.

Barter and market exchange, the latter involving money, seem based
on reciprocity. A house builder and shoemaker may exchange a house for
shoes, where each offers apparently equivalent value to the other. Of
course, it will usually take so many shoes to equal the value of a house
that direct barter is problematic and money is needed for exchange. And
similar sorts of products differ in quality, since one craftsman surpasses
another or puts more care into production of this item than another one,
making value differ (see 1133a12–14; Meikle 1995, 10–11, denies, however, that Aristotle here refers to differences in quality of products of the
same sort by κρεῖττον but only that one sort of product is worth more than
another sort). And services, such as medical treatment, can be exchanged
along with commodities. Money makes all such things readily commensurable. Of course, barter exchange is possible without money, so money
as measure does not make goods commensurable, but when extensive
exchange establishes markets and market pricing, money allows many
goods to be readily measured against each other (see Meikle 1995, 21–23).
More and less of the goods can be exchanged, and money somehow
becomes the intermediate (μέσον, 1133a19–22). Money thus facilitates
exchange, but what gives rise to exchange and keeps it going is the need
or use (ἡ χρεία) individuals have for the others' goods (1133a25–31 and
b6–20).[29] In the initial situation in which there is need, some amount of
the goods can be made proportionate for purposes of exchange.

Aristotle does not aim to determine how the price is set or products
made commensurable but merely to indicate that some proportion can
arise that leads to reciprocity and exchange. Money allows for commensurability of items, and the need of the parties leads to the exchange.
Someone might be desperately hungry, but the cost for food can be
relatively stable if there exists a sizable market in foodstuffs. If in a
large market the determination of price surely goes beyond the individual
participants in the exchange, still individual need leads to exchange.
Various factors not really specified by Aristotle (including at least the
need of the parties involved in the exchange), various levels of skill of
producers, time and effort expended in production, and the availability
and cost of productive inputs combine to set up a proportion for the
exchange. Aristotle introduces builder (A), shoemaker (B), house (C),
and shoe (D), with reciprocity and exchange occurring when somehow
A to B is proportionate as D to C (1133a7–33, esp. a22–24 and a32–33;

---

[29] Crisp translates ἡ χρεία, meaning use or need, as "demand," which is a term used in
modern economics and may contribute to misunderstanding.

cf. b4–5 and b23–26). Since each needs what the other has and exchanges for the goods of the other, the proportion and reciprocity is a diagonal or cross conjunction (ἡ κατὰ διάμετρον σύζευξις, 1133a5–7), that is, the builder is to the shoemaker as the product of the shoemaker is to the product of the builder.[30] When Aristotle sets up the "diagonal proportion" to reflect upon reciprocity in exchange, he does not intend this as a strict mathematical proportion as with the geometric proportion in cases of distribution. There he applied various mathematical manipulations to the ratios in proportion, which he does not do here (see 1131a30–b9). And though the ratio of merit of persons previously discussed can surely be a matter of dispute, he hardly conceded that it is somewhat arbitrary and "impossible that things differing to such a degree should become truly commensurable" as he does here concerning different goods evaluated monetarily (see 1133b18–20). Thus, Aristotle is not so much determining how price is set or what is a just price but merely establishing that some sort of reciprocity can arise permitting exchange.[31]

What establishes the proportion for the exchange is what the parties to the transaction value the goods at before the exchange takes place rather than afterward (1133b1–4). Aristotle assumes that the equality, proportion, and reciprocity that will satisfy the needs of the parties emerge prior to the exchange, while subsequent to the exchange, with needs satisfied, the goods may not seem to have the value they did previously. The need of the parties to the transaction, presumably in relation to the general prices in the market for the goods if there is a market, brings about exchange. And even when possessors of goods are not themselves immediately in need, money by its lastingness and usual stability in value serves as surety for future need and keeps exchange and community going (1133b10–18).

In clarifying how equality in barter and market exchange becomes possible, Aristotle shows that natural human need leads to the

[30] In 1133a22–24, in setting up the proportion of builder to shoemaker, Aristotle says, "so must the number of shoes be to a house [or to food]." Crisp leaves out "or to food." Probably Aristotle includes the food because a house is usually worth so many shoes that the exchange will not simply be a house for shoes, and we have a variety of needs.

[31] Meikle 1995, esp. 25–26 and 36–38, takes Aristotle to be trying to determine what allows for commensurability of goods, so when in 1133a19–20 he says that different goods cannot really be measured together, Aristotle is admitting defeat and giving up explaining it. But as Aristotle is not trying to explain how prices are set, neither is he trying to explain what gives rise to commensurability. It is enough for his purpose to mention some factors that contribute to treating goods as commensurable so that it can be clear that reciprocity can enter into exchange. My point that Aristotle does not press the mathematics here even as much as previously tells against Meikle's view that he tries to explain commensurability but fails. It is not the case, as suggested by Meikle, that Aristotle in NE v 5 "organizes his entire inquiry around" the question "how different products can be strictly commensurable."

introduction of money that facilitates trade. Money seems something by convention (νόμῳ) rather than by nature, as its very name νόμισμα (nomisma) indicates, and is displayed by the way humans can make it useless and reduce its value to nothing (1133a25–31). Yet money tends to hold its value and to measure and exchange for all goods (1133b10–18). Hence, despite varying denominations and valuations of money in different places, human community so much depends upon money for trade that it is not merely conventional. Serving the natural human need for exchange for self-sufficiency, money combines the natural and conventional. Treatment of money thus foreshadows the coming discussion in v 7 of whether the politically just can be by nature or merely by convention.

The reciprocity that enters into barter and exchange entailing no special area for justice of character, Aristotle can assert that so far in chapters 1–5 he has said what the unjust and the just are insofar as he needs them for explicating justice in character (1133b29–32). In light of what he has said about the just, just action (δικαιοπραγία) will be intermediate between doing the unjust and being unjustly treated (μέσον ἐστὶ τοῦ ἀδικεῖν καὶ ἀδικεῖσθαι), that is, between receiving or bestowing too much or receiving or bestowing too little (1133b29–32). Just action aims at the just, which is the intermediate in distribution or transaction. Justice in character is a mean of a sort (μεσότης τις), though in a way differing from the other moral virtues (1133b32–1134a1). Justice is a mean state (mesotēs) insofar as, like the other virtues, it aims at the intermediate (meson) in actions and passions, as Aristotle announced that "just action" (δικαιοπραγία) is intermediate; but whereas the other moral virtues are mean states between vices in the extremes, as courage is between rashness and cowardice, justice does not have two or more vices opposing it as do the other virtues, for only injustice opposes it.[32]

The treatments of the just and unjust have prepared for this account of justice of character:

And justice is the state in accordance with which the just person is said to be the kind of person who is disposed to do just actions in accordance with rational choice (πρακτικὸς κατὰ προαίρεσιν τοῦ δικαίου), and to distribute goods

---

[32] For the point that the other virtues, like justice, are mean states primarily aiming at the intermediate in action, but they are also mean states that are intermediate states between opposing vices, see Lesley Brown's contribution. I disagree with Curzer 1995, 218–222, who thinks Aristotle should have justice between two vices, and with Young 2006, 194, who thinks the proposal that justice is a mean aiming at the intermediate in action leaves in doubt why an art such as medicine is not also a mean state since it too aims at the intermediate. Yet in 1129a11–17 Aristotle contrasts medicine, which is a capacity for contraries, with a hexis that is a virtue that is not a capacity for contraries. The arts do not imply desire committed to attaining the intermediate as does moral virtue.

(διανεμητικός) – either between himself and another or between two others – so as to assign not more of what is worth choosing to himself and less to his neighbor (and conversely with what is harmful), but what is proportionately equal; and similarly in distributing between two other people. Injustice, on the contrary, is concerned with what is unjust, that is, a disproportionate excess or deficiency of what is beneficial or harmful. (1134a1–8)

Justice is the state or disposition directing the just person to choose the just. This maintains that justice is with respect to another and applies where the just person himself either receives some of what is distributed or serves as the judge of what other parties deserve. Though Aristotle speaks of capacity to *distribute*, this covers both distribution and transaction, since allocation for either should assign the appropriate and the fair to the involved parties, proportion determining the just. Injustice has the unjust person tending to choose quite inappropriately: if a party to the distribution, he takes for himself the excess of the useful or deficiency of the harmful and the contrary for the other, while, if not a party to the distribution, he still unfairly assigns excess and deficiency.

IV. DEFENSE OF THE ACCOUNT OF JUSTICE

Though Aristotle now has given accounts of justice and injustice and the just and unjust, and thus set out what he announced as his aim at the start of *NE* v, because there still may be difficulties about justice, and what sort of mean it is, he proceeds in the second half of the book to such further concerns. Thus v 1–5 defines justice of character, and v 6–11 defends the account. A person can do unjust actions without being unjust, so might no one ever *be* unjust? If so, justice and injustice as states of character have dubious status. And might the just be a legal and political matter applying to citizens, so there is no justice of noncitizens or between humans merely as humans? And is the politically just merely conventional rather than natural, and so justice has shaky standing? And the equitable seems superior to the just, thus diminishing the significance of the just. And if one can be unjust and just to oneself, then justice need not be in relation to others.[33] These issues about justice, seemingly disconnected, are linked because a problematic answer to any of them threatens the entire account of justice.[34]

[33] If one could be voluntarily unjust to oneself by giving oneself too little, justice would then after all be a mean between two extreme vices: the injustice of giving too much to oneself and the injustice of giving too little to oneself (see Hardie 1980, 183–184, and Curzer 1995, 218–222).

[34] I am motivating the topics discussed in the second half of *NE* v and the order of treatment. Many commentators have complained about the order and even rearranged sections of these chapters (Crisp's translation unfortunately does some rearranging of text).

Can justice or injustice of character be found in all interactions (6.1134a17–23)? Those not unjust may do unjust actions involuntarily, so commission of which actions involves injustice of character? Even theft, adultery, and piracy, clearly illegal and unjust actions, may not imply an unjust person. For instance, an act of adultery may arise from immediate passion and incontinence rather than choice, so not from the vice of injustice. Actions from deliberation and choice disclose and link with character (more on this in *NE* v 8).

In what looks possibly out of place, Aristotle now refers to reciprocity and the politically just (1134a23–26). How this may in fact connect with what preceded is that reciprocity in exchange can go well beyond relations of citizens, since noncitizens can be involved in trade. But if Aristotle's concern is with the simply just or politically just (τὸ ἁπλῶς δίκαιον καὶ τὸ πολιτικὸν δίκαιον), which might pertain merely to citizens, then perhaps only these can have justice of character and only in relation to fellow citizens. The actions of and relations to noncitizens will have little to do with justice of character, and justice tightly linked to citizenship may seem conventional rather than natural.

The politically just applies to persons associating for the sake of self-sufficient life, who are free and equal persons either according to proportion or according to number (1134a26–30). Democracy will have justice according to number since each free citizen is counted the same, whereas other kinds of constitutions will have various levels of citizens. And in antiquity female citizens have citizenship in some sort of proportion to male citizens. Those not fully citizens in political association – nonmales, noncitizen residents, slaves, or children – will not have the politically just in their relationships with citizens, though Aristotle assures us they have something according to similarity or approximation (καθ' ὁμοιότητα, 1134a28–30). Will it matter for being an unjust person whether the dubious action takes place with regard to a citizen or noncitizen? He has lined up interrelated queries: Is unjust action always deriving from an unjust person? And does the politically just apply to noncitizens? And these lead to further related questions: Is the politically just natural, and can one be unjust to oneself?

Aristotle suggests that the politically just extends to those who live under law (1134a30–b18). These can have their actions judged as just or unjust, and those doing unjust actions may or may not be unjust persons as previously indicated.[35] Unjust acts or unjust persons give more to themselves of the simply good things and less of the simply bad things. Where reason in the form of the just and law do not hold sway, but a

---

[35] Reference in 1134a32–34 to doing unjust actions without being unjust persons, which was the issue of 1134a17–23, shows the likely continuity of 1134a23–b18 with 1134a17–23.

human favoring himself rules, tyranny can result. Just rulers not favoring themselves serve the ruled, and so justice may seem another's good (cf. 1130a3–5). Rulers receive honor and privilege as compensation for not favoring themselves; those discontent with these become tyrants. The despotically just and paternally just, the relation of master with slaves and father with minor children, may be similar to tyranny but not the same. The tyrant acts unjustly toward those who should be fellow citizens, while the father-master oversees his own possessions and children (cf. 1138b5–8). If justice is in relation to another and those in the household are parts of the father and master, and no one chooses to harm himself, then the father is not unjust toward them. The just in familial relations is not the politically just and again offers the possibility of dubious actions without being an unjust person. Women lived more under law than possessions and children, so that the household just (τὸ οἰκονομικὸν δίκαιον) extending to them more resembles the politically just.³⁶

Reflection on the political just, its possible restriction to citizens and questionable relation with children and women, leads to inquiry about how it is natural or conventional (7.1134b18–30; cf. Plato Laws 889e–890a). If some of the politically just is natural, this supports the extension to all human relationships inasmuch as the just in other relationships approximates that of citizens and gives justice of character strong standing. What is naturally just should hold everywhere and not merely seem the case, while the legally or conventionally just is initially indifferent until specified by law. For example, what should be sacrificed and to which hero differs between communities, thus appearing conventional in its particularity. If what is politically just differs widely between communities, it may all be conventional, as some suppose, unlike the way fire by nature burns everywhere. Despite the variation in different communities and changeability, Aristotle affirms that there is the naturally politically just. If true, and what appears merely conventional and arbitrary instantiates the universally naturally politically just, then nothing politically just is simply purely conventional. He claims that among the gods there may be no variations, though all the human politically just things are changeable.³⁷

³⁶ Aristotle's discussion sounds quite dated to those in liberal countries. We still distinguish, however, between adults and children and citizens, foreign nationals, and noncitizens, and treat the just differently with respect to these. "Household" (οἰκία) was the center of economic life for individuals in antiquity (see Polanyi 1968 and Arendt 1958, ch. 2).

³⁷ In Meta. xii 7 and 9, God is eternally engaged in the same activity, thinking of thinking, but this cannot be appealed to directly in this practical context. Aristotle is considering the politically just, and strictly the gods have no moral virtue and justice does not pertain to them (see NE x 8.1178b8–18 and 1137a26–30).

Why he seems to say this is to allow that while all human instantiations of universal principles are changeable, the principles need not be. Some of the previous examples already suggest this. Religious sacrifice seems natural and universal for human communities, yet these engage in it differently. Communities offer diverse and changing instantiations of universal principles of the just.[38]

A less clearly political example, one close to the case of fire but also introducing choice, offers further support (1134b30–35). By nature the right hand is stronger, but all may become ambidextrous (contrast Plato *Laws* 794e). Among natural things generally some are necessary, such as fire burning everywhere, while others are only for the most part so, such as humans being for the most part right-handed. Yet work with the left arm can make it as strong as the right. This example shows changeability introduced by human choice even among natural beings and not merely political matters. Another example illustrates variation of the natural and conventional: measures for dry and liquid goods such as grain and wine differ between communities, but everywhere the wholesale measures are greater than retail (1134b35–1135a3). This example resembles the initial example of religious practices, and the previous discussion of money. Some things are universal and the same everywhere for humans, such as religious sacrifice, money to facilitate exchange, and larger wholesale measures, but the way these are instantiated in different communities differs without detracting from universality. This example of measures well displays universal stability with variation of instantiations but asserts nothing about naturalness. The final example is the most political: political constitutions (πολιτεῖαι) differ, yet one alone is everywhere by nature best (1135a3–8). That the same constitution is everywhere naturally best might refer to: (1) the very best possible, genuine aristocracy depending upon exceptional conditions (see *Politics* vii–viii), or (2) the constitution that is most practicable everywhere, that is, *politeia* or republic (see *Pol.* iv, esp. chs. 8–9), or (3) the fact that the distribution of offices according to merit is everywhere naturally just, or (4) Aristotle's position that

[38] Previously Aristotle affirmed that all agree that the just in distribution is according to merit, but different constitutions accept different sorts of merit for ruling (see 1131a25–27). So the same is somehow just everywhere and no mere appearance (cf. *Rhetoric* i 13.1373b4–20 where Aristotle says all agree there is law by nature, but he gives examples, such as the dispute of Antigone and Creon in Sophocles' *Antigone*, showing that they hardly agree about its instantiation). In thus contending that despite the changeability of all that humans set up as just, it has some basis in the politically just by nature, Aristotle approaches the Platonic view of the relationship of particular instances partaking of an intelligible form while allowing that what humans set up as politically just is a matter of interpretation and choice (cf. Destrée 2000).

everywhere the *polis* is natural for humans.[39] Actual constitutions and arrangements vary, but there is one universal standard of the just. The examples have been carefully selected.

The examples may contribute to inductive argument for the naturalness of the politically just or merely explicate the possibility of the naturally just despite so much political or other sorts of variation. The first two examples, about handedness and measures, might seem somewhat unlike the case of the politically just, since the first more definitely speaks of the natural and the second more dubiously, and the third example, about constitutions, may seem to beg the question. Of course, no science can strictly demonstrate its *first principles*, and that there is the politically just by nature has the status of a first principle. How Aristotle has made plausible the condition that where the politically just seems conventional, this is because it variably instantiates something universal and natural, amounts to some sort of an argument and leads to the conclusion that nothing politically just is exclusively conventional and completely detached from the politically just by nature. He can well say, "Each type of what is just and legal stands as a universal in relation to particulars; for the actions done in virtue of them are many, but each of them is a single entity, since it is a universal" (1135a5–8). As any well-formed law is universal and meant to apply to particular human actions, such laws may themselves be particular instantiations of even more universal natural standards of the politically just.[40]

The account of the politically just by nature supports all that Aristotle has developed about the just, and especially that the just extends beyond the relationships of citizens because the natural holds everywhere. He can then resume the question of when the person doing any unjust action, an *adikēma*, is an unjust person. A person acting voluntarily does something unjust or just (*dikaiopragei*), whereas a person acting involuntarily, compelled or through ignorance, does it merely accidentally (8.1135a15–b11). But even voluntary unjust action need not indicate an unjust person, that is, someone who does this sort of thing from a fixed character. A momentary passion leading to action makes it voluntary, but only voluntary action also chosen, deriving from prior deliberation and so premeditated, shows character since the

---

[39]   In *Politics* i Aristotle argues that humans are naturally political beings, though they can live only in more or less conventional Athens, Sparta, Corinth, and so on rather than in the simply natural *polis*.

[40]   In 1136b32–1137a Aristotle speaks of a judge making a decision in ignorance not thus acting unjustly legally or conventionally, but the decision is unjust in terms of what is simply or naturally just, "legal justice and primary justice being different" (ἕτερον γὰρ τὸ νομικὸν δίκαιον καὶ τὸ πρῶτον).

action is the actuality of a firm disposition or developed potentiality for such action (cf. 1136a1–5).[41]

Continuing consideration of questionable action, Aristotle distinguishes in associations of people three kinds of harm or injury (βλαβῶν) that need not entail being an unjust person (1135b11–27): all actions done in ignorance of to whom it is done, what is done, with what, or for the sake of what are errors (ἁμαρτήματα). Errors further divide into misadventure (ἀτύχημα) when the action is initiated outside the actor and the outcome is unexpected; and errors (ἁμαρτήματα) more narrowly when the action initiated by the actor has a not unexpected outcome, yet the action is not from vice.[42] The third sort of harm is an unjust action (ἀδίκημα) done knowingly, except not with prior deliberation but through some excusable passion.[43] Harming in these ways does not make the doer an unjust and wicked person (ἄδικος καὶ μοχθηρός) as are those who would do such actions from deliberation and choice. Wickedness, as indicated in 1121a25–30, is the sort of vice leading to harm of others. Being overgenerous is the vice of wastefulness but without being wickedness, since actions arising from it need not harm others. Justice and injustice relate to others with injustice such as to harm them: so injustice as a state of character makes doers wicked.

Aristotle has dealt with the questions he raised concerning justice, but he must consider a key point of his account, that justice is in relation to another. He begins by asking whether one can be voluntarily treated unjustly, which prepares for the pressing question of whether one can be unjust to oneself (9.1136a10–b14). Doing that which is unjust (ἀδικεῖν) is voluntary, but then is being treated unjustly (ἀδικεῖσθαι) voluntary, or must it be involuntary? Now even being treated justly need not all be voluntary, since few welcome being justly punished. And someone may suffer something unjust accidentally without being treated unjustly,

[41] Frede 2011, 22–24, argues that on Aristotle's account of desire and choice, when we act akratically and by appetite, this is against choice rather than according to choice since human desires are of various sorts and can work against each other. Aristotle generally divides desire into appetite (epithumia), spiritedness (thumos), and wish (boulēsis). Choice (proairesis) is a reasoned or deliberated desire.

[42] The terminology used for error or mistake (hamartēma) recalls that in the Poetics that explains tragic suffering by error (hamartia) of the protagonist, which causes the dramatic action generating fear and pity. Unexpected outcomes in misadventures come as complete surprises, as when the knife used is a real rather than the supposed pretend knife, while in erroneous action in the narrow sense the outcome is not unexpected. Oedipus expects his attack to result in death for the man at the crossroads; his error results from his ignorance that the man is his father.

[43] Talk of passions natural to humans (1135b21 and 1136a8) fits with the previous examples of natural superiority of the right arm and the naturally politically just. Whether anger that gives rise to harm is appropriate or excusable pertains to whether the act provoking it was just or not (1135b19–1136a9).

if harm was not done voluntarily. Being treated unjustly or justly requires that someone else voluntarily do this. But this is not restrictive enough, for an incontinent person may knowingly and so voluntarily mistreat himself or voluntarily allow himself to be harmed by another without suffering unjustly. To block the possibility of suffering unjust treatment from oneself or another voluntarily, Aristotle insists that even deliberately harming someone is not treating him unjustly if he wishes it. So one may be harmed voluntarily and thereby suffer something unjust (τἄδικα πάσχει), but nonetheless no one is voluntarily treated unjustly (ἀδικεῖται δ' οὐδεὶς ἑκών), for everyone wishes for what he supposes excellent (σπουδαῖον), which could hardly be being treated unjustly. The incontinent person harmed by himself or another is not harmed against his wish, and so not voluntarily treated unjustly. Aristotle concludes that being treated unjustly is *not voluntary* (οὐχ ἑκούσιον) rather than *involuntary* because it is inappropriate to speak of something's being involuntary when it can never be voluntary, as sound is more properly not visible than invisible.

Since being treated unjustly is not voluntary, entailing that one cannot treat oneself unjustly, the person acting unjustly is the one distributing unfairly rather than the recipient of the unfair distribution (1136b15–1137a4; see 1138a26–28). Voluntarily shortchanging oneself in distributing some good, as those who are moderate (οἱ μέτριοι) and equitable (ἐπιεικής) may do, cannot then be voluntary unjust treatment. And it seems they shortchange themselves and harm themselves according to their own wishes with the expectation of receiving some compensating good, such as honor or the noble. Similarly, the judge knowingly deciding unfairly has some expectation of reward. Aristotle by thus maintaining that one cannot be voluntarily treated unjustly by either another or oneself ensures that justice has to involve relation with another in accord with his whole account of justice. This keeps his account of justice straightforward rather than metaphorical like Plato's.

That we cannot voluntarily be unjustly treated or treat ourselves unjustly raises a question about what we can do (1137a4–30). People suppose that since they can act unjustly (τὸ ἀδικεῖν), being just is easy (τὸ δίκαιον εἶναι ῥάδιον). We readily enough engage in acts such as sex with the neighbor's spouse, punching someone, or putting money in someone's hand, but not as the unjust person does, from a firm state of character. In *NE* iii 5 Aristotle establishes that we are responsible for our state of character since from doing certain sorts of actions we become a certain sort of person, but we do not choose our character as we choose our actions. We cannot, then, simply elect to do the actions of unjust persons as unjust persons do them, and neither can one do what is just as the just person does without being a just person. Moreover, people suppose that familiarity with the laws secures insight into the just and unjust, but knowing what is appropriate for the particular situation requires astute application, as medical expertise requires being able to apply treatment to a patient as appropriate. The power to act as the just person does therefore demands the just state of character and practical intelligence. Then to suppose that the just person can readily do unjust as well as just things overlooks how a stable state of character is not in everyone's immediate power and that such a state tends to consistent actions.

Having shown that *being* just is not easy, since it requires the right character and understanding, and that the politically just in a community is a conventional instantiation of the naturally politically just, Aristotle tackles the difficulty of locating the just in particular situations (10.1137a31–1138a3). The laws of a community are universal, instantiating the even more universal politically just, so laws as applied to particulars may sometimes invite resort to the equitable (τὸ ἐπιεικές) and equity (ἡ ἐπιείκεια). Were the lawgiver present to the particular case, the equitable is what he would decide, a correction of the legally just (ἐπανόρθωμα νομίμου δικαίου). The universal law needs correction to fit the particulars of the case. The equitable can then be just while going outside the strict statement of the law, and excellent (σπουδαῖον) like the just and even superior to the just.[44] The equitable approaches the simply just. The equitable person will tend to choose and do what is equitable and not be fussy about his own share.[45] Equity is the disposition toward the equitable, and this is not a different disposition from justice.

---

[44] Previously in 1137a9–12 Aristotle indicated that the law in a community only accidentally happens to specify the just things since it is universal. That the equitable is in a way better than the just prepares for viewing friendship as better than justice (see 1155a22–28 and 1158b29–33). That the universality of law makes it possibly fit imperfectly with particular situations is a major topic in Plato's *Statesman* (see 294a ff.).

[45] That the equitable person tends to take less than his share (ὁ γὰρ ἐπιεικὴς ἐλαττωτικός ἐστιν), see also 1136b19–21. Brunschwig 1996, 117–135, traces Aristotle's bringing together two traditions: the popular sense of the equitable as indulgence that relaxes stern law and Plato's concern in *Statesman* 292d–303d and *Laws* 874e–875d with universal law poorly fitting particular situations, though Plato does not speak of the equitable in such contexts. Brunschwig contends that the equitable pertains only to the judicial setting, so he struggles to reconcile the possibly different meanings of the equitable in *NE* v 10. But the equitable is hardly limited to judicial settings since government officials may sometimes have to be equitable in applying law in their administration, and individuals can be equitable in accepting less than their strict share. Aristotle recognizes the multiple meanings of ordinary terms for virtues, and the equitable person who takes less than his share is correcting the law as it applies to his case since he does not wish to receive all the goods to which he is entitled, but apparently prefers the honor or the noble to the goods. It appears that the equitable can apply in nearly any area that the just applies to, and the just person is also equitable.

That a person cannot treat himself unjustly follows from the impossibility already shown of being voluntarily treated unjustly (see 1136a10–b14); Aristotle must further confirm his general claim that justice and the just are in relation to other persons rather than oneself (1138a4–28). Suicide, which the law forbids, seems problematic.[46] Harming voluntarily not in self-defense is unjust, but whom does the suicide treat unjustly? Not himself, because he wished for this and one cannot voluntarily be treated unjustly. The *polis* then receives the unjust treatment.[47] And regarding particular unjust actions in distributions or transactions, one cannot be unjust to *oneself* since one would then impossibly at the same time give the same thing to oneself and take it away. One would be doing and suffering injustice, which means voluntarily being treated unjustly, which was previously shown to be impossible (1136a10–b14). And one cannot commit particular unjust actions such as adultery, burglary, or theft against oneself, since one cannot do them against one's own wish, and Aristotle has already dealt with suicide.

Both doing and suffering unjust things are bad (φαῦλα), but doing them is worse since those doing them voluntarily are either completely unjust in character and blameworthy or approaching to this, but the sufferer need not at all have the vice of injustice (1138a28–b5). This parallels the famous claim in Plato's *Gorgias* 469b ff. that it is better to suffer than to do injustice, but with Aristotle's fascinating addition,

In itself, then, suffering injustice is less bad, but nothing prevents its being the greater evil in an incidental way (κατὰ συμβεβηκὸς δ᾿ οὐδὲν κωλύει μεῖζον εἶναι κακόν). What is incidental, however, is not the concern of an art (τέχνη); rather, the art says that pleurisy is more serious than a stumble (προσπταίσματος), even though the latter may turn out incidentally to be the more serious, if the fall it causes incidentally leads to one's being taken prisoner or put to death by the enemy. (1138a35–b5)

This states that the magnitude of some evils suffered may happen to outweigh evils done, while emphasizing that art as such does not concern itself with particulars like this since knowledge is directed at the universal rather than the particular. Why bother to make the point that seems

---

It should be clear, then, that equity and the equitable do not always have to mean loosening of the law, indulgence.

[46] Aristotle says that what the law does not allow it forbids (1138a7), so that even without a written law suicide is forbidden. The general point about law runs counter to modern political philosophy. Hobbes says, "The greatest liberty of subjects, dependeth on the silence of the law" (*Leviathan* ii 21). Nevertheless, Hobbes assumes and Locke argues that the "law of nature" prohibits suicide (*Second Treatise of Government* §§22–23).

[47] Whitehead 1993, 501, points out that Aristotle speaks of accomplished suicide. The dishonor will then be to the deceased, whether for bringing bloodguilt upon the *polis* or depriving it of the services of a subject. In *Phaedo* 62a–c Socrates gives the other classic argument: the suicide treats the gods unjustly for humans are their property.

innocent enough? He may merely be reaffirming like Plato, against creepy sophistical examples of possible suffering (see *Gorgias* 473b–d and *Rep.* 361c–362a), that one should never choose to do what is unjust.

But might Aristotle as he concludes his treatment of justice also glance at a pressing political question? While *art* as such, as universal knowledge, cannot observe particular situations, the *artisan* must pay attention to the particular. And art does not as does practical wisdom deal with the universal good, and especially with regard to the end of the *polis*. Aristotle may here coyly and unsettlingly observe that in political life circumstances arise in which the statesperson has to do something that borders on being unjust to allow the *polis* to avoid suffering something incidentally worse. The individual concerned with action and character should accept suffering the unjust rather than choosing to do the unjust, but will this hold for the *polis*?[48] This disturbing point is not loudly proclaimed, and he leaves it arguable that in dire or difficult circumstances what the statesman may have to do is not unjust.[49]

That much of Aristotle's account of justice is attentive to Plato's in the *Republic* receives confirmation in the way the book ends (1138b5–13). Aristotle still denies that a person is just with respect to himself, but he allows that metaphorically the parts within a person can have a just relationship. The Platonists grant the rational part a despotic or household just rule of the rest of the soul, and correspondingly they permit unjust treatment with respect to oneself, but to Aristotle this substitutes

---

[48] Only a few lines before in 1138a20–23 he had said, "In addition, an unjust act is voluntary and done from rational choice, and prior in the sense that a sufferer of injustice who retaliates in kind is not thought to be acting unjustly; but when a person harms himself, he suffers and does the same things at the same time." When a person retaliates after suffering unjust treatment, there is no injustice done, but what if a statesman can reasonably foresee the *polis* suffering something from others, might he then plausibly act to prevent it so that the community will not have to suffer even possible capture or destruction? Aristotle goes on in 1138b5–13 to indicate that the individual only metaphorically can be just with respect to himself, but the situation of the *polis* is likely rather different from that of the individual, and so different considerations may come into play.

[49] Recall the earlier passage discounting some questionable action as unjust action (1136a23–31), and the equitable goes outside the law without being unjust. These may now have additional significance. Plato also approaches this topic coyly by having Socrates state that he would prefer to suffer than to do injustice, though immediately he argues unfairly against Polus seemingly to defend suffering the unjust in preference to doing it. And in the *Republic*, the just city fights wars with dubious tactics (422c–423a) and abandons relatives captured in war (468a). Political philosophy must touch on the issue whether preserving the good sometimes justifies troublesome means or looseness regarding what is strictly right, and Aristotle discreetly enters this problematic terrain in the context of justice. This should make the political life less attractive than philosophy.

for the prominent justice among citizens, rulers and ruled, and the lesser type in the household, and between master and slave. The heart of Plato's account turns out merely figurative and leaves out the key sort of justice. In contrast with this Platonic approach, Aristotle supposes he gives justice as a state of character its due in his finely articulated and complete account.

WORKS CITED

Aquinas, St. Thomas. 1993. *Commentary on Aristotle's Nicomachean Ethics.* C. I. Litzinger, O. P. trans. Notre Dame, IN: Dumb Ox Books.

Arendt, Hannah. 1958. *The Human Condition.* Chicago: University of Chicago Press.

Bostock, David. 2000. *Aristotle's Ethics.* Oxford: Oxford University Press.

Brunschwig, Jacques. 1996. "Rule and Exception: On the Aristotelian Theory of Equity." 115–155 in Michael Frede and Gisela Striker eds. *Rationality in Greek Thought.* Oxford: Clarendon Press.

Burnet, John. 1900. *The Ethics of Aristotle.* London: Methuen.

Crisp, Roger trans. 2000. *Aristotle: Nicomachean Ethics.* Cambridge: Cambridge University Press.

Curzer, H. J. 1995. "Aristotle's Account of the Virtue of Justice." *Apeiron* 28: 207–238.

Destrée, Pierre. 2000. "Aristote et la question du droit naturel (*Eth. Nic.*, V, 10, 1134b18–1135a5)." *Phronesis* 46: 220–239.

Finley, M. I. 1977. "Aristotle and Economic Analysis." 140–158 in J. Barnes, M. Schofield, and R. Sorabji eds. *Articles on Aristotle.* Vol. 2. *Ethics and Politics.* London: Duckworth.

Frede, Michael. 2011. *A Free Will: Origins of the Notion in Ancient Thought.* Berkeley: University of California Press.

Gauthier, R. A., and J. Y. Jolif. 1959. *L'Éthique à Nicomaque.* Vol. 2, part 1. Louvain: Publications Unversitaires de Louvain.

Hardie, W. F. R. 1980. *Aristotle's Ethical Theory.* 2nd ed. Oxford: Oxford University Press.

Harrison, A. R. W. 1957. "Aristotle's *Nicomachean Ethics*, Book V and the Law of Athens." *Journal of Hellenic Studies* 77: 42–47.

Heath, T. 1949. *Mathematics in Aristotle.* Oxford: Clarendon Press.

Kussmaul, Peter. 2008. "Aristotle's Doctrine of Justice and the Law of Athens." *Dionysius* 26: 29–46.

Meikle, Scott. 1995. *Aristotle's Economic Thought.* Oxford: Clarendon Press.

Nussbaum, Martha C. 1986. *The Fragility of Goodness: Luck and Ethics in Greek Tragedy and Philosophy.* Cambridge: Cambridge University Press.

O'Connor, David. 1988. "Aristotelian Justice as a Personal Virtue." *Midwest Studies in Philosophy* 13: 417–427.

Polanyi, Karl. 1968. "Aristotle Discovers the Economy." 78–115 in George Dalton ed. *Primitive, Archaic and Modern Economies: Essays of Karl Polanyi.* Garden City, NY: Anchor.

Rawls, John. 1958. "Justice as Fairness." *Philosophical Review* 67: 163–193.

Sachs, Joe. 2002. *Aristotle Nicomachean Ethics.* Newburyport, MA: Focus.

Schumpeter, J. 1954. *History of Economic Analysis.* E. B. Schumpeter ed. New York: Oxford University Press.

Vlastos, Gregory. 1991. *Socrates: Ironist and Moral Philosopher*. Ithaca, NY: Cornell University Press.

Whitehead, David. 1993. "Two Notes on Greek Suicide." *Classical Quarterly* 43: 501–502.

Williams, Bernard. 1980. "Justice as a Virtue." 189–199 in A. O. Rorty ed. *Essays on Aristotle's Ethics*. Berkeley: University of California Press.

Young, Charles M. 2006. "Aristotle's Justice." 179–197 in R. Kraut ed. *The Blackwell Guide to Aristotle's Nicomachean Ethics*. Malden, MA: Blackwell.

9   The Book on Wisdom

I. THE ARGUMENT OF THE BOOK AND ITS CONNECTION TO THE TWO ARISTOTELIAN ETHICS

In the *Nicomachean Ethics*, a single book is dedicated to a single theme only in books 5 and 6. But in the case of book 6 there are doubts about its argument and also about its structure. Some think that the book is not well organized (Hardie 1968, 212; Kenny 1979, 100; Urmson 1988, 79), while others maintain that we can detect a clear plan at its base (Gauthier and Jolif 1970, ii 435–436; Rowe 1971, 113–114; Broadie and Rowe 2002, 357–358) or at least at the base of the central chapters, 2–11 (Greenwood 1909, 160–161). This difficulty about the book's structure derives from a deeper one, which is to establish what its main theme is. Is it that right reason (*orthos logos*) in particular determines the mean regarding moral virtue, or is the book dedicated to discussing intellectual virtues in general? There are arguments for both contentions.

The book begins with a reference to an already given definition of moral virtue: "Since we have already stated that one should choose the right mean (τὸ μέσον) and not the excess or the deficiency, and that the right mean is as the right reason says, let us determine this point" (1138b16–20).[1] This connects the present discussion of *orthos logos* to the previous treatment of moral virtue, with the intention to complete it (Rassow 1862, 19–20; Grant 1885, ii 144–145; Greenwood 1909, 170). A confirmation of this interpretation can be found at the end of the book, where Aristotle says:

Whenever people now define virtue, they all say what state it is and what its objects are, and then add that it is in accordance with right reason. Right reason is that which is in accordance with practical wisdom (φρόνησις); everyone, then, seems in some way to divine that the state like this, in accordance with practical wisdom, is virtue. (1144b21–28)

I would like to thank the editor, Ron Polansky, for revising my inadequate English and for suggesting many improvements to the content of this article, suggestions I followed only in part. Obviously, the responsibility for the content is totally mine.

[1]   In the quotations I use the Crisp 2000 translation with modifications.

But there is evidence going the other way. A little later, in chapter 1, Aristotle says:

When we had classified the virtues of the soul, we said that some are virtues of character, others intellectual virtues. We have already discussed the virtues of character; so let us now speak as follows of those that remain, having first made some distinctions about the soul. (1138b35–1139a3)

And toward the end of the book, in chapter 12, he takes up this indication, saying: "We have now said what practical wisdom and theoretical wisdom are, what each is concerned with, and that each is a virtue of a different part of the soul" (1143b15–17). In light of these passages, some suggest that there was a first version of book 6 that lacked the first and the last chapter, and this version was an analysis of intellectual virtues in general to correspond to the analysis of moral virtues in *NE* ii–iv (or in *EE* iii) and to complete the dichotomy of intellectual virtues and virtues of character described in *NE* 1103a5 and *EE* 1220a4–6. The later insertion by Aristotle of chapters 1 and 12, according to this interpretation, has changed the aspect of the whole book (Dirlmeier 1956, 441; Gauthier and Jolif 1970, i 77–78 and ii 435, 439–440).

Perhaps the safest way to interpret the evidence is to think that Aristotle aimed to kill two birds with one stone. Book 6 completes the list of virtues of soul with a description of the intellectual virtues, *and* it completes the discussion of moral virtue by clarifying the intellectual aspects of the virtue of the part of the soul irrational in itself but able to listen to reason. Since the *orthos logos* of virtue of character is an intellectual virtue, he uses the analysis of the intellectual virtues, vi 1 (second part)–12, as a way to find the answer to the question about *orthos logos* raised in vi 1 (first part) and definitively solved at vi 13. Such a procedure – that is, posing a problem, but then answering a preliminary question in order to reach the solution to the initial problem – is not uncommon in *NE*. There are other examples in *NE* i 10–11 and v 8–9.

Since *NE* vi is one of the so-called common books, the question arises of its relation to *NE* and *EE*. The book's opening passage connects chapter 1 to some preceding discussions, but it is not clear which, because both *NE* ii 2.1103b32–33 and *EE* ii 5.1222b7–8 promise a further discussion of the *orthos logos*. Also, the reference to a previous distinction between the virtues of the different parts of the soul does not help us to decide, because it could refer either to *NE* 1103a3–10 or to *EE* 1220a4–12. Is this book the answer to the questions of *EE*, as some suppose (Stewart 1892, ii 4; Kenny 1978, 50–59 and 161–189), or to those of *NE*, as others suggest (e.g., Burnet 1900, 251; Rowe 1971, 109–114)? Though some elements link book 6 to *EE*, in general more connections point to *NE*: the style, the quotations of known poets, and the use of commonplace examples, phrases that repeat nearly verbatim passages of *NE* i or are close to it.[2] Because of this I am inclined to consider book 6 to be closer to *NE* i–iv, even if it seems not to be written directly in the same vein.

II. THE STRUCTURE OF THE BOOK

If we admit that the aim of the book is to identify *orthos logos* with a virtue of the intellect, the book's structure seems rather plain. It divides into six sections:

1.   Statement of the problems (chapter 1)[3]
      (1a)   What is *orthos logos*?
      (1b)   What are the virtues of thought? (Solution of [1b] also solves [1a], implied.)
2.   The different characteristics of theoretical and practical thinking (chapter 2)
3.   A fresh start: distinction of five types of intellectual reasoning, the *ergon* of which is to be true; chapter 5 offers a first account and definition of *phronēsis* (Though *phronēsis* is clearly the best candidate for the role of *orthos logos*, this is not yet expressed.) (chapters 3–7.1148b8)
4.   Further remarks about *phronēsis* (chapter 7 from 1141b8 to chapter 8)
5.   Some forms similar to *phronēsis* and solution to problem a2 (chapters 9–11)
6.   Some final *aporiai* about *phronēsis* and solution to problem a1 (chapters 12–13)

Evidently, most of the book deals with practical thinking in general and *phronēsis* in particular. The main work of book 6 is the analysis of practical wisdom, and other intellectual capacities are described insofar as they can clarify by comparison the nature of practical wisdom (cf. Burnet 1900, 247–248 and 252; Greenwood 1909, 270–271; Broadie and Rowe 2002, 357–358). The only real structural problem is the double examination of *phronēsis*, in chapters 5 and 7–11, separated by a discussion of *nous* and *sophia* (chapters 6 to 7, first part). There are also some

---

[2] 1139b14, 1144a12–13 = 1095a13–14, b14, 1097a14–15; 1140a3 = 1102a26–27; 1142a11–20 = 1095a2–6; 1145a 6–11 = 1094a26–b7.

[3] There are two chapter divisions in *NE*, deriving from medieval or Renaissance translations. They are not by Aristotle and carry little weight for the interpretation of the text. Usually English-speaking scholars prefer the division adopted by Bywater and indicated by Roman numerals in the OCT edition. Continental scholars, however, prefer the other one, adopted by Bekker, and indicated by Arabic numerals. Here I will use Bywater's division, in order to be better understood by readers, even if I am convinced that for book 6 the other one is better.

repetitions, some philosophically difficult assertions, and some super-
ficial incoherencies. Let us examine the main sections of the book.

We already discussed 1a. In section 1b, 1138b34–1139a17 there is a
recapitulation of the main points established in NE i–ii: there are two
parts of the human soul, irrational (but able to listen to reason) and
rational, and two separate kinds of virtue, intellectual and moral, and
Aristotle gives definitions of intellectual virtue in general. In section 2
Aristotle divides the reasoning part of the soul according to the different
objects and establishes the virtues of each part.

Section 3 is a long examination of five capacities of the soul that
are necessarily truthful: art, science, practical wisdom, philosophical
wisdom, and intellectual understanding (τέχνη, ἐπιστήμη, φρόνησις, σοφία,
νοῦς). Aristotle introduces it with a formula (ἔστω δή, "let us say [or
assume]") that is employed here to refer to his own doctrine, and quotes
both his own scholarly works, such as the Analytics, and his more
popular or exoteric works (ἐξωτερικοὶ λόγοι). Mostly there is description
in these pages, and a few arguments, some of which are quite bad
(e.g., 1141a12–17). The section on nous in particular is very brief, and
very general in comparison with its treatment in Posterior Analytics
ii 19. We arrive at definitions of single intellectual capacities. The definitions provide answers to questions similar to the questions asked
regarding the moral virtues in NE iii 1115a4–5 (What is it? What sort of
things is it concerned with? Which part of the soul is each a virtue of?
Cf. 1143b15–17). First is the definition of epistēmē: "Science then is a
state by which we demonstrate, and has all the other distinguishing
characteristics we add in the Analytics" (1139b31–33); then we have
the definitions of technē: "Art, then, as we have said, is a productive
state involving true reasoning" (1140a21–22); and of phronēsis: "Practical
wisdom is a practical state, involving true reasoning, concerned with
what is good and bad for a human being" (1140b4–6, repeated at
b20–21).[4] About nous we have no proper definition, because it is included
in the definition of sophia: "It is clear that philosophical wisdom is
both science and intellectual understanding of what is by nature most
honourable" (1141b2–3). It is important to notice that Aristotle here
defines not only particular intellectual virtues but also other capacities,
such as epistēmē and technē, that are not virtues. Hence the standpoint of
this chapter is not identical to that of NE ii–iv.[5]

---

[4] At line 1140b5 I read ἀληθοῦς and not ἀληθῆ. At 1140b20–21 Aristotle adds that it is also
a state "concerned with action" (πρακτικήν).

[5] While some interpreters (e.g., Stewart, Zeller) consider all these five types of intellection
to be virtues, most think that only phronēsis and sophia are called virtues (e.g., Burnet,
Gauthier, Greenwood, Hardie, Joachim). I follow them on the basis of 1143b14–17.

Though brief, these analyses are crucial, and some of them, such as the description of science, claim to be accurate (ἀκριβολογεῖσθαι, 1139b19). Later we will learn that *sophia* is the virtue of one of the two subparts of intellectual soul (1143b17), but the conclusion is not explicitly drawn in this section. Yet it is said that practical wisdom is a virtue of intellectual soul (1140b24–25). The reticence in making his points clear is one of the most important causes of Aristotle's obscurity in book 6. In other books of the *NE* as well, Aristotle abstains from immediately explaining his view in order to slowly prepare the audience for his new conception, but here the strategy is not very effective.

Section 4 is dedicated again to practical wisdom, but it lacks a continuous line of argument; this fact makes it rather difficult to interpret the main points raised by Aristotle. In particular the final part of chapter 8 contains a series of scattered remarks, some of which are only of minor interest. This is a procedure typical of *NE* (see, e.g., the last part of *NE* v and ix).

In section 5 we find the description of some forms of knowledge similar to practical wisdom but not identical with it. It is a move frequent in the *NE*. We find it also in book 5, where besides general justice and special justice we find justice in exchange, political and domestic justice, and equity or reasonableness (v 5, 6, and 10), and in *NE* ix 5–6, where there is a discussion of concord and benevolence, two dispositions similar to friendship. At the end of section 5, Aristotle takes up some themes from section 4 and concludes the analysis of intellectual virtues. Here we are told for the first time that *sophia* is a virtue of the intellect, even if it was implied already in section 3.

Section 6 is limited to discussion of some final perplexities: the use of practical wisdom (1143b17–18) and the peculiar notion that *phronēsis*, practical wisdom, being inferior, commands *sophia*, philosophical wisdom (1143b33–34). But there is more in these concluding pages: often when Aristotle discusses a problem and gives us his solution, he uses it to introduce a new concept. In this way, he can simultaneously solve a difficulty and make his analysis progress toward the end he wants to reach (cf. Grant 1885, i 395). This happens here, and the solution of the first perplexity will give us the solution of the general problem of the book: What is right reason, that is, what is its standard?

III. PHRONĒSIS AND PRACTICAL THINKING

Here I concentrate on the sections about practical thinking, that is, chapters 1 (from 1138b35), 2, 5, 7 (from 1141b8), and 8. This is surely a crucial part of the entire book, because Aristotle describes his idea of practical thinking and practical wisdom, one of his best contributions to the history of Western philosophy. In fact, against Socrates and Plato, Aristotle thinks that human action is not simply the technical application of a truth discovered by theory or science (Gadamer 1960); rather there is a particular kind of human thinking that aims from the beginning at acting.[6] This kind of thinking connects with human virtues of character. We already know, from book 2, that moral virtue is a mean state concerned with pleasure and pain, and aimed at the intermediate in passions and actions. This state is relative to us and dictated by right reasoning. In book 1 the two kinds of virtues, intellectual and moral, may seem to run parallel to each other, as two completely distinct components of happiness. But now a close connection emerges of the virtue of character and one of the intellectual virtues (Joachim 1951, 69–70; Irwin 1999, 192), and there is some parallelism between the analysis of moral virtues in NE ii–iv and the analysis of intellectual virtues in NE vi.

Aristotle again divides the soul and says that intellectual soul has two parts, contemplative and calculative. He can distinguish them based on their different objects: "When the objects are different in kind, the part of the soul naturally related to each is different in kind, since they gain their understanding through a certain relationship and similarity between them and their objects" (1139a8–10). One deals with objects having unchanging principles and thus suited for theoretical science, while the other intellectual part deals with matters having changeable principles. The best intellectual state of each one is its virtue: "We must therefore grasp what is the best state of each sub-part, because this will be the virtue of each, and the virtue of a thing is related to its own proper activity" (1139a15–17). To locate its virtue is to find the state that enables a faculty to do its job in the best way. We thus arrive at the general definition of intellectual virtue: "The characteristic activity of each intellectual part of the soul, then, is truth; and so the virtues of each will be those states on the basis of which it will most of all arrive at truth" (1139b12–13).

The definitions of particular intellectual virtues will follow. In 1139a17–b13 Aristotle tells us the characteristics of the part of the reasoning soul capable of conversing with desiderative soul. Aristotle does not start from the logical form of practical reasoning, as a modern philosopher would, but from the faculties of the soul, because he considers practical

---

[6] Even in De Motu Animalium 7.701a7–8 Aristotle is cognizant of practical thinking: "Why is it that when someone is thinking, sometimes he acts and sometimes he does not, sometimes is in movement and sometimes not?" It is important to be clear that for Aristotle there is no problem of a specifically moral kind of reasoning distinguished from practical reasoning, as some suppose (Allan 1955). "Moral" reasoning in our sense seems to coincide for Aristotle with the perfection of practical thinking, i.e., to the practical thinking that aims at living well as a whole and to εὐπραξία.

reasoning a property of a living human being. Practical thinking is described as the result of the collaboration of two faculties, reason (referred to with the terms νοῦς, διάνοια at 1139a18 and 21) and desire (ὄρεξις). They function analogously and therefore can work together:

What affirmation and negation are in the sphere of thought, pursuit and avoidance are in desire. So, since virtue of character is a state involving choice, and choice is deliberative desire, the reasoning must be true and the desire correct, if the choice is to be good, and the desire must pursue what reason asserts. Such thought and truth are practical. In the case of thought concerned with contemplation, however, which is neither practical nor productive, what constitutes its being good or bad are truth and falsity.[7] (1139a21–26)

In practical reasoning, correctness of desire and true reasoning must go hand in hand if there is to be an action.[8] Desire and reason are united by the fact that they have an independent cognitive access to the same object, a good thing to be done, as is shown by the idea of a "natural virtue" to be discussed later.[9]

The notion of "deliberation" is the key concept in those passages, from which all the characterizations of *phronēsis* and practical thinking derive: deliberation is referred to in all the relevant passages.[10] It has two aspects. First, the product of deliberation is a choice (προαίρεσις), and in a choice we have a strict connection between reasoning and desire, because choice is a deliberative desire (1139a23). Second, in deliberation there is special relevance of the particular over and above the universal, since actions will be particular. The first aspect is dealt with in vi 2; the second aspect is examined in vi 7–9.

---

[7] A similar idea is in *De Anima* iii 7.431b8–12: "When [the faculty of thinking] affirms that it is pleasant or painful, immediately (ἐνταῦθα) it avoids or pursues, and generally in action. That which is apart from action, i.e. the true and false, is in the same genus as the good and bad; but these differ [i.e., true and false differ from good and bad] because to the last couple applies the distinction between being absolute and being relative to someone."

[8] Davidson 1963 seems to renew Aristotle's position when he explains human action causally as the product of a "pro-attitude" and a "belief." He has recognized his debt to his Greek predecessor in Davidson 2001, 300. But there is a difference between the Aristotelian and the Davidsonian notions of cause, because Aristotle works with a four-causes theory not accepted by contemporary philosophers.

[9] Cf. also *De Anima* iii 10.433a15–16: "The object of desire is the same as the principle of practical thinking." Desire is not limited to following the teachings of reason; it has its own access to reality. Fortenbaugh 1975, 70–75, is interesting but seems to go too far on the emotional side; see also Charles 2009, 65. About the difference between Aristotle's practical reason and Hume's concept of reason, which is never practical, see Broadie 1991, 215–219.

[10] 1139a13–14; a23; b8; 1140a25–26; b1; 1141b8–10; 1142a31–b33. In vi 12–13, the concept is absent.

(1) In vi 2 Aristotle discusses the relationship between reason and desire in the calculative element that connects directly with *praxis*: "Let us call ... [it] the calculative part, since deliberating and calculating are the same, and no one deliberates about what cannot be otherwise. So the calculative is one part, as it were, of the rational part of the soul" (1139a11–15), and he repeats the idea, already expressed in iii 5, that deliberation is a kind of calculation similar to a mathematical analysis (ἀναλύειν, 1112b20). Aristotle explains practical thinking from the point of view of the four causes:

The origin of action, its moving cause, not its goal (ὅθεν ἡ κίνησις ἀλλ᾽ οὐχ οὗ ἕνεκα), is choice; and that of choice is desire and goal-directed reasoning.[11] This is why choice involves not only intellect and thought, but also a state of character, for acting well and its contrary in acting require thought and character. Mere thought by itself moves nothing, but practical and goal-directed thinking does move (ἀλλ᾽ ἡ ἕνεκά του καὶ πρακτικήν) ... in fact good result (εὐπραξία) is the goal, and desire aims at this. (1139a31–b4)

A similar idea can be found in *De Anima* iii 10:

There are three things, one that which produces movement, second that whereby it does so, and third what is moved; and that which produces movement is twofold: that which is unmoved and that which produces movement and is moved. That which is unmoved is practical good, and that which produces movement and is moved is the faculty of desire. (433b13–17)

In the *NE* Aristotle calls, more precisely, "moving cause" and "final cause" that which in *De Anima* are called, respectively, "moved mover" and "unmoved mover." But the doctrine is the same. The same expression, διάνοια πρακτική, is used in both treatises to indicate practical reasoning (1139a36, 433a18). According to Aristotle, human movement in general, and *praxis* in particular, involve the complete human soul, both its intellectual and its emotional parts. *Praxis* in humans is the product of reasoning and habituation, that is, of an acquired moral character; because of that, action expresses the whole man and his living in a situation (cf. Heidegger 1992, 23–24 and 50–51; Sherman 1989, 56–58 and 156–199; Broadie 1991, 220–224).

The end of *praxis* is called εὐπραξία, a difficult term to translate. With its cognate εὐπραγία, it is a term of common language used to indicate either "success, good result" or the state of well-being that follows success.[12] It is the contrary of δυστυχία, δυσπραγία, κακοπραγία (failure).

[11] Cf. *De Anima* iii 10.433a13–14: "Intellect and desire can produce movement in respect of place, I mean intellect which reasons for the sake of something, and is practical."
[12] Pind. *Py.* vii, 18–20; *Ol.* viii 14; Herod. viii 54 etc. A man in the state of *eupraxia* can be an object of *phthonos*, envy. Aristotle uses the term in the usual meaning quite often;

The philosophers interpreted the idea of "success" in their own way: Xenophon (*Mem.* iii 9.14) and Plato (*Alc. I* 116b, and elsewhere) identify εὐπραγία with happiness and good acting. The distance from the popular morality lies in defining what success consists in, not in refuting the idea of success. Aristotle follows them, and identifies εὐπραξία with good life and good acting (εὖ ζῆν καὶ ... εὖ πράττειν, *NE* 1098b22; cf. *EE* 1246b37; *Pol.* 1325a22, b15, b21; *Rhet.* 1360b14). In my opinion, this identification is not about the meaning of the term but about the content of a successful life. Aristotle accepts the idea that the end of *prattein* is success, but he maintains that (well-understood) success is identical to the kind of happiness described in *NE* i. Some modern interpreters overstate the term when they translate *eupraxia* as "virtuous life" or "morally good behavior" and so on.

At vi 5 Aristotle describes *phronēsis* without any explicit reference to what he said in vi 2 about practical thinking. He starts with a *topos* for finding definitions (*Top.* 147a12 and *A.Po.* 97b15–17: "If definition is of the state of anything, look at what is in the state"), used also at the beginning of book 5 (1129a18–19), and says: "We may grasp practical wisdom by considering the sort of people we describe as practically wise" (1140a24–5). He next identifies wise people with those who can deliberate "about what conduces to living well as a whole" (1140a28), and repeats that the object of deliberation is what depends on the deliberator (αὐτῷ, 1140a32). Because of that, he distinguishes practical wisdom from science and art. Practical wisdom, in his view, has its own way to access reality and cannot be reduced to any other form of knowledge. Deliberation is its way of proceeding when searching how to act (1140a25–b4). We thus arrive at the definition of *phronēsis*, already quoted: "Practical wisdom is a practical state involving true reasoning, concerned with what is good and bad for a human being."

Aristotle adds some *endoxa* to confirm the definition. This is a move he uses often in his treatises. The confirmations derive from the fact that people such as Pericles are rightly judged to be practically wise (1140b7–11),[13] and also from an etymological argument: temperance, σωφροσύνη, has its name ὡς σῴζουσαν τὴν φρόνησιν, because it preserves practical wisdom, a form of knowledge that can be destroyed by pleasure and pain (b11–20). We have here a short reminder of the fundamental

---

cf. *NE* 1100a21, 1101b6–7, 1167a16; *EE* 1221a39, 1233b25, 1247a1; *Top.* 109b37, 110a3; *Rhet.* 1367a4, 1368b19, 1386b24, 1387a9, a18, b23. Wartelle 1982, 171, tries to differentiate too much between *eupraxia* and *eupragia*, but the texts do not confirm his position. See also Engberg-Pedersen 1983, 27–28.

13   Aristotle here reverses Plato's harsh judgment on Pericles; see *Gorgias* 515e–516a. Plato says that Pericles corrupted his fellow citizens, while Aristotle says that he looked for "both what is good for himself and what is good for people in general" (1140b9).

connection between reasoning and desire in practical wisdom. We can infer that *phronēsis* is one of the virtues of the rational mind. We have now part of the answer to the question, "What are the virtues of the rational part of the soul?" As a corollary Aristotle presents the thesis that practical wisdom is not a form of art (1140b21–25).

Phronēsis turns out to be a component of happiness in two ways: both as an intellectual virtue and as a central constituent of virtues of character that are, in turn, parts of happiness. But the two roles coincide, because *phronēsis* never operates alone: it works only in connection with moral virtue. What is new in this book is the idea that the standard (ὅρος) that determines the right middle is the operation of one of the intellectual virtues, and not some human good, such as wealth or some similar good (Urmson 1988, 81).[14] This has never been said before, and it is one of the main points of book 6.

(2) The presentation of practical wisdom is far from complete, however. Aristotle comes back to it in vi 7–8, after describing philosophical wisdom, or *sophia*. Having said that *sophia*, the best form of knowledge, is about the best object (an application of the principle established at 1139a8–11), and failing, for the moment, to express the conclusion that *sophia* is another virtue of rational soul, he makes a contrast with *phronēsis*, because *phronēsis*, he repeats, "is concerned with human affairs, namely with what we can deliberate about" (1141b8–9), and not with the best things in the world. He adds that the object of *phronēsis* is to deliberate tending to a πρακτὸν ἀγαθόν (1141b12), a good achievable by action, implicitly identifying *phronēsis* with practical thinking as described in chapter 2. But again the point is not expressed clearly.

Now a new point arises (1141b14): the objects of practical wisdom are both the universal and the particular, but the particular is the more important of the two. The result of deliberation is a particular action, concerned with a particular result (1141b16: ἡ δὲ πρᾶξις περὶ τὰ καθ᾽ ἕκαστα). As proclaimed at the beginning of the *Metaphysics* (981a12–24), he remarks that, for action, knowing only the particular is better than knowing only the universal. As in the *Metaphysics*, he appeals to a medical example: "If someone knows that light meats are digestible and wholesome, but does not know which kinds are light, he would not produce health; rather, the person who knows that chicken is light will be better at producing health" (1141b16–21). But, unlike the *Metaphysics*, here the idea of the knowledge of the universal and of the particular is expressed using the scheme of syllogism. He uses it more

---

[14] Here I accept the idea that *horos* in both 1138b23 and b34 means "standard," as Ross, Crisp, and others want; if, on the contrary, we translate the second occurrence of it as "definition" (proposed by Thomas Aquinas, Plebe, Defradas, Irwin, and others; cf. Bonitz 1870, 529b54 ff.), Aristotle's position will come out even more clearly.

than once, both in this book and in book 7, and also in *De Motu Animalium* 7 and *De Anima* iii 11. At some point Aristotle even uses the phrase συλλογισμοὶ τῶν πρακτῶν (1144a31–32) meaning "inferences about what we shall do," and not full-fledged "syllogisms" in the style of *Prior Analytics* (Barnes 1981, 23).

From such usage derives the idea of a special kind of syllogism admitted by Aristotle, the so-called practical syllogism. Many have discussed this kind of syllogism, and some try to make comparisons between it and modern analyses of practical thinking, as deontic logic and theories of practical inference. In my opinion Aristotle does not want to use the "practical syllogism" as a way formally to represent normative language and its laws, or to establish a kind of alethic deontic logic different from his standard logical theory. Aristotle often uses syllogistic vocabulary to represent various forms of human reasoning, from scientific explanation to dialectical and eristical encounters, to rhetorical argumentation and practical reasoning. He calls it Scientific, Dialectical, Eristical Syllogism, and Enthymeme. In *NE* vi syllogistic vocabulary is used to represent the psychic process that generates action, including deliberation in the process.

Aristotle seems very interested in maintaining that *phronēsis* is an independent form of reaching the truth. He already said that it is neither science nor art (1140b1), and he repeats here that it is neither a science (*epistēmē*) nor intellect (*nous*), because its main point of interest is the particular (1142a23–25; and see Heidegger 1992, 51–57). *Nous*, a very multifaceted word in Aristotle's vocabulary, is used here in the restricted sense of vi 6 and not in the general sense of vi 2, which included both theoretical and practical thinking (1139a18).

Now a possible objection to the claim that the particular is the most important aspect in practical reasoning is dealt with in vi 8. Someone might object that politics is the best form of practical thinking, and it has as its object some kind of universal good, the good of an entire city or a community (1094b10). In vi 8.1141b25, Aristotle answers that politics is a kind of ruling and coordinating (ἀρχιτεκτονική) practical wisdom, and distinguishing many forms of it, but never attributing to them the qualification of "universality." By using the adjective ἀρχιτεκτονική and not the expression καθόλου, he tries to avoid the contradiction deriving from the following ideas: (a) politics and legislation are the most important forms of practical wisdom, (b) legislation is necessarily general, and (c) the particular premise is the most important one in practical thinking. But elsewhere Aristotle identifies laws and universal commands (1137b12–14).

In the final part of chapter 8 three main points arise. First of all, Aristotle wants to distinguish between looking for one's own good in a vulgar way, as busybodies (πολυπράγμονες, 1142a2) do, and the life of wise men. He remarks that, when well understood, the good of the individual must include his family, friends, and fellow citizens (1142a9–10; cf. 1097b8–11).[15] Second, he says that there is an explanation why young people cannot be practically wise (1142a10–16): because wisdom is concerned with particular situations, and it takes time and experience of life to recognize the potentialities of a situation. Third, he adds that the error in practical reasoning could consist in assuming a wrong universal premise or a wrong particular premise (1142a20–24). This enumeration is incomplete, because in the following chapter we find other possibilities of being in error when we engage in practical reasoning. At the end he goes back to differentiating practical wisdom from science and intellect, as described in chapters 3 and 6. An important comparison between *phronēsis* and a special kind of perception appears here:

> Intellect (*nous*) is concerned with the first terms, of which there is no rational account to be given, while practical wisdom is concerned with the last things; and this is the object of perception (αἴσθησις) and not of scientific knowledge. This is not the perception concerned with objects peculiar to any particular sense, but like that with which we perceive that the last mathematical object is a triangle (ἀλλ᾽ οἵα αἰσθανόμεθα ὅτι τὸ ἐν τοῖς μαθηματικοῖς ἔσχατον τρίγωνον). But this is more perception than practical wisdom, though it is a perception of a peculiar kind. (1142a25–30)

The point will be taken up again in the following chapters.

IV. PRACTICAL WISDOM, GOOD DELIBERATION, AND SOME LOOK-ALIKES

Chapters 9–11 examine good deliberation (εὐβουλία), judgment, and good judgment (σύνεσις, εὐσυνεσία), discernment (γνώμη), and understanding (νοῦς), where νοῦς has the special sense that the word assumes in the phrase νοῦν ἔχειν, that is, "to have sense, to behave sensibly" (Burnet 1900, 280; Dover 1974, 235–236). This section follows the passage just quoted, where *phronēsis* is identified with a particular sort of perception (αἴσθησις). It has no clear connection with it, and it is very possible that there is a brief lacuna in the text, as indicated by Susemihl (1882, 135).

As I said before, here Aristotle lists and describes some forms of knowledge similar to practical wisdom but not identical with it. The sources of the list are opinions, common language (1142b20, 1143a12–13, a16, a21), and perhaps Plato's theories (Gauthier and Jolif 1970, ii 507–509). Aristotle

---

[15] Here a remark of Confucius's *Analects* IV 12 (11) corresponds to Aristotle's doctrine: "A gentleman cares about virtue (*de*), a petty man cares about gain (*tu*, earth); a gentleman cares about retribution (*xing*), a petty man cares about favouritism (*hui*)" (cf. IV 16).

follows in each case the same pattern: he looks for the definition of the faculty in question (τί ἐστίν, 1142a33), first asking about its kind (γένος, 1142a34) and, after, about its defining difference. Aristotle proceeds by elimination, and the kinds considered are identical to those listed in chapter 2: science (ἐπιστήμη), opinion (δόξα), and thought in general (διανοία), but there is also a new item, "good guesswork" (εὐστοχία). Good deliberation and good judgment are neither sciences (1142a34, 1143a1) nor opinions (1142b6–7, 1143a2), because of their object. Good deliberation and good judgment are about the typical objects of practical wisdom, what we deliberate and puzzle about (1143a6), that is, what depends on us and is not yet determined (1142b11–12). This is a subset of the particulars, and we already know that, for Aristotle, what depends on us is not an object of mere opinion but of another part of *doxastikon*, that is, of *deinotēs*, or of *phronēsis*.

This section does not use arguments from the preceding chapters – for instance, that opinion is not always right, whereas good deliberation is always good – but has arguments of its own and seems disconnected from what precedes. Good deliberation is no science because it is an inquiry, and no possessor of science inquires (1142a34–b2). It is no opinion because opinion can be true or false, whereas deliberation can be correct or incorrect (1142b6–12). It is no good guesswork because good guesswork is an ability to respond quickly to a given situation, whereas deliberation takes time (1142b1–6). Good judgment has the same object as practical wisdom, but it is not practical wisdom, because "practical wisdom gives commands ... while judgement only judges (κριτική μόνον)" (1143a8–10) – that is, good judgment lacks the essential connection to desire that characterizes practical wisdom. Discernment is discussed very briefly because, like good judgment, it is a capacity of judging but is limited to cases of equity (τὸ ἐπιεικές, 1143a19–24). The conclusion to which Aristotle arrives is that "all these states naturally tend in the same direction (as practical wisdom)" (1143a25) and are possessed by the same people. Consequently, we can infer some more features of practically wise people from some of them, especially from good deliberation and understanding.

Regarding deliberation we already know that it is the kind of reasoning (*logizesthai*) typical of practical wisdom. Aristotle qualifies deliberation as a kind of inquiry: "Inquiry is not the same as deliberation, since deliberation is a kind of inquiry (ζητεῖν τι ἐστίν)" (1142a32; cf. b14–16 and 1112b20–23). Aristotle compares deliberation to a procedure for the solution of geometric problems; but not, in our opinion, to the procedure of regressive analysis described in *A.Pr.* i 12.78a7–11 (as thinks Mignucci 1975, 283), because the search is not for a foundation of the given end by moving back to its antecedents, but rather for a certain specification of it, in order to prove its practicability. When one is deliberating, the inquiry proceeds not toward the first principles and supreme ends but rather toward particular premises and practical actualizations. An elucidation of this procedure can be found in *Metaphysics* ix 9, where Aristotle says: "It is by actualisation that geometrical relations are discovered: for it is by dividing the given figures (διαιροῦντες) that people discover (εὑρίσκουσιν) them" (1051a21–23). This passage illustrates a case of geometric constructions by which one can see on the blackboard the solution of a given problem, for example, if the angles of a triangle are equal to two rights. The procedure consists in dividing and decomposing geometric figures by drawing lines that divide lines and planes until the moment when the solution is evident at a glance. In both practical deliberation and geometric division a complex problem is subdivided until the moment the inquirer can "see" the solution (Cattanei 2009, 83–111). In practice, the analysis becomes the search for one or more intermediate terms that specify a given end and make it immediately practicable. The procedure terminates with the discovery of premises involving sense perception and the awareness of one's ability (Kenny 1979, 134–141; Broadie 1991, 225–229). The act in my power to do is discovered and recognized as a good act. Therefore it becomes the object of desire, as stated in vi 2.

Deliberation and inquiry could be long or short, whether about solving mathematical problems or locating the way toward happiness (1142b29). But the most important point raised about good deliberation in vi 9 is the idea of correctness (ὀρθότης). We already have seen that in the field of desire correctness corresponds to truth in the field of knowledge (1139a24); it could be an indication of the connection of desire and thinking in the operation of deliberation. But on a closer look "correctness" of deliberation seems rather connected to the idea of the ὀρθὸς λόγος defining ethical virtue.

Aristotle says that there is (a) the possibility of making an effective deliberation for bad results, either because one is bad or because one has weakness of the will (1142b17–21). This is correct but not good deliberation. Since the means are effective but the end is bad, no one would call "good deliberation" a deliberation that produces evil (Dirlmeier 1956, 462). It is to be noted that the use of "correct" here means "successful" rather than "good or right." But there is also (b) the possibility of doing the right thing for a bad reason:

Since there are various kinds of correctness, it is clear that good deliberation does not consist in every kind … it is also possible to achieve something good through false inference (ψευδεῖ συλλογισμῷ), that is, to achieve the right result, but not in the right way, the middle term being false. So this kind of correctness, on the basis of which we achieve the right result but not in the right way, is not yet good deliberation either. (1142b17–26)

This second kind of correctness has no connection with the idea of the purely logical correctness of a syllogism as in *A.Pr.* 53b26ff., as some think (Ramsauer 1878, 404; Bodéüs 2004, 325), but rather to an idea of book 2, according to which one has to do the act in accord with virtue in a deliberate way and for itself (1105a31–2).[16] When Aristotle says "the middle term being false," he does not refer to the wrong means because ineffective or morally unacceptable. He thinks of cases like the Spartans, described in *EE* 1248b36–1249a3, who do actions according to virtue, but for gain and to acquire wealth, rather than for the noble. They do the right thing for a not-quite-right reason (Irwin 1999, 248). So *orthos logos* in deliberation is related to the real good for man and not to apparent goods, such as wealth or celebrity.

Since practically wise people have as a defining characteristic the ability to deliberate well, "good deliberation will be correctness with regard to what is useful towards that end, of which practical wisdom is true supposition (οὗ ἡ φρόνησις ἀληθὴς ὑπόληψις ἐστίν)" (1142b33–34). This is the answer to the question "What is good deliberation?" (*ti estin euboulia;*) of line 1142a32. Aristotle repeats that good deliberation is about ways and means to achieve the supreme human goal, happiness. There is a long debate about the last phrase, because many scholars (from Thomas Aquinas to Bostock 2000, 85) say that here Aristotle attributes to practical wisdom a true apprehension of *eudaimonia*, that is, of the practical end, and others maintain that practical wisdom here is said only to be the true apprehension "of what is useful towards the end" (from Burnet 1900, 277, to Aubenque 1965), that is, of the means. We must remember that apprehension is a cognitive act of the soul, which can be true or false, as Aristotle already said (1139b17).[17] This is why he specifies "true" apprehension here. Without a doubt practical wisdom must have some supposition of the end, in order to deliberate about how to reach it (Berti 1993, 48–49); but the passage does not imply that practical wisdom posits the end, as some suppose (cf. Gauthier and Jolif 1970, ii 577; *contra* Bodéüs 2004, 146–147). It just says that practical wisdom must know it in order to deliberate well.

The practically wise man must have the ability to deliberate well, that is, "about the right thing, in the right way and at the right time" (1142b28). Good deliberation leads the agent to see what he or she should do when facing a practical problem. At the conclusion of the deliberation, the practicable action is viewed as the way to reach an end already given prior to deliberation. The situation is seen under a particular light: the

---

[16] In fact, *orthotēs* is not a term of the logical vocabulary of Aristotle and does not have an important role in the *Organon*.

[17] In *De Anima* iii 3.427b25, Aristotle specifies that practical wisdom has a particular type of apprehension.

so-called second premise of a practical syllogism describes the data in the light of the end to reach. Aristotle repeats this idea time and again, using different terms. This way of looking to the particulars allows desire to pass from the end to the means: even if the means seem a bitter medicine, as efficacious they are desired and taken.

We can now understand the peculiar use of the term νοῦς in these chapters. Aristotle used it in a very general way in vi 2.1139a18; in a very specialized way in vi 6 and following, when he opposed intellect to practical wisdom (1142a25–30). In chapter 11, from 1143a35, he tries to distinguish from the usage of vi 2 and vi 6 another sense of the term, and tells us about its difference:

Intellect is also concerned about the last things, and in both directions; there is intellection, and not rational account, of both the first terms and the last. The intellect related to demonstrations is concerned with the first and unchanging terms, while in practical questions intellect is concerned with the last term, which can be otherwise, that is, with the minor premise. For these last terms are first principles for achieving the end, since universals are arrived at from particulars. We ought, then, to have perception of these, and this is intellection. (1143a36–b5)

This type of practical νοῦς is acquired by experience (1143b6–9). It depends on a general knowledge of the facts of life and is similar to the kind of *empeiria* described in *Metaphysics* 981a8–12: "To formulate the assumption (ἔχειν ὑπόληψιν) that this particular thing benefited Callias, who had this particular disease, as well as Socrates and many men, is *empeiria*." In conclusion, Aristotle insists that the practically wise man is a person of judgment, of sound discernment, who knows how to judge situations because he has an experienced eye.

V. PUZZLES AND CONFIRMATIONS

The long discussion of the relationship between virtue and practical wisdom in chapters 12 and 13 leads to a clarification of the relationship between desire and reason described in chapter 2 and to an answer to the question about *orthos logos* asked in chapter 1. Aristotle writes these chapters in good style, lucidly expressing himself, similar to the style of *NE* i–iv, so that what he means comes out clearly. Nevertheless, these two concluding chapters have been much discussed in modern scholarship, mostly because modern readers do not happen to like what Aristotle prima facie is saying.[18]

---

[18]   A summary of more recent discussions is in Natali 2001, 183–189. Aristotle seems to have an agenda different from what we would expect (see my comments in Section VI).

The problem is what use *sophia* and *phronēsis* have for a good life (1143b17–18). In fact, *sophia* is not concerned with the good for man, and *phronēsis* seems perhaps dispensable. The possible objections to *phronēsis* are the following. First, ethical virtue suffices for action, and there is no need at all for a virtue of the intellect having human praxis as object. Second, if *phronēsis* is useful to one who wants to become an honest man, and not to one who is already honest, then it will be useless to one who already knows how to live. Lastly, although perhaps *phronēsis* is indispensable, maybe it is sufficient to obey another who possesses it, as one does in the case of medical science, without acquiring it oneself (b21–35). It is to be noted that Aristotle does not even examine the possibility that *phronēsis* by itself suffices to live a good life since virtue of character is for him an indispensable component of truly good action.

The initial answer to the objections to *sophia* and *phronēsis* is that it is not correct to approach the question by just asking what they are "useful" for. Their desirability stems not from their producing anything but primarily from the fact that each is the excellence and perfection of a "part" of the soul. Here Aristotle refers to the distinction of parts of the soul made in vi 2. Besides, both intellectual virtues do produce something, but in a different way. *Sophia* produces happiness by being part of it, the most important part, as we will discover in book 10 (1144a3–6). It produces happiness simply by its activity, being the virtue of the best part of man. Here, however, the activity of *sophia* is only a part of complete happiness, and not the whole of it; this passage opposes attempts to reduce Aristotle's happy life to intellectual activity alone. Theoretical wisdom and practical wisdom are two intellectual virtues, whose activity is part of the complex whole called the "happy life" (Cooper 1975, 112).

About the objection specifically to *phronēsis*, the answer is much longer. Aristotle makes a sort of double mental experiment. First he says that moral virtue by itself does not suffice because it does not find the means to act well: "Our characteristic activity (ἔργον) is achieved in accordance with (κατά) practical wisdom and the virtue of character, for virtue makes the aim right and practical wisdom the things toward it" (1144a6–9). Aristotle says the same even more clearly in *EE* ii 11.1227b22–36:

Does virtue make the aim or what is done in view of the aim correct? We establish that it is the aim, because for this there is neither syllogism nor reasoning (οὐκ ἐστι συλλογισμὸς οὐδὲ λόγος) ... therefore, the end is the starting-point of reasoning, and the conclusion of reasoning is the starting-point of action. And if it is true that the cause of every right choice is either λόγος or moral virtue, and it is not λόγος, then moral virtue must be the cause of the rightness of the end, though not of what leads to the end. (cf. Woods 1982, 163–164)

The theory presented here may seem different from what we saw in chapter 2. There Aristotle stated that desire and reasoning must collaborate having the same object; here he indicates that virtue of character and virtue of intellect must collaborate having different objects, the end and the means. But the second argument will also overcome this apparent difference.

The argument runs as follows. If practical wisdom makes us more capable of acting (πρακτικώτεροι, 1143b24, 1144a11–12), we must distinguish it from calculative ability in general or δεινότης (1144a20–28). Practical wisdom, as the ability to find the means to a good end, is not *deinotēs*, but it does not exist without that type of ability. It is linked to the virtue of character, and it is impossible to be φρόνιμος without being good:

Practical wisdom does not arise in that eye of the soul without virtue, as we have said and as is clear. For practical syllogisms that have as first principle: "since such-and-such is the end and the chief good...," whatever it is (let it be anything you like for the sake of the argument). And this is evident to the good person alone, since wickedness distorts (διαστρέφει) our vision and thoroughly deceives us about principles. Manifestly, then, one cannot be practically wise without being good. (1144a29–b1)

In other words, "possession of practical wisdom" encompasses "possession of ethical virtue." He repeats that the correctness of the end depends on moral virtue, and the correctness of the means to the end depends on practical wisdom (1144a20–22). Yet, as we said before, practical wisdom must have some supposition of the end in order to deliberate about how to reach it.

The third argument starts from the reverse side. Again Aristotle wonders what one of the pair of terms, moral virtue and practical wisdom, would be without the other, but starts from the nature of virtue to show that it is necessarily linked to practical wisdom. Without practical wisdom, moral virtue would be only "natural virtue," a spontaneous and generic tendency to do good, without knowing how to achieve it in practice:[19]

Each of us seems to possess the character he has in some sense by nature, since right from birth we are just, prone to temperance, courageous, and the rest. Nevertheless we expect to find that what is really (κυρίως) good is something different, and that we shall possess these qualities in another way. (1144b4–8)

The difference is in the capacity of being successful. Natural virtue is like a strong but sightless body that may fall headlong when it moves because it cannot see (1144b10–12). Sight in a strong body corresponds to practical wisdom in the soul. It determines how to give concrete actualization to

---

[19] On natural virtue, see now Viano 2007.

one's natural tendencies by enabling those already having natural virtue to find the means to act on their good tendencies (Kenny 1974, 188). In this way the parallelism with the previous argument is perfect. There it was said that whoever has *deinotēs* knows how to find the means and that when he has ethical virtue, he has the right ends, and therefore his *deinotēs* is practical wisdom. Here it is said that whoever has natural virtue tends toward a good end, and when he has practical wisdom, he is able to find out how to act in practice, and thus his moral virtue is authoritative (κυρία, 1144b16).

In vi 12–13 Aristotle wants to say that in order for there to be an action according to virtue, it is necessary that there should be both an immediate response of desire in the sphere of passions and an analysis of the situation made by practical reasoning. The role of desire is to indicate the direction in which one must move, through a reaction of pleasure and pain; the role of practical reasoning is to determine exactly what the result is that is to be reached and how to arrive at it. The former by itself could provide only a confused and ineffectual reaction; the latter by itself would not lead to action, as it consists only in a judgment concerning the facts relating to action, like the case of good judgment. The two elements, moral virtue and practical wisdom, cooperate in giving rise to a good action.[20]

In the last section of vi 13, Aristotle makes a comparison between his position, Socrates' position, and the theories of some unnamed contemporaries (νῦν πάντες, 1144b21). Socrates also admitted a strong connection between moral virtue and *logos*, and was right in doing so, but he understood it in a wrong way. He identified the two things, and even identified practical wisdom with ἐπιστήμη, science. Aristotle's contemporaries are closer to the truth:

> Even today, whenever people define virtue, they all they say what state it is and what its objects are, and then add that it is a state in accordance with (κατά) right reason (ὀρθὸς λόγος). Right reason is that which is in accordance with practical wisdom; everyone, then, seems in some way to divine that the habit like this, in accordance with practical wisdom, is virtue. (1144b21–25)

We are close to answering the problem posed in chapter 1. There is the need only of further explication. The relationship between reasoning and virtue of character must be made closer:

---

[20] See also *NE* x 8.1178a16–19: "[The two] are joined, both practical wisdom with a virtue of character, and virtue with practical wisdom, for the principles of practical wisdom are in accordance with (κατά) the ethical virtues, and the right reasoning of ethical virtues is in accordance with practical wisdom." In moral virtue, reason and desire join forces and become one, like water and wine; they do not merely mix, like water and oil.

Virtue is not merely the state in accordance with (κατά) right reason, but that which involves (μετά) it, and right reason in these things is practical wisdom. Socrates, then, thought that the virtues were forms of reason ... while we think that they involve reason. (1144b25–30)

Whereas merely acting according to the directives of another person could be acting *according* to right reason, only those who *themselves* are practically wise act according to virtue that *involves* right reason. This is what Aristotle means by *orthos logos*. The second puzzle is answered shortly in lines 1145a6–10: practical wisdom does not govern theoretical wisdom but only issues prescriptions for the sake of it. The *Magna Moralia* later presented the same idea more clearly: "It is a kind of steward of philosophy and procures leisure for it" (1198b18–20).

VI. SOME FINAL CONSIDERATIONS

We expect the study of *phronēsis* to disclose the foundations of Aristotle's ethical position. But he did not see things in this way. Inquiry into *phronēsis* has a definite place in the development of Aristotle's position, after the definitions of happiness and of human virtue, as a complement to them. *Phronēsis* is the quality of the practically wise man, which, to be understood, needs the preliminary clarifications of some more basic concepts.

If we ask what qualities Aristotle considers typical of the practically wise man, a most important one is the capacity to assess a given situation and to find what is the best and more effective way of acting in it. There is no doubt that Aristotle insists very much upon this point; but the modern reader can be disappointed, because he expects a clarification of how to deliberate about ends, rather than a description of what enables a person to act effectively. This seems to many too limited a reflection and undeserving a philosopher's attention. Consequently, many scholars try to explain away these passages and to credit Aristotle with a kind of deliberation about ends. In doing this, they often give the impression of struggling with the texts. It is better, in my opinion, to ask why Aristotle insists so much on the connection between desire and reasoning and on the knowledge of the particular action to be done, as defining characteristics of practical wisdom. This is because one of Aristotle's more profound teachings in *NE* vi is that in practical matters success is important. Aubenque is right when he comments: "Il n'est pas permis d'être maladroit, lorque la fin est bonne."[21] If we think it appropriate to do some action leading to our happiness, or for the best state of our family and our country, we cannot afford to fail. The practically wise man

---

[21] When the end is good, it is forbidden to be clumsy.

according to Aristotle is no Machiavellian or Hegelian "beautiful soul,"
but for Aristotle no end is good if not specified and made possible
(Aubenque 1963, 63 and 136). It is the opposite of the motto attributed
to Melanchthon, *fiat justitia, pereat mundus*, who says that one should
behave morally, and not care about what happens.

Besides, at 1140a28 Aristotle says that the practically wise man deliberates "about what conduces to living well as a whole," and recently
there has been a discussion whether the conception of happiness must be
a practical premise of the deliberation of the *phronimos* or not (Cooper
1975, 76–88; *contra* Broadie 1991, 198–212; a good report of the more
recent discussion is Bostock 2000, 82–99). In my opinion, what Aristotle
says in the passage about "living well as a whole" is clear, yet it seems
strange to conceive of Pericles deliberating the following way: "Since
happiness is activity of the soul in accordance with complete virtue ... ,
then I must declare war on Sparta." Aristotle can be understood as simply
saying that the practically wise man deliberates in a way that de
facto conduces to Aristotelian happiness, even if he has not read the
Nicomachean Ethics and perhaps thinks only that his choice is *pros to
kalon*, for the noble, and fails to identify "the noble" consciously with
Aristotelian happiness. In fact, Aristotelian practical philosophy aspires
to clarify and give a foundation to what is already in the opinion of the
person having virtue, though in a confused and unclear way:

For every man has something of his own to contribute to the truth ... beginning
with things that are correctly said but in an unclear way he will arrive at clear
ones, always exchanging what is expressed in a confused statement with more
clear ones. (*EE* i 6.1217a30–35)

WORKS CITED

Allan, D.J. 1955. "The Practical Syllogism." 325–340 in *Autour d'Aristote. Recueil
d'Études de Philosophie Ancienne et Médiévale Offert à Monseigneur A. Mansion.*
Louvain: Presses Universitaires de Louvain.
Aubenque, Pierre. 1963. *La prudence chez Aristote.* Paris: Presses Universitaires de
France.
1965. "La prudence aristotélicienne porte-t-elle sur la fin ou sur les moyens?" *Revue
des Etudes Grecques* 78: 40–51.
Barnes, Jonathan. 1981. "Proof and the Syllogism." 17–59 in E. Berti ed. *Aristotle on
Science: The "Posterior Analytics."* Proceedings of the Eighth Symposium
Aristotelicum. Padova: Antenore.
Bekker, Immanuel. 1831. *Aristotelis opera.* Berlin: Reimer. Reprint, Berlin: De Gruyter,
1960–1970.
Berti, Enrico. 1993. "*Phronēsis* et science politique." 436–459 in P. Aubenque and
A. Tordesillas. *Etudes sur la Politique d'Aristote.* Paris: Presses Universitaires
de France Reprint, E. Berti, Nuovi studi aristotelici 38–59. Milan: Morcelliana,
2008.

Bodéüs, Richard. 2004. *Aristote. Ethique à Nicomaque*. Paris: Flammarion.

Bonitz, Hermann. 1870. *Index aristotelicus*. Berlin: Akademie Verlag. Reprint 1955 Graz: Akademische Druck- Und Verlagsanstalt.

Bostock, David. 2000. *Aristotle's Ethics*. Oxford: Oxford University Press.

Broadie, Sarah. 1991. *Ethics with Aristotle*. Oxford: Oxford University Press.

Broadie, Sarah, and Christopher Rowe. 2002. *Aristotle. Nicomachean Ethics*. Oxford: Oxford University Press.

Burnet, John. 1900. *The Ethics of Aristotle*. London: Methuen. Reprint 1988 Salem, NH: Ayer Company Publishers.

Bywater, Ingram. 1894. *Aristotelis Ethica nicomachea*. Oxford: Clarendon Press (OCT).

Cattanei, Elisabetta. 2009. "L'immaginario geometrico dell'uomo che delibera." 83–111 in M. Migliori and A. Firmani eds. *Attività e virtù. Anima e corpo in Aristotele*. Milan: Vita e Pensiero.

Charles, David. 2009. "*Nicomachean Ethics* VII.3: Varieties of *Akrasia*." 41–71 in C. Natali ed. *Aristotle's Nicomachean Ethics Book vii. Symposium Aristotelicum*. Oxford: Oxford University Press.

Cooper, John. 1975. *Reason and the Human Good in Aristotle*. Cambridge, MA: Harvard University Press.

Crisp, Roger trans. 2000. *Aristotle: Nicomachean Ethics*. Cambridge: Cambridge University Press.

Davidson, Donald. 1963. "Actions, Reasons, and Causes." *Journal of Philosophy* 60: 685–700. Reprinted 3–20 in D. Davidson, *Actions, Reasons and Causes*. Oxford: Clarendon Press, 1980.

————. 2001. "L'action." 299–331 in *Quelle philosophie pour le XXIième siècle? L'organon du nouveau siècle*. Paris: Gallimard.

Defradas, Jean. 1992. *Aristotle. Ethique à Nicomaque*. Paris: Presses Pocket.

Dirlmeier, Franz. 1956. *Aristoteles. Nikomachische Ethik*. Berlin: Akademie Verlag.

Dover, K. J. 1974. *Greek Popular Morality in the Time of Plato and Aristotle*. Oxford: Blackwell.

Engberg-Pedersen, Troel. 1983. *Aristotle's Theory of Moral Insight*. Oxford: Oxford University Press.

Fortenbaugh, W. W. 1975. *Aristotle on Emotion*. London: Duckworth.

Gadamer, H. G. 1960. *Wahrheit und Methode. Grundzüge einer philosophischen Hermeneutik*. Tübingen: Mohr.

Gauthier, R. A., and J. Y. Jolif. 1970. *Aristote, L'Ethique à Nicomaque*. 2 vols. 2nd ed. Béatrice Nauwelaerts ed. Louvain-Paris: Publications Universitaires de Louvain.

Grant, Alexander. 1885. *The Ethics of Aristotle*. London: Longmans, Green. Reprint 2005 Boston: Elibron Classics.

Greenwood, L. H. G. 1909. *Aristotle: Nicomachean Ethics Book Six*. Cambridge: Cambridge University Press.

Hardie, W. F. R. 1968. *Aristotle's Ethical Theory*. Oxford: Clarendon Press.

Heidegger, Martin. 1992. *Platon. Sophistes*. Frankfurt am Main: Kostermann.

Irwin, Terence. 1999. *Aristotle. Nicomachean Ethics*. 2nd ed. Indianapolis: Hackett.

Joachim, Harold Henry. 1951. *Aristotle. The Nicomachean Ethics: A Commentary*. D. A. Rees ed. Oxford: Clarendon Press.

Kenny, Anthony. 1978. *The Aristotelian Ethics: A Study of the Relationship between the Eudemian and the Nicomachean Ethics of Aristotle*. Oxford: Clarendon Press.

————. 1979. *Aristotle's Theory of the Will*. London: Duckworth.

Mignucci, Mario. 1975. *L'argomentazione dimostrativa in Aristotele: commento agli Analitici secondi*. Padova: Antenore.

Natali, Carlo. 2001. *The Wisdom of Aristotle*. Albany: SUNY Press.

Plebe, Armando. 1965. *Aristotele. Etica Nicomachea*. Rome-Bari: Laterza.

Ramsauer, G. 1878. *Aristotelis ethica Nicomachea*. Leipzig: Teubner.

Rassow, Hermann. 1862. *Beiträge zur Erklärung und Textkritik der Nikomachischen Ethik*. Weimar: Druck der Hof-Buchdruckerei.

Ross, David trans. 1915. *Aristotle: Nicomachean Ethics*, in The Works of Aristotle Translated into English. Vol. 9. Oxford: Clarendon Press.

Rowe, Christopher. 1971. *The Eudemian and Nicomachean Ethics: A Study in the Development of Aristotle's Thought*. Cambridge: Cambridge Philological Society.

Sherman, Nancy. 1989. *The Fabric of Character: Aristotle's Theory of Virtue*. Oxford: Clarendon Press.

Stewart, J. A. 1892. *Notes on the Nicomachean Ethics of Aristotle*. 2 vols. Oxford: Clarendon Press. Reprint 1999 Bristol: Thoemmes Press.

Susemihl, Franz. 1882. *Aristotelis Ethica Nicomachea*. Leipzig: Teubner (BT).

Thomas Aquinas. 1969. *Sententia libri ethicorum*. Roma: St. Thomas Aquinas Foundation ad Sanctae Sabinae.

Urmson, J. O. 1988. *Aristotle's Ethics*. Oxford: Blackwell.

Viano, Cristina. 2007. "Aristotle and the Starting Point of Moral Development. The Notion of Natural Virtue." 23–42 in S. Stern-Gillet and K. Corrigan eds. *Reading Ancient Texts*, vol. 2. Leiden: Brill.

Wartelle, André. 1982. *Lexique de la "Rhétorique" d'Aristote*. Paris: Les Belles Lettres.

Woods, Michael. 1982. *Aristotle's Eudemian Ethics. Books I, II and VIII*. Oxford: Clarendon Press.

Zeller, Eduard. 1892. *Die Philosophie der Griechen in ihrer geschichtlichen Entwicklung*. Vol. 2/2. Leipzig: Reisland.

10 Phronesis and the Virtues (*NE* vi 12–13)

I want to focus on three related points in Aristotle's account in *Nicomachean Ethics* vi 12–13 of the relation between practical intelligence and the virtues of character. The first is Aristotle's view that the choices we make in trying to act according to virtue must all be guided by practical intelligence, or what he calls phronesis (*NE* vi 12).[1] Here it will be important to understand both what it is that he thinks phronesis contributes to decision making and why he thinks that that contribution is so important.

Second, Aristotle's emphasis on phronesis shapes his entire view of what sort of thing a virtue is in the first place (*NE* vi 13). In particular, by making phronesis central to the virtues, Aristotle clearly focuses on the virtues as involving certain patterns of practical reasoning and choice, ways of responding to reasons to act and to feel. We can contrast this with accounts of the virtues that treat them as, for instance, simple dispositions to engage in certain behaviors stereotypical of the virtues (e.g., giving a lot to the poor in the case of generosity).

The third feature of Aristotle's account is a surprising result of certain ideas that emerge in his discussions of the other two: since phronesis is inseparable from all the virtues (*NE* vi 12) and each virtue requires phronesis (vi 13), it follows that each virtue is inseparable from all the virtues – to have any virtue is to have them all (vi 13). This thesis is often called the reciprocity of the virtues, and it is a provocative thesis to say the least.[2] Can it really be true that one can have any virtue only if one

---

[1] The Greek word *phronēsis* is often translated as "practical intelligence" or "practical wisdom." However, it has become a familiar enough word among philosophers that one can now simply speak of "phronesis" without translating.

[2] Sometimes this thesis is called the unity of the virtues or simply the unity of virtue. Whatever we call it, we should distinguish it from the much stronger thesis that all the virtues are the *same*. I shall return to that stronger thesis later. The way that names are assigned to these two theses can be confusing. Scholars of ancient philosophy are usually careful to distinguish these theses, which both appear in ancient ethics, and to give them different names, typically "the reciprocity of the virtues" (or "the unity of the virtues") and "the unity of virtue," respectively. Among modern virtue theorists, however, it is usually only the weaker reciprocity thesis that is discussed, and in

also has all the virtues? What human being has ever been completely virtuous, virtuous in absolutely every way? Some have found the reciprocity of the virtues so implausible that they have denied the very idea that the virtues might require phronesis. Yet doing so would be to throw out Aristotle's entire way of thinking about the virtues, when in fact there seems to be a lot of merit in the idea that the virtues require phronesis.

I. WHAT PHRONESIS CONTRIBUTES

Suppose that a generous person comes across a friend in need and, being generous, wants to do something helpful for his friend. How should he decide what to do to help? For Aristotle, the process of making that sort of decision can be broken down (in thought, anyway) into three basic parts. The first part is the one just mentioned: the goal or end from which deliberation begins, such as helping a friend in need. As Aristotle says, one's end as a doctor is healing a patient, one's end as an orator is persuading an audience, and one's end as a statesman is governing well (*NE* iii 3.1112b12–14; cf. *EE* ii 10.1227a18–21). It is here that deliberation begins: doctors deliberate about *how* to heal, not *whether* to heal, and likewise for the others. The same is true, of course, of a person with a virtue of character; for instance, one's end as a generous person is helping others in need, and so a generous person deliberates about how to act generously, not whether to do so. So in the generous person's deliberation, this first part of the process can be taken as given: it is virtue (*aretē*), Aristotle says, that makes one's end the correct end (*NE* vi 12.1144a7–8).

If the decision-making process begins with an end, then clearly another part of the process must be the task of finding effective means to that end. And this is what Aristotle says: deliberation begins from ends taken as given and proceeds to look for "things that are conducive to ends" (*NE* iii 3.1112b11–12, b33–34; cf. *EE* ii 10.1226b9–12, 1227a5 ff.).[3] Now, we may have thought that looking for means to the end would exhaust the deliberative process, and in fact some scholars have held that this is all there is to "things that are conducive to ends" (e.g., Walter 1874; Fortenbaugh 1975, 71–78, and 1991; Tuozzo 1991). However, that thought implicitly assumes that the end in question is already determinate enough that *all* that remains is to work out the means to it, and that assumption is very awkward if we think again about Aristotle's examples of people who deliberate about ends. For instance, the doctor as such has

different authors it can appear under any of these names. Fortunately, context will usually indicate which thesis an author intends.

[3] Throughout I use the translation of the *NE* by Roger Crisp (2000).

the end of curing his patient, but before a doctor can work out how best to administer a cure to a patient, he would first have to determine what would *constitute* a cure for this patient, here and now, in the first place. And we can see that the same is true for the end of persuading an audience or governing well: clearly, before one could think about the means to such ends, one would first have to determine what would constitute achieving those ends in the first place (see also Pakaluk 2005, 137–140; Price 2005, 269–270). The same is true, of course, of the end of helping a friend: this end is indeterminate, and one cannot work out means to it until one has determined what would constitute genuinely helping one's friend in the case at hand. So it seems likely that deliberating about "things that are conducive to ends" includes thinking about not only means to an end but also the very *specification* of that end in more concrete terms.[4] So the decision-making process, for Aristotle, would seem to involve these three parts: the indeterminate end from which deliberation begins, making the end determinate in the case at hand, and working out effective means to that determinate end.

Phronesis is crucial to good deliberation, Aristotle believes, because phronesis is a virtue of practical intellect that makes ends determinate in an excellent and appropriate way. It is because of one's virtue that one has the right end, Aristotle says, and it is because of one's phronesis that one does the right things toward that end (*NE* vi 12.1144a7–9). This is important: for Aristotle, possessing a virtue is not just a matter of having one's heart in the right place; in fact, he makes this point about phronesis in order to answer the objection that virtue might make a person admirable but is not very useful or practical (1143b18–36). Virtue involves wishing to do well, but it also involves actually *doing* well, and this requires practical wisdom or (what is the same thing) phronesis.

Accordingly, Aristotle maintains that phronesis involves an understanding of the human good as a whole (*NE* vi 5.1140a24–31) with the aim of doing well (*eupraxia*, 1140b6–7).[5] This is because it is the job of phronesis to determine what it would mean for the achieving of an end to

---

[4] See, e.g., Allan 1953 and 1955; Hardie 1968, 216, 226–227, 235; Monan 1968, 6off.; Irwin 1985, 346; Sherman 1989, 87–89; McDowell 1998, 110; Russell 2009, 6–11.

[5] Here there is a controversy over exactly how this understanding of the human good comes into play in deliberation. In particular, there is disagreement as to whether this understanding yields a "grand end" or blueprint of the good life within which particular actions are chosen as its components. Proponents of such a view include Hardie 1968, 233; Cooper 1975, 96–97; Irwin 1975, 570; Sorabji 1980, 206–207; Wiggins 1980, 223–225, 236–237; MacIntyre 1988, 131–133; Reeve 1992, 69; and Kakoliris 2003, 192. For a concentrated attack on this view, see esp. Broadie 1991. Broadie argues instead that phronesis concerns deliberation about local ends, such as acting generously in one's present circumstances, without choosing one's actions as components in a grand, overall design or blueprint (see Broadie 2007, 123–126; see also Russell 2009, 27–30).

count as a genuine benefit. Return to our earlier example. Suppose that someone meant to help a friend in need and had found the means to collect some money to give (say) and the means to get the money to his friend, but had failed to ask whether giving his friend money would in fact be beneficial. His friend now has more money than he had before, but perhaps what his friend needed in the long run was not the money but the encouragement (say) to get the money himself, and perhaps in this case the best perspective was that of the long run. True generosity, then, will require not just a respectable end and handiness about means but also the wisdom to make that end more determinate within a broader understanding of what benefits people. That is exactly what phronesis contributes to deliberation: phronesis makes the things we do for the sake of an end correct *by* correctly grasping the nature of the human good.

The importance of the contribution that phronesis makes to deliberation can be seen in a number of other things that Aristotle says about phronesis. For one thing, Aristotle famously says that virtue lies in a "mean" and aims at what is appropriate in action and emotion (*NE* ii 6–9), but of course to say that one's end is to do what is appropriate is not at all to say just what one's end is. Rather, it takes "right reason" (*orthos logos*) to discern what in the circumstances would be appropriate and neither excessive nor deficient (ii 2.1103b31–34; vi 1.1138b18–25, b32–34), and Aristotle takes phronesis to be the same thing as right reason (see vi 13.1144b25–30). For another, Aristotle characterizes phronesis as a whole family of skills of the practical intellect: deliberative excellence (*euboulia*), by which one finds courses of action that are correct and beneficial (vi 9); good judgment (*sunesis, eusunesis*), by which one is insightful and perceptive in one's comprehension (vi 10); discernment (*gnōmē*), which makes one reasonable, equitable, and sympathetic (vi 11.1143a19–24); and intelligence (*nous*), by which one is appreciative of the particularity of the circumstances in which one chooses and acts (1143a25–b17).[6] Clearly, Aristotle thinks of phronesis as a family of skills that all aim in an intelligent, perceptive way at finding what it would be beneficial to do within the here-and-now. These are (the outlines of) just the deliberative skills one would need in order to make an indeterminate end more determinate in a genuinely beneficial way.

Not surprisingly, Aristotle also identifies an intellectual skill of finding effective and efficient means to one's end, a skill he calls cleverness (*deinotēs; NE* vi 12.1144a23–26). Of course, Aristotle recognizes that even persons without the virtues can be clever about finding means (1144a26–36; cf. vi 5.1140b21–22); not every clever person has phronesis. However, interestingly, Aristotle says that there is no phronesis without

---

[6] See Louden 1997 for discussion. See also Hursthouse 2006.

cleverness (vi 12.1144a28–29). This claim is important: evidently, Aristotle believes that a person with phronesis does not just *try* to do what is appropriate – even "bungling do-gooders" may do that – but also takes steps to acquire the know-how he needs in order to actually *do* what is appropriate.[7]

However, there is disagreement among Aristotle's readers about the more precise relation between phronesis and cleverness. Some scholars read Aristotle as making phronesis and cleverness distinct intellectual skills concerned with different parts of the deliberative process, phronesis being the skill of making ends determinate in an appropriate way and cleverness the skill of finding effective means. Put another way, on this interpretation phronesis and cleverness are distinct skills that concern different deliberative tasks. Moreover, on this view cleverness is the same skill both in people with and in people without the virtues; it is simply an aptitude for finding effective means to one's end, *whatever* that end may be. By contrast, other scholars maintain that a single intellectual skill concerns *both* the specification of the end *and* the means to it. In a person without the virtues of character, that skill is *mere* cleverness, but in a person with the virtues it is the same thing as phronesis. On this view, phronesis is cleverness that has been transformed by virtue of character and made a genuine intellectual virtue.[8] Unfortunately, Aristotle's text does not seem to me to settle decisively which of these views he intended.

So far we have focused on how phronesis enables one to specify what it would be to achieve an end considered in isolation, but phronesis must do more than that if one's action is to be genuinely according to virtue. Suppose that lending one's friend money would genuinely benefit the friend, but that the money one lends had already been promised to another in repayment of a debt. In Aristotle's view, this would be a failure with respect not only to the virtue of justice but also to the virtue of generosity. For Aristotle, the virtues are excellences of human nature and especially our nature as rational and intelligent creatures (*NE* i 7.1097b22–1098a20). In particular, virtues of character (like courage, patience, and fairness) are excellences of humans considered as beings that make choices and experience emotions and desires, where these can be shaped by sound practical reasoning (i 13). In that case, a specification of a generous end that is unjust can involve at most a partial or myopic grasp of the good and, in this respect, involves significantly hampered practical reasoning. Such an

---

[7] See also Foot 1978, 165–166; Hursthouse 1999, 118, 148–149; Swanton 2003, 27; Russell 2005.

[8] For the former view, see Urmson 1988, 83, and Russell 2009, 24–25. For the latter, see Bostock 2000, 89, and Natali 2001, 53. On this point, I have benefited from discussions with Ron Polansky (who favors the latter view).

act therefore could not come from the virtue of generosity, if a virtue is an excellence. This is a plausible thing to say. Even if there is some level on which we admire the intentions of a person who is "generous with other people's money," so to speak, still such "generosity" – note the irony of the term in this context – would still be a serious failure to reason properly about how to help others appropriately. For Aristotle, then, such "generosity" does not really deserve the name, at least not in any very strict sense of a virtue that is an excellence of a rational creature.[9]

In order for phronesis to specify the end of a virtue in a fully excellent way, therefore, it must specify such ends not merely one at a time but in concert with a wide array of other relevant ends and constraints. It is for this reason that Aristotle makes two further claims about the nature of phronesis in the final chapters of *Nicomachean Ethics* vi. One is that the phronesis involved in deliberation about the ends of the virtues is the same no matter which virtue is concerned. There is not one phronesis for generosity and another for justice, say, but the same phronesis for all the virtues – as Aristotle puts the point, phronesis is "one" (*NE* vi 13.1145a1–2). This means that no matter which virtue may be one's primary concern in deliberation, phronesis employs the same global understanding of the human good that is relevant to every virtue (see Broadie 1991, 259; Annas 1993, 78). The other claim Aristotle makes is that phronesis requires all the virtues of character. Because phronesis is global rather than myopic in its perspective on human goods, it makes the end of one virtue determinate in a way that also situates that end within the ends of all the other virtues as well. Since deficiency or "corruptness" with respect to any virtue compromises this global perspective, Aristotle says, phronesis requires all the virtues (vi 12.1144a29–b1).

We can summarize this section as follows. For Aristotle, phronesis is a family of skills of the practical intellect by which one determines what it would be to act according to virtue, which is to act in a way that is both genuinely beneficial and appropriate overall. For this reason, phronesis must employ a single, global grasp of the human good, and it would be jeopardized by the lack of any of the virtues. Aristotle employs the latter two ideas in his argument for the reciprocity of the virtues, so we shall return to them in Section III.

II. THE VIRTUES REQUIRE PHRONESIS

Aristotle holds that phronesis requires all the virtues, but does he think one can possess a virtue without phronesis? Yes – but the virtues that

---

[9] Aristotle also thinks that there are virtues that are not rational excellences. We shall come to these in Section II.

require no phronesis are not the excellences of our rational nature, and Aristotle's interest in them is at most a passing one. Aristotle recognizes that we sometimes think of virtues in a rather loose sense, as for instance when we say that a child is naturally generous or compassionate, or even that certain animals are naturally brave or loyal (see *NE* vi 13.1144b1–9). Aristotle does not pause to offer any theory of these traits – which he calls "natural virtues" – but says only that they do not involve phronesis; this is what we should expect, since we attribute such traits to young children and even animals. This is not to say that the natural virtues are necessarily mindless dispositions, only that one does not have to have phronesis in order to have virtues in this sense.

Because he passes over the natural virtues so quickly, Aristotle leaves unanswered many questions we will probably have about them. Aristotle suggests that natural virtues can develop into virtues in adulthood, when coupled with phronesis (*NE* vi 13.1144b12–14); is that how the virtues develop *generally*? Do the natural virtues of childhood develop into vices in adulthood, if they are not coupled with phronesis? If so, is that how vices form generally? Aristotle simply does not say. Rather, Aristotle's interest in the natural virtues extends only to contrasting them in this crucial respect with the sorts of virtues on which he does focus: whereas the natural virtues do not involve phronesis, virtues in the strict or "real" sense do (1144b3–4, b6–8, b13–17, b30–32).

What does Aristotle mean by "real virtue," that is, virtue in the strict sense (*kuriōs aretē, aretē kuria*), and why does such virtue require phronesis? According to Aristotle, the contrast between phronesis and cleverness is parallel to that between virtue in the strict sense and natural virtue (*NE* vi 13.1144b1–4, b14–17). As we saw in Section I, Aristotle holds that phronesis is always good, good without qualification, whereas in some cleverness is a bad thing. Likewise, Aristotle now says that natural virtue, like cleverness, can be a bad thing: since it is not guided by phronesis, natural virtue is as likely to go wrong as right, like a body moving without the guidance of sight (1144b8–12). This is not surprising, since it is phronesis that makes one reliable at specifying one's end correctly and in a balanced, unified way.[10] By contrast, virtue in the strict sense is always good, reliably resulting in good actions (1144b12–14). In other words, virtue in the strict sense is the sort of virtue we discussed in Section I: virtue that is an excellence of our nature as creatures who direct themselves by practical rationality. In that case, any virtue of character that would be an excellence without qualification in a human being must be an attribute by which one reliably conforms to sound practical reasoning in action and emotion. Such character virtues represent a complete

---

[10] See Annas 1993, 74, and 2005; Hursthouse 2013, §2, and 2006, 288–290.

union and harmony between the two basic parts of the human psyche: the capacity for intellect and reasoning, and the capacity for feeling and desiring (see i 13). Virtue in the strict sense is virtue that is an excellence without qualification in a human being.

For that reason, Aristotle maintains that virtue in the strict sense is inseparable from phronesis. As Aristotle puts the point, virtue in the strict sense must be reliable in doing what is appropriate in action and feeling and avoiding the myriad ways in which one might go wrong in action and feeling (see *NE* vi 6–9). Moreover, we have seen that Aristotle believes that reliably doing what is appropriate requires, first of all, correctly apprehending what is appropriate through right reason (ii 2.1103b31–34; vi 1.1138b18–25, b32–34), that is, phronesis (vi 13.1144b25–30). Likewise, for Aristotle, to be human is to live a life of activity,[11] and as we have seen, it is only the virtues that are paired with phronesis that issue reliably in action that is excellent. Therefore, since the reliability characteristic of virtue in the strict sense requires the guidance of phronesis in deliberating and choosing, virtue in the strict sense must be paired with phronesis.

Consider, by contrast, a person with only the "natural" virtue of generosity. A person acting from such a natural virtue may do the right thing on some occasions, but since he lacks phronesis, this success is fortuitous, and on other occasions his "generous" actions may be well intended but unfortunately bungling. Likewise, such a "generous" person may do things that are good in some way (e.g., helpful to some) but bad in another way (e.g., unjust to others). Action that is reliably excellent, and that in a complete and overall way, therefore requires those virtues that are inseparable from phronesis. For all of these reasons, then, it could only be such virtues that are human excellences in the fullest sense and without qualification.

We have focused on Aristotle's contrast between virtues in the strict sense and the so-called natural virtues, but it will also be useful to contrast Aristotle's view of the virtues with certain other conceptions of virtue as well. Aristotle makes one such contrast himself, as he rejects the view (which he attributes to Socrates) that the virtues are all species of phronesis: the virtues are inseparable from phronesis, he says, but they are not the same thing as phronesis (*NE* vi 13.1144b17–30).[12] It is not surprising that Aristotle should reject such a view, since he thinks that phronesis is a virtue of the practical intellect, whereas the various virtues of character all involve emotions and desires as well (see vi 1.1138b35–1139a17 with i 13). For that reason, he says that the virtues

---

[11]   See *NE* i 5.1095b31–1096a2; x 6.1176a33–b2; *Politics* vii 3.1325a32–34, 1325b12–16.
[12]   As I noted earlier, scholars of ancient philosophy often call this stronger view the "unity of virtue."

of character are "in accordance with phronesis" but are not forms of phronesis themselves (vi 13.1144b25–30).[13]

Aristotle also distinguishes the virtues in the strict sense from traits or qualities that are not necessarily active – that is, from the sort of thing that we might call just "being a good person." After all, someone could still be a "good person" even if he did not do anything – as Aristotle puts the point, even if he just slept all the time (NE i 5.1095b31–33). But for Aristotle, to be human is to be active, and a human life is a life of activity. Any sort of virtue that consists in just being, rather than in acting, cannot be a human excellence without qualification, and so is not the kind of virtue that he has in mind.

Aristotle's virtues in the strict sense show themselves in activity, but again we should not mistake these virtues for dispositions to engage in certain behaviors stereotypical of the virtues, as for instance we might think of giving freely to others as stereotypical of generosity.[14] After all, as we have seen, a person can give freely to others even when doing so is not in fact very helpful to them. Because generosity in Aristotle's sense is paired with phronesis, a generous person would be skilled in discerning what would be genuinely beneficial and helpful to the recipients of his generosity – that is, discerning what doing something "generous" would actually amount to in the case at hand. Likewise, a person can give freely to some even when doing so is unfair to others or ruinous to himself. Because phronesis discerns what is beneficial in an *overall* way, it seeks out what would be generous *within* the whole body of relevant concerns. Put another way, the genuine virtue of generosity aims at what is appropriate in giving – it aims not at giving a lot or on many occasions, but at giving what, when, to whom, and in the way in which it is appropriate to give (see NE ii 6; iv 1.1138b18–34).

For the same reasons, Aristotle does not think of the virtues as each aiming at some good in isolation from other sorts of goods.[15] For instance, Inspector Javert in Victor Hugo's Les Misérables aims at a single good – namely, "justice" in the sense of upholding the law – and he relentlessly pursues the outlaw Jean Valjean in the name of that good. But Javert aims at that good in a myopic way, ignoring all those goods that might be realized through mercy, compassion, and reasonability. Consequently, it could not be phronesis that leads Javert to act as he does, and therefore whatever "justice" there may be in him is no virtue, as Aristotle understands virtue.

---

[13] However, in saying this Aristotle seems to assume a much sharper division between the rational and affective parts of the soul than he does at NE i 13.1102b23–28.

[14] See, e.g., Wallace 1978; Brandt 1981. See Watson 1984 for discussion.

[15] See, e.g., Walker 1989. See Watson 1984 for discussion.

Virtues on Aristotle's account also have what we might call psychological depth. On some non-Aristotelian theories of the virtues, virtues are little more than placeholder dispositions. For instance, some philosophers begin by identifying certain groups of actions that are held to be right or admirable and then think of a virtue as whatever makes one regularly prone to do such actions (perhaps without one's even realizing it, as in Driver 2001; see also Thomson 1997). To say that someone has a virtue, on such a view, would be to say (for instance) that the things that person does regularly have certain sorts of good consequences, or are admirable in a particular sort of way. On this sort of view, we focus on the person's actions without making any particular commitments as to the nature of that person's inner character. By contrast, for Aristotle to say that a person has a virtue is to say something deep about the person's character: that he has a certain kind of emotional life and that there are certain things that he desires (NE ii 3), that he has certain ends (ii 4.1105a31–32; vi 12.1144a7–8), that he deliberates and chooses in accordance with right reason (ii 2.1103b31–34; vi 1.1138b18–25, b32–34), and that in all of this he is firm and reliable (ii 4.1105a32–33).

Lastly, it is again important to note that for Aristotle, possessing a virtue is not simply a matter of having one's heart in the right place, so to speak. After all, there is nothing to keep a person without phronesis from having his heart in the right place, but for Aristotle, a properly virtuous person is no "bungling do-gooder." Now, some have supposed that if one's heart were *truly* in the right place, then ipso facto one would be *so* beneficently motivated that genuinely excellent actions would flow naturally and phronesis would be unnecessary (see Slote 2001). However, we should recall Aristotle's distinction between the virtue that gives one the right end (puts one's heart in the right place) and the skill of practical reasoning – phronesis – that works out what it would mean to achieve that end in present circumstances. For Aristotle, one cannot jump from having the right end to looking for the best means, bypassing the work of phronesis; that would be like setting oneself in motion without really looking where one is going (NE vi 13.1144b10–12), and that is a hazardous maneuver however sterling one's intentions.

In sum, Aristotle holds that virtue in the primary or strict sense must be reliable in acting well, and that this reliability is impossible without phronesis. Even if there are other sorts of virtues that lack phronesis, still these are unreliable in practice and are not genuine human excellences. For that reason, it is impossible to possess a virtue in the strict sense without also having phronesis.

In the final paragraphs of *Nicomachean Ethics* vi, Aristotle proceeds to draw an important implication – namely, the reciprocity of the virtues – from his discussion of the relation between phronesis and the virtues, so we now turn to that.

III. THE RECIPROCITY OF THE VIRTUES

We have seen in Section I that Aristotle believes that phronesis requires all the virtues (*NE* vi 12.1144a29–b1) and that phronesis is the same in the case of every virtue (vi 13.1145a1–2). We have also seen in Section II that every virtue requires phronesis (1144b14–17, b20–28, b30–32). Readers will have noticed what follows from these claims: if every virtue requires phronesis, which is one, and phronesis requires all the virtues, then every virtue requires all the virtues. Not surprisingly, Aristotle makes this conclusion explicit:

It is clear from what we have said, then, that we cannot be really good without practical wisdom (*phronēsis*), or practically wise (*phronimos*) without virtue of character. Moreover, on these lines one might also meet the dialectical argument that could be used to suggest that the virtues exist in isolation from one another. The same person, it might be argued, is not best suited by nature for all the virtues, so that he will already have acquired one before he has acquired another. This is possible in respect of the natural virtues, but not in respect of those on the basis of which a person is said to be really good; for he will possess all of them as soon as he acquires the one, practical wisdom. (1144b30–1145a2)

The thesis that every virtue requires possession of all the virtues is the thesis we called the reciprocity of the virtues. Again, it is important to distinguish this thesis from the much stronger thesis that all the virtues are in fact the same thing, a thesis that scholars of ancient philosophy usually call the unity of virtue. Aristotle rejects the stronger unity of virtue thesis: he holds that every virtue is connected to every other virtue through phronesis, but as we saw in Section II, he denies that the virtues are the same thing as phronesis (*NE* vi 13.1144b17–30).

But, of course, even the relatively weaker reciprocity thesis is bold and striking enough. Interestingly, it is a thesis shared by every major ancient school,[16] but in modern times it has drawn heavy criticism. Perhaps the most obvious criticism is that no one could have virtue in every way: we can all think of people who have genuine virtues, but it is too much to expect anyone to have *every* virtue. Now, this criticism is not that Aristotle accepts nothing short of *perfect* virtuousness. On the contrary, Aristotle acknowledges that achieving what is appropriate with respect

---

[16] For Plato, see *Protagoras* 329b–334c, 349a–362a; *Gorgias* 506d–507c; *Republic* iv 428a–444e. For the Stoics, see Arius Didymus, in Stobaeus, *Anthology* ii 5b5; Diogenes Laertius, *Lives* vii 126; Plutarch, *On Stoic Self-Contradictions* 1046e–f. For Epicurus, see Diogenes Laertius, *Lives* x 132.

to a virtue is extremely difficult (*NE* ii 6.1106b28–35; ii 9.1109a24–30), and he even leaves room to suppose that people can be virtuous even if they are somewhat wide of that mark in certain ways (1109a30–b26). That would be a plausible supposition: even if moderation rather than abstinence is the mean with respect to food and drink (see iii 11), it is still plausible that temperance in a person who is susceptible to abusing food or alcohol would steer more toward abstinence than toward moderation. Moreover, Aristotle argues that becoming virtuous is a lengthy, gradual, and apparently "scalar" process, rather like learning a language or a musical instrument (ii 4). It seems clear, then, that Aristotle thinks one need not possess a virtue to a degree beyond improvement in order to possess that virtue in a bona fide and strict sense.[17]

Rather, the criticism is that Aristotle seems to accept nothing short of *complete* virtue – that is, that to possess *any* virtue one must possess *every* virtue. So, for instance, even if a less-than-perfectly generous person can be a bona fide generous person, apparently Aristotle thinks that one cannot possess the virtue of generosity at all unless one also possesses the virtues of temperance, courage, justice, and so on.[18] Because such a standard of virtue is so stringent, some modern virtue theorists have weakened or even rejected outright the connection that Aristotle makes between virtue and phronesis, and between virtue and appropriate action (e.g., Adams 2006, ch. 10). If it is the connection between virtue and phronesis that makes all the virtues require each other, the worry goes, then perhaps we should sever that connection.[19]

Another common criticism is that Aristotle's defense of the reciprocity of the virtues is inadequate anyway. As we saw in Section I, Aristotle argues that because phronesis is a global grasp of what is beneficial, it is incompatible with corruption in any area of life with which the virtues are concerned (*NE* vi 12.1144a29–b1). However, several scholars object that it does not follow from this that what phronesis requires is virtue. Even if a person with phronesis must be free of corruption where every virtue is concerned, nonetheless such an absence of corruption need not rise to the level of virtuousness in the strict sense, rather than to, say, basic moral decency of some more modest sort.[20] Again, then,

---

[17] For discussion of this way of thinking about the virtues, see Swanton 2003, 24–25; see also Russell 2009, ch. 4.

[18] For representative criticisms of this thesis, see, e.g., Foot 1983; Walker 1989, 1990, and 1993; Flanagan 1991, 33 and ch. 12; Wolf 2007.

[19] The only modern supporter of the full-blown reciprocity thesis known to me is McDowell 1997. For arguments for substantially qualified versions of the reciprocity thesis, see Badhwar 1996; Hursthouse 1999, 153–157; Swanton 2003, 286–288.

[20] See, e.g., Watson 1984, 59–60; Lemos 1993; Wolf 2007, 162.

perhaps we should question the connection between phronesis and the virtues, in particular the idea that phronesis requires all the virtues.

However, things are not quite so simple. After all, for reasons we discussed in Section I it seems clear that phronesis does require a global grasp of what is beneficial in all areas of human action. Because that grasp must be global, it seems that it would be compromised, at least potentially, by any shortcomings of character in any area of human action (cf. Telfer 1989–1990, 44–45). Moreover, avoiding failure without such a grasp requires luck to make up for that shortcoming, so that even one who avoids failure in this way still will not do so *as* the virtuous person does.[21] And also because it is global, that grasp of what is beneficial in human action must be the same grasp in the case of every virtue (cf. Badhwar 1996, 320). Likewise, for reasons we discussed in Section II it seems hard to deny that virtues that count as genuine human excellences must all be paired with phronesis.[22] If all that is so, then it seems that the virtues have to be reciprocally connected through phronesis – to have one is to have them all – just as Aristotle says. And yet that conclusion is a difficult one to accept. So we seem to be at an impasse.

But perhaps such a conclusion would be hasty. Notice that the objections discussed so far take it for granted that the reciprocity of the virtues is a thesis about what is required for any person to count as having a virtue: in order for you or me to have any virtue, we would have to have all of them. Alternatively, we might suppose that the reciprocity of the virtues is instead an ideal of virtue to which we should all aspire. Even if none of us can be completely virtuous, still we all have room for improvement and should try to become as virtuous as we can.

Whatever the merits of this idea, however, Aristotle nowhere suggests it. On the contrary, he holds that we acquire the virtues within a surrounding culture, and in particular by imitating other persons who are virtuous already (see esp. *NE* ii 4), but he says nothing about striving toward an idealized abstraction of virtue. And in any case, while one should not be complacent or slack about one's shortcomings in virtue, surely the alternative to such complacency is not a quixotic effort to rise ever closer to an unobtainable ideal. Indeed, for Aristotle virtue is important in human life because of its centrality to human well-being (*eudaimonia*; i 7–10), not for the sake of becoming as nearly perfect a human specimen as one can.

Another possibility is that the reciprocity of the virtues is a thesis about a model or "regulative ideal" of the virtues (see Ackrill 1981, 137; Russell 2009, ch. 11). This approach leaves it an open question how far

---

[21]   I thank Mark LeBar for this point.
[22]   Cf. Watson 1984; Hursthouse 1999, 154; Russell 2009.

one ought to emulate the ideal and instead focuses on what the reciprocity thesis reveals about the nature of the virtues. In particular, the reciprocity thesis interpreted as a regulative ideal reveals that improvement with respect to (say) generosity lies in the direction of increased practical intelligence not only with respect to the ends of generosity itself but *also* with respect to the connections between those ends and the ends of other virtues. This means that the development of any virtue must go hand in hand with an expanding sensitivity to benefit and appropriateness in a wide range of areas of practical concern. Given such an ideal or model, we should expect to find that improvements in any virtue should contribute over time to improvements in other virtues as well; in other words, our model of the virtues should hold that every virtue is such as to require every other virtue the more it matures. Furthermore, it is by reference to such a regulative ideal that we understand just what counts as a shortcoming, and why, and how much it matters overall. Even if we must sometimes be serene about our shortcomings, a regulative ideal reveals what our shortcomings are and requires us to accept that *shortcomings* are precisely what they are. Likewise, critical assessment of one's character is to be framed in terms of such an ideal, as is any response to such criticism.[23] But in any case, it is important to note that Aristotle's language in *Nicomachean Ethics* vi 12–13 does not make it obvious precisely what interpretation of the thesis he intended.

The reciprocity of the virtues raises one more puzzle that we should note, this time a puzzle internal to the *Nicomachean Ethics* itself. Elsewhere in the *Ethics*, Aristotle discusses a pair of large-scale virtues (*NE* iv 2–3): magnificence (*megaloprepeia*), which is restricted to virtuous persons of considerable wealth, and magnanimity (*megalopsuchia*), which is possessed only by virtuous persons of high social prominence.[24] Here Aristotle faces a dilemma. On the one hand, if he maintains the reciprocity of the virtues, then it seems to follow that only the wealthy and prominent can possess any virtues at all, since only they can possess magnificence and magnanimity. On the other hand, if Aristotle holds (plausibly) that there are other virtues (e.g., generosity and proper pride,

---

[23] For a discussion of these features of regulative ideals in the context of practical rationality, see Davidson 1985, Rovane 1999, and Davidson's reply to Rovane in the same volume. For regulative ideals in the context of the virtues, see Russell 2009, ch. 4.

[24] Some scholars (e.g., Pakaluk 2002) argue that while such virtues involve largeness of scale, they are not necessarily restricted to highly prominent persons. However, it is worth noting that Aristotle's discussion of magnificence is set mainly in the context of *leitourgia*, an Athenian institution whereby the very wealthy provided costly public goods as a sort of income tax (see esp. *NE* iv 2.1122a24–25, 1122b33, 1123a12, a20–24). The scale in question, then, seems tightly linked to social prominence. Moreover, Aristotle explicitly makes magnanimity and magnificence parallel to one another with respect to scale and grandeur (*NE* iv 4.1125b1–8; ii 7.1107b16–1108a1).

iv 1 and 4) that can be possessed by persons without any special wealth or prominence, then it seems that it is possible to possess some virtues without possessing some others, after all.[25] Aristotle himself seems not to have noticed this problem. Perhaps this is not entirely surprising, if the *Ethics* was cobbled together by later editors from scattered writings, and Aristotle may have held different views about the relations between the virtues at different times. Alternatively, perhaps, as some scholars have argued, this apparent tension in the *Ethics* is only illusory and disappears upon a more careful reading of the passages concerned. For these and other reasons, the reciprocity of the virtues remains a challenge and a puzzle for Aristotle's readers.[26]

IV. CONCLUSION

Nothing could be more essential to Aristotle's theory than the idea that every virtue of character in the primary sense must be paired with phronesis. The pairing with phronesis shapes Aristotle's entire understanding of the nature of the virtues. It is because of that pairing that the virtues are excellences of human nature, without qualification; that the virtues are reliably connected to good action; that the virtues are intelligent rather than haphazard; that the virtues are broad in compass rather than myopic; and that the virtues represent the harmony of the rational and affective sides of our nature. And as Aristotle's account of the virtues is one that refuses to be ignored in modern discussions of the virtues, it is his position on the nature and importance of phronesis, perhaps more than anything else in his account, that continues to demand to be reckoned with.

[25] For discussion of this problem, see Irwin 1988a and 1988b; Kraut 1988; Gardiner 2001; and Pakaluk 2002.

[26] We could raise yet further problems for Aristotle here. For instance, consider the *diversity* of his list of the virtues: even if it is easy to see how generosity might require justice, it is much more difficult to see how it might require, say, a good sense of humor or wit (*NE* iv 8; see Jacobs and Zeis 1990, 651). Another problem arises from the *multiplicity* of Aristotle's list of virtues: although all ancient schools maintained that every virtue requires all the virtues, "all the virtues" takes on rather alarming proportions in Aristotle's theory. Not only did Aristotle produce by far the longest catalog of virtues (i.e., basic or "cardinal" virtues), but even then it is not obvious either that Aristotle regarded that catalog as complete (although some take iii 5.1115a5 to suggest this; see, e.g., Reeve 1992, 169–170) or how one could determine when such a catalog was complete in the first place (see Russell 2009, ch. 7). It is likely that Aristotle thought that the virtues should cover all of the "key areas" of life (e.g., one's finances, emotions like fear and confidence, etc.), but it is far from obvious either that Aristotle's catalog does cover all such areas or that he thought it did. It is even less obvious how to identify such "key areas," how to individuate them, and how to know when they have all been identified.

WORKS CITED

Ackrill, J. L. 1981. *Aristotle the Philosopher*. Oxford: Oxford University Press.

Adams, R. M. 2006. *A Theory of Virtue: Excellence in Being for the Good*. Oxford: Oxford University Press.

Allan, D. J. 1953. "Aristotle's Account of the Origin of Moral Principles." *Actes du XIe Congrès International de Philosophie* 12: 120–127.

1955. "The Practical Syllogism." 325–340 in J. Moreau ed. *Autour d'Aristote: Recueil d'études offert à Mgr Mansion*. Louvain: Publications Universitaires.

Annas, J. 1993. *The Morality of Happiness*. Oxford: Oxford University Press.

2005. "Comments on John Doris' *Lack of Character*." *Philosophy and Phenomenological Research* 71: 636–642.

Badhwar, N. 1996. "The Limited Unity of Virtue." *Nous* 30: 306–329.

Bostock, D. 2000. *Aristotle's Ethics*. Oxford: Oxford University Press.

Brandt, R. B. 1981. "W. K. Frankena and the Ethics of Virtue." *Monist* 64: 271–292.

Broadie, S. 1991. *Ethics with Aristotle*. Oxford: Oxford University Press.

2007. *Aristotle and Beyond*. Cambridge: Cambridge University Press.

Cooper, J. 1975. *Reason and Human Good in Aristotle*. Cambridge, MA: Harvard University Press.

Crisp, R. trans. 2000. *Aristotle: Nicomachean Ethics*. Cambridge: Cambridge University Press.

Davidson, D. 1985. "Incoherence and Irrationality." *Dialectica* 39: 345–354.

Driver, J. 2001. *Uneasy Virtue*. Cambridge: Cambridge University Press.

Flanagan, O. 1991. *Varieties of Moral Personality*. Cambridge, MA: Harvard University Press.

Foot, P. 1978. "Morality as a System of Hypothetical Imperatives." 157–173 in *Virtues and Vices and Other Essays in Moral Philosophy*. Berkeley: University of California Press.

1983. "Moral Realism and Moral Dilemma." *Journal of Philosophy* 80: 379–398.

Fortenbaugh, W. 1975. *Aristotle on Emotion: A Contribution to Philosophical Psychology, Rhetoric, Poetics, Politics, and Ethics*. London: Duckworth.

1991. "Aristotle's Distinction between Moral Virtue and Practical Wisdom." 97–106 in J. P. Anton and A. Preus eds. *Essays in Ancient Greek Philosophy IV: Aristotle's Ethics*. Albany: SUNY Press.

Gardiner, S. 2001. "Aristotle's Basic and Nonbasic Virtues." *Oxford Studies in Ancient Philosophy* 20: 261–296.

Hardie, W. F. R. 1968. *Aristotle's Ethical Theory*. Oxford: Oxford University Press.

Hursthouse, R. 1999. *On Virtue Ethics*. Oxford: Oxford University Press.

2006. "Practical Wisdom: A Mundane Account." *Proceedings of the Aristotelian Society* 106: 283–307.

2013. "Virtue Ethics." http://plato.stanford.edu/archives/fall2013/entries/ethics-virtue/.

Irwin, T. 1975. "Aristotle on Reason, Desire and Virtue." *Journal of Philosophy* 72: 567–578.

1985. *Aristotle: Nicomachean Ethics*. Indianapolis: Hackett.

1988a. "Disunity in the Aristotelian Virtues." *Oxford Studies in Ancient Philosophy* 7: 61–78.

1988b. "Disunity in the Aristotelian Virtues: Reply to Richard Kraut." *Oxford Studies in Ancient Philosophy* 7: 87–90.

Jacobs, J., and J. Zeis. 1990. "The Unity of the Vices." *The Thomist* 54: 641–653.

Kakoliris, G. 2003. "Refuting Fortenbaugh: The Relationship between *Ethike Arete* and *Phronesis* in Aristotle." *Philosophia* (Athens) 33: 183–193.

Kraut, R. 1988. "Comments on 'Disunity in the Aristotelian Virtues.'" *Oxford Studies in Ancient Philosophy* 7: 79–86.

Lemos, J. 1993. "The Unity of the Virtues and Its Recent Defenses." *Southern Journal of Philosophy* 31: 85–106.

Louden, R. 1997. "What Is Moral Authority? Εὐβουλία, σύνεσις, and γνώμη vs. φρόνησις." *Ancient Philosophy* 17: 103–118.

MacIntyre, A. 1988. *Whose Justice? Which Rationality?* Notre Dame, IN: University of Notre Dame Press.

McDowell, J. 1997. "Virtue and Reason." 141–162 in R. Crisp and M. Slote eds. *Virtue Ethics*. Oxford: Oxford University Press.

    1998. "Some Issues in Aristotle's Moral Psychology." 107–128 in S. Everson ed. *Companions to Ancient Thought, 4: Ethics*. Cambridge: Cambridge University Press.

Monan, J. 1968. *Moral Knowledge and Its Methodology in Aristotle*. Oxford: Oxford University Press.

Natali, C. 2001. *The Wisdom of Aristotle*. G. Parks trans. Albany: SUNY Press.

Pakaluk, M. 2002. "On an Alleged Contradiction in Aristotle's *Nicomachean Ethics*." *Oxford Studies in Ancient Philosophy* 20: 201–220.

    2005. *Aristotle's Nicomachean Ethics*. Cambridge: Cambridge University Press.

Price, A. W. 2005. "Aristotelian Virtue and Practical Judgment." 257–278 in C. Gill ed. *Virtue, Norms, and Objectivity*. Oxford: Oxford University Press.

Reeve, C. D. C. 1992. *Practices of Reason: Aristotle's Nicomachean Ethics*. Oxford: Oxford University Press.

Rovane, C. 1999. "Rationality and Identity." 463–482 in L. E. Hahn ed. *The Philosophy of Donald Davidson*. La Salle, IL: Open Court.

Russell, D. C. 2005. "Aristotle on the Moral Relevance of Self-Respect." 101–121 in S. Gardiner ed. *Virtue Ethics, Old and New*. Ithaca, NY: Cornell University Press.

    2009. *Practical Intelligence and the Virtues*. Oxford: Oxford University Press.

Sherman, N. 1989. *The Fabric of Character*. Oxford: Oxford University Press.

Slote, M. 2001. *Morals from Motives*. Oxford: Oxford University Press.

Sorabji, R. 1980. "Aristotle on the Role of Intellect in Virtue." 201–219 in A. O. Rorty ed. *Essays on Aristotle's Ethics*. Berkeley: University of California Press.

Swanton, C. 2003. *Virtue Ethics: A Pluralistic View*. Oxford: Oxford University Press.

Telfer, E. 1989–1990. "The Unity of Moral Virtues in Aristotle's *Nicomachean Ethics*." *Proceedings of the Aristotelian Society* 91: 35–48.

Thomson, J. J. 1997. "The Right and the Good." *Journal of Philosophy* 94: 273–298.

Tuozzo, T. 1991. "Aristotelian Deliberation Is Not of Ends." 193–212 in J. P. Anton and A. Preus eds. *Essays in Ancient Greek Philosophy IV: Aristotle's Ethics*. Albany: SUNY Press.

Urmson, J. O. 1988. *Aristotle's Ethics*. Oxford: Blackwell.

Walker, A. D. M. 1989. "Virtue and Character." *Philosophia* 64: 349–362.

    1990. "Character and Circumstance." *Moral and Social Studies* 5: 39–53.

    1993. "The Incompatibility of the Virtues." *Ratio* 6: 44–62.

Wallace, J. D. 1978. *Virtues and Vices*. Ithaca, NY: Cornell University Press.

Walter, J. 1874. *Die Lehre von der praktischen Vernunft in der griechischen Philosophie*. Jena: Mauke's Verlag.

Watson, G. 1984. "Virtues in Excess." *Philosophical Studies* 46: 57–74.

Wiggins, D. 1980. "Weakness of Will, Commensurability, and the Objects of Deliberation and Desire." 241–265 in A. O. Rorty ed. *Essays on Aristotle's Ethics*. Berkeley: University of California Press.

Wolf, S. 2007. "Moral Psychology and the Unity of the Virtues." *Ratio* 20: 145–167.

11   Was Aristotle a Humean?
      A Partisan Guide to the Debate

I. THE DEBATE

How much power does Aristotle grant to practical reason? He seems to characterize it as purely instrumental: as on Hume's view, our passions and desires set our goals, and reason is relegated to working out how to achieve them. And yet the whole tenor of his discussion of practical reason, and in particular of its virtue, *phronēsis*, seems distinctly un-Humean: practical reason has an authority and an ethical significance that no Humean would allow. What then is his view?

The prima facie evidence for a Humean interpretation is strong. First, Aristotle argues repeatedly that practical reasoning – deliberation – is never about which goals to pursue but only about "things toward" goals (*ta pros ta telē*) – that is, about ways to achieve them (see especially *NE* iii 3 and *EE* ii 10). Second, when he does address the question of how we get our goals – which he does in a series of passages that I will call the Goal passages – he attributes that function not to any kind of reasoning but instead to our ethical characters:

Virtue makes the goal right, *phronēsis* [the excellence of practical reason] the things toward the goal.[1] (*NE* vi 13.1144a7–9)

Decision (*prohairesis*) won't be right without *phronēsis* nor without virtue: for the one makes us do the end and the other the things toward it. (vi 13 1145a4–6)

Virtue and vice respectively keep healthy, and corrupt, the starting point, and in actions the that-for-the-sake-of-which [i.e., the goal] is the starting point, just as in mathematics the hypotheses are. Neither indeed in that case is the *logos* [reasoned account] instructive of the starting points, nor in this case, but virtue either natural or habituated [is instructive] of right belief about the starting point. (vii 8.1151a15–19)

For discussion of this material I am grateful to John Cooper, Cian Dorr, Terry Irwin, Hendrik Lorenz, Anthony Price, Kieran Setiya, Ralph Wedgwood, and audiences at Oxford and Cambridge; for very helpful comments on this contribution I thank Rachel Barney, Cian Dorr, and Kristen Inglis.

[1]   Here, as he often does, Aristotle uses *aretē* as shorthand for *ēthikē aretē* – character virtue, in contrast with intellectual virtues like *phronesis*; I follow suit by using "virtue" on its own to mean character virtue. Translations are my own unless otherwise noted.

Does virtue make the goal right or the things toward the goal? We suppose the goal, because there is no syllogizing or *logos* about this. Instead, this must just like a starting point be laid down. (*EE* ii 11.1227b23–25)

Character, not reasoning, gives us our goals. Moreover, character is evidently a state of the nonrational part of the soul, the seat of the passions (*NE* i 13, *EE* ii 1). Therefore it would seem that our emotions and desires set our goals, and reason's task is only to work out how to achieve them. And therefore some scholars have argued – or assumed – that Aristotle is indeed a Humean (e.g., Walter 1874 and Fortenbaugh 1964).

But this turns out to be only half the story. For there are a number of excellent reasons to think that Aristotle cannot be a straightforward Humean.

First and most strikingly, far from agreeing that reason "is and ought only to be the slave of the passions," Aristotle argues that passion can and should be a slave to reason – or rather, a willing servant, pupil, or child (see *NE* i 13, iii 12, and vii 6). Second, he describes the kind of desire we have for things *qua* goals not as a nonrational passion but instead as something distinctively rational – or at least distinctively human, not shared with lower animals: wish (*boulēsis*). So deliberative reason evidently serves not passions but something itself rational. Third, he distinguishes *phronēsis* from mere cleverness (*deinotēs*) – efficiency in instrumental reasoning (*NE* vi 12), and fourth, he endows *phronēsis* with enormous ethical import: without it, one cannot have any of the character virtues, and with it one has them all (*NE* vi 13). Both of these claims imply that excellent practical reasoning is something more than merely figuring out how to get what one happens to desire.

Finally, there are a number of passages that have been thought to confirm this by attributing to *phronēsis* the very role the Goal passages apparently attributed to character virtue: the setting of ends. Most of these passages are in fact easily accommodated by the Humean reading, and I will ignore them here,[2] but one is much harder to dismiss: in *NE* vi 9 he evidently calls *phronēsis* "true supposition of the end" (1142b31–33). Ends, it would now seem, are the province of practical reason after all. And so scholars – probably a majority at this point – have argued that Aristotle is more of a Kantian about practical reason: that on his view we reach our goals through reasoning, and the job of nonrational passion and desire is simply to follow along.[3]

---

[2] For detailed arguments, see Moss 2011 or 2012.

[3] See Allan 1953; Gauthier and Jolif 1958–1959; Irwin 1975; Sorabji 1973–1974; and Cooper 1975 among others. For extended discussion of Humean and anti-Humean elements in Aristotle's thought, and attempts to reconcile them, see among others Irwin 1975 and Smith 1996.

Was Aristotle then a Humean, or was he not? Or was he simply confused, or inconsistent? My aim is to canvass various strategies for reconciling the opposing evidence, in hopes of showing the best way forward. We will see that neither the straightforward Humean reading nor the stark anti-Humean reading can accommodate all the textual evidence, and we will see the outlines of a reading that can. On Aristotle's view, nonrational character does indeed fix our ends, but practical reasoning nonetheless plays a very un-Humean role with respect to the end, in two ways. First, it is reason's job to grasp what one's character has fixed as a goal, and also to recognize it *as* a goal. Second, the reasoning that goes into figuring out how to achieve the virtuous person's goal requires an ethical sensitivity totally lacking in mere instrumental efficiency. And this, I will argue, allows us to reconcile the claim that nonrational virtue supplies our goals with the claim that reason can be passion's master rather than its slave.

Elsewhere I have addressed in detail the apparent textual evidence for the stark anti-Humean reading and provided extensive arguments for the quasi-Humean reading I defend in its place.[4] My project here is to show in broader strokes that this quasi-Humean view does the best job of accommodating Aristotle's texts, and moreover to show that it is a view that we should attribute to him gladly, for it is one worth holding.

II. ANTI-HUMEAN STRATEGIES

How do those impressed by the un-Humean elements in Aristotle's ethics propose to address the apparent evidence for the Humean view? Let us recall that evidence and consider possible strategies for accommodating it.

1. *Deliberation Is Not of Ends*

Aristotle says this so often and so clearly that there can be no doubt that he means it. But perhaps he does not mean it precisely as the Humean takes it. Perhaps he means that deliberation has to start from an undeliberated end but that in many cases that end is hopelessly general, so that in working out the "things toward the end" we are specifying the *components* of the end. Thus, most of our ends – including crucially our ultimate end, whatever we take to be *eudaimonia* (e.g., pleasure or the life of virtue) – are after all chosen through deliberation.

---

[4] Moss 2011; see also chapters 7 and 8 of Moss 2012. I have at a few points repeated short excerpts from those works here.

Can this be the right reading of Aristotle? It is hardly a charitable one. For if we take this line, we wind up dismissing as massively overstated the distinction to which Aristotle draws so much attention in his discussion of deliberation, and especially in the Goal passages, between being right about ends and being right about things toward them: on this view – as its proponents explicitly acknowledge – *phronēsis* is actually in charge of both.[5]

There is another strategy available, however: perhaps Aristotle means simply that in any episode of deliberation one must take something as one's end, and one cannot deliberate about whether or not that is one's end at the same time as deliberating about how to achieve it. This seems plausible in its own right, although it does saddle Aristotle with a failure to say clearly what he means. Unfortunately, however, it runs seriously afoul of the analogies he draws between practical reasoning and theoretical reasoning.

The starting points (*archai*) from which we reason in the theoretical realm are postulates or definitions from which we produce (in the highest case) demonstrations; the starting points of deliberation are the goals that we deliberate about how to achieve. The starting points of demonstration, Aristotle frequently argues, are not themselves the product of any demonstration: demonstration must begin from something indemonstrable. The analogy between the two forms of reasoning drawn, for example, in two of the preceding Goal passages thus implies that the starting points of deliberation – goals – are the sort of thing that *could* not be the products of deliberation.

This same analogy, however, may seem to suggest a third and more promising anti-Humean strategy: a way to give reason dominion over our ends while taking Aristotle's restrictions on deliberation at face value. For although the starting points of theoretical reasoning are not products of reasoning in the strict sense, they are nonetheless a function of intellect, and indeed of intellect in its highest form: *nous*. Thus, many have argued that – despite his evident silence on the point – this is Aristotle's account of practical reasoning too. Our goals – the starting points of deliberation – are set by reason in a nondeliberative capacity: they are the product of *nous*.[6]

The first strategies have to argue that Aristotle did not mean what he said about how we get our ends (since he seems to deny that we get them through deliberation); this one has to argue that he did not say

---

[5] "Practical intellect is not concerned with means *as opposed to* ends. Insofar as it is concerned with constituent 'means,' it is also concerned with ends" (Irwin 1975, 571); compare Wiggins 1980.
[6] See Cooper 1975; Dahl 1984; and Reeve 1992.

what he meant (since he never attributes them to *nous*).[7] All three, however, also face a far more formidable objection: as we have already seen from the Goal passages, Aristotle has plenty to say about how we *do* get our ends, and here the credit goes neither to deliberation nor to *nous* nor to any other form of reason, but instead to character virtue. It is not just that he explicitly denies that there is *logos* or *sullogismos* (reasoning) about the starting points of deliberation, and neglects to mention that there is *nous* of these starting points instead; it is also that he explicitly and repeatedly claims that it is character virtue that "makes the goal right," or "is instructive of the goal" (*NE* vi 13, vii 8, and *EE* ii 11, quoted earlier).

Indeed, in addition to the explicit claims of the Goal passages, there are other passages that strongly imply that one's view of ends is a feature of the kind of character one has:

Suppose someone said that everyone longs for the apparent good, but they are not in control of the appearance: whatever sort of person one is, in that way the end appears to one.[8] (*NE* iii 5.1114a31–b1)

Should we say that what is wished for without qualification is the good, but for each person the apparent good? For the virtuous person, then, what is wished will be what really is [good/to-be-wished-for], while for the base person what is wished for is some chance thing. ... For the virtuous person discerns each thing rightly, and in each case the truth appears to him. For distinctive things are fine and pleasant in accordance with each character state, and the virtuous person presumably excels the most at seeing the truth in each case, being like a standard and measure of these things. (iii 4.1113a23–33)

Practical syllogisms have a starting point: "Since the end and the best is of such a sort. . . ." And this does not appear except to the good man. For vice perverts, and makes us be deceived about the practical starting points. (vi 12.1144a31–36)

You aim in life for what appears good to you, but what appears good to you is fixed by the kind of character you have: if you are vicious, base things will appear good to you, and you will therefore have bad ends; if you are virtuous, fine things will appear good to you, and your ends will therefore be correct. One way to put the point is: if all you want is for your child to aim at the right ends, do not waste time on her reasoning skills but shape her character instead. Guiding her to do

---

[7] Some take 1143a35–b5 as evidence that ends are grasped by *nous*, but as Cooper (despite his embrace of the view) rightly argues, this is a misreading (1986, 42n).

[8] This is part of a complicated argument for the conclusion that we should be held responsible for our characters. For my purposes, what is crucial is the correlation of the way the end appears with the kind of ethical character one has, and it is clear that Aristotle takes this as established: what is up for debate in the passage is whether we have control over our characters, which would give us indirect control over the appearance of the end.

certain kinds of actions habitually will shape her character (*NE* ii 1–4) and thereby give her her view of the end:

The many and most vulgar seem not unreasonably to suppose *on the basis of their lives* that the good, that is, *eudaimonia*, is pleasure.[9] (*NE* i 5.1095b14–19, emphasis added)

It would be superfluous to examine all the beliefs that people have about *eudaimonia*. ... For it is absurd to apply reasoning (*logos*) to those who have need not of reasoning but of experience (*pathos*). (*EE* i 3.1214b28–1215a3)

It is experience (upbringing, habituation) and character, not deliberation, argument, or any other intellectual exercise, that fixes our ends.

Is all this decisive against the anti-Humean reading? No: there are two broad strategies for attempting to reconcile the claim that "virtue makes the goal right" with the anti-Humean view that reason sets our end. One could deny that Aristotle holds that character virtue literally supplies the goal, or one could deny that he thinks character virtue wholly nonrational. Let us consider these points in turn.

2. *Virtue Supplies the Goal*

Perhaps "virtue makes the goal right" does not mean that virtue literally supplies our goals. Some argue that the claim of the Goal passages is instead simply that virtue makes us *want* the goal that reason supplies, or that without virtue, nonvirtuous desires will corrupt reason, making it choose bad ends.[10]

These strategies too, however, wind up accusing Aristotle of not saying what he meant, and of implying a good deal that he did not mean. Consider again the passage on parallels between practical and theoretical reasoning from *EE* ii 11.1227b23–30:

Does virtue make the goal right or the things toward the goal? We suppose the goal, because there is no syllogizing or *logos* about this. Instead, this must just like a starting point be laid down.... For just as in theoretical sciences the hypotheses are our starting points, so in the productive ones the end is a starting point and hypothesis.

---

[9] The point is made more general if we follow Irwin in transposing 1095b16 with what follows (b17–19): he translates "people quite reasonably reach their conception of the good, i.e., of happiness, from the lives [they lead]; for there are roughly three most favored lives: the lives of gratification, of political activity, and, third, of study. The many, the most vulgar, would seem to conceive the good and happiness as pleasure."

[10] For the former strategy, see, e.g., Allan 1953; for the latter, see, e.g., Irwin 1999, in his commentary on *NE* vi 5.1140b11–19.

Virtue "lays down" (*hupokeisthai*) the starting points for deliberation, just as the starting points of demonstration are "laid down." Aristotle emphasizes the analogies between starting points in the two realms, and makes no mention of any disanalogies. The very strong implication is that just as the starting points of mathematics are literally supplied by something distinct from mathematical reasoning – induction resulting in *nous* (see *Metaphysics* i 1 and especially *Posterior Analytics* ii 19) – so too the starting points of practical reasoning are literally supplied by something distinct from practical reasoning: virtue. (We will see more on this parallel below.)

Moreover, this is the overwhelmingly straightforward reading of the Goal passages. After all, they describe parallel roles for *phronēsis* and virtue: whatever it is that *phronēsis* does in relation to the things toward the goal ("make them right," "make us do them"), virtue does in relation to the goal itself. And surely what *phronēsis* does in relation to the things toward the goal is literally to identify them – tell us what they are. Thus the clear implication of the Goal passages is that virtue dictates what the goal is. This is all but explicit in the passage from *NE* vii 8: virtue is *didaskalikos* of – instructive of, teaches us – the goal.

3. *Virtue Is Nonrational*

We have seen strong evidence that character virtue literally gives us our ends. If character virtue is as usually thought a state of the nonreasoning part of the soul, then Aristotle now looks very Humean indeed. But perhaps it includes intellectual elements, and it is these rather than the nonrational elements that fix our ends.[11] Perhaps the habituation that shapes character involves not merely doing certain actions and feeling certain passions, but also reflecting and reasoning about what one is doing and feeling, and perhaps the character virtue that results is correspondingly a partly intellectual state.[12]

If this is Aristotle's view, however, he seems to go out of his way to obscure it. Throughout the ethical works he repeatedly insists on a sharp distinction between ethical virtues and intellectual virtues, and an equally sharp distinction between the habituation that produces the former and the teaching that produces the latter (see especially *NE* i 13–ii 1, and *EE* ii 1 and ii 4). To doubt the fixity of these distinctions is to accuse Aristotle of systematically misleading his readers. The textual evidence against this particular strategy is consistent and strong; the textual

[11] For the view that character has intellectual components and thus overlaps with *phronēsis*, see, e.g., Irwin 1975 and Lorenz 2009; for extensive arguments against this view, addressing the putative textual evidence in detail, see Moss 2011 or 2012.

[12] For this view, see, e.g., Sorabji 1973–1974.

evidence in favor of it is sparse and weak.[13] If we can find another way to make sense of Aristotle's ethics, we should.

To sum up: there are various anti-Humean strategies for accommodating Aristotle's apparent Humeanism, but they do so at the cost of undermining the distinctions and analogies most central to Aristotle's moral psychology. Aristotle sharply distinguishes nonrational character virtue from rational *phronēsis*, sharply distinguishes ends from things toward them, and consistently attributes the ends to character virtue, reserving only the things toward them for *phronēsis*. It is no accident that anti-Humeans often wind up accusing Aristotle of being "misleading," of "lapses," or of being simply inconsistent in his claims.[14] The stark anti-Humean reading is distinctly uncharitable to Aristotle: if the Humean reading can do better we should embrace it.

III. HUMEAN STRATEGIES

Can the Humean reading accommodate the various elements of Aristotle's ethics that seem so un-Humean? Let us take these in turn, and consider possible responses.

1. Reason Is Passion's Master Rather than Slave

The true Humean interpreter is in fact something of a straw man: I know of no one who actually argues that Aristotelian reason is a slave to passion. But if the role of reasoning is simply to achieve the goals firmly fixed by nonrational character, what room could there be for reason to be passion's master? Perhaps one might argue that even Humean instrumental reason often commands passion to delay its gratification, or to seek it in somewhat different objects. Can this be what Aristotle has in mind? Surely not. When he says that the nonrational part should listen, obey, be persuaded by, and agree with the rational part, or do "as the *logos* commands (*tattei*)," that the virtuous person wishes "not to be led by passion, but as the *logos* commands," or that "courage is attendance (*akolouthēsis*) on the *logos*, and the *logos* orders (*keleuei*) one to choose

---

[13] Perhaps the main textual argument for the view of character virtue as partly rational is Aristotle's description of it as a *hexis prohairetikē*, disposition to make decisions: since decisions are the result of deliberation, this might imply that deliberation is a function of character virtue. But a passage from the *EE* makes clear what Aristotle means by this characterization: virtue is a *hexis prohairetikē* in that it provides the *goal* for the deliberation that yields a decision, not the whole process (iii 1.1230a27–29 with ii 11.1227b8–1128a3); see also *Rhet.* 1417a18–19, discussed by Fortenbaugh 1991, 101.

[14] See, e.g., Cooper 1975 [1986], 64; Hardie 1968, 213; Joachim 1951, 218; Greenwood 1909 [1973], 51; Irwin 1975, 578.

the fine," surely he implies that *logos* tells passion more than simply how to achieve what it already wants (*NE* i 13.1102b26–28, b33–34; iii 12.1119b13–18; iv 5.1125b34–35; *EE* iii 1.1229a1–2).

The prospects for a direct denial of this point thus look very dim. Perhaps however there is a modification of the Humean position that can find a way to accommodate reason's dominion: in Section V, I will show that there is. In the meantime, let us consider how the Humean reading handles Aristotle's other apparently un-Humean claims.

2. Desires for Ends Are Rational

The desire for something as an end is not a nonrational passion but instead a wish (*boulēsis*). Therefore, it seems, reason must have some role after all in setting our ends. Can the Humean accommodate this point?

The rationality of wish is not as straightforward as some claim: although Aristotle does call wish rational (*logistikē*) at *Rhetoric* 1369a3, the ethical works deny that it is the product of reasoning (since wishes are for ends, which are not deliberated), and *Politics* 1334b17–25 and *De Anima* 432b4–8 imply that it belongs to the nonrational part of the soul. So perhaps the Humean could show that wishes are passions in the relevant sense after all. But this will not do: even if Aristotle denies that wishes depend on deliberative reason, he must think they depend on some kind of reason, for he denies that beasts have wishes (*EN* iii 2.1111b12–13). Our goals cannot depend entirely on our nonrational capacities, for in that case nonrational animals would have goals, and therefore wishes, too. Here too the straightforward Humean position is at a loss.

3. Phronēsis *Is Distinct from and Ethically Superior to Cleverness*

If *phronēsis* is nothing more than means-end efficiency, why does Aristotle bother distinguishing it from cleverness (*deinotēs*), which clearly is precisely the ability to reason well about how to achieve any given goal (*NE* vi 12)? Perhaps, the Humean can reply, the distinction between *phronēsis* and cleverness is merely terminological: Aristotle's point is just that we do not dignify cleverness with the name of an intellectual virtue if it is in the service of bad ends.

This response may seem initially promising, but it looks much weaker when we consider that Aristotle also attributes to *phronēsis* a very important trait that cleverness lacks: without *phronēsis* one cannot have strict character virtue, and with it one has all the character virtues. On the terminological-difference reading, *phronēsis* (rather than cleverness) entails and is entailed by character virtues simply because to say that someone has *phronēsis* is already to imply that she has character virtue too: the mutual entailment claims are trivial and analytic. And this seems a very strained reading indeed.

The anti-Humean has to hand a much more substantive explanation of *phronēsis*'s difference from and superiority to cleverness: *phronēsis*, she can say, is what gives one the right end. And in the face of all the evidence we saw already that that task falls to virtue instead, she will point to the passage that seems to call *phronēsis* "true supposition of the end." If her reading of that passage is correct, then perhaps, all the difficulties with the anti-Humean view notwithstanding, we should retreat to it after all. Let us then consider that passage.

4. Phronēsis *Is Supposition of the End*

Good deliberation is the rightness that accords with what is advantageous toward the end, of which *phronēsis* is true supposition (*hupolēpsis*). (*NE* vi 9.1142b31–33)

There is in fact an established Humean reading of this passage: the traditional translation has the antecedent of the "of which" (*hou*) wrong; Aristotle is saying not that *phronēsis* is about the end but instead (reaching a bit further back) about "what is advantageous toward the end" – in keeping with the Goal passages after all.[15]

Is this admissible? Anti-Humeans argue against the reading on textual and contextual grounds: it is a less natural reading of the grammar, or it ignores the distinction Aristotle is drawing in the wider passage between qualified and unqualified *phronēsis* (see, e.g., Cooper 1987, 64n). I think these arguments are doomed to be inconclusive: the passage is a compressed one, and both readings can be defended. How then should we settle the dispute?

As it turns out, help is forthcoming from another text: a discussion of deliberation in the *EE* – so far as I know overlooked in this connection – uses very similar wording. Attention to that passage will confirm the traditional translation of our vi 9 passage: Aristotle is calling *phronēsis* "true supposition of the end." It will not, however, confirm the anti-Humean reading thought to be entailed by that translation. Instead it will suggest a modified Humean reading that addresses several – although not yet all – of the objections we have seen in this section.

IV. REASON AND ENDS

The passage that concerns us is Aristotle's explanation of why deliberation (and thus also decision [*prohairesis*], the desire that results from

---

[15]   The reading originates with Walter 1874, 470–472.

deliberation) is distinctively rational. The Humean answer would be: only through reason can one work out the means to one's ends. Although Aristotle surely thinks this part of the answer, what he emphasizes here is something different: only through reason can one *have* ends. And he puts this by saying that only those with reason have *"supposition"* of the end:

Decision is not present in the other animals, nor in people of every age nor of every state. For neither is deliberation [present], nor *supposition of the that-on-account-of-which (hupolēpsis tou dia ti)*, but nothing prevents many from being able to opine whether something is to be done or not to be done, while not yet doing this through reasoning (*dia logismou*). For the deliberative capacity of the soul is the capacity contemplative of a certain cause (*to theōrētikon aitias tinos*). For the that-for-the-sake-of which (*hē hou heneka*) is one of the causes, because the that-on-account-of-which (*to dia ti*) is a cause. . . . Wherefore those for whom no goal (*skopos*) is laid down are not able to deliberate. (*EE* ii 10.1226b20–30, emphasis added)

Animals, children, and wantons do not make decisions because they do not deliberate: they can opt for one course of action rather than another, but not on the basis of reasoning. Why not? Because they have no "supposition of the that-on-account-of-which" – that is, no supposition of the end. (The passage equates the that-on-account-of-which (*dia ti*) with both the that-for-the-sake-of-which (*hou heneka*) and the goal (*skopos*) – two terms interchangeable in Aristotle's vocabulary with *telos*, end.) What these nondeliberative types lack is "supposition of the end" – precisely what *phronēsis* guarantees the truth of, according to the traditional translation of *NE* vi 9.[16]

What is such a supposition, according to the present passage? The strong suggestion is that it is simply *the recognition that one is working toward a given end* – that one's actions are worth choosing because they will contribute to that end, rather than just because they are immediately attractive, or for no particular reason. A crucial part of what it is to do something through deliberation is to recognize what one is doing as being for the sake of an end, and to use that end to guide one's deliberations: as Aristotle puts it a few lines later,

before the process [of deliberation] begins there will be the that-on-account-of-which (*to di ho*), and this is the that-for-the-sake-of-which. . . . For the one who deliberates, if he has carried his inquiry back from the end, deliberates about what is toward it, in order to bring the process back to himself, or what he can do himself toward the end. (*EE* ii 11.1227a13–18, based on Woods's translation)

---

[16] I have been giving the *Nicomachean* numbering for books 5–7, but it is worth emphasizing that these books are shared with the *EE* (where they form books 4–6): these two passages on supposition would both have appeared in the *EE*, fairly close together.

Thus "supposition of the end" in our *EE* passage evidently means not the thought that goes into *supplying* the end (e.g., choosing the life of virtue rather than the life of pleasure as one's goal), but rather the grasping of the end *qua* end, that is, the using of the end to guide deliberation.

Given the similarity in language ("supposition of the end," "supposition of the that-on-account-of-which"), and the similarity in context (both are discussions of deliberation), we have excellent reason to take it that this is precisely what Aristotle means in *NE* vi 9's "supposition" passage as well. *Phronēsis* is, as Aristotle tells us repeatedly, excellence in deliberating about the things toward the end; in order to do this, as this passage reminds us, it has to grasp what the end is. Being good at working out how to achieve the end involves correctly grasping the end as one's end, and that is a job for reason rather than for character.

If this is right, then the anti-Humean's strongest piece of textual evidence, even when translated in the anti-Humeans' preferred way (with *phronēsis* as supposition of the end, rather than of "what is advantageous toward it"), turns out not to support the anti-Humean view at all. For the claim that reason grasps the end as an end is perfectly consistent with the claim – so strongly implied by the Goal passages and others – that it is not reason's task, but rather character's, to supply the content of the end.

This might seem too trivial a role for *phronēsis* for Aristotle to bother emphasizing, but the contrast with nonrational agents in *EE* ii 10 shows that it is not. Aristotle wants to point out that there is a distinctive kind of relation that rational creatures can have toward something that appeals to us: we can have it as an end. Why should this be distinctively rational? Aristotle is not explicit on this point, but has in mind I think several related explanations.

First, and most obviously, to understand the notion of an end one must understand means-end relations, that is, must be able to engage in means-end reasoning – the sort of thing captured in practical syllogisms. Merely wanting *x* while also doing something *y* that in fact contributes to *x* does not yet count as having *x* as your end: you must be able to reason *that* doing *y* is for the sake of *x*, and thus must be able to reason full stop. As the characterization of deliberation as "contemplation of the final cause" emphasizes, Aristotelian reasoning is essentially an understanding of causal relations, and the means-end relation is one such relation: only someone who understands that relation can aim at an end.[17]

Moreover, Aristotle equates ends with practical goods (see especially *EE* i 8) and thus holds that, to understand something as being your end,

---

[17] On the relation between practical rationality and the means-end relationship, see, e.g., Lorenz 2006, 179–181.

you must endorse it as *good*.[18] Animals and akratics can plot about how to achieve the objects of their appetite, but the result is not a decision, and thus *EE* ii 10 implies that the process does not strictly count as deliberation toward an end. One must explicitly endorse something as good in order to "lay down an end" that can guide one's actions (and at the limit one's whole life) – and thus in order to have a wish for it rather than a mere passion. Only humans can have the thought "*x* is my goal – that which is *worth* pursuing, that is, that for the sake of which it is worth doing other things."

Finally, in grasping something as one's end, one has to do what one previously could get away without, which is to recognize precisely what it is that one is aiming at. If the face-value interpretation of "virtue makes the goal right" is correct, then a good upbringing is what makes you value virtuous activity: it makes you, for example, admire people who act generously, enjoy acting generously yourself, and in situations that call for acting generously tend to aim at doing just that. You can do all this, however, without any articulate awareness of precisely what it is that you value. This does not mean that you are valuing generous actions for the wrong reasons: that is true only of those who lack even the nonintellectual aspects of virtue.[19] Rather, it means that you are only implicitly aware of what you are valuing. And if you cannot explicitly identify the generous as what it is that you value, then you cannot deliberately aim at it, cannot have it as the end that structures your explicit deliberations. Thus you need *phronēsis* in order to grasp what it is that you are valuing: *phronēsis* must grasp the end, although virtue supplies it.

This last point may seem speculative, but it gains strong support from analogies with Aristotle's account of reasoning outside the practical sphere – theoretical and productive reasoning. In all three cases, as we saw previously, reasoning begins from "starting points" – assumptions – that are not themselves the product of reasoning. Just as deliberation begins from the laying down of an end that was not itself reached through deliberation, so demonstration begins from the laying down of postulates or definitions that were not themselves reached through demonstration, and productive reasoning from the laying down of an end definitive of the craft. In the practical case, as we have seen, the starting points are provided by character. What about the

---

[18] Only humans can think that we should (*dein*) do something or, equivalently, think something good (*agathon*); these are beliefs presupposed by wish (see, e.g., *EE* ii 10.1226a6 on *dein*, and *NE* iii 4–5 on *agathon*).

[19] See *NE* x 9.1179b20–31: well-habituated people who are not yet strictly virtuous already "love the fine (*kalon*)," by contrast with those who "live according to passion."

theoretical case? Aristotle says that these are grasped by *nous*, intellectual understanding (*Post. An.* ii 19). But *nous* does not grasp the starting points out of thin air: instead, it gets them by conceptualizing material provided by repeated perceptual experience (i.e., through induction). The same is true in the productive realm: the doctor who has the medical art (*technē*) deliberates from an intellectual grasp of health that his merely experienced counterpart lacks, but that intellectual grasp emerges precisely from experience (*empeiria*). In all three cases, then, we can distinguish the intellectual grasp of starting points from the experience-based process that provided the materials for that grasp. In the theoretical and productive cases, this process is induction or experience; in the practical case, we can infer, it is habituation. As Aristotle puts it at *NE* i 7.1098b3–4, "of starting points, some are grasped by induction, some by perception, some by *some sort of habituation*, and others in other ways" (emphasis added).[20]

Thus Aristotle has good reason to hold that only intellect can grasp something as an end, for only through intellect can one (i) recognize precisely what it is that one has been inarticulately aiming at, and (ii) give it the status of an end – a good for the sake of which one does other things. And this is perfectly compatible with the view (indeed, given the analogies with other forms of reasoning, fits exceptionally well with the view) that the *content* of one's ends – the nature of the things one values – is dictated entirely by one's nonrational upbringing and character. It is intellect that grasps ends, and so *phronēsis* is "true supposition of the end," but it is character that provides the material for its grasp, and so it is virtue that "makes the goal right."

Now we have a modified Humean interpretation: reason does not set our ends, but it does play a crucial role in grasping them. This position is clearly a marked improvement over the pure Humean one: it can accommodate the traditional reading of the "true supposition" passage (point 4), as well as Aristotle's distinction between rational wishes and nonrational passions (point 2).

As to the central and most important un-Humean elements in Aristotle, however, our modification lends no help. If reason's only role

---

[20] I give an extended argument for this interpretation in Moss 2012, ch. 8, where I argue that habituation has a cognitive (but not intellectual) aspect: through taking pleasure in certain actions, we *perceive* them as good, and this forms the cognitive basis for our eventual intellectual judgment of them as good. For related interpretations, see Tuozzo 1991; Achtenberg 2002; and Burnet 1900 (introductory note to book II). Note that this account has something in common with the anti-Humean account on which *nous* grasps ends (see Section I, under point 1), but differs in assigning the content of ends to virtue, and on not insisting on calling the intellectual grasp *nous* (for Aristotle calls it *phronesis* instead).

in deliberation is to grasp what the passionate part of the soul is already aiming at, then reason may be a very sophisticated servant to passion, but it is still not its master (point 1): it does not "command one to choose the fine" (*EE* iii 1, quoted earlier) but only articulates that the fine is what one has already chosen. Likewise, if *phronēsis* is confined to "making right the things toward the end" – with the caveat only that in order to do this it needs to grasp what the end is, and that it is an end – then it is intrinsically no different from cleverness, and cannot merit the ethical import that Aristotle so clearly grants it (point 3). Our modified Humean position is better than its predecessor at accommodating the un-Humean elements in Aristotle but still not good enough.

V. NON-HUMEAN DELIBERATION

That *phronēsis* is necessary for character virtue does indeed strongly imply that it is excellence at something that goes beyond ordinary means-end reasoning. Someone merely efficient at putting his plans into action may be smarter and more effective than his bumbling friends, but we would be very wary of calling this an ethical difference – and would find little reason to call his reason the master of passions. But must deliberation always be a matter purely of instrumental reason? Must "things toward ends" always be instrumental means?

We have already seen one interpretation that makes Aristotelian deliberation go beyond instrumental reasoning: the interpretation on which deliberation specifies components or constituents of ends (see Section II, under point 1). This interpretation does indeed account for the ethical significance of *phronēsis* and shows how reason can "command" passion even while being only of "things toward ends": if it is reasoning that tells us that the life of virtue is *eudaimonia*, then it is reasoning that tells us to pursue virtue. As I argued previously, however, this interpretation is a very tenuous fit with Aristotle's sharp distinction between being right about ends and being right about things toward them.

There is however another and more promising version of the view that Aristotelian deliberation – or at least excellent deliberation – is something more than instrumental reasoning. Russell in this volume, and elsewhere Hursthouse and others, argue that the *phronimos* has a special deliberative task because she has a special end: her goal is to "do the right thing," or the appropriate thing, and figuring out how to achieve that kind of end calls on skills very different from means-end efficiency. I want to show that this view is not merely consistent with or suggested by Aristotle's texts but is strongly supported by his characterization of the virtuous person's goal as something that must be made determinate (hōrismenon) and by his treatment of deliberating as a form of defining or determining (horizein).[21]

Up to now I have been speaking about virtue making the goal right without mentioning what the right goal is. On this point, however, Aristotle is very explicit. He tells us repeatedly that virtue aims at the fine (to kalon, iii 7.1115b13–14, iv 1.1120a23–24, and EE iii 1.1230a27–29). He also famously tells us that it aims at "the intermediate" (to meson): virtue aims at (is stochastikē of) the intermediate in actions and passions, that is, what is most appropriate (ii 6.1106b28, ii 9.1109a22–23); for a virtuous person, the intermediate is the that-for-the-sake-of-which, the goal (EE ii 11.1227b36–38). We can charitably – and plausibly – assume that these descriptions are meant to be equivalent: virtue has one characteristic aim, the intermediate, that is, the fine. (Of course ultimately the virtuous person aims at eudaimonia: the point is that her habituated character disposes her to see eudaimonia as consisting in fine activity – which in the practical sphere is activity that hits the intermediate in actions and passions.)

Virtue ensures that we aim at the intermediate and the fine. But it can be difficult to know – to define or determine, as Aristotle frequently puts it – just what the intermediate, fine thing is in any given situation. For example:

Getting angry belongs to everyone and is easy, and so is giving and spending money; but to whom and how much and when and for the sake of what and in what way no longer belongs to everyone, nor is easy; hence doing this well is rare and praiseworthy and fine (kalon). ... Presumably hitting the intermediate is difficult, and especially in particulars: for it is not easy to determine (diorisai [from horizein]) how and to whom and about what sort of things and for how long one should be angry. (NE ii 9.1109a26–30, b14–16)

Nothing counts as the intermediate unless it is determinate: not too much and not too little, but precisely the right amount. (See also the claim that there is a horos [boundary – the noun cognate with horizein] of mean states, at NE vi 2.1138b23). Notably, in his most explicit definition of the fine Aristotle describes this too as determinate: the three greatest species of the fine are order, symmetry, and "the determinate" (to hōrismenon; Meta. xiii 3.1078a36–b1).[22] A painter makes something fine (or beautiful – another translation of kalon) when she correctly determines the right

---

[21]   The view is in fact suggested by Zeller, who is usually condemned as a stark Humean interpreter: "Virtue consists in preserving the proper mean, which can only be determined by [the phronimos]. ... But, if this be so, [phronesis] cannot be limited to the mere discovery of means for the attainment of moral ends: the determination of the true ends themselves is impossible without it" (1897 [1962], 188).

[22]   For a good discussion of the connection between this notion of the fine and Aristotle's ethics, see Lear 2006.

proportions in colors and shapes; likewise, an ethical agent achieves something fine when she correctly determines the right proportion in actions and passions. But this means that getting things right in action is at least as difficult as getting things right in art.

A nonvirtuous person can reason about how to enjoy lots of pleasures, for example, without worrying about what would count as doing this in the right way, at the right time, as one should, and so on – that is, without worrying about the precise right way in which it should be done, for there is no such thing as the precise right way that alone counts as achieving that kind of goal. But if your goal is to enjoy the right pleasures at the right times in the right way, and so on – to hit the intermediate in pleasures, that is, to pursue them in a way that is fine – then to be determinate enough, the course you choose must be very determinate indeed.[23]

Hence, there is the tendency of those without *phronēsis* to go wrong – to overreact to minor slights, for example, or to spend ostentatiously when aiming to be generous. And hence there is the need for *phronēsis* – for just like craft (*technē*) for painters or doctors, its function is precisely to provide the *logos* (reasoning or account) that determines (*horizein*) the intermediate:

Virtue is a state issuing in decisions, consisting in a mean (*mesotēs*) relative to us, determined by *logos* and as the *phronimos* would determine it (*hōrismenē logōi kai hōs an ho phronimos horiseien*).[24] (*NE* ii 6.1106b36–1107a2)

We have said earlier that one should choose the intermediate ... and that the intermediate is as the right *logos* says; the right *logos* is the one in accordance with *phronēsis*. ... *Phronēsis* is the right *logos*. (vi 1.1138b18–20; 13.1144b23–28)

In fact, Aristotle frequently describes deliberation as a process of determination: deliberation is about things that are as yet "undetermined" (*adioriston*, iii 3.1112b9), and hence good deliberation cannot be identical with belief because "everything that is the object of belief is already determined (*hōristai*)" (vi 9.1142b11); "The object of deliberation and the object of decision are the same, but the object of decision is already

---

[23] It is worth noting that in his doctrine of the intermediate Aristotle embraces the Pythagorean notion, prominent also in Plato's *Philebus* and the Hippocratic medical treatises, that the good is determinate or bounded, the bad indeterminate or unbounded (see especially *NE* ii 6.1106b28–30). It certainly seems possible that someone could pursue a highly determinate form of vicious or ethically neutral action, but Aristotle seems explicitly to rule this out. At any rate, what is crucial for our purposes is that good action *must* be determinate, rather than that bad action cannot be.

[24] (Following the manuscript, against Aspasius's emendation.) The passage in fact says that the *logos* determines the mean state (*mesotēs*) that virtue *is*, but since virtue is a mean state precisely because it aims at the intermediate (ii 6.1106b27–28, ii 9.1109a20–23), we can put the point as I have done here.

determined (*aphōrismenon*)" (iii 3.1113a3–4), that is, through the preceding deliberation.

If deliberation is a process of making an indeterminate end sufficiently determinate to be acted upon, and if the ends of the virtuous person (the intermediate, or the fine) intrinsically demand to be made especially, precisely, appropriately determinate, then while mere instrumental reasoning can suffice for ordinary deliberation about how to achieve ordinary goals, for excellent deliberation about how to achieve excellent goals it cannot.

Is this enough to show that *phronēsis* has ethical import even while being confined to "things toward the goal"? Surely yes. Reasoning poorly about how to go about eating three pieces of cake at 3 pm is probably not an ethical failing, but reasoning poorly about how to go about eating the *right* amount of cake at the *right* time and in the *right* way (etc.) arguably is an ethical failing – because it of necessity involves determining what the right amount, time, and way are, that is, what counts as hitting the intermediate, what counts as being temperate rather than self-indulgent or ascetic. Or to take an example based on one from Hursthouse, reasoning poorly about how most efficiently to protect someone from a hurtful truth out of kindness may not be an ethical failing, but reasoning poorly about whether on this particular occasion protecting them from that truth *is* kind – about whether it is in fact a correct implementation of one's wish to do the kind thing – is an ethical failing, for someone who tends to get this sort of thing wrong will not in fact be kind at all, but instead overprotective and officious.[25] (Note that this does not show that character virtues like kindness are after all in part intellectual; instead it shows that the state of one's nonrational soul will not really be character virtue if the rational prescriptions it receives from the rational part, about what to do and how to feel, are flawed.)

Finally and most crucially, is this enough to show that reason is passion's master rather than its slave? I think it is – particularly when we recall that Aristotle describes reason not only as passion's master but also as its father or friend (*NE* i 13.1102b32) and pedagogue (iii 12.1119b13–15). A Humean nonrational part obeys reason only in the minimal way that someone obeys another when she says "I want *x* but I don't know how to get it; therefore I will heed the advice of my clever servant." But an Aristotelian virtuous person's nonrational part is different. It is well habituated and so wants the fine and the intermediate, but it also knows that this means waiting to hear what reason prescribes.

---

[25]   Hursthouse 1991, 231. Cf. Hursthouse 2013: "Quite generally, given that good intentions are intentions to act well or 'do the right thing,' we may say that practical wisdom is the knowledge or understanding that enables its possessor, unlike the nice adolescents, to do just that, in any given situation."

Thus it obeys reason in the much more substantive way that someone obeys another when she says "I want *F* things, but I don't know what kinds of things are really *F*, and so I don't know if I want *x* or *y* or *z*; therefore I will defer to the counsel of my wise parent, friend, or teacher."

VI. QUASI-HUMEANISM

Was Aristotle, then, a Humean about practical reasoning? Not precisely. One element of our modified picture still looks very Humean: reason never has the job of setting our ends. That can be done only by our upbringing, for it is our habituated pleasure in doing certain kinds of activities that makes us aim at them. Is this a crude, objectionable view of human nature on which we are slaves to our brute desires? No: translate *telos* and *skopos* not as "end" or "goal" but instead as "value," and we get what I suspect is a commonsense picture both for the Greeks and for us. Your upbringing dictates your values, and it does so by making you into a certain kind of person – the kind who cares about certain kinds of things. If your parents spoil you with excessive pleasures, and never encourage you to do generous or just acts, you will (i) become a spoiled, self-indulgent person, and (ii) as an aspect of having that character, value your own pleasure and comfort above other goods. If your parents consistently encourage you to do generous, just acts, you will (i) become a generous and just person, and (ii) as an aspect of having that character, value others' well-being and rights on an equal footing with your own. Moreover, this is not an intellectual process: the main mechanism is that you come to enjoy and appreciate the things you habitually do, and dislike their opposites (see especially *EE* vii 2.1237a1–7 and *NE* ii 3.1104b8–12, and Burnyeat 1980). Perhaps your parents explain what they are doing to you as they do it, but it seems that the process could work entirely without intellectual reflection: if you raise a child on a consistent diet of self-indulgence, she will come to value her own comfort whether or not she can put it in those words.

To deny that reasoning plays a crucial role in this process is not to place a harsh and arbitrary limit on its powers. It is simply to say that values are not the sort of thing you can reason yourself into having. For what it is for something to be one of your values is for caring about it to be bound up with your emotion, desires, and dispositions to action – part of your character – and you can therefore only come to have values by coming to have a character, and only come to have new values by coming (through a change in way of life – a rehabituation) to have a new character.[26]

---

[26] Or rather, this is the normal and natural way for us to acquire values, even if things can happen otherwise. Consider the context for the most famous Goal passage. Aristotle is addressing the objection that *phronēsis* is useless; the response is that it plays an

Reason does not give us our goals, then; but it does have the role of grasping what precisely they are, and of recognizing them as goals. Thus we, unlike lower animals, can live lives guided by our conception of the good.

Moreover, in the virtuous among us reason has the further very difficult job of determining what counts as achieving the goal. Thus, excellence in practical reasoning is hard to come by, requires ethical sensitivity, and is necessary for the virtues of character; and thus also reason can and should command the passions, rather than obey them.

Now we have a modified Humean reading that addresses all four un-Humean elements in Aristotle's ethics (points 1–4 in Section III), and that offers an attractive picture of goal acquisition and of ethically excellent practical reasoning. If this is not enough to save Aristotle from the charge of Humeanism, then we should not bother trying to save him from that charge.

WORKS CITED

Achtenberg, D. 2002. *Cognition of Value in Aristotle's Ethics: Promise of Enrichment, Threat of Destruction.* Albany: SUNY Press.

Allan, D. J. 1953. "Aristotle's Account of the Origin of Moral Principles." 120–127 in *Actes du XIe Congres Internationale de Philosophie*, vol. XII. Reprinted in J. Barnes, M. Schofield, and R. Sorabji eds. 1977. *Essays on Aristotle*, vol. 2, 72–78. *Ethics and Politics.* London: Duckworth.

Anton, J., and A. Preus eds. 1991. *Essays in Ancient Greek Philosophy IV: Aristotle's Ethics.* Albany: SUNY Press.

Burnet, J. 1900. *The Ethics of Aristotle.* London: Methuen.

Burnyeat, M. F. 1980. "Aristotle on Learning to be Good." 69–91 in Rorty ed. 1980.

Cooper, J. M. 1975. *Reason and Human Good in Aristotle.* Cambridge, MA: Harvard University Press.

Dahl, N. O. 1984. *Practical Reason, Aristotle, and Weakness of the Will.* Minneapolis: University of Minnesota Press.

important functional role: "The [human] function is achieved in accordance with *phronēsis* and character virtue: for virtue makes the goal right, *phronesis* the things toward it" (*NE* vi 12.1144a6–9). These are the natural, teleological roles for virtue and *phronesis* – it is for the sake of their performing these roles that we are by nature equipped to have them. Perhaps sometimes it is not character virtue but instead some form of reasoning that gives us our goals: arguably this is what happens to akratic and enkratic (weak-willed and self-controlled) types, who have the right goal without having good characters (vii 8). But that is not how we are meant by nature to get our values, and if you do get your values this way – as, for example, someone does when she is proselytized into a new religion or ethos or moral philosophy – there will be tension between your character and your values that may keep you from acting on your values (and thus from really having them as values), and certainly will keep you from living a well-functioning, *eudaimōn* life.

Fortenbaugh, W. W. 1964. "Aristotle's Conception of Moral Virtue and Its Perceptive Role." *Transactions and Proceedings of the American Philological Association* 95: 77–87.

1991. "Aristotle's Distinction between Moral Virtue and Practical Wisdom." 97–106 in Anton and Preus eds. 1991.

Gauthier, R. A., and J. Y. Jolif. 1958–1959. *L'Ethique à Nicomaque: Introduction, Traduction et Commentaire.* 3 vols. Louvain: Publications universitaires.

Greenwood, L. H. G. 1909. *Aristotle: Nicomachean Ethics Book Six.* Cambridge: Cambridge University Press. Reprinted New York: Arno Press, 1973.

Hardie, W. F. R. 1968. *Aristotle's Ethical Theory.* Oxford: Oxford University Press.

Hursthouse, R. 1991. "Virtue Theory and Abortion." *Philosophy and Public Affairs* 20: 223–246.

2013. "Virtue Ethics." http://plato.stanford.edu/archives/fall2013/entries/ethics-virtue/.

Irwin, T. 1975. "Aristotle on Reason, Desire and Virtue." *Journal of Philosophy* 73: 567–578.

Joachim, H. H. 1951. *Aristotle: The Nicomachean Ethics.* Oxford: Oxford University Press.

Lear, G. R. 2006. "Aristotle on Moral Virtue and the Fine." 1116–136 in R. Kraut ed. *The Blackwell Guide to Aristotle's Nicomachean Ethics.* Oxford: Blackwell.

Lorenz, H. 2006. *The Brute Within: Appetitive Desire in Plato and Aristotle.* Oxford: Oxford University Press.

2009. "Virtue of Character in Aristotle's *Nicomachean Ethics*." *Oxford Studies in Ancient Philosophy* 37: 177–212.

Moss, J. 2011. "'Virtue Makes the Goal Right': Virtue and *Phronesis* in Aristotle's Ethics." *Phronesis* 65: 204–261.

2012. *Aristotle on the Apparent Good: Perception, Phantasia, Thought and Desire.* Oxford: Oxford University Press.

Reeve, C. D. C. 1992. *Practices of Reason: Aristotle's Nicomachean Ethics.* Oxford: Clarendon Press.

Rorty, A. O. ed. 1980. *Essays on Aristotle's Ethics.* Berkeley and Los Angeles: University of California Press.

Smith, A. D. 1996. "Character and Intellect in Aristotle's *Ethics*." *Phronesis* 41: 56–74.

Sorabji, R. 1973–1974. "Aristotle on the Role of Intellect in Virtue." *Proceedings of the Aristotelian Society* n. s. 74: 107–129. Reprinted in Rorty ed. 1980, 201–220.

Tuozzo, T. 1991. "Aristotelian Deliberation Is Not of Ends." 193–212 in Anton and Preus eds. 1991.

Walter, J. 1874. *Die Lehre von der praktische Vernunft in der griechischen Philosophie.* Jena: Mauke's Verlag.

Wiggins, D. 1980. "Deliberation and Practical Reason." 221–240 in Rorty ed. 1980.

Zeller, E. 1897. *Aristotle and the Earlier Peripatetics.* 2 vols. B. F. C. Costelloe and J. H. Muirhead trans. London: Longmans, Green.

12 Aristotle's Analysis of Akratic Action

I. INTRODUCTION

The question whether akratic action is possible, for Aristotle, is first and foremost the question whether it is possible for people to understand that they should not perform some specific action (e.g., to have the drink that they are being offered) and nevertheless to act against that understanding.[1] Aristotle's analysis of akratic action in *NE* vii 3 is one of the most-discussed passages in Aristotle's corpus. Its interpretation has been, and continues to be, highly controversial. The present chapter offers a reconstruction of Aristotle's train of thought in that chapter. Some parts of that reconstruction may be familiar; other parts may not. We shall focus on the central passage that deals with the manner in which the akratic person, while she acts akratically, understands that she should not do what she is doing. Before turning to that passage, we should consider two passages in the chapter that precedes Aristotle's analysis of akratic action, in which he articulates the difficulty that his analysis is meant to resolve. They may offer some clues as to how Aristotle conceives of akratic action.

The first passage (*NE* vii 2.1145b22–31) is one in which Aristotle briefly discusses Socrates' position about akrasia. According to Aristotle, Socrates thought that nobody acts contrary to what is best, while holding the appropriate correct supposition. Rather, acting contrary to what is best is always a matter of acting because of ignorance, where this must mean not only lack of understanding but also lack, at the time of action, of the correct supposition concerning what is best. Aristotle points out, reasonably enough, that Socrates' conception manifestly conflicts with what appears and is widely held to be the case. Nonetheless, Aristotle is notably prepared to take seriously the possibility that the affection in question, by which he means the defeat of understanding or correct supposition at the hands of some passion,

---

[1] Throughout the present chapter, "to understand" and "understanding" will be used to translate the Greek words ἐπίστασθαι and ἐπιστήμη. This decision will be explained in Section II.

comes about because of ignorance. "One should investigate," he says, "about the affection, if it does come about because of ignorance, what manner of ignorance that turns out to be" (1145b28–29).

Before the akratic experiences an episode of akrasia, Aristotle notes, she plainly thinks that she should not do the bad thing in question (1145b30–31), thus holding the correct supposition. A tentative and, at this point, still hypothetical picture that emerges at this early stage in Aristotle's discussion is a diachronic one in which the akratic, prior to the episode of akratic action, thinks that she should not perform the act in question, whereas at the time of the akratic action she experiences a certain form of ignorance, which in a way explains why her knowledge or correct supposition is mastered by some passion or other. On the interpretation I offer in the present chapter, that is precisely the kind of diachronic picture that Aristotle himself wants to present.

In another passage worth calling attention to (NE vii 2.1145b31–1146a7), Aristotle envisages akratic action as arising from a motivational conflict in which a powerful appetite pulls the person one way (1146a2–3) while something else – belief, *phronēsis*, or whatever – pulls him the other way. Aristotle speaks of belief and *phronēsis* pulling the other way (*antiteinein*: 1146a1, a4), resisting the appetitive impulse until that resistance is abandoned or overcome and the person acts on appetite.

This is the language of motivational conflict, recalling the picture of enkratic and akratic conflict presented in NE i 13.1102b14–18 (cf. 1102b21), and of course the psychological conflicts by appeal to which the Socrates of Plato's *Republic* seeks to establish the theory of the tripartite soul.[2] That Aristotle here envisages akratic action as arising from motivational conflict in which appetite prevails is an important point of detail. According to some interpretations of Aristotle's analysis of akratic action in NE vii 3, that analysis leaves no room for motivational conflict, in that it takes the akratic to remain unaware of the fact that the object he is impelled to pursue is also one he has decided, or wishes, to stay away from.[3] That Aristotle thinks of akratic action as arising from motivational conflict not only in NE i 13, but also in articulating difficulties about akrasia in the chapter that immediately precedes the analysis in NE vii 3, is a consideration in favor of interpretations that leave room for motivational conflict.

[2] The verb ἀντιτείνειν ("pull the other way") is used for psychological conflict at *Republic* x 604a2 and a10.

[3] E.g., Ross 1995, 229–230; Cooper 1975, 49–50.

II. THE CENTRAL PASSAGE: NE VII 3.1146B31–1147B19

Aristotle offers three distinctions concerning how people can correctly be said to understand something. These distinctions yield a number of ways in which one might interpret the Socratic claim that it is impossible to act against one's own understanding of what one should or should not do.

1. NE 1146b31–35

According to the first distinction, presented at 1146b31–35, understanding something may be a matter of having understanding without employing it, or it may be a matter of both having and employing the understanding in question. On the basis of this distinction, Aristotle says that it seems, or is held, to be a terrifying thing to act as one should not, while one is contemplating – that is, employing one's understanding – that one should not do the thing at issue. However, acting against understanding when one is not contemplating the matter in question, Aristotle adds, does not seem to be a terrifying thing. It is not immediately clear what the distinction between merely having and employing understanding is meant to come to. Many have thought that Aristotle means to distinguish between knowing something but not currently attending to it, on the one hand, and attending to it, on the other: for instance, one knows one's social security number, but only on occasion does one call it to mind.[4]

I shall argue for an alternative interpretation of what the distinction is meant to come to.[5] The Greek verb *epistasthai* denotes having expertise or expert knowledge concerning something or other, and Aristotle follows the Socrates character of Plato's *Meno* in conceiving of such expertise in terms of grasping something in a way that rests on having identified, and being able to provide, the cause or proper explanation of the matter in question. "To understand" is a reasonably close English equivalent of the Greek verb *epistasthai*, at any rate as that verb is used in the writings of Plato and Aristotle.[6] It is also along those lines that understanding (*epistēmē*) as a state is explicated in Aristotle's discussion

---

[4]   E.g., Ross 1995, 228; Hardie 1968, 274. Irwin 1999 translates θεωρεῖν at 1146b33–34 as "attend."

[5]   The present interpretation is similar to, but should be distinguished from, Charles 2009, according to which what Aristotle means by employing understanding is contemplating a truth "as part of a relevant body of knowledge." The notion I am introducing is more specific than this.

[6]   As Burnyeat 1981, 102, says, "Explanation and understanding go together in a way that explanation and knowledge do not."

of the topic in *NE* vi 3. That discussion, which itself refers to the explication of understanding that is given in *Posterior Analytics* i 2, defines understanding as a demonstrative state, a state that is suited to providing demonstrations of certain truths by reference to appropriate starting points or principles. Those demonstrations identify the proper explanations why the proposition in question is true.

Now, one thing to note about this is that in *NE* vi 3 understanding is defined as a state (*hexis*) of a certain kind, rather than as an activity: as something that one *has* rather than as something that one *does*. Merely being in that state, without putting it to use, is to understand in the sense of having understanding without employing it. The discussion in *NE* vi 3 suggests what employing that state might come to: understanding something is a state suited to demonstrating it, and plainly one way in which one might put such a state to use is by demonstrating the truth of the proposition that one understands, whether by stating the demonstration in speech or by thinking it through. For Aristotle, doing so will crucially involve calling to mind the propositions that constitute the demonstration and employing them as premises of an argument for the truth of the proposition that is being demonstrated.

In our passage from *NE* vii 3, Aristotle switches from speaking of employing understanding to speaking of contemplating (*theōrein*). He uses this word, and the cognate noun *theōria*, in several other places so as to denote the activity that comes about when understanding (*epistēmē*) is put to use.[7] Given that the state of understanding something, for Aristotle, is a matter of knowing something on the basis of knowing its cause or explanation, it is natural to think that the activity that comes about when understanding is put to use is an activity of grasping something to be true by grasping its cause or explanation. For example, being in the state of understanding that triangles have interior angles equal to two right angles consists in knowing that fact based on knowing its explanation, and the activity that corresponds to that state is occurrently grasping that triangles have angles equal to two right angles by occurrently employing appropriate propositions as premises of an argument for the truth of that proposition about triangles.

Given the strict notion of understanding that Aristotle means to explicate in *NE* vi 3, and also in the *Posterior Analytics*, understanding concerns only propositions that are true by necessity. And the relevant propositions about individuals and particular objects or actions, such as the proposition that I should not have any more to drink, are not true by necessity. So it may seem clear that the notion of understanding that Aristotle explicates in *NE* vi 3 is unsuited to understanding propositions

---

[7]   E.g., *De Anima* ii 1.412a22–23; ii 5.417b28–29.

such as the ones that are at issue in the analysis of akratic action. However, in *NE* vi 3 Aristotle notes that the notion he is explicating is a strict one, and he implicitly recognizes a looser notion, or looser notions, based on similarities with understanding conceived of strictly (1139b18–19). Now in *NE* vii 3 Aristotle distinguishes between what seems to be understanding conceived of strictly, and perceptual understanding, which concerns propositions that feature a particular term, such as the proposition that this chocolate bar should not be eaten (1147b13–17). Such perceptual understanding, it seems reasonable to suppose, is a case of understanding conceived of loosely, based on similarities with understanding conceived of strictly.

In what way might perceptual understanding resemble understanding conceived of strictly? Given the close connection in Aristotle's usage between understanding something and knowing its cause or explanation, one point of similarity should be that perceptual understanding crucially involves knowing the reason or explanation why the proposition in question is true. Given that the propositions that are subject to perceptual understanding will include many that are not true by necessity, the premises on whose grasp perceptual understanding rests need not be true by necessity, either.

Moreover, particular terms such as "this chocolate bar" must feature in some of those premises, given that they must yield conclusions in which such particular terms feature. Nonetheless, Aristotle thinks that there really are reasons and proper explanations why a given agent in a specific situation should or should not perform some action, and so it seems reasonable for him to operate with a relaxed notion of understanding, with the result that one can in a way understand that, say, one should not have this drink that one is being offered. This will be a matter of grasping a truth in a distinctive way, namely, by grasping the reason why the proposition in question is true.

The upshot of these comments on Aristotle's conception of understanding is an alternative interpretation of the contrast between merely having understanding and employing understanding, which Aristotle also refers to as contemplating the matter in question. On this interpretation, employing understanding so as to contemplate something is not only a matter of attending to it. It is also, and crucially, a matter of grasping its reason. More precisely, it is a matter of grasping the truth of a proposition on the basis of grasping the reason why the proposition is true. This conception is much more specific than the standard conception of what is involved in contemplating a given proposition, for instance, the proposition that one should not act in some particular way. As we will see, that greater specificity has considerable advantages for understanding what goes on in the Central Passage overall.

2. NE 1146b35–1147a10

Aristotle's second distinction concerning how people can be said to understand something, presented at 1146b35–1147a10, is based on a distinction between two modes of propositions, universal and particular. "Nothing prevents a person from acting against understanding when they have both and are employing the universal, but not the particular one" (1147a1–3). Having distinguished between universal and particular propositions, Aristotle adds a further distinction, which concerns the constituents of universal propositions. One constituent concerns the person, the other one concerns a given object. His example is the universal proposition that dry food is good for every human. This concerns a certain kind of object, dry food, and it concerns the person in question, given that it concerns every human being. Aristotle envisages a case in which someone knows that dry food is good for every human, and hence for him, and also that such-and-such food (say, cereal) is dry, but either lacks or fails to employ the proposition that this is cereal.[8]

Aristotle concludes abruptly that the difference between "these two manners" is enormously large, so that knowing in this way seems to be nothing strange, but knowing in another way seems astonishing (1147a8–10). The two manners in question must be two manners of knowing, which presumably are meant to amount to two manners of understanding.[9] What Aristotle takes to be astonishing would then seem to be acting against understanding when one understands the thing in question in one of the two ways of understanding that he means to introduce, whereas there is nothing strange, he thinks, in acting against understanding when one understands whatever it may be in the other way. One way of understanding that this triangle has internal angles equal to two right angles, Aristotle holds elsewhere,[10] is by understanding that triangles have angles equal to two right angles, without knowing of this triangle. This is a matter of understanding universally that this

---

[8]   1147a7: ἀλλ' εἰ τόδε τοιόνδε, ἢ οὐκ ἔχει ἢ οὐκ ἐνεργεῖ ("but if this is a thing of this kind, the person either does not have or does not employ"). It may well be significant that Aristotle is saying that this proposition is not employed, rather than that it is not contemplated. He may mean to leave room for the idea of employing a proposition (say, as a premise in an argument) without thereby contemplating it. Contemplating is the activity that corresponds to the state of understanding, and the object of understanding at issue in the situation that Aristotle has in mind is not the proposition that this particular thing is cereal, but the proposition that this particular thing is good for me. That this is cereal is part of the reason why this is good for me.

[9]   The Greek word translated as "to know" is εἰδέναι. According to a proposal by Burnyeat 1981, 104 (which rests on results presented in Lyons 1963), one use of εἰδέναι is as a synonymous replacement for ἐπίστασθαι.

[10]   Posterior Analytics i 1.71a24–29; cf. Prior Analytics ii 21.67a14–21.

triangle has angles equal to two right angles. Aristotle contrasts this with unqualified understanding that this triangle has angles equal to two right angles, which comes about when someone recognizes that this figure is a triangle and applies to it his understanding that triangles have angles equal to two right angles. The distinction between two ways of knowing that is in play in our passage seems to be that same distinction.[11] Someone who understands that cereal is good for people in a way understands that this portion of cereal is good for people, even if she does not know of this portion of cereal. This is to be distinguished from cases in which someone knows that this is cereal, applies to it her understanding that cereal is good for people, and so understands in a different way that this portion of cereal is good for people. Those latter cases are cases of unqualified understanding that this portion of cereal is good for people.

So Aristotle's main point in our passage seems to be that there is nothing perplexing about cases of acting against understanding in which a person understands only universally, but does not understand without qualification, that they should pursue or avoid some particular object – say, this portion of cereal. For example, a person may understand that he should now eat cereal, and he may put that understanding to use in grasping the fact on the basis of grasping the appropriate explanation. Now it might be that he just does not know that the stuff in that container in the refrigerator is cereal, or it might be that he does know that but fails now to think of it, so that he also fails to employ this knowledge so as to grasp both the fact that he should now eat this and the reason why that fact obtains. If he did so employ the proposition that this is cereal, then he would count as unqualifiedly understanding, in the sense of contemplating, that he should now eat this. He would be grasping the fact in a distinctive way, by grasping the reason why it obtains. For anyone to grasp in this way that he should now eat this portion of cereal and nonetheless to act against that understanding, Aristotle is saying, would be bizarre.

In effect, in providing this second distinction between ways of understanding something, Aristotle is calling attention to a way in which one can act against one's own understanding even when that understanding is in a way active. He is calling attention to unproblematic cases in which someone acts against understanding when he understands universally, though not without qualification, that he should pursue or avoid some particular thing. Jones is at a party and understands that he should not have any more alcohol, given that he will be driving home. He grasps that

---

[11] Morison 2011 offers a detailed explanation and philosophical defense of Aristotle's distinction, and also a fuller account of its application in our passage than can be provided here.

fact and the reason why it obtains. Moreover, he employs that understanding in selecting a bottle of what he takes to be nonalcoholic beer, rather than some other beer. He is wrong about the beer he selects: that beer contains about 5 percent alcohol. He either simply does not know this or knows it but fails to put this knowledge to use, perhaps because he is distracted by the conversation he is having. As he is drinking the beer, he is acting against understanding. He understands that he should not have any more alcohol. So in a way he understands that he should not have the alcoholic drink he has selected. Moreover, he is employing that understanding. Partly on the basis of that understanding, he selects the beer that he does select, in preference to some other beer. Nevertheless, this is an unproblematic case of acting against understanding. It is unproblematic because Jones is at the time of action simply unaware of the key fact that he is having an alcoholic drink.

3. NE *1147a10–18*

In the third distinction, presented at 1147a10–18, Aristotle introduces a special way of having understanding that he takes to be different from the ways that have been spoken of. Within having but not employing understanding, he adds, there is a distinctive state, "so as both in a way to have and not to have [i.e., understanding], like people who are asleep, experience fits of insanity, or are drunk." People who are in certain emotional states, he says, are in this kind of condition: anger, sexual desire, and some other such states change also the condition of the body, as well as (he thinks) the condition of their understanding. "It is clear, then," he concludes, "that we should say akratics are in the same state as these people" (1147a17–18). So with this distinction, between a special way of having but not employing understanding and other cases of having but not employing understanding, Aristotle has finally focused in on the cognitive condition in which he takes the akratic to act against understanding when she acts akratically.

This cognitive condition is not simply a matter of having but failing to employ understanding that one should not do the thing in question. It is supposed to be a different way of having understanding from the ones that have already been spoken of, and of course having understanding without employing it was spoken of in the first distinction Aristotle offered. The cognitive condition in which people act akratically should also be different from understanding something by having and employing a suitable universal proposition without employing, or having, some relevant particular proposition. That, too, is a way of having understanding that has already been spoken of. Rather, both the examples Aristotle uses and the fact that he says that this condition is a matter of having understanding in a way, and also of not having understanding, indicate that he has in mind a condition of having understanding that is temporarily compromised by the psychological or physiological condition that one is in.

Elsewhere Aristotle says that a sleeping geometer is further removed from being in fulfillment than a waking one.[12] A geometer who is awake can right away achieve fulfillment as a geometer by activating her understanding of geometry. By contrast, a sleeping geometer is temporarily prevented from putting her understanding to use by the condition in which she currently is. In waking up, she gets a step closer to the fulfillment of what she is. She is now in a state of full preparedness for exercise.

Aristotle characterizes the cognitive condition in which akratics act akratically as a matter of having understanding in a way, but also of failing to have understanding. So far as ordinary cases of having but not employing understanding are concerned, he never says that these are cases of not having understanding. And why would he? After all, he conceives of having understanding as being perfectly consistent with not currently employing it. Why then is he saying this about the particular cognitive condition in which akratics act akratically?

Elsewhere he makes clear that he takes it to be characteristic of having understanding that the person in question is able to exercise it at will, unless she is prevented by something external – external to the person, that is, as when, say, a brick hits her on the head (*De Anima* ii 5.417a27–28). We can therefore make sense of the idea that the akratic while acting akratically in a way lacks understanding by supposing that she exemplifies a special case of having but failing to employ that understanding. What is characteristic of that special case is that the person in question is temporarily prevented from employing her understanding, given the psychological or physiological condition she is in.[13]

The idea that emerges is that it is only in an expanded or relaxed sense of having understanding that the akratic, while acting akratically, counts as having understanding. Being in that condition, Aristotle quite obviously thinks, also counts as a way of temporarily not having understanding. This is an important point, since it enables us to make sense of the evident fact that he takes the akratic to revert from ignorance to understanding at some time after the akratic action (1147b6–9). He plainly thinks that there is a sense in which akratics, when and while they act akratically and against their own understanding, act in ignorance

---

[12]   *Generation of Animals* ii 1.735a9–12. Cf. *Physics* vii 3.247b13–16: "When someone, from being drunk, asleep, or sick is changed into the opposite condition, we don't say that they have again come to be a person who has understanding, even though before they were unable to make use of their understanding."

[13]   Similarly, Ross 1995, 229; Kenny 1966, 174; and Pickavé and Whiting 2008, 343.

of the fact that they should not act in the way that they do. And we can make sense of this: it is because although there is a sense in which they have understanding, they are not, while acting against that understanding, in a position to employ it.

4. A Supplementary Comment: NE 1147a18–24

Aristotle has now identified the specific cognitive condition in which he thinks akratics act against their own understanding when they act akratically. This answers the question in what way the akratic knows that he should not do the thing in question when he acts akratically (1146b8–9). Before approaching the explanation of akratic action in a different way, namely in the manner of the natural philosopher, Aristotle wraps up the present part of the discussion by adding a supplementary comment. This comment concerns the fact that when people act akratically, they may well say things that seem to express their own understanding that they should not act in the way that they do. Someone may act akratically in, say, having a much bigger meal than she should, and while hugely enjoying every bit of it say that she really should not be eating this much, given that her doctor told her that she risks having a heart attack unless she loses twenty pounds. So, one might object to Aristotle that when people act akratically, they often show every sign of understanding that they should not do the thing in question and, in fact, of making use of that understanding so as to state both the fact and the reason why.

Aristotle's response is that saying the things that come from understanding is no reliable indication that the person in question is currently employing the relevant piece of understanding. In fact, the example of learners who do not yet have understanding but who can already recite the explanations proves that people can say things that come from understanding (that is to say, they can state suitable facts and the explanations why those facts obtain) without yet even having that understanding. In saying the things that come from understanding, people may simply be relying on memory, without at the time making use of their understanding so as to grasp the inferential and explanatory connections between the facts and explanations that are at issue. In fact, they might not have mastered those connections, and so they might not even *have* the understanding from which the things they say come.

5. The Natural Philosopher's Explanation: NE 1147a24–b9

The next section, which begins at 1147a24, seems best understood as an explanation of akratic action that employs principles or terminology specific to the philosophy of nature. The preceding discussion was conducted at a more general level, relying for the most part on terms that are familiar from discussions meant to apply to all branches of knowledge alike, such as the *Analytics*.[14] Aristotle gives no indication that he means to modify or correct the preceding account of the specific cognitive state in which people act akratically. We should try to interpret the natural philosopher's explanation so that it supplements the account that has already been given, in a way that employs principles or terminology belonging specifically to the philosophy of nature. In fact, this can be done.

Aristotle begins with a comparison between theoretical thought and practical thought. In so doing, he relies on the earlier distinction between universal and particular propositions, except that beliefs now take the place of propositions. Aristotle also adds that it is perception that controls the cognition of particulars. These and other references to psychological capacities, acts, and states apply terminology that belongs to the study of ensouled beings, and therefore, for Aristotle, to the philosophy of nature. Whenever one belief arises from a suitable pair of universal and particular beliefs, Aristotle says, then in theoretical cases "it is necessary for the soul to assert what is concluded, and in practical cases right away to do it" (1147a26–28). He adds an example: "if one should taste anything that is sweet, but this, being one of the particulars, is sweet, it is necessary for a person who is able to, and is not prevented, to do this at once" (1147a29–31).

Two details in this passage call for comment. First, it is not immediately clear what Aristotle has in mind in speaking of one belief arising from a suitable pair of other beliefs. He might have in mind belief in the conclusion that is entailed by the universal and particular beliefs in question; for instance, the belief that one should taste this particular thing. That is unlikely, though, because Aristotle says that whenever one belief arises in this way, it is, in theoretical cases, necessary for the soul to assert what is concluded. By this comment, he seems to mean that the formation of the single belief, in theoretical cases, necessarily leads to acceptance of the conclusion, in parallel to the way it necessarily leads, in practical cases, to enactment of the conclusion. But if by the single belief in question Aristotle just means belief in the conclusion, then the formation of that single belief already includes acceptance of the conclusion. So it seems better to think that the single belief in question is a composite belief that combines a universal and a suitable particular belief.[15] The idea then is that whenever people form such combined

---

[14] Burnyeat 2001, 19–24, clarifies what Aristotle means by discussing some matter *phusikōs* ("in the manner of the natural philosopher"), namely, to discuss it in a way that relies on principles appropriate to (some subject matter in) natural philosophy.

[15] This suggestion is due to Michael Frede. *Contra* Charles 2009, 53.

beliefs in which suitable universal and particular propositions are accepted and thought of together, then in theoretical cases one necessarily accepts the conclusion, while in practical cases one necessarily enacts the conclusion, provided that one is able to and is not prevented.

Second, what kinds of possible preventers does Aristotle have in mind in saying that in practical cases, once someone forms the appropriate single belief, it is necessary for him to do the thing in question, provided that he is able to and is not prevented? Those possible preventers, one might think, include nonrational desires (Charles 2009, 54–55). This, however, seems wrong. If desires were included among possible preventers, Aristotle would be envisaging cases in which someone has and employs both the relevant universal proposition and a suitable particular proposition, and so would count not only as understanding but also as contemplating the fact that he should not do the particular thing at issue. Aristotle would then be committed to thinking that in such cases the person in question may act against his own fully active understanding, being prevented from acting on that understanding by a nonrational desire, for instance an appetite.

But note that Aristotle said earlier (at 1147a8–10) that it would be astonishing for someone to act against understanding when she understands the thing in question by having and employing both the relevant universal proposition and a suitable particular proposition. So, if possible preventers included desires, Aristotle would now leave open as a possibility something that a short while ago he said would be astonishing, without explaining or even acknowledging as dramatic a change as this.[16] So it seems best to understand Aristotle as having in mind only factors outside the person's psychological makeup as possible preventers of action on fully active understanding. The idea, then, is that once someone forms a unified practical belief by putting together a suitable pair of universal and particular beliefs, she is bound to act on the conclusion, provided that she is able to do so – that is to say, provided that she is not externally prevented from doing so.

We now come to the central sentences of Aristotle's analysis: "Whenever then the universal belief is in the person preventing him from tasting, and on the other hand the belief that everything sweet is pleasant, and that this is sweet (and this one is active), and an appetite happens to be present, then belief says to avoid this, but the appetite drives the person on. For it can move each of the parts. As a result, it so happens that people act akratically in a way under the influence of reason and belief, although belief is not in itself opposed to correct reason, but only incidentally; for the appetite, not the belief, is opposed to correct reason" (1147a31–b3).

---

[16] This argument is due to Jozef Müller.

Aristotle is describing a conflict between correct reason and an appetite. He says that it is the appetite that is opposed to correct reason, whereas belief is opposed to correct reason only incidentally, not in itself. The belief under whose influence the person acts akratically is the belief that this is pleasant. This belief, Aristotle thinks, is not in itself opposed to correct reason, presumably because it does not as such conflict with correct reason. Correct reason does not deny that this is pleasant. Reason insists only that it should be avoided. The belief is opposed to correct reason incidentally, in that it triggers and supports an appetite to pursue the thing in question. And that appetite is opposed, and opposed in itself, to correct reason.

For the appetite to be opposed, and opposed in itself, rather than incidentally, to correct reason, the occurrent expression or deliverance of reason that is at issue should be an impulse that is exactly opposed to the appetitive impulse that drives the person to the particular sweet thing. This in fact seems to be what Aristotle has in mind: the person holds a universal belief that prevents him from tasting, and as the appetite drives him to some particular sweet and therefore pleasant thing, belief says to avoid this thing.[17] By this, Aristotle means that the person has formed the belief that he should now avoid this particular thing, on the basis of believing that he should now avoid having any food, and that this particular thing is food. The universal belief that he should now avoid food is a decision not to eat now.

Given Aristotle's moral psychology, whenever a person realizes that a decision she has made applies to her present circumstances, she is impelled to act on the decision. In fact, as our passage makes clear, Aristotle takes it that when someone combines the universal content of a decision with a suitable perceptual belief so as to form a single but composite belief, she will necessarily enact the conclusion of that belief, provided that she is able to – that is to say, provided that she is not externally prevented from doing so. So, as long as the person in question is employing both members of a suitable pair of universal and particular beliefs – say, the universal belief that she should not have any food now, and the particular belief that this is food – she will find herself with a single, composite belief with which she will comply, provided that she is not externally prevented from doing so. In our passage, Aristotle also envisages a belief that this particular thing is sweet, and therefore pleasant, and, based on that belief, an appetite to eat this particular sweet thing. So at this stage the person experiences precisely the kind of motivational conflict that Aristotle takes to be characteristic of akratics.

---

[17]   The most natural way of construing τοῦτο is as picking up τουτί, which is the closest neuter subject in what precedes.

The appetitive impulse will prevail and get the person to act on it. Now we know that, setting aside external prevention, Aristotle takes it to be impossible for a person to act against his own understanding, if he both has and employs the relevant universal proposition (say, "I should not now have any food") and has and employs a suitable particular proposition (say, "this is food"). How then can the person whose thoughts Aristotle is describing in our passage act against his own understanding, as he must do if they are to act akratically? The answer should be obvious. Aristotle has already told us in what cognitive condition akratics act against their own understanding when they act akratically. As we have seen, he takes their cognitive condition to be one in which their understanding that they should not act in the relevant way has been temporarily incapacitated. Aristotle has also told us that emotional states such as certain appetites and anger put people in this kind of condition. So his idea must be that appetite eventually prevails over correct reason by putting the person in the kind of cognitive condition that was described earlier as the condition of understanding or quasi-understanding in which akratics act akratically.[18]

It is important to bear in mind that it is no part of Aristotle's conception of that cognitive condition that people who are in it are completely deprived of their cognitive powers. They may be fully aware of the particulars they are facing (contra Rowe 1971, appendix). They may know perfectly well that this is a chocolate bar. They are definitely in a position to engage in voluntary action, given Aristotle's conception of the voluntary. As is well known, Aristotle operates with a rather relaxed notion of what kind of cognition is required for voluntary action. He takes even infants and nonhuman animals to be able to act voluntarily. Provided that a dog is aware that it is your hand that it is biting, rather than a sausage that you are holding in your hand, the dog, Aristotle thinks, is acting voluntarily in biting your hand. When Aristotle describes the cognitive condition in which people act akratically as ignorance, as he does in a passage to which we will turn presently, he is relying on a specific notion of ignorance that he has introduced quite carefully.

What he has in mind is a form of ignorance that consists specifically in temporarily not having understanding. As we saw, he conceives of having understanding as a matter of having some acquired piece of understanding ready for use. People who experience an episode of akrasia do not,

---

[18] Thus Aristotle envisages two distinct stages of episodes of uncontrol: a stage of motivational conflict between appetite and active understanding, and a stage of action on appetite, during which understanding is temporarily incapacitated. An interpretation along these lines was suggested by Rowe 1971, appendix. Müller 2008 has more recently drawn attention to the possibility of reading the passage in this way.

strictly speaking, have understanding. They are temporarily unable to engage in the activity of understanding ("to contemplate") that they should not do this particular act. In other words, they are temporarily unable to grasp that fact in a certain distinctive way, namely, by grasping the reason why it obtains. So in this specific sense they are at that time ignorant of the fact that they should not do the act in question.

Nonetheless, in an extended or relaxed sense, they do have that understanding. After all, once they calm down, they will again be able to make use of their understanding and contemplate the relevant facts at will. They will not have to regain that understanding by learning the relevant facts and explanations all over again. Given the removal of the relevant physiological obstacles, they will once again be able to employ the understanding that in a way they had all along.

Aristotle declines to tell us how it is that the akratic person's ignorance subsides and how she again comes to have understanding (1147b6–9). That account, he says, is not specific to the phenomenon of akrasia, as it applies likewise to the transitions from drunkenness to sobriety and from sleep to waking. Moreover, it is, he adds, the task of physiologists to provide such an account. Aristotle's idea seems to be that certain emotional states, drunkenness, and sleep bring with them agitated physiological conditions that render the person temporarily unable to employ whatever understanding she may have. This remark implicitly answers the question why Aristotle has nothing to say, for present purposes, about how it is that the cognitive condition in which people act akratically comes about: how this form of temporary ignorance arises is not a question specific to the phenomenon of akrasia, but applies likewise to drunkenness and sleep; and in any case it belongs to the physiologist, not to the philosopher, let alone the practical philosopher, to discover the material processes that lead to the temporary incapacitation of understanding.

6. Two Supplementary Comments: NE 1147b9–17

"Given that the last proposition is a belief about what is perceptible and controls action, this the person either does not have while she is in the emotional state, or she has it in the way in which, as was said, having isn't understanding but only saying, as the drunk person has the verses of Empedocles." Most commentators have thought that in speaking of the last *protasis* (1147b9), Aristotle has in mind the minor premise of the good practical syllogism described in the preceding passage (at 1147a31–34). This is because of the widespread, but mistaken, opinion that, in Aristotle's usage, the word *protasis* just means "premise." However, it is in fact clear that the word, which occurs frequently in the *Analytics*, means "proposition" (Charles 2009, appendix 1). Given that this is what the word means, there are three reasons for thinking that in speaking of the last proposition in our passage, Aristotle has in mind the conclusion of the bit of practical thought with which he credited the akratic just before his appetite drove him to act against that conclusion.

First, that proposition – namely, that this should be avoided[19] – is in fact the last proposition that Aristotle mentioned. Second, that proposition is an object of understanding (epistasthai) in a way that the minor premise of the akratic person's good practical syllogism is not. The minor premise, for example, that this is food, is not grasped on the basis of grasping suitable reasons or explanations. It is grasped just by looking at what one is up against (NE iii 3.1112b33–1113a2). By contrast, the conclusion of the good practical syllogism is grasped on the basis of a suitable reason or explanation. It is grasped precisely on the basis of grasping the two premises of the good practical syllogism. By employing those two propositions as premises of an argument, one grasps the reason why the proposition that is the conclusion is true.

And third, Aristotle is telling us that the last proposition controls action. It is hard to see why he might want to say that the minor premise of the good practical syllogism (i.e., "this is food") controls action. That some particular object is food is by itself neither here nor there so far as action is concerned. On the other hand, it is easy to see how it is that the conclusion of the good practical syllogism is the kind of proposition that controls action. That some particular object should be avoided is a determinate, situation-specific prescription, and as long as such a prescription is an item of occurrent, active understanding ("contemplation"), Aristotle thinks, the person in question will necessarily act on it, unless she is externally prevented from doing so. In fact, this is what he said just a short while ago, pretty much in so many words (at 1147a25–31). So, the idea that such practical conclusions control action is not only by itself readily intelligible. It also has been carefully prepared for in the immediate context of our passage.

What this first supplementary comment comes to, then, is that akratics, while they act akratically, do not have, in the sense that they do not have understanding of, the kind of proposition that, if and as long as it is an item of active understanding or contemplation, controls action. In saying that they do not have that proposition, Aristotle is relying on what he said earlier about the cognitive condition in which akratics act akratically.

He said earlier that this condition is a matter of having understanding in a way.[20] The point crucial for his current purposes is that it is also a

---

[19]   ἡ μὲν οὖν λέγει φεύγειν τοῦτο ("opinion then says to avoid this"), 1147a34.
[20]   ὥστε καὶ ἔχειν πως, 1147a12–13.

matter of not having understanding.[21] Having understanding without employing it is a matter of having that understanding ready for use, so that one can employ it at will, unless one is externally prevented from doing so. In this strict sense of having understanding, the akratic does not, at the time of akratic action, have understanding that he should not do the particular act in question. In now saying that, while they are in their emotional condition, akratics do not have the proposition that is the conclusion of the good practical syllogism, Aristotle is simply insisting on the strict notion of what is involved in having some piece of understanding.

Alternatively, an akratic, while being in some suitable emotional state, may have the last proposition not by having understanding of it but by being in a position to say it. This idea also has been carefully prepared for: saying the words that come from understanding is no reliable sign that the speaker is employing understanding, or even that he has understanding. One can say these things from memory, without at the time employing, and in fact without even having, understanding of the facts in question.

In a last supplementary comment, Aristotle revisits Socrates' refusal to accept that understanding can be defeated by some other psychological force. "And because the last term does not seem to be universal," Aristotle says, "or suited to understanding in the same way as the universal, what Socrates was looking for seems to come about: for that in spite of whose presence the affection comes about is not what seems to be understanding in the strict sense of the term, but perceptual understanding, nor is it understanding in the strict sense of the term that is dragged about on account of the affection" (1147b13–17).

The last term that features in the piece of practical thought that Aristotle has just described (at 1147a31–34) is the term "this particular thing," denoting some particular object in the person's environment. Aristotle plainly has in mind a syllogism of the form: A holds of B. B holds of C. Therefore: A holds of C. A stands for "to be avoided," B stands for "food," and C stands for "*this* particular thing." In English: this particular thing is to be avoided because food is to be avoided and this particular thing is food.

So the idea is that the term "this particular thing," which (in Aristotle's schematic depiction) is the last term to enter into the person's practical thinking, is not a universal term, and not suited to understanding in the way universal terms are. If all the three terms featuring in the syllogism were universal, the premises might be such as to impart complete, nondefective understanding of the conclusion that follows

---

[21] καὶ μὴ ἔχειν, 1147a13.

from them. But as things stand, one of those terms, the last one, is not suited to understanding in the way that the others are.

Furthermore, the nonuniversal term in question features in the conclusion, and must do so, since the conclusion is such as to control action and therefore must be about some particular object of pursuit or avoidance. Because the nonuniversal term needs to feature in the conclusion, it must also feature in one of the premises. So it cannot be eliminated and replaced with some universal term. Given the ineliminable presence in the argument of a nonuniversal term, the proposition that is the conclusion is not open to being understood in a complete, nondefective way. Any understanding that one may have concerning such a proposition will therefore fail to amount to understanding in the strict sense of the term. Since such understanding is tied to particulars that are objects of perception, it makes sense for Aristotle to describe this compromised form of understanding as perceptual understanding.

The upshot is that as long as one limits oneself to the narrow conception of understanding that corresponds to the strict use of the term, it turns out that it is never understanding that is defeated by any other psychological force when someone acts akratically. As Aristotle says, that, in spite of whose presence akrasia comes about, is not what seems to be understanding in the strict sense of the term, but is perceptual understanding.[22] Aristotle's idea is that it is understanding concerning particulars, understanding that one should pursue or avoid this or that particular object, that controls action. Since it is this and no other form of understanding that is such as to control action when things go as they should, it seems reasonable for Aristotle to think that it is this and no other form of understanding that gets defeated when people act akratically.

III. CONCLUDING COMMENTS

It is appropriate to end by saying a bit more than has so far been said in defense of what may be the most unorthodox idea that has been presented in the chapter: that what Aristotle means by *epistasthai* throughout the whole discussion is knowing a fact in a distinctive way, namely, knowing it on the basis of knowing the reason or explanation why that fact obtains. Once that idea is adopted, it becomes clear that the distinction between understanding and contemplating is not the distinction between

---

[22] This seems the best way of interpreting the difficult words οὐ γὰρ τῆς κυρίως ἐπιστήμης δοκούσης παρούσης γίνεται τὸ πάθος ... ἀλλὰ τῆς αἰσθητικῆς at 1147b15–17. Stewart's rather popular conjecture of περιγίγνεται instead of παρούσης γίγνεται (adopted, for instance, by Broadie and Rowe) is unnecessary. The present translation assumes that the participle παρούσης has concessive force.

knowing and attending to, but that between dispositional and occurrent cases of grasping the truth of a suitable proposition on the basis of grasping the reason or explanation why the proposition is true.

One reason to accept this interpretation of what Aristotle in our discussion means by *epistasthai* is that it reflects Aristotle's own explication of what the verb and its cognates mean. By way of explicating what understanding (*epistēmē*) is in *NE* vi 3, he says that it is a state suited to demonstrating, and for Aristotle to demonstrate the truth of a given proposition is just to give a rigorous statement of the reason or explanation why the proposition is true. In *Posterior Analytics* i 2, he says that "we think that we understand each thing without qualification ... when we think we know the explanation on account of which the thing in question is" (71b9–11).[23]

Second, interpreting what Aristotle means by *epistasthai* in this way has the important advantage that it makes it easy to see why he thinks that when people act akratically, they do the base thing in question voluntarily.[24] If Dan is unaware of the fact that the woman he is having sex with is his friend's wife, then having sex with his friend's wife is not, for Aristotle, something that Dan does voluntarily. If the akratic person's temporary inability to employ *epistēmē* were a temporary inability to call to mind what he dispositionally knows (for instance, that Sarah is a married woman, and in fact is Jack's wife), then one might reasonably worry that in his emotional condition he cannot be aware of the particulars of the situation in the way that is required for voluntarily doing the bad thing in question. However, being temporarily unable to grasp facts on the basis of grasping the explanations why those facts obtain leaves one in a position to recognize individuals and particular objects in one's environment, which is what is required for voluntary action.

It also leaves one in a position to grasp normative facts. For example, while Dan is akratically having sex with Jack's wife, Sarah, he may be aware not only of the fact that Sarah is Jack's wife but also of the fact that he should not be having sex with her. But in such cases, Dan's awareness that he should not be doing what he is doing does not rest on his active knowledge of the reason why he should not be doing it. It is not connected to his more general practical commitments in the way that it would be if his actions were guided and controlled by active understanding.

---

[23] Cf. also *Physics* i 1.184a10–16; *Posterior Analytics* ii 19.100b5–14: ἐπιστήμη δ' ἅπασα μετὰ λόγου ἐστι ("every form of understanding is with an account"), which is why understanding does not pertain to the indemonstrable principles of a science; likewise *NE* vi 6.1140b31–1141a1.

[24] As he states at *NE* vii 2.1146a6–7, and at *NE* vii 10.1152a15–16.

Third, and last for now, Aristotle is notoriously unclear about just which proposition it is of which the akratic, while in the grip of his emotional condition, is ignorant in the special way of being ignorant that pertains to akrasia. Hence the long debate in the secondary literature about whether the akratic, according to Aristotle's analysis, is ignorant of the minor premise of the good syllogism,[25] or only of its conclusion.[26] The present interpretation of what Aristotle means by *epistasthai* explains why it is reasonable for him to leave it implicit to which proposition the ignorance that is characteristic of akrasia pertains. The ignorance in question consists in a special way of not having precisely the piece of understanding against which akratics act when they act akratically. This is also the piece of understanding that Aristotle has in mind in speaking of the understanding in spite of whose presence akrasia comes about. He describes this understanding as perceptual understanding, because it features a particular term, and perception is responsible for the cognition of particulars.

So, if *epistasthai* in our discussion means what we have taken it to mean, Aristotle gives us all the information we need to work out just which proposition he has in mind in saying that the akratic, while in the grip of the emotional condition, is ignorant of something or other (1147b6), does not have understanding of something or other (b10–11), and acts akratically in spite of the presence in him of perceptual understanding of something or other (b15–17). The proposition in question is not the proposition that is the major premise of the good syllogism, since that proposition does not feature a particular term. Nor is it the minor premise, since it is not an object of understanding at all. It is grasped by perception, not on the basis of grasping an explanation.[27] So the proposition in question must be the conclusion of the good syllogism. The salient piece of understanding that the akratic in a way has but also lacks at the time of akratic action is understanding that he should now stay away from the particular object that he is pursuing.

[25] E.g., Ross 1995, 229–30; Cooper 1975, 49–50.

[26] E.g., Joachim 1951, 226–229; Charles 2009, 61–62.

[27] It is probably no coincidence that in the whole discussion Aristotle never uses the verbs *epistasthai* or *theōrein* with regard to the kind of proposition that constitutes the minor premise of the good syllogism (e.g., "this is sweet"). Relatedly, he freely switches between "employ" (χρᾶσθαι) and "contemplate" (θεωρεῖν) in speaking of what it is that people understand (i.e., that they should not do something, or that certain things are base: 1146b32–34, 1147a12), but in speaking of employing the kind of proposition that constitutes the minor premise of the good syllogism (at 1146b35–1147a3; at 1147a7; and at 1147a33), he uses only "employ" or "be active" (ἐνεργεῖν), but never "contemplate."

WORKS CITED

Broadie, S., and C. Rowe. 2002. *Aristotle: Nicomachean Ethics*. Oxford: Oxford University Press.

Burnyeat, Myles. 1981. "Aristotle on Understanding Knowledge." 97–139 in E. Berti ed. *Aristotle on Science: The Posterior Analytics*. Padova: Editrice Antenore.

2001. *Map of Metaphysics Zeta*. Pittsburgh: Mathesis Publications.

Charles, David. 2009. "*Nicomachean Ethics* VII.3: Varieties of *Akrasia*." 41–71 in C. Natali ed. *Aristotle's Nicomachean Ethics, Book VII*. Oxford: Oxford University Press.

Cooper, John. 1975. *Reason and Human Good in Aristotle*. Cambridge, MA: Harvard University Press.

Hardie, W. F. R. 1968. *Aristotle's Ethical Theory*. Oxford: Oxford University Press.

Irwin, T. 1999. *Aristotle: Nicomachean Ethics*. Indianapolis: Hackett.

Joachim, H. 1951. *Aristotle: The Nicomachean Ethics*. Oxford: Oxford University Press.

Kenny, A. 1966. "The Practical Syllogism and Incontinence." *Phronesis* 11: 163–184.

Lyons, J. 1963. *Structural Semantics – An Analysis of Part of the Vocabulary of Plato*. New York: Blackwell.

Morison, B. 2011. "An Aristotelian Distinction between Two Types of Knowledge." *Proceedings of Boston Area Colloquium in Ancient Philosophy* 27: 29–57.

Müller, Jozef. 2008. "Aristotle on Decision and Uncontrolled Action." Ph.D. dissertation, Princeton.

Pickavé, M., and J. Whiting. 2008. "*Nicomachean Ethics* 7.3 and Akratic Ignorance." *Oxford Studies in Ancient Philosophy* 34: 323–371.

Ross, W. D. 1995. *Aristotle*. 6th ed. New York: Routledge (first published 1923).

Rowe, Christopher. 1971. *The Eudemian and Nicomachean Ethics: A Study in the Development of Aristotle's Thought*. Cambridge: Cambridge University Press.

Stewart, J. A. 1892. *Notes on the Nicomachean Ethics of Aristotle*. vols. 1–2. Oxford: Clarendon Press.

13   Philosophical Virtue
In Defense of the Grand End

I. DOES ARISTOTELIAN VIRTUE OF CHARACTER REQUIRE PHILOSOPHY?

According to the account of happiness that Aristotle develops in *NE* i, happiness is a life of virtuous activity adequately supplied with external goods (i 7, i 8). A consequence of this account, Aristotle says, is that happiness will be "widely shared" (*polukoinon*, *NE* i 9.1099b15–20). Virtue comes through human effort (and not from, say, divine grace), and so if happiness is based in virtue, it should be accessible to anyone who is not deformed in her capacity for virtue.[1]

But just how widely shared does Aristotle think virtue-based happiness is? Does he think that most decent citizens of fourth-century Athens are plausible candidates for virtue-based happiness? Or does his comment about the wide extension of virtue assume improved social and cultural conditions, his point being that in those *improved* conditions many citizens can achieve virtue-based happiness?[2]

How one answers these questions depends, in part, on how one interprets Aristotelian virtue of character and, in particular, how one interprets practical wisdom (*phronēsis*) – the intellectual excellence required for and expressed in virtue.[3] If, as some commentators maintain, the *phronēsis*

I would like to thank James Allen, Andrew Chignell, Jessica Moss, Alice Phillips Walden, and the editor of this volume for their detailed and helpful comments on drafts of this contribution.

[1]   "[Virtue-based happiness] would also be something widely shared, since everyone who was not incapacitated with regard to virtue could attain it through some kind of learning and personal effort" (1099b15–20). All translations of the *Nicomachean Ethics* are from Crisp 2000 unless otherwise indicated. Translations of Aristotle's other works are my own.

[2]   Assuming ideal conditions would not render the claim pointless, since we can understand the claim as a comparative one. Aristotle would be saying that in ideal social conditions, virtue-based happiness will be widespread, whereas happiness that depends on divine favor (a possibility that Aristotle has just entertained) will not.

[3]   Aristotle often uses "virtue" (*aretē*) as an abbreviation for "virtue of character" (*ēthikē aretē*), and I will occasionally follow him by using "virtue" as shorthand for "virtue of character."

required for virtue requires an articulate and reasoned picture of the human good, one resembling the account Aristotle presents in his ethical works, then only in a society rather different from Aristotle's (one that facilitates for the masses reflection about the human good) will virtue-based happiness be a real possibility for most citizens. After all, an articulate, reasoned, *Nicomachean Ethics*–style blueprint of the good does not emerge automatically from a good upbringing or common sense but depends on a person's finding herself in the privileged intellectual and cultural conditions that enable her to wrestle with questions of ethical philosophy. But if *phronēsis* does not require a reasoned grasp of the universal principles that organize the best life – if it simply requires good behavior based in a prereflective appreciation of the conventional virtues of character – then virtue-based happiness may be a plausible possibility for any nondeformed person in fourth-century Athenian conditions who has been well brought up.

Broadie 1991 argues that it would go against common sense for Aristotle to envision the ethical agent as a kind of ethical philosopher who has a reasoned blueprint of the good. We regularly and rightly ascribe virtue of character to people who lack grand visions of the good, Broadie says, and so out of charity we should not saddle Aristotle with a view that restricts virtue to an enlightened few who have reflected on *Nicomachean Ethics*–style questions. In her words, "The conditions for assigning these predicates ['courageous person' and 'temperate person'] become utterly unrealistic if, in addition to moral virtue's entailing practical wisdom, practical wisdom entails possession of a true, comprehensive articulate picture of the human good" (Broadie 1991, 201).

I argue that Aristotle's virtuous person necessarily and essentially possesses a reasoned *Nicomachean*-style blueprint of the good. *Politics* iii 4 and iii 18 imply that the *phronēsis* required for virtue closely approximates political science (*politikē*), the intellectual excellence of the statesman whereby he correctly grasps the nature of the human good and figures out what to do to bring it about. I also argue that attributing to Aristotle such an intellectually exalted conception of virtue does not make him vulnerable to Broadie's objection from common sense.[4] This is because Aristotle recognizes a *secondary* kind of virtue that has less exalted conditions and so can be possessed by non-philosophers. This secondary kind of virtue is both praiseworthy and ethically salient, and in this way Aristotle's ethical philosophy makes room for common sense.

---

[4] As for her other objections against intellectually exalted readings of virtue, see the excellent discussion in Kraut 1993.

II. TWO READINGS OF PHRONĒSIS

Let us begin with what is uncontroversial about Aristotelian virtue of character. According to Aristotle, the virtues of character – temperance, courage, generosity, justice, and the like – are excellent states of a person's capacity to reason, where this capacity includes the capacity not only to engage in deliberations issuing in rational choices (*prohairesis*) about what to do but also to have nonrational desires and emotions that harmonize with these rational choices.[5] The virtuous person possesses a stable disposition to respond appropriately in feeling and action to a wide variety of situations, in each case rationally choosing the *kalon* (noble, honorable, admirable) action for its own sake and carrying out that decision with the support of her nonrational desires.[6]

Virtue of character is inseparable from *phronēsis*, the intellectual virtue that ensures correct deliberation and thus correct rational choices (ii 6.1107a1, vi 1.1138b18–34, vi 13.1144b14–1145a2). *Phronēsis* distinguishes "real" or "full" (*kuriōs*) virtue from mere "natural" (*phusikē*) virtue, the nonthinking desiderative disposition possessed by animals and children to mimic virtuous behavior (1144b1–17). Someone who possesses *phronēsis* (a *phronimos*) "deliberates nobly about what is good and beneficial for [himself], not in particular respects such as what conduces to health or strength, but about what conduces to living well as a whole" (vi 5.1140a28), and these reasonings instruct her in what is *kalon* and motivate *kalon* action. Thus, the person with "real" or "full" (*kuriōs*) virtue differs from the possessor of mere natural virtue, since the latter's actions do not rest on or express deliberation.

The controversial aspect of Aristotelian virtue that is my focus is the nature of the virtuous person's deliberation (or, what amounts to the same thing, the nature of *phronēsis*). According to what has become

---

[5] The rationality relevant to virtue of character comes in two forms, corresponding to two parts or aspects of the rational part of the soul (*to echon logon*). One part of to echon logon actually thinks (*dianooumenon*, NE i 7.1098a3–5) and in particular deliberates (*bouleuesthai*, vi 1.1139a 12–13). The other part (*the alogon*) does not itself think but rather desires; this part is the seat of nonrational desires and emotions, and it counts as derivatively rational or rational "in a way" (*pēi*, 1102b4) insofar as it can respond to the strictly rational part by "obeying" (*peitharchei, peitharchikon*), "listening" (*euēkoōteron, katēkoon*), or harmonizing with (*homophōnei*) reason (1102b13–1103a1). Virtue of character is thus that state of the soul whereby a human being expresses well her two types of rationality: the rationality of her deliberative part and the rationality of her nonrational part (her *alogon* or emotional part) *qua* that part's ability to "listen to" or "obey" reason.

[6] For my purposes, I will leave *kalon* untranslated, though the reader may substitute any of the translations I offer herein – "noble," "honorable," or "admirable." For a discussion of the proper translation of *kalon*, see Irwin 2010.

known as the "Grand End" reading of *phronēsis*, the *phronimos* deliberates with a view to an articulate and reasoned vision of the good
(a "Grand End"). In the case of the *phronimos*, this Grand End will be
the picture of the human good that Aristotle sketches in the
Nicomachean Ethics – the picture whereby happiness is the active life
of complete virtue. While this blueprint need not be easy to apply to
every particular situation – applying it will sometimes require some
sort of separate ethical perception, for example – this Grand End
nonetheless plays a critical role in both explaining and justifying the
phronimos's rational choices.[7] If the *phronimos* is asked why in a
particular situation she did action X rather than action Y, her answer
will necessarily reference her Grand End by showing the link between
her chosen action and her conception of happiness as virtuous activity.
While this Grand End need not figure explicitly in the deliberations
immediately leading up to her choices, it nonetheless stands *implicitly*
in the background as the goal explaining her action.

By insisting that *phronēsis*-informed deliberation begins from a
Nicomachean-style blueprint of the good, the Grand End reading of
phronēsis envisions the virtuous agent as someone concerned with the
same general questions about the structure of the human good that
Aristotle addresses in the ethical works. In the *Nicomachean Ethics*,
Aristotle says that such an inquiry is part of "political science" (*politikē*),
the science concerned with delineating the human good and bringing it
about for a community.[8] As Grand Enders interpret *phronēsis*, the ethical
agent or *phronimos* and the philosopher-statesman with *politikē* are
importantly similar insofar as both have an articulate grasp of the constituents of happiness.[9] Where the virtuous agent's *phronēsis* and the
statesman's *politikē* differ is primarily in their scope: *politikē* aims at the
good of all citizens, whereas *phronēsis* strictly speaking aims at the good

[7] By "ethical perception" I mean something different from ordinary sensory perception,
though I am not taking a specific position here on what this ethical perception consists
in. Aristotle discusses ethical perception at *NE* vi 8.1142a23–30.

[8] Aristotle on the connection between political science and the good: "Knowledge of the
good would seem to be the concern of the most authoritative science (*kuriōtatēs*), the
highest master science (*architektonikēs*). And this is obviously the science of politics,
because it lays down which of the sciences there should be in cities, and which each
class of person should learn and up to what level. And we see that even the most
honourable of faculties, such as military science, domestic economy, and rhetoric,
come under it. Since political science employs the other sciences, and also lays down
laws about what we should do and refrain from, its end will include the ends of the
others, and will therefore be the human good" (i 2.1094a27–b7; cf. vii 11.1152b1–3).

[9] In support of this view of *phronēsis* that strongly assimilates it to the political science
we see on display in the ethical works, some commentators appeal to the following
passage: "Political science and practical wisdom are the same state, but their being is
different" (vi 7.1141b14).

of its possessor (vi 8.1141b30–1142a8). But even this difference between *phronēsis* and *politikē* is potentially a small one, since an individual's good requires the good of that individual's community (1142a9–12, i 2.1094b7), and so the *phronimos* can achieve his good only if he achieves the good of his community as well.

Regardless of how big or small that particular difference is, the important point for Grand Enders is this: the *phronimos*, like the philosopher-statesman with *politikē*, deliberates with a view to a substantive, comprehensive, and articulate picture of happiness of the sort sketched in the *NE*'s political science lessons. The *phronimos* aims at a life of virtuous activity, where the content of "virtuous activity" is fleshed out in the universal terms we find in the ethical works. The *phronimos* aims not at temperance but at temperate activity and knows that temperate action involves not complete suppression of non-rational desires but rather the harmony of nonrational desire and reason under reason's control. And she aims at just activity, knowing that just activity accords with not just any sort of equality but with equality for equals. According to Grand Enders, these principles set the terms for the *phronimos*'s deliberation no less than they do for the philosopher-statesman's, so that only those who grasp these principles can have *phronēsis*.

Opposed to the Grand End reading of *phronēsis* is what we might call the "Ground Level" reading. Broadie has given the most fleshed out account of this reading, so I focus on her account.[10] On her view, virtuous

---

[10]   Price articulates and defends what he describes as a non–Grand End view of deliberation and asserts that it is very close to Broadie's view. I am not sure that he is right that his favored view is in fact an alternative to the Grand End view as I describe Grand End views here; for the same reasons, I am also not sure that he is right that his view is shared by Broadie. On Price's view, deliberation tests the acceptability of one's current project not just by evaluating it against one's other current and future projects but by testing it against one's conception of the good, understood as one's distinctive values that makes the agent the sort of person she is: "Wondering, for example, in a situation which permits me either to φ or χ, which would best serve my *eudaimonia* amounts to comparing the pros and cons of φ'ing with those of χ'ing in a manner that is open to whatever considerations, relevant in the context, really matter to me as the person that I am with the character that I have. It is to attempt to make a choice that I can stand by and live with" (235). I agree with Meyer 2013 that, if Price is construing the deliberator as choosing an action with a view to some substantive picture of the sort of person – or the sort of life – the deliberator wants to be or to have, Price's view (whether he realizes it or not) is actually very close to the Grand End view; both give a Grand End a guiding role in deliberation. Price seems to think that for a conception of the good to be a Grand End, it must be the sort of thing that can be grounded in a desire-independent manner; he also seems to think that it must be so exhaustive that it can be applied to circumstances without the need to exercise judgment. Like Meyer, I do not think that Grand End views are committed to these claims.

deliberation begins not with a substantive blueprint of the good that the virtuous person seeks to instantiate (on the Ground Level view, the *phronimos* need not have any conception of the good at all) but rather with some specific and ordinary end like making a business contact that arises when an opportunity to achieve that end arises in a person's situation (Broadie 1991, 234). When this opportunity for achieving the end arises – call the end *O* – she forms a provisional wish (*boulēsis*) for *O*, and deliberation sets in to determine whether, and if so how, she can achieve *O* in a way that does justice to the other concrete goals that she has at the time. (I say "provisional" wish, because deliberation may end up showing that obtaining *O* requires too great a sacrifice to the other specific goals that the agent has at the time.) Broadie calls this "Ground Level" deliberation and its corresponding excellence "Ground Level" *phronēsis*, because it is essentially concerned with pursuing the specific, ordinary ends that we acquire when we confront something in our immediate environment and not with pursuing some comprehensive end or vision of happiness.[11]

On Broadie's view, what distinguishes the *phronimos* from vicious agents or otherwise less impressive moral agents is the *phronimos*'s deliberative ability consistently to read individual ethical situations well so as to act correctly, where reading well is perceiving the extent to which she should pursue the concrete objective *O*. The *phronimos*, but not the vicious person, will pursue *O* in that situation when pursuing *O* does justice to all the other things she cares about, but crucially the wise agent's choice of *O* or her choice of *O* over *P* need not rest on her acceptance of an ethical blueprint or universal principles that make clear the values of the goods at stake.[12]

Broadie grants that there is a kind of *phronēsis* – "architectonic" (*architectonikē*) *phronēsis* (vi 7–8) – that is concerned with large blueprint questions about the structure of the human good, but she insists

---

[11]   "Hence on what I am calling the basic level, the virtuous individual, acting day to day in response to particular situations, aims at this, that and the other goal, short term and long: to get his harvest in, to educate his children, to help a friend in difficulties, to run for office, prepare himself for a military campaign etc., etc. He might, if asked on any occasion, acknowledge that, yes, he pursues his various ends 'for the sake of happiness' (it would be odder to say 'No' than 'Yes'). This does not mean that he equates any one of them with happiness in a universal definition, or that he equates them all (a questionable totality, in any case) with happiness in that way. Nor does it mean that he defines happiness to himself as something else specific to which all these others are means" (Broadie 1991, 46–47).

[12]   "The deliberator explains his choice of *A* by saying, e.g., 'I wanted *O*, and this was the situation, but at the same time it was important not to jeopardise *P*.' But it does not follow that he can or should be expected to justify the priorities implied in wanting *O* on these terms" (Broadie 1991, 248).

that what is essential to virtue of character is Ground Level *phronēsis* and not architectonic *phronēsis*. While an especially reflective ethical agent at a mature point in her ethical career might acquire architectonic *phronēsis* and the *NE*-style blueprint of the good it implies, this development happens *after* the agent has already established herself as a *phronimos* deliberator and so cannot be a prerequisite for a person having the *phronēsis* required for virtue.[13]

In insisting that wise choice-making does not require a reasoned Grand End to serve as a lodestar, Broadie envisions the virtuous agent as, at least potentially, radically different from the wise philosopher-statesman who has mastered *politikē*. While the latter necessarily has a concern with general questions about the structure of the human good, the former need not have inquired into that domain at all.[14] So whereas on the Grand End reading the *phronēsis* required for virtue is intellectually very similar to *politikē*, since both integrally involve a *Nicomachean Ethics*-style conception of the good, on the Ground Level view *phronēsis* and *politikē* are substantially different kinds of intellectual capacities: the latter, but not the former, involves *Nicomachean*-style thinking about the human good.

III. EVIDENCE FOR THE GRAND END READING OF PHRONĒSIS

Having sketched these two readings of *phronēsis*, I want to argue for the Grand End reading. As we shall see, *Politics* iii 4 and iii 18 closely connect the *phronēsis* required for virtue with a grasp of *politikē*, and specifically the kind of *politikē* that implies a *Nicomachean*-style grasp of the human good. But before looking at *Politics* iii 4 and iii 18 I want to look first at a passage from *NE* v 2 that shares some of their themes and

[13] "We gain philosophical understanding of the practicable end by reflection on our experience of particular achieved instances. There is therefore a basic level of virtuous activity and happiness which is logically and often chronologically prior to such reflection. On that basic level the [*phronimos*] has not articulated to himself a single specific goal which in general he equates with happiness. For many people this may be the only level. It has to come first because whatever one reflectively decides that happiness is – pleasure, honour, fine action – that which it is must first occur and be a familiar element in human life before it can be grasped as a universal and become a topic" (Broadie 1991, 46–47).

[14] Aristotle shows "no sign of holding that practical virtue itself, which includes practical wisdom, necessarily presupposes a command of philosophical ethics. ... The ground-level practical wisdom that keeps us decently going as human beings precedes philosophical ethics (which comes on the scene at leisure), hence cannot depend upon it" (Broadie 1991, 199–200). Cf. "It is clear that someone can have ground-level wisdom without having architectonic wisdom (and likewise administrative political expertise without legislative expertise)" (Broadie 2002, 373).

so has the potential to supplement our analyses of them. It will not be my aim to *argue* for a particular interpretation of the *NE* v 2 passage, as it is a difficult passage and allows for a variety of readings; instead I will present a reading that, *if* correct, entails that *NE* v 2 raises as a hypothesis a claim that *Politics* iii 4 and iii 18 later explicitly accept, namely, that the *phronēsis* that is integral to virtue of character is something very close to the political science we see on display in the ethical works. Even if one rejects my interpretation of v 2, however, my argument concerning *Politics* iii 4 and iii 18 will still stand; considered on their own, these two chapters connect *phronēsis* with *NE*-style political science in a way that supports the Grand End over the Ground Level reading of *phronēsis*.

1. NE *v* 2

Aristotle at *NE* v 2 distinguishes two kinds of justice: general justice and particular justice. He says that general justice is coextensive with the virtues of character, whereas particular justice extends only to that domain of virtue that governs "graspingness" (*pleonexia*) in apportioning oneself external goods. Moreover, insofar as general justice is coextensive with the virtues of character, it is also identical to what is lawful, since law prescribes actions that accord with all the virtues; particular justice, by contrast, is coextensive only with the laws regulating *pleonexia*.

In the following passage, Aristotle summarizes the connections between general justice, virtue, and lawfulness, and then turns to a question about moral education:

[1] For most lawful actions are those prescribed by virtue as a whole. For the law prescribes living in accord with each virtue and prohibits living in accord with each vice. And the things that are productive of virtue as a whole are those laws that have been enacted in relation to education with a view to the common good. [2] Concerning the education of the individual that makes him without qualification (*haplōs*) a good human being, we must determine later whether it belongs to political science or to some other [science]. [3] For perhaps (*ou gar isōs*) it is not the case that being a good person and being a good human being are the same, for every citizen. (v 2.1130b22–27, my translation)

Here I present a possible interpretation of this passage, one that differs from that of many commentators.[15] Aristotle's earlier discussion (summarized at [1]) of general justice as both lawfulness and virtue as a whole prompts Aristotle in this passage to distinguish (i) being disposed to obey laws that command virtuous behaviors from (ii) being virtuous without

---

[15]   As their translations make clear, Broadie 2002, Crisp 2000, Kenny 2011, and Irwin 1999 interpret the passage as raising a question about the scope of political science.

qualification. He needs to distinguish these two because, having just identified general justice *both* with lawfulness *and* with virtue as a whole, someone might conclude that being disposed to obey the law *is* to be virtuous without qualification or to have virtue of character.[16] But this identification would be a mistake: when Aristotle said that general justice is virtue as a whole and so also lawfulness, he meant only that the actions prescribed by law are *coextensive* with the actions done by the person with virtue of character; he did not mean that the disposition to obey the law is identical to possessing virtue of character. To guard against this potential mistake and point out the distinction between (i) and (ii), Aristotle suggests at [2] that what is essential to someone satisfying (ii), but not essential to someone satisfying (i), is an education in political science – an education in the doctrines of the *NE*, for example.

At [3] Aristotle notes that this suggestion about political science as the distinguishing feature of virtue of character is plausible only if one accepts that the virtue of a good human (i.e., virtue of character, or the virtue of someone good without qualification) is different from the virtue of a good citizen (i.e., the virtue whereby one preserves the constitution by, e.g., obeying its laws [*Pol.* iii 4.1276b26–29]).[17] Someone might confuse these two types of virtues for the same reason that one might confuse (i) and (ii): given that Aristotle has just identified general justice *both* with lawfulness *and* with virtue as a whole, it would be easy to think that possessing citizen virtue – preserving the constitution through one's disposition to obey the law – just *is* possessing the virtue of a man, or virtue without qualification. So Aristotle is urging us at [3] to distinguish the virtue of a citizen from virtue of character and to consider the possibility that possessing political science is essential to virtue of character but not to the virtue of a citizen. He promises to discuss later the distinction between citizen virtue and character virtue and suggests that that discussion will help assess [2]'s hypothesis about political science as distinctive of the latter.

[16] To be virtuous without qualification is to possess *phronēsis*-informed virtue of character or "real" or "full" (*kurios*) virtue (vi 13.1144b31–1145a1).

[17] Aristotle on the importance of obeying the constitution-specific laws to preserve a given constitution: "The most important of all the things that have been said for the preservation of constitutions, which all men now belittle, is to be educated with a view to the constitutions. For there is no benefit in the most beneficial laws, even when they have been accepted by all those who are politically active, unless people are habituated and educated in the constitution (democratically if the laws are democratic, oligarchically if they are oligarchic)" (*Pol.* v 9.1310a12–18). Here, Aristotle suggests that for an oligarchic constitution to be preserved, it is not enough that its rulers prescribe oligarchic laws. It requires in addition that citizens be habituated and educated in the constitution's goals and policies so that they obey the laws the rulers correctly prescribe.

2. Politics *iii 4*

Politics iii 4 addresses whether the virtue of a good human is the same
(*tēn autēn*) as that of the good citizen (1277a21–23, 1276b15–17), thus
fulfilling *NE* v 2's promissory note to discuss in detail the relation
between citizen virtue and virtue of character. *Politics* iii 4 gives
two arguments that citizen virtue and the virtue of the good human
being (i.e., virtue of character) are not the same, and it is the second
argument that is the more important one for our purposes. As we shall
see, the argument strongly implies a close relationship between possessing virtue of character and possessing political science.

Aristotle asks us to imagine the best (*aristēs*) city (1276b37). In that
city all the citizens will have the virtue of a good citizen (this is part of
what it is to be the best city), but not all of them will have the virtue of a
good human being:

> For if it is impossible that the [best] city be made up of excellent [human beings], it
> is at any rate necessary that each do his own job well, and do it out of virtue. But
> since it is impossible for the citizens to be all alike, there would not be one single
> virtue of a citizen and a good man (*mia aretē politou kai andros agathou*). For the
> virtue of the excellent citizen must belong to them all (only so can the city be the
> best), but it is impossible that the virtue of a good man belong to them all, unless
> all the citizens in the excellent city must necessarily be good [human beings].
> (1276b37–1277a5)

If in the best city every citizen has the virtue of a good citizen but not
every citizen has the virtue of a good man, then the virtue of a good
citizen is not identical with the virtue of a good man. The premises
straightforwardly entail the conclusion, but why should we (or
Aristotle) accept the premises? Why cannot the best city consist of
citizens who are all virtuous men? Indeed, is the best city not one in
which all citizens are virtuous men?[18]

There are several interpretations of the ethical hierarchy that Aristotle
insists on here.[19] For our purposes it is not important that we decide

---

[18] When Aristotle says that not all the citizens can be good men, he cannot simply be
pointing out that a city must contain craftsmen and other laborers who lack the leisure
to develop virtue of character. In *Pol.* iii 5.1278a8–11 Aristotle implies that a craftsman
can never be a good citizen. Since *Pol.* iii 4 asserts that in the best city all the citizens
have the virtues of a citizen, *Pol.* iii 4 is not including craftsmen as necessary citizens of
the best city.

[19] According to Keyt 2007, Aristotle's point is that in every city – and so in the best city too –
there will be young people who, being too immature yet to have *phronēsis* and so virtue,
must be ruled by virtuous adults. While these young boys can have citizen virtue, they
cannot yet have virtue of character. According to Frede 2005, the ethical hierarchy
reflects the need for a true whole like a city to contain a ruling and ruled element.

between these interpretations, since all interpretations agree on the point that is relevant for my argument: namely, that there is an ethical hierarchy in *Politics* iii 4's best city consisting of (on the one hand) rulers who have both virtue of character and citizen virtue and (on the other hand) subject citizens who merely have citizen virtue.

After setting out the ethical hierarchy in the best city and using it to show that virtue of character and citizen virtue are not the same, Aristotle then makes an important qualification. He says that while the virtue of a good citizen and that of a good man are not the same "without qualification" (*haplōs*), there will be one case – the case of the good ruler in the best state[20] – where these virtues will be the same:

> Thus it is clear from these considerations that the virtue of a human being and a citizen are not without qualification (*haplōs*) the same (*hē autē*). But will there be anyone whose virtue as an excellent citizen and an excellent human being will be the same? We say that the excellent ruler is good and practically wise (*phronimon*), but that the citizen need not be *phronimon*. (1277a12–16)

A few lines later, Aristotle confirms this point about the identity of character virtue and citizen virtue in the specific case of the best state's good ruler:

> But if the virtue of good ruler and good human being is the same, and if also a subject is citizen, then the virtue of a human being and a citizen would not without qualification (*haplōs*) be the same (*hē autē*) – though it would be in the case of a certain citizen. (1277a22)

So a special kind of citizen – the ruler in the best state – has both the virtue of a good man and the virtue of a citizen, and in his case these two virtues are the same (*hē autē*). That is to say, the condition of this good ruler's soul that makes him good at preserving his city's constitution (and so makes him a good citizen) is in some way the same condition that

---

As a kind of whole, even the best city will have a hierarchical structure and so need, in addition to good rulers, good subjects who have a special "moral outfit" that makes them suited for passive roles. Because the virtue that makes them suited for passive roles does not make use of *phronēsis*, subjects fail to express virtue of character. According to Kraut 2002, when Aristotle says that the best city cannot consist of all good men, he is expressing a realism about most citizens' chances of attaining virtue of character in typical social conditions. On Kraut's view, Aristotle is saying that, without a radical transformation of the *polis*, even the best cities will have citizens who lack virtue of character. As I say herein, all interpretations agree on the point that is important for my argument: viz., that there is an ethical hierarchy in *Pol.* iii 4's best state.

[20] At *Pol.* iii 18.1288a32–39 Aristotle mentions his "earlier discussions" where he argues that the virtue of a man is the same as that of a citizen in the best (*aristēs*) city. "Earlier discussions" clearly refers back to the iii 4–5 discussion, and this makes it clear that the restricted context of the best state is continuous throughout *Pol.* iii 4.

makes him perform well his human capacity to reason (and so makes him a good human being, or a human being with virtue of character).

A city's constitution (*politeia*) is its particular structure of political offices and corresponding goal (*telos*, *Pol.* iv 1.1289a15–18). Differences in constitution mark out aristocratic cities (ruled by the most virtuous and aiming at virtue, iii 7.1279a35–37, 9.1280b5–7, 18.1288a32–b1) from oligarchic cities (ruled by the wealthy and aiming at wealth, v 10.1311a9–11, iii 8.1279b34–1280a6, 9.1280a25–30) from democratic cities (ruled by the masses and aiming at freedom, vi 1.1317a40–b14). Later Aristotle explicitly says that the best city in *Politics* iii 4 is an aristocracy (iii 18.1288a32–41), which is not surprising given that its rulers have the distinction of possessing virtue of character and given that an aristocracy is ruled by an elite few who possess such virtue.[21] Now because the *Politics* iii 4 constitution is an aristocratic one, it follows that its rulers will express citizen virtue by preserving the city's distinctively aristocratic government, and this means that their citizen virtue will lie in their dispositions to prescribe laws and education practices that promote virtue among the constitution's citizens. In legislatively promoting virtue (and not, say, the accumulation of wealth), the

---

[21]   In conversation, Ron Polansky has suggested that the "best state" in *Pol.* iii 4 (later described as an "aristocracy" at iii 18.1288a32–41) does not refer to an aristocracy in the sense that I have sketched here (a government ruled by virtuous human beings and aiming at virtue) but rather refers to the polity (*politeia*) form of government that Aristotle describes in detail in *Pol.* iv. A polity is a mix of an oligarchy and democracy (iv 9.1294b14–18), and in it the multitude govern for the common advantage. While this might result in a kind of virtue (1295a35), it will not be full or complete (*kuriōs*) virtue, as Aristotle says that it is hard for a large number to reach complete virtue and emphasizes that what the multitude can have is *military* virtue (iii 7.1279a40–b1; cf. iii 17.1288a13, where the manuscripts say *polemikon* [military]). Because some of the multitude that rule the polity lack full virtue (they possess mere military virtue), and because a polity is ruled by the many and not by a few, a polity cannot be aristocratic in the sense I developed here. Regarding Polansky's suggestion, it is true that Aristotle suggests at *Pol.* iv 2 that there is a loose sense in which a polity is aristocratic (iv 2.1289b15–17). However, *contra* Polansky, we should assume that when at *Pol.* iii 18.1288a32–41 Aristotle calls the *Pol.* iii 4 constitution aristocratic, he is operating with a sense of "aristocratic" that *distinguishes* aristocracies from polities; "aristocratic" in the passage refers to constitutions ruled by a few people who have the distinction of possessing full virtue. In support of this reading of "aristocratic" in *Pol.* iii 18, note that just one chapter earlier in iii 17 Aristotle is thinking of polity as a form of government *distinct from* aristocracy and kingship (1288a6–15; cf. iv 8.1294a10–11). Note also *Pol.* iv 7.1293b1–21, where Aristotle, referring to his "earlier discussions" in *Pol.* iii 4, says that in an aristocracy alone can the same person have the virtue of a human being and that of a citizen. "Aristocracy" here cannot refer to a polity, because the multitude who rule in a polity are not all virtuous without qualification (iii 7.1279a40–b1; cf. iii 17.1288a13); "aristocracy" must refer to a community ruled by an elite few who have full virtue.

rulers prevent the aristocratic constitution from turning into an oligarchy or some other sort of constitution. But to promote virtue, the rulers must have legislative *politikē* *(nomothetikē, NE* x 9.1180b13–29, vi 8.1141b25). Legislative *politikē* takes as its starting point a clear grasp of the human good (i 2.1094a22–25; cf. *Pol.* 1321a14–16).[22] So these rulers' citizen virtue consists – in part at least – in their possession of and acting in accordance with the correct and articulate conception of human happiness that we find in the *NE*'s political science lessons.[23]

We have seen what makes the rulers in the *Pol.* iii 4 city good citizens. What makes them good human beings? *Pol.* iii 1277a12–16 and 1277b25–26 make clear that it is their possessing *phronēsis; NE* vi 13.1144b30–1145a2 implies this as well.[24] Now, we have seen that in *Pol.* iii 4's best city what makes the ruler a good citizen is the same as what makes him a good man (1277a12–16, a20–23) and also that what makes the ruler a good citizen is his prescribing in accordance with the political science lessons of the *Nicomachean Ethics.* We also know that in *Pol.* iii 4's best city *phronēsis* makes the ruler a good human being, a person with virtue of character. Putting these ideas together, it follows that the *phronēsis* that makes a ruler in the best city a good man is the same condition as the *politikē* in virtue of which he is a good citizen. In other words, the *phronēsis* integral to the ruler's virtue of character is in some way the same disposition as *politikē*. And since virtue of character does not change across constitutions (*Pol.* iii 4.1276b33–34; *NE* vi 13.1145a2), Aristotle must think that in any and all constitutions the *phronēsis* pertinent to virtue of character is in some way the same disposition as *politikē*.

This perfect coincidence between *phronēsis* and *politikē* coheres well with the Grand End view. On the Grand End view the *phronēsis* of the virtuous person and the *politikē* of the statesman provide their possessors with equipment that in its essentials is the same: both outfit their possessors with – among other things – an accurate, action-guiding conception of the good as a life of virtuous activity. By contrast, the

---

[22] The universal laws that the lawmaker crafts in light of this target then guide the jurors and assemblymen charged with making a particular decree *(psēphisma)* on individual legal cases. Aristotle calls the *phronēsis* pertinent to adjudicating such cases "deliberative" *(bouleutikē)* and "judicial" *(dikastikē) phronēsis (NE* vi 8.1141b25–30). Because it essentially concerns particular cases, it differs from the universal legislative *politikē* that is on display in the ethical works.

[23] The rulers will also express citizen virtue by obeying the laws they prescribe.

[24] "It is clear from what we have said, then, that we cannot be really good without practical wisdom, or practically wise without virtue of character ... one will possess all of [the virtues of character] as soon as he acquires the one, practical wisdom" (1144b30–1145a3).

Ground Level view has no obvious explanation for the identity or perfect coincidence of *politikē* and virtue of character that Aristotle insists on in *Politics* iii 4, since on the Ground Level view the practical thinking that characterizes *politikē* plays no essential role in the *phronēsis* pertinent to virtue of character. Though on the Ground Level view *phronēsis* might be a necessary condition of *politikē*, it is a truly weak one, since many (if not most) of the people with so-called Ground Level *phronēsis* lack *politikē*. Such a weak necessary condition is not likely to ground the seeming identity claim that we see in *Politics* iii 4.[25]

3. Politics *iii 18*

A passage from *Politics* iii 18 poses a similar problem as *Politics* iii 4 for the Ground Level view. In *Politics* iii 18 Aristotle, apparently referring to the discussion in *Politics* iii 4, says that the man with virtue of character is educated in something that is "nearly" the same as political science:

Since we showed in our first discussions that the virtue of a human being must be the same as that of a citizen of the best city, it is clear that the way and the means by which a human being becomes excellent (*spoudaios*) are the same as those by which someone constructs an aristocratic or kingly city, with the result that the education and the character traits that make a human being excellent will be practically (*schedon*) the same as those that make him political (*politikon*) and kingly (*basilikon*). (*Pol.* iii 18.1288a37–b2)

[25] To explain the tight connection between virtue of character and political science in *Pol.* iii 4, Broadie might give a similar explanation as she gives when commenting on Aristotle's claim that *phronēsis* and political science are the same state (*hexis*) though different in being (*einai*, vi 8.1141b23–24). In her commentary, she explains this as the claim that "the same upbringing fosters both" (Broadie 1991, 204). If "upbringing" here includes *all* the developmental materials that go into having these two states, then Broadie cannot consistently hold that the same upbringing fosters both *phronēsis* and political science, since she makes clear elsewhere that political science is developed only in the context of high cultural and knowledge conditions that foster philosophical reflection, whereas *phronēsis* requires no such exalted conditions (Broadie 1991, 47–48). Perhaps, then, by "upbringing" she means "*pre-reflective* upbringing," and Broadie's point is that both *phronēsis* and political science require the same upbringing in pleasure and pain training. Were Broadie to make this response, it would be a weak one, since on Broadie's view a good prereflective upbringing is at best a very weak necessary condition of political science – so weak that in her view one can have a good upbringing and yet have a view diametrically opposed to political science. This is the condition of the Spartans, who in Broadie's view have virtue of character (and thus a good upbringing) but also falsely identify the human good with external goods (Broadie 1991, 379). By weakening the connection between *phronēsis* and political science to such an extent that Ground Level *phronēsis* is compatible not only with political science but also with political ignorance, it is very difficult for Broadie to explain the strong connection Aristotle makes in *Pol.* iii 4 between political science and *phronēsis*.

What goes into constructing an aristocratic (or kingly) city?[26] Rulers in an aristocratic government are outstanding in virtue and aim to bring about virtue in the city. But bringing about virtue in others requires, we have seen, a grasp of the political science lessons in the *NE*. So Aristotle is saying in the preceding passage that the education and character traits of the human being with virtue of character are practically (*schedon*) the same as the ones that would make him an aristocrat, where the latter is a mastery of political science.

Again, this close connection between *phronēsis* and political science coheres nicely with the Grand End view, since according to the Grand End view the same training and character traits that give someone political science gives someone *phronēsis*. The Ground Level interpretation, by contrast, sees at best a weak connection; even if *phronēsis* is a necessary condition of having political science, it is far from being integral, and so we should be surprised to see Aristotle making what appears to be a wholly general claim about the identity of the *phronimos*'s education and the statesman's education.[27]

If the foregoing discussions of *Politics* iii 4 and iii 18 are correct, then Aristotle thinks that acquiring the *phronēsis* relevant to virtue requires engaging in the philosophy of human affairs. And if this is right, then, *contra* the Ground Level reading, having virtue requires having, on the basis of reflection, an articulate and comprehensive grasp of the best principles for organizing human life. It requires being an ethical philosopher of sorts.

IV. SECONDARY VIRTUE IN NE III 8

Most citizens whom we think decent do not have a deep philosophical insight into the *NE*'s doctrines about the human good, and many will not have the opportunities to develop such insight. And yet, as Broadie points out, we tend to regard many people who lack ethical philosophy to be praiseworthy and living lives of ethical significance. If Aristotle is to answer Broadie's objection from common sense, he must make room in his ethical theory and moral psychology for a type of virtue that such nonphilosophers can possess, and this virtue must go beyond the "natural

---

[26] Kingship is essentially an aristocracy in which only one person has virtue of character and so rules. "Kingship, then, as we said, is a structure that accords with aristocracy. For it accords with worth, whether this be peculiar (*idian*) virtue of that of a family" (*Pol.* v 10.1310b33).

[27] The close relationship between virtue and political science explains why Aristotle says that any reasonable person wants "*politikoi*" sons (*NE* x 9.1181a1–7). Any true *politikos* will be a good man, since the same education produces both. Keyt 2007, 239, makes this point.

virtue" of children or those who do what is virtuous for instrumental reasons alone.

In the remainder of the chapter, I argue that *NE* iii 8 briefly sketches a portrait of a secondary virtue that Aristotle assigns to the decent citizen. His account there is brief, but by looking at it in light of some of his moral psychology – particularly, his account of shame (*aidōs*) – we shall see that this secondary virtue involves the agent's having true motivating beliefs about the intrinsic value of virtue. To the extent that the decent (but non-*phronimos*) citizen can have these beliefs and a disposition to act in accordance with them, she has a virtue that is ethically salient enough, I will argue, to answer Broadie's objection from common sense. Because this secondary virtue includes an intrinsic appreciation for actions that are, for example, just or courageous, Aristotle's ethics does justice to the commonsense conviction that nonphilosophers can lead praiseworthy and ethically meaningful lives.

NE iii 8 discusses five kinds of pseudoforms of bravery – behavioral dispositions that resemble genuinely virtuous behavior but nonetheless fall short. It is worth quoting much of the relevant passage:

> Bravery, then, is something of this sort. But other states are also called bravery, according to five ways. [1] First there is civic (*politikē*) bravery, for it is most similar [to real bravery]. [2] For (*gar*) citizens seem to endure dangers on account of the penalties prescribed by laws and censures, and on account of the honors (*timas*); and on account of this they seem to be the bravest, among whom the cowardly are dishonored and the courageous honored. ... In such a way also Homer describes, for example when he says of Diomede and Hector: "Polydamas will be the first to throw up disgrace on me," and "For Hector speaking among the Trojans will say, "By me the son of Tydeus." [3a] This is the most similar to the bravery described earlier, [3b] since it comes about on account of virtue. [3c] For it comes about on account of shame and on account of a desire for something fine (*kalou*) (because for honor) and by aversion from disgrace, which is something shameful. [4] Into this group someone might also put those forced by their superiors. [5a] But they are worse, [5b] insofar as not by shame but on account of fear they do brave things, [5c] and they flee not the shameful but the painful. (1116a16–33, translation mine)

Aristotle lists "civic" (*politikē*) bravery as the pseudoform of bravery that is closest to real bravery ([1], [3a]). To explain its privileged status, he says that it results on account of virtue [3b], a claim he glosses by saying that the person with civic bravery acts from shame and a desire for something fine [3c]. The "virtue" referenced in [3b] cannot be the full virtue of the ethical works. However, as we shall see, it is a good basis for understanding Aristotle's view on the virtue capacities of the decent but unphilosophical citizen. So what is the nature of civic bravery?

We should begin by examining the motivational attitudes that Aristotle connects to civic bravery: shame and a desire for fineness [3c].

Elsewhere Aristotle describes a sense of shame or disgrace (*aischunē*) as the fear of dishonor (*adoxias*).[28] A person with a sense of shame is sensitive to public opinion:

They are more ashamed of things that are done in front of people's eyes and in the open; whence the saying, "The eyes are the dwelling of shame." That is why people feel more shame before those who will be with them and before those attending them, because in both cases they are in their eyes. (*Rhet.* ii 6.1384a33–b1)

Sensitivity to public opinion has a proper role in the life of the genuinely virtuous person.[29] Specifically, the virtuous person is sensitive to *good* people's opinions and only good people's opinions of her; this is the praiseworthy mean between indifference to any and all public opinion (the deficient state "shamelessness" – *anaischuntias*) and a concern with the opinion of everybody (the excessive state "bashfulness" – *kataplēxeōs*).[30]

Shame presupposes that the person actually identifies with and endorses the ethical standard that she has violated. This is evidenced by the fact that one can feel shame even when external observers and possibilities for public honors and dishonors are absent; it is also evidenced by the *discriminating* aspect of shame – the fact that we feel shame not just in front of anybody, but in front of those people whom we trust to speak the truth.[31] Shame, then, implies a concern not simply for good reputation, but an intrinsic concern for the ethical standards themselves.

Shame's origins in spirited desires (*thumoi*) supports this thesis that shame implies a noninstrumental concern for ethical standards, for

[28] Aristotle does not explicitly equate shame (*aidōs*) and disgrace (*aischunē*), but he does so implicitly. For example, in *NE* iv 9 his argument about shame works only under the assumption that the two are equivalent.

[29] "For some things, like dishonor (*adoxias*), it is right and *kalon* to fear, and shameful not to fear: the person who fears this is good and properly disposed to feel shame, and the one who does not is shameless" (iii 6.1115a12–15). At *NE* iv 9 Aristotle argues that shame is not proper to a decent person, since shame is a response to bad actions and the decent person does not do bad actions. This conception of shame as a strictly reactive attitude to one's actual base activity is not the conception of proper shame in operation in *NE* iii 6. According to the *NE* iii 6, one has a proper sense of shame if the thought that a particular action would be shameful restrains that person from thinking of that action as a real possible action for her.

[30] Though shame is praiseworthy, it lacks reasoned choice and thus falls short of being a virtue (*EE* iii 7.1233b26–27, 1234a23–25, *NE* ii 7.1108a32–35).

[31] "Now since shame is the impression of dishonor (*adoxias*), in which we shrink from it itself and not from its consequences, and since no one cares what opinion is held of him except because of the people who form that opinion, it follows that the people before whom we feel shame are those whose opinion of us matters to us. Such persons are: those who admire us, those whom we admire, those by whom we wish to be admired, those with whom we are competing, and those whose opinion of us we respect" (*Rhet.* ii 6.1384a22–27).

spirited desire has a social dimension that explains how one might develop an intrinsic appreciation of ethical standards.[32] Spirit is the nonrational desire through which we form friendship and form attachments to others,[33] and Aristotle describes early friendships between children and their parents as based on the child's perception of them as familiar, benevolent, and superior.[34] This loving perception of the parent as superior and benevolent makes it reasonable to think that the child comes to admire the parent and noninstrumentally to desire to be the sort of person her parent exemplifies. She will desire not just to receive praise from the parent but take her parent's standards to be right. Supposing that the parent upholds a life of virtuous activity, a child will acquire at an early age a noninstrumental concern to do what her parent upholds – just, courageous, and temperate action. When she acts contrary to this desire, she will feel shame.

The fact that shame implies an internalization of ethical principles is important, because it shows that when someone does virtuous actions from a sense of shame, she does not do virtuous actions simply for external reasons – to get honor or a good reputation – but rather because she believes that *such actions are good in themselves*.[35] If we apply this account of shame to iii 8's account of civic bravery, then (given [3c]) it follows that the civically brave have a noninstrumental concern to do

[32] Aristotle never explicitly says that shame is a spirited desire, but the striking similarities he draws between shame and the spirited emotion of anger (*orgē*) strongly suggest that shame too is spirited. Like shame, anger essentially involves judgments about how oneself measures up against an internal evaluative standard: the angry person believes that the slanderer has treated her as though she lacks the honorable characteristics she upholds and believes herself to possess. In shame, it is ourselves, not someone else, who has failed to respect our true worth: when we do something shameful, we have acted contrary to our potentially honorable selves, our selves when we are at our best.

[33] "[Thumos] is the capacity of the soul by which we feel friendship (*philoumen*). A sign of this is that one's spirit is roused more against those with whom one is familiar (*sunētheis*) and against friends (*philous*) than against those whom one does not know (*agnōtas*) when one takes oneself to be slighted. Thus Archilochus, for example, when reproaching friends, correctly addresses his spirit with the following: 'For surely thou are plagued on account of friends'" (*Pol.* vii 6.1327b38–1328a6). In connecting spirit with attachments for the familiar, the passage is reminiscent of a similar connection that Plato draws. In *Rep.* ii, Socrates says that the guardians must be spirited if they are to be brave, and then stresses that this spirited nature must combine gentleness toward those who are familiar to them (*tous oikeious*) and harshness toward their enemies.

[34] Aristotle on the child's attitudes toward her parents: *NE* viii 12.1161b17–1162a9, x 9.1180a30–b7; *Pol.* vii 1336b30–35. Aristotle parallels the relationship between parents and children and that between rulers and subjects (*NE* viii 11.1161a10–20, 10.1160b25–26); presumably, he thinks that similar feelings of kinship and admiration develop between citizens and the lawmakers of their communities.

[35] Rawls 1999, 407, shares this picture when he describes the "morality of authority" – a primitive sort of morality that consists in love-based obedience to authoritative persons:

what is *kalon*; they do not simply do what is brave to receive a good reputation or pubic honors. Presumably this is one reason why Aristotle indicates that acts of civic bravery, but not acts of the other pseudoforms, come about from "virtue" [3b]: unlike people with "compelled" bravery who do what is virtuous only because of instrumental reasons [5a–5c], people with civic bravery regard virtue as worth doing for its own sake – worth doing just because it is the *kalon* thing to do. And indeed, this noninstrumental concern to do what is *kalon* is exactly what we find at [3c] where Aristotle speaks of their desire for something *kalon*.[36]

So far I have argued that those with *NE* iii 8 civic bravery do virtuous actions because they believe that courageous actions are *kalon*. But there is an obvious objection to this interpretation of civic bravery. If we look at the *NE* iii 8 passage, Aristotle also says that people with civic bravery act because of censures (*epitimia*) and honors (*timas*) (1116a19), and the emphasis on honors seems to suggest that external honors play an important role in the civically brave person's choice to do virtuous actions. We might conclude from this that even if civically brave people have a sense of shame and thus a belief that the action in question is *kalon*, they must have an equally strong, if not stronger, motivation based in good

> The child's having a morality of authority consists in his being disposed without the prospect of reward or punishment to follow certain precepts that not only may appear to him largely arbitrary but which in no way appeal to his original inclinations. If he acquires the desire to abide by these prohibitions, it is because he sees them as addressed to him by powerful persons who have his love and trust, and who also act in conformity with them. He then concludes that they express forms of action that characterize the sort of person he should want to be.

36 Irwin 1996, 163, disagrees with my claim that those with civic bravery in *NE* iii 8 do what is brave because brave action is *kalon*. As he interprets civic bravery, they do brave actions because they hope to get honor, an external good that (Irwin says) is *kalon*: "The brave person is not moved primarily by considerations of honor and shame, but by the fact that brave action is itself [*kalon*], whether or not it wins him honor. While those who have the bravery of citizens are concerned for something that is [*kalon*], they do not choose brave action for its own sake and because it is [*kalon*]." In denying that the citizen does the brave action because such action is *kalon*, Irwin fails to take seriously the internalization of values that is presupposed in shame. But putting that point aside, his interpretation faces another problem. Irwin says that those with civic bravery do not act for the *kalon* but pursue something *kalon*, viz., honor. But in *EE* viii 3.1249a4–10 Aristotle suggests that external goods like honor are kalon *only when they are possessed by a person who is motivated by the kalon as such*. This distinguishes external goods from virtuous actions that are *kalon* by nature. While external goods like health, strength, and honor are good by nature, they become *kalon* only when they come into the possession of the virtuous person who acts for the sake of the *kalon*. It follows that the honor that people with civic bravery seek will not be *kalon* unless they already act for the sake of the *kalon*. Irwin's reading requires Aristotle to assume that people with civic bravery are motivated by the *kalon* as such, which is precisely the claim Irwin wants to reject. Thus, we should accept my reading of [3c] according to which those with civic virtue pursue the *kalon* as such (and not simply something – honor – that happens to be *kalon*).

reputation. If a good deed will not be rewarded with honors, then perhaps, depending on the situation, the person of civic bravery will not do it.

I think we should reject this more instrumental reading of civic bravery. Recall [3a]–[3c]:

[3a] This is the most similar to the bravery described earlier, [3b] since it comes about on account of virtue. [3c] For it comes about on account of shame and on account of a desire for something fine (*kalou*) (because for honor) and by aversion from disgrace, which is something shameful. (1116a16–33)

At [3c] Aristotle says that brave citizens pursue the *kalon* as such, and he glosses this by explaining that they pursue honor (see note 36). This suggests that Aristotle's references to honors and censures should be interpreted in such a way that pursuit of honors expresses their intrinsic concern with the *kalon* as such. There seem to be two interpretive possibilities that respect this constraint. First, perhaps Aristotle mentions honors because the citizen relies on honors to know which actions count as *kalon*. Not knowing what makes something genuinely *kalon*, citizens use honors and public disgrace, both enshrined in legal enactments and public censuring practices, to know what actions count as *kalon* in a particular situation.[37]

---

[37] Burnyeat 1980 suggests this interpretation. In support of his reading, consider the following passage from *NE* i 5, where Aristotle discusses people who choose the political life:

> Sophisticated people, men of action, see happiness as honour, since honour is pretty much the end of the political life. Honour, however, seems too shallow to be an object of our inquiry, since honour appears to depend more on those who honour than on the person honoured, whereas we surmise the good to be something of one's own that cannot easily be taken away. Again, they seem to pursue honour in order to convince themselves of their goodness; at least, they seek to be honoured by people with practical wisdom, among those who are familiar with them, and for their virtue. So it is clear that, to these people at least, virtue is superior. (1095b27–31)

Although sophisticated people want to be honored, they do not want to be honored by just anyone and for just anything; they want to be honored only by practically wise people and for their good deeds. Aristotle takes this to be an indication that such people want honor only coincidentally: what these people *really* seek is virtue, and honor is instrumentally useful to them by making them confident that they have successfully done what virtue requires. A similar idea surfaces later at *NE* viii 8 where Aristotle contrasts a person who seeks honor to be sure that he will receive future benefits with the person who seeks honor to reassure herself that she is a good person: "But it does not appear to be for its own sake that people choose honour, but incidentally. For the masses enjoy being honoured by those in high office because of their expectations (they think that they will get anything they want from them, and enjoy the honour as a sign of future indulgence). Those, however, who desire honour from good people familiar with them are seeking to have their own opinion of themselves confirmed; they enjoy honour, then, because they are confident of their own goodness on the strength of the judgement of those who say they are good" (1159a17–25).

Alternatively, the reference to honor might be meant to highlight a more specific deficiency in the brave citizen's conception of the *kalon*. Perhaps the person with civic bravery mistakenly thinks that what makes a type of action or character *kalon* is some extrinsic property – specifically, its tendency to be approved and esteemed by the community.[38] In the brave citizen's mind, to be a *kalon* action just is to be a type of action that generally provokes honor and praise. Such a mistake is understandable, given that honor is a prize for virtue and *kalon* achievements (iv 3.1123b35).

Either way we interpret *NE* iii 8's references to honor, unlike the other "brave" characters discussed in *NE* iii 8, those with civic courage do not require promises of external goods like wealth or good reputation to act virtuously; they will do a brave action even if they do not expect to be honored for it on that occasion. For this reason they differ from those who do courageous actions out of fear; such people flee not the shameful but the painful ([5b], [5c]).[39] They are like the slavishly virtuous in the *Phaedo* who act courageously only because that behavior minimizes pain over a lifetime. While both kinds of pseudobravery fall short of full bravery, civic bravery is superior, insofar as the person of civic bravery shares with the fully virtuous person the belief that just (temperate, courageous, etc.) activity is valuable for its own sake.

Aristotle makes clear that civic courage is not full courage (1116a15–16), and on our analysis of civic courage it is not hard to see why. Those with civic courage have not arrived at their conception of the good through their own reasoning; they identify their good with just, courageous, and temperate activity because at an early age they internalized these values from their community. This dependence on the reasoning of others displays their lack of *phronēsis*.

---

[38]   This view of the *kalon* would be similar to the view of the pious in the *Euthyphro* as what the gods love. Taylor 2006, 187, seems to take this sort of interpretation of civic bravery's deficiency: "The person of civic courage thinks that facing the enemy toe to toe in the battle line is a fine thing to do because that is what wins one honor, and that flight is ignoble because it brings disgrace. The person of true courage thinks that those acts deserve respectively honor and disgrace because they are, respectively, intrinsically splendid and intrinsically disgraceful."

[39]   "For the masses naturally obey fear, not shame, and abstain from shameful acts because of the punishments associated with them, not because they are disgraceful. For, living by their feelings as they do, they pursue their own personal pleasures and the means to them, and avoid the opposed pains; and they do not have even an idea of what is noble and truly pleasant, since they have never tasted it" (*NE* x 9.1179b11–16). That people who act out of fear have an overriding concern with pleasure and pain is not surprising, given Aristotle's definition of fear. The definition specifies a special relationship between fear and pleasure and pain. Fear is "a pain or disturbance due to imagining some destructive or painful evil in the future" (*Rhet.* 1382a21–22).

V. SECONDARY VIRTUE BEYOND NE III 8

The foregoing discussion of civic bravery shows that non-*phronimoi* can have motivations that give them a meaningful approximation of full virtue. Like those philosophers who have full virtue, non-*phronimoi* can be motivated to pursue the *kalon* as such. Moreover, provided that they are brought up with correct rules and honor practices – rules that proceed from *phonēsis* and *nous* (*NE* x 9.1180a22) – they will internalize a correct ethical code that recommends virtuous actions and prohibits vicious ones. Education (*paideia*) will instill in them a concern with courage, justice, and temperance; it will also instill rules of good conduct like "justice requires that I keep my promises" or "bravery requires that I not leave the battle line." These principles will help develop ordinary citizens' conceptions of what the virtues are and what value priorities the virtues imply.

In the *Politics*, Aristotle outlines the beginning of an educational program consisting of musical and athletic training, one that aims at "civic" (*politikē*) virtue (*Pol.* vii 6.1341a1) and at the *kalon* (vii 6.1338b29). This educational program will help tame appetitive desires that might compromise young people's spirit-based desire to do what is *kalon*. Musical education in songs about virtuous characters will inculcate and reinforce in children true beliefs about which characters and action types are worth exemplifying. Physical training will help solidify friendships with others and strengthen young people's relationship to the community from which they internalize their values. In this way, Aristotle's educational program in the *Politics* is geared at producing the secondary virtue that many citizens never go beyond: thus from moral *paideia*, non-*phronimoi* citizens acquire true beliefs about the good, beliefs that underlie the feelings of shame that they experience when they act against virtue. Because of these true beliefs and a corresponding disposition to act in accordance with them, they can approximate, in an ethically salient way, the rational excellence that full virtue constitutes.[40]

There will be important practical limitations to this secondary virtue of the ordinary citizen. As we have seen, those with civic virtue depend

---

[40] The training required for full virtue will go beyond musical and athletic training and will presumably include training in the political science lessons of the *Nicomachean Ethics*. While Aristotle never explicitly describes this training in the *Politics*, he may allude to it at *Pol.* viii 3.1338a30–34 where he speaks of the need for a liberal education; though he promises to give an account of such an education later, it is not clear that he fulfills this promise. It is possible that his more detailed discussion of musical education in viii 6–7 is the promised account of liberal education, but it is also possible that he thinks that after the age of seventeen – the age where his explicit remarks on public education come to an end – students go on to study political science.

on the law and honor practices to know what counts as *kalon* activity. But because law and moral principles do not apply in every case, reliance on them inevitably brings about occasional mistakes. In nonstandard situations where the typically honored act – say, returning what one owes – is not the correct action, non-*phronimoi* may act inappropriately. What is more, should these citizens come under the rule of nonvirtuous rulers, they may not be able to continue to act virtuously. For as non-*phronimoi* they will be susceptible to erroneous arguments that purport to show that the human good is, for example, pleasure or honor, and so should new rulers take power in the *polis* and perpetuate such arguments, non-*phronimoi* may come to adopt false views of the human good.

These weaknesses highlight the important difference between ordinary citizens and *phronimoi* philosopher-statesmen. Only lawmakers who are fully acquainted with the political science lessons of the *NE* know what courage is and why it contributes to happiness; only they know, for example, that it is because courage serves reason and because happiness lies in fulfilling the human function of reasoning that courage is part of happiness. Ordinary citizens may grasp that the virtues have some sort of relation to reason (vi 13.1144b22–23, ii 2.1103b31–33). But because they lack a detailed account of the virtues and an understanding of reason's relationship to human goodness, they fail to understand what courage essentially is and why it is always worth having and exercising.

Still, the non-*phronimos* with civic virtue has an approximation of full virtue that is much more ethically salient than the approximation possessed by the slavish person whose actions mimic virtuous behavior but rest on the false belief that the external goods are the only ends worth seeking for their own sakes.

VI. CONCLUSION

I began with the question of how widely shared Aristotle thinks virtue of character is and, in particular, whether he thinks that most decent citizens of fourth-century Athens are plausible candidates for virtue. I argued that having *phronēsis* requires having political science and therefore that the virtuous person necessarily has a reasoned, articulate, and comprehensive grasp of the best principles for organizing human life. Unless we attribute this view of virtue to Aristotle, we cannot make sense of the close connection between possessing virtue of character and possessing architectonic political science. This means that only citizens who have the economic and intellectual resources to devote themselves to Aristotle's political science lectures are plausible candidates for *phronēsis*, a restriction that undoubtedly entails that a good number of decent citizens are not candidates for virtue of character. So when Aristotle says that virtue-based happiness will be widely shared (*NE* i 9.1099b15–20), he must be assuming ideal social and cultural conditions and indicating that in such improved conditions virtue-based happiness will be widely shared. But since Aristotle recognizes an approximation of virtue that is available to ordinary people, he agrees with common sense that nonphilosophers can lead praiseworthy and ethically meaningful lives.

Aristotle's exalted conception of full virtue rests on his reasonable assumption that the best practical life requires the full development of a human being's practical rational capacities, a development that involves a reflective appreciation of reason's central place in the good life. In response to his relegating ordinary citizens to secondary virtue, we should feel an invigorated social commitment to creating conditions that allow each and every person to develop a similar appreciation, thus allowing her to reach her full potential.

WORKS CITED

Broadie, Sarah. 1991. *Ethics with Aristotle*. Oxford: Oxford University Press.

    2002 *Aristotle: Nicomachean Ethics; Translation, Introduction, and Commentary*. Oxford: Oxford University Press.

Burnyeat, M. F. 1980. "Aristotle on Learning to Be Good." 69–92 in Amelie Rorty ed. *Essays on Aristotle's Ethics*. Berkeley: University of California Press.

Crisp, Roger trans. 2000 *Aristotle: Nicomachean Ethics*. Cambridge: Cambridge University Press.

Frede, Dorothea. 2005. "Citizenship in Aristotle's *Politics*." 167–184 in Richard Kraut and Steven Skultety eds. *Aristotle's Politics: Critical Essays*. Lanham, MD: Rowman and Littlefield.

Irwin, Terence. 1996. "Ethics in the *Rhetoric* and in the *Ethics*." 142–174 in Amelie Rorty ed. *Essays on Aristotle's Rhetoric*. Berkeley: University of California Press.

    1999. *Aristotle: Nicomachean Ethics*. 2nd ed. Indianapolis: Hackett.

    2010. "The Sense and Reference of 'Kalon' in Aristotle." *Classical Philology* 105: 381–402.

Kamtekar, Rachana. 1998. "Imperfect Virtue." *Ancient Philosophy* 18: 136–160.

Kenny, Anthony. 2011 *Aristotle's Eudemian Ethics: Translation*. Oxford: Oxford University Press.

Keyt, David. 2007. "The Good Man and the Upright Citizen in Aristotle's Ethics and Politics." *Social Philosophy and Policy* 24: 220–240.

Kraut, Richard. 1993. "In Defense of the Grand End." *Ethics* 103: 361–374.

    2002. *Aristotle: Political Philosophy*. Oxford: Oxford University Press.

McDowell, John 2001. "Deliberation and Moral Development in Aristotle's Ethics." *Mind, Value, and Reality*. Cambridge, MA: Harvard University Press.

Moss, Jessica. 2011. "Virtue Makes the Goal Right." *Phronesis* 56: 204–261.

Meyer, Susan Sauvé. 2013. Review of A. W. Price *Virtue and Reason in Plato and Aristotle. Ethics* 123: 572–577.

Polansky, Ronald 2000. "*Politeia* Is Aristotle's 'Best Constitution.'" *Iphitos* 1: 59–70.

Price, A. W. 2011. *Virtue and Reason in Plato and Aristotle*. Oxford: Oxford University Press.

Rawls, John. 1999. *A Theory of Justice*. Rev. ed. Oxford: Oxford University Press.

Simpson, Peter L. Phillips. 1997. *The Politics of Aristotle*. Chapel Hill: University of North Carolina Press.

Taylor, C. C. W. 2006. *Aristotle: Nicomachean Ethics Books II–IV*. Oxford: Oxford University Press.

14   The *Nicomachean Ethics* on Pleasure

Pleasure is an important component of the discussion of many different topics in the *NE*, including, but not limited to, virtue, *eudaimonia*, and *akrasia*. Pleasure is also the focus of two extended discussions in its own right, in *NE* vii 11–14 and *NE* x 1–5. That Aristotle should demonstrate this level of interest in pleasure, given the ethical project of the *NE*, is not surprising, both in general and in the specific historical context of Aristotle's work. Contemporary theorists had taken a diverse range of positions on the relation between the (human) good and pleasure, as is clear from Aristotle's own surveys of the views taken, in *NE* vii 11 and *NE* x 1–2: views that range from the hedonist identification of goodness with pleasure to the denial that any pleasure is good, let alone "the good." No matter what their position, however, it is clear that any contemporary ethical theorist could be expected to take some position on the standing of pleasure as regards the human good.

For Aristotle's part, it might seem that the standing of pleasure is doomed from the start. True, in *NE* i 5, a "life of pleasure" is one of three types of life – along with the "political" and "theoretical" lives – introduced as the three main candidates for identification as *eudaimonia*. But, unlike its counterparts, the life of pleasure is apparently immediately and decisively dismissed: it is "a life for beasts," and those who choose it are "slavish" (1095b19–20). After this condemnation, it may seem surprising when, in *NE* x 7, Aristotle offers as evidence that the life of reflective wisdom is the chief sort of *eudaimonia* that its guiding activity – activity in accordance with wisdom (*sophia*) – is agreed to be the most pleasant among activities in accordance with virtue, philosophy being thought to involve pleasures "most amazing with respect to their purity and stability" (1177a22–27). The surprise here is not just the claim said to be "agreed" to regarding philosophy's pleasures. Agreed by whom?

Thanks to the students in my seminar on pleasure in Plato and Aristotle (Yale, Spring 2009), where much of the preparatory work for this piece was done. For discussion of the issues or comments on a draft of this material, I am especially grateful to Joachim Aufderheide, Ursula Coope, Dorothea Frede, and Gabriel Lear. For this, and patience, thanks to the editor, Ron Polansky.

one might ask. Given the dismissal of the "life of pleasure" in *NE* i 5, it seems no less surprising that being pleasant should be taken by Aristotle to be a criterion of *eudaimonia* at all.

   This apparent privileging of pleasure is not restricted to Aristotle's most intellectual conception of *eudaimonia*. While *theōria* may be "the most pleasant among activities in accordance with virtue" (1177a23–24), Aristotle's conception of activity in accordance with virtue quite generally centrally involves pleasure on the part of the virtuous agent.

   We must take as an indication of a person's states the pleasure or pain consequent on what he does, because the person who abstains from bodily pleasures and finds his enjoyment in doing just this is temperate, while the person who finds doing it oppressive is intemperate; and the person who enjoys facing up to danger, or at least does not find it painful to do so, is courageous, while he who does find it painful is a coward. For virtue of character is concerned with pleasures and pains: it is because of pleasure that we do bad actions, and pain that we abstain from noble ones. It is for this reason that we need to have been brought up in a particular way from our early days, as Plato says, so we might find enjoyment or pain in the right things; for the right education is just this.[1] (*NE* ii 3.1104b3–13)

   Here we see the complexity of Aristotle's attitude to pleasure: pleasure is the cause of bad actions, but pleasure found in refraining from (the wrong sort of) pleasures or engaging in the right sort is a hallmark of virtue of character. Indeed, according to Aristotle, "our whole inquiry" into virtue "must be concerned with [pleasure and pain], because whether we feel enjoyment and pain in a good or bad way has great influence on our actions" (1105a5–7).[2]

   Though complex, Aristotle's attitude toward the relation between pleasure and *eudaimonia* reflects two natural intuitions about pleasure. The first is that pleasure as such – or, at least, certain types of pleasure – should not be the main focus of a human life if that life is to be the kind of life that could constitute *eudaimonia*, and that this is so irrespective of whether the person living such a life would express his or her satisfaction and pleasure in it. The second is that the kind of life that could constitute *eudaimonia* – the kind of life that parents wish for their children, for example – will be such that the person living the life would express his or her satisfaction and pleasure in it.

   Aristotle cites Plato as precursor to his view of the importance of early education in regard to what one enjoys and disdains. In fact, Plato is an important historical predecessor with respect to this whole set of

---

[1]   Extended quotations from the *NE* are from Crisp 2000, with modifications where noted. The text translated is the OCT edition of Bywater 1894.

[2]   Aristotle's view of the role of pleasure and pain in virtue is the focus of Frede 2006. See also Frede 2009.

attitudes toward pleasure. Consider, for comparison, Plato's *Republic*, in which pleasure is rejected as a candidate for the good (505c) and is often the villain of the piece as regards ethically problematic behavior, but where two supplementary proofs of the *Republic*'s contention that the best and most just person is the most *eudaimōn* person, each turn on demonstration that the best and most just person's life is the one that is *most pleasant* (*Rep.* ix 583a1–3; precisely 729 times more pleasant, according to 587d12–e4).

Plato, or possibly Platonists, are also, we may surmise, responsible for the alleged agreement concerning the superiority of intellectual pleasures. The maximal "purity" (*kathareiotēs*) and "stability" (*bebaiotēs*) that Aristotle attributes to philosophy's pleasures, in *NE* x 7.1177a25–26, recall two Platonic criteria for privileged pleasures appealed to both in the *Republic* and in the *Philebus*: purity in *Rep.* ix 583b4, 585b11 and *Phlb.* 52c2, d6, e1, e2, 53c1; and stability in *Rep.* ix 585e3, 586a6, where it is paired with purity, and such pleasures are contrasted with those of the vulgar, fit for "beasts" (with *Rep.* ix 586a7: βοσκημάτων, compare *NE* i 5.1095b20).[3]

Nor are these the only points of comparison between Aristotle and Plato. To make sense of his complex attitude toward pleasure, Aristotle must – and we shall see that he does – suppose that there are different types of pleasure, and that the differences between types of pleasure make a difference in regard to their value as pleasures. In doing so, Aristotle is adopting the position that Socrates puts forward, against his hedonist opponent Protarchus's initial objections, in Plato's *Philebus* (12c4–d6, with 13a6–b5); using one of the very same examples (temperance: *NE* ii 3.1104b5–6 and *Phlb.* 12d1–2).

There is, nevertheless, one very fundamental disagreement between Aristotle and Plato about the role and value of pleasure. Both Plato and Aristotle treat pleasure as something experienced by both humans and other animals. Both engage with a hedonist position in which the (purported) fact that all animals seek pleasure is offered as evidence that pleasure should be identified as the (human) good. This is the position of the hedonist Academician, Eudoxus,[4] as reported in *NE* x 2.1172b9–11; and of Philebus, the (probably fictional) hedonist antagonist of the dispute between Socrates and Protarchus in Plato's *Philebus* (see 11b4–6 for

---

3 Stability is not found in the *Philebus* as a criterion for evaluating pleasure. It is, however, found together with purity in the *Philebus*'s parallel discussion of knowledge: 56a7, 59b4–5, 59c2. If the *Philebus* is in Aristotle's sights, then, as we will see, this is not the first time in the *NE* that Aristotle treats the *Philebus*'s premium types of knowledge as being the premium pleasures.

4 Eudoxus, who lived ca. 390–340 BCE, was known for his work in mathematics and astronomy as well as his hedonism; see Taub 1998.

Philebus's position and 67b1–7 for the implication that the behavior of animals is part of the evidence for his thesis).[5] Where Plato's rejection of this line of argument is unequivocal (*Phlb.* 67b1–7), Aristotle seems, if anything, to endorse it.[6]

   Their different responses reflect their location of pleasure in one or other aspect of Janus-faced human nature, which looks toward animals, but also toward the divine. In Plato, the inclusion of certain pleasures in the good human life – and as good-making features of it – reflects the ways in which the animal side of human nature falls short by comparison with gods. For Aristotle, by contrast, human experience of the most valuable pleasures – like *eudaimonia* in general, at least according to *NE* x 7 – is a respect in which humans exceed their animal nature and share in the life of gods. The disagreement finds a focus – whether as cause or effect – in their disagreement as to whether or not gods experience pleasure. In the *Philebus*, Plato has his protagonists agree that it would be unreasonable to think that they do (33b7–11). Aristotle no less clearly takes for granted that they do, ascribing to god(s) the enjoyment of a "single, simple pleasure" in *NE* vii 14.1154b26. For Aristotle, it is precisely because of sharing, in a limited way, in the divine activity *noēsis*, which has its own proper pleasure (*NE* x 7.1177b19–21), that a person who lives such a life is *eudaimōn*. The person lives such a life, he says, not in virtue of his humanity, but in virtue of something divine within (1177b26–28).[7]

   This fundamental disagreement about whether pleasure is a symptom of human inadequacy or a mark of its transcendence is the context for the apparently highly technical dispute as to the metaphysical status of pleasure that dominates the *NE*'s two extended treatments of pleasure.

I. A TALE OF TWO DISCUSSIONS OF PLEASURE

One historically puzzling feature of the *NE* is that it contains *two* extended treatments of pleasure: *NE* vii 11–14 and *NE* x 1–5. Pleasure is the only topic among those singled out for special attention in the *NE* that receives two separate treatments in this way. Already in 1936, Festugière argued convincingly, on purely formal grounds, that the two discussions could not both belong to (the same version of) the *Nicomachean Ethics*. Despite significant differences in emphasis and focus (and setting aside, for the moment, the question of their

---

[5] Eudoxus's impact on the Academy has often been seen as an influence upon Plato's writing of the *Philebus*. See, e.g., Gosling 1975, 139–141.

[6] See the excellent discussion in Broadie 1991, esp. 346–353, to which I am also more generally indebted for the contrast I draw here.

[7] Cf. *Metaphysics* xii 7.1072b16, where the activity in which god's way of life consists – the activity *noēsis* – is identified as pleasure.

consistency of view), each reads as – and presents itself as – the self-contained discussion of pleasure in the context of the *NE* inquiry; neither makes any reference to – or shows any evidence of knowledge of the contemporaneous existence of – the other.[8]

Since the treatment of pleasure in *NE* vii 11–14 is part of the common books and since the *Eudemian Ethics*, unlike the *Nicomachean Ethics*, would be without a separate treatment of pleasure, absent this one, it is natural to suppose that the treatment in *NE* vii 11–14 originally belonged to the *Eudemian Ethics* and became part of the *Nicomachean Ethics* by whatever the process by which the common books came to be included therein. This view – in essence, the view of Festugière 1936 – remains the majority opinion, often combined with the view that the treatment of *NE* x 1–5 – and the *Nicomachean Ethics* in general – is later and philosophically more mature.[9] In favor of the association of *NE* vii 11–14 with the *Eudemian Ethics* is the apparent fit between its treatment of pleasure and the kind of treatment canvassed prospectively at *EE* i 5.1216a29–37 and retrospectively at *EE* vii 15.1249a17–21 (cf. Festugière 1936, 31–33 and 39–44). However, given the looseness of fit between each pleasure treatment and its immediate surroundings, without knowing very much more than we do about the history of the manuscripts of the *NE*, *EE*, and the corpus in general, little can be said with any great confidence about the original venue and relative dating of either treatment of pleasure.[10] Plainly, each of Aristotle's extended treatments of pleasure and their relation to each other must be considered independently on their merits.

1. NE *vii 11–14*

The explicit, main focus of the discussion of pleasure in *NE* vii 11–14 is to establish that the arguments that have been offered in defense of three antihedonist theses do not in fact suffice to establish these theses. The antihedonist theses are: (i) no pleasure is good, whether in itself or incidentally; (ii) although some pleasures are good, the majority are bad; and (iii) even if all pleasures are good, pleasure cannot be the chief good

[8] For a different view, see Pakaluk 2005, ch. 10, and Warren 2009.
[9] Though the majority view, it is not universal, nor need this combination of views be held *in toto* if at all. Webb 1977 takes the discussion of pleasure in *NE* vii 11–14 to be the philosophically superior treatment and, on these grounds, the one that properly belongs to the *NE*, understanding the discussion of *NE* x 1–5 to be a separate piece written at some time between the composition of *EE* and *NE*. Kenny 1978 takes the discussion of *NE* vii 11–14 to be the superior, if either is, but locates it – and the common books in general – in the *Eudemian Ethics*, which he takes to be the ethical work of Aristotle's maturity. And see Lawrence Jost's contribution in this volume.
[10] For looseness of fit, see *NE* vii 11.1152b1–8 and vii 14.1154b32–34; and ix 12.1172a14–x 1.1172a16 and x 6.1176a30–33.

(1152b8–12). *NE* vii 11 offers a list of arguments in support of these theses. *NE* vii 12 announces its intention to establish that the arguments considered do not support the conclusions that pleasure is not good or the chief good (1152b25–26).[11]

Given this negative ambition – and the dialectical focus of the chapters overall – there is, in principle, no reason why the discussion in these chapters should provide any evidence for Aristotle's own views of pleasure and of its relation to goodness. Nevertheless, at least the elements of an Aristotelian view as to the nature of pleasure and its relation to goodness emerge from the chapters' critical engagement with a view about pleasure that is said to underlie two of the three antihedonist theses targeted – theses (i), 1152b12–15, and (iii), 1152b22–23 – the view that pleasure is a *genesis*, that is, a "becoming" or "coming-to-be."

Aristotle says little by way of explanation of the *genesis* theory of pleasure. But what he does say makes clear that the identification of pleasure as *genesis* is intended to bring out a contrast between pleasures and "ends" (*telē*), where, for his opponent, as also for Aristotle, "ends" are the (primary) locus of value. Thus, the reason given by the defender of antihedonist thesis (i), no pleasure is good, is "that every pleasure is a perceived *genesis* (becoming) in the direction of nature, but no *genesis* (becoming) is in the same class as ends (*telē*); for example, no instance of house-building is in the same class as a house" (1152b13–15).

The idea, very roughly, appears to be this: pleasure – pleasures in general – are associated with the establishment – the coming-to-be – of goods (good natures, the ends to which the pleasures are in some way directed, as house building is directed toward the existence of houses).[12] But the ends to which these pleasure establishments are directed are distinct from the establishments by means of which they come into being. When the end exists, the process by which it was established has ceased: (an instance of) house building has ceased once the house to whose existence it is directed has come into being. But ends – the opponent supposes – are the (primary) locus of value. If, then, pleasures, being establishments of ends, are necessarily distinct from the ends they establish, then, it might seem, pleasures cannot be valuable, at least cannot be valuable in just the same way as the ends to whose establishment they are directed.

Regarding the structure of value, this view has something intuitive about it. At least prima facie, the value of house building is dependent on the value of houses. Hence, house building does not have the same sort of

---

[11] *NE* vii 11–12 are given detailed, insightful discussion by Frede 2009.
[12] I shall return to the nature of the association.

(independent) value that houses (might) have.[13] It is, in addition, something Aristotle himself believes (*NE* i 1.1094a5–6: distinct products are better than the activities whose products they are). But it is not yet clear how the view could be supposed to justify the thesis that no pleasure is good (i). After all, one thing the value of houses seems to secure is the *value* of house building: but this means that house building can at least be something good.[14]

Aristotle cites the *genesis* view of pleasure in support of both antihedonist thesis (i): that no pleasure is good, and antihedonist thesis (iii): that pleasure is not the chief good. But the thesis does better in defense of thesis (iii) than (i). Indeed, it is possible that, in defense of *both* antihedonist theses, the *genesis* view of pleasure has as object the explicit conclusion of antihedonist thesis (iii): that pleasure is not the chief good. This is because Aristotle's characterization of thesis (i) at 1152b8–10 offers as reason for the denial that pleasure is *good* that pleasure is not the same as *the* good (b9–10). Of course, it is not at all clear how the thesis that pleasure is not *good* is supposed to follow from the thesis that pleasure is not *the* good. Nevertheless, it is possible that the *genesis* view of pleasure is introduced as an argument for antihedonist thesis (i) because it is used to deny that pleasure is *the* good on the way to a denial (by means of additional argument) that pleasure is *good*.

Of course, the plausibility – such as it is – of the use of the *genesis* view of pleasure in support of the conclusion that pleasure is, at least, not the chief good depends entirely on the plausibility of the identification of pleasure as being (exclusively) associated with the *coming-to-be* of goods. Why think this? Aristotle does not say; he will, in fact, reject this exclusive association. We can, however, get some idea of his opponent's position from our other main source of evidence regarding the *genesis* theory of pleasure: Plato's *Philebus*. In the *Philebus*, Socrates attributes to certain "subtle folk" (53c6) an argument according to which pleasure, because it is a *genesis* and is thus always "for the sake of something" (*to heneka tou*, *Phlb.* 54c9) and not "that for whose sake" (*to hou heneka*, *Phlb.* 54c9), cannot be placed "in the lot [or: rank] of the good" (*Phlb.* 54c10, d2). With the language of "for the sake of which" reframed into Aristotelian talk of "ends" (*telē*), we have here precisely the position cited in support of antihedonist theses (i) and (iii).

Whether or not Aristotle, in *NE* vii, is targeting the *Philebus* directly – or some other Academic theorist with a similar argument as well or

---

13   Of course, this is only an example of a certain kind of value structure. The good of houses is itself, presumably, dependent on the good of other things, e.g., of shelter for people and their possessions.

14   As Gabriel Lear points out (pers. comm.), this securing of value depends on a teleological conception of value, which the opponent may not share.

instead – the *Philebus* can be used to give some indication as to *why* one might think that pleasure is correctly viewed as *genesis*, independently of the value conclusions to be drawn from this view of it. In the *Philebus*, the *genesis* view of pleasure is at least initially motivated by identifying one type of pleasure or pain as consisting in restorations or destructions of an animal's natural harmonious condition.[15]

SOC: I say that when we find the harmony being destroyed in animals, there comes to be at the same time, both a destruction of the nature and an occurrence of pains. PRO: What you say is very plausible. SOC: And, in turn, when the harmony is being restored and is returning to its own nature, pleasure must be said to occur, if we must speak as economically and swiftly as possible regarding the most important things. (*Phlb.* 31d4–10)

In this view of pleasure, a significant amount of work is done by the normative notion of harmony, prepared for, earlier in the *Philebus*, by a fourfold ontological division of things. To illustrate this picture of pleasure, Socrates begins with what seem its best-case examples: the pleasures of eating and drinking (or, better: eating-when-hungry and drinking-when-thirsty) (31e3–32a1).

Such bodily pleasures are readily taken as canonical. Indeed, as Aristotle will protest, they have often hijacked the name of pleasure as though the only sort there is (*NE* vii 13.1153b33–1154a1). The intuitive picture of restorative pleasure that the *Philebus* builds up on the basis of these examples is one in which there is, for animals, an optimal condition to be in (e.g., satiety of one's hunger or thirst); the occurrence of pains indicates the disruption of this optimal condition; the occurrence of pleasures its restoration.

Many parts of this picture seem open to challenge. But, in objecting to the pleasure as *genesis* view in *NE* vii, Aristotle does not challenge the general shape of the model: the existence of normative natures and the association of pleasure with the restoration of such natures when they are disrupted. Instead, what Aristotle challenges is the understanding of the way in which pleasure is involved in such restorative pleasures and, in connection with this, the standing of such restorative pleasures as paradigmatic in building a general theory of pleasure.

His main argument in *NE* vii is found in 12.1152b33–1153a7. It is part of a sequence of arguments, probably connected.[16] Aristotle has just

---

[15] The only other type of pleasure/pain the *Philebus* explicitly identifies as such is one involving the pleasures and pains of expectation of pleasures/pains of the first mentioned type (*Phlb.* 32b9). For an argument that the *Philebus* takes these two kinds of pleasure, when suitably expanded, to exhaust the terrain, see Delcomminette 2006, 289–347.

[16] After the first (*prōton*, 1152b6), each new member of the series is marked in a characteristic Aristotelian fashion by *eti* ("again," "further") (1152b33, 1153a7).

argued (1152b26–33) that, once one distinguishes between calling some-thing "good" without qualification and calling something "good" in a qualified manner: good for someone, in some circumstance, at some time, most of pleasure's opponents' candidate "bad pleasures" will dis-appear. Most: those that do not – "such ['pleasures'] as occur together with pain and for the sake of healing, such as those of the sick – are not in fact pleasures, but merely appear so" (1152b31–33). Thus far, then, he has argued, there is no reason to dispute (all) pleasures' claim to be good. Next comes his main argument:

> Again, since one kind of good is an activity, while another is a state, the processes that restore a person to his natural state are only incidentally pleasant. The activity in the appetites is the activity of the state and nature that remain, since there are also pleasures that do not involve pain and appetite, such as those of contemplation,[17] in which case one's nature is not lacking in anything. An indication of this is the fact that people do not enjoy the same pleasure when their natural state is being replenished, as they do when it has been restored. Once it is restored, they enjoy things pleasant without qualification; but while it is being replenished they enjoy even quite the contrary. They even enjoy sharp and bitter things, none of which are pleasant either by nature or without qualification; nor, therefore, are the pleasures, since as pleasant things differ from each other, so also do the pleasures arising from them. (1152b33–1153a7)

The *Philebus*'s restorative pleasures, Aristotle argues, though they are indeed pleasant, are "only incidentally pleasant." This means, at least, that such pleasures should not be taken as a basis for building a general theory of pleasure. Incidentally, Aristotle would say, a doctor might build a house, through happening to have both medical and house-building expertise. Still, examining doctors as such is not going to tell us anything very informative about house building.

Instead, Aristotle prefers to consider examples of pleasure that – unlike restorative pleasures – do not involve pain or appetite. His example is the pleasure of contemplation – understood, in the Aristotelian way, as putting to use the possession of knowledge or understanding (and not as the difficult and sometimes painful endeavor to acquire it). So understood, it would be hard to construe on the restorative model.

Pleasures of this sort are to be understood as arising from the *activity* (*energeia*) of natures, not from their restoration. So understood, pleasure corresponds to one of the two kinds of good that this argument initially distinguished. Aristotle wants, then, to extend this same view of pleasure

---

[17] Crisp's translation follows Bywater here in secluding ἐνέργειαι at 1153a1, on the possible authority of Aspasius. The idea of activities (plural) of contemplating is certainly odd. Bywater reports Kᵇ as reading the whole phrase in the singular: ἡ τοῦ θεωρεῖν ἐνέργεια.

to the, incidentally, pleasant restorative cases, making the claim that, in such pleasant restorations, the pleasure in fact *consists* in "the activity of the state and nature that remain."

How does Aristotle defend his view? He begins with the association of good with activity and state. But can he expect his opponent to agree with this? Yes, insofar as the state that he mentions seems to coincide with the normative harmonious condition that the opponent's own *genesis* model of pleasure treats as the locus of value. The opponent need not obviously balk at the Aristotelian proposal that we can distinguish, on the one hand, the dispositional *possession* of such a state ("a state," *hexis*) and its active engagement ("an activity," *energeia*).

But how does Aristotle seek to persuade his opponent that pleasure itself belongs, not with the restoration of such states or activities, but with their active engagement? Aristotle's argument is driven by a unifying principle. Once we accept that the pleasures of contemplation cannot be conceived on the model of restoring some good nature as opposed to its active engagement, then there is pressure to view the restorative pleasures as being in some way captured by the activity view. Arguably, Aristotle's opponent – at least in the *Philebus* – is also committed to unifying pleasures by means of a single theoretical framework. For the opponent, this leads to the claim that "true pleasures" – those that, in the *Philebus*, satisfy Aristotle's characterization of the pleasures of contemplating as "without pain or appetite" – are indeed *restorations* (fillings), but of unfelt lacks (e.g., *Phlb.* 51b3–7).[18]

If this helps us see what Aristotle is up to, we may still ask what he means when he says that, in restorative pleasures, we find the activity of "the state and nature that remain." Perhaps the thought is this: it is part of being a healthy animal that, for example, when hungry or thirsty, the animal seeks out and takes pleasure in appropriate nourishment; doing so is itself an expression of the animal's nature. Similarly, it is part of the life of a generally healthy animal that, when nevertheless suffering from some (curable) ailment, the animal seeks out and takes pleasure in appropriate remedies. Is it plausible to suppose the animal takes pleasure on such occasions? The thought may be similar to that behind claims one still hears today regarding the body "knowing what it needs," whatever that means, and citing cravings for unusual, but, as it turns out, nutritionally appropriate foods, for example.[19]

---

[18] Tellingly, though the *Philebus* speaks in this context of the pleasures of learning (*manthanein*) (51e7–52a3), it is not at all clear where, if anywhere, the pleasures of exercising knowledge fit into its picture.

[19] Possible too is a kind of confusion between doing something gladly and finding pleasure in doing so. As we will see, this is a confusion that may bedevil Aristotle in any case.

That this is Aristotle's line of thought is supported by the "indication" that he points to as part of his argument (contrast Frede 2009, 195–196). It is, Aristotle suggests, a feature of people who are in need of (and in reach of) recovery of the optimal condition that they sometimes take pleasure in things that, once recovered and under optimal circumstances, they would not take pleasure in. To the extent that the example of enjoyment of "sharp and bitter things" may prompt us to think of the example as medical and not just eating-when-hungry, we may question how well this argument fits together with Aristotle's earlier claim that (at least some) so-called pleasures that are accompanied by pain and undertaken for the sake of healing are not in fact pleasures at all (1152b31–33). Perhaps the identification of restorative pleasures as being "only incidentally pleasant" is meant to be consistent with them not being pleasures (without qualification) at all (so suggests Aubry 2009, 253–254). Or perhaps the two separate stretches of argument have different sorts of medical examples in view. The *Philebus* considers pleasures that, rooted in pathological conditions of soul or body, have a special intensity and which, far from relieving the root cause of illness, if anything entrench it (*Phlb.* 45c1–47b9; see discussion in Frede 1997, 275–279). It is possible that these are the kinds of pleasure that Aristotle regards as not pleasures at all.

In a second main line of argument in *NE* vii 12, Aristotle argues again that pleasures consist in activities (*energeiai*) as opposed to comings-to-be (*geneseis*); and he uses this argument as the basis for offering a new way to speak about pleasure:

Again, it is not necessary that there be something else better than pleasure, as the end, according to some, is better than the coming-to-be (*genesis*). For pleasures are not comings-to-be, nor do they all even involve coming-to-be, but they are activities (*energeiai*) and constitute an end; nor do they result from our coming to be something, but from our exercising our capacities. And not all pleasures have an end distinct from themselves, but only those of people who are being led to the completion of their nature. This is why it is wrong to say that pleasure is a perceived coming-to-be. What we should rather say is that it is (an) activity of one's natural state, and that it is unimpeded rather than perceived. (1153a7–15, Crisp translation; parenthesis around "an" mine)

In place of his opponent's characterization of pleasure as a "*genesis* (coming-to-be) in the direction of nature" (1152b13), Aristotle offers its characterization as "(an) activity of one's natural state"; where his opponent adds that such comings-to-be are "perceived," Aristotle substitutes talk of the activity in question as "unimpeded." This substitution of "unimpeded" is puzzling. It has not been prepared for by the previous argument; and lack of impediment is not obviously an exclusive alternative to being perceived. Aristotle would not deny that activity-pleasures involve perceptual awareness, at least to the extent that they cannot occur without our being aware of them.

Further, what is the view of pleasure to which Aristotle is committed in light of this legislation as to how one should speak? He is not committed to the view that every pleasure is an unimpeded activity of one's natural state – incidentally pleasant restorative processes need not be since they are not necessarily unimpeded. Is he committed to the view that every unimpeded activity counts as (a kind of) pleasure? The passage does not settle this question. In the preceding translation, the inclusion of "an," marked by parenthesis, though permissible, does not correspond to anything explicit in Greek (cf. Irwin 1999, 270 ad loc.). It is possible that Aristotle means to say that pleasure is unimpeded activity, with the implication that, wherever there is unimpeded activity, there is pleasure and not that pleasure is simply to be understood as one activity of this kind. If so, this raises an additional question of what Aristotle would make of bad but apparently unimpeded activities, given the context of his dispute with his opponent as to whether pleasures are (always/ever) good.

A decision on the relation between unimpeded activity and pleasure makes a difference as to how one inclines to understand a later argument in *NE* vii 13, where Aristotle argues, contra antihedonist (iii), that some kind of pleasure either may or must be the chief human good. Unfortunately, this passage too may be read in one of two ways. Here is Crisp's translation:

And even if certain pleasures are bad, there is no reason why some pleasure or other should not be the chief good, just as one kind of knowledge might be, though some kinds are bad. And if there are unimpeded activities of each state, whether the activity of all of them or of one in particular constitutes happiness when unimpeded, that one must presumably be the most worthy of choice. But pleasure is an unimpeded activity, so the chief good might be some kind of pleasure, even if it so happens that most pleasures are bad without qualification. (1153b7–14)

On Crisp's reading, the claim about pleasure picked up here is that pleasure is *an* unimpeded activity, not unimpeded activity *tout court*. Since happiness (*eudaimonia*), on Aristotle's understanding, is one or more unimpeded activities, it follows that it is at least *possible* that some kind of pleasure should turn out to be the chief good. It is possible, but not necessary, because it is also possible that the kind of unimpeded activity that happiness is, is distinct from the unimpeded activity that is pleasure.

But there is another possible reading of this passage. First, where Crisp has "But pleasure is an unimpeded activity," the Greek has merely something equivalent to "But pleasure is *this* (*touto*)," leaving open the option to substitute whichever understanding of pleasure's relation to unimpeded activity one takes from the earlier passage. Second, the relevant sentences can just as legitimately be read as having Aristotle argue that, on his understanding of pleasure, the chief good not merely *might*, but *will be* some kind of pleasure.[20] To see the alternative, consider Rowe's translation of the key parts of the very same passage (in Broadie and Rowe 2002):

Given that there are unimpeded activities of each disposition, then whether happiness is the activity of all of them or of one of them, it is perhaps even a necessary conclusion that this activity, provided it is unimpeded, be most desirable; but this is pleasure. In that case the chief good will be a kind of pleasure, even if most pleasures turned out to be bad, even without qualification. (1153b9–14)

Note that, even if Aristotle is, in his own person, asserting that *eudaimonia* is some kind of pleasure, he is emphatically not suggesting the hedonist thesis that pleasure *as such* is the chief human good (cf. Rapp 2009, 219–220). At best, *eudaimonia* would be *some kind of* pleasure; and it would be so only in virtue of the (prior) identification of *eudaimonia* as consisting in certain unimpeded activities. As we have seen, the indeterminacy of the passage is such that it does not make certain Aristotle's own view. Nevertheless, together with something that Aristotle immediately goes on to remark, we can identify two important points about the significance of the talk here and earlier of activities being unimpeded.

Immediately following this argument, Aristotle goes on to say:

And this is why everyone thinks that the happy (*eudaimōn*) life is pleasant, and weaves pleasure into happiness (*eudaimonia*) – reasonably enough, since no activity is complete/perfect (*teleios*)[21] when it is impeded, and happiness (*eudaimonia*) is something complete/perfect (*teleios*). (1153b14–17, Crisp trans. modified)

If we combine this comment on impediment with Aristotle's earlier, and puzzling, insistence that, in reframing his opponents' characterization of pleasure, their talk of "being perceived" should be replaced by talk of "being unimpeded," we can identify the following claims:

1.   An activity is only even a candidate for being pleasure if that activity is unimpeded.
2.   An activity is complete/perfect (*teleios*) only if that activity is unimpeded.

These claims do not settle the question of how Aristotle views the relation between pleasure and unimpeded activity. But they will, nevertheless, stand us in good stead when it comes to comparing his view here in *NE* vii 11–14 with the treatment of pleasure in *NE* x 1–5.

[20]   For a defense of this reading, see Rapp 2009, 214–220.
[21]   The Greek word *teleios* has both these connotations.

2. NE x 1–5

Like *NE* vii 11–14, Aristotle's second discussion of pleasure in *NE* x 1–5 includes substantial engagement with the views of other theorists about pleasure, including additional criticism of the *genesis* view of pleasure, together with consideration of arguments for and against a *positive* view of pleasure, the Academician Eudoxus's identification of the good with pleasure.[22] Unlike *NE* vii 11–14, Aristotle's second discussion of pleasure in *NE* x 1–5 also departs from such dialectical treatment of pleasure, when, beginning in *NE* x 4, Aristotle indicates that he is taking up the question of pleasure once again "from the beginning" (1174a13–14). Here, if anywhere, do we find Aristotle's own views on "what [pleasure] is and what it is like" (1174a13) clearly expressed.

As in *NE* vii 11–14, in *NE* x 4–5 Aristotle associates pleasure with activities (*energeiai*), where these activities are set in contrast to comings-to-be (*geneseis*) or, here at least, also changes (*kinēseis*).[23] In fact, pleasure is apparently associated with certain very specific activities, those of perceiving and thinking. Why Aristotle should limit the scope of pleasure in this way – if that is his intention – requires consideration. First, however, there are interpretative questions about the nature both of the association between pleasure and activity and of the contrast between (such) activities and changes.

Aristotle begins his fresh start in *NE* x 4 with a comparison between pleasure and the perceptual activity of seeing.

> Seeing seems at every moment to be complete/perfect (*teleia*),[24] because it does not lack anything that will come to be later and complete/perfect its form. And pleasure seems to be like this as well, since it is a whole, and at no time can one find a pleasure such that, if it comes to be for a longer time, its form will become complete/perfect. (1174a14–19, Crisp trans. modified)

This feature of pleasure, this respect in which pleasure is like seeing, is offered as a reason for thinking that pleasure (and, presumably, seeing) is not a change (*kinēsis*) or coming-to-be (*genesis*). According to Aristotle, a *change* – Aristotle's example is an event of building – is not complete at any or every moment. A change is made up of dissimilar temporal parts,

---

[22] For excellent discussion, see Warren 2009.

[23] *NE* x 4.1174b10 indicates that Aristotle is here treating change (*kinēsis*) and coming-to-be (*genesis*) as interchangeable (cf. x 3.1173a28–31).

[24] We find here again the occurrence of this Greek word *teleios*, also found in *NE* vii 11–14, and which has connotations of both completeness and perfection. While I agree with Crisp 2000 that the translation "complete" better captures the thought here, it is worth marking the fact that the same Greek word occurs here – and will come up in an important context later in this same chapter.

which together constitute the completion of the change in question, but which, considered individually, are distinct both from each other and from the whole.

An event of house building, for example, consists of such distinct and dissimilar events as the laying of the foundation and the construction of the frame. Neither of these constituent events is itself an event of house building considered on its own. During the temporal periods in which these constituent events are occurring, the event of house building is in progress, but is not complete. It is complete, if at all, only when all such constituent events have taken place (1174a27–29). By contrast, what it is for pleasure – like seeing – to be *complete* at any or every moment is for it to be an event such that, when it occurs and no matter what specific duration it may occupy, no (temporal) part of the event is such that it cannot itself be described as an event of pleasure. Events of seeing or of pleasure are not put together from parts that are unlike themselves; temporally speaking, they are what Aristotle elsewhere characterizes as homoiomerous: their (temporal) parts are uniform all the way through.

The distinction Aristotle draws here is independently interesting, although there are questions as to how – and how well – it divides up examples. For present purposes, it is more important to consider what Aristotle *does not* say, though he has often been taken to. First, Aristotle does not here say that pleasure is itself an activity (*energeia*); in fact, he does not even say this explicitly of seeing, although it is clear from the remainder of this chapter that seeing should be thought of as an activity, one that pleasure will be said to "complete" or "perfect." To say that pleasure is *like* an activity such as seeing in terms of being complete at every time does not commit Aristotle to saying that pleasure is itself an activity (cf. Bostock 2000, 154–155). Second, although it is often assumed that in contrasting seeing – and pleasure – with changes (*kinēseis*), Aristotle means to draw an exclusive contrast between change and activity (*energeia*), nothing he says in this chapter commits him to denying that changes are also some kind of activity, one that is incomplete.[25] In principle, this leaves open the possibility that, when pleasure is subsequently identified as something that "completes" or "perfects" an activity (*energeia*), there is a wide range of possible activities that it could complete or perfect. However, this possibility is put in doubt by Aristotle's subsequent explanation of

[25]   The belief that Aristotle is here committed to this stems from bringing into the interpretation of this chapter a distinction drawn in *Metaphysics* ix 6, according to which there is a use of "activity" (*energeia*) reserved for activities that are not also changes. For an argument as to the anomalous nature of the *Metaphysics*'s passage's terminology and its inapplicability to *NE* x 4, see Burnyeat 2008.

the relation between pleasure and activity, in which his focus remains squarely on activities of the complete variety, activities of perceiving and thinking.

Here is how Aristotle characterizes the relation between pleasure and activities of perceiving and thinking in *NE* x 4:

> Every sense engages in activity in relation to its object, and its activity is complete/perfect (*teleios*)[26] when it is in good condition in relation to the noblest of its objects. ... In the case of each sense, then, the best activity will be that of the subject in the best condition in relation to the best of that sense's objects. And this activity will be the most complete/perfect and the most pleasant. For there is a pleasure corresponding to every sense, just as there is to thought and contemplation; and it is most pleasant when it is most complete/perfect, and most complete/perfect when the subject is in good condition and it occurs in relation to the best of its objects. Pleasure completes/perfects the activity, but not in the same way as the object of the sense and the sense complete/perfect it when they are both good, just as health and the doctor are not responsible in the same way for one's being healthy. (1174b14–26, Crisp trans. modified)

When Aristotle says that pleasure completes or perfects an activity such as seeing, what does he mean? He uses forms of the same Greek term as he used in the previous passage (quoted above) when he characterized pleasure, like seeing, as something "complete" at every moment it occurs. Despite the awkwardness, there is reason to think that Aristotle does not mean to claim that pleasure *completes* or *perfects* an activity of seeing in just the same sense of "completeness" or "perfection" in which seeing has already been said – without mention of pleasure – to be complete. Here, unlike there, there are degrees of completeness or perfection. Here, unlike there, there are value conditions involved, so that "perfect" seems the better English term to choose for translation.

Aristotle here makes two claims about the relation between pleasure and perceptual (and, presumably, intellectual) activity:

1. When a sense (or intellectual power) that is itself in the best condition engages in activity in relation to the best or noblest sort of sense – (or intellectual) object, the sense-activity (or intellectual activity) will be most perfect and most pleasant.
2. Pleasure perfects the activity, though the way in which it does so is distinct from the way in which the sense (or intellectual power) and object, when good, perfect the activity.

Shortly hereafter, Aristotle makes one further claim about this perfecting by pleasure:

[26] Aristotle uses the Greek word *teleios* again, which, as before, has connotations both of completeness and of perfection.

3. Pleasure perfects the activity "not as an inherent state, but as a kind of supervenient end, like the bloom on those in their prime" (1174b31–33).[27]

This last claim might seem the most promising for clarifying Aristotle's thought. However, this appearance is deceptive. The Greek phrase underlying the identification of pleasure as "a supervenient end" can just as easily point to pleasure as simply (an) end that the activities perfected arrive at as fulfillment (see LSJ s.v. ἐπιγίγνομαι II); the modern philosophical connotations of "supervenient" are, then, potentially misleading. Likewise, although, in the example of the "bloom of those in their prime," the terms here translated "bloom" and "prime" may indicate two related but distinct features of the persons considered, they can also be understood as two different ways of picking out the very same feature, the "primeness," as it were, of those in their prime (Bostock 2000, 156–158). Simply on the basis of claim 3, then, it is unclear whether Aristotle means to identify pleasure as being itself the perfection of an activity as the activity it is or as an additional perfection, but one that is intimately related to the perfection of the activity as such.

No more help is to be drawn from the analogy that Aristotle gives in the passage quoted previously from which 1 and 2 are drawn, an analogy as to the different ways in which doctors and health are causes of being healthy. Although commentators have exercised themselves greatly, without resolution, over whether pleasure should be thought of as cause in relation to an activity in terms of formal or final causation,[28] it seems just as plausible that the analogy with cause is not meant to suggest that pleasure is itself a cause, but simply to illustrate a comparable ambiguity. The term "perfects" – like the term "cause" – can be used in different ways so that, with respect to one and the same item, two different things can (in different ways) perfect it, just as health and a doctor are each (different kinds of) causes of being healthy (see Broadie's comment ad loc. in Broadie and Rowe 2002).

This leaves us with 1 and 2, which, taken separately, give a certain amount of information. If a sense-activity is most perfect when the sense and its object are in certain conditions, then being in the relevant conditions constitutes a way in which sense and object perfect an activity independently of pleasure. What is this way? It cannot be simply that sense and object are what makes the activity a *seeing*, though this is no doubt true. This cannot be Aristotle's meaning, because the way of perfecting by sense and object that Aristotle wishes to distinguish is the

[27] For the point that *hoi akmaioi* are those in their *prime* (not the young, as commonly supposed), see Bostock 2000, 156.
[28] See, e.g., Gauthier and Jolif 2002, II.2 838–41; Gosling and Taylor 1982, ch. 13.

way in which sense and object perfect that activity *when they are good.* Let us say, then, that sense and object perfect an activity of seeing in this way by making it the best kind of seeing, in the sense in which one might think that, when one is seeing, it is better to see good things – things good to be seen – than not.

Aristotle says of this best kind of seeing – the seeing that occurs when the sense and object are both good – that it is "most perfect" and "most pleasant" (claim 1). To say of some activity that it is "most pleasant" is to say that this is an activity from which one can derive the maximal pleasure. It is not – or not yet – to say that pleasure is taken therein. But it might seem intuitive to say that for the seer to take pleasure in such a most perfect and pleasant activity of seeing is itself a way to improve the seeing. It is so, at least, if it is better to enjoy seeing things good to be seen than not. This does not change the character or quality of the seeing in terms of what is seen and what sort of seeing it is; but it does change the character and quality of the experience for the seer. This, I argue, is the kind of distinctive perfection that Aristotle points to in claim 2.[29]

Although pleasure and the goodness of sense and object perfect a sense or intellectual activity in different ways, which could in principle come apart, Aristotle may suppose that, in practice, the two kinds of perfection always co-occur. At least, his discussion in *NE* x 4 gives the impression that, for perceptual and intellectual activities, he thinks it inevitable that, when the activity is perfect in the way that sense/intellectual power and object can make it, pleasure will occur (1174b26–31, 1174b33–1175a3). Outside the chapter, we might look for an example of activity and pleasure occurring separately by appeal to another passage in which pleasure is described as "supervenient" upon acts, *NE* ii 3.1104b3–13 (quoted earlier).[30]

In *NE* ii 3, the temperate person is distinguished from the intemperate person by the "supervenient" pleasure the temperate person finds in abstaining from bodily pleasures. The intemperate person does not find such pleasure in abstention. Indeed, being intemperate, such a person will abstain from such pleasures only in rather unusual circumstances. But, although not mentioned in this passage, there is a third type of person in Aristotle's schema of virtue who regularly abstains, but who, like the intemperate person, does not find pleasure in doing so. This is the continent person. Here is a case in which there is an act – abstaining when

---

[29] In arriving at this view, I found it helpful to reflect on the (somewhat different) view developed in doctoral work by Joachim Aufderheide (St. Andrews) and in Aufderheide's unpublished manuscript.

[30] Where Crisp translates "consequent" in place of "supervenient," although the same Greek term ἐπιγίγνομαι is involved. I am indebted to Aufderheide's unpublished manuscript for attention to this passage for comparison purposes.

appropriate to do so – in the absence of the pleasure that (in the virtuous person) supervenes on it. Notice, however, that, even if such abstention is, in itself, an example of *some* perfect activity (which seems unclear), it is not an example of the perfect intellectual activity of *phronēsis* (practical wisdom), for such practical wisdom does not exist in Aristotle's view in the absence of the appropriate affective responses, in this case, the enjoyment of abstention.

Whether or not Aristotle's two sorts of perfection can come apart in practice, we have some feel for their distinction. But, one may ask, is the perfecting pleasure something additional to the otherwise perfect activity it perfects or not? I have argued that the otherwise perfect activity is in principle, though perhaps not on Aristotle's view in practice, separable from the perfecting pleasure taken therein. In this sense, but in this sense only, that perfecting pleasure is additional. However, since the perfecting pleasure in the otherwise perfect activity has its character as the pleasure it is fixed by being pleasure *therein*, such pleasure does not – and could not – occur independently of the otherwise perfect activity it perfects.

Aristotle calls the perfecting pleasure an "end" (claim 3, 1174b33). This cannot mean that pleasure is, for example, the end of one's seeing, in the sense that one undertakes the seeing for the sake of the pleasure it involves. Especially when it comes to underwriting the connection between *eudaimonia* and pleasure, it will be crucially important that the intellectual activities that constitute *eudaimonia* of the principal sort are activities that are themselves engaged in for their own sake and not (not also) for the sake of anything else (see the discussion in *NE* x 7, introduced previously). Pleasure too – for example, the pleasure of seeing when that seeing is perfect in the way that sense and object can make it – is something engaged in just for its own sake, as Aristotle pointed out in *NE* x 2.1172b20–23. Identifying pleasure as an end may pick up on this feature of it. Alternatively, it may pick up on the linguistic relation in Greek between pleasure's characterization as an end – a *telos* in Greek – and its role in making an activity perfect – *teleios* ("end-y") in Greek.

This latter alternative suggests a possible answer to an important question Aristotle does not explicitly address: *Why* suppose that pleasure perfects – makes better – at least the relevant sorts of activity? Is there more to this than the intuition that pleasure makes things better? Perhaps Aristotle's thought is that pleasure in the relevant sorts of activity is a way of ensuring that the activity in question has the appropriate endlike character that Aristotle – like both hedonist and antihedonist opponents – takes to be necessary in any candidate for the good.

Discussing Eudoxan hedonism, Aristotle said about pleasure that "everyone agrees" that it is something chosen neither because of nor for the sake of something else, "since no one asks for the justification of anyone's being pleased, on the assumption that pleasure is worthy of choice in itself" (*NE* x 2.1172b21–23). Unlike Eudoxus, Aristotle does not take this to show that pleasure itself is the end. However, when appropriately informed by the relevant otherwise perfect activity, he may take pleasure to help to make that activity suitably endlike for that activity to be good in itself. If this is Aristotle's view, it contrasts nicely with the antihedonist opponent he has been most keen to criticize, the *genesis* theorist. The *genesis* theorist rejected pleasure's claim as the good because of his view of pleasure as oriented toward but distinct from any end. Aristotle, by contrast, would take pleasure's endlike character to be a crucial component of its perfecting the activities it does as ends.

Of course, Aristotle does not think that any and every activity perfected by pleasure is thereby a candidate for being the good any more than is pleasure itself. In *NE* x 5, Aristotle turns to consideration of the differences in species or kind (*eidos*) among pleasures by focusing, as he had in x 4, on the pleasures of perceiving and thinking.

For this reason [i.e., for the reason that it perfects an activity], pleasures also seem to differ in species, because we assume that things of different species are completed/perfected by different things. This is apparently what happens with natural and artificial objects, such as animals, trees, a picture, a statue, a house or a tool. Similarly, we assume that activities that differ in species are also completed/perfected by things differing in species. The activities of thought differ in species from those of the senses, and both differ among themselves, so therefore do the pleasures that complete/perfect them. (1175a21–28, Crisp trans. modified)

Aristotle goes on to argue that the close relation between pleasure and the activity that it perfects provides evidence of this variety among pleasures. This close relation is seen in two facts about pleasure: first, that the pleasure proper to a given activity enhances that activity; second, that the pleasure proper to another activity will hinder engagement in distinct activities. To illustrate these facts, Aristotle appeals to four (or possibly five) main examples: the enjoyment of geometry, music, and building in support of fact one (1175a31–36); the enjoyment of flute playing (contrasted with the enjoyment of argument or reasoning, of *logoi*) in support of fact two (1175b3–6).[31]

---

[31] Aristotle also mentions as at least candidate pleasures: eating sweets and enjoying the performance of tragedies in the theater. I separate these from the main examples, because they perform a merely subordinate role in relation to fact two, to illustrate the related fact that we engage in two (candidate-enjoyable) activities at once only when neither one is sufficiently engaging as to distract us from the other in the manner that fact two appeals to.

Does Aristotle mean to associate pleasure exclusively with perceptual and intellectual activities, as the predominant focus of *NE* x 4–5 might suggest?[32] This question might be thought answered, in the negative, by the inclusion, in *NE* x 5's list of examples, of the pleasure of "lovers of building" (1175a34–35; cf. Bostock 1988, esp. 254–255, and Bostock 2000, 160–161). Since building is Aristotle's example, in *NE* x 4, of a change in contrast to a complete activity such as seeing, it is natural to think not only that Aristotle does not mean to focus only on pleasures of perceiving or thinking but also that he does not mean to exclude an association between pleasure and changes, whatever *NE* x 4 has sometimes been taken to mean.[33]

There is, however, an important feature of Aristotle's chosen examples that has been neglected. Each has a parallel in Plato's *Philebus* in Socrates' discussion of types not of pleasure, but of *knowledge*: geometry (56e8), music (56a3), building (56b8), flute playing (56a5). (We also find a parallel for the activity associated with *logoi* in "dialectic" [*dialegesthai*], 57e6–7.) Given its extent, it seems to me unlikely that this overlap in choice of examples is unintentional, occurring in a context in which the *Philebus* has been very much in view. But with the *Philebus* background in mind, it seems that, when Aristotle gives the example of enjoyment of building, here as elsewhere in the discussion of *NE* x 4–5, he has in mind a pleasure associated with, in this case, an intellectual activity. Aristotle no less than Plato *can* think of building as an intellectual activity, as he does, for example, in *NE* vi 4.1140a6–10, when he identifies building as "one of the skills, [being] essentially a productive state involving reason."

If he is using the *Philebus* examples of kinds of knowledge, Aristotle is being polemical. The *Philebus* allows that certain perceptual and intellectual pleasures are candidates for inclusion in the good human life. It identifies these as "true pleasures" – and, as with the other kinds of pleasure it recognizes – regards them as processes of restoration of optimal conditions, fillings, in the case of true pleasures, of *unfelt* lacks (*Phlb.* 51b–53c). Examples of true pleasures include: seeing beautiful colors and shapes; hearing beautiful sounds; learning (at least when unaccompanied by pain). The *Philebus* also includes in the good human life *all* the kinds of knowledge it distinguishes in *Philebus* 55c–59d.

---

32   Yes, according to Bostock 2000, ch. 7, who also concludes that, for Aristotle, "*what* we enjoy is always either a thought or a perception" (2000, 163). For agreement that rejects this account of *what* is enjoyed, see Taylor 2003. Of course, as a conscious experience, any kind of pleasure will involve perception or intellection. But that is not the issue here, which is rather the *scope* of the pleasures there are.

33   Burnyeat 2008, 269–270. Note, however, that I do not mean here to embrace the view that Burnyeat is mainly concerned to reject.

But such examples of (achieved) knowledge are not identified as pleasures.[34] Hence, in showcasing perceptual and intellectual pleasures that include *both* what the *Philebus* would call "true pleasures" *and* the *Philebus* examples of types of knowledge, Aristotle would be pointedly demonstrating that, once one abandons the *Philebus* conception of pleasure as *genesis* (coming-to-be) (or *kinēsis*, change), one can identify *as pleasures* all the activities that the *Philebus* itself recognizes as good by including them in its picture of the good human life.

In *NE* x 5, like *NE* x 4, Aristotle's focus thus remains on the pleasures of perceptual and intellectual activities. However, this need not mean that these are the only pleasures he thinks there are, nor the only activities that pleasure could, in principle, perfect. Aristotle's treatment of pleasure comes in the context of an investigation into the nature of the good human life (*eudaimonia*). This context – and not his theory of pleasure – best explains his restriction of focus to the pleasures of perceptual and intellectual activities. It is (certain) perceptual and intellectual activities (including the intellectual activities of practical wisdom, the virtues) that, in light of the "function argument" of *NE* i 7, remain in contention for identification as *eudaimonia*. In this connection, it is notable that *NE* x 5 will itself be concerned with the "function" or "work" (*ergon*) of animal types, associating the pleasure proper to each type of animal with the pleasure related to the activity of its proper function (1176a3–5).

II. THE RELATION BETWEEN ARISTOTLE'S TWO TREATMENTS OF PLEASURE

Each of Aristotle's two treatments of pleasure has associated pleasure with activity. Is the relation between pleasure and activity in *NE* x 4–5 the same as, or at least consistent with, the relation between pleasure and activity envisaged in *NE* vii 11–14? At least prima facie they are not the same. In *NE* vii 11–14, Aristotle appeared to argue that pleasure is itself (an?) unimpeded activity. In *NE* x 4–5, Aristotle says that pleasure *perfects* certain activities; he does not say that pleasure is itself an activity. These two conceptions can, however, be placed in a coherent relation, if we recall the claims that were made in *NE* vii 12–13 regarding impediment and perfection and if we exploit a distinction used for a quite different purpose in this connection by G. E. L. Owen.

---

[34] They cannot be, since the *Philebus* is committed throughout to the possibility of an intellectual life without pleasure as exemplifying the good life, not of humans, but gods (33a8–c4; 55a5–8).

Recall, first, the claims that were identified regarding the relation between impediment and perfection on the basis of arguments in *NE* vii 12 and 13. These were:

1. An activity is only even a candidate for being pleasure if that activity is unimpeded.
2. An activity is complete/perfect (*teleios*) only if that activity is unimpeded.

These two claims combine to give the view of *NE* vii: (some) unimpeded activity is pleasure, where this is equivalent to the claim that (some) complete/perfect activity is pleasure. To this, the treatment of pleasure in *NE* x 4–5 adds the claim that:

3. Pleasure perfects (makes complete/perfect [*teleios*]) an activity (doing so in a different way from the way in which the sense/intellectual power and object, being good, perfect the activity).

Can we make sense of the claim that pleasure both *perfects* (3) and is itself the very thing perfected – (1) and (2)? We can, if we think of the perfecting pleasure as the *enjoyment* of the person engaged in the perfect activity, but the perfect activity in focus as pleasure in *NE* vii as not this, but the location or source of the enjoyment in question. Owen (1971–1972) appealed to a distinction much like this, to argue, *not* that Aristotle's two treatments of pleasure in *NE* can be made compatible with one another, but that, since they are focused on different questions, the question of their compatibility does not arise.

Owen's thesis starts from an ambiguity in "pleasure" – and its Aristotelian Greek correlates – according to which "pleasure" can be used to refer both (i) to that in which I take pleasure and (ii) to the pleasure I take therein. For example, running is one of my pleasures (i), so that, when I run, I experience the pleasure (ii) of running. Owen argued that, in *NE* vii 11–14, Aristotle is focused on the nature of pleasure as what is enjoyed or enjoyable (i); in *NE* x 1–5 by contrast, Aristotle is focused on the nature of enjoyment (ii). The arguments that Owen offered in defense of his thesis were, rightly, subjected to serious criticism, particularly his contention that the arguments of *NE* x 1–5 turned on features of verbs.[35]

Cautiously applied, Owen's distinction can, nevertheless, be useful. *If* one thinks – as many in the history of philosophy have thought – that pleasure, in the sense of enjoyment, is a detachable *feeling*, the same – or at least in principle commensurable – across all cases of experiencing it, then pleasure in the sense of enjoyment and in the sense of that in which

---

[35]   See esp. Gosling 1973–1974 and Gosling and Taylor 1982, 204–224.

the enjoyment or pleasure is taken will seem quite distinct.[36] But Aristotle does not have this view of pleasure. In Aristotle's view, differences in the activity with which pleasure is – somehow – associated make a fundamental difference of both nature and value in the pleasure to be found therein. This means that, although the referents of the two uses of "pleasure" can be distinguished, they are parts of a single package, more closely related to each other than to different examples of pleasure. On such a picture, it may seem perfectly natural to move from claims about that in which pleasure is taken to claims about the pleasure taken therein.

In fact, we have seen this happening already, even in *NE* x 4, though without describing what was happening in this way. I have argued that, in *NE* x 4, when Aristotle says of pleasure that it perfects activities, he is pointing to the way in which a person engaged in an otherwise perfect activity can (and will) nonetheless perfect that activity in a different way, by taking pleasure in her engagement in it. That is to say, the pleasure that perfects in *NE* x 4 is enjoyment (pleasure type ii). What it perfects is an activity that Aristotle describes, in *NE* x 4.1174b19–20, as "most perfect and *most pleasant*." Such an activity is *already* perfect, inasmuch as the sense (or intellectual) power and the sense – (or intellectual) object involved in the activity – are in optimum condition. But to say of such an activity that it is "most pleasant" is just to say that it is a source or location of maximal pleasure (a pleasure type i).

Does this mean that, if I enjoy seeing, for example, it is *seeing* itself that I experience as pleasant? It could mean this, and this is one understanding of what Aristotle means, in *NE* x 4, when he says that so long as sense/intellectual power and object are "as they should be," "there will be pleasure in the activity" (1174b33–1175a1). But Aristotle could also be saying, not that the activity of seeing is the *object* of my enjoyment of seeing, but that it is the location or source of that enjoyment, so that *what* I enjoy is whatever (perfect) objects of sight I am enjoyably seeing. This latter understanding is supported by Aristotle's casual, but on the alternative reading surely puzzling, mention of it being our practice to identify *objects* of sight and of hearing as *pleasant* by way of (incomplete) support for his association of pleasure with each specific sense (1174b27–29).[37]

---

[36] See, e.g., the account of "sensory pleasures" in Feldman 2004, 25–26. Feldman himself prefers to formulate his hedonism in terms of "attitudinal pleasures," but these too are assumed commensurable (ibid., 55–66). Annas 1980, 292–293, stresses the significance of Aristotle's departure from this common modern assumption about pleasure.

[37] I thus side with Taylor 2003 over Bostock 2000, ch. 7. The conviction that Aristotle is focused exclusively on pleasure *in* seeing etc. may be driven in part by the conviction that, in associating pleasure with *activity*, he must mean to exclude it from any connection with *change*; for rejection of the legitimacy of such motivation, see Burnyeat 2008, esp. 265–272.

In turn, this removes the danger of an intolerably smug account of the virtuous agent's enjoyment of acting in accordance with virtue. When the temperate person takes pleasure in acting temperately, the object of his pleasure is not as such *his temperance*, as if the person might say "Here I am, acting temperately. Isn't that great!" Rather, the enjoyment of acting temperately will consist, at least in part, in the enjoyment of those acts that *constitute* temperance: eating and drinking moderately, for example.[38]

My proposal for reconciling the claims that are made about pleasure in Aristotle's two treatments of pleasure is that, in *NE* vii 11–14, Aristotle makes only one of the two points he makes about pleasure in *NE* x 4–5. In both, he identifies as *source* or location of pleasure certain perfect/unimpeded activities. In *NE* x 4, but not in *NE* vii 11–14, he goes on to characterize the enjoyment component of such a pleasure as something that itself perfects an activity in a distinct, though apparently inevitable, manner. The proposal offers an intelligible, even natural reading of the key passages of argument in *NE* vii 12–13 that I picked out for discussion. The dispute between Aristotle and his Platonist opponent in *NE* vii 12 is a dispute as to whether restorative bodily processes such as eating-when-hungry or nonrestorative, unimpeded or perfect activities such as the activity of contemplating are the paradigmatic *sources* of pleasure. Since, on Aristotle's view, perfect activities are the sources of pleasure, but one or more such perfect activities are also *eudaimonia*, then, as *NE* vii 13 suggests, such perfect activity or activities may – or will – be precisely what Aristotle takes the *eudaimonia*-constituting perfect activity of contemplating to be, in *NE* x 7: "the most pleasant of activities in accordance with virtue," involving those pleasures of philosophy "most amazing with respect to their purity and stability" (1177a22–27).

Note, however, that this way of understanding the material is not compelled. Nor is it clearly demanded by principles of charity. Though each discussion of pleasure is concerned with its metaphysical character, the focus of each discussion is not this, but the relation between pleasure and the human good. Since we have independent grounds for thinking that the two discussions were never intended for a single work, we are not under the same interpretative pressure to reconcile them.[39]

---

[38]   More needs to be said here, however. See the suggestive remarks of Frede 2009, 185–188 and 201–203, contrasting Aristotle's "adverbial" and "adjectival" uses of pleasure in connection with virtue.

[39]   We would be under such pressure if Owen 1971–1972, 146, were right to think that, in *NE* x 5.1175b33–35, Aristotle declares "absurd" the view that pleasure is the same as the activity, where this is to be understood as a characterization of the view of *NE* vii 11–14. Even if the treatments represented different stages in Aristotle's thought about

III. VARIETIES OF PLEASURE AND VALUE

In *NE* x 5, Aristotle uses the close relation between pleasure and activity to argue, first, that perfecting pleasures – like the activities they perfect – differ in species or kind (1175a21–28, quoted earlier) and, second, that differences in the value of the activities perfected lead to differences in the value of the correlative pleasures.

Since activities differ in their goodness and badness, and some are worthy of choice, some to be avoided, others neither, the same goes for pleasures, each activity having its own proper pleasure. Thus the pleasure proper to a virtuous activity is good, and that proper to a wicked one bad, because appetites for noble objects are to be praised, those for disgraceful things blamed. (1175b24–29)

Just as the value of pleasure depends on the value of the activity in which the pleasure is sourced, so Aristotle thinks that the value of pleasure is sourced in the value of things that are actually pleasant and not in the taking of pleasure therein. This move is complex. It is not that Aristotle supposes that some things are actually pleasant, irrespective of whether somebody would ever find them so. But he does deny that the simple fact of *someone* finding something pleasant is reason to agree that what the person finds to be pleasant is pleasant *tout court*. One example of such thinking is found in *NE* vii 12 in the "indication" that Aristotle offers in support of his claim that his opponent's restorative pleasures are only "incidentally pleasant":

An indication of this is the fact that people do not enjoy the same pleasure when their natural state is being replenished, as they do when it has been restored. Once it is restored, they enjoy things pleasant without qualification; but while it is being replenished they enjoy even quite the contrary. They even enjoy sharp and bitter things, none of which are pleasant either by nature or without qualification; nor, therefore, are the pleasures, since as pleasant things differ from each other, so also do the pleasures arising from them. (1153a2–7)

Aristotle here identifies some things as pleasant "by nature or without qualification" and sources the difference among pleasures in the difference between what things are pleasant and how.

One kind of difference among what things are pleasant, according to *NE* x 5, differentiates the pleasures that are to be found in different species of animal.

pleasure, it would be surprising to find him characterize as "absurd" at one time a view he himself holds at another time. However, what Aristotle declares absurd is the idea that pleasure could be identified just with the activities of seeing or thinking. Neither *NE* vii nor *NE* x 4 canvasses *this* sort of identification. Each identifies as (the source or location of) pleasure *perfect* or *unimpeded* activities of seeing or thinking, not seeing or thinking *tout court*.

A horse, a dog and a human being have different pleasures; and, as Heraclitus says, a donkey would choose sweepings over gold, since donkeys find food more pleasant than gold. (1176a5–8)

However, at least among humans, the variety among pleasures does not cease at the species level. If it did, then humans would be in the position that Aristotle may take other animals to be in. They would be able to pursue the natural human good by pursuing pleasure, just as Eudoxus suggested they do (*NE* x 2). But this is not Aristotle's view of the human situation. Human beings differ greatly in the things they experience as pleasant. What one finds pleasant is a subjective matter. Actually being pleasant, however, is not a (strictly) subjective matter, according to Aristotle. Although being pleasant is a function of being (at least potentially) pleasant to someone or other, not any old someone will do. The standard for being actually pleasant – pleasant without qualification, that is – is set by the good person. Aristotle here treats *pleasant* by analogy with (other) perceptual qualities like *sweet* or *hot*.

This happens too with sweet things. For the same things do not seem sweet to a feverish as to a healthy person, or hot to a sick as to a fit person; and the same thing happens in other cases. But in all such things, it seems that what is so is what appears so to the good person. If this is right, as it seems to be, and virtue – that is, the good person in so far as he is good – is the measure of each thing, then pleasures will be what appear so to him, and pleasant things will be what he enjoys. And if things that he finds disagreeable appear pleasant to someone, that is not surprising, since there are many ways for people to become ruined and perverted. The things are not pleasant, except to these people with this disposition. (1176a12–22)

Since the standard for actual pleasantness is the good person, then, although this kind of actual pleasantness is an indicator of value, it is not an indicator of value that anyone who needs it could use. The person for whom it might act as an indicator of value is the good person, that is, the person who has already achieved the value in question. The value of pleasure is effect and not source of the value in question. This reversal of the relation between pleasure and value is, in the end, the key point of difference between Aristotle and a hedonist such as Eudoxus (see Annas 1980, esp. 296–298).

IV. DIFFICULTIES FOR ARISTOTLE'S THEORY

In closing, I mention some difficulties that arise for the theory of pleasure and for the relation between value and pleasure that Aristotle puts forward.

First, Aristotle's view that it is the good person alone who is the standard of what things are pleasant challenges a rather natural intuition that things are pleasant just in case someone (anyone) finds them so. Clearly, Aristotle's view is deeply bound up with his conception of pleasure, not as a detachable feeling, but as closely bound up with – and informed by – the activity enjoyed. Aristotle's comparison of pleasant with sweet is useful insofar as perceptible qualities such as sweet are plausibly construed as "response-dependent," that is, as essentially involving a disposition to produce a specific response in an observer.[40] Further, when we evaluate the truth of claims about perceptible qualities, not any observer will do. However, it is one thing to take as authoritative in determining what is sweet or what is pleasant the healthy observer in normal conditions. It is quite another to give such authority to the *good* person, as Aristotle does in *NE* x 5.1176a12–22 (quoted previously), doing so, apparently, for pleasant, but also for secondary qualities such as sweet or hot.[41] This assimilation of – or slide between – a robust conception of natural health and value is a symptom of bigger issues in Aristotle's thinking that I shall not attempt to address.

Next, Aristotle's close association of pleasure with perfect activity – in particular, his apparent assumption, in *NE* x 4–5, that when a perceptual or intellectual activity is itself perfect, the person engaged in the activity must experience pleasure – raises two further difficulties. The first is that it might seem that perfect perceptual activity and pleasure can and will come apart. As Kenny (1963, 49) memorably observed, "the most sensitive nose in the world put in front of the most powerfully smelling manure in the world will not necessarily find the experience pleasant." The objection is that Aristotle has confused being perfectly perceptible with being (a) perfect and (b) perceptible.

Aristotle can meet this objection, if he can give an account of standards of perfection for sense and object that involve more than being in good working order perceptually speaking, and that, on pain of circularity, do not include the giving of pleasure. The discussion in *NE* x 4–5 gives two indications that Aristotle is thinking in this way. The first is his statement, in *NE* x 4, that a sense engages in the kind of perfect activity that pleasure perfects when it is engaged in that activity "in relation to the *noblest* of its objects" (1174b14–16). The characterization of the

---

[40] Relying on such a comparison with secondary qualities, some philosophers have offered response-dependent theories of value: McDowell 1985 and Wiggins 1991. In identifying pleasure as response-dependent, Aristotle is not offering a response-dependent theory of value: value is already presupposed in his account of the kind of observer on whose response the pleasant (without qualification) depends.

[41] This is the clear implication of 1176a15–16, unless the *spoudaios* here can be understood as that person who has the excellence relevant to each specific sphere (taste, temperature, etc.).

sense objects in question as "noblest" or "most fine" or "most beautiful" (*kalliston*) is an indication that the objects are being evaluated in normative terms that need not collapse into those that best provoke the senses' ordinary perceptual functions. The second indication is Aristotle's statement in *NE* x 5 that "sight differs from touch in purity (*kathareiotēs*), as do hearing and smell from taste" (1175b36–1176a2). It is not clear what Aristotle means by this statement, but "purity" too seems to function here as a normative standard.

The second difficulty that arises from Aristotle's association of pleasure with perfect activities – and the final difficulty for his theory that I shall consider – is this. Grant that pleasure occurs when there is relevantly perfect activity, there seem to be cases in which the occurrence of pleasure is inconsistent, or at least in tension, with the characterization of the associated activity as perfect. Consider the required enjoyment of perfect virtuous activity, especially on the "non-smug" understanding of this that I have given, where the enjoyment consists not in the satisfaction of knowing oneself to be acting in accordance with the relevant virtue, but in what one does. While there may be examples of virtuous activity in which it is a fault in the performance of the activity that one does not take pleasure in what it involves, there seem also to be examples in which the taking of pleasure would be a fault.[42]

Take, for example, the virtuous agent acting courageously on the battlefield, engaged in a just killing of an enemy in a just war.[43] It is not difficult to agree with Broadie (2003, 23) that if we take Aristotle to mean that "the agent enjoys what he is doing, or, as we might say, has a good time doing it, then the claim is ... ethically grotesque." But if this is *not* what Aristotle means – if he means only that the agent does the action willingly – then Aristotle seems, in offering a theory of *pleasure*, to be guilty of a confusion between doing something gladly and doing it with pleasure.

Aristotle appears to recognize that the pleasure involved in courage raises difficulties, since he addresses it himself (discussed by Frede 2009, 202–203).

People are called courageous for enduring what is painful; so courage involves pain, and is justly praised, since it is more difficult to endure what is painful than to abstain from what is pleasant. Nevertheless, the end that courage aims at would seem to be pleasant, but to be obscured by what else is happening. For the end for boxers – their reason for doing what they do, namely, the crown and the honours – is pleasant, but since they are flesh and blood, being hit is distressing

---

[42] Broadie 2003, 22–24, and cf. discussion in Broadie 1991, 316–324.

[43] Whatever we may think about the possibility of just killings or just war, Aristotle would surely subscribe to their existence.

and painful, as is all the hard exercise they do; and because of the number of these painful things, what they are aiming at, being small, seems to have nothing pleasant in it. And so, if this is true of courage as well, death and wounds will be painful for the courageous person, and he will face them involuntarily, but he will stand his ground against them because it is noble, or shameful not to. (*NE* iii 9.1117a32–b9)

It is not clear what Aristotle means when he identifies what is pleasant in courage as "the end that courage aims at," but it seems to be distinct both from simply *being courageous* in the way that invited the "smug" understanding and from doing those acts that courage in the context involves, at least to the extent that these are the cuts and thrusts of battle. Associating the pleasure of acting in accordance with virtue with the end of the action ties in with my proposal that the way in which pleasure perfects an activity is in helping to make it suitably endlike. But this is not yet enough to give a clear picture of the relation Aristotle envisages between pleasure and virtue and to determine whether he has the resources to defuse this kind of objection.

WORKS CITED

Annas, Julia. 1980. "Aristotle on Pleasure and Goodness." 285–299 in Amélie Oksenberg Rorty ed. *Essays on Aristotle's Ethics*. Berkeley: University of California Press.

Aubry, Gwenaëlle. 2009. "*Nicomachean Ethics* VII.14 (1154a22–b34): The Pain of the Living and Divine Pleasure." 238–263 in Natali ed. 2009.

Aufderheide, Joachim. "Pleasure as the Bloom on the Cheek of Youth." Unpublished manuscript.

Bostock, David. 1988. "Pleasure and Activity in Aristotle's Ethics." *Phronesis* 33: 251–272.

2000. *Aristotle's Ethics*. Oxford: Oxford University Press.

Broadie, Sarah. 1991. *Ethics with Aristotle*. Oxford: Oxford University Press.

2003. "Reply to C. C. W. Taylor." 21–27 in Heinaman ed. 2003.

Broadie, Sarah, and Christopher Rowe. 2002. *Aristotle: Nicomachean Ethics; Translation, Introduction and Commentary*. Oxford: Oxford University Press.

Burnyeat, M. F. 2008. "*Kinēsis* vs. *Energeia*: A Much-Read Passage in (but Not of) Aristotle's *Metaphysics*." *Oxford Studies in Ancient Philosophy* 34: 219–292.

Bywater, I. 1894. *Aristotelis Ethica Nicomachea*. Oxford: Clarendon Press.

Crisp, Roger trans. 2000. *Aristotle: Nicomachean Ethics*. Cambridge: Cambridge University Press.

Delcomminette, Sylvain. 2006. *Le Philèbe de Platon. Introduction à l'Agathologie Platonicienne*. Leiden: Brill.

Feldman, Fred. 2004. *Pleasure and the Good Life*. Oxford: Clarendon Press.

Festugière, A. J. 1936. *Aristote. Le Plaisir*. Paris: Librairie Philosophique J. Vrin.

Frede, Dorothea. 1997. *Platon Philebos*. Göttingen: Vandenhoeck & Ruprecht.

2006. "Pleasure and Pain in Aristotle's Ethics." 255–275 in R. Kraut ed. *The Blackwell Guide to Aristotle's Nicomachean Ethics*. Oxford: Blackwell.

2009. "*Nicomachean Ethics* VII.11–12: Pleasure." 182–207 in Natali ed. 2009.

Gauthier, Rene Antoine, and Jean Yves Jolif. 2002. *L'Éthique à Nicomaque*. Louvain-la-Neuve: Éditions Peeters.

Gosling, J. C. B. 1973–1974. "More Aristotelian Pleasures." *Proceedings of the Aristotelian Society* 74: 15–34.

———. 1975. *Plato: Philebus*. Oxford: Clarendon Press.

Gosling, J. C. B., and C. C. W. Taylor. 1982. *The Greeks on Pleasure*. Oxford: Oxford University Press.

Heinaman, Robert ed. 2003. *Plato and Aristotle's Ethics*. Aldershot: Ashgate.

Irwin, Terence. 1999. *Aristotle: Nicomachean Ethics*. 2nd ed. Indianapolis: Hackett.

Kenny, Anthony. 1963. *Action, Emotion and Will*. London: Routledge and Kegan Paul.

———. 1978. *The Aristotelian Ethics*. Oxford: Clarendon Press.

McDowell, John. 1985. "Values and Secondary Qualities." 110–129 in Ted Honderich ed. *Morality and Objectivity*. London: Routledge.

Natali, Carlo ed. 2009. *Aristotle's Nicomachean Ethics, Book VII: Symposium Aristotelicum*. Oxford: Oxford University Press.

Owen, G. E. L. 1971–1972. "Aristotelian Pleasures." *Proceedings of the Aristotelian Society* 72: 132–152.

Pakaluk, Michael. 2005. *Aristotle's Nicomachean Ethics: An Introduction*. Cambridge: Cambridge University Press.

Rapp, Christof. 2009. "Nicomachean Ethics VII.13–14 (1154a21): Pleasure and Eudaimonia." 209–235 in Natali ed. 2009.

Taub, Liba. 1998. "Eudoxus." In E. Craig ed. *Routledge Encyclopaedia of Philosophy*. London: Routledge. Retrieved March 19, 2010, from http://www.rep.routledge.com/article A126.

Taylor, C. C. W. 2003. "Pleasure: Aristotle's Response to Plato." 1–20 in Heinaman ed. 2003.

Warren, James. 2009. "Aristotle on Speusippus on Eudoxus on Pleasure." *Oxford Studies in Ancient Philosophy* 36: 249–281.

Webb, Philip. 1977. "The Relative Dating of the Accounts of Pleasure in Aristotle's Ethics." *Phronesis* 22: 235–262.

Wiggins, David. 1991. "A Sensible Subjectivism." 185–211 in his *Needs, Values, Truth*. 2nd ed. Oxford: Blackwell.

15   Finding Oneself with Friends

Some relationships we inherit, others we choose. Above all, we inherit our family. Finding ourselves with a native love for those who care for us in our early years, we may later revoke it, but if so we are not deciding that our initial criteria for loving were not satisfied. There were no such criteria. We simply loved. By contrast, we choose our friends, and thus have reasons for doing so. Our criteria are often inarticulate, especially when we are young, but they are nonetheless there; otherwise we would befriend people randomly. But what are these criteria? And what should they be? If we look for virtue in a friend, as Aristotle recommends, we will seek someone who matches our understanding of goodness. Perhaps the good seem too dull, though, and we would prefer instead a companion who excites; if so, our criterion of friendship is pleasure. Yet if merely exciting people seem a waste of our time, and it is wealth or power that guides our associations, we will choose instead the company of the rich and powerful. Such a choice may seem too calculating to deserve the title of friendship, let alone family, but Aristotle is not worried about our modern affective categories.[1] Instead, he wishes to explain a Greek notion broader than any of ours – namely, *philia* – and show not only how it includes all of the relationships just mentioned but also how it should be integrated into the best life.

To account for this breadth, with its consequent complexity, Aristotle devotes nearly a fifth of the *Nicomachean Ethics* to *philia*, more text than he assigns to any other ethical topic save moral virtue. Although we cannot survey his whole account here, we can nevertheless highlight some of its main points, focusing on four of the interesting problems raised, and then

---

Like all philosophical work, this chapter would not have been possible without *philia*, and four virtuous *philoi* in particular: Ronald Polansky, C. D. C. Reeve, David V. Orbison, and Sarah Alison Miller.

[1] Nehamas 2010. Following Nehamas, we shall leave *philia* (pl. *philiai*) and its cognates (*philos*, sg.; *philoi*, pl.) untranslated. The common translations–"love" and "friendship"–tend to prejudice interpretations, making it difficult to incorporate into them such *philoi* as business partners.

investigating how, if at all, Aristotle solves them.[2] The first of these problems we shall call the problem of instrumentality. Aristotle insists that in *philia* the participants (*philoi*) experience goodwill toward each other for the other's sake. In other words, they do not exploit one another. But how is this possible within versions of *philia* whose bases are utility or pleasure? Aristotle includes these versions within his account, after all, so we should try to interpret him in a way that allows *philoi* in these relationships to preserve some mutual respect. This can be done, but the way in which we shall do it here merely refocuses the problem: the highest version of *philia*, whose basis is virtue, requires *philoi* to use each other in order to maximize this virtue. Thus, even if *philoi* of the highest type direct their goodwill to each other for their own sake, are they not still using one another to accomplish an ulterior goal?

Aristotle solves this first problem, as we shall see, by showing how the *philoi* of the highest type – but only these *philoi* – do not use one another to accomplish anything ulterior because their ultimate goal is the self properly understood, the self perfectly actualized, the virtuous and happy self that is the same for each. But this solution generates a second problem, the problem of self-sufficiency. From the first book of this treatise, Aristotle stipulates that the happy person, the person who has perfectly actualized himself, will be self-sufficient (1097b7–13). Despite his insistence that "self-sufficiency" applies "not to a person on his own, living a solitary life," however, the impression lingers eight books later that a self-sufficient person will not need *philia*. Aristotle rejects this impression with a series of complex arguments designed to show how the activities of virtuous and happy *philoi* are enhanced by living together. But in order to accomplish their purpose, these arguments must stretch the notion of *philia* so far that a third problem arises: narcissism. In the end, true *philia* is not a relationship with another, as it would appear, but instead a relationship with oneself. As surprising as this result may seem, it nonetheless fulfills Aristotle's own premise that "the origin of relations of friendship towards our neighbors, and of the characteristics by which we distinguish the various kinds of *philiai*, seems to be in our relations with ourselves" (1166a1–3).[3]

Whether or not Aristotle saw narcissism as a problem, ethical or otherwise, we shall conclude that it makes him unable to account for the love of a particular person in her difference or otherness. Apparently he was not concerned with this aspect of love, although many philosophers since, and many of us nowadays, consider it fundamental. This fourth and final

---

[2]   Pakaluk 1998 provides a comprehensive commentary.
[3]   All translations of the *Nicomachean Ethics* are from Crisp 2000, unless otherwise noted. Crisp's translations of *philia* and some of its cognates have been replaced with the Greek originals, for the reason mentioned in note 1.

problem – which we shall call the problem of alterity – is not an accident of peculiar choices in his account of love and friendship. On the contrary, as we shall argue, it follows inevitably from his solutions to the first two problems (instrumentality and self-sufficiency), his subordination of *philia* to the criteria of knowledge. His epistemology precludes knowledge of a particular person as such: knowledge of anything, including a different person, must be knowledge of its essence, which it necessarily shares with all other instances of its kind.[4] "No craft examines the particular," he writes elsewhere (*Rhetoric* 1356b31–33), because "the particular is unlimited and not an object of scientific knowledge." Because he submits *philia* to the criteria of knowledge, Aristotle must circumscribe it by the same limit. We cannot know a different individual as such, so neither can we love her as such. We must love her as we know her: essentially. Symptomatic of his failure to recognize the contribution of alterity to love, we shall ultimately conclude, is Aristotle's inability to incorporate family love into his account. The unknowable individual becomes the unlovable other.

I. TWO DEFINITIONS: VIRTUE AND PHILIA

Philia requires, as Aristotle says, a certain feeling: goodwill (*eunoia*).[5] With goodwill toward someone, you wish good things for her. But this unqualified wish hardly guarantees *philia* between the two of you. He therefore adds several qualifications to this necessary feeling. To be *philia*, first of all, there must be "reciprocated goodwill" (1155b33). Second, this goodwill must be mutually acknowledged (1155b35–1156a6; see also 1166b30–33). Although *philia* is a very broad category from our modern perspective, it is nonetheless narrower in this way than our own notion of love. Star-crossed characters who smolder for each other in unknowing silence upon a thousand screens may share love, by our lights, but not *philia*, by Aristotle's. Nor do oenophiles and their wine,

---

[4] *Metaphysics* 1040a1–5 and 1031b19–22. Knowledge, for Aristotle, is of what is universal (see *De Anima* 417b22–33). Matter is what makes something particular, but "matter is unknowable in itself" (*Meta.* 1036a8). Unless otherwise noted, all translations of Aristotelian texts aside from the *Nicomachean Ethics* are from Barnes 1995.

[5] See 1156a9–10, and 1166b30–1167a21. Most translators render *eunoia* as "goodwill," that is, a volition or feeling. Hadreas 1995 argues that it is instead a cognition or judgment, better rendered as "recognition of another's worthiness," or "thinking favorably of another." His main argument is that the "definition" of *philia* (1156a3–5) mentions *eunoia* and then wishing well, so that wishing well (a feeling) would be redundant unless it were different from *eunoia* (a thought). As Hadreas acknowledges, however, it could also be the same as *eunoia* and offered not as an addition but instead as an explanation. This seems to be Aristotle's intent because in the lines right before this "definition" he uses *eunoia* and wishing well interchangeably (1155b32–34).

thanks to his third, most important, and ultimately most problematic qualification.

When we wish good to our fellow *philos*, he writes, "we ought to wish good things to a *philos* for his own sake *(ekeinou heneka)*" (1155b31). The well-wishing we have toward our *philos*, for example, is very different from that which we have toward some inanimate objects (1155b28–29). You may wish well toward a bottle that is aging in your cellar but only so that it may benefit you when you uncork it. Every wish you have for it, in fact, refers to the utility or pleasure it gives *you*; none is a wish for *its* own sake (1155b29–32). No matter how much you love wine, then, you cannot be its *philos*. Correlatively, you cannot be the *philos* of anyone you exploit, whether you treat him as an inanimate object or an animate tool (Aristotle's description of a natural slave).[6] To do so would be to measure your every wish for his welfare against your own, and such calculation falls afoul of the third qualification of the necessary goodwill. To summarize these three qualifications, Aristotelian *philia* requires a feeling of goodwill that is reciprocal, mutually acknowledged, and for the other's sake.[7] Although this precise feeling is a necessary condition of *philia*, however, it is not its definition. For Aristotle, *philia* is a state *(hexis)* rather than a feeling *(pathos)* (1157b29–33). To define it properly, therefore, we should know something about states and then identify the sort of state that is *philia*.

Aristotle presents the notion of state earlier in the treatise, when he defines virtue *(aretē)* by saying twice that it is "concerned with feelings" (1106b17–25), but that "neither virtues nor vices are feelings" (1105b29). Feelings come and go, after all, whereas virtues are stable dispositions, or states, both to feel and to act in the right way. Consider the virtue of courage. It is concerned with the feeling of fear, especially in battlefield action, but it is not that feeling alone (1116b24–1117a5). Someone with courage must have the right degree of fear – neither its excess nor its

---

[6] The notorious Aristotelian passage on natural slavery is in *Politics* i 5–6. But in a lesser-known passage from these two books on *philia* (*Nicomachean Ethics* viii and ix), he writes: "There is neither *philia* nor justice towards soulless things. Nor is there any towards a horse or cow, or towards a slave, in so far as he is a slave. For master and slave have nothing in common, since a slave is a tool with a soul, while a tool is a slave without a soul. In so far as he is a slave, then, there is no *philia* with him" (1161b2–6). Nevertheless, he does mention *philia* between master and slave at *Politics* 1255b12–15. If he is consistent, he must mean it here in a loose sense, unless *philia* is possible between a master and a slave insofar as he is something other than a slave (i.e., a human).

[7] As Cooper 1999, 313, observes, *Rhetoric* ii 4 defines *to philein* (liking or loving) as "wanting for someone what one thinks good, for his sake and not for one's own, and being inclined to do such things for him" (1380b35–1381a2). Like Cooper, we shall focus on the more precise discussion of *philia* found in books viii and ix of *Nicomachean Ethics*.

deficiency – and this feeling must be felt and acted upon "at the right time, about the right things, towards the right people, for the right end, and in the right way" (1106b20–23). To have this virtue, or for that matter its vicious alternatives, then, one must be in a state "in respect of which we are well or badly disposed in relation to feelings" (1105b27). Likewise for the other virtues. Being well off in relation to feelings generally, being in the state that is intermediate in relation to them, is thus virtue's genus (1106a13). But without its specific difference, or differentia, we do not yet have its definition, because Aristotelian definitions are by genus and differentia.[8]

Aristotle has already argued that human virtue perfects the human function, "activity of the soul in accordance with reason" (1098a7). This rational activity, he now adds, determines what is appropriate for feeling (and action) in complex circumstances, just as craftsmen determine what is appropriate to their materials and products (1106b13–15). "Virtue," according to the resulting definition, "is a state involving rational choice, consisting in an intermediate relative to us and determined by reason" (1106b36–1107a2). In sum, its genus is a state; its differentia, rational choice; its aim, the intermediate relative to us in feeling and action. Aristotle appears to define *philia* similarly.[9] "Affection [*philēsis*] seems to be a feeling," he writes, "but *philia* is a state" (1157b29). Though not a feeling, *philia* is nonetheless concerned with feeling, as we have seen, the feeling of goodwill triply qualified. Being well off in relation to this feeling should be its genus, therefore, if the parallel with virtue's definition holds, just as its specific difference should be the rational choice that actualizes this state in particular circumstances. Evoking this parallel, accordingly, Aristotle writes that "mutual friendship [*antiphilein*] involves rational choice [*prohairesis*], and rational choice comes from a state" (1157b31–32; cf. 1164b2).

In his definition of virtue, rational choice aims at the intermediate, but Aristotle's discussion of *philia* does not rely on this notion at all. Indeed, he mentions it there only once, in passing: "Desire is for the intermediate" (1159b21). And yet, he writes, "in all the states of character we have mentioned, and in the others as well, there is a sort of target, and it is with his eye on this that the person with reason tightens or loosens his string" (1138b22–23). What, then, is the target of reason in the case of *philia*? The *philēton* (roughly, the lovable). Like its closest English equivalent, this

[8] *Categories* 2a17–19, *Topics* 102a31–35, *Metaphysics* 1038a5–9. For an introduction to Aristotelian definition, see Shields 2007, 98–105. For a fuller discussion of Aristotle's doctrine of the intermediate and the definition of virtue it yields, see the Brown chapter in this volume. Heeding her conclusions, quotations of Crisp's translation have been emended to substitute "intermediate" for "mean."
[9] About the precise relationship between virtue and *philia*, Aristotle is vague: "It is a virtue or involves virtue" (1155a1).

Greek word is ambiguous between two senses: what is loved (descriptive), and what should be loved (normative). Sensitive to this important ambiguity, as well as to the great variety of things people do in fact love, Aristotle distinguishes three types of *philēton*: the good, the pleasant, and the useful (1155b18–19).[10] As quick illustrations, food is lovable because it is pleasant to eat; money, because it is useful for buying such pleasant things; and virtue, finally, because it is good. The same can be said about *philoi*: some are lovable because they make pleasant company, others because they are useful, and still others because they are virtuous.[11] Upon this distinction between three types of *philēton*, then, Aristotle bases another between three types of *philia* (1156a6–b36). For if *philia* is the use of reason to actualize our feelings of goodwill toward other people – thus helping to stabilize them through the changing circumstances of life (1167a11–13) – our choice of *philoi* will depend on our *philēton*.[12]

II. A FIRST PROBLEM: INSTRUMENTALITY

If our *philēton* is the useful, for example, we shall choose our *philoi* for the sake of their utility to us.[13] You are a politician who ensures that

[10] "The good" translates *agathon*, "the pleasant" or "pleasure" translates *hedu* or *hēdonē*, and "the useful" translates *chrēsimon*. Speaking precisely, Aristotle eliminates the useful as a distinct object: "What is useful is the source of some good or some pleasure; hence what is good and what is pleasant are lovable as ends" (1155b19–21). He nonetheless discusses utility *philia* as a distinct type (1156a22–31, 1158a18–37, 1162b5–20, and 1163a10–22), so we shall preserve the useful as an object in this discussion. (For a similar distinction, see also *Topics* 118b27–28.)

[11] To be precise, *philoi* are lovable because they *seem* pleasant, *seem* useful, or *seem* to have virtue, whether or not they really are. Aristotle is aware of this paramount distinction in human relationships, but he is concerned with it only when appearance and reality come apart – that is, when the reality of one *philos* turns out to be different from how she appeared to the other (e.g., 1163a24–36, 1164a13–22, and 1165b5–31).

[12] Aristotle's main account treats types of *philia* that are pure, wherein the two *philoi* share the same *philēton*. "Each gets from each the same or similar benefits," he writes of the best type, "as ought to happen among *philoi*" (1156b34–1157a1). But mixed types are possible, wherein the *philoi* seek different types of object from each other. He devotes several pages to these, especially *philia* between unequals (1158b7–1159b25) or between family members (1161b11–1162a34). The clearest example of mixed *philia* is the sort of pederasty not uncommon among the elite of his era, wherein an adolescent boy (the *philoumenos*, or beloved) offered the pleasure of sexual favors to a mature *erastēs* (or lover), who in return initiated his boy into the benefits of political life. Aristotle mentions this sort of relationship to show how mixed *philia* often dissolves because the participants have divergent goals (1164a3–22). That said, he does not deny its claim to be *philia* (1158b1–5).

[13] Aristotle believes that *philia* of utility is more common among the old (1156a24–26), whereas the cause of *philia* among the young is more often pleasure, "since they live in accordance with their feelings, and pursue in particular what is pleasant for themselves and what is immediate" (1156a33–34).

investigators connive at my illegitimate business, for which I contribute handsomely to your political campaigns. By using each other in this way, by choosing each other for the sake of utility, are we wishing each other well for each other's sake? It would appear that neither we, nor any others who choose each other for utility's sake, could be *philoi* properly speaking. This is most clear when the supposed *philoi* are no longer useful to each other: you cannot protect my business because of a popular corruption investigation, or I have diverted my interests to a legitimate business; in each case, the basis of our *philia* disappears. Aristotle recognizes this as a common feature of this type of *philia* (1165b1–4), acknowledging that "those who love one another for utility love the other not in himself, but only in so far as they will obtain some good for themselves from him" (1156a11–13). Here, then, is the first problem for Aristotle's account: on one hand, it distinguishes three types of *philia*, including one for utility's sake; on the other hand, this account seems to exclude this type because it lacks the necessary goodwill.[14]

The contradiction appears still more serious when we consider how it may extend beyond just this one type of *philia*. For as Aristotle himself writes elsewhere, "that because of which we love is better loved."[15] In other words, if you love someone because of something else, that something else is better loved by you than he is. When we share *philia* with each other, and thus experience goodwill toward each other, this is because of the *philēton* we seek from one another. Are we not, then, using each other to achieve that *philēton*? When two people are *philoi* because they enjoy each other, for example, is this *philia* not as instrumental as the type based on utility? "Aristotle's own examples," observes Nehamas, "are much more often cases of passion, erotic and sexual – primarily pederastic and matrimonial – than the witty conversationalists so common among his interpreters."[16] Accordingly, let us imagine a

---

[14] The contradiction may be irreconcilable if every passage is given equal weight, for although Aristotle has said that *eunoia* is necessary for every form of *philia* (1156a3–5), adding later that it "seems to be the first principle of *philia*" (1167a3; 1156a1 mentions its role in the origin of the utility type in particular), he nevertheless writes elsewhere that *eunoia* "does not, however, become *philia* for utility or pleasure, since goodwill does not arise for these reasons" (1167a13–14). The account of *philia* given in this chapter attempts to reconcile this contradiction by interpreting Aristotle as writing sometimes of *philia* or *eunoia* when in fact he means their paradigmatic forms, the *philia* of virtue or the *eunoia* found therein. In the inferior types of *philia*, accordingly, there are inferior forms of *eunoia*.

[15] *Posterior Analytics* 72a32. In the translation of Irwin and Fine 1985: "if, for instance, we love y because of x, x is loved more than y."

[16] Nehamas 2010, 231. Note 40 lists the examples and categorizes them as "pederastic," "matrimonial," and "pleasant companions." Pederastic: 1156b1–2, 1157a6–14, 1158a10–15, 1159b15–16, 1164a2 ff.; matrimonial: 1162a16 ff.; pleasant companions: 1156a13, 1157a6, 1158a31.

sexual relationship between two carefree youths. If this pleasure were the
basis of their relationship, as would be clear once they became bored of
each other in bed, would they not be using each other to achieve it? If so,
can each one truly wish the other well for his own sake? If not, the *philia*
of pleasure would prove as spurious as that of utility. Both would lack the
necessary goodwill. According to one interpretation, this is Aristotle's
intent – to distinguish authentic *philia* (wherein *philoi* wish good to each
other for each other's sake) from its instrumental imitations (see Pakaluk
1998, 61–63).

There is at least one comment that seems to support this interpretation. Speaking of relationships whose *philēton* is utility or pleasure,
Aristotle writes that "they do not appear to be *philiai* – that is, because
of their dissimilarity to *philia* based on virtue" (1158b11–12). The whole
passage surrounding this comment, however, highlights the ways in
which the *philiai* of utility or pleasure – let us call them, with Aristotle,
the inferior types – seem not only dissimilar to that superior type but also
similar to it (1158b1–12). *Philia* of virtue is more enduring and immune to
slander than they are, he observes, but it is often useful and pleasant too.
"It is because of their similarity and dissimilarity to the same thing,"
Aristotle therefore adds, "that they seem both to be and not to be *philiai*"
(1158b5–6). His emphasis in this passage is thus on the appearance of
philia, not its nature. Concerned more with its nature, by contrast, many
other passages treat relationships based on utility or pleasure as genuine
philiai.[17] Heeding these passages, then, another interpretation shows
how even *philoi* of the inferior types wish each other good for each other's
sake, once this sort of wish is properly understood.[18]

According to this interpretation, when Rosencrantz and Guildenstern
share a *philia*, whatever it is that each seeks in this relationship, whether
it be pleasure, utility, or virtue, each wishes the other to achieve this
philēton, so long as it does not compromise the achievement of his own.
Thus, if the *philēton* of both is pleasure, Rosencrantz wishes Guildenstern
to achieve it so long as this pleasure does not compromise Rosencrantz's
own. Correlatively, Guildenstern wishes the same for Rosencrantz. The
interpretation becomes more complicated, as we should expect, in the
case of a mixed *philia*. Let us imagine that Rosencrantz pursues pleasure
while Guildenstern pursues utility. Rosencrantz will wish Guildenstern to
achieve utility so long as it does not compromise Rosencrantz's pursuit of
pleasure, whereas Guildenstern will wish Rosencrantz to secure pleasure,
so long as it does not compromise Guildenstern's pursuit of wealth and

[17] See, e.g., 1156a3–1156b5, 1158a2–36, 1162a34, 1165b2–4, and 1170b25–30. For a fuller
discussion and critique of Pakaluk's interpretation, see Nehamas 2010, 220–221.
[18] Thanks to Ron Polansky for helping me to clarify this interpretation *contra* the one
shared by Konstan 1997, 68–69, Cooper 1999, 312–335, and Nehamas 2010, 222n25.

power. In neither case is the *philia* a case of exploitation – the way a master treats his slave, or an oenophile his bottle of wine – for in both cases each *philos* wishes well to the other for his own sake (*ekeinou heneka*, 1155b31).

In neither case, however, do the *philoi* wish well to each other in themselves (*kath' hautous*). This was precisely how Aristotle described their inferiority: "Those who love one another for utility love the other not in himself" (1156a11). For even though *philoi* of the inferior types wish well to the other for his own sake, their goodwill is directed by thoughts of pleasure or utility. That is to say, it is oriented toward the other's pleasure or utility, and it is limited by threats of compromise to one's own pleasure or utility. In sum, Aristotle argues, it is determined by qualities that each has only incidentally (*kata sumbebēkos*: 1156a16–17, 1157b4). When politicians and businessmen share a utility *philia*, for instance, the *philēton* that regulates their participation is incidental because neither wealth nor honor is essential to their humanity. Regular sex pleases both of the youths in the relationship imagined previously, moreover, but the pleasure that determines their participation in this hedonistic *philia* is also incidental to who (or what) they essentially are. Both inferior types of *philia*, Aristotle thus writes, are "incidental, since the person is loved not in so far as he is who he is," but insofar as he provides some benefit or pleasure (1156a16–17).

If any *philia* is instrumental as long as the reciprocal good-wishes of its *philoi* are regulated by the *philēton* they pursue together, should not the best type of *philia* be no less so? It would appear so, at first glance, because this type also has a *philēton*, virtue, that regulates the wishes of its participants. Suppose, for example, that a good man and woman choose to marry each other because they cherish virtue above all.[19] So they wish each other well, reciprocally and with mutual acknowledgment, but do they do so for the other's own sake? The husband wishes that his wife win a promotion at work, say, not so much because he will profit from her raise as because she will flourish with the additional responsibility. His wishes are therefore for her sake – just as the wishes of the politician, businessman, and carefree youths were for the sake of their *philoi* – but these wishes are likewise regulated by the *philēton* that is the basis of

[19] Those familiar with Aristotle's views on women (*Politics* 1260a13) may be surprised to learn that he counts such a union among the best sort. But he does, with qualification: "It may also be *philia* for virtue, if they are good, since each has his or her own virtue" (1162a25–27). At the risk of anachronism, we shall ignore this qualification for the purpose of our example and its wider purpose. Marriage is one of the only common relationships in our era that involves, at least in principle, commitment not only to character but also to living together over a long period of time. For many people, then, it will be the closest point of contact between Aristotle's *philia* of character and their own lives. Some of our era's other, less common examples include the friendships forged over prolonged cohabitation in the military or religious orders.

their relationship. The only difference now is that this *philēton* is virtue, at least as he understands it. He does not wish her to succeed, after all, if her success requires her to steal.[20] By regulating his goodwill toward her according to virtue, however, he is not doing so according to something foreign to her self. In Aristotle's technical vocabulary, he is regulating his goodwill according to who or what she is, that is, according to the human essence. If she does likewise, it is a *philia* of the best type.

It is not that inferior *philoi* know the human essence but choose to ignore it when they form their *philiai*. They know it no more in the case of their *philoi* than they do in their own case, because "whatever some-one regards as his being [*einai*], or the end for which he chooses to live, that is what he wishes to pursue with his friend" (1172a1–3).[21] *Philoi* of the superior type love each other for who they are – in other words, for their essence – because they know who they are. Like *philoi* of the inferior types, then, they wish well to the other for his own sake and regulate their goodwill toward each other by the *philēton* that determines their *philia*. But the superiority of this *philēton* makes all the difference. Virtue perfects their selves – who they most of all are, their essence (1169a1). Consequently, each limits his goodwill toward the other by one thing only: who that other really is. But this is not really a limit. Aristotle thus calls their *philia* perfect or complete (*teleia*: 1156b6). "Complete *philia* is the *philia* of good people similar in virtue," he writes, "for they wish goods in the same way to each other in so far as they are good, and they are good in themselves" (1156b7–9). Unlike the inferior types of *philia*, then, the relationship of superior *philoi* is in no way instrumental – they love each other not because of anything else, but because of who they really are. "Only good people," Aristotle writes, "can be *philoi* for the sake of the other person himself" (1157a20).

Unlike the incidental qualities of pleasure and utility that often fluctuate with circumstance, Aristotle thinks virtue typically survives the vicissitudes of life, so that complete *philia* lasts longer than its incomplete imitations (1156b13 and 1159b3–12). But we should not imagine this long *philia* as long-suffering. Aristotle goes on to argue that the pleasures enjoyed by good people are superior, insofar as they are pleasant unconditionally (x 1–5; see esp. 1176a10–29).[22] According to

---

[20]   Theft Aristotle forbids categorically, along with other actions (adultery and homicide), and some feelings (spite, shamelessness, and envy). "In their case," he says, "one can never hit the mark, but always misses" (1107a14–15).

[21]   This translation is not from Crisp but instead from Reeve 1992, 175, nearly matching the one in Irwin and Fine 1985, 265. Reeve mentions a similar passage (*Rhetoric* 1381a9–10) and provides a brief commentary.

[22]   More will be said about Aristotle's account of pleasure in what follows. A fuller treatment can be found in Harte's chapter in this volume.

this argument, the value of a pleasure depends on the value of the activity it completes. Because virtuous activity is the best of all activities, the pleasures completing it are likewise best. Hence, *philoi* of virtue share the best pleasures, strengthening their bond still further (1156b18–24). Moreover, they may also share the pleasures and benefits that characterize inferior *philia*. In the domestic life of the husband and wife we imagined earlier, they may enjoy each other sexually, while profiting from each other's talents: she from his cooking, he from her financial prudence. Despite the strength these incidental qualities add to their bond, however, "they are disposed in this way towards each other because of what they are, not for any incidental reason" (1156b10–12).

Needless to say, such a relationship does not appear overnight; it takes time to flower, first putting down roots in a mutual regard for virtue, then growing through the countless interactions of life together. For "nothing is as proper to *philoi*," observes Aristotle, "as living together" (1157b20, 1158a9, 1170b11–13). This is not so much because they enjoy and profit from each other's company, as because "a sort of training in virtue emerges from good people's living in each other's company" (1170a11–12). The goal of this training is to realize their essence; the virtues are simply the character traits that permit them to do so. Exercising these virtues, and enjoying the superior pleasures such superior activities afford, their mutual goodwill must surely grow. Whereas many marriages lose their appeal after a while – when the pleasure or the utility from which they grew dries up, so that the mutual goodwill of their participants withers – this one will become more appealing over time.

III. TWO TYPES OF VIRTUE: MORAL AND INTELLECTUAL

The good of each thing, according to Aristotle (1097a15–26; see also 1139a17–18), is the performance of its characteristic activity or function (*ergon*). His examples are craftsmen – first, a flute player and a sculptor; later, a tanner and a carpenter – whose characteristic activities are obvious. But if there is a characteristic activity for each of the human craftsmen, must there not be one for the human being as such? He now reverses direction, turning from the many activities performed by individual humans to the many functions performed by the parts of an individual human body.[23] For if there is a characteristic activity or function for the eye, the hand, the foot, and each of our other bodily parts, then surely there must be one for the human being as a whole? Taken together, these two rhetorical questions place the individual in between the many

---

[23] Reeve 2012, 238–239. See also Reeve's chapter in this volume.

activities he may exercise as a craftsman and the many activities upon
which his bodily survival depends. Only if the human being has a function as such, Aristotle assumes, would it be possible for human parts to
have subservient functions (promoting indirectly the ultimate activity of
the whole), and for human beings to exercise different craft-activities
(fulfilling their human function in some particular way). "Whatever the
human function turns out to be," Reeve (2012, 239) thus writes, "it must
be something we can intelligibly think of as explaining the functions of
the parts of the human body, and how it is that human beings can be
craftsmen, subject to the rational principles or norms of their craft."

With these constraints in mind, it seems, Aristotle argues that this
function cannot be the life of nutrition and growth, which we share with
plants, or of perception, which we share with other animals. "What
remains is a life," he quickly concludes, "of the element that possesses
reason" (1098a4: *logos*). Although he does not make the argument
explicit, it cannot rely upon the isolation of something unique to
humans, otherwise using grammar or telling jokes would also be viable
candidates. Even if he seems here to be grasping something unique, he is
not choosing reason because it is unique. Uniqueness is a necessary but
insufficient criterion of essence. More fundamentally, our essence must
explain who we are, accounting for all of our unique qualities. Rationality
alone, according to Aristotle, does this. It may not be evident when we
sleep, but we are nevertheless potentially rational even then, insofar
as we are human (1102b4–9). This is not to say that we are perfectly so.
On the contrary, we typically behave foolishly when we are young, and
maturation is difficult (1095a2–11). The perfection of our characteristic
activity requires a lifetime of effort, years of practice in the virtues that
perfect it (1098a8–21).

Virtues, recall, are the traits of character that help one accomplish a
characteristic activity. The virtues of a lyre player (e.g., perfect pitch and
dexterity) help her accomplish her function: playing the lyre. The virtues
of a general (e.g., foresight and ingenuity) help him accomplish his function: winning battles. The virtues of a human being (e.g., temperance and
courage) are the character traits that help him accomplish the human
function: "the activity of the soul and actions in accordance with reason"
(1098a12–13: *logos*). In *philia* of virtue, therefore, the *philoi* strive to help
each other function well, actualize their essence, and thereby become
more fully who they most of all are. But who are they? Reason is the
answer provided by Aristotle's sketch of the human function, but he
qualifies it immediately. The rational element in the soul is divided, so
that "one part has reason in being obedient to reason, the other in
possessing it and engaging in thought" (1098a3–5). He elaborates the
distinction shortly thereafter (i 13), where he says he has treated the

soul more carefully in other works, adding that "we should make use of these" (1102a27–28). Some of their theoretical complexities will not be relevant to a practical work, he concedes (1102a28–33), but the complex role of reason in the human soul is not among them.

Indeed, the role of reason in the soul provokes Aristotle to invoke his division of the soul into three parts – more fully articulated in *De Anima* – hoping thereby to make it clearer. The lowest part, which we have in common with plants as well as other animals, is responsible for nutrition and "has no share at all in reason" (1102a32–b7, b29–30). As such, it is deaf to ethical injunctions, let alone philosophical arguments. Aristotle ignores it "because there is nothing it has the power to do or not do" (1144a10–12). Plants lack the next part, which we nonetheless have in common with other animals. As far as its relationship to reason, this part "consisting in appetite and desire in general does share in it in a way, in so far as it listens to and obeys it" (1102b30–32). He compares it to a son who can heed his father's advice, sharing in paternal wisdom although lacking it in himself. This middle part of the human soul is thus rational, but only with qualification (1102b32–34). It is capable of following the unqualified rationality – the wisdom – of the highest part, which has reason "in the strict sense, possessing it in itself" (1103a3–4).[24] There are, then, two distinct roles for reason in the human soul. One is impure, so to speak, wherein the part of the soul that lacks reason but can obey it does so. A second role, by contrast, is pure: the part that has reason in itself activates it.

"Virtue," Aristotle adds, "is distinguished along the same lines" (1103a4). For virtue is whatever perfects the human function – that is, the activity of reason – so that if there are two varieties of human rationality, pure and impure, there must be two varieties of virtue as well: "intellectual, such as wisdom, judgement, and practical wisdom, while others are virtues of character, such as generosity and temperance" (1103a5–7). Inasmuch as it is complete, *philia* of virtue should be valuable to the *philoi* in both ways, as training for their intellects as well as their characters. For whatever reason, Aristotle does not make the distinction explicit when he celebrates *philia*'s value to the *philoi* of virtue. "They seem to become even better through their activity and their improving each other," he writes vaguely, "because each takes impressions from the other of what meets with his approval" (1172a10–13). Yet the omission is

---

[24] Despite this division of the soul into three parts, Aristotle nevertheless heeds the simpler distinction of his popular works and continues to speak of two major parts of the soul: the rational and the part without reason. Because the middle part distinguished earlier has this ambiguous relationship to reason, he wavers in his assignment of it to one major part or the other (1102b28–1103a4). For a practical work, apparently, his decision makes no difference.

hardly noticeable: whether a situation demands virtue of character or virtue of intellect, moral or intellectual virtue, it is easy enough to imagine *philoi* of virtue checking their choices with one another. They will seek each other's approval, but not in the manner of those who fish for compliments, assuaging their insecurity by extorting the endorsement of others. Rather, they are prepared to hear that they are making a mistake, ready to respect contrary advice, correction, or even reproof. One hallmark of the best sort of *philia* is that it not only withstands such moments; it is fortified by them.

When temperance seems required, for example, a wife may avail herself of the dispassionate distance of her husband – both from the situation itself and from her own particular character flaws – in order to assess whether she really should abstain or whether, in fact, her self-restraint conceals some unwarranted self-effacement. Another example: when action on the battlefield would seem rash, a soldier may seek the advice of his comrade-at-arms to help him decide whether his assessment of the risk is not in fact a shield for his cowardice. And so on for the other virtues of character. Accordingly, the discussion of *philia* that occupies the eighth and ninth books of this treatise follows neatly from its seventh book's discussion of *akrasia* (incontinence). After learning there how self-deception works, *philia* of virtue now enters Aristotle's ethics as the best practical insurance against it.

Similarly, in a situation more intellectual – say, when someone must choose how to review an unconventional book – he may consult the complementary expertise of his colleague in order to deepen his acquaintance with the relevant facts or surmount the prejudices of his own perspective (1172a5). For in intellectual matters, too, a *philos* can help compensate for our flaws. Indeed, *philia* of virtue is still our best practical insurance against parochial philosophy. One of the advantages of the contemplative over the practical life, according to Aristotle, is that when we exercise the virtues of character we require other people to be "associates in and objects of" our actions, whereas in the exercise of intellectual virtue, "the wise person can contemplate by himself, the more so the wiser he is." This contrast seems to undermine the value of complete *philia* for intellectual activity. "Maybe," Aristotle nevertheless concedes, "he can do it better with collaborators" (1177a30–b1).[25] If so,

---

[25]   The problem is discussed more thoroughly later in the chapter. See also Hitz 2011, who emphasizes the value of collaboration but ignores Aristotle's comment, central to our interpretation, that "those who have knowledge will pass their time more pleasantly than those who are still in search of it" (1177a25–27). Aristotle enjoins the ultimate pleasure, not the penultimate; when he speaks of the pleasure of contemplation, accordingly, he must mean the pleasure of knowledge already acquired, not the pleasure of seeking knowledge (whether alone or with the collaboration of philosophical *philoi*).

the discussion of *philia* that occupies the eighth and ninth books anticipates nicely the tenth book's discussion of contemplation (*theōria*).

IV. A SECOND PROBLEM: SELF-SUFFICIENCY

Aristotle's most sustained treatment of *philia*'s value (ix 9) alludes to such benefits, as we saw earlier, by claiming that "a sort of training in virtue emerges from good people's living in each other's company" (1170a11–12). However integral it may be to the daily life of *philoi* who seek to perfect their virtue together, this training merits only one sentence in his long and complex presentation of *philia*'s value. In order to comprehend the rest of this value, then, we should interpret the entire treatment, which begins with a fundamental problem first posed by Plato in *Lysis*: the happy person (*eudaimōn*) is supposed to be self-sufficient (*autarkēs*), so why should he have any *philoi* at all (1169b2–7; cf. 1097b7–16)?[26] Aristotle appears to exacerbate this second problem for his account by writing that the *philos* is "another self" (*heteros autos*), an ambiguous phrase that he will use later to solve it, but which he glosses here problematically as someone who "provides what a person cannot provide by himself." As such, after all, *philoi* seem of no use to the happy person. He is self-sufficient, and so needs nothing he cannot provide by himself, including pleasure: "He will have no need, or little need, of friends for pleasure (because his life is pleasant, it has no need of imported pleasure)" (1169b26–27; cf. 1158a23–24).

Before interpreting Aristotle's solution to this problem, we should emphasize its precise target: the happy person. To the less-than-happy, after all, *philia* of pleasure or utility could still be of value. They are not self-sufficient and often lack virtue, so *philoi* of utility could offer them benefits they cannot provide by themselves, while *philoi* of pleasure could bring to their lives enjoyment that is absent from their own activities. This is the condition of the masses, who accordingly view *philia* only in terms of pleasure or utility (1169b24). Their narrow view focuses the problem: the happy person needs neither pleasure nor utility from his *philoi*, so he should have no need of *philia* whatsoever. Aristotle's view is broader, of course, with complete *philia* (of virtue and character) distinguished from its incomplete imitations (of pleasure or utility). That said, his concern with this second problem is narrow in its own way. Rather than focusing on the incomplete imitations, as the masses do, he focuses instead on complete *philia* and its value for the *philoi* involved. Generally, he argues that these *philoi* also enjoy pleasure from each other's company and help, giving their *philia* value, but these pleasures

---

[26] For a discussion of the parallel with *Lysis*, see Hitz 2011, 4–5.

are not "imported" (*epeisakton*), whereas those available in the incomplete imitations are.

The distinction implied here, between imported and not imported, anticipates the distinction Aristotle makes explicit soon afterward, in his account of pleasure, between those that are "foreign" and those that are "proper" (*allotrion* and *oikeion* respectively; 1175a29–b24). "Each of the pleasures," he begins, "is closely related to the activity it completes." For example, the pleasure of philosophical conversation is closely related to the activity of philosophical conversation – so closely, in fact, that it cannot be obtained any other way; it is the pleasure proper to this activity. While conversing, one may also enjoy the pleasure of music, but because this pleasure can be obtained otherwise, it is a pleasure foreign to philosophical conversation. "The pleasure proper to an activity enhances it," Aristotle adds, whereas "foreign pleasures produce much the same result as pain, since they ruin the activity." This same distinction seems to underwrite his first two arguments for the value of *philia* to virtuous activity. In short, both show that the pleasures enjoyed together by *philoi* of virtue are proper to the activity that is the *philēton* of their *philia*.

One of these arguments – let us call it the continuity argument – claims that "it is not easy by oneself to continuously engage in activity; but with others and in relation to them it is easier" (1170a5–7). If someone wishes to engage as continuously as possible in virtuous activity, as every *philos* of virtue does, he will benefit from the help of the other. A soldier courageously defends his camp from the enemy's siege, but even the most courageous soldier must sleep. If he were his camp's lone defender, this virtuous activity would be in vain; by replacing him on the barricade when he must sleep, his *philos* makes this activity more continuous, giving it a chance to succeed. Such help makes it thereby more pleasant as well, not by importing a pleasure foreign to the activity, but instead by enhancing it with a pleasure proper to it. "His activity will be more continuous, and will be pleasant in itself," Aristotle thus concludes, "which is what ought to happen in the case of a blessed person" (1170a7–8: *makarios*). To emphasize that this is proper pleasure, and not a distraction, let alone an impediment, he adds that this person "enjoys actions that are in accordance with virtue."

Another argument for the value of *philia* to virtuous activity – let us call it the transparency argument – likewise assumes the distinction between proper and foreign pleasure, stressing this time not the additional pleasure available thanks to the continuity made possible by someone else's participation in the virtuous activity, but instead the additional pleasure available upon the contemplation of his participation in that same activity. "The activity of the good person is good and pleasant in itself," so our soldier's valiant defense of his camp is good and pleasant in itself, whether he notices it or not. In the heat of battle, however, he may become so absorbed in this activity as to lose sight of its proper pleasure. By contrast, when he looks upon his *philos* engaged in the very same defense, the shared activity of their virtue, he might perceive this pleasure more clearly. "We are better able to contemplate our neighbors than ourselves," Aristotle writes, "and their actions [*praxeis*] than our own" (1169b33–35). Consequently, "the blessed person will need friends like this," friends with whom he shares his virtuous activity, "since he rationally chooses to contemplate actions [*praxeis*] that are good and his own, and the actions of a good person who is his friend are like this" (1170a1–4).[27]

After these two arguments – a first about the continuity of pleasure, a second about its transparency – Aristotle offers a third. "The argument is extremely obscure," writes Pakaluk (1998, 208–209), "and has tended to be dismissed by commentators." Gauthier and Jolif (1970), for example, object that "it pretends to be more profound, but is only more laborious" than what comes before it.[28] In what follows, the aim is to offer an interpretation of it that illuminates its obscurity by showing it to be laborious but nonetheless profound. In order to motivate this interpretation, though, we should first recall the heavy burden of the argument it interprets. With it, and the two arguments that precede it, Aristotle is trying to solve a fundamental problem with his account of *philia*: the happy person is supposed to be self-sufficient, so why should he have any *philoi* at all? Both of the arguments we have just considered reason that the virtuous person will need *philoi* in order to enhance his virtuous activity and thereby augment its proper pleasure. In the first, the *philos* made this activity more continuous; in the second, he made it more transparent. In both arguments, then, the value of the *philos* was made

---

[27] In this argument about contemplating the actions of a *philos*, Aristotle may have in mind not only the advantage for pleasure just explicitly mentioned but also the advantage for the "sort of training in virtue" he will mention shortly thereafter (1170a11–12). "For if it is even slightly easier to study a friend's actions than one's own," Reeve 1992, 180, observes, "say because 'most people are bad judges of their own' (*Pol.* 1280a15–16), that should be sufficient for Aristotle's purposes." In order to help us see ourselves and our own actions more clearly, however, the actions contemplated cannot be those of someone unrelated to us, or even the friend's actions if they are unrelated to our own. Otherwise the lessons would have no bearing on our own life. Our friend's actions must somehow involve us but also be available for a contemplation more impartial than the biased one we turn directly upon ourselves. Reeve navigates between these poles on pages 180–182.

[28] Before offering her own interpretation of this third argument, Hitz 2011, 8, surveys the puzzlement it has engendered among previous commentators, citing not only Gauthier and Jolif but also Cooper 1977b, 341.

to depend on imperfections in the activity of virtue: in the first case, its imperfect continuity; in the second, its imperfect transparency.[29]

V. TWO TYPES OF ACTIVITY: MORAL AND INTELLECTUAL

Although these imperfections afflict the activities of moral virtue, as Aristotle argues in the next book (1177a11–1178a8), the happiest life is devoted not to them but rather to the activity of the intellect (*nous*), specifically the wisdom (*sophia*) available in philosophical contemplation (*theōria*).[30] When he argues for intellectual over moral virtue near the end of the treatise, in fact, he invokes the hierarchical nature of the soul articulated near its beginning: reason that can initiate thinking (*nous*) above and a part that is able to follow it below. Indeed, on each of these occasions, as well as in the defense of *philia*'s value they bracket, Aristotle not only invokes the nature of the soul, with its actively thinking part, but also reminds us that happiness is an activity (*energeia*: 1098a3–7, 1169b29–32, 1176a33–b2). As such, it is perfect or complete when it has its end within itself, unlike an incomplete or imperfect process (*kinēsis*), which aims toward an end it itself lacks.[31] This distinction, between activity and process, is both subtle and crucial to Aristotle's argument. Fortunately, he himself explains it.

"Every process – building, for example – takes time and has an end," Aristotle writes, "and is complete when it has produced what it aims at" (1174a19 –21). The end of building a temple, for example, is a finished temple. "Placing stones together" is a step toward the actualization of this end, as is "fluting a column" and establishing "the foundation and

[29] At the beginning of ix 9, before he develops these two arguments, he produces three quick reasons why the happy person will need *philoi*. Each of these reasons suffers from the weakness of the first two main arguments, namely, they do not imagine the *perfectly* happy person. These three reasons are as follows. First, *philoi* are among the greatest external goods, so the happy person should not be deprived of them any more than he should be deprived of other external goods, such as wealth and honor (1169b8–10). Second, the happy person is virtuous, and so needs people upon whom to exercise his virtues, such as generosity and justice (1169b11–16). Third, "a human is a social [*politikos*] being and his nature is to live in the company of others," so that if happiness were to require us to forego our *philoi*, it would require us to transcend our human nature (1169b17–22). These reasons also suffer the defects mentioned by Pakaluk 1998, 202–204.
[30] Wisdom (*sophia*) Aristotle defines as "scientific knowledge [*epistēmē*], combined with intellect [*nous*], of what is by nature most honorable" (1141b2–3). Soon thereafter, he says that it "produces happiness, not as medicine produces health, but as health does" (1144a4–5).
[31] *Metaphysics* 1048b20–37. For a fuller analysis and defense of the distinction, see Reeve 2000, 137–147.

the triglyph," but none of these steps is complete because individually they fall short of the end (1174a24–26). Each actualizes some of the potential in the materials at hand, but only some. Moreover, "each process is incomplete during those processes that constitute its parts – the time it takes, in other words – and these parts differ in form from the whole and from each other" (1174a22–23). Building is a process, in sum, because it is incomplete, heterogeneous, and divisible. Activities, by contrast, prove to be complete, homogeneous, and indivisible. As examples of them, Aristotle chooses seeing and thinking (*Meta.* 1048b23–24). "It is the same thing that at the same time has seen and is seeing," he observes, "or is thinking [*noei*] and has thought [*nenoēken*]" (1048b33–34). Seeing has no distinguishable parts: each resembles the others, and they all possess at every instant the end of seeing, which is vision itself.[32] This is still more true of pure thinking (*noein*), which does not rely, as seeing does, on any bodily organ.[33]

"Contemplation [*theōria*] alone seems to be liked for its own sake," Aristotle thus writes, "since nothing results from it apart from the fact that one has contemplated, whereas from the practical virtues, to a greater or lesser extent, we gain something beyond the action" (1177b2–4). Several other shortcomings keep the life of moral (or practical) virtue from achieving perfect happiness. Notable for our purposes are two: its inferior continuity and self-sufficiency. Of all activities, philosophical contemplation is "the most continuous, since we can contemplate more continuously than we can *do* anything" (1177a22–23; emphasis added). As for self-sufficiency, philosophy no less than political action requires the necessities of life: food, water, shelter, and so on. But none of these are Aristotle's concern here, external as they are to both sorts of activity. "Provided with such things," however, "the just person will need people as associates in and objects of his just actions."[34] Other people are integral to his activity, as they are for those of the other moral virtues: the generous person needs recipients of her generosity, the courageous person needs fearsome adversaries, and even the witty person needs someone to laugh at her jokes. "The wise person," by contrast, "can contemplate even when he is by himself" (1177a28–b1). Recognizing the value of others when someone seeks knowledge, Aristotle concedes that "maybe he can do it

---

[32] This is not to say that seeing cannot be used for ulterior ends, such as learning. But Aristotle distinguishes between *internal* and *external* ends (1094a3–5) and here intends internal ones.

[33] *De Anima* iii 4, esp. 429a30–b6. See also *Generation of Animals* 736b27–29.

[34] Aristotle elaborates this feature of justice in v 1 as follows: "Justice in this sense, then, is complete virtue, not without qualification, but in relation to another person" (1129b27–28; see also 1129b32–33). For a fuller discussion of this and other aspects of justice, see Polansky's chapter in this volume.

better with collaborators," but his celebration of intellectual pleasure makes it clear that the concession is inconsequential.

"The most pleasant of activities in accordance with virtue," he writes, is not any activity in accordance with moral virtue, but instead "that in accordance with wisdom [sophia]"; it is "most pure" (kathareiotēton) (1177a24–26). This is not at all surprising, inasmuch as intellectual activity is superior to practical action, and pleasures are always ranked by the perfection of the activities they attend (1174b21–24). What is remarkable here is Aristotle's claim that "those who have knowledge will pass their time more pleasantly than those who are still in search of it" (1177a25–27). The blessed person he imagines as enjoying this perfect wisdom, therefore, is not someone who needs philoi as collaborators in the search for knowledge. He already knows everything. If he is to enjoy the company of philoi at all, then, he must enjoy their participation in his omniscience. But what is the value of philoi to such a person? What, in other words, is the value of philia to the perfectly virtuous? Answering this question is the heavy burden carried by the laborious yet profound argument (1170a13–b8) that Aristotle advertises as "more from the point of view of nature" (phusikōteron).

Commentators debate the precise meaning of this term, some interpreting it as a reference to human nature, others as a reference to metaphysical considerations.[35] Our interpretation straddles their debate by showing how this phusikōteron argument relies on the conception of human nature that has been alluded to already in this treatise, in the function argument (i 7), but is elaborated elsewhere, in his work on psychology (De Anima). Accordingly, we agree with Terence Irwin and Gail Fine, who write that "something's nature indicates its function and the final cause or end to which it tends," so that when Aristotle argues here "'from the natural point of view' (phusikōs)," he is appealing "to human nature, especially to human psychology."[36] This argument has seemed obscure and puzzling to commentators, then, because its premises, like those of the function argument it assumes, are explained elsewhere, in a work that is itself phusikōteron. It is beyond the scope of this volume, focused as it is on the Nicomachean Ethics, to elaborate an interpretation of Aristotle's psychology in De Anima. Yet a statement of its relevant conclusions about human nature – especially our highest activity – might nonetheless illuminate the psychological background against which he here draws ethical inferences.

[35] For a list of references, and the main reasons given on each side, see Hitz 2011, 8n23.

[36] Irwin and Fine 1985, 416, enumerate two meanings of phusis, or "nature," in the Nicomachean Ethics, but only the relevant one is quoted herein. They list many passages for each meaning, but the one in question here (1170a13) is mentioned as an example of an appeal "to human nature, especially human psychology."

This statement relies on some highly controversial readings of some famously obscure passages.[37] Our goal is not to resolve scholarly debates about Aristotle's psychology, however, but instead to see whether one interpretation of it might shed some light on this *phusikōteron* ethical argument. More specifically, we wish to gain a better understanding of the activity that is philosophical contemplation because "this is the highest activity, intellect [*nous*] being the highest element in us" (1177a20–21). This activity is perfect happiness, and perfect happiness has emerged as the precise target of the fundamental problem for Aristotle's account of *philia*. For it is the philosopher alone, actively living the life of wisdom and thus bringing human life itself to perfection, who will be so self-sufficient as not to need *philoi*. Or so it seems. With a better understanding of this activity, we can return to this *phusikōteron* argument with an appreciation of its assumptions about understanding (*noēsis*). Then we shall be in a better position to evaluate whether it truly solves this fundamental problem, as Aristotle thinks it does, saving the life of his blessed philosopher from loneliness.

VI. A FINAL SOLUTION: ONE SELF

"Intellect" (*nous*), Aristotle writes, "more than anything else, constitutes humanity" (1178a8–9). Yet in the same passage he also calls it the divine element (1177b28–29).[38] One way to cut this knot is to see Aristotle as fundamentally a Platonist on the question of our identity: humans are compounds of divine *nous* and base matter. In the technical terms of his metaphysics, we are compounds of form and matter, soul and body.[39] But just as compounds are most of all their form, and especially the supreme part of that form, so too are humans most of all *nous*, the supreme element of our souls (1169a1–3; see *Meta.* 1035b12–14, b18–20). Elsewhere he concludes that the best condition of this supreme element is disembodiment, when "it is alone just what it is" (*De Anima* 430a23–24). For only "when separated" is it "unaffected, unmixed, since in its essential nature it is activity." The argument that leads to this dense conclusion is complex, drawing on Aristotle's psychology as well as his metaphysics, but we can extract from it a lesson for *philia* by recalling the distinction between process and activity.

If *nous* is in its essential nature an activity, its object – what it thinks about – could not be distinct from itself, otherwise it would have its end outside of itself, making it a process. The same as its object, then, it

---

[37] For a full commentary on these and other passages, along with a sense of their interpretive complexity and scholarly controversies, see Polansky 2007.
[38] See also *Generation of Animals* 736b27–28.
[39] *De Anima* 412a3–413a10; see also *Parts of Animals* 641a16–33.

must think itself. Indeed, as essentially active, this self-contemplation must also be continuous: complete, homogeneous, and indivisible. Accordingly, "it does not sometimes think and sometimes not think"; on the contrary, it is "immortal and eternal" (*De Anima* 430a24). Pure of all embodiment, this perfect self-contemplation is god's own.[40] Someone who theologizes this well, thinking perfectly of god's perfect self-contemplation, should likewise become identical to it. Such a theologian, in other words, would become god. This may not be possible for embodied humans. With their importunate limitations, our stubborn bodies frustrate our efforts to know ourselves. But we nonetheless have a share of that divinity, so that "we ought not to listen to those who exhort us, because we are human, to think human things, or because we are mortal, think of mortal things." Instead, recognizing who we most of all are, "we ought rather to take on immortality as much as possible, and do all that we can to live in accordance with the highest element within us." This is *nous*, and "even if its bulk is small, in its power and value it far exceeds everything" (1177b33–1178a3).

Living in accordance with our best element, devoting ourselves purely to its pure self-contemplation, is thus our best and most pleasant activity. "So this life," Aristotle concludes, "will also be the happiest" (1178a8). But this happiness transcends that available to a human being, insofar as he is human. "Such a life is superior to one that is simply human," Aristotle asserts, "because someone lives thus, not in so far as he is a human being, but in so far as there is some divine element within him" (1177b27–28). As human, he is doubly compound: of soul and body, at one level, of *nous* and the lower capacities of the soul, including that which obeys reason, at another. It is not as a compound of either type that he thinks divinely, however, but as *nous* alone. "The activity of this divine element is as much superior to that in accordance with the other kind of virtue," namely moral or practical virtue, "as the element is superior to the compound" (1177b28–31). When we devote ourselves to moral virtue, on one hand, we are "happy in a secondary way, since the activities in accordance with it are human" (1178a8–10). When we live the contemplative life, on the other, consummating it with the perfect self-knowledge of philosophical theology, we do not live a human life, properly speaking, but instead one that is divine.

Before applying the lessons of this quick interpretation of Aristotle's *nous* to the fundamental problem faced by Aristotle's *philia*, let us recall this problem again. Here is how we put it earlier, in terms that had not yet

---

[40]   *Metaphysics* 982b29–983a10, 1026a18–20, 1074b34–1075a11. See also *On the Heavens* 286a9–10.

been investigated: the happy person is supposed to be self-sufficient, so why should he have any *philoi* at all (1169b2–7)? We can now formulate the same problem more precisely with our account of the highest happiness – the perfect and divine activity of *nous*: self-contemplation. Why should the philosopher who enjoys this activity – living a divine life – have any *philoi*?

The earlier arguments, whatever their other merits, cannot solve this precise problem because they understood *philoi* as remedies for the defects of the happy person's activity. When it was thought to be imperfectly continuous, they were proposed as a way to make it less so by helping out (1170a4–11). Or when it was thought to be imperfectly transparent, they were proposed as a way to make it less so by performing it at an appropriate distance (1169b29–1170a3). "We are better able to contemplate [*theōrein*] our neighbors than ourselves," Aristotle observed there, "and their actions [*praxeis*] than our own" (1169b33–35). But in the highest happiness that is now revealed as contemplation (*theōria*), and more exactly the perfect activity of self-contemplation, this is manifestly false. At the summit of intellectual virtue, we are able to contemplate ourselves and our perfect activity of self-contemplation perfectly well. When we are truly happy, in other words, we are fully transparent to ourselves – continuously so. If we still need friends at that summit, then, they must supply some other advantage. What is it? Articulating this other advantage is the heavy burden of the *phusikōteron* argument for the value of *philoi* (1170a13–b14).

As written, to be sure, the argument appears laborious, not to mention invalid, but this appearance is chiefly due to Aristotle's refusal to enter into intricate theoretical discussion in the midst of his practical works, even as he adduces an argument that is explicitly theoretical (*phusikōteron*). Its three main premises nonetheless receive their explanation and support, if anywhere, in the theoretical works briefly summarized earlier. The first of these premises is that "living in the real sense seems to be perceiving [*aisthanesthai*] or thinking [*noein*]" (1170a18–19). As Aristotle presents it here, this premise is the subconclusion of a cramped subargument that loosely summarizes his more rigorous identification of the human essence elsewhere. Here he mentions how people define "human life by the capacity for perception or thought," but even in this treatise he has dismissed perceiving as external to the human essence because it is shared with the other animals (1098a2–3). When he writes here of "perceiving or thinking," then, he seems to be alluding to his exact identification of our essence elsewhere as *nous* and its activity (*noēsis*).

The second premise is likewise presented as a subconclusion to a similarly cramped subargument, this time to the effect that our essential activity is self-reflexive. Crisp translates this subconclusion as follows:

"To perceive that we perceive or to think is to perceive that we exist [einai] (since we say that to exist [einai] is to perceive or think)" (1170a34–35). But this is a mistranslation. With his use of einai here, Aristotle is concerned not with bare existence but instead with essence.[41] Socrates *exists* as a particular individual because he is some form in some matter; he exists as a human being because this form (essence or being) is human. A translation of this second premise that is consistent with the first's invocation of human essence, therefore, adapts Crisp's as follows: "To perceive that we perceive or think is to perceive our being (since we saw that our being is to perceive or think)." Keeping in mind that Aristotle is still speaking loosely of the human essence as perceiving or thinking, whereas in fact it is thinking and thinking alone, he seems to be summarizing his more rigorous reasoning elsewhere to the effect that this contemplative essence is self-reflexive.[42]

Unlike the first two premises, the third is unique to the *Nicomachean Ethics*. Upon it turns the whole account of *philia*. "The good person is related to his *philos* as he is related to himself," Aristotle writes, "because his *philos* is another self" (1170b6–7). This premise is not, however, unique to this argument. It appears earlier in the same chapter, in the preliminary arguments for the value of *philoi* to a happy person, specifically the practitioner of moral virtue: "A *philos*, since he is another self, provides what a person cannot provide by himself" (1169b6–7). The words of the apothegm are the same – *philos heteros autos* – but they are being used in a secondary sense. There, the *philos* is another self in the sense of a helper: someone who "provides what a person cannot provide by himself." You would need such a *philos* only if you needed help. But the perfect self-contemplator needs none. When Aristotle uses these same words here – in his final argument for the value of *philoi*, where he concludes that they are valuable even to this supremely happy person – they cannot mean the same thing.

To find their primary meaning, we should examine the first of their three occurrences in the treatise (1166a32).[43] Aristotle begins this crucial passage by tracing "the origins of relations of friendship [philika] towards our neighbors, and of the characteristics by which we distinguish the

---

[41] Smith (Barnes 1995, 1849) makes the same mistake: "To perceive that we perceive or think is to perceive that we exist (for existence was defined as perceiving or thinking)." Irwin and Fine 1985, 260, render it vaguely: "Perceiving that we are perceiving or understanding is the same as perceiving that we are, since we agreed [in (4)] that being is perceiving or understanding."

[42] *De Anima* 429b6–9. For an illuminating commentary on this and related passages, see Gerson 2005, 148–152.

[43] Quoted in the introduction to this chapter. Kahn 1981, 30, epitomizes this strategy as follows: "In IX.4 Aristotle seems to be preparing the way for these later developments by his emphasis on the self as *nous*, just as he is laying the basis for IX.8 and IX.9 by his doctrine of the friend as a second self."

various kinds of *philia*," to something more fundamental: "our relations with our self" (1166a1–3).[44] This self, as the passage says no less than three times, is *nous* (1166a17–23). Putting these two claims together, we get the view that *philia* arises from our relation with our *nous*. Those who do not identify themselves with intellectual activity, confusing their self with their lower psychological capacities, not to mention their body, will seek *philoi* who make the same mistake. "Whatever being consists in for each, or whatever the end for which each chooses to live," recall, "it is this that they wish to pursue in the company of their *philoi*" (1172a2–4). Those who identify with their bodies will pursue bodily pleasure in the company of others who make this mistake. Better will be those who identify with the compound of body and soul. For in the company of others who make this all-too-human mistake, they will pursue the moral virtues. "Since they are also united with the feelings," Aristotle argues, "the virtues of character must be concerned with the compound," and, "the virtues of the compound are human" (1178a19–22).[45]

Only the blessed person Aristotle imagines at the end of this ethical treatise identifies fully with his *nous*. He alone knows himself, and so he alone is capable of the complete *philia* whose activity is most pleasant: the perfect self-contemplation available only in philosophical theology. This activity appears lonely only when we forget that his self-contemplation is also the contemplation of any *philos* with whom he is united in eternal divinity. Many will object to this theological twist, agreeing with Nussbaum (2001, 376) that "wishing for the good, both for ourselves and for another, must remain within the confines of our species identity." But the objection relies upon a passage that is easily misunderstood (1159a3–13). Aristotle himself speaks of "the puzzle whether *philoi* really wish one another the greatest good – to be gods – because they will no longer have them as *philoi*." The puzzle arises because *philoi* must remain roughly equal, above all in their achievement of virtue (1158b33–1159a2). Thus, if two *philoi* are equally human, the ascension of one to divinity without the other would destroy their *philia*. "If, then, we were right to say that one friend wishes goods to the other for the other's sake," Aristotle argues, "the latter must remain as he is, whatever that may be." Consequently, "it is to the other as a human being [*anthrōpos*] that a *philos* will wish the greatest goods."

Apparently, therefore, we must wish our friends the goods of human, not divine, life. A second passage seems to corroborate this anthropocentric interpretation (1166a19–23). "Being [*einai*] is a good to the good

---

[44] Crisp's translation has been revised here to represent the singular *heauton* as the singular "our self" rather than the plural "ourselves."

[45] *De Anima* 403a15–28 explains the association between feelings and the compound (of body and soul).

person, and each person wishes for what is good for himself," Aristotle begins, adding that "no one chooses to have everything if he has first to become someone else (since as things are god possesses the good), but only if he remains whatever he is." If he were a human being, then, he could not reasonably choose the good of divine life, for that would require being something else, something with a different being or essence. As Aristotle says in the next sentence, however, he is not a human being: "And each person would seem to be the intellectual part [nous], or primarily this." Recognizing his authentic being, thinking, he should wish for the good of this life above all. Because a philos is another self, moreover, he should wish the same for him as well. This passage makes explicit the peculiar doctrine that the anthropocentric interpretation of Aristotle's ethics must overlook: we are above all nous.

Still, the problem of lonely self-sufficiency remains: unless the divine self-contemplator has need of philoi, it seems, he will inhabit the citadel of self-knowledge alone. Alone, that is, unless there is another such person. For if there were, his retreat to this citadel would find him there too. Is there another such person? Yes and no. Our answer depends on what we mean by "person." No, there is not another such person there, if by "person" we mean a unique individual, for the perfect activity of nous is the same in you as it is in me. As perfect activity and pure form – none other than the god at the summit of philosophy – it lacks the matter required to individuate anything, including people (Meta. 1075a1–7). But yes, there is another such person there; indeed, we are all there, inasmuch as "each person would seem to be nous, or primarily this" (1166a23). For nous is there preeminently and eternally: "As human thought, or rather the thought of composite objects, is in a certain period of time," Aristotle writes, "so throughout eternity is the thought which has itself for its object" (Meta. 1075a7–11).

Your nous is eternally there; so too is mine. In that citadel, in an eternal now, we enjoy the same activity. Most pleasant of all, this activity is the self-contemplation of the divine essence we share. There, as philoi properly understood, we are each to the other another self – not as helpers but as one. Here in time, Aristotle recognizes, our self-contemplation is compromised in myriad ways by our embodiment.[46] Here, then, the best philos merely approximates complete philia. He is a helper in embodied intellectual activity, whenever such help is needed, but more importantly he shares in the unity of its sporadic achievement. "He ought therefore at the same time to perceive the being [einai] of his philos," Aristotle concludes, "and this will come about in their living together

---

[46]   Aristotle compares the dual presence of the best good (i.e., God) both inside and outside the temporal cosmos to a general who is present both in himself, outside of the army, and within it, in the order he makes possible (Meta. 1075a12 –16).

and exchanging words and thoughts" (1170b10–12). But the goal of these temporal conversations will be one eternal being: the divine self. *Philia* is a way to find oneself with friends; with their help, what one finds is that there is only one self.

VII. TWO FINAL PROBLEMS: NARCISSISM AND ALTERITY

The result of this account of *philia* will appear odd, paradoxical, and even narcissistic to many readers. According to it, the proper goal of relationship with another turns out to be the self. Rather than ignoring this consequence, let alone balking at it, Aristotle embraces it. After enumerating the features of *philia*, he states that "all of these apply most of all to a person's relationship to himself, because he is most of all a *philos* to himself and so ought to love himself most of all" (1168b8–10). He nevertheless recognizes that others will balk at this view, "for people criticize those who like themselves most, and call them by the derogatory term 'self-lovers'" (1168a29–31; "self-lover" translates *philautos*). But their criticism of self-love is based ultimately upon a misunderstanding of the self. Those reproached by the masses as self-lovers are "those who assign themselves the larger share of money, honours and bodily pleasures" (1168b16–18). In other words, things that are incidental to who they are. As such, they do not really love or benefit themselves. On the contrary, as Aristotle observes, the wicked person who makes this mistake about who he really is "will harm himself and those around him by following his evil feelings" (1169a13–14).

The true self-lover, by contrast, is the person who benefits himself and others because he knows himself and assigns to himself things – or, more accurately, activities – that are essential to his self. "*Nous* always chooses what is best for itself," Aristotle asserts, "and the good person obeys his *nous*" (1169a17–18). Indeed, he identifies the self with intellect three different ways in this short chapter: with *nous* (in the sentence just quoted, and earlier at 1168b35); with reason (*logos*, 1169a1–6); and also as "the most authoritative element" (*kuriōtaton*, 1168b29–34). "Someone who likes this part and gratifies it," Aristotle infers, "is most of all a self-lover" (1168b33–34). The good person loves himself most of all because intellect is the most lovable of love objects, the primary *philēton*, and the good person, the one who has achieved the summit of intellectual activity, knows himself as this very activity. Lest this seem lonely, recall the central premise of Aristotle's whole treatment of *philia* – that the *philos* is another self – and thereby remember that the good person loves his *philos* no less. For when we understand this apothegm properly, we recognize no distinction at all between complete *philoi*: they each identify fully with *nous* and its perfect activity (*noēsis*). "We ought to be self-lovers," Aristotle thus concludes, "but in the way the masses are, we should not" (1169b1–2).

Even if he manages to acquit his account of vulgar self-love, however, it remains vulnerable to a charge of narcissism nonetheless. To see why, let us recapitulate the main points of our interpretation, gradually returning as we proceed to English translations of *philia* and its cognate terms in order to manifest the deep significance of this account, whether or not we accept it, for love and friendship in our own day.

It is a relationship between two people who share a feeling of goodwill that is reciprocal, mutually acknowledged, and for the other's sake. This feeling is necessary but insufficient for *philia* because *philia* involves rational choice. With the involvement of rational choice, then, there arise three types, for there are three types of love object: the pleasant, the useful, and the good. Each type of love object imposes a limit on its respective *philia*, making at least the inferior types of love instrumental to some extent, whereas the highest type escapes this charge because of the connections in Aristotle's wider philosophy between goodness and essence, virtue and function. Appreciating these connections, we saw how the highest type of love would not be using the *philos* to obtain a distinct love object because the love object in that type of love is the essence of the *philos* himself. Equipped with an interpretation of that essence, we saw how it was intellect – not an intellect unique to the *philos*, mind you, but one that is shared with all other thinking beings, and especially god. The result, then, is that in love and friendship we love nothing unique to our beloved friend, but instead something that is generic to all beings like him, including ourselves. Quite literally, according to Aristotle's account, when we love another, we love none other than our own self. Love of another just is self-love.

Stated in this order, reducing other-love to self-love, the account does seem narcissistic. To be fair, however, its equation can be reversed to emphasize its altruism: love of self just is love of another.[47] This peculiar feature is shared with mysticism of any sort, which makes your self the same as mine. But this version, rational mysticism, achieves this result by submitting love to reason. By making love a matter of rational choice – that is, by articulating for it criteria of any kind – this philosophy of love, and arguably any other that submits it to reason, privileges a criterion over the person who is supposed to be its object. This was the problem of instrumentality, and Aristotle solved it in what appears to be the only way: identifying the love object with the criterion, that is, identifying the other with reason. But the terminus of this solution, or so we have argued

---

[47]   Thanks to Thomas Ball for this observation.

in this chapter, is identity between the reason of the rational chooser and the reason of the object chosen rationally. In short, Aristotle's solution to the problem of instrumentality discussed in the first half of this chapter creates the problem of alterity we now pose at the end of its second half. If a philosophy of love privileges reason over love, in other words, it faces a dilemma between a failure to love the other without using him for one's own purposes, on one hand, and a failure to love him without conflating him with one's self, on the other.

The quickest way out of this dilemma is to renounce its basic approach, subverting its implicit hierarchy, making love supreme instead of reason. Such an approach would have been anathema to Aristotle, but it was perhaps Plato's, and it certainly came to the fore at the end of antiquity, first with Plotinus, then more radically with Augustine. All three wrote as if the transport of love took us above reason.[48] Plato testified to the power of the particular in love with the love story of Alcibiades and Socrates (*Symposium* 212d2–222b1). The role of this power in Plato's "theory" of love is ambiguous to say the least: if he has a theory, and Socrates reports it, then perhaps individuality is transcended as one climbs the ladder of love toward the Form of Beauty. Plotinus writes both less ambiguously and less beautifully, preserving individuality until the final rung of this ladder, when he enjoins the lover finally to "cut away everything."[49] Fusing this Greek tradition of rational mysticism with biblical Christianity, which distinguishes more sharply between human individuals and their divine creator, Augustine preserved his devotion to the alterity of the beloved from beginning to end.[50] Whatever its historical lineage, however, something like this approach – privileging love over reason, and respecting the alterity of the beloved – is needed to explain the love of family.

It is no coincidence that Augustine begins his love story with an account of his infancy, and particularly his love of his mother (see *Confessions* i 5–6). Finding ourselves with a native love for those who succor us in our early years, we may later revoke it, but if so we are not deciding that our initial criteria for loving were not satisfied. There were

---

[48] For Plato, see *Phaedrus* 249c3–250a8, *Symposium* 210e1–212a7, *Republic* 509b4–7; for Plotinus, *Enneads* i 6.7, iv 8.1, vi 7.34–36, vi 9.2–4; for Augustine, *Confessions* i 1, i 4, ix 10, x 6, x 27, xi 31.

[49] v 3.17. Individuality is effaced within the ineffable One, but it remains at the level of Intellect. Indeed, Plotinus develops the notion of Forms of Individuals in order to account for the importance of diversity to Its beauty. See *Enneads* v 7 and Gerson 1994, 72–78.

[50] For the distinction between God and everything else, see *Confessions* x 6.9. For the preservation of individuality from the beginning of life through his eschatological vision, see i 5.9–10 and ix 10.

no such criteria. We found ourselves among these people, and we simply loved them. This approach is also adopted in our era by Freud and the psychoanalysts, who try to separate it from its ancient teleology (the ladder of love), and the notion of perversion it underwrites.[51] Whether or not they succeed, what they share with Augustine highlights the contrast with Aristotle's own approach to love. Faithful to it, he cannot really accommodate family love, although he does mention it occasionally (1161b12–1162a16, 1166a9, 1168a24–26). Kahn (1981, 22n1) notes the shortcoming, first suggesting that "birth and kinship should have been added as a fourth basis for *philia*," adding that "presumably Aristotle neglected this in his formal theory, because his theoretical concern with *philia* was oriented towards problems that involve *prohairesis* or deliberate choice: an affection based upon family connection or childhood experience is not *chosen*."

What Aristotle does say about family love reveals the depth of his commitment to rational choice: "A parent, then, loves his children as himself, since what has come from him is, as it were, another self" (1161b27–29; see also 1161b19). Some parents love this way, of course, but they are narcissists. Their variety of love dooms children to a lifetime of insatiable craving for the attention of another who will love them not as a self-extension but for who they are in themselves. Such a love requires loving the child not despite his differences from oneself but rather because of those differences. This is not to say that such children, or the adults they become, know who they are in themselves, nor that an account of their true self could escape the rationalist trap that subordinates lovable idiosyncrasies to intelligible universal criteria. However we have been raised, though, we all know to some extent their irrational craving. Montaigne expresses it best in his essay "On Friendship," which accordingly eschews a generic account in favor of a tribute to a particular friend.[52] "Beyond all my understanding," he admits, "beyond what I can say about this in particular, there was I know not what inexplicable and fateful force that was the mediator of this union." As frustrating as this admission may be to philosophers, who seek an explanation or account of this ineffable force, it has the virtue of honesty. This virtue, so important in love, is rivaled by another that is never dreamt of in Aristotle's philosophy: poetic beauty. "If you press me to tell why I loved him, I feel that this cannot be expressed," Montaigne confesses, "except by answering: Because it was he, because it was I."

---

[51]   *Three Essays on the Theory of Sexuality*. For the genesis of all love from the relation between a particular mother and her baby, see 2.5; for the critique of the notion of perversion, see 1.7.

[52]   Pakaluk 1991, 187–199; quotations are from page 192.

WORKS CITED

Barnes, J. 1995. *The Complete Works of Aristotle: The Revised Oxford Translation* (6th printing, with corrections). Princeton: Princeton University Press.

Cooper, J. M. 1977a. "Aristotle on the Forms of Friendship." *Review of Metaphysics* 30: 619–648. Reprinted 312–335 in *Reason and Emotion*.

  1977b. "Friendship and the Good in Aristotle." *Philosophical Review* 86: 290–315. Reprinted 336–355 in *Reason and Emotion*.

  1999. *Reason and Emotion*. Princeton: Princeton University Press.

Crisp, R. trans. 2000. *Aristotle: Nicomachean Ethics*. Cambridge: Cambridge University Press.

Gauthier, R. A., and J. Y. Jolif. 1970. *L'Éthique à Nicomaque*. Paris-Louvain: Publications Universitaires.

Gerson, L. P. 1994. *Plotinus*. New York: Routledge.

  2005. *Aristotle and Other Platonists*. Ithaca, NY: Cornell University Press.

Hadreas, P. 1995. "*Eunoia*: Aristotle on the Beginning of Friendship." *Ancient Philosophy* 15: 393–402.

Hitz, Z. 2011. "Aristotle on Self-Knowledge and Friendship." *Philosophers' Imprint* 11: 1–28.

Irwin, T., and G. Fine, trans. and eds. 1985. *Aristotle: Nicomachean Ethics*. Indianapolis: Hackett.

Kahn, C. H. 1981. "Aristotle and Altruism." *Mind* 90: 20–40.

Konstan, D. 1997. *Friendship in the Classical World*. Cambridge: Cambridge University Press.

Lawson-Tancred, H. trans. 1987. *Aristotle: De Anima (On the Soul)*. London: Penguin.

Nehamas, A. 2010. "Aristotelian *Philia*, Modern Friendship?" *Oxford Studies in Ancient Philosophy* 39: 213–247.

Nussbaum, M. C. 2001. *The Fragility of Goodness*. 2nd ed. Cambridge: Cambridge University Press.

Pakaluk, M. 1991. *Other Selves: Philosophers on Friendship*. Indianapolis: Hackett.

  1998. *Aristotle: Nicomachean Ethics Books VIII and IX*. Oxford: Oxford University Press.

Polansky, R. 2007. *Aristotle's De Anima*. Cambridge: Cambridge University Press.

Reeve, C. D. C. 1992. *Practices of Reason: Aristotle's Nicomachean Ethics*. Oxford: Clarendon Press.

  2000. *Substantial Knowledge*. Indianapolis: Hackett.

  2012. *Action, Contemplation, and Happiness*. Cambridge, MA: Harvard University Press.

Shields, C. 2007. *Aristotle*. New York: Routledge.

16 Competing Ways of Life and Ring Composition (*NE* x 6–8)

The closing chapters of Aristotle's *Nicomachean Ethics* x are regularly described as "puzzling," "extremely abrupt," "awkward," or "surprising" to readers.[1] Whereas the previous nine books described – sometimes in lavish detail – the multifold ethical virtues of an embodied person situated within communities of family, friends, and fellow citizens, *NE* x 6–8 extols the rarified, godlike, and solitary existence of a *sophos* or sage (1179a32).[2] The ethical virtues that take up approximately the first half of the *Ethics* describe moral exempla who experience fear fighting for their communities, are sensitive to the esteem and recognition of others, and feel desire to live together with a wide variety of kinds of friends. Such good people take pleasure in prudently expending sums to improve their communities – communities in which they exchange goods and participate in ruling and being ruled in a cooperative fashion. The exemplum of x 7–8, by contrast, is a person whose activity consists almost entirely in exercising his or her mind (*nous*) – a part of one's soul that Aristotle explicitly notes is disconnected from human emotions and that can be exercised, insofar as one is wise, in a wholly solitary fashion (1178a15–16, a19–20; 1177a33–34).

Although Aristotle's claim that a "life in accord with the mind" is best and most pleasant (1178a6–7) may jar the intuitions of many people – he himself endorses Anaxagoras's claim that the happy person will appear as "someone who is absurd" (*atopos*, 1179a15) to most people – it is false to claim that his conclusions in *NE* x 6–8 are unexpected or unanticipated,

I am grateful to David Reeve and Eric Brown for providing me copies of their forthcoming works on the *Nicomachean Ethics*. I am especially grateful to Ron Polansky for the invitation to contribute this chapter to his volume and his helpful discussion of it.

[1] Such claims are legion. Among recent exclamations, Pakaluk 2005, 316, characterizes parts of the account as "puzzling"; Long 2011, 109, characterizes the account of contemplation as "extremely abrupt"; and Brown 2013, 137, claims the disconnect between *NE* i 5 and x 6–8 is "awkward" and "surprising."

[2] Parenthetical references within the text unaccompanied by abbreviations refer to the OCT Greek text of the *Nicomachean Ethics* (Bywater 1894). Translations of the Greek text are my own, although much indebted to the translations of Reeve forthcoming; Broadie and Rowe 2002; and Irwin 1999.

or that the text is discontinuous with what precedes it. The *Nicomachean Ethics* exhibits aspects of ring composition both within the work as a whole and within book 10.[3] In *NE* i 5 Aristotle introduces his rendition of a trope that he inherits (most immediately) from Plato – namely, that the problem of the good can be considered like a contest between three different kinds of life – the life of enjoyment (*apolaustikos*), the life of politics (*politikos*), and the life of contemplation (*theōrētikos*).[4] *NE* x 6–8 returns to that contest, rendering a verdict about which life takes first, second, and third place. As the opening lines of *NE* x 6 note, that verdict presupposes central claims articulated between the first and last books of the *Ethics*, specifically about the nature of the virtues, the nature of friendship, and the nature of pleasure. *NE* i 5 and x 6–8 thus serve as "bookends" that encase arguments and propositions located between them.

Book 10 exhibits a similar ring composition.[5] *NE* x opens with methodological reflection on the gap between the theoretical positions that thinkers articulate and the way they live their lives (especially in the case of scolds who simultaneously criticize pleasure on a scientific level but seek it on a practical level [1172a33–b8]). Chapter 8 concludes with an explicit reiteration of the methodological point, a reiteration that underscores how Aristotle's treatment of the contest of lives incorporates central aspects of the discussion of pleasure in *NE* x 1–5. Aristotle's reiteration of the problem of a gap between theory and practice also draws attention to the centrality of his treatment of pleasure in his adjudication of the three lives. Although the life of pleasure takes a distant third in the contest of lives, the contemplative life wins the contest in part because it itself is the most pleasant form of life.

---

[3] On the phenomenon of ring composition in Plato's *Republic* and elsewhere in Aristotle's corpus, see Barney 2010 (esp. at 36–37); on the phenomenon more generally in ancient literature, see Douglas 2007.

[4] For the trope of the three competing ways of life, see Joly 1956; Lawrence 1993, 33–34; Crittenden 1996; and Brown 2013. Nightingale 2004, 17–26, shows (contra Joly) that fourth-century thinkers may be projecting aspects of the competition on to their predecessors (like Pythagoras) for rhetorical effect; see further Gottschalk 1980, 23–26, for the case of Heraclides of Pontus. On the relationship between the trope and Aristotle's *Protrepticus*, see Hutchinson and Johnson in this volume. Morrison 2001 considers the notion of politics as a way of life. Aristotle makes reference to the contest of the best life in *Eudemian Ethics* (*EE*) i 4–5 and *Politics* (*Pol.*) vii 1–2, albeit with far less conclusive results than in *NE*.

[5] In discussing ring composition in *NE* x, I sidestep the place of x 9 – a chapter that prepares for the transition between the *NE* and the *Politics* – and focus on the structure within x 1–8. But x 9 is itself a part of the ring composition of the *Ethics* as a whole, since it revisits the claim that ethics is a part of political science, a claim made in the first three chapters of *NE* i.

The central philosophical problem looming behind Aristotle's treatment of the contest of lives concerns the relationship between the notion of activity (*energeia*) and the notion of a way of life (*bios*).[6] In the past four decades, much of the scholarship on *NE* x 6–8 has sought to address the question of what activities a certain way of life includes or excludes. "Monistic" or "dominant" end interpretations of the best life have viewed it as including only contemplative activities, whereas "inclusivist" end interpretations of the best life have viewed it as including noncontemplative activities.[7] Although this chapter largely sidesteps this debate – partially because there are ample recent first-rate introductory treatments of the debate, partially because I have addressed the question elsewhere in my own writing[8] – I argue that focusing solely on the contest between the two best ways of life overshadows the way that Aristotle incorporates insights from the third way of life into the best way of life.[9] Although the notion of a contest among different kinds of lives presupposes that the lives are mutually exclusive, Aristotle has no problem saying that the contemplative life trumps the life of pleasure because the contemplative life is more pleasant.

[6]   Reeve 2012 notes that two Greek words – *zōē* and *bios* correspond to the English word "life." Although Aristotle does not always distinguish them (consider *EE* ii 1.1219a38–39 or *NE* x 1.1172b3–7), Reeve suggests that *zōē* often refers to the sort of "life processes studied by biologists, zoologists, and other scientists," whereas *bios* "refers to the sort of life a natural historian or biographer might investigate – the life of the otter, the life of Pericles" (239). Stewart 1982, ii 443–445, and Gauthier and Jolif 1970, ii 862, argue that in x 6–8, by *bios* Aristotle meant "aspects" of a life; in response, Cooper 1975, 160, argues that *bios* "means always '(mode of) life,' and in any one period of time one can only have one mode of life. One cannot be said to have both a religious *bios* and a social *bios* ... as we might say someone has an active religious life and an interesting social life" (compare Keyt 1989). Critically building on Hadot 1995 and 2002, Cooper 2012 expands on the notion of ways of life both in Aristotle and in other ancient philosophers.

[7]   Literature on interpretations of the highest good is formidable. Hardie 1965 initiated the debate and occasioned Ackrill 1980, which remains the preeminent defense of the inclusivist position (although Keyt 1983; Whiting 1986; Crisp 1994; and Cooper 1999 provide noteworthy variants). Prominent defenders of the dominant end interpretation include Hardie 1979; Kraut 1989; Heinaman 1988 and 2007. Charles 1999; Scott 1999; and Lear 2004 provide a compromise position of sorts that explains noncontemplative goods as approximations of the highest good. For a bit of a backlash against the interpretive problem in general, see Bush 2008 and Long 2011.

[8]   Recent surveys of the debate between inclusive and dominant end interpretations include Irwin 2012 and Lear 2009; I have addressed the question in light of Aristotle's account of the need for friendship in Lockwood forthcoming.

[9]   For instance, I take it that Reeve in this volume is mistaken to say that the life of enjoyment is "set aside" or that the contest is really one between two different lives. Scholars who discuss the contest of lives sometimes seem to omit discussion of x 6 entirely. For instance, Cooper 2012 entitles his chapter on Aristotle "Philosophy as Two Ways of Life"; he claims that as early as i 5, "Aristotle immediately sets aside the life of pleasure as not worth taking seriously as a candidate for the happy life" (95).

I proceed in two parts. In the first part I examine what I will call the "outer" ring of the *Ethics*, namely the relationship between the contest of lives proposed in *NE* i 5 and its overall resolution in x 6–8. I show how i 5 and x 6 establish the framework for the contest, how x 7 adjudicates that contest in large part by relying upon premises articulated in the interim between books 1 and 10, and how x 6 and x 8 determine the second and third place positions in the contest. In the second part I focus on what I will call the "inner" ring of *NE* x. More than half of *NE* x struggles with the nature of pleasure, its role in a happy life, and the methodological problems of examining pleasure within a practical science. I show how x 1 and x 8 are "bookends" that underscore the methodological problem of examining pleasure and how the contest of lives draws upon the proximate conclusions concerning the nature of pleasure in *NE* x 1–5.

I. CONTEMPLATION AND THE OUTER RING OF NE I AND X

Although the argument for the highest good in *NE* x 6–8 clearly makes use of the framework of the contest of lives articulated in i 5, it remains to say what Aristotle's use of ring composition adds to his argument. Chapters i 5 and x 6 are "bookends" of a sort, each of which sheds light on the ultimate conclusion of the argument.[10] In i 5 Aristotle makes use of the contest of lives to consider possible candidates for the good, but in doing so, he alters the traditional slate of contestants. The preliminary analysis of i 5 also underscores central concepts – such as that intrinsic choiceworthiness is a characteristic of any possible candidate for the good and that the victor of the contest needs to explain how the good "belongs" (*oikeion*) to its possessor. In x 6 Aristotle reformulates the framework of the contest in a more sophisticated fashion, drawing upon several of the central discussions that have taken place between the first and tenth books but also echoing aspects of the original formulation in i 5. Thus i 5 is proleptic – it problematizes the question of the highest good initially in anticipation of a solution to the problem at the end of the

---

[10] Pakaluk 2005, 320–322, argues that it is wrong to view *NE* x 6–8 as proposing a comparison of lives that is continuous with the contest presented in i 5. His main arguments are that (1) the depiction of the lives in i 5 and x 6–8 are inconsistent (e.g., the life of pleasure in i 5 is the life of bodily pleasure, whereas in x 6 it is the life of amusement), (2) by the end of i 5 there is no further reason to consider the lives of pleasure and practical activity, and (3) the lives depicted in either section are fragmentary (e.g., the political life fails to recognize the superior nature of wisdom described in vi 13 while the contemplative life is potentially unjust). I think (1) and (2) are rare instances of Pakaluk misreading Aristotle's text (which I hope to show in the remainder of part 1 of the chapter); (3) is a more general problem about the integrity of a way of life, one that I address briefly in my conclusion.

Ethics.[11] A closer examination of the bookends illustrates the transformation that takes place between them.

NE i provides a preliminary examination of the good, and i 5 contributes toward that examination by considering what objects or *telē* (1095b31, 1096a80) people have valued according to the way people have lived their lives. There are three most favored lives – the lives of enjoyment (*apolaustikos*), political activity (*politikos*), and "contemplation" (*theōrētikos* [1095b17–19]).[12] Although the first two lives are articulated clearly in the chapter – the first takes bodily pleasure as the good and the second takes honor (*timē*) or excellence (*aretē*) as the good – Aristotle fails to characterize the *theōrētikos bios* (or its object) in i 5, except to note that it will be examined subsequently (1096a4–5). Aristotle uses the term *theōria* (and its cognates) rather broadly in the *Ethics* – sometimes capturing its etymological sense of "viewing" and "beholding" (*theōreō*) or being a spectator (*theōros*) – but also in the "mundane" sense of considering one's own interest (for which he reports Pericles was famous [vi 5.1140b7–10]).[13] Terms such as *theōria* and *philosophia* were contested in the fourth century – Aristotle's contemporary Isocrates, for instance, offered a different and competing take on both terms – and its use in i 5 is cautiously neutral, anticipating its discussion in x 7–8.[14]

Although it would be incautious to burden the term *theōrētikos* with too much meaning in i 5, all three lives and objects that Aristotle identifies as possible candidates for the good stand in contrast to the life of money making (*chrēmatistēs*) and its object – wealth – which

---

[11]   The proleptic anticipation that Kahn 1996 locates within the early and middle Platonic corpus, I suggest, also takes place within the *Ethics* (both with the work as a whole and within [at least] the tenth book).

[12]   Although I use the term "contemplation" to translate *theōria* (and its cognates), the activity that the term represents is very different from modern notions of scientific discovery or research. As Kraut 1989, 16n2, observes, to "contemplate" in its narrow sense "is not to be seeking knowledge but to be bringing to mind the knowledge one already has." Larmore 1992, 189, claims that Aristotle's use of the term *theōria* is "very different from how we understand theory today. It meant going over what is already known, beholding it and appreciating it. Learning was no part of Aristotelian *theōria*, except as a precondition. I am not sure that we today can attach much sense to valuing this sort of activity. It has no role in modern science, which learns, not in order to contemplate, but to learn more. Perhaps the idea of *theōria* still resonates with certain kinds of religious experience."

[13]   For elaboration of the breadth of Aristotle's use of *theōria* in the *Ethics*, see Rorty 1980 and Roochnik 2008. Nightingale 2004, 40–71, chronicles the original sense of the *theōros* as one who visits oracular centers, goes on pilgrimages to religious festivals, or journeys abroad for the sake of learning.

[14]   See Nightingale 2004, 20–21, 232–235, and Broadie and Rowe 2002, 76–77, for the cultural context of the late fourth-century debates with respect to characterizations of *theōria*.

Aristotle dismisses as unworthy of consideration (1096a5–8). Aristotle's predecessors – most immediately Plato – had joined the life of money making and pleasure into a single life and presented as a contestant for the best way of life one characterized by consumption and material gain.[15] But Aristotle refashions the slate of candidates and replaces the life of money making with the life of enjoyment. The move is a critical one on his part and draws attention to the new candidate that Aristotle includes in his contest, namely the life of enjoyment. Aristotle's initial description of it is unpromising: its advocates are characterized as "most vulgar," and "utterly slavish"; the life itself is likened to that of grazing cattle (1095b16, b19–20). And yet, he notes that proponents of such a life have some "argument" (logos)[16] in their defense since many people in power feel similar to the legendary Assyrian king Sardanapallus (Ashurbanipal) – a ruler whom Athenaeus reports as having said "eat, drink, and play (paize), since all else is not worth the snap of the fingers" (see Stewart 1892, i 63–64). Aristotle's revision of the candidates for the best way of life reflects his belief that it is a "fact of life" (or more accurately, a fact about the way people lead their lives that cannot be dismissed by practical philosophy) that pleasure is a central component of happiness, a topic upon which I will elaborate in the second part.

Aristotle's discussion of the three lives and their requisite objects also underscores and anticipates two criteria that he will use in his adjudication of the best way of life in x 6–8. The first criterion emerges when Aristotle dismisses wealth as a good because it is not desired for its own sake but chosen for the sake of something else, whereas pleasure, the object of the political life, and the object of the theōrētikos bios are intrinsically desirable (di' hauta agapatai [1096a8–9]). The second criterion emerges because determining the object of the political life is problematic: initially, its proponents believe it is honor. Yet since honor

---

[15] The closest parallel to the contest of three lives in Plato is Republic 581c, which asserts that there are three primary classes of human beings: the wisdom-loving, the victory-loving, and the gain-loving (philokerdes). But in the subsequent contest between them, Socrates twice characterizes the lover of gain as a moneymaker (chrēmatistikos [581d1, 583a9]). Phaedo 68b–c contrasts three lives and places the philochrēmatos alongside the philosophos and the philotimos. Philebus 21d–22b envisions a contest between the life of pleasure (hēdonē), the life of wisdom (phronēsis), and the life that combines the two (the koinos), but that contest seems radically different from the "three lives" contest found in the Ethics. Aristotle's identification of the third candidate as the life of enjoyment and his dismissal of the life of money making are his own innovations to the trope. For the relationship between Plato and Aristotle on this question, see Joly 1956, 114–115.

[16] Burnet 1901, 20, notes that tugchanousi de logou (1095b21) has the sense of "they get a hearing"; he writes that the "whole passage is dominated by the metaphor of the diadikasia," or suits among several persons.

depends on the person giving the honor rather than the honored, it cannot be the good of the political life for the good is *"oikeion ti"* or "something belonging" or "akin" to the good person (1095b25–26). Aristotle infers that the real object of the political life is "virtue" (*aretē*) since that is the reason why practically wise people (*phronimoi* [1095b28]) honor its possessors. "Belonging" and "intrinsic desirability" thus emerge as preliminary criteria of the good in i 5.

NE i 5 explores different ways of life to elucidate happiness and the good; x 6 commences with the claim that "since we have discussed the subjects of virtue, friendship, and pleasure, it remains to treat of happiness in outline ... our account will be more concise if we first take up what was said earlier" (1176a30–33). Aristotle's list of previous subjects is not random: central premises in x 6–8 derive from *NE* vi, ix, and x, as I will articulate. Chapter x 6 establishes the framework for setting up and adjudicating the contest, but the framework ultimately derives from the core criteria of i 5. The account of happiness in outline establishes two claims that will guide the choice of candidates: first, happiness is an activity rather than a state (*hexis*), since a state might be possessed by someone asleep or suffering the greatest misfortunes (1176a33–35). Although the distinction between *energeia* and *hexis* is something that Aristotle elaborates upon later in the *Ethics*, the core insight – that happiness is "activity" – is first stated in i 5 (using precisely the counter-examples of sleep and great misfortune [1095b32, 1096a1]).[17]

Aristotle's second claim that sets up the contest is that happiness is one of the activities chosen for its own sake (*tōn kath' hautas hairetōn* [1176b4]), which he further characterizes as meaning that it lacks nothing, is self-sufficient (*autarkēs* [1176b5–6]), or is an activity "from which nothing is sought beyond the activity" (1176b6–7). Aristotle elaborates upon criteria of the good – especially that of self-sufficiency – elsewhere (especially in i 7.1097b6–21), but the formulation of self-sufficiency in x 6 seems explicitly indebted to the preliminary formulation of intrinsic desirability in i 5.[18] Both ground rules – that happiness is an activity

---

[17]   In i 5 Aristotle criticizes the claim that *aretē* is the good because it is "too incomplete" (*atelestera* [1095b32]); he subsequently goes on to argue that one can possess *aretē* while being asleep, being inactive, or suffering great evils. At i 5, Aristotle has yet to identify *aretē* as a *hexis*, but his argument in i 5 presupposes such a claim (a claim Aristotle will ultimately argue for in 1106a10–12). In i 8.1098b31–1099a7, Aristotle elaborates on the claim that happiness is an *energeia* rather than a *hexis*. In x 6.1176b1–2, he notes that it has previously been said that happiness is an *energeia*; the reference may be to i 8 or to i 7.1098a5–7 (within the "function" argument).

[18]   Scholars have queried whether Aristotle uses criteria of the good consistently in *NE* i and x; see Curzer 1990 and Brown 2013. Regardless of inconsistency, the core notion at play in x 6 – that something is chosen or desired for its own sake – is the same as that articulated in i 5.

and that it is intrinsically choiceworthy – ultimately derive from the initial formulation of the contest of lives in i 5. Further confirmation that x 6–8 is indebted to i 5 can be found in the candidates for happiness that the two ground rules pick out: actions in accord with virtue, namely doing noble and fine things (*ta kala kai spoudaia prattein* [1176b7–8]), pleasant amusements (*tōn paidiōn hai hēdeiai* [1176b9]), and contemplative activity (1177a18).[19] Having thus established the ground rules and slate of contestants, the remainder of x 6–8 consists in adjudication of the contest started in i 5.

The overall structure of the adjudication of the contest is as follows: the rest of x 6 rejects the claim that happiness consists in amusements, substantially drawing upon the premise that the good person is the standard for what is truly pleasant (an argument that derives from the discussion of pleasure in x 5). *NE* x 7 stipulates that contemplative activity is in accord with its own virtue (*kata tēn oikeian aretēn* [1177a17]); defends the superiority of contemplative activity by explicitly drawing upon premises that derive from the prior discussions of friendship, virtue, and pleasure; and marks the crucial transition from showing what is the highest activity to showing what is the best way of life. *NE* x 8 confirms the superiority of the contemplative life over the practical life through three comparisons between them; but it also renders the verdict that the practical life is nonetheless a happy life, even if it is one that is second behind the contemplative life. Although substantial elements of the contest were on the table in a preliminary fashion in i 5, an examination of the arguments at each stage in x 6–8 shows that the adjudication of the contest requires premises that derive from intermediate discussions in the *Ethics*, specifically those concerning the nature of the self, the psychic nature of intellectual and ethical excellences, and the nature of pleasure – which is precisely what Aristotle claims in the first line of x 6 (1176a30–31).[20] Let me highlight the "borrowing" at each stage of the adjudication of the contest to underscore the textual integrity of what is discussed between i 5 and x 6–8 and its relationship to the overall conclusions of *NE* x.

[19] Although Aristotle does not mention contemplative activity in the initial list of intrinsically chosen activities in x 6 (it emerges for the first time in x 7), it too follows from the two criteria. One is reminded that the chapter break between x 6 and x 7 is the result of editorial decisions made over a millennium after the text was composed.

[20] Brown 2013, 137, insists that there is "awkwardness in the way that Aristotle touches on the traditional choice of lives, postpones his treatment of that choice, and then articulates a surprising position." Aristotle's extensive borrowing from *NE* vi, ix, and x in his adjudication of the contest shows that he is in no position to resolve that contest prior (at least) to his accounts of self-love and pleasure.

In the first stage of the adjudication, Aristotle shows that although pleasure is an integral part of a happy life, it is nonetheless wrong to claim that a life of pleasant amusement or "play" (*paidia*) is the happiest life.[21] In i 5, Aristotle claimed that proponents of pleasure deserved a hearing for whether a life devoted to eating, drinking, and play includes the most valuable activities, and x 6 presents such a hearing. Arguments in favor of a life of amusement seem to take the form of "people in power pursue amusing activities, people in power know what most contributes to happiness, therefore happiness consists in amusing activities." Aristotle presents several clusters of arguments against such a claim, but most of them are grounded in a premise that Aristotle points out has been repeated numerous times (1176b25), most recently in the account of pleasure in x 5, namely that "what is honored and pleasant is what is so to the decent person and for each type of person, the most desirable activity is the one that accords with his own state; for the decent person as well, then, the most desirable activity is one that is in accord with that person's excellence" (1176b25–27). Aristotle uses wordplay throughout x 6 to underscore the point: it is childish (*paidikon* [1176b33]) to point to the example of children (*paides* [1176b22]) to ground the claim that the activity of amusement (*paidia*) is best; rather, the pleasures that appear to the decent person will be pleasures, and the things he delights in will be pleasant (1176a17–19).[22] Aristotle quotes the sage Anacharsis – presumably such a decent person – who claims that one should "amuse oneself (*paizein*) so as to engage in serious matters" (1176b33). Pleasant amusement is a form of recreation (*anapausis*) and thus valuable in a well-ordered life; but x 6 concludes that the happy life (*ho eudaimōn bios*) seems to be in accord with excellence, and that involves serious matters; it does not consist in amusement (1177a1–3).

The second stage of the contest, in x 7, rather seamlessly picks up on the conclusion of x 6 by stating that "if happiness is in accord with excellence, it is quite reasonable that it should be in accord with the one that is best, and this will be the virtue of the best element" (1177a12–13). But rather abruptly, Aristotle now stipulates not only that *theōrētikē* is just such an activity but that such a point has already been stated (1177a18).[23] If such a claim has not been made with sufficient

---

[21] Aristotle's account of pleasant amusement as a *diagōgē* (or intellectual pastime) is usefully compared with his account of music as a preeminent educational *diagōgē* in *Politics* viii.

[22] The claim that the *spoudaios* or "decent person" is the measure of what should be honored or pleasing is also stated at iii 4.1113a25–33, ix 4.1166a12–13, and ix 9.1170a14–16.

[23] As commentators note, there is no passage that explicitly states that theoretical activity of the divine part within a person consists in complete happiness; nonetheless,

explicitness, nonetheless Aristotle is quite right to state that such a conclusion seems to agree with what has been said previously and with the truth (1177a18–19). *NE* x 7 presents six arguments in support of the claim that contemplative activity is activity "in accord with that virtue that belongs to one" (1177a17), and thus is complete happiness. All six of the arguments are based on premises articulated in the books on virtue, friendship, and pleasure. The arguments can be succinctly stated:

1. Since mind is the highest part of us, its activity is best (1177a19–21).
2. Since we can contemplate more than acting, the activity of contemplation is more continuous (1177a21–22).
3. Activity in accord with *sophia* is the most pleasant of activities in accord with virtue (1177a22–27).
4. The activity of contemplation is most self-sufficient because it is least dependent upon others (1177a27–77b1).
5. Contemplative activity is the only activity that seems to be intrinsically desirable (1177b1–4).
6. The activity of contemplation is most leisurely (1177b4–6).

The claim that mind is highest within us derives from Aristotle's discussion of self-love (ix 8.1168b28–1169a3, 1169a15–18); that contemplation is the most continuous activity follows the claim that it is divine (since the interruptions of activity are the result of human elements [x 4.1175a3–5]); the superlatively pleasant nature of contemplation follows from the analysis of *sophia* as an intellectual virtue and the claim that activities are perfected – and thus most pleasant – when they are directed at the highest objects (vi 7.1141a20–22, x 4.1174b20–23); and that the activity of contemplation is most self-sufficient and desired for its own sake follows from the account of self-sufficiency as lacking nothing in x 6 (1176b5–6). Although x 7 is the first place that Aristotle takes up the relationship between leisure (*scholē*) and contemplation (and thus it receives the most extended discussion in x 7), the other five arguments have firm bases in previous discussions. The result is a sort of crescendo: *NE* i 5 identified the contest's candidates, crucial passages in *NE* vi, ix, and x establish the premises for adjudicating the contest, and the first half of x 7 pulls all these pieces together to show that contemplative activity will be the "complete happiness of a human being, if it receives a complete

that the contest of lives in i 5 provides no criticism of the contemplative life may imply a preliminary endorsement. In numerous places in *NE* vi (e.g., 1141a18–b3, 1143b33–1144a6, and 1145a6–11) Aristotle makes clear that both the object and the activity of *sophia* is higher than *phronēsis*. As Burnet 1901, 461, aptly puts it, the claim about *theōrētikē* "follows at once from the proof given in book VI that *sophia* is the highest form of goodness."

span of life" (1177b24–25). The remainder of x 7 considers the claim that a life based in such activity is itself the best life.

The second half of x 7 presents a somewhat otherworldly account of the divine nature of mind – a substance that elsewhere in his writings Aristotle identifies with the divine.[24] Whereas the arguments in x 6 and x 7 previously had been concerned almost entirely with the question of what is the best activity, Aristotle's discussion of the divine nature of mind addresses the question of what is the best form or way of life.[25] He begins by noting that a "complete life" including the activity of contemplation will be superior (*kreittōn* [1177b26]) to one lived in accord with the human element since it is not insofar that one is human that one will live such a life (*biōsetai* [1177b27]); rather, insofar as the divine element is superior to the compound, to that degree will its activity, too, be superior to that in accord with the other sort of virtue. Aristotle concludes: "If, then, mind is something divine in comparison with the human, so also is a life in accord with that divine in comparison with human life" (1177b30–31). Implicitly recollecting the discussion of self-love, he asserts that each person would seem to be that divine part (1178a2; cf. ix 8.1168b28–1169a6) and that it would be absurd if a person chooses "not his own life" but that of something else (1178a3–4). Explicitly recollecting the discussion of pleasure in x 5,[26] Aristotle concludes that since what properly belongs (*oikeion* [1178a5]) to each thing by nature is best and most pleasant for it, the life of the mind (*ho kata ton noun bios* [1178a6–7]) is best and most pleasant for humans, given that a human is mind most of all; such a life will be superlatively happy.

It is difficult to address succinctly all the philosophical challenges raised by Aristotle's discussion of such a divine life.[27] But it is clear that the account is grounded in previous texts and thus brings together familiar material now cast in an unfamiliar light. The account of a divine life of happiness for the life in accord with the mind applies to the contest of lives, the claims that *sophia* is mind of the highest objects (*NE* vi 7), that we are most what is best in us (*NE* ix 8), and that the highest pleasures are those that most "belong to" or are akin to us (*NE* x 5). Such a life may

---

[24] For a recent review of the relationship between mind and the divine in Aristotle's philosophy, see Long 2011. Mind is divine, but Polansky 2007, 466–467, rejects identifying mind with God.

[25] Lawrence 2004, 130–137, distinguishes between "activity monism" and "life monism." The second party of x 7 ground the transition from one to the other.

[26] *to lexthen proteron* (1178a4–5) is most plausibly construed as a reference to x 5.1176a3–9, where Aristotle discusses *hēdonē oikeia*, namely the claim that creatures and activities have pleasures that "belong to" them. See further Stewart 1892, ii 449; cf. Burnet 1900, 464.

[27] For sustained discussion and criticism, see Lawrence 2004, 146–156, and Lawrence 2006, 64–73.

appear "strange" (as Anaxagoras put it), but it should not appear strange to one familiar with these central tenets from the major discussions of virtue, friendship, and pleasure.

If x 7 is a heavenly ascent of sorts, the final stage of the contest in x 8 returns to earth both to identify the life of human virtue as happy in a secondary way and to contrast it with the best life. Structurally, x 8 presents three comparisons between the divine life of contemplation and what the chapter calls the happiness of a life "in accord with all the other virtues the activities of which are human" (1178a9–10);[28] the chapter concludes with a more general reflection about the relationship between happiness and external goods (an issue first raised problematically in NE i 10–12).[29] The first contrast (1178a9–23) elevates the activities of the mind over those of the other virtues because the former is separable from the human compound (including connections to pathēmata or "emotions") whereas the latter are necessarily connected to the body and nonrational parts of the soul – an argument that draws heavily on the account of soul division in NE vi 1–2.[30] The second contrast (1178a23–b7) grounds the claim that contemplative activities require fewer external goods than the activities of the other ethical virtues. In this contrast, Aristotle invokes the examples of the political person (ho politikos), the generous person (ho eleutheros), the just person (ho dikaios), the brave person (ho andreios), and the temperate person (ho sōphros) as contrasts to the sketch of the person who leads the life of the mind in x 7. The argument is hardly rigorous, although its rhetorical strength derives from the force of the examples that Aristotle has fleshed out in his account of the individual virtues and the contrast they offer to the divine life fleshed out in x 7. Like the first comparison, Aristotle's examples derive from

---

[28] Aristotle calls such happiness "secondly" (deuterōs), a term he uses elsewhere in the Ethics in contrast with kuriōs (at x 5.1176a20) and in contrast with prōtos (at viii 7.1158b31). Lawrence 1993, 7–15, argues persuasively that the difference between the two lives is that the first is an ideal or utopian life under perfect condition whereas the second is a "however circumstanced ideal." Although Lawrence does not invoke the distinction, it is very similar to that which Aristotle makes between the best regime as a "city of one's prayers" and as "the most universally practically one" (Pol. iv 1.1288b21–24, b37–40).

[29] The final lines of x 8 (1179a22–32) take up the claim that the wise person (sophos) is most loved by the gods. As Broadie 2003 argues, the passage has troubled commentators since it seems out of place. Plausible are her claims that the passage is meant to articulate Aristotle's notion of piety. See also Broadie and Rowe 2002, 447–449.

[30] The argument also presupposes something like the account of nous in De Anima iii 4–5 – an account that x 8 explicitly sidesteps on the grounds that such metaphysical accuracy is not germane to the argument at hand. As Ron Polansky has pointed out to me, such remarks (a similar one can be found in i 13.1102a28–33) suggest that although Aristotle's analyses in the Ethics are compatible with his more rigorous theoretical treatises, they are not dependent upon them to establish the truth of the Ethics.

earlier passages in the work (namely, the illustrations of individual virtues in iii–v).

The third and final passage (1178b7–23) contrasts the lives of the gods – which exemplify happiness – with the lives of beasts, which have no share in happiness. Since the only activity it is plausible for the gods to perform is *theōria*, it follows that humans will be most happy insofar as they have the most affinity (*suggenestatē* [1178b23]) with the gods. The passage concludes that happiness itself is a sort of *theōria* and that other activities are happy insofar as they possess something similar (*homoiōma ti* [1178b27]) to *theōria*.[31] Just as in the first two comparisons in x 8, the structure of the argument presupposes that the contest for the best life is solely between two mutually exclusive forms of life, namely, the life of contemplation and that of practical activity. But the concluding passage on the problem of external goods blurs the contrast between the two forms of life. On the one hand, even while Aristotle elevates the contemplative life over the practical life in x 8, he acknowledges that "the one who is happy will also need external prosperity, insofar as he is human" (1178b5). Indeed, Aristotle claims that "insofar as such a person is a human being and shares his life (*suzē(i)* [1178b5]) with others, he chooses to do deeds that accord with excellence" (1178b5–7).[32] Worries that Aristotle's contemplative sage is potentially an "evil genius" – namely, someone who devotes his or her life to contemplation at all costs, including doing terrible actions – seems unwarranted.[33] On the other hand, the concluding passages of x 8 also claim that the demands of external goods are minimal, since private individuals (*idiōtai* [1179a6–7]) seem to perform decent actions no less than those with political power, and "a person's life (*bios*) will be happy if he is active in accordance with excellence" (1179a8–9). It is possible to do fine things and live a happy life without embracing (at least) the explicitly political existence of the *politikos*. Although the contest of lives adjudicates between lives as mutually exclusive ideal types, the contest also provides for a continuum of happy lives, including the divine contemplative life, the human political life, and the private life of activity in accord with virtue.

---

[31]   As Broadie and Rowe 2002, 78, notes, "resemblance is the key to the fact that both [lives] are forms of happiness." The claim that other activities can resemble *theōria* is the basis of the analyses in Charles 1999 and Scott 1999: the former locates an analogical likeness between primary and secondary forms of happiness whereas the latter locates the likeness in terms of a paradigm and its copies.

[32]   Aristotle's use of *suzēn* or "communal living" invokes his discussion of communal living as a necessary condition of friendship in *NE* ix 12.1171b33 ff.

[33]   Keyt 1983, 368, most forcefully raises the problem of whether the contemplative life may be "immoral"; see also Lear 1988, 314–316. Lawrence 1993, 30, aptly dissolves the concern.

Although the contest presupposes mutually exclusive lives, the text also makes clear that there is overlap between lives. As noted earlier, Aristotle holds without contradiction that the contemplative life is superior to the life of amusement but that the contemplative life also includes the pleasure that belongs (oikeion) to it. Although the best life clearly includes pleasure, pleasure is not its goal or aim. Aristotle's claim that the contemplative life includes action in accord with ethical excellence (1178b6) makes a similar point. There is no contradiction in claiming that the contemplative life is superior to the life of practical activity and that the contemplative life includes actions in accord with excellence. The contemplative life can include pleasure and practical activity without being defined by those activities.[34] But the parallel between the subordinate inclusion of pleasure and practical activity is obscured when the contest is presented as solely between two contestants.

II. PLEASURE AND THE INNER RING OF NE X

The "outer ring" of NE i 5 commences with Aristotle's observation that it is not unreasonable to apprehend what is the nature of the good and happiness "from people's lives" (1095b14–15). But the tenth book of NE as a whole exhibits an inner ring that concerns a related question, namely the relationship between the way people live their lives and philosophize about practical matters. In numerous places throughout the Ethics, Aristotle makes clear that the aim of the work is eminently practical rather than theoretical.[35] The practical consideration of pleasure poses a dilemma for the account of the best way of life: on the one hand, Aristotle believes that since humans are especially inclined toward the enticements of pleasure, they must proactively guard against pleasure in ethical habituation. But on the other hand, the best way of life is a happy life, and a happy life must include pleasure. Aristotle uses a ring composition at the beginning and the end of NE x to underscore the textual integrity of the tenth book and highlight a desideratum for his own account – namely, that it be consistent with the way people in fact do live their lives. Having surveyed the main arguments in NE x 6–8, it is unnecessary to reexamine all of that terrain. Instead, I would like to analyze two intersecting threads running through the tenth book – namely the methodological problem of keeping practical thought consistent with the way people live and the problem that pleasure poses for such consistency.

---

[34] Is the position I am ascribing to Aristotle inclusivist or dominant end? Like Curzer 1991, I would suggest that both interpretations miss something in the claims about the good that they ascribe to Aristotle.

[35] That ethics is practical rather than theoretical is the subject of the last chapter of NE x (1179a35–b4). See also ii 2.1103b26–31.

Warrant for yoking together the nature of pleasure and the contest of
the best life is provided in Aristotle's remarks reflecting on the nature
of practical truth that serve as "bookends" framing the entire discussion
of book 10 (leaving aside x 9, which is its own bookend of sorts to the
discussion of ethics and politics in *NE* i 2–4). In x 1, Aristotle notes that
some thinkers claim that it is better to regard pleasure as a bad thing with
respect to how we live (*pros ton bion* [1172a30])[36] – even if pleasure is not
bad – since they believe people are inclined toward it and are slaves to
pleasure (1172a29–32).[37] Aristotle cautions that

> surely it is not fine to say that. For the accounts that people give of things in the
> sphere of feelings and actions carry less conviction than the facts (*tōn ergōn*). ...
> True accounts (*hoi alētheis tōn logōn*), then, are what seem to be most useful not
> only with regard to knowledge, but also with regard to how we live (*pros ton bion*).
> For since they are in tune with the facts (*tois ergois*), they carry conviction, and
> so they encourage those who comprehend them to live (*zēn*) in accord with them.
> (x 1.1172b3–7)

Aristotle closes x 8 with a very similar sentiment. After reporting the
endoxa of Solon and Anaxagoras supporting the view that the happy
person requires minimal external goods, Aristotle notes that although
their opinions carry some conviction (*pistis*)

> in the practical sphere, the truth is determined from the facts of one's life
> (*ex tōn ergōn kai tou biou*), for that is decisive. When we examine what has
> been previously said, one must bring it to bear on the facts of one's life (*ta erga
> kai ton bion*), and if it is in harmony with the facts, accept it, but if it clashes, we
> should suppose it mere arguments. (1179a18–22)

Both passages – with their references to the way people live their lives –
seem to echo the contest of lives in i 5.1095b15. What is the purpose of
such a ring composition?

I submit that Aristotle uses such a nonargumentative literary device in
the tenth book to underscore a deeper tension in the work as a whole
about the nature of ethical thought. Speusippus's antihedonistic views
about the good are hardly an outlier; at the end of ii 9.1109b7–12,
Aristotle himself had counseled that "in everything, we must guard
against the pleasant and pleasure itself; for we are already biased in its
favor when we come to judge it. We must react to it as the elders reacted

[36] Aristotle's use of *pros ton bion* or "with respect to how one lives" echoes the same use
of the phrase in i 2.1094a22, where Aristotle asks whether knowledge of the good
promotes such a thing.

[37] *NE* x 1–3 rhetorically situates its account of pleasure between those of Eudoxus (who
praises pleasure as the good) and Speusippus (who denied that it was a good), almost as if
it were a Platonic dialogue between Aristotle and two members of the Academy. For the
rhetorical sophistication of the passage, see Warren 2009.

to Helen, and on each occasion repeat what they said." Among other things, the Trojan elders said of Helen, "beauty, terrible beauty. ... Ravishing as she is, let her go home in the long ships and not be left behind" (*Iliad* iii 156–160, Fagles trans.) And yet, as I have shown in my analysis of the outer ring of the *Ethics*, Aristotle argues that contemplation is the best activity, the basis for the best way of life, and what is best and most pleasant because it most completely belongs to us (x 7.1178a5–8; cf. 1177a22–27). *NE* x straddles this dilemma, and Aristotle's use of ring composition signals his sensitivity to it.

Aristotle is clear that the good is not reducible to pleasure. Although taking pleasure in the proper objects is crucial for ethical habituation, Aristotle believes that most people lack a sense of such pleasures and instead live by emotions and pleasures more suited to beasts (1179b8–16). What Aristotle wants to avoid is the hypocrisy he ascribes to the anti-hedonist who dismisses pleasure as bad for purposes of propaganda, as it were, for the many. Aristotle notes about such a project that "if someone who puts the blame on pleasure is ever seen seeking it, he is taken to be inclining towards it on the supposition that to him every sort of pleasure is worth seeking" (1172b1–3). As noted earlier, Aristotle himself had chastised pleasure (ii 9) but then gone on to endorse the purity and supreme pleasure of philosophy and contemplation. Why is the *Nicomachean Ethics* not guilty of a similar hypocrisy?

I submit that the answer is found in the way that the contest of the best way of life draws liberally from the account of pleasure in the first half of the tenth book and takes seriously the life of amusement as a candidate in the contest of lives. For instance, Aristotle's displacement of the life of material gain for the life of pleasure in the traditional formulation of the contest reflects his belief that the way people live their lives in search of pleasure indicates the fundamental importance of pleasure as a good, even if pleasure is not the good.[38] The defeat of the life of amusement was grounded in the claim that the decent person is the measure or standard of what is truly pleasant (x 6.1176b24–27), a claim made earlier in the account of pleasure in x 5.1176a15–19. Finally, the claim that the life of the mind is that which by nature "properly belongs" (*oikeion*) to a person and is most pleasant for such a person (x 7.1178a4–8) is grounded in the claim that activities and ways of life have their own "proper pleasures" (*oikeia hēdonē* [1176a3–5]), which is another claim of x 5. The adjudication of the contest in x 6–8 incorporates the account of pleasure in x 1–5 into an understanding of the best way of life as the most pleasant life. Discussions of the contest that focus on only two ways

---

[38] Compare Aristotle's treatment of the Eudoxan argument that pleasure is the good because all people seek it (x 2.1172b9–15).

of life fail to notice the important role that pleasure plays in the contest –
both methodologically and in its adjudication.

The bookend discussions on keeping accounts consistent with actions
appears to be Aristotle's way of highlighting the difference between his
own position and that of the hypocritical antihedonist described in x 1.
Aristotle agrees with the antihedonist that a life of bodily pleasure is
slavish and something more suited for cattle than humans – points made
in the adjudication of the contest of lives both in its original formulation
and in the critique of the life of amusement (i 5.1095b19–22, x 6.1177a6–9).
But Aristotle's decision to give the life of enjoyment a fair hearing and his
qualified endorsement of hedonistic amusements as sources of relaxation
(i 5.1095b21, x 6.1176b33–1177a1) distinguish him from the hypocritical
antihedonist. Aristotle and the antihedonist may ultimately share the
same qualified endorsement of pleasure as a good – namely, one according
to which not all pleasures but only those that the excellent person feels are
truly pleasant are good – but when Aristotle applies such a view to the
contest of lives, his account is consistent with the way that people live
their lives. In everyday life people express preferences for different things,
exercise delayed gratification, and seek what they really enjoy rather than
just any old pleasure. The account of pleasure in x 1–5 is able to make sense
of such "facts of life" and the adjudication of the best way to live draws
upon the account repeatedly. By the close of x 8, Aristotle has clearly
distinguished himself from the hypocritical antihedonist in x 1, albeit an
antihedonist with whom Aristotle shares some concerns.

III. CONCLUSION: MODERN PROBLEMS WITH ANCIENT LIVES

More jarring, of course, is the gap between the way people live their lives
and the quasi-divine life that x 6–8 elevates as the pinnacle of human
happiness. Anaxagoras is indeed correct to say that a person living such a
life is *atopos* or "a strange sort" to most people (x 8.1179a15). One is
reminded, in the *Symposium* 175a5, of Agathon's claim that Socrates also
was "strange" (*atopon* [cf. 221d]) – that he was someone who stops in
midconversation or in the middle of a journey to stand still and contemplate for hours. The very notion of a way of life – a mode of existence
singularly focused on one sort of activity – is an affront to modern tastes
that in practice enact a balancing act of multiple aspects of life – family
life, work life, social life, civic life, and so forth. But that there is a gap
between our lived experience of aspects of life and Aristotle's presentation of singular ways of life does not by itself offer an argument against his
view. Aristotle might respond that the modern view of life as comprising
an unending balancing act is a bit chaotic (if not downright Sisyphean).

Adjudicating between ancient and modern views of the integrity of a life goes beyond my scope. But regardless of what we think of Aristotle's awarding victory to the *bios theōrētikos* as the most happy form of life, the careful use of ring composition and the synthesis of previous arguments into the adjudication of lives in *NE* x 6–8 supports the claim that the *Nicomachean Ethics* exhibits an artistic and philosophical unity.[39] Developmental readings of Aristotle have treated the account of the contemplative life in x 6–8 as the outgrown vestige of an earlier Platonic stage in Aristotle's intellectual biography.[40] Nussbaum (1986, 376–377) went so far as to claim that *NE* x "seems to be oddly composed, giving rise to suspicion that chapters 6–8 are not originally part of the same whole" and that "there is no reason to rule out forgery" in the case of those sections, since they do not fit in the argument of the *Ethics* (and indeed she claims that they "represent a line of ethical thought that Aristotle elsewhere vigorously attacks").[41] My discussion should show that scholars who wish to excise x 6–8 from the *Ethics* will need to excise other significant passages as well.

WORKS CITED

Ackrill, J. L. 1980. "Aristotle on *Eudaimonia*." 15–34 in Rorty ed. 1980.
Barney, R. 2010. "Platonic Ring-Composition and *Republic* 10." 32–51 in M. McPherrran ed. *Plato's Republic: A Critical Guide*. Cambridge: Cambridge University Press.
Broadie, S. 2003. "Aristotelian Piety." *Phronesis* 48: 54–70.
Broadie, S., and C. Rowe. 2002. *Aristotle: Nicomachean Ethics; Translation, Introduction and Commentary*. New York: Oxford University Press.
Brown, E. 2013. "Aristotle on the Choice of Lives: Two Concepts of Self-Sufficiency." 135–158 in P. Destrée and M. Zingano eds. *Theoria: Studies on the Status and Meaning of Contemplation in Aristotle's Ethics*. Louvain-la-Neuve: Peeters.
Burnet, J. 1900. *The Ethics of Aristotle*. London: Methuen.
Bush, S. 2008. "Divine and Human Happiness in the *Nicomachean Ethics*." *Philosophical Review* 117: 49–75.
Bywater, I. 1894. *Aristotelis Ethica Nicomachea*. Oxford: Clarendon Press.
Charles, D. 1999. "Aristotle on Well-Being and Intellectual Contemplation." *Proceedings of the Aristotelian Society*, Supplement 73: 205–223.
Cooper, J. M. 1975. *Reason and the Human Good*. Cambridge, MA: Harvard University Press.

[39] My study thus augments the arguments that Pakaluk 2011 gives for the textual unity of the *Nicomachean Ethics* as a whole; it also responds to a problem with the unity of the text raised in Pakaluk 2005, 320–322.
[40] The grandfather of such readings is Jaeger 1948, which treats the account of a divine life in the *Nicomachean Ethics* as remnants from Aristotle's youthful Platonism (articulated most clearly in the *Protrepticus*).
[41] Labarrière 2002 presents an alternative to Nussbaum based on the possibility of *nous* in x 7 being practical.

1999. "Contemplation and Happiness: A Reconsideration." 212–236 in his *Reason and Emotion: Essays on Ancient Moral Psychology and Ethical Theory*. Princeton: Princeton University Press.

2012. *Pursuits of Wisdom: Six Ways of Life in Ancient Philosophy from Socrates to Plotinus*. Princeton: Princeton University Press.

Crisp, R. 1994. "Aristotle's Inclusivism." *Ancient Philosophy* 12: 111–136.

Crittenden, P. 1996. "Aristotle and the Idea of Competing Forms of Life." *Philosophical Inquiry* 18: 88–100.

Curzer, H. J. 1990. "Criteria for Happiness in *Nicomachean Ethics* I 7 and X 6–8." *Classical Quarterly* 40: 421–432.

1991. "The Supremely Happy Life in Aristotle's *Nicomachean Ethics*." *Apeiron* 24: 47–69.

Douglas, M. 2007. *Thinking in Circles: An Essay on Ring Composition*. New Haven, CT: Yale University Press.

Gauthier, R. A., and J. Y. Jolif. 1970. *L'Ethique à Nicomaque*. 4 vols. 2nd ed. With a new introduction and updated bibliography. Paris-Louvain: Publications Universitaires.

Gottschalk, H. B. 1980. *Heraclides of Pontus*. Oxford: Clarendon Press.

Hadot, P. 1995. *Philosophy as a Way of Life: Spiritual Exercises from Socrates to Foucault*. M. Chase trans. Oxford: Blackwell.

2002. *What Is Ancient Philosophy?* M. Chase trans. Cambridge, MA: Harvard University Press.

Hardie, W. F. R. 1965. "The Final Good in Aristotle's Ethics." *Philosophy* 40: 277–295.

1979. "Aristotle on the Best Life for a Man." *Philosophy* 54: 35–50.

Heinaman, R. 1988. "*Eudaimonia* and Self-Sufficiency in the *Nicomachean Ethics*." *Phronesis* 33: 35–41.

2007. "*Eudaimonia* as an Activity in *Nicomachean Ethics* 1.8–12." *Oxford Studies in Ancient Philosophy* 33: 221–253.

Homer. 1990. *The Iliad*. R. Fagles trans. New York: Penguin.

Irwin, T. H. 1999. *Nicomachean Ethics*. 2nd ed. Translation with introduction and notes. Indianapolis: Hackett.

2012. "Conceptions of Happiness in the *Nicomachean Ethics*." 495–528 in Shields ed. 2012.

Jaeger, W. 1948. *Aristotle, Fundamentals of the History of His Development*. 2nd ed. R. Robinson trans. Oxford: Oxford University Press.

Joly, R. 1956. *Le Thème philosophique des Genres de vie dans l'Antiquité Classique*. Brussels: J. Duculot.

Kahn, C. 1996. *Plato and the Socratic Dialogue: The Philosophical Use of a Literary Form*. Cambridge: Cambridge University Press.

Keyt, D. 1983. "Intellectualism in Aristotle." 364–387 in J. Anton and A. Preus eds. 1991. *Essays in Ancient Greek Philosophy IV: Aristotle's Ethics*. Albany: SUNY Press.

1989. "The Meaning of *Bios* in Aristotle's Ethics and Politics." *Ancient Philosophy* 9: 15–21.

Kraut, R. 1989. *Aristotle on the Human Good*. Princeton: Princeton University Press.

Labarrière, J. L. 2002. "De l'unité de l'intellect chez Aristote et du choix de la vie la meilleure." 221–243 in M. Canto-Sperber and P. Pellegrin eds. *Le style de la pensée*. Paris: Les Belles Lettres.

Larmore, C. 1992. "The Limits of Aristotelian Ethics." 185–196 in J. Chapman and W. Galston eds. *Virtue (Nomos XXXIV)*. New York: New York University Press.

Lawrence, G. 1993. "Aristotle and the Ideal Life." *Philosophical Review* 102: 1–34.

2004. "Snakes in Paradise. Problems in the Ideal Life." *Southern Journal of Philosophy*, Supplement 43: 126–165.

2006. "Human Good and Human Function." 37–75 in R. Kraut ed. *The Blackwell Companion to Aristotle's Nicomachean Ethics*. Malden, MA: Blackwell.

Lear, G. R. 2004. *Happy Lives and the Highest Good: An Essay on Aristotle's Nicomachean Ethics*. Princeton: Princeton University Press.

2009. "Happiness and the Structure of Ends." 387–403 in G. Anagnostopoulos ed. *A Companion to Aristotle*. Chichester: Wiley-Blackwell.

Lear, J. 1988. *The Desire to Understand*. Cambridge: Cambridge University Press.

Lockwood, T. forthcoming. "The Value of Contemplation and Friendship." In K. Nielsen ed. *Friendship in the Aristotelian Tradition*. Cambridge: Cambridge University Press.

Long, A. A. 2011. "Aristotle on *Eudaimonia, Nous,* and Divinity." 92–114 in Miller ed. 2011.

Miller, J. ed. 2011. *A Critical Guide to Aristotle's Nicomachean Ethics*. Cambridge: Cambridge University Press.

Nightingale, A. W. 2004. *Spectacles of Truth in Classical Greek Philosophy: Theōria in Its Cultural Context*. Cambridge: Cambridge University Press.

Nussbaum, M. C. 1986. *The Fragility of Goodness: Luck and Ethics in Greek Tragedy and Philosophy*. Cambridge: Cambridge University Press.

Pakaluk, M. 2005. *Aristotle's Nicomachean Ethics: An Introduction*. Cambridge: Cambridge University Press.

2011. "On the Unity of the *Nicomachean Ethics*." 23–44 in Miller ed. 2011.

Polansky, Ronald. 2007. *Aristotle's De Anima*. Cambridge: Cambridge University Press.

Reeve, C. D. C. 2012. *Action, Contemplation, and Happiness*. Cambridge, MA: Harvard University Press.

2014. *Aristotle Nicomachean Ethics*. Indianapolis, IN: Hackett.

Roochnik, D. 2008. "What Is *Theōria? Nicomachean Ethics*, Book 10.7–8." *Classical Philology* 104: 69–81.

Rorty, A. O. 1980. "The Place of Contemplation in Aristotle's *Nicomachean Ethics*." 377–394 in Rorty ed. 1980.

ed. 1980. *Essays on Aristotle's Ethics*. Berkeley: University of California Press.

Scott, D. 1999. "Aristotle on Well-Being and Intellectual Contemplation: Primary and Secondary *Eudaimonia*." *Proceedings of the Aristotelian Society*, Supplement 73: 225–242.

Shields, C. ed. 2012. *The Oxford Handbook of Aristotle*. Oxford: Oxford University Press.

Stewart, J. A. 1892. *Notes on the Nicomachean Ethics of Aristotle*. 2 vols. Oxford: Clarendon Press.

Warren, J. 2009. "Aristotle on Speusippus on Eudoxus on Pleasure." *Oxford Studies in Ancient Philosophy* 36: 249–282.

Whiting, J. 1986. "Human Nature and Intellectualism in Aristotle." *Archiv für Geschichte der Philosophie* 68: 70–95.

17   The Relationship between
      Aristotle's Ethical and Political
      Discourses (*NE* x 9)

I. OVERVIEW OF NE X 9 AND OUR QUESTIONS

In the closing chapter of the *Nicomachean Ethics* (x 9), Aristotle reminds his audience that while his discourse has provided an account of happiness as virtuous activity, and of the contributions to the happy and good life made by virtue, practical wisdom, pleasure, friendship, and so on, their goal (*telos*) is not knowledge but *becoming* good (1179a31–b4; cf. 1103b26–29, 1095a5). How does one become good? Aristotle reviews two further points from earlier in the *NE*: first, that arguments, which is what Aristotle's discourses provide, are not sufficient to make us good, for they motivate (*protrepsasthai kai parormēsai*) only those who already love the fine (*philokalon*, 1179b7–10; cf. 1095a10). Second, this love for the fine is produced by habits (*ethesi*, 1179b24–26; cf. ii 1 and 4). Only at this point does Aristotle introduce the main idea of x 9, which is that law is the best means for the formation of character.

Why law? Aristotle explains that right habits are not easy for the majority or the young (1179b31–34), and the law's prescriptions combine reasoning with compulsion without incurring resentment, as would an individual who opposed our impulses (1180a15–25). Aristotle seems to think that we need laws because virtuous conduct requires us to do things that conflict with some of our natural desires, and until and unless we become used to doing this so that it no longer brings us any pain, we need the threat of punishment – greater pain – from the law. But Aristotle also thinks that virtue, which involves acting for better reasons than the fear of punishment, can be inculcated in at least some people by the right laws. Further, Aristotle maintains that in states that leave the inculcation of virtue up to the family (1180a25–32), the private individual would do well to study legislation to guide his attempts to make others, say the members of his household, virtuous – just as one would want to know the universals in medicine (and not just rely on experience) whether one was responsible for the health of a few or many (1180a32–b3, 1180b20–28).

I would like to thank Stephen Menn and Ron Polansky for their comments on previous drafts of this contribution.

The chapter concludes with a call for the study of legislation. Even though legislation is a part of political expertise, one cannot learn it from the politicians, for they do not have the intellectual grasp of legislation that would enable them to teach it (if they had such a grasp, they would teach legislation, given its great value – cf. Plato, *Meno* 93b–94d). The sophists are no better for teaching legislation, for they lack experience, as is evident from their identification of legislation with rhetoric and their view that legislation is a simple matter of choosing among the laws of existing constitutions (1180b35–1181a17; cf. Isocrates, *Antidosis*). Choosing laws well requires comprehension (*sunēsis*, 1181a18) and discrimination, but these are based on the very political experience that the sophists lack (cf. Plato, *Timaeus* 19e). Aristotle here distinguishes between the experienced person's knowledge of the means by which an end is produced and the inexperienced person's ability to judge only the end product. Thinking of laws as the means by which virtue is produced, Aristotle supposes that it is the experienced person who will be best able to choose which laws bring about the end. A parallel with medicine illustrates his point: not just anybody, but the trained doctor, can put to good use texts that collect diseases and cures (1181b2–10).

With the verdict that his predecessors have left the subject of legislation unexamined (*anereunēton*, 1181b11), Aristotle announces a program for an inquiry into legislation and of constitutions (or, in the translation below, "political systems") in general:

[1] First, then, if any part of what has been said by those before is plausible, let us try to go through it. Then, in the light of the political systems we have collected, [2] let us try to consider what sorts of things preserve and destroy cities and each type of political system, and what causes some cities to be well run, and others badly. For when these issues have been considered, we shall perhaps be more likely [3] to see which political system is best, how each must be arranged, and what laws and habits it should employ. (1181b15–22, Crisp trans., numbers inserted by me)

This agenda seems to point to sections of Aristotle's *Politics*: [1] roughly corresponds to *Politics* ii, [2] to *Politics* iii 6–vi, and [3] to *Politics* vii–viii. (*Politics* i, which considers the city and its constituent parts, is not part of this agenda, and neither is *Politics* iii 1–5, which is concerned with defining the citizen.) Does the puzzling clause "how each must be arranged" in [3] refer to different best constitutions (perhaps for different conditions) or back to the different existing constitutions considered in the middle books of the *Politics*? Scholars argue about whether the text of the *Politics* represents work from different stages in Aristotle's intellectual life or mostly fits together into a single, if not fully executed, plan. They also disagree about the order of composition of the *Nicomachean*

Ethics and *Politics*, with Kraut 2002 taking the position that the *NE* was written later, so it is not even clear whether *NE* x 9's closing agenda points forward or backward.

Aristotle's remarks in *NE* x 9 tell us in a general sense that in his view the contributions of the *Nicomachean Ethics* are in the service of the project of making those for whose upbringing one is responsible virtuous. However, we can deepen our understanding of this idea by investigating some questions raised by his remarks: Why is it legislation, in particular, that one should study if one is interested in making others virtuous, especially if one is acting only as a private individual, and how does this square with Aristotle's insistence in *Politics* i that political expertise and the expertise involved in running a household are distinct? What exactly are the defects of previous work on legislation, and how does Aristotle's *Politics* improve on this previous work? It cannot be that the subject has not been broached; after all, Plato's *Laws* is a massive work about legislation that provides a rationale for the laws it prescribes.

To pursue these questions, we begin with a review of Aristotle's various remarks about the relationship between legislation and his discussions in earlier books of the *NE*, about virtue, friendship, and so on (Section II). Next, we compare Aristotle's way of thinking about the relationship between legislation and virtue to his predecessors', especially Protagoras's, Thrasymachus's, and Plato's, to illuminate how they failed to investigate legislation properly (Section III). We also examine Aristotle's idea that law habituates us to virtue and how exactly this works. Finally, we consider why, given Aristotle's claim that expertise in ruling the household and the *polis* are distinct, both private individuals and public officials should study legislation (Section IV).

II. LEGISLATION AND VIRTUE

It sounds odd to modern ears, accustomed as we are to a sharp boundary between the private and the political, that the discussions of the *Nicomachean Ethics*, about happiness, virtue, friendship, and so on, belong to political expertise (*politikē*); odder still that they are meant to contribute to legislation (*nomothetikē*). But Aristotle repeats this claim throughout the *NE*. In the *NE*'s "preamble" (*pephroimiasthō*, 1095a9–10), Aristotle argues that the best good, the end aimed at in all our practical affairs, would have to be the object of "political expertise" (*politikē*), the architectonic expertise (1094a27), which "makes use of the other practical expertises ... and ... legislates (*nomothetousēs*) about what one must do and what things one must abstain from doing" (1094b5–6). The end at which the political expert aims (for the citizens) is the same as the end at which any private individual aims (for himself or herself), namely, happiness. In the course of book 1, Aristotle's audience learns that happiness is activity in accordance with virtue, and Aristotle closes book 1 with a reference forward to book 2's discussion of virtue, saying that the true student of politics studies virtue because he wishes to make his fellow citizens virtuous. He gives the lawgivers of Crete and Sparta as examples because, even if they do not get it quite right, these states, unlike most states, are concerned with citizens' virtue (1102a11ff.). At the beginning of the book 2 account of virtue through habituation, Aristotle says that legislators make citizens good by forming habits in them (1103b3). Aristotle introduces book 3's discussion of the voluntary and involuntary by saying that it will prove useful to legislators who must assign praise and blame (1109b34). In his book 5 discussion of justice, he explains that "justice" and "injustice" in the sense of "lawful" and "unlawful" refer to the whole of virtue in relation to others, for the law prescribes acts productive of such virtue (1129b11–1130b13; cf. 1130b20–27). He introduces the topic of pleasure in book 7 by saying that the person inquiring philosophically into political expertise, who is to be the architectonic craftsman of the end, must inquire into pleasure and pain, since moral virtue and happiness involve pleasure (1152b1–7). Finally, he introduces the discussion of friendship in book 8 with the observation that lawgivers care more for friendship than justice, for when people are friends they have no need of justice (1155a23).

While such repetitions attest to Aristotle's seriousness about the topics of the *NE* belonging to political expertise, they do not explain what he has in mind. A little historical background helps. First, in Greek culture generally, the scope of "law" is wide, including not only written laws but also customs. Aristotle himself extends it to take into its purview the education of the young (viii 1). Second, Aristotle's idea that the goal of political expertise and its highest branch legislation is the happiness of the citizens goes back to the sophist Protagoras, to whom Plato's *Protagoras* specifically attributes the claim that the political expertise (*politikē technē*) he teaches leads to success in private and public affairs (318e–319a, with Socrates undermining this claim in the rest of the dialogue). The parallel between political expert and doctor that Aristotle draws in *NE* x 9 (1181b2–10; cf. 1180b27) seems to go back to Protagoras as well: in the *Theaetetus*, Plato puts in the mouth of a fictionally resurrected Protagoras the claim that the political expert makes healthy things appear just to a city in the way that a doctor or a gardener makes a sick animal or plant have good and healthy appearances.[1] While

---

[1] "The wise and efficient politician is the man who makes wholesome things seem just to a city instead of pernicious ones. Whatever in any city is regarded as just and admirable is just and admirable in that city and for so long as that convention maintains itself;

these texts point to a Protagorean connection between political expertise and happiness, it is quite likely that Protagoras drew a connection specifically between legislative expertise and happiness as well, since he took the position that the law defines justice in each constitution and he himself was engaged in legislating for colonies.

Plato's dialogues assume Protagoras's connection between political expertise and happiness and seek to determine what this happiness-producing expertise consists in, sometimes criticizing someone's claims to have it, sometimes specifying criteria by which it may be identified. Political expertise is directive (*Statesman* 260b–c) and architectonic in that it makes use of the other expertises (*Euthydemus* 291c ff.); it makes people virtuous (*Republic* 500d; *Statesman* 309b–c), because their happiness depends on their virtue (*Gorgias* 470e). In the *Gorgias*, in the course of criticizing rhetoric, the so-called expertise that Gorgias claims brings "the greatest good for humankind" (452d; cf. 451c), as a false imitation of corrective justice (*dikaiosunē*), Socrates maps out the expertises and their domains in a way that builds on the legislator-doctor analogy. Political expertise (*politikē technē*) as a whole aims at the good of the soul; corrective justice is its inferior branch, and legislation (*nomothetikē*), of which sophistry is a false imitation, is its superior branch (464b–465e). (This distinction is not the same as the distinction drawn by Aristotle in *NE* v between the two domains of specific justice, distribution and rectification.) These two branches of politics, corrective justice and legislation, correspond to medicine and gymnastics, the two expertises that care for and aim at the good of the body. Legislative expertise seems to be the expertise that produces and maintains the happiness of citizens. This idea is fleshed out in the *Republic* and much more fully in the *Laws*, which explores concretely which laws result in the happiness of the citizens.

Plato's interest in law reflects a concern with a way in which Protagoras's relativism about justice is appropriated by a younger generation of sophists. While Protagoras emphasizes the relativity of justice due to the variability of law, Thrasymachus adds that not only is justice law-dependent but the laws themselves serve the interests of the powerful (*Republic* i; cf. *Laws* iv 714b–d). Plato responds by denying that laws and a political system that benefit only a part rather than the whole of the city are genuine laws and a genuine constitution (*Laws* 715b), and describing, in both the *Republic* and the *Laws*, what laws that serve the common good and produce virtue in citizens would be like. Following Plato's lead, Aristotle too distinguishes between true and perverted

but the wise man replaces each pernicious convention by a wholesome one, making this both be and seem just" (*Theaetetus* 167c, trans. Levett).

constitutions by whether they aim at the good of the whole or of a part (*Politics* iii 6.1279a17–21), and deems the laws that conform to the former just and those that conform to the latter unjust (iii 11.1282b8–13).

Aristotle joins the battle with Plato against Thrasymachus and Protagoras in recognizing a natural justice that is the same everywhere, in addition to the conventional justice that is due to legislation and depends on the legislation's scope (1134b17–35a5). However, unlike Plato, Aristotle prepares for his account of the best constitution by making a study of actual constitutions with a reputation for good laws and ideal constitutions described by previous thinkers (*Politics* ii 1.1260b27–36). Apart from providing some of the experience that he has claimed develops the judgment (*sunēsis*) needed for choosing correctly among possible laws, the review of constitutions enables Aristotle to evaluate laws in light of their constitutional context – for Aristotle has absorbed this grain of truth from Thrasymachus, that laws maintain the constitution within which they are framed, and they are supposed to. Maintaining the constitution is not just what corrupt laws, not worthy of the title, do when they maintain the advantages of the ruling class; rather, all laws, insofar as they function well as laws, maintain the constitution to which they belong. Thus, to judge whether a law is a good law, Aristotle considers first what constitution it belongs to. This allows him to evaluate laws both relative to the constitution they are supposed to preserve and absolutely, that is, relative to the constitution that achieves the happiness of all the citizens.

We can see the fruits of Aristotle's approach in his criticisms of Plato's ideal constitutions. For example, in discussing the ideal constitution of Plato's *Republic*, Aristotle first points out that the degree of unity appropriate for a city is different from the degree of unity appropriate for a family or individual (ii 2), but then, granting that the ideal city is to be maximally unified, argues that far from unifying the citizens, the community of private property and the family results in diffusion of responsibility (ii 3.1261b32–40) and the dilution of family feeling (1262a13–14). Aristotle's approach also allows for the evaluation of constitutions in the light of legislation required for their maintenance. It is a shortcoming of a constitution if realizing it requires the rustication of everyone over the age of ten (*Republic* 540e–541a). Looking at laws and constitutions in light of each other reveals what laws are conducive to what good constitutional goals and what laws are not, but also what constitutional goals would be unacceptable given the legislation that would be required to bring them about.

III. HABITUATION AND LAW

How does law habituate us to virtue? Aristotle identifies virtue as a disposition in relation to the affections (*NE* ii 5 1105b25 ff.; cf. *Physics* vii 3.246a10–247a19) and says that we acquire virtue by habituation (*ethismos*). He does not say much about what this process consists in, however, only that by performing actions of a certain kind, we acquire a corresponding disposition: thus, it is by how we act in frightening situations, through becoming habituated to feeling fear or confidence, that some of us become courageous and others of us become cowardly (*NE* ii 1.1103b15–20). Ideally, habituation results not just in acting in conformity with the law but also (in those for whom this is possible) of feeling the right way as one acts, for this is the mark of virtue as opposed to mere continence. However, action in conformity with the law is no small goal, for this is the best the many and the young can achieve. This too requires habituation: the law cannot command obedience except through habituation (*Politics* ii 8.1269a20), and a state cannot achieve the goal of lawfulness (*eunomia*) unless its good laws are obeyed (iv 8.1294a3–7).

The case of how habituation results in virtue is, of course, the most interesting. Burnyeat (1980) proposes that in the process of performing certain sorts of actions (e.g., the brave or temperate sort), one comes to discover their intrinsic value, so that one acquires the disposition to perform actions of that type for their own sake and to take pleasure in them. For part of what it is to have a virtuous disposition is to value such actions for their own sake and take pleasure in doing them.

This raises at least two questions, one philosophical and psychological, and the other textual. First, simply performing an action of the right sort for the circumstances cannot ensure that the agent focuses on the good-making features of an action. So, for example, a hoplite who stands his ground in battle may have his motives to avoid punishment and blame reinforced rather than learning anything about the intrinsic value of protecting his comrades in battle.[2] Indeed, contemporary psychological research on motivation suggests that, whether one sees one's activity as intrinsically valuable or as instrumental to some further end, it is sensitive to reward and praise (and so, it is reasonable to suppose, also to punishment and blame) in surprising ways. For example, in a landmark study by Lepper, Greene, and Nisbett (1973), children who were given rewards for drawing with markers proved less likely to draw with markers when no reward was in the offing, as compared with children who were given the opportunity to draw with markers but for no reward. In a review of thirty years of work on the effects of praise on motivation, Henderlong and Lepper (2002) found that unless it is specific, informational, and given for things in the agent's control, praise often

---

[2] Although Aristotle discusses courage in one context where it is most salient – military action – it does not follow that the habituation to courage requires military experience (or indeed that nonmilitary contexts do not call for courage). I am grateful to Ron Polansky for his thoughts on this point.

undermines intrinsic motivation, especially in the long term. This suggests that since the law brings about behavioral conformity by punishing nonconformity, it might actually undermine the development of intrinsic motivations to conform by making the extrinsic reasons salient.

However, we should note a significant asymmetry between reward and praise on the one hand and punishment and blame on the other. Reward and praise may be given for ability whether the ability is thought to be due to natural capacity or effort, whereas punishment and blame are given for things that are thought to be in the agent's control. So even if praise and reward undermine intrinsic motivation – for example, when the praised agent encounters difficulty and concludes that he is lacking in ability after all – there may not be a similar effect with blame and punishment, which carry a clearer message that the desired behavior is in the agent's control. Despite this asymmetry it seems that both punishment and blame can distract the agent from the intrinsic disvalue of his actions unless he takes them as giving him information about what was wrong with his actions. But what draws the agent's attention to the intrinsically good- or bad-making features of actions?

Perhaps Aristotle thinks it is the law itself that does this: because what is important for the development of a virtuous disposition is acting as virtue would prescribe and, furthermore, doing so for its own sake, perhaps law provides the correct and illuminating description of the behavior one is to avoid. When Aristotle says that the virtuous person chooses fine actions for their own sake (NE 1105a32), he likely means, "under the description that makes them the fine actions they are," rather than specifically "as an end rather than a means."[3] (This removes the apparent conflict between choosing the actions for their own sake and choosing them because they contribute to the agent's happiness.) Aristotle also does not think of law as especially operating by forbidding, since he thinks that legislation should cover the upbringing of the young and himself describes laws pertaining to education (v 9.1310a13–20, viii 1.1337a10–11).

Although Aristotle frequently points to the educative function of law, we have seen there is a puzzle about the mechanism(s) by which people are supposed to end up valuing actions for the right reasons as a result of habituation by the law. Aristotle's remarks raise a second, textual, issue: while discovering the intrinsic value of virtuous acts by performing them is surely an important step in the acquisition of virtue, many of the passages on habituation seem to point to something more basic. In NE ii 3 Aristotle says that the person who resists temptations or withstands frightening things cheerfully or anyway without distress is or becomes moderate or courageous, for it is because of pleasure that we do base

---

[3] I owe this reading of di' auta to Terry Irwin.

things and because of pain that we hold back from doing fine things (1104b5–11). His point seems to be that the performance of (some) virtuous actions requires that we overcome our natural aversions to pain and propensities to pleasure. Standing firm in battle requires overcoming a natural flight response in the face of danger; staying awake throughout one's night watch requires overcoming a natural desire to sleep when tired. Aristotle's examples of habituation in the education of his best constitution (*Politics* vii–viii) also point to habituation's role in changing our response to our natural pleasures and pains. Here, Aristotle recommends exposing young children to cold so that they become accustomed (*sunethizein*) to it, the idea being that in later life we more easily endure those things we have had to endure since childhood (1336a14–20). The first stage in habituation seems to be getting people accustomed to experiencing certain bodily or emotional states (the point of exposing the child to cold may be so that the body does not fall ill on exposure to cold, or so that the child gets used to feeling cold and no longer thinks of the discomfort as so bad or to be avoided or feared). Aristotle generalizes from this example to strictures on the games children should play and the kind of talk they should hear (1336a25–35, 1336b5). He seems to hold that repeated experience of certain uncomfortable states reduces the motive to escape them. This is the sense in which contemporary psychologists speak of habituation: the diminution in response to a stimulus when it is repeated. It is this aspect of habituation that Aristotle emphasizes in *NE* x 9 when he says that people will not find their nurture and occupations painful when they have become habituated (*sunēthē genomena*, 1179b34–1180a1).

In *Politics* viii 5 Aristotle prescribes for the best constitution certain modes and rhythms for citizens to listen to on the assumption that music produces in its listeners certain emotional states that it somehow also represents (1340a10–b12). The idea seems to be that one mode represents, say, anger (presumably appropriate anger) and another courage, and these modes also produce anger and courageous feelings in their audience, so that the audience gets practice with these feelings during its musical education and so is disposed to feel them in similar real-life situations. Virtue is a disposition in relation to how we are affected as well to how we act, and how we are affected also influences how we act. But here, habituation is not a matter of diminishing responses to things that we are initially averse to, or to things we are initially strongly attracted to; rather, it seems to involve developing positive and active responses to these things – new pains and pleasures, for example.

It is also interesting that we are supposed to practice being in frightening situations for the development of courage, but apparently not being in tempting situations in order to develop moderation. For moderation,

Aristotle recommends veering in the direction of abstention. (In this he differs from Plato, whose *Laws* [671a–672a] recommends drinking parties for testing and developing the moderation of old men.) Aristotle's reasoning is that we need to counteract our natural propensities, so our propensity to cowardice by erring in the direction of rashness, and our propensity to self-indulgence by erring in the direction of abstention (*NE* ii 8.1109a1–19). Perhaps it is because of these different natural propensities that habituation does not look like a unitary phenomenon when we examine it in detail.

The pleasures in the discovery of intrinsic value described by Burnyeat are pleasures that we have to develop our abilities to enjoy. Possibly this value is obscured by our first feelings of pleasure and pain. In any case, the pleasures in the intrinsic value of virtuous actions are likely to involve reflection and so belong to the development of practical wisdom. One can see how reflection on one's law-inculcated behavior could take in the reasons for laws to direct us as the laws do, and so to create intrinsic motivation for virtuous actions.

All this bears directly on our particular question about the way in which law makes people virtuous. By threatening punishment for actions contrary to virtue, law motivates behavioral conformity with virtue; by being the subject of reflection, it helps those few that are capable of it to think about the goals of virtuous action and legislation, that is to say, about the chief good.

IV. POLITICAL AND PRIVATE VIRTUE-INCULCATION: SAME EXPERTISE OR DIFFERENT?

We turn, finally, to Aristotle's claim about the value to the private individual of studying legislation. In *Politics* i Aristotle argues that the content and value of *politikē*, the expertise in ruling over a community of equals, is distinct from and superior to that of expertise in ruling over inferiors (e.g., the members of a man's household). He is arguing against Plato's view, expressed in the *Statesman* (258e–259c), that political expertise is an art of ruling – whether over few (as in a household) or many (as in a city). And in *NE* vi 8 Aristotle describes legislation as the controlling part of political expertise – having to do with the universals, while the issuing of edicts has to do with particulars (1141b25–26). But if legislation belongs to political expertise, which is a distinct expertise from that needed by the head of a household, why should a private individual study legislation?

This question bears upon another, and more contentious, one about the relationship between the *Nicomachean Ethics* and the *Politics*. It is quite natural for us to read the former as Aristotle's specification of human happiness and virtue and the latter as his discussion of the constitutional arrangements that do and do not aid in the development of such happiness and virtue. There is nothing wrong with this so long as we do not import modern public-private distinctions into our reading of the *NE*. The *NE* is not concerned exclusively with individual happiness, for the goal of the architectonic expertise mentioned in the beginning and end of the work is the city's happiness. There is every reason to construe the happiness of the city individualistically, as at least largely constituted by the happiness of individual citizens, but the *NE* does not seem to be written as if individual happiness is achievable no matter what the social circumstances. This is not to say that no one can be happy except in Aristotle's ideal constitution, but rather to say that the *NE* is addressed to those who would make *others* virtuous and thereby happy.

Bodéüs 1993 argues that the *NE* is addressed to would-be legislators (3, 45, 57–62). Considerations favoring this proposal include (in addition to the textual indications of *NE* i 1 and x 9) the inadequacy of the *Politics* for the student of legislation, given that it lacks the *NE*'s general account of the end and of the contribution to it of virtue, activity, friendship, and so on, which a legislator would have to know in order to choose good laws and ensure that they are obeyed, and the repeated remarks (cited at the start of Section II herein) that the political and, in particular, the legislative expert should understand the topics discussed in the *NE*. One might object to this that it makes the text of the *NE* irrelevant to the majority of its readers who are not in a position to legislate for a constitution aimed at the development of virtuous and happy human beings (as does Schütrumpf 1997). A way out of the irrelevancy worry is suggested by Curren 2000, which proposes that the arguments of the *NE* and *Politics* address self-interested legislators as well as those aimed at the good of the whole (99–100).

But Aristotle is quite clear in *NE* x 9 (cf. i 3.1095a1–11) that arguments and perhaps speeches more generally can have the desired effect only on people who have been brought up to love the fine and to desire and act in accordance with reason. So to whom is the *NE* addressed, and to whom is it relevant?

We can make progress on this question by considering our narrower question about the value to a private individual of studying legislation. Aristotle points out that because many constitutions, unfortunately, leave education in the hands of the family (*NE* x 9.1180a24–29), it is left to the head of the household to prescribe the conduct that shapes those in his care so they will be virtuous (the conversation between Socrates and Ischomachus in Xenophon's *Oeconomicus* is an example). Because the problem for the father is how to motivate and direct virtue-inspiring conduct in children who are led by pleasure and pain, he has to formulate rules of action and provide a rationale as well as punishments for non-compliance, just as the laws would in a good constitution. But this means his task is to legislate for his children, and he will do so better if he is guided by legislative expertise than if not. Although Aristotle mentions that the situation of the head of the household is in some ways preferable to that of the legislator – his children obey him out of affection; he can tailor his prescriptions to the individuals in his charge – these do not do away with the need for legislative expertise.

Yet legislative expertise suggests a kind of generality that may seem unnecessary in the household. One might wonder: Why can a father not, as Protagoras imagined, "strive to make him [viz. the child] as good as possible, teaching and showing him by every word and deed that this is right and that wrong, this good and that bad, this holy and that unholy, 'do this' and 'don't do that'" (Plato, *Protagoras* 325d, Taylor trans.)? There might be several reasons: even though the facts of kinship and paternal beneficence dispose children to obey their father (1180b5–6), still, children might be less resentful and rebellious if their father coerces them by means of rules whose consistency they can see and whose rationale they understand or will come to understand. Further, a man's children are only temporarily his inferiors; when they grow up, they will be his equals and the equals of other citizens, and being ruled by even homemade laws prepares them for that. Even private education needs to prepare children for citizenship.

These thoughts can help us reconcile some apparently contradictory remarks Aristotle makes about the practical expertises: that on the one hand, political expertise is distinct from economic expertise – namely, the expertise required for running a household well (*Politics* i) – but on the other hand, that political wisdom and practical wisdom are the same disposition (*hexis*), although what it is to be them is different (*NE* vi 8.1141b23–25). Presumably by the last comment Aristotle means that political wisdom and practical wisdom are related to different things, the city as a whole in the case of the former and one's life as a whole in the case of the latter. *Politics* iii 4 echoes this point about sameness of disposition by claiming that the distinctive virtue of the ruler is practical wisdom, which is the same as the virtue of a good man. (In context, Aristotle is distinguishing the constitution-relative sense of a good citizen and a good ruler – defined in terms of preservation of the constitution – from the absolute sense, one who rules and is ruled by equals.) This should not be understood as saying there are two expertises, one for ruling over others and one for running one's own life, which converge. Rather, there is one, architectonic, expertise, and it equips one to rule over and be ruled by equals for the sake of the common good, whether the equals in association are the members of a family or co-citizens, where the time of equality may still lie in the future.

382   RACHANA KAMTEKAR

WORKS CITED

Adkins, A. W. 1991. "The Connection between Aristotle's *Ethics* and *Politics*." 75–93 in D. Keyt and F. Miller eds. *A Companion to Aristotle's Politics*. Malden, MA: Blackwell.

Bodéüs, R. 1993. *The Political Dimensions of Aristotle's Ethics*. J. E. Garrett trans. Albany: SUNY Press.

Burnyeat, M. 1980. "Aristotle on Learning to Be Good." 69–92 in A. O. Rorty ed. *Essays on Aristotle's Ethics*. Berkeley: University of California Press.

Cashdollar, S. 1973. "Aristotle's Politics of Morals." *Journal of the History of Philosophy* 11: 145–160.

Crisp, R. trans. 2000. *Aristotle: Nicomachean Ethics*. Cambridge: Cambridge University Press.

Curren, R. 2000. *Aristotle on the Necessity of Public Education*. Lanham, MD: Rowman and Littlefield.

Henderlong, J., and M. Lepper. 2002. "The Effects of Praise on Children's Intrinsic Motivation: A Review and Synthesis." *Psychological Bulletin* 128: 774–795.

Kraut, R. 2002. *Aristotle: Political Philosophy*. Oxford: Oxford University Press.

Lepper, M., D. Green, and R. Nisbett. 1973. "Undermining Children's Intrinsic Interest with Extrinsic Reward: The Overjustification Hypothesis." *Journal of Personality and Social Psychology* 28: 129–137.

Levett, M. J. 1990. *Theaetetus*. Rev. M. F. Burnyeat. Indianapolis: Hackett.

Menn, S. 2005. "On Plato's ΠΟΛΙΤΕΙΑ." *Proceedings of the Boston Area Colloquium in Ancient Philosophy* 21: 1–51.

Miller, F. 2006. "Aristotle's Philosophy of Law." Chapter 4 in F. Miller and C. -A. Biondi eds. *History of the Philosophy of Law, Treatise of Legal Philosophy and General Jurisprudence*, vol. 6. New York: Springer/Kluwer.

Schofield, M. 2006. "Aristotle's Political Ethics." 305–322 in R. Kraut ed. *A Companion to Aristotle's Nicomachean Ethics*. Malden, MA: Blackwell.

Schütrumpf, E. 1997. Review of Bodéüs, *The Political Dimensions of Aristotle's Ethics*. *Gnomon* 69: 13–16.

Taylor, C. C. W. trans. 1976. *Plato: Protagoras*. Oxford: Oxford University Press.

18 Protreptic Aspects of Aristotle's *Nicomachean Ethics*

In order to reach the fullest understanding of Aristotle's *Nicomachean Ethics*, we would do well not only to study the details of his argumentation but also to appreciate the various purposes that these details serve. Aristotle tries to inform his audience about his own ethical and social standpoint and how it is founded on arguments consistent with his wider philosophical commitments; but he also tries to motivate members of his audience to engage in their own philosophical inquiries, as applied not only to concrete moral and political questions but also to the most abstract and inapplicable forms of philosophy.

We hope to show that the overall protreptic plan of Aristotle's ethical writings is based on the plan he used in his published work *Protrepticus (Exhortation to Philosophy)*, by highlighting those passages in his ethical writings that primarily offer hortatory or protreptic motivation rather than dialectical argumentation and analysis, and illustrating several ways that Aristotle's ethical works adapt certain arguments and examples from his *Protrepticus*.[1] We confine our attention in this contribution to the *Nicomachean Ethics*.

The most explicit references to Aristotle's audience and his purpose in writing any of his ethical discourses are found in *NE* x. Early in the book, he writes this: "True arguments, then, seem to be the most useful, not only in the acquisition of knowledge, but in how we live. For since they are in harmony with the facts, they are believed, and for that reason they exhort (*protrepontai*) those who understand them to live

---

We would like to acknowledge written comments from the editor, from two anonymous readers for the press, and from our friends Jonathan Barnes, Philip Horky, and Matthew Walker.

[1] We have argued in Hutchinson and Johnson 2005 that Aristotle's *Protrepticus* can be reconstructed on the basis of the authentication of the major excerpts (amounting to at least five hundred lines) contained in chapters VI–XII of the *Protrepticus* of Iamblichus. In our work in progress on an edition, translation, commentary, and reconstruction (continually published at www.protrepticus.info), we show how the other pieces of evidence can be related to the framework recoverable from these seven authenticated chapters of Iamblichus's *Protrepticus*.

in accordance with them" (1.1172b3–7).[2] Toward the end of the book, however, he focuses on the qualification "those who understand them" rather more: "As things are, though they [sc. philosophical arguments] appear to have the power to influence and exhort (protrepsasthai) those young people who possess generosity of spirit, and perhaps to make susceptible to virtue a character that is well bred and truly loves what is noble, they seem unable to exhort (protrepsasthai) the masses in the direction of what is noble and good" (9.1179b7–10, modified). For the majority of people, then, politics and laws are called for, not ethics and philosophy.

But then whom does Aristotle expect to influence by his philosophical ethics, if not the masses, and how? The answer is given in the same passage: he aims to *exhort certain students*, those students who possess maturity of mind and character. At the most general level, Aristotle's *Eudemian* and *Nicomachean Ethics* should be interpreted as particular modes of protreptic discourse. In the *Rhetoric*, Aristotle defines protreptic as a kind of deliberative speech, employed either in private counsel or in public assemblies: deliberative discourses aim to encourage (protrepein) or discourage (apotrepein) something (i 3.1358b8–10). If and when these works were lectures delivered to students in the Lyceum, they were protreptics for a private assembly; when the *EE* and the *NE* began to circulate publicly in written copies, they began to function as protreptics giving public counsel to everyone.

What hortatory counsel does Aristotle offer? In the first chapter of *NE* x, Aristotle urges the study of pleasure and pain, because of its centrality in the development of virtue; we "educate the young by steering them in the right direction with pleasure and pain" (1.1172a20–21). The knowledge of pleasure and pain is valuable in the scientific study of legislation, which in the last chapter Aristotle earnestly recommends for mature young men who are going to be responsible for children in private households, as well as for those who plan a career of public service (9.1180b23–28).

In this context, Aristotle mentions "some people" who think that "legislators ought to summon people (parakalein) to virtue and exhort them (protrepsasthai) to act for the sake of what is noble – on the assumption that those who have been trained well in their habits will respond" (1180a5–8, modified), referring to a remarkable claim made by Plato in *Laws* iv: codes of laws should not be bare prohibitions provided with penalty clauses but should first make an attempt, in literary preambles to each law, to persuade the citizens by intelligent considerations

---

2 Crisp trans., modified. Unless otherwise indicated, all translations from the *NE* are cited unmodified from the Cambridge University Press translation by Roger Crisp; all other translations are ours.

that motivate them to obey (718c–723e).[3] For example, to someone tempted to rob temples, in the preamble "you might talk to him and exhort him (*protrepsasthai*) as follows" (ix 854a), and then Plato offers some sample considerations.

For Aristotle, however, such preambles seem to be useless, and laws motivate citizens directly, without any need for motivating preambles, by punishing wickedness and rewarding virtue, "as if exhorting (*protrepsontes*) the one while deterring the other" (iii 5.1113b25–26, modified). It would seem that Aristotle has little faith in the power of protreptic discourse when presented to most people, either by philosophers or by legislators in their preambles; as we shall see, he saves his protreptic speeches mainly for the purpose of exhorting talented and well-raised young adults to adopt scientific attitudes of study and research, not using protreptic discourse much for the purpose of exhorting them to virtue.[4]

Early in his career, while still a member of Plato's Academy and during the time that Plato was working on his *Laws*, Aristotle wrote a work entitled *Protrepticus (Exhortation to Philosophy)*,[5] and that work, now lost, had as its goal to encourage the youth to the conclusion that one should do philosophy.[6] The dramatic scenario seems comparable to those found in the Platonic dialogue *Rival Lovers* and in Plato's *Euthydemus*, where young men form the audience to a lively debate about the nature and value of philosophy. In the background of Aristotle's *Protrepticus* is the intense rivalry for students between Isocrates and the Academy; as evident in Isocrates' *Antidosis*: "It is not about small things, either the argument or the judgment in which we are engaged, rather it is about the greatest of things. For you are going to cast a vote not about me alone, but also about an occupation to which many of the youth are applying their mind" (*Antidosis* 173). Aristotle in the *Rhetoric* gives as an example of a

---

[3]　See Bobonich 2002, 97–105, for a useful discussion of the preludes and several more examples.

[4]　Cf. Burnyeat 1980, 81: "He [Aristotle] is not attempting the task so many moralists have undertaken of recommending virtue even to those who despise it: his lectures are not sermons, nor even protreptic argument, urging the wicked to mend their ways. ... Rather, he is giving a course in practical thinking to enable someone who already wants to be virtuous to understand better what he should do and why."

[5]　On the ancient Greek lists of Aristotle's writings, *Protrepticus* is the twelfth title on the list of Diogenes Laertius (v 22), and the fourteenth on the list appended to the Vita Hesychii. Both lists indicate that the work was one book in length. See Gigon 1987, 22, 26.

[6]　Alexander of Aphrodisias reports that "one should do philosophy... as he says in the *Protrepticus*" (*Commentary on Aristotle's Topics*, CIAG II:2, 149.9–15; cf. Olympiodorus, *Commentary on Alcibiades*, 144.15–17 Westerink). Later commentators add the detail that a group of boys is being exhorted: "as Aristotle says in his writing entitled *Protrepticus*, in which he exhorts the youth to do philosophy" (Elias, *Prolegomena to Philosophy*, CIAG XVIII:1, p. 3.19; cf. David, *Prolegomena*, CIAG XVIII:2, p. 9.2–12); these appear to be references to the scene of a dialogue.

rhetorical argument: "You are going to judge not about Isocrates but about an occupation, whether one must do philosophy" (ii 3.1399b9–11).

Aristotle's *Protrepticus* was apparently a dialogue that involved at least three speakers, one being "Isocrates," a character whom Aristotle has constructed out of Isocrates' writings, somewhat as Plato had earlier constructed for his own purposes characters such as "Protagoras" and "Gorgias" and composed speeches for them that were more or less based on what was known about their teachings from their writings.[7] This "Isocrates" defends a rhetorical and political conception of philosophical education, one that is highly critical of the Academy's preoccupation with abstruse theoretical speculation in subjects like astronomy and geometry.

Another character in Aristotle's *Protrepticus* seems to have been "Heraclides," based on the Academic philosopher Heraclides of Pontus, a contemporary of Aristotle. Heraclides had intellectual inclinations opposite to those of Isocrates: he was interested in the mathematical, astronomical, and cosmological speculations of the Pythagoreans, and even in their more mysterious and secretive traditions. Aristotle appears to have played these characters off one another, but also offered a grand synthesis of their practical and theoretical enthusiasms in the voice of a character called "Aristotle." He reaches the inclusive conclusion that, whatever one's ultimate commitments, whether to pleasure or virtue or knowledge, "one should do philosophy."

How different is this conclusion of the *Protrepticus* from that of the *Nicomachean Ethics*? The argument in *NE* x as a whole is essentially an expansion of the structure of argument that was the culmination of the *Protrepticus*: whether your goal is pleasure or political and social prominence or intellectual activity, in all three cases you should do philosophy. After the rhetorically charged conclusion of x 8, Aristotle adds a transition section (ch. 9), to exhort students to the topic of his next lecture course, on politics and legislation; this does not seem to mirror the ending of *Protrepticus*,[8] and yet it shows him returning to the attack against Isocrates and reworking material from his earlier *Protrepticus*. The whole of *NE* x, then, is most clearly viewed through protreptic

---

[7] Plato never portrayed Isocrates as a character, but he does mention him at *Phaedrus* 278e. Aristotle shows intimate knowledge of Isocrates' published works and frequently refers to them in the *Rhetoric*. For more on the rivalry between Plato and Isocrates (and Aristotle), see Nightingale 2004. On ramifications in later polemics, see Blank 2007.

[8] Nor does any such "transition-to-legislative science" section seem to be part of the *Eudemian Ethics* course, though the concluding part of those lectures, corresponding to *NE* x, is missing; one of the most recognizable differences between the *Eudemian* and the *Nicomachean* is that the ethics is part of politics in the *NE* but not in the *EE* (see Hutchinson 1995, 202 and n5).

lenses, with protreptic themes and *Protrepticus* passages in mind. This is also true to a lesser extent of the entire *NE*, so the plan for the rest of our treatment is to pass in review the protreptic aspects of all the discussions in the other *Nicomachean* books, before returning to a close study of *NE* x, by which time our better polished protreptic lenses ought to help us see its protreptic aspects in better focus.

When we look more widely at Aristotle's ethical writings, we find protreptic aspects of all the books of the *EE* and *NE* but unevenly distributed. The richest lode of protreptic argumentation is in *NE* x, but we also find an important "protreptic to intelligence" in the discussion of intellectual virtues in *EE* v = *NE* vi,[9] and many framework and methodological passages near the start of both treatises are clearly recycled from Aristotle's *Protrepticus*, especially the device of the "three (or four) lives" and the "function" argument that structures Aristotle's analysis of the moral and intellectual virtues. On the other hand, there are scant protreptic elements in *EE* vi = *NE* vii, the book on weakness of will and pleasure, and only a few traces in *NE* viii–ix and *EE* vii, the books on friendship. As for Aristotle's discussions of the moral virtues in *EE* iii and *NE* iii 6–iv and justice in *EE* iv = *NE* v, to a certain limited extent he provides motivations for embracing the virtues, but his main focus is to provide motivations and guidelines for thinking philosophically about the virtues, in showing us by example how we can make progress in developing our own independent and responsible conceptions of private and public morality.

I. FRAMEWORK AND METHODOLOGICAL PASSAGES (NE I)

The rhetorical strategy of the *Protrepticus* is to convince the young that on any reasonable view of what a successful life would be, they should do philosophy. But, as we read in *NE* x 9, only youths of a certain advanced moral character can be expected to benefit from doing moral philosophy. Aristotle had made the same point in greater detail in *NE* i 3, a connected chapter in which Aristotle specifies the task that he sets himself and the students that he is addressing.

He begins by asserting that "our account will be adequate if its clarity is in line with the subject matter, because the same degree of precision is not to be sought in all discussions, any more than in works of craftsmanship" (1094b11–14). No further detail is offered here, but a parallel

---

[9] In this study we have chosen to limit our scrutiny to the books that are definitely part of Aristotle's *Nicomachean Ethics*, not relying on evidence from the common books that might be native to the *Eudemian Ethics* instead.

passage from the *Protrepticus* provides concrete examples and evidently seems to be an earlier formulation of the same idea.

Just as we put up with plausible reasoning from an orator, so it is necessary to demand from the mathematician demonstrations that are necessary. And one must not seek the same necessity everywhere, nor, similarly, the same precision in everything, but just as we divide the technical fields by their underlying materials, not seeking precision similarly in gold and tin and bronze, nor in cork and box and lotus, in the same way this is so in the theoretical sciences.[10]

It is at most a different formulation of this *Protrepticus* idea when Aristotle comments that "accepting from a mathematician claims that are mere probabilities seems rather like demanding demonstrations from an orator" (*NE* i 3.1094b25–27, modified). Regarding the degree of precision appropriate to ethical arguments, Aristotle recommends that "We should be content ... to demonstrate the truth sketchily and in outline" (b19–21). "The details of our claims, then, should be looked at in the same way, since it is a mark of an educated person to look in each area for only that degree of precision that the nature of the subject permits" (b22–25).

When the demonstrations are sketchy outlines, this calls for judgment on the part of the audience, and this excludes those who are immature (1094b27–1095a8).

Each person judges well what he knows, and is a good judge of this. So, in any subject, the person educated in it is a good judge of that subject, and the person educated in all subjects is a good judge without qualification. That is why a boy is not fitted to hear lectures on political science, since our discussions begin from and concern the actions of life, and of these he has no experience. Again, because of his tendency to follow his feelings, his studies will be useless and to no purpose, since the end of the study is not knowledge but action. It makes no difference whether he is young in years or juvenile in character, since the deficiency is not related to age, but occurs because of his living and engaging in each of his pursuits according to his feelings.

The two reasons that young boys *in general* are, unfortunately, not good hearers of political discourses are because they are led by their feelings instead of reason, and because they have not been experienced in practical affairs or generally educated. Not being generally educated, they are

---

[10] Aristotle's *Protrepticus*, apud Iamblichus, *De Communi Mathematica Scientia* (*DCMS*), chapter XXVII, page 86, lines 4–12 (Festa). We now attribute to Aristotle's *Protrepticus* several excerpts contained in chapters XXII–XXVII of Iamblichus's *DCMS*, building on and extending the work of previous scholars. In the *DCMS*, Iamblichus does not explicitly name his sources, using the same techniques as in his *Protrepticus*. In what follows, references to passages of Aristotle cited in the *DCMS* will be given in condensed form, such as *DCMS* XXVII 86.4–12.

incapable of judging the wide-ranging demonstrations that relate to political science.

Interestingly, the problem for these boys is not that the demonstrations are too complex or detailed – in fact, as Aristotle argues in the *Protrepticus*, youths are *better* suited than the old to judge difficult mathematical proofs. Rather it is because undereducated youths do not generally have the experience that allows them to judge arguments *less* precise than mathematical proofs, those based not on necessities but on probabilities, which involve uncertainty and particulars. Aristotle does not make the point about boys being good judges of mathematical proofs in the *Nicomachean Ethics*, but he had highlighted this issue (in a passage in the *Protrepticus* or his work *On the Pythagoreans*) in the context of describing how Pythagoras instructed older and younger students differently: "To the ones who were senior and without leisure because they were involved in political affairs ... he talked in a simple style ... but with those who were younger and [more] capable of working and learning he conversed using demonstrations and mathematics" (*DCMS* XXV 77.7–17). We can thus get a fairly clear idea of the kind of students to whom Aristotle addressed his *Protrepticus* and his *Eudemian* and *Nicomachean Ethics*, and for what purpose he addressed them: they were relatively older students, not young boys, with some life experience already; and Aristotle's purpose was to motivate them to acquire some of his philosophical tools of analysis, so that they would be able to develop their own practical philosophies based on his outline account, not to motivate them to become morally better.

Both the *Nicomachean Ethics* and the *Eudemian Ethics*, like the *Protrepticus*, are structured around the traditional theme of the alternative "ways of life" that Aristotle asserts everyone would agree are viable candidates for the good life. In *Nicomachean Ethics* i 5, Aristotle mentions three especially prominent ways of life, the life of pleasure, of politics, and the life of contemplation. The theme of the three (or four) ways of life has its roots in the earliest Greek philosophy, even earlier, in lyric poetry (see Joly 1956). An especially influential and vivid contribution to this theme was made by Aristotle's contemporary Heraclides of Pontus, when he compared the ways of life to the different kinds of people attending the Olympic Games: some come to make money selling concessions (like those who devote their lives to making money), and others to compete and gain victory (like those who devote their lives to noble and virtuous activity), but some come just to observe the spectacle (like the philosophers). Aristotle himself made use of the analogy of the Olympic Games in his discussion of the three-lives argument in the *Protrepticus*.[11]

---

[11] Aristotle's *Protrepticus*, apud Iamblichus, *Protr.* chapter IX, page 53.19 to 54.5 (Pistelli). In what follows, references to passages of Aristotle's *Protrepticus* cited in Iamblichus's

Almost as an afterthought, Aristotle in the *Nicomachean Ethics* dismisses out of hand the "life of making money," a way of life rejected as a candidate for the good life because, according to Aristotle, it is not undertaken voluntarily but only under compulsion. The life of contemplation, he announces, will be examined "in what follows," after briefly mentioning some complexities in connection with the ways of life devoted to pleasure and politics or noble causes. He does not get into the details here but announces his intention to move on "because these issues have been sufficiently dealt with in our circulated (*enkukliois*) discussions" (i 5.1096a3–4, modified), probably referring to his earlier *Protrepticus*.

When we examine the evidence of this lost work, we find that the order of its discussion of "ways of life" seems to have been this: wealth (the subject of an Oxyrhynchus papyrus fragment of the lost work),[12] practical intelligence (preserved in Iamblichus, *DCMS* XXVI and *Protr.* VI), virtue (*Protr.* VI–IX), political intelligence (*Protr.* X), and then pleasure (*Protr.* XI). The overall protreptic conclusion of the work is that, whatever way of life one prefers, one should do philosophy. "Thus we take the position that success is either intelligence and a certain wisdom, or virtue, or great enjoyment, or all [of] these. Thus if it is intelligence, it is evident that living successfully would belong to the philosopher alone; and if it is virtue of the soul or enjoyment, even so it will belong to them either alone or most of all" (*Protr.* XII 59.26–60.4).

The same general topics are discussed in roughly the same order in the *Nicomachean Ethics*, though with much greater detail in most cases. Thus, virtue is discussed in books 2–5, practical and political intelligence in book 6, and pleasure in book 10 (after the discussion of friendship in books 8–9, which seems to have no parallel in *Protrepticus*). The conclusion of the *NE* is more exclusive than that of the *Protrepticus*, insofar as Aristotle argues that the life of contemplation is demonstrably the best one available to a human being, and that the other ways of life, even the one devoted to cultivating moral virtues like justice, cannot compare to the godlike activity of contemplation and philosophy. In the *Protrepticus*, Aristotle pursues a more inclusive strategy; attempting to co-opt the other ways of life by showing that philosophy can make the best of any of them, by making one more virtuous, more politically wise and effective at leadership, or even more capable of enjoying higher and more continual pleasures.

> *Protrepticus* will be given in condensed form, viz. *Protr.* IX 53.19–54.5. For Heraclides' use of the three-lives theme and the Olympic Games analogy, see Cicero, *Tusculan Disputations* v 3.8–9. There is also a little-noticed parallel to the Cicero passage in Iamblichus, *On the Pythagorean Life* XII 31.20–32.10.
>
> 12 P.Oxy 666 (overlapping with Stobaeus, *Eclogues* iii 3.25, where it is ascribed to Aristotle).

The strategy employed by Aristotle to resolve the question as to which way of life is the best in *Nicomachean Ethics* i 7 is the so-called *ergon* argument, in which Aristotle attempts to deduce an overall *function* for a human being. This argument, which continues to inspire much commentary, appears in two other well-known versions in the corpus of Aristotle: in *EE* ii 1 and *Politics* vii 1. But its original version was probably the one in his *Protrepticus*, cited by Iamblichus in chapter IX of his work of the same name. Whereas in the *NE* we have the examples of "a flute-player, a sculptor, or any practitioner of a skill" (1097b25–26), in the *Protrepticus* the examples are medicine, architecture, writing, farming, and shipbuilding (IX 49.17–50.12 and 50.26–27); in the *Nicomachean Ethics* "the eye, the hand, the foot and <the> other parts of the body" (1097b30–31) have replaced the detailed example of the eyelid in the *Protrepticus* (50.19–26, an account that adds details not found in the biological works). The examples of the life of "the horse, the ox," and of every animal (1098a2–3) correspond to a comment in the *Protrepticus* about the *ergon* of "the animals, either absolutely all of them or the best and most honorable of them" (50.27–51.2), but in both works it seems that Aristotle is focused on humans, commenting on nonhuman animals primarily to offer insight into human nature.

After Aristotle has established his preliminary outline definition that the human good turns out to be "activity of the soul in accordance with virtue, and if there are several virtues, in accordance with the best and most complete" one (1098a16–18), his next task would be to delve into the topic of virtues, find out how many there are, and evaluate them. This is exactly what he does do, starting at i 13, and the beginning of that discussion contains both protreptic elements and a reference to *Protrepticus* (see Section II). But before he begins that discussion of virtue, he takes the opportunity to offer a variety of considerations that corroborate his analysis and his outline definition (i 8–12). And before he even gets to the corroborations, he offers a rather significant "protreptic to further philosophy," which will repay brief study.

Without apologizing for the fact, Aristotle says that what he has achieved so far is only a preliminary outline; this is a necessary way of proceeding, and enables others to "carry on and complete the details," and "in this task time will bring much to light or else offer useful assistance. This is how skills have come to advance, because anyone can fill in the gaps. But we must bear in mind what we said above [sc. i 3], and not look for the same precision in everything, but in each case whatever is in line with the subject-matter and the degree appropriate to the inquiry" (1098a22–29). We are reminded of the earlier comments on precision that themselves came from *Protrepticus*; we are invited to take part in the collective advance of knowledge, a process that was discussed in the dialogue, and we are encouraged to take responsibility for filling in and developing these outlines over the course of future time. This protreptic to further philosophy is further specified a few lines later, as a protreptic to dialectic: "Some first principles we see by induction, some by perception, some by a kind of habituation, and others in other ways. We must try to investigate each type in the way appropriate to its nature, and take pains to define each of them well, because they are very important in what follows" (i 7.1098b3–7). There is no mistaking that this is a protreptic passage, and it attempts to motivate us to philosophy.

The section containing corroborations occupies *NE* i 8–12, and it begins with *Protrepticus* material being re-presented, up to near the end of i 8, though there seems little reason to believe that anything in i 9–12 had any antecedent discussion in the dialogue. The inscription at Delos, which Aristotle interprets here (8.1099a24–31), made a prominent appearance in the *Eudemian Ethics*, right at the beginning of that work. It is unclear to us at this point whether it was borrowed for the *EE* from the *Protrepticus*, as is the case with much in *EE* i. However that may be, it seems clear to us that everything in chapter 8 up to this point has been recycled from his earlier dialogue. This set of corroborations, which is the next passage after the preceding protreptic to further philosophy, starts with a division of goods into external activities of the body and of the soul; this is also to be found in *Protrepticus*, and the same is true of the next two basic statements, that the end resides in activities, and that the successful man lives and acts well (1098b12–22).

These three basic points are followed by three more substantial discussions, of which the first is that Aristotle's analysis is properly inclusive, in that it satisfies all the desiderata that fit the concept of success: some think it is "virtue, some intelligence (*phronēsis*), others a certain wisdom (*sophian tina*), while others think it is a combination of these or one of these along with more or less pleasure" (1098b22–25, modified). The most exact parallel to this way of putting the point occurs near the end of *Protrepticus*: "We take the position that success is either intelligence and a certain wisdom (*sophian tina*), or virtue, or great enjoyment, or all these" (XII 59.26–60.1). The equivocation between "intelligence and a certain wisdom" is a highly significant indication of the very formulation used in the *Protrepticus*; it is a formulation that Aristotle used in that dialogue in order to co-opt the Isocratean leitmotif "intelligence" for his own purposes.[13]

---

[13] Jaeger's developmental hypothesis rested in part on a mistaken view of the prominence of *phronēsis* in the formulations of Aristotle's ideals. Jaeger took the view (1932 [1948] Engl. trans., 2nd ed., 81–85, 239–240) that this was evidence of an earlier "Platonic" stage of Aristotle's thought, which was superseded by one in which *sophia* was the highest cognitive virtue. On the contrary, our reading of the *Protrepticus* fragments indicates that Aristotle is careful there, in the passages where he agrees with Isocrates

Two more substantial discussions complete the set of corroborations, of which the next one starts this way: "Our account of success is in harmony with those who say that success is virtue or some particular virtue ... it makes a great difference whether we conceive of the chief good as consisting in possession or in use" (1098b30–33, modified). This discussion is highly consistent with the *Protrepticus* evidence, and the next detail about the Olympic Games reminds us that there was a prominent use of the Olympic Games metaphor already in the dialogue;[14] and yet there is no solid parallel, although its position among other protreptic arguments suggests recycling.

The final corroboration is probably but not certainly recycled from Aristotle's earlier dialogue. "It is also the case that the life of these [sc. virtuous] people is pleasurable in itself. For experiencing pleasure is an aspect of the soul, and each person finds pleasure in that of which he is said to be fond." For example, horse fanciers enjoy horses, and "a lover of justice finds it [sc. pleasure] in the sphere of justice" (1099a7–11). We do not find an exact parallel to this in *Protrepticus*, only a related thought that "everybody chooses most of all what conforms to their own proper dispositions (a just man choosing to live justly, a man with bravery to live bravely, likewise a self-controlled man to live with self-control)" (VI 39.20–23).

II. THE MORAL VIRTUES (NE I 13 AND II–IV)

After Aristotle establishes and corroborates the main lines of his inquiry into successful human living, he begins an analysis, from *Nicomachean Ethics* i 13 to iii 5, of the concept of virtue and the common features of virtues and of virtuous actions. This specialized analysis takes him beyond the territory he needed to enter in the more general work *Protrepticus*, and overall we see very few signs of common ground between the two works. One of two main exceptions is at iii 4, where Aristotle is suggesting a way out of relativist disputes; he argues that "the good person stands out a long way by seeing the truth in each case, being a sort of standard and measure of what is noble and pleasant" (1113a32–33; cf. ix 4.1166a12–13). It follows that the wise person is the standard of the good, a position that Aristotle had earlier established by asking and

about the importance of *phronēsis*, to keep open the possibility that *sophia* is a higher virtue than *phronēsis*, the position that is explicitly argued in *EE* v = *NE* vi. An insightful recent discussion of these issues with full bibliography is available in Bobonich 2006, 16–23.

[14] "Just as we travel to Olympia for the sake of the spectacle itself, even if nothing more is going to accrue from it ... and as there are many other spectacles we would choose instead of lots of money, so the observation of the universe, too, is to be honored above all things that are thought to be useful" (*Protr.* IX 53.19–26).

answering a rhetorical question posed in the *Protrepticus*: "Again, what standard do we have, what criterion of good things <,> that is more precise than the intelligent man? For all that this man will choose, if the choice is based on his knowledge, are good things, and their contraries are bad" (*Protr.* VI 39.16–20).[15]

The other passage where we notice protreptic aspects in this discussion is at its very outset, at *NE* i 13, where Aristotle tries to motivate the future political leaders in his audience to acquire at least some knowledge of human psychology, since they should be concerned to promote virtue. "The true politician is thought to have taken special pains over this, since he wants to make citizens good and obedient to the laws" (1102a8–9), as in Crete and Sparta. "If this inquiry is a part of political science, pursuing it will clearly accord with our original purpose" (1102a12–13). Since human virtue is in the soul, "the politician clearly must have some understanding of the sphere of the soul. ... The politician, then, must consider the soul, and consider it with a view to understanding virtue, just to the extent that is required by the inquiry, because attaining a higher degree of precision is perhaps too much trouble for his current purpose" (1102a18–26). As we will see repeatedly, Aristotle reserves his protreptic discourse mainly for the purpose of motivating those in his audience to an in-depth study of a certain scientific topic that is relevant to their ambitions to become successful politicians.

It is a telling detail that the very next words of Aristotle are a reference back to his *Protrepticus*: "Some aspects of the soul have been dealt with competently in our popular works as well, and we should make use of these.[16] It is said, for example, that one element of the soul has reason,

---

[15] A similar application of this *Protrepticus* idea, that the intelligent and good man provides the authoritative answer to the question what the true pleasures are, is found in the discussion of pleasure at x 5.1176a10–22.

[16] Bernays speculated that Aristotle's references to *exoterikoi logoi* were references to the popular works of Aristotle, including his dialogues (1863, 91); the passage in *NE* i 13 he took to be a reference to the *Eudemus* (63–69). Diels (1883, 477) later cast doubt on this by arguing that the *exoterikoi logoi* were most likely "discourses external to Aristotle's school" (1883, 492), although he also concluded that the term *exoterikoi logoi* has no univocal sense. Jaeger reviewed the previous scholarship (1932 [1948], Eng. trans., 246–258) and found good reasons to support Bernays's position: "there is no longer anything against Bernays' conjecture that the exoteric discussions were definite writings, and in fact the literary works of Aristotle" (249). Although Jaeger did not comment specifically on the reference to *exoterikoi logoi* at *NE* i 13, he argued that all of the references to *exoterikoi logoi* in the *EE* refer to the *Protrepticus*, and implies that the *NE* reference should be interpreted in line with this. Rees 1957, 117–118, reviewed the issue and argued specifically that *NE* i 13.1102a26–28 is a reference to *Protrepticus* VII 41.27–42.1. Moraux 1960, 115–118, argues that the reference is likely to the *Protrepticus*, though not exclusively (it could at the same time be a reference to the *Eudemus* and *On Justice*, dialogues in which a similar view about the soul was probably discussed). Gauthier and Jolif 1970,

while another lacks it" (1102a26–28). Although this could have been stated in other popular works as well, it definitely was stated in *Protrepticus*: "Part of us is soul, part body; and the former rules, the latter is ruled; the former uses the latter, which supports it as a tool. Further, it is always with reference to the ruler and the user that the use of that which is ruled and the tool is coordinated. And of the soul one part is reason, which by nature rules and judges our affairs; the other part is a follower and is naturally ruled" (VII 41.15–22). On this basis, Aristotle builds his fundamental division between intellectual and moral virtues, and in his ensuing discussion of the moral virtues makes virtually no further use of *Protrepticus* material or protreptic speech.

Aristotle's discussions of the moral virtues from *NE* iii 6–iv would be a natural place to look for protreptic strategies, such as those employed by Prodicus in his famous "Choice of Heracles" story, which was adapted for Socrates to use against Aristippus by Xenophon at *Memorabilia* ii 1; but no, we simply do not find anything like the exhortations to courage and temperance that persuaded Heracles to choose his life of heroic virtue. On the contrary, Aristotle assumes that his audience is already committed to these virtues and does not need further motivation. What he does instead is provide an analytical framework for understanding the virtue in question: "Let us now resume consideration of the virtues, and one by one say what each is, what sorts of things it is concerned with, and in what way; at the same time it will be clear how many there are" (iii 5.1115a4–5).

How many virtues are there, in fact? The canon of the four cardinal virtues – wisdom, justice, temperate self-control, and courage – which had been solidly established in the Academy by Plato, was evidently a tidy simplification of a wider and more complex field of traits or virtues. Aristotle shows himself aware of the centrality of these four virtues and also unwilling to reduce the other virtues to these four. He sometimes argues by eliminations based on these four virtues as if they were the core of the conceptual field (x 7.1177a31–32), and sometimes he refers to these four plus liberality (x 9.1178a28–33); but there are actually quite a few more moral virtues. We see the same tendency in the *Protrepticus*, which bases one of its key arguments on the Platonic quartet of main virtues: "Since everybody chooses most of all what conforms to their own proper dispositions (a just man choosing to live justly, a man with bravery to live bravely, likewise a self-controlled man to live with self-control), it is clear that the intelligent man will choose most of all to be intelligent" (VI 39.20–24). Yet since other virtues also make a prominent appearance there, such as liberality (IX 53.7) and *kalokagathia*

II.i, 93–94, while accepting the attractiveness of that line of argument, conclude that the reference is most likely to the *Protrepticus* (see also their commentary on vi 4.1140a2–3).

(see subsequent discussion), Aristotle's consistent view would seem to be that the four main virtues are central but not cardinal.

We see no signs of protreptic motivation in the direction of either self-control or courage. What we do see, however, is *apotreptic* language about lack of self-control, when Aristotle says in iii 11 that those who stuff themselves are "utterly slavish" and that some of what the intemperate man enjoys is "detestable" (1118b25 and b20–21), after having said in iii 10 that his status is "brutish" (1118b3–4), since the bodily sense he particularly enjoys, the sense of touch, is essentially part of our animal, not our human, nature. To repel the minds of his listeners and readers from this vice, Aristotle deliberately focuses on the most disreputable pleasures. This *apotreptic* to vice is the only one in all of Aristotle's discussion of the virtues and vices (there is not even any *apotreptic* to the extravagant wasting of money in the discussion of liberality, which would have been an easy rhetorical exercise), and there are no protreptics to any of the cardinal virtues.

When it comes to the noncardinal virtues, which Aristotle discusses in *NE* iv, we see the same pattern generally confirmed: Aristotle's main focus is to encourage his students to acquire his well-tested analytical tools so that their understanding of the virtue can be more intelligent and productive, not so that their commitment to the virtue can be deeper and better motivated.

If there is any protreptic orientation to any virtue in Aristotle's ethics, any virtue that he particularly attempts to motivate, it would be the virtue of self-respect, or rather to its large-scale counterpart *megalopsuchia*, being "great souled." In his *NE* discussion of *megalopsuchia*, Aristotle subsumes *kalokagathia* within *megalopsuchia*, saying "Greatness of soul, then, seems to be a sort of crown of the virtues, because it makes them greater and does not occur in isolation from them. This is why it is hard to be truly great souled, since it is not possible without a noble and good character (*kalokagathia*)" (iv 3.1124a1–4). This term is very prominent in Xenophon's Socratic works; and Isocrates criticized Socratic teachers for pretending to be able to foster *kalokagathia* (*Against the Sophists* 6; *Helen* 8). The term *kalokagathia* features in a prominent way three times in the Isocratean speech of advice *To Demonicus* (6, 13, 51), to whom the character "Aristotle" replies in his *Protrepticus*, accusing "Isocrates" of having no idea what *kalokagathia* actually amounts to (IX 52.28–53.2). Aristotle thought he knew better than Isocrates what *kalokagathia* is, and devoted discussions to it, which are preserved in the Aristotelian *Magna Moralia* ii 9 and in the fragment (vii 3) that was placed by ancient editors at the end of the *EE*. At the start of *NE* x 9, as we have already seen, arguments of moral philosophy are incapable of exhorting the many (*hoi polloi*) to *kalokagathia* (1179b10), which is a politician's virtue par excellence.[17] In his focus on the "crown of the virtues," we see Aristotle occupying the same dialectical and rhetorical territory as he had occupied in his earlier *Protrepticus*.

III. FRIENDSHIP (NE VIII–IX)

We find Aristotle's extended discussion of friendship in *NE* viii–ix to be virtually free of protreptic aspects. There is a brief self-contained pro-treptic to friendship at the opening of that discussion, describing it as not only most necessary but also noble, highly beneficial, totally natural, and as being a type of social glue that is the truest form of justice. Having assembled this rather conventional protreptic to friendship (to which there is no parallel in his *Protrepticus*, as far as we can judge from the limited evidence), Aristotle briskly proceeds to an enumeration of the debates on the topic.

The one clear case in which Aristotle redeploys a line of thought that he had deployed in the *Protrepticus* for protreptic purposes is his resolution (ix 9.1170a13–b19) of one of the current debates about friendship, about whether a successful man would need to have friends; Aristotle argues that he would, employing a line of thought he had already deployed in his *Protrepticus*. Only by means of a friend is the good human being able to perceive goodness in action and perceive that "life itself is good and pleasant" (1170a19–20). And "people define animal life by the capacity for perception, and human life by the capacity for perception or thought, so living in the real sense seems to be perceiving or thinking" (1170a16–19). In the *Protrepticus* he had argued that "living is distinguished from not living by sensing, and living is defined by its presence and power, and if this is removed life is not worth living, as though life itself were removed along with sensation" (VII 44.9–13). This is a key line of argument that also structures Aristotle's discussion of pleasure, to which we now turn.

IV. PLEASURE (NE X 1–6)

As he reminds us at the beginning of *NE* x 6, Aristotle aims to take up the discussion about which way of life was the best, from the point he had left it in i 7. There were three candidates left in the running: the lives focused on pleasure, virtue, and science, and of these three candidate lifestyles,

---

[17] It counts as an argument in favor of elections to high office, rather than selection by lot, that as a result "prominent people will practice *kalokagathia*" ([Aristotle], *Rhetoric to Alexander* 1424a17–18).

the one focused on pleasant amusements is briefly and decisively rejected by three arguments in x 6. The second of these three arguments for rejection is based on a line of thought probably already articulated in *Protrepticus*: the activity of the better person (or better part of a person) is more virtuous, hence superior, hence more conducive to happiness, together with a premise that may not have been in that earlier dialogue, that a life of virtue consists of serious things, not amusements (1177a1–6). It is hard to say whether any elements of the first and third arguments may have also been derived from *Protrepticus*.

Aristotle's highly analytical treatment of pleasure itself in x 1–5 divides neatly into three parts: a protreptic to the objective study of pleasure and pain (x 1), a review of the contemporary range of arguments on the value of pleasure and pain (x 2–3), and an outline of Aristotle's preferred analysis and evaluation of pleasures (x 4–5). Some of the Academic arguments that all pleasure is bad (x 3.1173a13–b31) may have featured in *Protrepticus*,[18] and at least one of the arguments for Aristotle's view that not all pleasures are good was recycled from that dialogue. In both works we are asked to conduct a thought experiment, to assess the value of a life richly provided with pleasure but entirely deprived of intelligence; in the *NE* version, "no one would choose to live the whole of his life with the mind of a child, even if he were to take the utmost pleasure in what pleases children" (*NE* x 3.1174a1–3). This can be seen as being a brief version of this *Protrepticus* argument, put into the mouth of the character "Heraclides": nobody would choose a life deprived of intelligence, "not even if they were going to live enjoying the wildest pleasures, in the way that some people carry on who are out of their right minds" (VIII 45.9–11); "even if someone had everything, but has some affliction affecting his intelligence, that way of life would not be valuable, for none of his other goods would be of any benefit. Hence everybody, insofar as they have some perception of being intelligent and are capable of having a taste of this thing, think other things to be nothing; and this is the reason why not a single one of us would put up with being either drunk or infantile up to the end of our life" (VIII 45.18–25).

Given the great swarm of arguments hostile to pleasure in Plato's Academy, Aristotle found it necessary to protest against a certain unscientific mixture of ideological and factual communication. In *NE* x 1

---

[18]   The first two arguments are capped by an extremely brief third argument, a counterfactual claim that pleasure cannot be the only good thing, because cognitive and moral activities would still be worth choosing even if pleasure did not accompany them (1174a4–8). This is entirely consistent with Aristotle's reasoning in *Protrepticus*, indeed it is a logical consequence of it, but it is unlikely that any version of it occurred there, as Aristotle would be undermining his main motivational message there if he were to take time to explore the idea that cognition might not be pleasant.

Aristotle urged his audience to enter into the scientific study of pleasure and pain, the correct application of which is crucial to education and to quality of life. It is right to dissuade the young from certain pleasures; but to say that all pleasures are bad is either an honest misunderstanding or else a deliberately ideological communication on the part of those who think it "is better with a view to how we live to represent pleasure as a bad thing, even if it is not" (1172a29–33), persuading us away from temptation toward moderation. Aristotle rejects this approach, saying that arguments lose their credibility when they conflict with the evident experience of those who hear them, and the arguments that have real power to motivate and exhort people to virtue are the true ones that are in harmony with the facts.

The most significant exploitation of *Protrepticus* arguments for the purpose of Aristotle's discussion of pleasure comes in his positive account in chapters 4–5, where he tries to show how the cognitive pleasures are good and have their proper place in the good life. It seems that Aristotle is here adapting a line of thought he had previously articulated in his *Protrepticus*. The best way to display this adaptation is to translate the last three paragraphs of chapter XI (58.1–59.13) of the *Protrepticus* of Iamblichus, a passage quoted literally by Iamblichus from near the end of Aristotle's *Protrepticus*.

Someone who uses a thing correctly is using it more, for the natural objective and mode of use belong to someone who uses a thing in a beautiful and precise way. Now the only function of the soul, too, or else the greatest one of all, is thinking and reasoning. Therefore it is now simple and easy for anyone to reach the conclusion that he who thinks correctly is more alive, and he who most attains truth lives most, and this is the one who is intelligent and observing according to the most precise knowledge; and it is then and to those that living perfectly, surely, should be attributed, to those who are using their intelligence, that is, to the intelligent. *But if what it is to live is the same, for all animals at least, it is clear that an intelligent person would surely exist most and in the most authoritative sense, and most of all at that time when he is being active and happens to be observing the most knowable of existing things.*[19]

[...]

Furthermore, there is a difference between enjoying oneself while drinking and enjoying drinking; for nothing prevents someone who is not thirsty, or has not been brought the drink he enjoys, from enjoying himself while drinking, not

[19]   This sentence at XI 58.10–14 is, we think, a "fast-forward paraphrase" by Iamblichus of (part of) the content of the intervening part of the dialogue, as it seems to condense into one sentence several ideas that would have been elaborated more carefully by Aristotle, to judge from the careful elaboration in the citations that can be firmly established. For other examples, see Hutchinson and Johnson 2005, 227–229.

because he is drinking but because he happens at the same time to be seeing or being seen as he sits there. Thus we will say that this fellow enjoys himself, and enjoys himself while drinking, but not because he is drinking, and not because he enjoys drinking. Thus[,] in the same way we will also say that walking and sitting and learning and every process is pleasant or painful, not insofar as we happen to feel pain or pleasure in their presence, but insofar as we all feel pain or pleasure by their presence. So, similarly, we will also say that a life is pleasant if its presence is pleasant to those who have it, and that not all to whom it happens that they enjoy themselves while living are living pleasantly, only those to whom living itself is pleasant and who enjoy the pleasure that comes from life.

Thus we attribute living more to the one who is awake rather than to the one who is asleep, and to the one who is being intelligent more than to the one who is unintelligent; and we say the pleasure that comes from life is the one that comes from the uses of the soul, for this is being truly alive. Further, even if there are many uses of the soul, still the most authoritative one of all, certainly, is the use of intelligence to the highest degree. Further, it is clear that the pleasure that arises from being intelligent and observant must be the pleasure that comes from living, either alone or most of all. Therefore living pleasantly and feeling true enjoyment belong only to philosophers, or to them most of all.

This subtle and masterful analysis deserves far more study than it has received; there have been two outstanding studies, but these have investigated Aristotle's analysis with respect to some aspects of his logic, not ethics (Owen 1960; de Strycker 1968). Without doing justice to it here, we do need to note for our purposes that the first protreptic conclusion is linked intimately to the second conclusion, that the pleasure of intellectual activity is the only true enjoyment (or at least is the most authentic one), by means of the premises that intellectual activity is the authentic expression of human vitality, and that the pleasure that intrinsically accompanies authentic human vitality is ipso facto the intrinsically authentic pleasure.

Aristotle finds his analysis of pleasure in terms of cognitive activity to be confirmed by a number of corroborating considerations: the weakening of pleasure over time is explained by the weakening of the corresponding cognitive activity (1175a5–10); this analysis explains why it is hard to say whether we aim at life for the sake of pleasure or vice versa (1175a10–21), and it explains why the pleasure involved in an activity strengthens it (1175a29–b1), and why the pleasure involved in a competing second activity weakens the pleasure of the first (1175b1–13). The third of these corroborating considerations claims that those who enjoy intellectual activities do them better, with more precision (1175a29–b1); this has a good chance, based on circumstantial evidence, of being derived from the *Protrepticus*, though there is no direct parallel to be found in the surviving evidence of that lost dialogue.

V. POLITICIAN VS. PHILOSOPHER (NE X 7–8)

We are now closing in on our objective, the protreptic payload in *NE* x 7–8. Before entering into a discussion of political theory, Aristotle takes the trouble to remind the ambitious men in his audience that there is a yet higher form of human life than the one to which his next lectures are going to prepare them; the philosopher leads a higher life than the politician. The lecture audience of the *NE* was focused on political science,[20] which is why Aristotle finds it opportune to stress this point here, in the hopes that some of these young men would turn to philosophy instead, and that the others who became politicians would support or at least tolerate philosophy. In order to argue this point and stimulate motivation in these would-be politicians to do philosophy, Aristotle reached back to his *Protrepticus* and recycled some of its contents for this new purpose.

In fact, the entire content of *NE* x 7–8 seems to have been recycled from Aristotle's earlier work, except for one line of argument. The line of argument that did *not* occur in *Protrepticus* is the one that opens x 8, clarifying that the political life can be successful "in a secondary way" because it is the virtue of the compound human person, not the "virtue of intellect" that is "separate"; this political life is secondary both because it is the virtue of a lower entity and because it has a lower degree of self-sufficiency (1178a9–b7). This line of argument did not occur there, not because Aristotle had a different view then, but because he had a different purpose: to recommend philosophy in an inclusive way to everybody who might read his book, by arguing that philosophy makes a valid contribution in practical life, both personally and politically. It was not part of his rhetorical strategy in *Protrepticus* to stress the inferiority of the political life to that of the philosopher, as this would alienate some of his readers; but here in the *NE* he is addressing students who have chosen to study philosophy in the Lyceum, perhaps because they were convinced by arguments in *Protrepticus* that it would be valuable for their political careers. They could benefit from a narrow protreptic to pure philosophy.

The preceding line of argument, that the politician leads a secondarily excellent life, is also absent from the parallel passages in *Politics* vii 1–2, which are themselves largely recycled from the *Protrepticus*. Among those who accept Aristotle's framework and agree that the life of virtue is the best life, a question is still to be settled: "whether the practical and political life is or is not more desirable than one which is wholly independent of external goods, for example a life devoted to theory, which some say is the only one for a philosopher. For these are pretty much the two human lives that appear to have been decided upon by those who

---

[20] On this difference between *EE* and *NE*, see note 8.

have been ambitious in the pursuit of excellence, both in past ages and in our own. Which is true is a question of no small moment" (vii 2.1324a26–33). Aristotle visibly refrains from pushing the point in this *Politics* context that the political life is secondary; but he does do this in the *Nicomachean Ethics*, where we find the strongest surviving expression, in all his surviving works, of this valuation of philosophy over politics.

If we now remove from consideration the preceding line of argument and examine the rest of Aristotle's reasoning in *NE* x 7–8, we can tell that most or all of it is derived from arguments of the *Protrepticus*.[21] In some cases, Aristotle refers to his earlier work, and we possess citations of the parts of the dialogue to which he refers; in other cases we see obvious parallels between surviving parts of the two works, though there is no reference on Aristotle's part; in still other cases, there is no surviving part of the *Protrepticus* with which to make the comparison, but its location within this large borrowing and the terms in which it is expressed support the conclusion that some such argument was present in the lost work. It would take far too long to enter into all the details here, and this is a task for future research for other scholars. We limit ourselves to comments on several key passages where there are surviving parallels to study, starting with those passages where Aristotle explicitly says that he is recycling.

The first key passage is the one opening the discussion, in which Aristotle says that he has "already said" that the activity of the best element in us (whether it is intellect or something else, and whether it is divine or just the most divine element in us) will be contemplation, and that this agrees with "our earlier discussion" (sc. *NE* i). Where had Aristotle "already said" this? He had already said this in the following passage of his *Protrepticus* (VII 41.22–42.4):

Everything is well disposed when it is in accordance with its own proper (*oikeios*) virtue, for to have obtained this is good. Moreover, it's when a thing's most authoritative and most estimable parts have their virtue that it is well disposed; therefore the natural virtue of that which is better is naturally better. And that which is by nature more of a ruler and more commanding is better, as a human is than the other animals; thus soul is better than body (for it is more authoritative), as is the part of the soul which has reason and thought, for this kind of thing is what prescribes and proscribes and says how we ought or ought not to act. Whatever, then, is the virtue of this part is necessarily the virtue most valuable of all in the strict sense, both for everything in general and for us; in fact, I think one might actually take the position that we are this part, either alone or especially.

---

[21]   The one comment in x 8 that probably has no parallel in *Protrepticus* is 1179a17–22, where Aristotle appeals to the touchstone of experience in the facts of life as a more reliable indicator than the beliefs of the wise; the older, more experienced members of Aristotle's audience are encouraged by him to rely more on their own insights than on impressive stories about wise men published in some book, even his own.

As René Gauthier said, presenting a longer version of this passage in his commentary, "it is in fact impossible not to recognize" this fragment of the *Protrepticus* as the subject of Aristotle's reference.[22]

And it is important to see that Aristotle's reference to his earlier *Protrepticus* not only refers to the general theses just now articulated but also indicates the provenance of all the remarks that follow. The very next claim in *NE* x 7, that contemplative knowledge is the highest activity (1177a19–21), is probably also a restatement of a *Protrepticus* thesis,[23] and the last claim in the chapter contains another explicit reference[24] to the earlier work: "What we said previously (*proteron*) will apply here as well" (1178a4–5, modified), namely that since it is proper (*oikeios*) for humans to act with intelligent guidance, and what is proper to any living thing is what is best and pleasantest for it,[25] then this is the best and most pleasant activity for us. Since part of this thought was expressed at the beginning of the previously quoted *Protrepticus* passage, and since the other part (on intelligent activity being very pleasant) was expressed in the passages quoted by Iamblichus in chapter XI of his *Protrepticus*, this would seem to be either a new combination of ideas that had been separate in *Protrepticus* or else a recycling of a (now lost) passage that combined these two ideas together in the dialogue.

Since the beginning and the end of this chapter are new exploitations of familiar *Protrepticus* material, it stands to reason that everything else

[22] As far as we know, the first identification of *Protrepticus* as the work referred to by "already said" was made by Gauthier in Gauthier and Jolif 1970, ii 876–878, on the basis of a suggestion made to him by R. P. Dubois. This identification, says Gauthier, "resolves a question debated for a long time," and we agree that it should have resolved this question. S. Broadie, in Broadie and Rowe 2002 ad loc., not seeing a convincing parallel in the *NE*, suggests "the reference might be to the *Protrepticus*."

[23] At the end of a sequence of linked arguments, Aristotle contends that, "according to the most authoritative judgment, intelligence is supreme among goods" (VI 39.26–40.1); this is an answer tailored to respond to the concerns of Isocrates, and in his own voice Aristotle is likely to have expressed the matter in his own preferred terms, that intelligent activity is the highest activity.

[24] It seems that we are the first to recognize this as a reference to the *Protrepticus*. Commentators before Gauthier and Jolif were not much aware of the significance of the *Protrepticus*, nor has there actually been any attempt to settle this reference, not even in the most recent commentary by Broadie 2002. Perhaps the connection had been noticed by Gauthier, who was the first to bring *Protrepticus* passages into evidence in an *NE* commentary (see note 22); but unfortunately his commentary at this point (1970, ii 883) is damaged by what appears to be the accidental loss of all comments on the text from 1177b1–1178a31.

[25] For another example of a general thesis being expressed in terms of "propriety" in the *Protrepticus*, it is instructive to compare an earlier passage (*DCMS* XXIII 70.18–21): "what is similar in nature to each thing is what is proper (*oikeios*) to it, and to the man of free status (*eleutheros*) the dominant end of the activity in accordance with his proper way of life has its reference to himself and to nothing else external."

in the chapter would also be recycled, absent contrary considerations. Therefore we can expect more insight into Aristotle's much-debated remarks by studying them in the light of their argumentative background in the *Protrepticus*, rather than in earlier books of the *NE* (or the common books). This detailed work for x 7 has yet hardly been undertaken,[26] let alone finished, since the requisite comparison[27] would require a fuller presentation of the available *Protrepticus* evidence than has yet been published. Here we can only start.

Consider Aristotle's remark on self-sufficiency (*autarkeia*), "The self-sufficiency that is spoken of will belong to the activity of contemplation most of all" (1177a27–28), because the practice of wisdom needs fewer resources and can even be done alone. Where was this self-sufficiency spoken about? This cannot be a reference to the *NE* i 7 discussion, in which self-sufficiency and ultimate finality were the two marks of being the chief good, because Aristotle explicitly says that he has a different meaning in mind. "We are applying the term 'self-sufficient' not to a person on his own, living a solitary life … we take what is self-sufficient to be that which on its own makes life worthy of choice and lacking in nothing" for a person, whether or not they are socially self-sufficient (1097b8–15). The answer is again that we need to look to the *Protrepticus* to find the right parallels; in that work, Aristotle argues that it scores in favor of philosophy that doing it does not need special resources, unlike other activities. "Its practice differs greatly from all others: philosophers need neither tools nor special places for their job; rather, wherever in the inhabited world the mind runs, it latches onto the truth equally everywhere as if it were present everywhere" (VI 40.24–41.2). This makes a point about philosophers being free of need for technical and local resources, whereas the *NE* x 7 point was about philosophers being free of need for social network resources; these are two allied points in one larger argument, part or all of which was argued in the *Protrepticus*.

Issues of self-sufficiency and free status occur in several other contexts in the fragments of this lost dialogue; in fact, it seems to have been one of the central themes of the dialogue, if we are right in seeing *Rhetoric* i 5, on protreptic discourse, as deriving from and providing evidence for

---

[26] A good start was made by Romeyer-Dherbey 1975. He compared the *Protrepticus* to an island rising from the sea, "still covered in seaweed" (414), but at the time that he did his work interest in *Protrepticus* was plunging, after Düring's 1961 attempted reconstruction, and the island sank back into obscurity for decades.

[27] Hermeneutical dividends can also be expected from the effort of studying the various parts of the evidence of the *Protrepticus* and comparing them to certain other parts of Aristotle's corpus where he visibly recycled themes from that earlier dialogue, especially these: *EE* i and *EE* v (= *NE* vi), *Politics* vii 1–2, *Rhetoric* i 5–7, *Metaphysics* i 1–3, ii 1–3, and *De Part. An.* i 1 and 5.

Aristotle's own *Protrepticus*. It is highly believable that in that earlier dialogue there was a similarly broad list of candidates for the meaning of *eudaimonia* (success): "Let's define success as good conduct combined with excellence, or as self-sufficiency in life, or as the most pleasant life that can be enjoyed securely, or as good condition of property and body, together with the ability to preserve and make use of them. That success is one or more of these things, pretty well everyone agrees" (1360b14–18). For an example of how this focus on self-sufficiency comes into play in the rhetoric of the dialogue, consider this: Aristotle, at a rhetorically charged part of one of his speeches, argues (against Isocrates) that the philosopher is the only producer who lives by looking at nature and the divine; like "some good helmsman who hitches the first principles of his life onto things that are eternal and steadfast, he moors his ship and lives life on his own terms" (X 55.27–56.2).[28]

Much more could be said about the fascinating details of *NE* x 7 with the help of *Protrepticus* perspectives, but let us notice just one more thing, that this is where the gods make their entrance into the argument. The whole protreptic climaxes at the end of x 8 with the claim that the wise person's activity is the one most closely related to that of the gods, and he must be the one dearest to the gods; but this movement of thought is first begun here. The philosopher will lead a life that is "superior to one that is simply human, because someone lives thus, not in so far as he is a human being, but in so far as there is some divine element within him." So "we ought not to listen to those who exhort (*protrepein*) us, because we are human, to think of human things, or because we are mortal, think of mortal things. We ought rather to take on immortality as much as possible, and to do all that we can to live in accordance with the highest element within us; for even if its bulk is small, in its power and value it far exceeds everything" (7.1177b26–1178a2). This last comment is so rhetorically perfect, and so unusual in its literary texture in the context of the *NE* that it should be considered not a revised exploitation of the earlier work but a literal citation from it.

We do not have this exact passage in any other *Protrepticus* evidence, but we do find rhetorically polished expressions of allied thoughts. "When perception and intellect are removed, a human becomes pretty much like a plant; when intellect alone is removed, he turns into a wild animal; when the irrational element is removed but he retains the intellect, he bears a resemblance to a god" (V 35.14–18). "Animals too have some small glimmers of reason and intelligence, but have absolutely no allotment of the intellectual wisdom of contemplation; this is present among the gods alone,

---

[28] And see note 23; see also an interesting passage in favor of using dialectical analysis of principles in empirical science: "nature itself is able to guide us by itself to the principles, but is not self-sufficient in judging each thing without taking up a different understanding" (*DCMS* XXVII 87.9–11).

just as a human actually falls short of many animals in the precision and power of its perceptions and impulses" (V 36.9–13). Both the preceding remarks seem to have been made by the speaker "Aristotle," and a rhetorically supercharged version of this idea was also put into the mouth of the "Heraclides" (VIII 48.9–21):

So nothing divine or happy belongs to humans apart from just that one thing worth taking seriously, as much intellect and intelligence as is in us, for, of what's ours, this alone seems to be immortal, and this alone divine. And by being able to share in such a capacity, our way of life, although naturally miserable and difficult, is yet so gracefully managed that, in comparison with the other animals, a human seems to be a god. For "intellect is the god in us"– whether it was Hermotimus or Anaxagoras who said so – and "the mortal phase has a portion of some god." One ought, therefore, either to do philosophy or say goodbye to life and depart hence, since all of the other things anyway seem to be a lot of nonsense and foolishness.

This seems to have been at the climax of Heraclides' speech, in just the same way that divine considerations come in at the climax of Aristotle's protreptic speech in *NE* x.

The gods are the topic still when Aristotle resumes his *Protrepticus* recycling at x 8.1178b7 (after putting it down for a different purpose at 1178a9–b7, as noted earlier). Aristotle asks rhetorical questions to force us to see that the only virtuous activity the gods would engage in is intellectual activity, because it makes no sense to conceive the gods having human moral virtues such as justice, courage, and generosity; nor could we imagine the gods to be inactive or asleep like Endymion. This passage triggered the interest of Jakob Bernays (1863, 116–122), who originally postulated that it was a recycling from the lost *Protrepticus*, on the basis of a report by Augustine about Cicero's lost dialogue *Hortensius*, which was known to have been modeled on Aristotle's dialogue. "Cicero in his dialogue *Hortensius* argues thus: 'If we, when we depart this life, were permitted to live for ever, as the fables say, in the Isles of the Blest ... we should not need courage, where no task or danger was prescribed to us, nor justice, where there was no property of another for us to seek. ... We should be blessed by the possession of one thing only – science and knowledge of nature, for which alone the life of the gods is to be praised'" (*De Trinitate* 14.9.12 = *Protrepticus* fr. 12 Ross, Ross trans.). This was the beginning of the modern resurrection of the *Protrepticus*, because it inspired Ingram Bywater to search for traces of this lost work, which he found in 1869 in the *Protrepticus* of Iamblichus.[29] He confirmed the speculation of Bernays by discovering

---

[29]   Bywater 1869, 55, gave due credit to Bernays: "The exceeding blessedness of a speculative life was maintained by a line of argument not unlike that in the Tenth Book of the *Ethics*. Guided by such hints as these Prof. Bernays of Bonn has reconstructed the

this rhetorical passage (IX 53.2–10): "One might see that what we say is all the more true if someone conveyed us in thought, as it were, to the Isles of the Blest, for in that place neither use nor benefit would be produced in anything else, and only thinking and observation remains, which we say even now is an independent way of life. If what we say is true, would not any of us be rightly ashamed if when the right was granted us to settle in the Isles of the Blest, we were by our own fault unable to do so?"

As the protreptic ramps up to its climax, we find mention of famous sages of the past, such as Solon and Anaxagoras (*NE* 1179a9–17), of whom the former may have been held up as an example of wisdom in *Protrepticus*, and the latter certainly was; not only does "Heraclides" invoke Anaxagoras in the previously quoted speech, but "Aristotle" also invokes his wisdom in the speech that follows (X 51.11–15). It is not quite clear whether this mention is derived from the earlier dialogue, but when we consider the absolute climax of the protreptic, all signs point to that conclusion: "If the gods feel any concern for human affairs, as they seem to, it would be reasonable for them to find enjoyment in what is best and most closely related to them – namely intellect – and to reward those who like and honour this most, on the assumption that these people care for what is loved by the gods, and act rightly and nobly. And it is quite clear that all of these qualities belong most of all to the wise person; he, therefore, is dearest to the gods" (1179a24–30).

VI. PROTREPTIC TO SCIENTIFIC LEGISLATION (NE X 9)

After the rhetorical high point that ends *NE* x 8, one gets the impression that the end of the work has been reached, and nothing is left to do but applaud. This may have been the way the *Eudemian Ethics* ended, but indications in *NE* i show that the *NE* was part of a two-part course in ethics *and* politics, unlike the *EE*, for which reason Aristotle takes this opportunity to effect a transition to the new subject. And this transition both takes the form of a protreptic and harks back to his *Protrepticus*.

Virtually the first comment in *NE* x 9 is the one with which we started this investigation, in which Aristotle proceeds from the finding that philosophical arguments have protreptic effects on only some people, not most (1179b7–10). The approach that is effective for all is training and education under good laws, so if we wish to put these philosophical ideas into practice, we must understand what makes good legislation

Aristotelian Dialogue ... with the critical tact and poetical insight into the mind of antiquity by virtue of which he stands so completely alone among living scholars."

good; and this is true not only for aspiring politicians but also for those who only need to learn how to govern their own households.

Having motivated his audience to study this subject in general, Aristotle proceeds, in what are virtually his last comments, to distinguish his particular approach from that of "those of the sophists" who "advertise (*epaggellomenoi*) that they teach politics, but appear very far from actually doing so "being completely ignorant about what kind of thing it is and what its sphere of concern is. Otherwise, they would not have classed it with rhetoric or even as inferior to it" (1181a12–15, modified); this is a comment that is aimed squarely at Isocrates, who had declared that imitating and adapting existing laws were easy and sufficient procedures (*Antidosis* 81–84). In attacking Isocrates here, Aristotle revisits his criticism of Isocrates in his *Protrepticus*, where Aristotle recommends direct and scientific study of the realities of social and political life, not the imitative procedures recommended by Isocrates (*Protr.* X).[30] This is ultimately the study to which Aristotle is primarily exhorting his *NE* students, in all its complexity and difficulty, not to the moral virtues.

WORKS CITED

Barnes, J. ed. 1995. *The Cambridge Companion to Aristotle*. Cambridge: Cambridge University Press.

Bernays, J. 1863. *Die Dialoge des Aristoteles in ihrem Verhältniss zu seinen übrigen Werken*. Berlin: Wilhelm Hertz.

Blank, D. 2007. "Aristotle's 'Academic Course on Rhetoric' and the End of Philodemus, On Rhetoric VIII." *Cronache Ercolanesi* 37: 5–48.

Bobonich, C. 2002. *Plato's Utopia Recast: His Later Ethics and Politics*. Oxford: Oxford University Press.

2006. "Aristotle's Ethical Treatises." 12–36 in Kraut ed. 2006.

Broadie, S., and C. Rowe. 2002. *Aristotle's Nicomachean Ethics: Translation, Introduction, and Commentary*. Oxford: Oxford University Press.

Burnyeat, M. 1980. "Aristotle on Learning to Be Good." 69–92 in Rorty ed. 1980.

Bywater, I. 1869. "On a Lost Dialogue of Aristotle." *Journal of Philology* 2: 55–69.

de Strycker, É. 1968. "Prédicats univoques et prédicats analogiques dans le *Protreptique* d'Aristote." *Revue Philosophique de Louvain* 66: 597–618.

Diels, H. 1883. "Über die exoterischen Reden des Aristoteles." *Sitzungsberichte der Berliner Akademie der Wissenschaften* 19: 447–494.

Düring, I. 1961. *Aristotle's Protrepticus: An Attempt at Reconstruction*. Studia Graeca et Latina Gothoburgensia XII. Göteborg: Acta Universitatis Gothoburgensis.

Düring, I., and G. E. L. Owen eds. 1960. *Aristotle and Plato in the Mid-Fourth Century*. Göteborg: Elanders Boktryckeri Aktiebolag.

---

[30] Another indication that Aristotle is revisiting the same territory is this: near the end of x 9 law is described as "discourse (*logos*) proceeding from a certain intelligence and insight" (1180a21–22, modified), a comment also found in his *Protrepticus*: "the law is a kind of intelligence, i.e. a discourse (*logos*) based on intelligence" (VI 39.15–16).

Gauthier, R. A., and J. Y. Jolif. 1970. *L'Éthique à Nicomaque*. 3 vols. Louvain and Paris: Publications Universitaires de Louvain.

Gigon, O. 1987. *Librorum deperditorum fragmenta* = vol. iii of *Aristotelis Opera*. Berlin: De Gruyter.

Hutchinson, D. S. 1995. "Ethics." 195–232 in Barnes ed. 1995.

Hutchinson, D. S., and M. R. Johnson. 2005. "Authenticating Aristotle's *Protrepticus*." *Oxford Studies in Ancient Philosophy* 29: 193–294.

Jaeger, W. 1923. *Aristotle*. R. Robinson trans. 1948. Oxford: Oxford University Press.

Joly, R. 1956. *Le Thème de genres de vie dans l'Antiquité Classique*. Brussels: Palais des Académies.

Kraut, R. ed. 2006. *Blackwell Guide to Aristotle's Nicomachean Ethics*. Malden, MA: Blackwell.

Moraux, P. 1960. "From the *Protrepticus* to the Dialogue *On Justice*." 113–132 in Düring and Owen eds. 1960.

Nightingale, A. 2004. *Spectacles of Truth in Classical Greek Philosophy*. Cambridge: Cambridge University Press.

Nuyens, F. 1948. *L'Évolution de la psychologie d'Aristote*. Louvain: Institut supérieur de philosophie.

Owen, G. E. L. 1960. "Logic and Metaphysics in Some Earlier Works of Aristotle." 163–190 in Düring and Owen eds. 1960.

Rees, D. 1957. "Bipartition of the Soul in the Early Academy." *Journal of Hellenic Studies* 77: 112–118.

Romeyer-Dherbey, G. 1975. "Vie bienheureuse et philosophie: les traces du *Protreptique* dans le Livre X de *l'Ethique de Nicomaque*." *Les Études Philosophiques* 4: 399–414.

Rorty, A. O. ed. 1980. *Essays on Aristotle's Ethics*. Berkeley: University of California Press.

19   The *Eudemian Ethics*
      and Its Controversial Relationship
      to the *Nicomachean Ethics*

In his 1900 edition of Aristotle's *Ethics*, John Burnet chose to print the parallel passages from the *Eudemian Ethics* below his text of the *Nicomachean*, claiming that in the *EE* we have "the most authoritative commentary on the" *NE*. He went on to urge that "Eudemos [*sic*] gives us the thought of Aristotle as he understood it, as faithfully as he can, though it is plain enough that he has added a good deal from other Aristotelian sources in order to bring out more clearly what he took to be the meaning, and even that he has here and there given a turn of his own to what Aristotle had said" (Burnet 1900, xiv). He was thus summing up the then-dominant view of the relationship between these two treatises as it had emerged in the last half of the nineteenth century while simultaneously showing his high regard for the lesser-known treatise. Burnet thought that the *EE* had been "too much neglected" heretofore, especially given the close proximity of the student and (later) colleague (Eudemus) to his teacher (Aristotle), a relationship so close that the student can be assumed to have attended all the *NE* lectures and talked over "all the difficulties with the master" (p. xv).

A mere decade later, this confident assignment of the authorship of the *EE* to Eudemus and its status as a later work than Aristotle's own *NE* was importantly challenged by Thomas Case in his pioneering article,[1] and he

I would like to thank Fred Miller, Anthony Kenny, and John Cooper for many conversations and some helpful correspondence over the years about the *EE-NE* connection but, especially, Ron Polansky for his critical suggestions on this contribution. None of these scholars, of course, should be held accountable for any mistakes I have made herein nor for the specifics of the overview offered here. The Taft Committee of the University of Cincinnati has generously supported academic leaves and related professional travel over the years during which I have tried to get a better fix on the controversial relationship between these two ethical works, for which I am grateful.

[1] Case 1910/1996. I shall refer to the reprinted version when quoting. The author later expressed some annoyance (in Case 1925) at having his own early, substantial work (comparatively) neglected by readers and its being overshadowed by Jaeger's more influential tome. Case does not suggest that Jaeger borrowed from him, and they seem to have arrived independently at very similar conclusions. Both, for example, reversed the tendency to treat the *EE* as due to Eudemus and not Aristotle and both saw it as an earlier,

was followed, of course, in this respect by Werner Jaeger thirteen years later, whose large-scale study dominated the field for years.[2] Case complained about the "Chorizontes" ("Dividers," "Separators") for offering up various unconvincing hypotheses about the relationship between the two works, especially the crucially important question about how to solve the "problem of the common books," which stems from the fact that the three central books – those treating, in order, justice, intellectual virtue, and moral weakness/pleasure – have always from ancient times been said to be identical in both works. Giving understandable pride of place to the *NE*,[3] almost all editors save time and space by printing the common books as books 5, 6, and 7 of that work, with a brief mention that they are also equivalent to books 4, 5, and 6 of the *EE*.

more Platonist work, with "a strong theological bias" derived from Plato (Case 1996, 32). Both treat the common books as *Nicomachean* doctrine in the main and, along with the undisputed books, a distinct philosophical development away from Platonism, containing new and improved thoughts on ethics and practical as opposed to purely theoretical reasoning. Jaeger devoted more attention to the early *Protrepticus* than Case did, but in essentials their view of Aristotle's ethical development are clearly compatible.

[2] Jaeger 1923/1948. The original German edition sparked a long-running series of attempts to chart the chronology of Aristotle's philosophical writings, which efforts seem of late to be "running on empty." See, e.g., Jonathan Barnes's dyspeptic reflections on "Jaegerianism" in Barnes 1990. Even more recently Barnes has observed that "we often lose interest in a question after a few years or months or minutes of research. *I used to worry about the comparative dating of Aristotle's works. I got nowhere, and neither did anyone else. I don't worry about the matter any more*" (Barnes 2007, 328, emphasis added). I recall many scholarly friends during the 1980s who would readily register their clear disinterest in "playing the dating game" that I was still fond of at the time. I am more sympathetic to their point of view now. On the other hand, I remember John Cooper's clear admonition to keep in mind that either the *EE* preceded the *NE*, or the other way round: "*tertium non datur*." This, of course, assumes that each was a more or less complete course of lectures aimed at similar audiences who attended at different times. This, as we shall see, is not necessarily the only way to assess the matter.

[3] It is noteworthy that study of Byzantine scholarship on the Aristotelian corpus reveals some twenty medieval manuscripts of the *NE* while only two survive for the *EE* from that period. The result is that the text of the *EE* is in much more need of repair and emendation than that of the *NE*, which too often forces editors to emend the text in an effort to make sense of what has come down to us. If one compares the *apparatus criticus* of each of these works in the editions of Franz Susemihl (assuming editorial practice of this one editor to be fairly consistent), we find that on average the "basement" on an *EE* page is usually two or three times as full as that of an *NE* sample and sometimes even more than that. Some of this disparity may be due to a reluctance seriously to perform the task of making sense of the manuscript readings before attempting to amend or athetize lines or phrases that present difficulties. Sir Anthony Kenny, however, in preparing his new translation (see next note) has found that in many cases sufficient sense can be made of the manuscript reading if one tries hard enough while, of course, there will still remain numerous places where we cannot be sure of what we should print.

A striking exception to this practice is the edition published in 1851 by Fritzsche, who printed the common books as belonging together with the so-called undisputed books, namely 1–3 and 7–8, and commented in detail (in Latin) on them all as forming one integrated whole, which he attributed, however, to Eudemus of Rhodes, a younger colleague of Aristotle.[4] Case, for his part, concluded that Aristotle wrote the *EE* and *Magna Moralia* "more or less together as rudimentary first drafts of the mature *Nicomachean Ethics*" (Case 1910/1996, 27); the "*truth*" about the *EE* "in general is that it was an earlier rudimentary sketch written by Aristotle, when he was *still struggling, without quite succeeding, to get over Plato's view that there is one philosophical knowledge of universal good*" (31, emphasis added). This very supposition, of course, appears to overlook the fact that the critique of Plato's Form of the Good in *EE* i 8 is every bit as harsh as that of *NE* i 6, perhaps even more so,[5] lacking as it does the formal, presumably sincere, apology for preferring truth over friendship, with which *NE* i 6 opens:

Such an inquiry turns out to be difficult going because those who introduced the Forms are friends. It will presumably be thought better, indeed one's duty, to do away with what is close to one's heart in order to preserve the truth, especially when one is a philosopher. For one might love both, but it is nevertheless a sacred duty to prefer the truth to one's friends. (1096a12–17, Crisp trans.)

Compare this *NE* passage[6] with the seemingly more dismissive remarks of *EE* i 8, following an introductory exposition of Plato's views:

---

[4] Fritzsche 1851. One factor inhibiting study of the *EE* has been the lack of editions or translations that include all eight books. Fortunately, there will soon be one in the World's Classics Series published by Oxford University Press, translated in its entirety by Anthony Kenny. A similar full-book version is forthcoming from Cambridge University Press as well. Their imminent publication augurs well for future study of the *EE*.

[5] For discussion of the very similar, yet intriguingly dissimilar, critiques of Plato's thoughts on the Form of the Good in both ethical treatises, see Flashar 1977, 1–16, especially the important summary of their differences on p. 11. The original German version of his paper, which featured more annotation, appeared in Flashar 1965. While one could make entirely too much of this tonal difference, when combined with the five key differences he finds between the two chapters, Flashar's remark that the *EE*'s critique shows "eine kuehle Reserve" (Flashar 1965, 233), "a cool reserve" that contrasts with the *NE*'s fervent expression of "a personal bond between himself and the advocates of the theory of Ideas" (1977, 11, trans. M. Schofield), seems salient. Later papers by Berti, Robinson, Verbeke, and Brunschwig, all to be found in the seminal proceedings of the 5th Symposium Aristotelicum (Moraux and Harlfinger 1971), are also well worth consulting on *EE* i 8.

[6] Ron Polansky reminds me that this preliminary apology for criticizing Plato, perhaps, is a reminder of *Republic* 595b9–c3, 607c6–7 (cf. *Phaedo* 91c1–7) and may well not bear the weight I am placing on it as any sort of marker of a closer connection to his teacher than that presupposed by the *EE*'s similar critique. I take the point but agree with Flashar that the fairly "formal apology" found in the *NE* suggests "an outside audience"

So the good-itself (*auto to agathon*) is the Form of the good, and, indeed, like the other Forms, the Form of the Good is separate from the things that share in it. . . . To speak in a summary fashion, let us say first that *the thesis that there is a Form of good or indeed of anything else is verbal and vacuous.* The matter has been studied in many places, both in the external discussions, and in the work *On Philosophy.* (1217b14–16, 19–23, Woods trans., emphasis added)

This *EE* passage suggests unmistakably a pronounced, almost harsh, distancing from Plato's views, a note not sounded in the *NE*; its tone seems out of tune with any assumption that the *EE* dates from Aristotle's *early discipleship* in the Academy and *eo ipso* exhibits Platonic loyalties. The *EE* refers us to earlier writings where Forms had been attacked quite generally on a variety of grounds while the *NE* seems content to raise difficulties peculiar to the Form of the Good and does not go out of its way to remind its readers that Aristotle has no truck at all with Platonic Forms. Neither Case nor Jaeger, it may be said, took sufficient account of the details of these particular parallel chapters, as Flashar (1965/1977) has shown.[7]

More generally, it can be said that too much is made by both writers, but especially by Jaeger, of psychological speculation about the young Aristotle's presumed, suppressed (almost Oedipal?) rivalry with his *Meister*, especially on metaphysical issues, an approach that seems in retrospect to be an anachronism projected back from turn of the century

for this work, whose members would be aware of Plato's Form of the Good and thus appreciative of the student's tribute to his teacher in spite of the ensuing disagreement. The more technical treatment in the *EE* of "number theory," presumably based on "discussions within the Academy" of Xenocrates' theory "in the first instance," appears to support the contention that the audience of the *EE* was more "esoteric" than "exoteric" (Flashar 1977, 13, 11). This impression is controversial, to be sure, but the differences between the two treatises on this and other important matters need to be accounted for somehow and not necessarily on chronological grounds. In his own paper on the comparison of the critical arguments in *NE* i 6 and *EE* i 8, Allan 1964, 281, observes that the *EE* "is throughout more demonstrative and didactic in its tone, and assumes on the part of the hearers fuller knowledge both of the Academic background and of Aristotle's system. It borrows more freely than *N.E.* does from other treatises in the corpus." Along with Kenny I share Allan's general appraisal of the overall differences in style and argument between the two works but confess that others, with good reason, may not agree.

[7] For an accessible, even if somewhat dated, critique of Jaeger's main arguments in defense of his "Urethik" picture of the *EE*, which he sees as heavily dependent on Platonic theology, see Monan 1968. Fr. Monan's work was heavily influenced by D. J. Allan's pioneering investigations into the relationship between the *EE* and the *NE*, which were also influential in steering Kenny and his followers away from the "Case-Jaeger-Rowe" consensus, which can still be called (I think) the "received view." Irwin and Cooper, for example, and many other scholars continue to defend it, stoutly, against Kenny's animadversions.

Berlin onto mid-fourth-century Athens.[8] That is, Jaeger sought to show that earlier identification with Platonism in the first book of the *Metaphysics*, as it has come down to us, by speaking often in the first-person plural about Forms and numbers as a faithful member of the Academy, must reflect an earlier stage of his thought, since duplication of this material in later books is expressed in the third person, suggesting a later distancing.[9] An important restatement or refurbishment of the "Case-Jaeger" approach is Rowe 1971b.[10] Rowe's monograph updates their arguments, consolidating the view that the *EE* was an early work of Aristotle's, destined to be replaced by the "later and better" *NE*, including, of course, the common books, which *may* (except for the book on *phronēsis* in Rowe's opinion) have had earlier versions in their *EE* context. In particular, Rowe concluded that the treatment of pleasure in the third common book was clearly improved upon in *NE* x 1–5 and that the two discussions of pleasure are, in fact, not compatible. The occurrence of two (seemingly) distinct discussions of the same general topic has long proved a stumbling block for commentators.[11] Hence, a decision to award these central books to the *EE*, whether it is regarded as earlier or later, has often been defended, although the cost to the original integrity of the familiar ten-book *NE* would be presumably high, on almost any reckoning. Thus, most commentators who favor a later date for the *NE* but suspect the "common books" began as *EE* ones, postulate a

---

[8] A very trenchant comment along clearly "Freudian" lines can be seen in Jonathan Lear's acid account of 1096a11–17: "It is precisely here that Aristotle launches an *explicit attack on his philosophical father. . . . One might wonder: Why the need to appeal to truth and piety to justify an aggressive attack?*" (Lear 2000, 169n21, emphasis added). While this remark seems over the top in suggesting quasi-Oedipal aggression in the *NE*, it is clear that Aristotle does not find the Form of the Good very helpful in ethical theory for reasons laid out quite dispassionately, most of which are also found in the *EE*.

[9] See Code 1996 for a recent and balanced discussion of Jaeger's general theory as applied especially to Aristotle's alleged development in metaphysics.

[10] This work, a revised version of his 1969 Cambridge PhD thesis, opens with a brief but very insightful overview of the "history of the problem" since Schleiermacher's time. One of Rowe's chapters is also to be found in Moraux and Harlfinger 1971, 73–92.

[11] Our earliest surviving (partial) commentary on the ethics – that by Aspasius (c. 100–150 CE) – considered the later discussion of pleasure as a sign that the earlier one was not written by Aristotle for this complete work, but, perhaps, by another author. Aspasius writes that "he [Aristotle] speaks as though he had not yet discussed it." Barnes 1999, 20–21, remarks that "it is as certain as such things can be that the two accounts of pleasure, which we read in *EN* VII and *EN* X, were not designed by Aristotle to appear between the covers of the same book; it is certain, in other words that our *Nicomachean Ethics* is a hybrid." For an attempt to forestall such doubts about the two discussions of pleasure belonging to the same work, see Owen 1986, 334–346. For a rather thorough exposition of the problem posed by the two accounts of pleasure, more favorable to Kenny's hypotheses, see Gosling and Taylor 1982, 193–300. See also Verity Harte's contribution in this volume.

later revision of them to make them cohere with the more mature work, whether that insertion was due to Aristotle himself, his son Nicomachus, or even some later editor. (The problem presented by the very existence of the common or disputed middle books will be seen to be at the heart of Kenny's pioneering effort to overcome the Case-Jaeger-Rowe consensus, a scholarly "game-changer," to be sure.) This consensus, still the majority view among scholars, embodies what I will term henceforth "the received view." It sees the relationship between the two works as follows: the *EE* as an early, inferior, more Platonically influenced, set of lectures on ethics, superseded by the later and superior *NE*; the common books may well have been part of the earlier *EE* but even if so, they were later revised to fit in with the surrounding *Nicomachean* books in order to form the canonical ten-book whole familiar from late antiquity forward. The existence of two seemingly independent discussions of pleasure in *NE* vii and x is to be explained, on this view, perhaps by an incomplete attempt to integrate the earlier material into its newer context.

There can be little doubt that Anthony Kenny's work on the *EE* has been the strongest force in getting scholars to consider seriously its claim to be an important source in its own right for Aristotle's mature ethical theorizing. He challenged the "received view" directly by arguing that the arguments for the *EE*'s being an early, immature work were for the most part based on a failure properly to interpret the situation presented by the common books if they are automatically understood as belonging primarily to the ten-book *NE*. In so doing, Kenny (as he readily acknowledges at Kenny 1992, 113) may have given the impression in his first book that he thought the *EE* later and better than the *NE*, surely an impression with which many of his early readers, both critics and sympathizers, were left. An important retrospective statement about Kenny's earlier, insufficiently clear expression of his overall comparison of the two works follows:

What I did try to do in my book was to show that the arguments for the opposite view, that the *EE* is inferior and earlier, were wholly inadequate to support the almost universal conviction that they have carried. There is, I maintained, no evidence which will stand examination that the *NE* is later than the *EE*. . . . There is a big difference between saying 'There is no evidence that *p*' and flatly asserting 'Not-*p*'. There is also a difference between saying 'There is some evidence that not-*p*' and going on to conclude that not-*p*. The last section of my [1978] book was full of warnings against going on, without further ado, to draw such conclusions. *The explanation of the differences between the NE and the EE may well be other than chronological.* (Kenny 1992, 114, emphasis added)

Among the differences between the two treatises Kenny has highlighted the "inclusivism" of the *EE* as opposed to "intellectualism" (see my note 18 for this distinction) as well as its relatively greater sophistication on selected topics, most notably in the philosophy of mind and its treatment of the topic of voluntariness and responsibility. In Kenny 1979, he points to the discussion of "mixed actions" at *NE* iii 1110a1–b9, for example, seamen forced to jettison cargo during a dangerous storm, where such action is assimilated to the class of voluntary action on the grounds that, although they are not performed *haplōs* (simply, so described without qualification), they are such as any sane sailor would do in such circumstances. Kenny then compares *EE* ii 8 where this sort of case is dealt with more successfully insofar as it invites us to distinguish "between duress which is itself voluntary [you are blameworthy for having set sail in the face of ominous weather] and duress which is involuntary" [e.g., a sudden freak storm that no one had predicted]; he concludes that the "*EE* is more lenient than the *NE*" and thus more in line with what we ourselves might want to say about "mixed actions" (Kenny 1979, 47–48).

Now this sort of defense of the *EE* on philosophical grounds, even when combined with Kenny's careful sifting of the ancient evidence, sparse as it is, about the reception of the two treatises, and the preferences of their earliest readers, cannot be expected to carry the day with critics who react differently to these two sorts of evidence. This is why so much hangs on Kenny's treatment of the problem of the "common books" and his use of the computer to find a neutral tool for settling disputes over them. Even when the dust has settled, it must be said from the apparent standoff between Kenny and his critics about chronology that we should not be confident that one work is earlier or later than the other, one better or worse than the other. Whether the differences we do find suggest different audiences or, rather, different editorial choices made early on in the transmission of these works, or some combination of both factors, these are complicated questions that surely need sorting out in future work. It might be the case, for example, that Aristotle regularly gave two sets of lectures, one for would-be *politikoi* who are urged to stay in their seats for the *Politics* to follow at the very end of the *NE*, while the *EE* was, perhaps, geared for a somewhat more select or seasoned audience.[12] There are a number of possibilities still to be explored, and yet most will agree that the strong and renewed interest in the *EE* in its own

[12] If so, it has to be admitted that its opening with the literary quotation from the Delian inscription (1214a1–8) is somewhat unusual when contrasted with the more typical general or universalizing statement at *NE* 1094a1 ff., which is similar to the opening of other well-known treatises. Yet since the same inscription appears at *NE* 1099a24–28, it may well have been brought to the fore in the *EE* for special emphasis, as an early indication of the literary quality of its first six chapters, which sought to avoid hiatus, a stylistic goal of works meant to be read and not just heard, in imitation of Isocrates' practice. A careful study of these first six chapters can be found in Gigon 1971.

right initiated by Kenny's "game-changing" scholarship since 1978 is still in its early stages.

Before moving on to Kenny's main case for assigning the common books (CB) to the *EE* in more detail, however, it is well worth stressing that much good work employing the *EE* as setting the table for (assumed) further progress in the *NE* has been done in recent years. Cooper (1975) offers a good example of this positive deployment of the received view.[13] The main idea here was to use the *Eudemian* discussion of a topic as a presumably earlier one that might set a stage for later and fuller development of that very topic, especially if one can interpret the *NE* discussion as an advance on the *EE*. Using the *Poetics*, for example, as a possibly intermediate text, Freeland (1996, 345) sums up her own "triangulating" investigation as follows: "The *EN* presents a better, clearer definition of voluntariness and a more complex, textured account of the possibility of fortune impeding virtuous activity in its work toward a happy, flourishing life"; thus, she sides with "the majority view on the *general* greater maturity and sophistication of the *EN*." Hence, those who agree with her can use the *EE* to help shed light on Aristotle's ethical views while resisting most of Kenny's claims about the relative dating of the treatises and being more or less open to his arguments for the original home of the common books being the *EE* environs.

Well, stepping back from the "received view" for a moment, how should we characterize the relationship between these two treatises? The strong overlap between the two works, both in the general order of discussion and in shared doctrines, strikes almost any reader as salient and pervasive, while the *EE*, for the most part, is more concise in its treatments of many topics, especially the various virtues.[14] The virtue of "even (or good) temper," "mildness," "gentleness" (*praotes*), for example, merits sixty-six lines in Bekker's edition of *NE* iv 5 while *EE* iii 3 allows only twenty-one. The *NE*, of course, has two whole books devoted to friendship (1155a3–1172a15), while the corresponding one book of the *EE* runs from 1234a18 to 1246a25. Similar ratios between comparable stretches can be easily constructed, with the *NE* being relatively more expansive, chatty, and digressive than the *EE*, more accessible to a wider audience perhaps, fuller in discussion of various points and more generous with examples than its more austere sibling, on the whole. This may well be due to a difference in intended audience for the two (different?)

---

[13] Meyer 1993 (on the voluntary) is another example in this genre, as are comparative studies of particular virtues such as Young 1988 (on temperance), Mills 1980 (on courage), or Irwin 2003, replied to by Kenny himself in the same volume.

[14] See Miller 2003, 188 (table 10.1), for a handy summary of the contents and relative ordering of all three of the ethical treatises attributed to Aristotle.

lecture courses, if that is what they were. We will return to the question of their intended audiences later.

Still, in spite of the general pattern of *NE* discussions being more discursive than their *EE* counterparts, there are important exceptions to this typical pattern. The famous "function-argument" of *NE* i 7.1097b22–1098a20 – hereafter the NFA – is markedly shorter and sketchier, more preemptive,[15] perhaps, than that found at *EE* ii 1.1218b31–1219b25. The *NE*'s main arguments are put in the form of rhetorical questions and not deductive arguments,[16] while Woods (1992, 85) observes that the EFA (*Eudemian* Function Argument) is "clearly presented as a formal argument" and is "considerably more elaborate than the corresponding argument" of the NFA. It has multiple premises – twenty-six steps on Woods's reading – leading to a similar conclusion as that of the NFA while the EFA, by contrast, is clearly a deductive argument, assessable for both validity and soundness, perhaps. One of the best discussions of both arguments, Hutchinson 1986, finds the NFA to be "a cryptic and compressed version of a more elaborate and persuasive argument in the *EE*" (= EFA).[17] While this assessment is not shared by every scholar who has examined and compared the NFA to the EFA, it is worth noting that the EFA's conclusion, when compared to that of the NFA, not only varies in its "inclusivist" flavor,[18] not leaving much room for the "dominant-end"

[15] Crisp 2000, xiii, notes: "Of course, it is *too swift of him* to expect us to just accept that exercising rationality well is exercising it in accordance with the virtues" (emphasis added).

[16] "Well, do the carpenter and the tanner have characteristic activities and actions, and a human being none? Has nature left him without a characteristic activity to perform? Or, as there seems to be characteristic activities of the eye, the hand, the foot, and generally of each part of the body, should one assume that a human being has some characteristic activity over and above all these? What sort of thing might it be then?" (1097b28–34).

[17] Hutchinson 1986, 40. His third chapter (39–72) contains a probing account of both arguments. Hutchinson finds the EFA to be "an impressively sustained argument, valid throughout, with true or at least plausible premises. It is, furthermore, a unified argument" (*contra* Woods 1992, 45).

[18] While this is not readily clear in the EFA by itself, Cooper 1975, 99, notes that "as I argue at length below, Aristotle's own account of flourishing in the *Eudemian Ethics* clearly conforms to the inclusive, rather than to the dominant pattern": see also p. 119. By an "inclusivist" reading I mean one that interprets the final good sought throughout the *NE* as a complex, composite good consisting of all sorts of activities, including the practice of all the virtues, intellectual and moral, accompanied by sufficient, external goods such as family and friends, a life with appropriate pleasures in wholesome activities, and so on. As opposed to this sort of interpretation, which tries to take the whole arc of the *NE* into account, a "dominant-end" or "intellectualist" reading insists that x 6–8 singles out the activity of *theōria* or contemplation as the highest good for man, and thus happiness of the first rank while the life of virtue and social involvement

reading of the *NE*'s final account of *eudaimonia* – but also goes so far as to employ the technical terminology of *genos* and *horos* (in the sense of "definition") in characterizing its conclusion at 1219a39.[19] In this and in other respects the *EE* strikes many as somewhat more "scholastic" in its style, assuming more in the way of technical background in its audience.

This leads to a general question of the possibly different audiences for these two lecture courses, if that is what they were, one perhaps pitched at "graduate students," the other at "undergraduates," to use an obviously anachronistic and yet suggestive comparison to our own practices. The *Eudemian* employment of quasi-technical terminology is one of the main considerations that led D. J. Allan to posit what he termed the *EE*'s "quasi-mathematical method," most notably, perhaps, in connection with Allan's discussion of the EFA, which he finds employing various forms of *hupokeisthai*, a verb often translated by Woods with a rather colorless "assume" when it could easily bear the somewhat stronger signification of "hypothesize" in "the Euclidean way in which reference is made to the assumptions" or "hypotheses," which the *EE* "says are derived either from popular reasoning or from induction" (Allan 1961, 309). Allan, then, sees the *EE* as employing "a mathematical pattern of deduction ... without holding that the precision of mathematics can be reproduced in the ethical sphere" (307). In saying this, of course, Allan wishes to avoid running afoul of the familiar warning against expecting precision at *NE* i 3.1094b19ff., an admirable admonition that does not seem to show up as such in the *EE*.[20]

One crucial assumption that might enable us to sidestep some nasty, perhaps intractable, difficulties about the relative dating of our treatises is to approach them with the understanding that the audiences of the two works might be differently constituted. The *NE*, for its part, seems to be

provides at best a secondary kind of *eudaimonia*. For many decades now commentators have differed over which side to come down on when evaluating the argument of the *NE* as a whole, whereas most commentators see the *EE* as "inclusivist" throughout, with the possible exception of its last chapter. The issues are too complex and controversial to be dealt with here, but see Kenny 1992, 92ff., for a brief overview of the position I accept. A recent exchange between Cooper 2003 and Kenny 2003b also reflects their (to a degree) shared position that the *NE* privileges the intellectual virtue of contemplation in its last book, while the "*EE* regards *eudaimonia* as the exercise of all the virtues, not just of a single dominant virtue: it includes the exercise of the moral virtues, and of both the intellectual virtues, wisdom and understanding" (Kenny 2003b, 151).

[19] The verb for "defining" (*horizein*) occurs eight times in the *EE*, not even once in the *NE*.
[20] See Jost 1991, 32–36, for some brief speculation as to why the methodological warning about precision sounded so clearly in the *NE* is not as clearly heard in the *EE*. A quite comprehensive and very thorough discussion of Aristotle's thoughts about the degree of *akribeia* to be expected in his ethical theory can be found in Anagnostopoulos 1994.

directed at a (relatively) untutored group while it could be argued that the *EE* seeks to convince those with some background in other areas of philosophy. Miller (2003, 191), for one, finds the integrated "philosophy of human affairs"[21] (*NE* x 9.1181b15) quite generally to be a fit subject for a certain group of hearers: "Ethics and politics can be studied by educated persons who have not been trained in the more technical branches of philosophy"; such a conception of the subject leaves room for criticism that Aristotle's arguments are relatively weak insofar as they rest on "common sense or ordinary language." This sounds about right, which is why the *NE* lectures are pitched at young men with just this sort of educational level and with political ambitions, perhaps, even if they are warned rather early on that they will need much more experience really to understand what they are being told (1094b27–1095a3). This seeming swipe at the immaturity of some in the seats is quickly softened, perhaps, because "the deficiency is not related to age" and it "makes no difference whether he is young in years or juvenile in character" (a6–7). This paragraph ends with a statement that this "preamble" shall stand as to the nature of the audience (*akroatou*) and how the present inquiry is to be

---

[21]   Most modern scholars take this phrase – a *hapax legomenon* in the Corpus – to be Aristotle's way of signaling at the very end of the *NE* a tight connection to the *Politics* to follow, reminding his hearers of what he had been maintaining all along since the very first book, to wit, the essential unity of ethics and politics; this was highlighted in i 2.1094a27–28 by clearly invoking the most authoritative (*kuriōtatēs*) and architectonic of the practical disciplines, viz., *hē politikē*, as the immediate subject under investigation. Bodéüs 1993, somewhat surprisingly given his general argument, contends to the contrary that the "philosophy of human affairs" is not to be thought of as Aristotle's special way of referring to his own creation but, rather, to the completion of "*the enterprise of all those who have striven to give intellectual guidance to human development*" (77–81, esp. 81, where the italicized [by the author] description occurs). It is puzzling why Bodéüs is so intent on interpreting Aristotle here as merely "passing the torch" of political inquiry in an intellectual relay race (79). The dichotomy he offers between a young Platonist bent on reaffirming the master's doctrine in a gesture of solidarity *and* the mature empirical political scientist of Jaeger's imagination (78) is a false one. The note struck at the end of the *NE*, then, seems just the right one to link the ethical and political dimensions of the architectonic science promised way back in *NE* i. Many commentators have followed the lead of John Burnet, who stressed the unity of ethics and politics in his introduction to his edition and argued for a very tight connection between the *NE* and the *Politics*, while the connection between the *EE* and the *Politics* is much looser. Indeed, the latter seems to refer back to the former in many places, although cross references in our corpus should never be assumed to be original with Aristotle. Fred Miller, in conversation, has suggested to me that it was only after composing the *EE* and going on to write the *Politics* that Aristotle realized he should go back and rewrite the ethical *logoi* to bring them into line with the newly conceived architectonic science bridging what no longer seemed to him to be two disciplines. This unification proposal is a plausible addition to the "received view" and one that would need to be satisfactorily dealt with by those of us in the "Kenny camp."

conducted (a11–13).[22] Allan (1961, 305) notes that the *EE*, by contrast, "is not meant for the statesman, but is designed to assist the individual in such deliberation" as is clearly called for at *EE* i 2.1214b6–14:

> Taking note of these things, everyone who can live according to his own choice should adopt some goal for the fine life, whether it be honour or reputation or wealth or cultivation [*paideian*] – an aim that he will have in view in all his actions; for, not to have ordered one's life in relation to some end is a mark of extreme folly. But, above all, and before everything else, he should settle in his own mind – neither in a hurried nor in a dilatory manner – in which human thing living well consists, and what those things are without which it cannot belong to human beings. (Woods trans.)

This early passage seems to leave open the possibility that various members of the audience might well make different choices as to what goal to adopt and that these choices might well depend on individual proclivities, such things as temperament, perhaps, or talent even. Making such a case for the *EE* as a whole is a tall order and one that cannot be undertaken here. Still, recalling the consensus about the *EE*'s being inclusivist in its approach to *eudaimonia* (see note 18), as opposed to the intellectualist, "dominant-end" conception that many find at the end of the *NE*, it is not unreasonable to read the *EE* as more amenable to a qualified type of individualism than the *NE*, one that does not sharply privilege the theoretical life over the practical.

The crucial problem Kenny set himself in his first book on the *EE-NE* relationship was that presented by the presence of the common or disputed books. He attempted to "settle in a definitive manner the original context of the disputed books" (Kenny 1978, 4–5), most strikingly by a pioneering statistical study of machine-readable versions of the three separate sections of the Greek text,[23] that is, the seven uniquely *NE* books, namely, i–iv, viii–x, those to be found only in the *EE* (i–iii, vii–viii) as well as the middle books themselves, cheerfully admitting up front his status at that time "as a complete novice" in the still rather untrodden field of computer-assisted stylometrics (v). Since Attic Greek is rich in its stock of particles and connectives, small words that provide shading and considerable nuance to prose works, they provide an important, "topic-neutral" vocabulary, whose usage would not be as tightly tied to its subject matter as adjectives, nouns, verbs, and other

---

[22] It is worth pointing out that Bekker has everything from the beginning lines to this point in his edition as forming just the initial chapter, instead of the three individual chapters that modern editors break this material up into.

[23] At that time Kenny used Susemihl's 1884 edition of the *EE* alongside Bywater's 1894 OCT of the *NE*. I doubt that significant differences would emerge if the 1991 OCT of the *EE* co-edited by Walzer and Mingay were used instead, but future work might yet show some. Quotations in the text are drawn from the first of the "trilogy," viz. Kenny 1978.

content-full expressions would be. Examples familiar to readers with Greek would be *men, de, gar, ge, eti, hoion,* and the like. Kenny chose to study thirty-six of these and count their occurrences in the undisputed *NE*, the common books, and the remaining *EE* books, making pairwise comparisons of their relative frequencies. Dropping those five that occur most frequently, he produced two "scattergrams" comparing the thirty-one left over, with the CB frequency on the y-axis compared with the *NE* on one page (80) and again compared with the *EE* on the facing page (81), both on their respective x-axes. A straight diagonal line is drawn on each graph, which would represent a perfect match between the relative frequency of a particular particle or connective as we find it in the CB and the corresponding portions of the undisputed or unshared books. If the two texts being compared exhibited absolutely homogeneous usage, the crosses indicating actual times a given expression occurred would exactly coincide. When the actual numbers are plotted, however, and we compare the "bombing patterns," so to speak, of the two charts, we see at once that the *NE*'s crosses are on average further away from the diagonal than are the *EE*'s. That is, the "bombing pattern" of the *EE* when compared to the CB is tighter than that of the *NE* when compared to the same text. Kenny reports his findings as follows: "If one wished to predict the frequency of a word in the [CB], information about its frequency in the *EE* would be much more useful than information about its frequency in *NE*" (82). Kenny went on in later chapters to compare increasingly more "topic-sensitive" words (e.g., expressions of doubt or tentativeness such as *isōs* 'perhaps' or technical terms such as logical words) in the three texts, finding similar patterns. Eight metaphysical terms, for example, cluster more closely around the diagonal for the CB in the graph with the *EE* (144) than that for the *NE* (143).

The general results of Kenny's pioneering stylometric work have been welcomed by many scholars, and even "diehard" fans of the *NE*-side of the controversy routinely accept that the linguistic environment provided by the *EE* as a whole has been shown to be more "ecologically friendly" to the common books than the *NE* surround. A good example of this tendency, although perhaps not "diehard" in light of important early work he did in checking Kenny's results that I will return to, is provided by Christopher Rowe. In his "Historical Introduction" to the fresh translation of the *NE* with commentary by Sarah Broadie, he agrees with the "received view" that "the balance of opinion, and of the evidence, makes the *Eudemian* earlier" but also adds straightway that "*there is also something like the same balance in favour of an Eudemian origin for the 'common books,' particularly in light of some stylistic evidence*" (Broadie and Rowe 2002, 4, emphasis added). Rowe surmises, then, that they were revised for the *NE*, with the result that we can safely take them to be doctrinally compatible with, even needed by, the *NE*. The strength, however, of Kenny's conclusions about the common books as well as the crucial lessons that we should continue to draw from the case made in 1978–1979 as updated in the first appendix to his 1992 book, have been not fully appreciated.[24] In particular, we should not quote a common book passage against the *EE* as though it comes from the other work, supposedly trumping the earlier one. Indeed, the shoe is on the other foot, so to speak, and this means that we should explore more carefully than heretofore how the common books and the undisputed *EE* tend to cohere. A good example of this is how the last chapter of the *EE* can be used to shed light on a question left hanging in *EE* v, namely, how to specify the *horos* or standard of right reasoning.[25] This vexing problem, explored in detail in Kenny 1992, has now received a fresh and insightful discussion in Broadie 2010.

One of Kenny's main (surely justified) complaints against the received view was that it often pitted a doctrine derived from the common books against an undisputed *Eudemian* book, as though foreign to the *EE*, and thus its adherents missed many opportunities to solve difficulties raised in a disputed book by turning to the *EE* for possible solutions. Of course, much of Kenny's case depends on a thorough appreciation of his original statistical arguments for the common books being significantly closer in style to the *EE* than the *NE*, and in his 1992 appendix Kenny tried to meet the harsh critiques of his most noteworthy early critics, for example, T. Irwin and J. Cooper. It is certainly worth observing that Rowe (1983, 74, with n108) decided to check by hand Kenny's results for three different books, namely, *NE* iv, *EE* iii, and *NE* v (= *EE* iv), the first of the common books (= *AE* A in Kenny's original designation). Rowe starts by detailing the varying uses

[24] In his insightful review of Kenny 1992, Pakaluk 1995 usefully divides up Kenny's statistical arguments into four distinct types, registering some understandable surprise that, in the extensive appendix devoted to updating and expanding his earlier results along with rebuttal of the relatively few critics who bothered to address the stylometry in any detail, Kenny now appears to put more stock in the account of context-sensitive vocabulary (e.g., the words of doubt and certainty) than in the comparison of particles and connectives, those "topic-neutral" words studied so closely in his first book (Pakaluk 1995, 242; cf. Jost 1983, 334ff., for an early account of this).

[25] See Kenny 1978, 181ff.; Broadie 1991, 433nn10 and 11, seems to follow Kenny's lead here: "If the book on practical wisdom belongs, *as now seems more probable, with the Eudemian rather than the Nicomachean Ethics, we should positively expect the two passages* [= 1249b3–4 and 1138b18 ff.] *to be making different, though no doubt related points*" (emphasis added). Von Fragstein 1974, 399, goes so far as to claim that the question about the *orthos logos* at CB 1138b34 is dealt with *only* (*nur*, his emphasis) in *EE* viii 3, citing Dirlmeier's admission that the *NE* fails to give an answer to "die *Frage* ... was ist der *horos*," leaving "*eine innerliche Tension*" at the end of *NE* x.

of twenty-four particles and connectives that can be distinguished when we bring in the subtleties of Greek grammar. He distinguishes ten different uses of *ei* in conditional sentences, those with different tenses of the verb, for example, as well as its use in indirect questions, making for an eleventh use. The problem of homography is that since the vast majority of the words Kenny counts have distinguishable uses, statistics gathered for tokens of a word type that fail to note which distinct use is involved face "the theoretical possibility of false signals" (Rowe 1983, 6). To study the actual usage and then sum up the results is Rowe's task, which he carries out as assiduously as one could hope for, although he limits himself to only three books, one from each set. He concluded his study with the admission that Kenny's stylometric study as a whole – in spite of some significant quibbles about details – had dealt "a near lethal blow" to his earlier "intuition" that the *NE* was an "organic whole" with the common books "being written of a piece with it"; in his last footnote to his series of installments Rowe stated: "To the degree that I am now inclined to accept Kenny's solution to the problem of AE [= CB], I must reject my own" (as developed in Rowe 1971b). He continues to agree with that portion of the received view that sees the *EE* as earlier than the *NE*, however, as do most scholars, perhaps, while granting that the common books are more at home in the *EE* on stylistic grounds and that they required considerable reworking when brought in to fill the yawning gap between *NE* iv and viii–x. Those of us who are inclined to go further with Kenny's conclusions about the *EE* as a whole when its doctrines are compared to those of the *NE* where they seem to differ can always withhold a firm judgment about chronology and attribute such variation as we find to differences in audience and their level of sophistication, as suggested earlier.

Much work is being done these days on such topics as the treatment of friendship in *EE* vii that does not see its contribution as earlier than, or inferior to, the parallel treatment of *NE* viii–ix. A very good example of this can be found in Osborne 2009. An even more ambitious attempt to show that *Eudemian* discussion of self-love and friendship represents an advance on the *Nicomachean* treatment can be found in Green 2010. The plain fact is that much work remains to be done on the *EE*, some of which will help shed light on the arguments of the *NE* and some just to clarify what important differences there might be, without prejudging the question one way or the other as to which is earlier or later, jejune or mature, philosophically inferior or superior to the other. We should celebrate, then, the richness afforded by our having at hand two lecture courses on ethics from the Lyceum and not be forced to choose one over the other as the only genuinely Aristotelian contribution.

WORKS CITED

Alberti, A., and R. Sharples eds. 1999. *Aspasius: The Earliest Extant Commentary on Aristotle's Ethics*. Berlin: De Gruyter.

Allan, D. J. 1961. "Quasi-mathematical Method in the *Eudemian Ethics*." 303–318 in S. Mansion ed. *Aristote et les problems de methode*. Louvain: Publications Universitaires.

   1964. "Aristotle's Criticism of Platonic Doctrine concerning Goodness and the Good." *Proceedings of the Aristotelian Society* 64: 273–286.

Anagnostopoulos, G. 1994. *Aristotle on the Goals and Exactness of Ethics*. Berkeley: University of California Press.

Barnes, J. 1990. Review of J. Rist 1989. *The Mind of Aristotle. Notes and Queries* 37: 318–319.

   1999. "An Introduction to Aspasius." 1–51 in Alberti and Sharples eds. 1999.

   2007. "Sextan Scepticism." 322–334 in Scott ed. 2007.

Bodéüs, R. 1993. *The Political Dimension of Aristotle's Ethics*. J. Garrett trans. Albany: SUNY Press.

Broadie, S. 1991. *Ethics with Aristotle*. Oxford: Oxford University Press.

   2010. "The Good, the Noble, and the Theoretical in *Eudemian Ethics* VIII.3." 3–25 in J. Cottingham and P. Hacker eds. *Mind, Method, and Morality: Essays in Honour of Anthony Kenny*. Oxford: Oxford University Press.

Broadie, S., and C. Rowe. 2002. *Aristotle: Nicomachean Ethics*. Oxford: Oxford University Press.

Burnet, J. 1900. *The Ethics of Aristotle*. London: Methuen.

Case, T. 1910/1996. "Aristotle." 501–522 in *Encylopaedia Britannica* 11th ed. Vol. 2. Reprinted (in part) in Wians ed. 1996, 1–40.

   1925. "The Development of Aristotle." *Mind* 34: 80–86.

Code, A. 1996. "Owen on the Development of Aristotle's Metaphysics." 303–325 in Wians ed. 1996.

Cooper, J. M. 1975. *Reason and Human Good in Aristotle*. Cambridge, MA: Harvard University Press.

   1981. Review of A. Kenny, *The Aristotelian Ethics. Nous* 15: 366–385.

   2003. "Plato and Aristotle on 'Finality' and '(Self-)Sufficiency.'" 117–147 in Heinaman ed. 2003.

Crisp, R. trans. 2000. *Aristotle: Nicomachean Ethics*. Cambridge: Cambridge University Press.

Flashar, H. 1965/1977. "'Die Kritik der Platonischen Ideelehre in der Ethik des Aristoteles." 223–246 in H. Flashar and K. Gaiser eds. *Synusia Festgabe fuer Wofgang Schadewaldt*. Reprinted (in part) in English as "The Critique of Plato's Theory of Ideas in Aristotle's Ethics." 1–16 in J. Barnes, M. Schofield, and R. Sorabji eds. *Articles on Aristotle*. Vol. 2. *Ethics and Politics*. London: Duckworth.

Freeland, C. 1996. "Aristotle's *Poetics* in Relation to the Ethical Treatises." 327–345 in Wians ed. 1996.

Fritzsche, A. T. H. 1851. *Aristotelis Ethica Eudemia*. Regensburg: Mantz.

Gigon, O. 1971. "Das Prooimion der *Eudemischen Ethik*." 93–133 in Moraux and Harlfinger eds. 1971.

Gosling, J. C. B., and C. C. W. Taylor. 1982. *The Greeks on Pleasure*. Oxford: Clarendon Press.

Green, J. 2010. "Self-Love in the Aristotelian Ethics." *Newsletters for the Society for Ancient Greek Philosophy* 11:12–18.

Heinamen, R. ed. 2003. *Plato and Aristotle's Ethics*. Aldershot: Ashgate.

Hutchinson, D. 1986. *The Virtues of Aristotle*. London: Routledge & Kegan Paul.

Inwood, B., and R. Woolf. 2013. *Aristotle: Eudemian Ethics*. Cambridge: Cambridge University Press.

Irwin, T. 1980. Review of A. Kenny, *The Aristotelian Ethics*. *Journal of Philosophy* 77: 338–354.

    2003. "Glaucon's Challenge: Does Aristotle Change His Mind?" 87–108 in Heinaman ed. 2003.

Jaeger, W. 1923/1948. *Aristoteles: Grundlegung einer Geschichte seiner Entwicklung*. Berlin: Weidmann. Reprinted in English trans. by Richard Robinson as *Aristotle: Fundamentals of the History of His Development*, 2nd ed. Oxford: Clarendon Press.

Jost, L. J. 1983. "Aristotle's Ethics – Have We Been Teaching the Wrong One?" *Teaching Philosophy* 6: 331–340.

    1991. "Eudemian Ethical Method." 29–40 in J. P. Anton and A. Preus eds. *Essays in Ancient Greek Philosophy IV: Aristotle's Ethics*. Albany: SUNY Press.

Kenny, A. 1978. *The Aristotelian Ethics: A Study of the Relationship between the Eudemian and Nicomachean Ethics of Aristotle*. Oxford: Clarendon Press.

    1979. *Aristotle's Theory of the Will*. New Haven, CT: Yale University Press.

    1992. *Aristotle on the Perfect Life*. Oxford: Clarendon Press.

    2003a. "Reply to Irwin." 109–116 in Heinaman ed. 2003.

    2003b. "Reply to Cooper." 148–152 in Heinaman ed. 2003.

    2011. *Aristotle: The Eudemian Ethics*. Oxford: Oxford University Press.

Lear, J. 2000. *Happiness, Death and the Remainder of Life*. Cambridge, MA: Harvard University Press.

Meyer, S. S. 1993. *Aristotle on Moral Responsibility: Character and Cause*. Oxford: Blackwell Publishers.

Miller, F. 2003. "Aristotle: Ethics and Politics." 184–210 in C. Shields ed. *The Blackwell Guide to Ancient Philosophy*. Oxford: Blackwell.

Mills, M. J. 1980. "The Discussion of *ANDREIA* in the *Eudemian* and *Nicomachean Ethics*." *Phronesis* 25: 198–218.

Monan, D. 1968. *Moral Knowledge and Its Methodology in Aristotle*. Oxford: Clarendon Press.

Moraux, P., and D. Harlfinger eds. 1971. *Untersuchugen zur Eudemischen Ethik: Akten des 5.Symposium Aristotelicum*. Berlin: De Gruyter.

Osborne, C. 2009. "Selves and Other Selves in Aristotle's *Eudemian Ethics* vii 12." *Ancient Philosophy* 29: 349–371.

Owen, G. E. L. 1971/1972. "Aristotelian Pleasures." *Proceedings of the Aristotelian Society* 72: 133–152. Reprinted in M. Nussbaum ed. 1986. *Logic, Science, and Dialectic: Collected Papers in Greek Philosophy*, 334–346. Ithaca, NY: Cornell University Press.

Pakaluk, M. 1995. Review of A. Kenny 1992. *Aristotle on the Perfect Life*. *Ancient Philosophy* 15: 233–245.

Rowe, C. 1971a. "The Meaning of *Phronesis* in the *Eudemian Ethics*." 73–92 in Moraux and Harlfinger eds. 1971.

    1971b. *The Eudemian and Nicomachean Ethics: A Study in the Development of Aristotle's Thought*. Proceedings of the Cambridge Philological Society, supp. no. 3.

1983. "De Aristotelis in tribus libris Ethicorum dicendi ratione: Participles, Connectives, and Style in Three Books from the Aristotelian Ethical Treatises." *Liverpool Classical Monthly* 8: 4–11, 37–40, 54–57, 70–74.

Scott, D. ed. 2007. *Maieusis: Essays in Ancient Philosophy in Honour of Myles Burnyeat*. Oxford: Clarendon Press.

Von Fragstein, A. 1974. *Studien zur Ethik des Aristoteles*. Amsterdam: B. R. Gruener.

Wians, W. ed. 1996. *Aristotle's Philosophical Development*. Lanham, MD: Rowman and Littlefield.

Woods, M. 1992. *Aristotle: Eudemian Ethics: Books I, II, and VIII*. 2nd ed. Oxford: Clarendon Press.

Young, C. M. 1988. "Aristotle on Temperance." *Philosophical Review* 97: 521–542. Reprinted in Anton and Preus eds. 1991, 107–125.

20 Topical Bibliography to Aristotle's *Nicomachean Ethics*

BOOK-LENGTH STUDIES

Baracchi, C. 2008. *Aristotle's Ethics as First Philosophy*. Cambridge: Cambridge University Press.

Bostock, D. 2000. *Aristotle's Ethics*. Oxford: Oxford University Press.

Broadie, S. 1991. *Ethics with Aristotle*. Oxford: Oxford University Press.

Burger, R. 2008. *Aristotle's Dialogue with Socrates: On the Nicomachean Ethics*. Chicago: University of Chicago Press.

Crubellier, M., and P. Pellegrin. 2002. *Aristote. Le philosophe et les savoirs*. Paris: Seuil.

Curzer, H. 2012. *Aristotle and the Virtues*. Oxford: Oxford University Press.

Düring, I. 1966. *Aristoteles. Darstellung und Interpretation seines Denkens*. Heidelberg: Winter.

Echeñique, J. 2012. *Aristotle's Ethics and Moral Responsibility*. Cambridge: Cambridge University Press.

Garver, E. 2006. *A Confrontation with Aristotle's Ethics: Ancient and Modern Morality*. Chicago: University of Chicago Press.

Gottlieb, P. 2009. *The Virtue of Aristotle's Ethics*. Cambridge: Cambridge University Press.

Hardie, W. F. R. 1980 [1968]. *Aristotle's Ethical Theory*. 2nd ed. Oxford: Clarendon Press.

Höffe, O. 1996 [1971]. *Praktische Philosophie: Das Modell des Aristoteles*. 2nd ed. Berlin: Akademie.

Hughes, G. J. 2013. *The Routledge Guidebook to Aristotle's Nicomachean Ethics*. London: Routledge.

Irwin, T. H. 2007. *The Development of Ethics: A Historical and Critical Study*. Vol. 1. *From Socrates to the Reformation*. Oxford: Oxford University Press.

Kontos, P. 2002. *L'action morale chez Aristote*. Paris: Presses Universitaires de France.

Kraut, R. 1989. *Aristotle on the Human Good*. Princeton: Princeton University Press.

May, H. 2010. *Aristotle's Ethics: Moral Development and Human Nature*. London: Continuum.

Natali, C. 2013 [1991]. *Aristotle: His Life and School*. D. S. Hutchinson ed. Princeton: Princeton University Press.

Pakaluk, M. 2005. *Aristotle's Nicomachean Ethics: An Introduction*. Cambridge: Cambridge University Press.

Reeve, C. D. C. 1992. *Practices of Reason: Aristotle's Nicomachean Ethics*. Oxford: Clarendon Press.

  2012. *Action, Contemplation, and Happiness*. Cambridge, MA: Harvard University Press.

Salem, E. 2010. *In Pursuit of the Good: Intellect and Action in Aristotle's Ethics*. Philadelphia: Paul Dry Books.

Shields, C. 2007. *Aristotle*. New York: Routledge Press.

Smith, T. 2001. *Revaluing Ethics: Aristotle's Dialectical Pedagogy*. Albany: SUNY Press.

Tessitore, A. 1996. *Reading Aristotle's Ethics: Virtue, Rhetoric and Political Philosophy*. Albany: SUNY Press.

Urmson, J. 1988. *Aristotle's Ethics*. Oxford: Blackwell.

Wolf, U. 2002. *Aristoteles Nikomachische Ethik*. Darmstadt: Wissenschaftliche Buchgesellschaft.

EDITIONS OF THE NICOMACHEAN ETHICS

Greek Editions

Bywater, I. 1894. *Aristotelis Ethica Nicomachea*. Oxonii: e typographeo clarendoniano.

Susemihl, F., and O. Apelt eds. 1912 [1882]. *Aristotelis Ethica Nicomachea*. 3rd ed. Leipzig: Teubner.

Translations

Apostle, H. G. 1984. *Aristotle's Nicomachean Ethics*. Translated with commentaries. Grinnell: Peripatetic Press.

Bartlett, R. C., and S. D. Collins. 2011. *Aristotle's Nicomachean Ethics*. Chicago: University of Chicago Press.

Bien, G. 1985. *Aristoteles Nikomachische Ethik*. 4th ed. Hamburg: Felix Meiner.

Bodéüs, R. 2004. *Aristote: Ethique à Nicomaque*. Traduction et présentation. Paris: GF Flammarion.

Broadie, S., and C. Rowe. 2002. *Aristotle: Nicomachean Ethics; Translation, Introduction, and Commentary*. New York: Oxford University Press.

Crisp, R. 2000. *Aristotle: Nicomachean Ethics*. Translated and edited. Cambridge: Cambridge University Press.

Dirlmeier, F. 1983. *Aristoteles, Nikomachische Ethik*. 2nd ed. Translated, with introduction and commentary. Berlin: Akademie Verlag.

Gauthier, R. A. 1972–1974. *Aristoteles ethica nicomachea* [in Latin]. Leiden: E. J. Brill.

Gigon, O. 2000. *Aristoteles. Die Nikomachische Ethik*. With revisions by R. Nickel. Dusseldorf: Artemis and Winkler.

Irwin, T. H. 1999. *Nicomachean Ethics*. 2nd ed. Translation with introduction and notes. Indianapolis: Hackett.

Natali, C. 1999. *Aristotele. Etica nicomachea*. Translation, introduction, and notes. Rome-Bari: Laterza.

Ostwald, M. 1986 [1962]. *Nicomachean Ethics*. Translated with notes. New York: Macmillan.

Rackham, H. 1990 [1926]. *Aristotle: The Nicomachean Ethics*. Loeb Classical Library. Cambridge, MA: Harvard University Press.

Ross, W. D. 2009 [1915]. *Aristotle: The Nicomachean Ethics*. Oxford World's Classics. Revised with an introduction and notes by L. Brown. Oxford: Oxford University Press. Also printed in J. Barnes ed. *The Complete Works of Aristotle*, the revised Oxford translation. Princeton: Princeton University Press.

Sachs, J. 2002. *Aristotle: Nicomachean Ethics*. Translation, glossary, and introductory essay. Newburyport, MA: Focus Publishing.

Thomson, J. A. K. 2004 [1955]. *The Ethics of Aristotle*. Revised by H. Tredennick, with new introduction and further reading by J. Barnes. London: Penguin.

Tricot, J. 1959. *Éthique à Nicomaque*. Translation, introduction, notes, and index. Paris: J. Vrin.

Wolf, U. 2006. *Aristoteles, Nikomachische Ethik*. Reinbek: Rowohlt.

Zanatta, M. 1986. *Aristotele. Etica Nicomachea*. Introduction, translation, and commentary. Milan: Biblioteca Universale.

ARISTOTLE'S ETHICAL CORPUS AND THE COMPOSITION OF THE NICOMACHEAN ETHICS

Allan, D. J. 1957. "*Magna Moralia* and *Nicomachean Ethics*." *Journal of Hellenic Studies* 77: 7–11.

Allan, D. J. 1961. "Quasi-Mathematical Method in the *Eudemian Ethics*." 303–318 in S. Mansion ed. *Aristote et les problems de method*. Louvain: Publications Universitaires.

Barnes, J. 1997. "Roman Aristotle." 1–70 in J. Barnes and M. Griffin eds. *Philosophia Togata ii: Plato and Aristotle at Rome*. Oxford: Oxford University Press.

Bobonich, C. 2006. "Aristotle's Ethical Treatises." 12–36 in R. Kraut ed. *The Blackwell Guide to Aristotle's Nicomachean Ethics*. Malden, MA: Blackwell.

Bodéüs, R. 1973. "Contribution a l'histoire des oeuvres morales d'Aristote: Les Testimonia." *Revue philosophique de Louvain* 71: 451–467.

Cooper, J. M. 1999 [1973]. "*Magna Moralia* and Aristotle's Moral Philosophy." 195–211 in his *Reason and Emotion: Essays on Ancient Moral Psychology and Ethical Theory*. Princeton: Princeton University Press.

Jaeger, W. 1948 [1923]. "The Original Ethics." 228–258 in his *Aristotle: Fundamentals of the History of His Development*. R. Robinson trans. 2nd ed. Oxford: Oxford University Press.

Kenny, A. 1978. *The Aristotelian Ethics: A Study of The Relationship between the Eudemian and Nicomachean Ethics of Aristotle*. Oxford: Oxford University Press.

Pakaluk, M. 2011. "On the Unity of the *Nicomachean Ethics*." 23–44 in J. Miller ed. *Aristotle's Nicomachean Ethics: A Critical Guide*. Cambridge: Cambridge University Press.

Rowe, C. J. 1971. *The Eudemian and Nicomachean Ethics: A Study in the Development of Aristotle's Thought*. Cambridge: Cambridge University Press.

1975. "A Reply to John Cooper on the *Magna Moralia*." *American Journal of Philology* 96: 160–172.

EDITIONS AND COMMENTARY ON THE EUDEMIAN ETHICS

Buddensiek, F. 1999. *Die Theorie des Glücks in Aristoteles' Eudemischer Ethik*. Göttingen: Vandenhoeck und Ruprecht.

Decarie, V. 1978. *Aristote. Ethique à Eudème*. Introduction, translation, notes, and indices, with the collaboration of R. Houde-Sauvé. Paris: J. Vrin.

Dirlmeier, F. 1969. *Aristoteles, Eudemische Ethik*. 2nd ed. Berlin: Akademie Verlag.

Donini, P. 1999. *Etica Eudemia*. Translation, introduction, and notes. Rome: GLF Editioni Laterza.

Inwood, B., and R. Woolf. 2013. *Eudemian Ethics*. Cambridge: Cambridge University Press.

Kenny, A. 2011. *Aristotle, The Eudemian Ethics*. Oxford: Oxford University Press.

Leigh, F. ed. 2013. *The Eudemian Ethics on the Voluntary, Friendship, and Luck*. The Sixth S. V. Keeling Colloquium in Ancient Philosophy. Leiden: Brill.

Moraux, P., and D. Harlfinger eds. 1971. *Untersuchugen zur Eudemischen Ethik: Akten des 5 Symposium Aristotelicum*. Berlin: De Gruyter.

Rackham, H. 1992 [1935]. *Aristotle, Athenian Constitution, Eudemian Ethics, Virtues and Vices*. Loeb Classical Library. Cambridge, MA: Harvard University Press.

Simpson, P. 2013. *The Eudemian Ethics of Aristotle*. New Brunswick, NJ: Transaction.

Solomon, J. *Eudemian Ethics*. 1984 [1915]. In *The Complete Works of Aristotle, the revised Oxford translation*. J. Barnes ed. Princeton: Princeton University Press.

Walzer, R. R., and J. M. Mingay. 1991. *Aristotelis Ethica Eudemia*. Oxonii: e typographeo clarendoniano.

Woods, M. 1991. *Aristotle: Eudemian Ethics, Books I, II, and VIII*. 2nd ed. Oxford: Clarendon Press.

EDITIONS AND COMMENTARY ON THE MAGNA MORALIA

Armstrong, G. C. 1990 [1935]. *Magna Moralia*. Loeb Classical Library. Cambridge, MA: Harvard University Press.

Dalimier, C. 1995. *Aristote. Les grands livres d'éthique*. Paris: Arléa.

Dirlmeier, F. 1958. *Aristoteles, Magna Moralia*. Darmstadt: Wissenschaftliche Buchgesellschaft.

Donini, P. 1965. *L'etica dei Magna Moralia*. Turin: Giappichelli.

Stock, St. George. *Magna Moralia*. 1984 [1915]. In *The Complete Works of Aristotle, the revised Oxford translation*. J. Barnes ed. Princeton: Princeton University Press.

EDITIONS AND COMMENTARY ON THE PROTREPTICUS

Barnes, J., and G. Lawrence. 1984 [1915]. "Fragments: Dialogues." 2403–2417 in *The Complete Works of Aristotle, the revised Oxford translation*. J. Barnes ed. Princeton: Princeton University Press.

Berti, E. trans. 2000. *Protreptico: Esortazione alla filosofia*. Turin: UTET Università.

Bywater, I. 1869. "On A Lost Dialogue of Aristotle." *Journal of Philology* 2: 55–69.

Chroust, A. H. 1964. *Protrepticus: A Reconstruction*. South Bend, IN: University of Notre Dame Press.

Düring, I. 1961. *Aristotle's Protrepticus: An Attempt at Reconstruction*. Studia Graeca et Latina Gothoburgensia 12. Göteborg: Acta Universitatis Gothoburgensis.

Hutchinson, D. S., and M. R. Johnson. 2005. "Authenticating Aristotle's *Protrepticus*." *Oxford Studies in Ancient Philosophy* 29: 193–294.

Rabinowitz, W. G. 1957. *Aristotle's Protrepticus and the Sources of Its Reconstruction*. Berkeley: University of California Press.

Ross, W. D. 1955. *Aristotelis fragmenta selecta*. Oxford: Clarendon Press.

COMMENTARIES ON INDIVIDUAL BOOKS
OF THE NICOMACHEAN ETHICS

Dahl, N. No date. *Nicomachean Ethics, Book III*. Project Archelogos. http://archelogos.com/xml/toc/toc-eniii.htm.

Gadamer, H. G. 1998. *Nikomachische Ethik VI*. Translated with commentary. Frankfurt am Main: Vittorio Klostermann.

Gottlieb, P. No date. *Nicomachean Ethics, Books I–II*. Project Archelogos. http://archelogos.com/xml/toc/toc-eni.htm.

Greenwood, L. H. G. 1909. *Aristotle: Nicomachean Ethics Book Six.* Cambridge: Cambridge University Press.

Jackson, H. 1879. *Peri Dikaiosunes – the Fifth Book of the Nicomachean Ethics of Aristotle.* Cambridge: Syndics of the University Press.

Konstan, D. 2001. *On Aristotle's Nicomachean Ethics 8 and 9.* (Aspasius, Anonymous, and Michael of Ephesus). Ithaca, NY: Cornell University Press.

2007. *Aspasius: On Aristotle's Nicomachean Ethics 1–4, 7–8.* London: Duckworth.

Natali, C. No date. *Nicomachean Ethics, Books X.* Project Archelogos. http://archelogos.com/xml/toc/toc-enx.htm.

Pakaluk, M. 1999. *Nicomachean Ethics VIII and IX.* Oxford: Clarendon Press.

Reeve, C. D. C. 2013. *Aristotle on Practical Wisdom: Nicomachean Ethics VI.* Cambridge, MA: Harvard University Press.

Taylor, C. C. W. 2006. *Aristotle: Nicomachean Ethics Books II–IV.* Oxford: Clarendon Press.

Wilson, J. Cook. 1912. *On the Structure of Book Seven of the Nicomachean Ethics.* Oxford: Oxford University Press.

ANCIENT GREEK COMMENTARY TRADITION

Alberti, A., and R. W. Sharples eds. 1999. *Aspasius: The Earliest Extant Commentary on Aristotle's Ethics.* Berlin: De Gruyter.

Alexander of Aphrodisias. 1990 [1887]. Questiones Ethicae. In *Commentaria in Aristotelem Graeca.* Supplementum Aristotelicum, vol. 2, pt. 1. I. Burns ed. Berlin: Reimer. Translated as *Ethical Problems*, by R. W. Sharples. Ithaca, NY: Cornell University Press.

Anonymous. 1892. *Eustratii et Michaelis et Anonyma in Ethica Nicomachea.* In *Commentaria in Aristotelem Graeca.* vol. 20. G. Heylbut ed. Berlin: Reimer. Translated in part as D. Konstan. 2001. *On Aristotle's Nicomachean Ethics 8 and 9. (Aspasius, Anonymous, and Michael of Ephesus).* Ithaca, NY: Cornell University Press.

Aspasius. 1889. *Aspasii in Ethica Nicomachea quae supersunt commentaria.* In. G. Heylbut ed. *Commentaria in Aristotelem Graeca*, vol. 19. Berlin: Reimer. Translated in part as Konstan, D. 2007. *Aspasius: On Aristotle's Nicomachean Ethics 1–4, 7–8.* London: Duckworth.

Gottschalk, H. B. 1990 [1987]. "The Earliest Aristotelian Commentators." 55–81 in R. Sorabji ed. *Aristotle Transformed: The Ancient Commentators and Their Influence.* Ithaca, NY: Cornell University Press.

Heliodorus (the Paraphrist). 1889. *Heliodori in Ethica Nicomachea Paraphrasis.* In *Commentaria in Aristotelem Graeca*, vol. 19. G. Heylbut ed. Berlin: Reimer.

Mercken, H. P. F. 1990 [1973]. "The Greek Commentators on Aristotle's Ethics." 407–443 in R. Sorabji ed. *Aristotle Transformed: The Ancient Commentators and Their Influence.* Ithaca, NY: Cornell University Press.

Michael of Ephesus. 1892. *Michaelis Ephesii in librum quintum Ethicorum Nicomacheorum commentarium.* In G. Heylbut ed. *Commentaria in Aristotelem Graeca.* vol. 22. Berlin: Reimer.

PHILOLOGICAL AND ANALYTICAL COMMENTARIES

Aquinas, T. 1993 [1964]. *Commentary on Aristotle's Nicomachean Ethics.* C. I. Litzinger trans. Notre Dame, IN: Dumb Ox Books.

Burnet, J. 1900. *The Ethics of Aristotle*. London: Methuen.

Dirlmeier, F. 1999 [1956]. *Aristoteles Nikomachische Ethik*. Berlin: Akademie.

Gauthier, R.A., and J.Y. Jolif. 1970 [1958–1959]. *L'Ethique à Nicomaque*. 2nd ed. With a new introduction and updated bibliography. Paris-Louvain: Publications Universitaires. Reprinted in Louvain and Paris: Peeters, 2002.

Grant, A. 1885. *The Ethics of Aristotle*. 4th ed. rev. London: Longmans, Green.

Joachim, H.H. 1955. *Aristotle – The Nicomachean Ethics*. D.A. Rees ed. Oxford: Clarendon Press.

Sparshott, F. 1994. *Taking Life Seriously: A Study of the Argument of the Nicomachean Ethics*. Toronto: University of Toronto Press.

Stewart, J.A. 1892. *Notes on the Nicomachean Ethics of Aristotle*. Oxford: Clarendon Press.

Zanatta, M. 1986. *Aristotele Etica Nicomachea*. 2 vols. Milan: Biblioteca Universale.

BIBLIOGRAPHIES

Barnes, J., M. Schofield, and R. Sorabji. 1995. Bibliography. 295–384 in J. Barnes ed. *The Cambridge Companion to Aristotle*. Cambridge: Cambridge University Press.

Everson, S. 1998. Bibliography. 241–283 in S. Everson ed. *Companion to Ancient Thought*, vol. IV: *Ethics*. Cambridge: Cambridge University Press.

Gauthier, R.A., and J.Y. Jolif. 1970. "Bibliographie 1912–1958." 917–940 in *L'Ethique à Nicomaque*. 2nd ed. Vol. II, pt. 2. Paris-Louvain: Publications Universitaires.

1970. "Bibliographie 1958–1968." 315–334 in *L'Ethique à Nicomaque*. 2nd ed. Vol. I, pt. 1. Paris-Louvain: Publications Universitaires.

Ingardia, R. *The International Aristotle Bibliography*. http://www.brill.nl/publica tions/online-resources/international-aristotle-bibliography.

Lockwood, T. "Aristotle's Ethics." *Oxford Bibliographies in Classics*. D. Clayman ed. New York: Oxford University Press. [http://www.oxfordbibliographies.com/view/ document/obo-9780195389661/obo-9780195389661-0079.xml?rskey=NdrSbm& result=15&q=]

Natali, C. 2002. "Gli studi italiani sull'*Etica Nicomachea* dalla fine del sec. XIX a oggi." *Elenchos* 23: 89–138.

LEXICA

Bonitz, H. 1961 [1870]. *Index Aristotelicus*. Berlin: De Gruyter.

Bywater, I. 1892. *Contributions to the Textual Criticism of Aristotle's Nicomachean Ethics*. Oxford: Clarendon Press.

Höffe, O. ed. 2005. *Aristoteles Lexikon*. Stuttgart: Alfred Kröner.

Kieran, T.P. ed. 1962. *Aristotle Dictionary*. With an introduction by Theodore James. New York: Philosophical Library.

Organ, T.W. 1949. *An Index to Aristotle*. Princeton: Princeton University Press.

Rassow, H. 1874. *Forschungen über die Nikomachische Ethik des Aristoteles*. Weimar: Hermann Böhlau.

Urmson, J.O. 1990. *Greek Philosophical Vocabulary*. London: Duckworth.

COLLECTIONS OF ARTICLES

Alberti, A. ed. 1990. *Studi sull' Etica di Aristotele*. Naples: Bibliopolis.

Anton, J.P., and A. Preus eds. 1991. *Essays in Ancient Greek Philosophy IV: Aristotle's Ethics*. Albany: SUNY Press.

Barnes, J., M. Schofield, and R. Sorabji eds. 1977. *Articles on Aristotle*. Vol. 2. *Ethics and Politics*. London: Duckworth.

Chateau, J.-Y. ed. 1997. *La Vérité pratique, Ethique à Nicomaque Livre VI*. Paris: J. Vrin.

Destrée, P. ed. 2003. *Aristote: Bonheur et vertus*. Paris: Presses Universitaires de France.

Destrée, P., and M. Zingano eds. 2013. *Theoria: Studies on the Status and Meaning of Contemplation in Aristotle's Ethics*. Louvain-la-Neuve: Peeters.

Heinaman, R. ed. 1995. *Aristotle and Moral Realism*. Boulder, CO: Westview Press.

    ed. 2003. *Plato and Aristotle's Ethics*. Burlington, VT: Ashgate.

Höffe, O. ed. 1995. *Aristoteles: Die Nikomachische Ethik*. Berlin: Akademie Verlag.

Irwin, T. ed. 1995. *Classical Philosophy, Collected Papers. Aristotle's Ethics*. Vol. 5. New York: Garland.

Kraut, R. ed. 2006. *The Blackwell Guide to Aristotle's Nicomachean Ethics*. Cambridge: Blackwell.

Miller, J. ed. 2011. *Aristotle's Nicomachean Ethics: A Critical Guide*. Cambridge: Cambridge University Press.

    ed. 2012. *The Reception of Aristotle's Ethics*. Cambridge: Cambridge University Press.

Moraux, P., and D. Harlfinger eds. 1971. *Untersuchungen zur Eudemischen Ethik*. Berlin: De Gruyter.

Müller-Goldingen, C. ed. 1988. *Schriften zur aristotelischen Ethik*. Hildesheim: Georg Olms.

Pakaluk, M., and G. Pearson eds. 2011. *Moral Psychology and Human Action in Aristotle*. Oxford: Oxford University Press.

Romeyer-Dherbey, G., and G. Aubry eds. 2002. *L'Excellence de la Vie: sur L'Ethique à Nicomaque et L'Ethique à Eudème d'Aristote*. Paris: J. Vrin.

Rorty, A. O. ed. 1980. *Essays on Aristotle's Ethics*. Berkeley: University of California Press.

Sherman, N. ed. 1999. *Aristotle's Ethics: Critical Essays*. Lanham, MD: Rowman and Littlefield.

Sim, M. ed. 1995. *The Crossroads of Norm and Nature: Essays on Aristotle's Ethics and Metaphysics*. Lanham, MD: Rowman and Littlefield.

TOPICS WITHIN ARISTOTLE'S ETHICS

BOOK I: HAPPINESS AND THE HUMAN GOOD

The Method of Ethics

Barnes, J. 1980. "Aristotle and the Method of Ethics." *Revue Internationale de Philosophie* 133/134: 490–511.

Höffe, O. 1995. "Ethik als praktische Philosophie – Methodische Überlegungen (I 1, 1094a22–1095a13)." 13–38 in O. Höffe ed. *Aristoteles: Die Nikomachische Ethik*. Berlin: Akademie Verlag.

Irwin, T. H. 1981. "Aristotle's Methods of Ethics." 193–224 in D. O'Meara ed. *Studies in Aristotle*. Washington, DC: Catholic University of America Press.

Kraut, R. 2006. "How to Justify Ethical Propositions: Aristotle's Method." 76–95 in R. Kraut ed. *The Blackwell Guide to Aristotle's Nicomachean Ethics*. Malden, MA: Blackwell.

Natali, C. 2010. "*Posterior Analytics* and the Definition of Happiness in *NE* I." *Phronesis* 55: 304–324.

Salmieri, G. 2009. "Aristotle's Non-dialectical Methodology in the *Nicomachean Ethics*." *Ancient Philosophy* 29: 311–335.

Whiting, J. 2001. "Strong Dialectic, Neurathian Reflection, and the Ascent of Desire: Irwin and McDowell on Aristotle's Methods of Ethics." *Proceedings of the Boston Area Colloquium in Ancient Philosophy* 17: 61–116.

Zingano, M. 2007. "Aristotle and the Problems of Method in Ethics." *Oxford Studies in Ancient Philosophy* 32: 297–330.

The Accuracy of Ethics

Achtenberg, D. 2002. *Cognition of Value in Aristotle's Ethics: Promise of Enrichment, Threat of Destruction*. Albany: SUNY Press.

Anagnostopoulos, G. 1994. *Aristotle on the Goals and Exactness of Ethics*. Berkeley: University of California Press.

Bolton, R. 1991. "Aristotle on the Objectivity of Ethics." 59–72 in J.P. Anton and A. Preus eds. *Essays in Ancient Greek Philosophy IV: Aristotle's Ethics*. Albany: SUNY Press.

Irwin, T.H. 2000. "Ethics as an Inexact Science: Aristotle's Ambitions for Moral Theory." 130–156 in B. Hooker ed. *Moral Particularism*. Oxford: Clarendon Press.

Natali, Carlo. 2007. "Rhetorical and Scientific Aspects of the *Nicomachean Ethics*." *Phronesis* 52: 364–381.

Roche, T.D. 1988. "On the Alleged Metaphysical Foundation of Aristotle's Ethics." *Ancient Philosophy* 8: 49–62.

1992. "In Defense of an Alternative View of the Foundation of Aristotle's Moral Theory." *Phronesis* 37: 46–83.

Winter, M. 1997. "Aristotle, *hos epi to polu* Relations, and a Demonstrative Science of Ethics." *Phronesis* 42: 163–189.

The Rationality of Ethics

Irwin, T.H. 1978. "First Principles in Aristotle's *Ethics*." *Midwest Studies in Philosophy* 3: 252–272.

Kraut, R. 1998. "Aristotle on Method and Moral Education." 271–290 in J. Gentzler ed. *Method in Ancient Philosophy*. Oxford: Clarendon Press.

Lännström, A. 2006. *Loving the Fine: Virtue and Happiness in Aristotle's Ethics*. Notre Dame, IN: University of Notre Dame Press.

McDowell, J. 1980. "The Role of *Eudaimonia* in Aristotle's *Ethics*." 359–376 in A.O. Rorty ed. *Essays on Aristotle's Ethics*. Berkeley: University of California Press.

Price, A.W. 2005. "Aristotelian Virtue and Practical Judgement." 257–278 in C. Gill ed. *Virtue, Norms, and Objectivity: Issues in Ancient and Modern Ethics*. Oxford: Clarendon Press.

Vasiliou, I. 1996. "The Role of Good Upbringing in Aristotle's *Ethics*." *Philosophy and Phenomonlogical Research* 56: 771–797.

Whiting, J. 2001. "Strong Dialectic, Neurathian Reflection, and the Ascent of Desire: Irwin and McDowell on Aristotle's Methods of Ethics." *Proceedings of the Boston Area Colloquium in Ancient Philosophy* 17: 61–116.

Williams, B. 1985. *Ethics and the Limits of Philosophy*. Cambridge, MA: Harvard University Press.

The Doctrine of Three Lives

Brown, E. 2013. "Aristotle on the Choice of Lives: Two Concepts of Self-Sufficiency." 135–158 in P. Destrée and M. Zingano eds. *Theoria: Studies on the Status and Meaning of Contemplation in Aristotle's Ethics*. Louvain-la-Neuve: Peeters.

Cooper, J. M. 2012. *Pursuits of Wisdom: Six Ways of Life in Ancient Philosophy from Socrates to Plotinus*. Princeton: Princeton University Press.

Crisp, R. 2003. "Socrates and Aristotle on Happiness and Virtue," with reply by C. Rowe. 55–86 in R. Heinaman ed. *Plato and Aristotle's Ethics*. Burlington, VT: Ashgate.

Crittenden, P. 1996. "Aristotle and the Idea of Competing Forms of Life." *Philosophical Inquiry* 18: 88–100.

Joly, R. 1956. *Le Thème philosophique des genres de vie dans l'Antiquité Classique*. Brussels: J. Duculot.

Labarrière, J. L. 2002. "De l'unité de l'intellect chez Aristote et du choix de la vie la meilleure." 221–243 in M. Canto-Sperber and P. Pellegrin eds. *Le style de la pensée*. Paris: Les Belles Lettres.

Morrison, D. 2001. "Politics as a Vocation, According to Aristotle." *History of Political Thought* 22: 221–241.

Tessitore, A. 1988. "Aristotle's Political Presentation of Socrates in the *Nicomachean Ethics*." *Interpretation* 16: 3–22.

Aristotle's Criticisms of the Platonic Notion of the Good

Ackrill, J. L. 1977 [1972]. "Aristotle on 'Good' and the Categories." 17–24 in J. Barnes, M. Schofield, and R. Sorabji eds. *Articles on Aristotle*. Vol. 2. *Ethics and Politics*. London: Duckworth.

Allan, D. J. 1963–1964. "Aristotle's Criticism of Platonic Doctrine concerning Goodness and the Good." *Proceedings of the Aristotelian Society* 64: 273–286.

Flashar, H. 1977 [1965]. "The Critique of Plato's Theory of Ideas in Aristotle's Ethics." M. Schofield trans. 1–16 in J. Barnes, M. Schofield, and R. Sorabji eds. *Articles on Aristotle*. Vol. 2. *Ethics and Politics*. London: Duckworth.

Gadamer, H. G. 1986. "Aristotle's Critique of the Idea of the Good." 126–158 in his *The Idea of the Good in Platonic-Aristotelian Philosophy*. P. C. Smith trans. New Haven, CT: Yale University Press.

Kosman, L. A. 1968. "Predicating the Good." *Phronesis* 13: 171–174.

Nussbaum, M. C. 1980. "Shame, Separateness, and Political Unity: Aristotle's Criticisms of Plato." 395–435 in A. O. Rorty ed. *Essays on Aristotle's Ethics*. Berkeley: University of California Press.

Segvic, H. 2004. "Aristotle on the Varieties of Goodness." *Apeiron* 37: 151–176.

Happiness as the Human Good

Ackrill, J. L. 1980 [1974]. "Aristotle on *Eudaimonia*." 15–34 in A. O. Rorty ed. *Essays on Aristotle's Ethics*. Berkeley: University of California Press.

Aubenque, P. 1978. "Die Kohärenz der aristotelischen *Eudaimonia*-Lehre." 45–57 in G. Bien ed. *Die Frage nach dem Glück*. Stuttgart-Bad: Cannstatt.

Austin, J. L. 1967 [c. 1938]. "*Agathon* and *Eudaimonia* in the Ethics of Aristotle." 261–296 in J. M. E. Moravcsik ed. *Aristotle: A Collection of Critical Essays*. Garden City, NY: Anchor Books.

Bartlett, R. C. 2008. "Aristotle's Introduction to the Problem of Happiness." *American Journal of Political Science* 52: 677–687.

Broadie, S. 1999. "Aristotle's Elusive 'Summum Bonum.'" *Social Philosophy and Policy* 16: 233–251.

Charles, D. 1999. "Aristotle on Well-Being and Intellectual Contemplation." *Proceedings of the Aristotelian Society*, Supplement 73: 205–223.

Cleemput, G. Van. 2006. "Aristotle on *Eudaimonia* in *Nicomachean Ethics* 1." *Oxford Studies in Ancient Philosophy* 30: 127–157.

Cooper, J. M. 1986 [1975]. *Reason and the Human Good in Aristotle*. Indianapolis: Hackett.

 1999 [1987]. "Contemplation and Happiness: A Reconsideration." 212–236 in his *Reason and Emotion: Essays on Ancient Moral Psychology and Ethical Theory*. Princeton: Princeton University Press.

 2003. "Plato and Aristotle on 'Finality' and '(Self)sufficiency'" with reply by A. Kenny. 117–152 in R. Heinaman ed. *Plato and Aristotle's Ethics*. Burlington, VT: Ashgate.

Crisp, R. 1994. "Aristotle's Inclusivism." *Ancient Philosophy* 12: 111–136.

Curzer, H. J. 1990. "Criteria for Happiness in *Nicomachean Ethics* I 7 and X 6–8." *Classical Quarterly* 40: 421–432.

 1991. "The Supremely Happy Life in Aristotle's *Nicomachean Ethics*." *Apeiron* 24: 47–69.

Devereux, D. 1981. "The Essence of Happiness." 247–260 in D. O'Meara ed. *Studies in Aristotle*. Washington, DC: Catholic University of America Press.

Farwall, P. 1995. "Aristotle and the Complete Life." *History of Philosophy Quarterly* 12: 247–263.

Glassen, P. 1957. "A Fallacy in Aristotle's Argument about the Good." *Philosophical Quarterly* 66: 319–322.

Gurtler, G. 2003. "The Activity of Happiness in Aristotle's Ethics." *Review of Metaphysics* 56: 801–834.

Hardie, W. F. R. 1965. "The Final Good in Aristotle's Ethics." *Philosophy* 40: 277–295.

Heinaman, R. 1988. "*Eudaimonia* and Self-Sufficiency in the *Nicomachean Ethics*." *Phronesis* 33: 35–41.

 1993. "Rationality, *Eudaimonia*, and *Kakodaimonia* in Aristotle." *Phronesis* 38: 31–56.

 2002. "Improvability of *Eudaimonia* in the *Nicomachean Ethics*." *Oxford Studies in Ancient Philosophy* 23: 99–146.

 2007. "*Eudaimonia* as an Activity in *Nicomachean Ethics* 1.8–12." *Oxford Studies in Ancient Philosophy* 33: 221–253.

Irwin, T. H. 2012. "Conceptions of Happiness in the *Nicomachean Ethics*." 495–528 in C. Shields ed. *The Oxford Handbook of Aristotle*. Oxford: Oxford University Press.

Kenny, A. 1991. "The Nicomachean Concept of Happiness." *Oxford Studies in Ancient Philosophy*, Supplemental Volume: 67–80.

Kraut, R. 1989. *Aristotle on the Human Good*. Princeton: Princeton University Press.

 1995. "In Defense of the Grand End." *Ethics* 103: 311–374.

Lawrence, G. 1993. "Aristotle and the Ideal Life." *Philosophical Review* 102: 1–34.

 2005. "Snakes in Paradise: Problems in the Ideal Life." *Southern Journal of Philosophy* 43, Supplement: 126–165.

Lear, G. R. 2004. *Happy Lives and the Highest Good: An Essay on Aristotle's Nicomachean Ethics*. Princeton: Princeton University Press.

Long, A. A. 2011. "Aristotle on *Eudaimonia*, *Nous*, and Divinity." 92–114 in J. Miller ed. *Aristotle's Nicomachean Ethics: A Critical Guide*. Cambridge: Cambridge University Press.

McDowell, J. 1980 [1980]. "The Role of *Eudaimonia* in Aristotle's *Ethics*." 359–376 in A. O. Rorty ed. *Essays on Aristotle's Ethics*. Berkeley: University of California Press.

 1995. "Eudaimonism and Realism in Aristotle's *Ethics*." 201–218 in R. Heinaman ed. *Aristotle and Moral Realism*. Boulder, CO: Westview Press.

Meyer, Susan Sauvé. 2011. "Living for the Sake of an Ultimate End." 47–65 in J. Miller ed. *Aristotle's Nicomachean Ethics: A Critical Guide*. Cambridge: Cambridge University Press.

Nagel, T. 1980 [1972]. "Aristotle on *Eudaimonia*." 7–14 in A. O. Rorty ed. *Essays on Aristotle's Ethics*. Berkeley: University of California Press.

Roche, T. D. 1995. "The Ultimate End of Action: A Critique of Richard Kraut's Aristotle on the Human Good." 115–138 in M. Sim ed. *The Crossroads of Norm and Nature: Essays on Aristotle's Ethics and Metaphysics*. Lanham, MD: Rowman and Littlefield.

Scott, D. 1999. "Aristotle on Well-Being and Intellectual Contemplation: Primary and Secondary *Eudaimonia*." *Proceedings of the Aristotelian Society*, Supplement 73: 225–242.

Vranas, P. 2005. "Aristotle on the Best Good: Is *Nicomachean Ethics* 1094a18–22 Fallacious?" *Phronesis* 50: 116–128.

Walker, M. 2011. "Aristotle on Activity 'According to the Best and Most Final' Virtue." *Apeiron* 44: 91–110.

Whiting, J. 2002. "*Eudaimonia*, External Results, and Choosing Virtuous Actions for Themselves." *Philosophy and Phenomenological Research* 65: 270–290.

Wilkes, K. 1980 [1978]. "The Good Man and the Good for Man in Aristotle's *Ethics*." 341–358 in A. O. Rorty ed. *Essays on Aristotle's Ethics*. Berkeley: University of California Press.

Human Ergon or Function

Achtenberg, D. 1989. "The Role of the *Ergon* Argument in Aristotle's *Nicomachean Ethics*." *Ancient Philosophy* 9: 37–47.

Barney, R. 2008. "Aristotle's Argument for a Human Function." *Oxford Studies in Ancient Philosophy* 34: 293–322.

Brüllmann, P. 2012. "Ethik und Naturphilosophie Bemerkungen zu Aristoteles' *Ergon*-Argument (EN I 6)." *Archiv für Geschichte der Philosophie* 94: 1–30.

Destrée, P. 2002. "Comment démontrer le propre de l'homme? Pour une lecture 'dialectique' de EN, I, 6." 39–62 in G. Romeyer-Dherby and G. Aubry eds. *L'Excellence de la vie: Sur l'Ethique à Nicomaque et l'Ethique à Eudème d'Aristote*. Paris: J. Vrin.

Gomez-Lobo, A. 1989. "The *Ergon* Inference." *Phronesis* 34: 170–184.

Korsgaard, C. 1986. "Aristotle on Function and Virtue." *History of Philosophy Quarterly* 3: 259–279.

Kraut, R. 1979. "The Peculiar Function of Human Beings." *Canadian Journal of Philosophy* 9: 467–478.

Lawrence, G. 1997. "Nonaggregatability, Inclusiveness, and the Theory of Focal Value: *Nicomachean Ethics* I.7 1097b16–20." *Phronesis* 42: 32–76.

2001. "The Function of the Function Argument." *Ancient Philosophy* 21: 445–475.

2006. "Human Good and Human Function." 37–75 in R. Kraut ed. *The Blackwell Guide to Aristotle's Nicomachean Ethics*. Malden, MA: Blackwell.

Nussbaum, M. C. 1990. "Aristotle on Human Nature and the Foundations of Ethics." 83–131 in J. Altham and R. Harrison eds. *World, Mind, and Ethics: Essays on the Ethical Philosophy of Bernard Williams*. Cambridge: Cambridge University Press.

Purinton, J. 1998. "Aristotle's Definition of Happiness (*NE* I.7, 1098a16–18)." *Oxford Studies in Ancient Philosophy* 16: 259–298.

Roche, T. D. 1988. "*Ergon* and *Eudaimonia* in *Nicomachean Ethics* I: Reconsidering the Intellectualist Interpretation." *Journal of the History of Philosophy* 26: 175–194.
Whiting, J. 1988. "Aristotle's Function Argument: A Defense." *Ancient Philosophy* 8: 33–48.

Happiness, Chance, and External Goods

Brown, E. 2005. "Wishing for Fortune, Choosing Activity: Aristotle on External Goods and Happiness." *Proceedings of the Boston Area Colloquium in Ancient Philosophy* 21: 57–81.
Cashen, M. 2012. "The Ugly, the Lonely, and the Lowly: Aristotle on Happiness and the External Goods." *History of Philosophy Quarterly* 29: 1–19.
Cooper, J. 1999 [1985]. "Aristotle and the Goods of Fortune." 292–311 in his *Reason and Emotion: Essays on Ancient Moral Psychology and Ethical Theory*. Princeton: Princeton University Press.
Farwall, P. 1994. "Aristotle, Success, and Moral Luck." *Journal of Philosophical Research* 19: 37–50.
Gooch, P. W. 1983. "Aristotle and the Happy Dead." *Classical Philology* 78: 112–116.
Irwin, T. H. 1985. "Permanent Happiness: Aristotle and Solon." *Oxford Studies in Ancient Philosophy* 3: 89–124.
Lear, J. 1995. "Testing the Limits: The Place of Tragedy in Aristotle's *Ethics*." 61–84 in R. Heinaman ed. *Aristotle and Moral Realism*. Boulder, CO: Westview Press.
Nussbaum, M. C. 1986. *The Fragility of Goodness: Luck and Ethics in Greek Tragedy and Philosophy*. Cambridge: Cambridge University Press.
1998. "Political Animals: Luck, Love, and Dignity." *Metaphilosophy* 29: 273–287.
Pritzl, K. 1983. "*Nicomachean Ethics* I.10–11: Aristotle on the Happiness after Death." *Classical Philology* 78: 101–111.
Scott, D. 2000. "Aristotle on Posthumous Fortune." *Oxford Studies in Ancient Philosophy* 18: 211–230.
Stemmer, P. 1992. "Aristoteles' Glücksbegriff in der *Nikomachischen Ethik*: Eine Interpretation von *EN* I 7, 1097b2–5." *Phronesis* 37: 85–110.
White, S. A. 1992. *Sovereign Virtue: Aristotle on the Relationship between Happiness and Prosperity*. Stanford, CA: Stanford University Press.

BOOK II: ETHICAL VIRTUE

The Nature of Agency

Ackrill, J. L. 1980 [1978]. "Aristotle on Action." 93–102 in A. O. Rorty ed. *Essays on Aristotle's Ethics*. Berkeley: University of California Press.
Balaban, P. 1986. "Aristotle's Theory of *Praxis*." *Hermes* 114: 163–172.
1990. "*Praxis* and *Poiesis* in Aristotle's Practical Philosophy." *Journal of Value Inquiry* 24: 185–198.
Charles, D. 1984. *Aristotle's Philosophy of Action*. London: Duckworth.
Coope, U. 2007. "Aristotle on Action." *Proceedings of the Aristotelian Society* 81, Supplement: 109–138.
Ebert, T. 1976. "*Praxis* und *Poiesis*. Zu einer handlungsthoretischen Unterscheidung bei Aristoteles." *Zeitschrift für philosophische Forschung* 30: 12–30.
Freeland, C. A. 1985. "Aristotelian Actions." *Noûs* 19: 397–414.

Hagen, C. T. 1984. "The *Energeia/kinēsis* Distinction and Aristotle's Theory of Action." *Journal of the History of Philosophy* 22: 263–280.

Natali, C. 2004. *L'action efficace. Études sur la philosophie de l'action chez Aristotle.* Louvain and Paris: Peeters.

Politis, V. 1998. "Aristotle's Advocacy of Non-Productive Action." *Ancient Philosophy* 18: 353–379.

Segvic, H. 2009 [2002]. "Aristotle's Metaphysics of Action." 111–143 in her *From Protagoras to Aristotle: Essays in Ancient Moral Philosophy.* Princeton: Princeton University Press.

Vasiliou, I. 2011. "Aristotle, Agents, and Actions." 170–190 in J. Miller ed. *Aristotle's Nicomachean Ethics: A Critical Guide.* Cambridge: Cambridge University Press.

Williams, B. A. O. 1995. "Acting as a Virtuous Person Acts." 13–23 in R. Heinaman ed. *Aristotle and Moral Realism.* Boulder, CO: Westview.

Nature, Habit, and the Acquisition of Ethical Virtue

Balaudé, J.-F. 1997. "Nature et norme dans les traités éthiques d'Aristote." 95–129 in P. M. Morel ed. *Aristote et la notion de nature.* Bordeaux: Presses Universitaires de Bordeaux.

Bowditch, N. 2008. "Aristotle on Habituation: The Key to Unlocking the *Nicomachean Ethics.*" *Ethical Perspectives* 15: 309–342.

Burnyeat, M. 1980. "Aristotle on Learning to be Good." 69–92 in A. O. Rorty ed. *Essays on Aristotle's Ethics.* Berkeley: University of California Press.

Curzer, H. 1996. "Aristotle's Bad Advice on Becoming Good." *Philosophy* 71: 139–146. 2002. "Aristotle's Painful Path to Virtue." *Journal of the History of Philosophy* 40: 141–162.

Di Muzio, G. 2000. "Aristotle on Improving One's Character." *Phronesis* 45: 205–219.

Everson, S. 1998. "Aristotle on Nature and Value." 77–106 in S. Everson ed. *Companion to Ancient Thought 4: Ethics.* Cambridge: Cambridge University Press.

Hursthouse, R. 1988. "Moral Habituation." *Oxford Studies in Ancient Philosophy* 6: 201–219.

Kraut, R. 2007. "Nature in Aristotle's Ethics and Politics." *Social Philosophy and Policy* 24: 153–175.

Lawrence, G. 2011. "Acquiring Character: Becoming Grown-Up." 233–283 in M. Pakaluk and G. Pearson eds. *Moral Psychology and Human Action in Aristotle.* Oxford: Oxford University Press.

Lennox, J. 1999. "Aristotle on the Biological Roots of Human Virtue." 10–31 in J. Maienschein and M. Ruse eds. *Biology and the Foundation of Ethics.* Cambridge: Cambridge University Press.

Lockwood, T. 2013. "Habituation, Habit, and Character in Aristotle's *Nicomachean Ethics.*" 19–36 in T. Sparrow and A. Hutchinson eds. *A History of Habit, from Aristotle to Bourdieu.* Lanham, MD: Lexington Books.

London, A. J. 2001. "Moral Knowledge and the Acquisition of Virtue in Aristotle's *Nicomachean* and *Eudemian Ethics.*" *Review of Metaphysics* 54: 553–583.

Morel, P. M. 1997. "L'habitude: une seconde nature?" 131–148 in P. M. Morel ed. *Aristote et la notion de nature.* Presses Universitaires de Bordeaux.

Sherman, N. 1989. *The Fabric of Character: Aristotle's Theory of Virtue.* Oxford: Clarendon Press.

Smith, A. D. 1996. "Character and Intellect in Aristotle's *Ethics.*" *Phronesis* 41: 56–74.

Vasiliou, I. 1996. "The Role of Good Upbringing in Aristotle's *Ethics*." *Philosophy and Phenomenological Research* 56: 771–797.

Verbeke, G. 1990. *Moral Education in Aristotle*. Washington, DC: Catholic University of America Press.

Ward, J. K. 2005. "Aristotle on *Physis*: Human Nature in the *Ethics* and *Politics*." *Polis* 22: 287–308.

The Definition and Nature of Ethical Virtue

Audi, R. 1995. "Acting from Virtue." *Mind* 104: 449–471.

Collins, S. 1999. "The Moral Virtues in Aristotle's *Nicomachean Ethics*." 131–158 in R. C. Bartlett and S. D. Collins eds. *Action and Contemplation: Studies in the Moral and Political Thought of Aristotle*. Albany: SUNY Press.

Curzer, H. J. 2005. "How Good People Do Bad Things: Aristotle on the Misdeeds of the Virtuous." *Oxford Studies in Ancient Philosophy* 28: 233–256.

Gottlieb, P. 2009. *The Virtue of Aristotle's Ethics*. Cambridge: Cambridge University Press.

Hutchinson, D. S. 1986. *The Virtues of Aristotle*. London: Routledge and Kegan Paul.

Kraut, R. 1976. "Aristotle on Choosing Virtue for Itself." *Archiv für Geschichte der Philosophie* 58: 223–239.

Lorenz, H. 2009. "Virtue of Character in Aristotle's *Nicomachean Ethics*." *Oxford Studies in Ancient Philosophy* 37: 177–212.

Nussbaum, M. C. 1988. "Non-Relative Virtues: An Aristotelian Approach." *Midwest Studies in Philosophy* 13: 32–53.

Sherman, N. 1997. *Making a Necessity of Virtue: Aristotle and Kant on Virtue*. Cambridge: Cambridge University Press.

Walker, A. D. M. 1989. "Virtue and Character." *Philosophy* 64: 349–362.

White, S. A. 1992. "Natural Virtue and Perfect Virtue in Aristotle." *Proceedings of the Boston Area Colloquium on Ancient Philosophy* 8: 135–186.

The Notion of What Is "Fine" (To Kalon)

Irwin, T. H. 2010. "The Sense and Reference of *Kalon* in Aristotle." *Classical Philology* 105: 381–396.

    2011. "Beauty and Morality in Aristotle." 239–253 in J. Miller ed. *Aristotle's Nicomachean Ethics: A Critical Guide*. Cambridge: Cambridge University Press.

Korsgaard, C. 1986. "Aristotle and Kant on the Source of Value." *Ethics* 96: 486–505.

    1996. "From Duty and for the Sake of the Noble." 203–236 in S. Engstrom and J. Whiting eds. *Aristotle, Kant, and the Stoics*. Cambridge: Cambridge University Press.

Kosman, A. 2010. "Beauty and the Good: Situating the *Kalon*." *Classical Philology* 105: 314–357.

Lännström, A. 2006. *Loving the Fine: Virtue and Happiness in Aristotle's Ethics*. Notre Dame, IN: University of Notre Dame Press.

Lear, G. R. 2009. "Aristotle on Moral Virtue and the Fine." 116–136 in R. Kraut ed. *The Blackwell Guide to Aristotle's Nicomachean Ethics*. Malden, MA: Blackwell.

Owens, J. 1981. "The *Kalon* in Aristotelian *Ethics*." 261–278 in D. O'Meara ed. *Studies in Aristotle*. Washington, DC: Catholic University of America Press.

Rogers, K. 1993. "Aristotle's Conception of *To Kalon*." *Ancient Philosophy* 13: 355–371.

Tuozzo, T. M. 1995. "Contemplation, the Noble, and the Mean: The Standard of Moral Virtue in Aristotle's Ethics." *Apeiron* 28: 129–154.

The Doctrine of the Mean

Bosley, R. 1991. *On Virtue and Vice: The Metaphysical Foundations of the Doctrine of the Mean.* New York: Peter Lang.

Bosley, R., R. Shiner, and J.D. Sisson eds. 1995. *Aristotle, Virtue and the Mean.* Kelowna, BC, Canada: Academic Printing and Publishing (= *Apeiron* 28.4).

Brown, L. 1997. "What Is the 'Mean Relative to Us' in Aristotle's *Ethics*?" *Phronesis* 42: 77–93.

Curzer, H.J. 1996. "A Defense of Aristotle's Doctrine of the Mean." *Ancient Philosophy* 16: 129–139.

    2006. "Aristotle's Mean Relative to Us." *American Catholic Philosophical Quarterly* 80: 507–519.

Gauthier-Muzellec, M.-H. 1998. *Aristote et la juste mesure.* Paris: Presses Universitaires de France.

Hardie, W.F.R. 1977 [1964–1965]. "Aristotle's Doctrine that Virtue Is a 'Mean.'" 33–46 in J. Barnes, M. Schofield, and R. Sorabji eds. *Articles on Aristotle.* Vol. 2. *Ethics and Politics.* London: Duckworth.

Hursthouse, R. 1980–1981. "A False Doctrine of the Mean." *Proceedings of the Aristotelian Society* 81: 57–72.

    2006. "The Central Doctrine of the Mean." 96–115 in R. Kraut ed. *The Blackwell Guide to Aristotle's Nicomachean Ethics.* Malden, MA: Blackwell.

Hutchinson, D.S. 1988. "Doctrines of the Mean and the Debate concerning Skills in Fourth-Century Medicine, Rhetoric, and Ethics." *Apeiron* 21: 17–52.

Leighton, S.R. 2011. "Inappropriate Passion." 211–236 in J. Miller ed. *Aristotle's Nicomachean Ethics: A Critical Guide.* Cambridge: Cambridge University Press.

Losin, P. 1987. "Aristotle's Doctrine of the Mean." *History of Philosophy Quarterly* 4: 329–341.

Peterson, S. 1988. "*Horos* (limit) in Aristotle's *Nicomachean Ethics*." *Phronesis* 23: 233–250.

Rapp, C. 2006. "What Use Is Aristotle's Doctrine of the Mean?" 99–126 in B. Reis and S. Haffmanns eds. *The Virtuous Life in Greek Ethics.* Cambridge: Cambridge University Press.

Urmson, J. 1980 [1973]. "Aristotle's Doctrine of the Mean." 157–170 in A.O. Rorty ed. *Essays on Aristotle's Ethics.* Berkeley: University of California Press.

Wolf, U. 1988. "Über den Sinn der aristotelischen Mesonlehre." *Phronesis* 33: 54–75.

Young, C.M. 1996. "Aristotle's Doctrine of the Mean." *Topoi* 15: 89–99.

Overviews of Aristotle's Moral Psychology

Cooper, J. 1999 [1988]. "Some Remarks on Aristotle's Moral Psychology." 237–252 in his *Reason and Emotion: Essays on Ancient Moral Psychology and Ethical Theory.* Princeton: Princeton University Press.

Grönroos, Gösta. 2007. "Listening to Reason in Aristotle's Moral Psychology." *Oxford Studies in Ancient Philosophy* 32: 251–272.

Irwin, T.H. 1980. "The Metaphysical and Psychological Basis of Aristotle's *Ethics*." 35–53 in A.O. Rorty ed. *Essays on Aristotle's Ethics.* Berkeley: University of California Press.

McDowell, J. 1998. "Some Issues in Aristotle's Moral Psychology." 107–128 in S. Everson ed. *Companion to Ancient Thought 4: Ethics*. Cambridge: Cambridge University Press.

Pearson, G. 2011. "Non-Rational Desire and Aristotle's Moral Psychology." 144–169 in J. Miller ed. *Aristotle's Nicomachean Ethics: A Critical Guide*. Cambridge: Cambridge University Press.

2012. *Aristotle on Desire*. Cambridge: Cambridge University Press.

Price, A. W. 2012. *Virtue and Reason in Aristotle and Plato*. Oxford: Oxford University Press.

The Voluntary and the Involuntary

Curren, R. 1989. "The Contribution of *Nicomachean Ethics* III.5 to Aristotle's Theory of Responsibility." *History of Philosophy Quarterly* 6: 261–277.

Dudley, J. 2012. *Aristotle's Concept of Chance: Accidents, Cause, Necessity, and Determinism*. Albany: SUNY Press.

Flannery, K. 2006. "Force and Compulsion in Aristotle's Ethics." *Proceedings of the Boston Area Colloquium in Ancient Philosophy* 22: 41–61.

Furley, D. J. 1977 [1967]. "Aristotle on the Voluntary." 47–60 in J. Barnes, M. Schofield, and R. Sorabji eds. *Articles on Aristotle*. Vol. 2. *Ethics and Politics*. London: Duckworth.

Irwin, T. H. 1980. "Reason and Responsibility in Aristotle." 117–156 in A. O. Rorty ed. *Essays on Aristotle's Ethics*. Berkeley: University of California Press.

Kenny, A. 1979. *Aristotle's Theory of the Will*. New Haven, CT: Yale University Press.

Klimchuk, D. 2002. "Aristotle on Necessity and Voluntariness." *History of Philosophy Quarterly* 19: 1–19.

Madigan, A. 1986. "Dimensions of Voluntariness in *EN* III.12, 1119a21–33." *Ancient Philosophy* 6: 139–152.

Meyer, S. S. 2009. "Aristotle on the Voluntary." 137–157 in R. Kraut ed. *The Blackwell Guide to Aristotle's Nicomachean Ethics*. Malden, MA: Blackwell.

2011 [1993]. *Aristotle on Moral Responsibility: Character and Cause*. Oxford: Oxford University Press.

Moline, J. N. 1989. "Aristotle on Praise and Blame." *Archiv für Geschichte der Philosophie* 71: 283–302.

Natali, C. 1998. "Aristotele: azione e responsabilità." 85–103 in C. Vigna ed. *La libertà del bene*. Milano: Vita e Pensiero.

2000. "Responsabilità e determinismo nell'etica aristotelica." 481–510 in M. Migliori ed. *Il dibattito etico e politico in Grecia tra il V e il IV secolo*. Naples: La Città de sole.

Nielsen, K. 2007. "Dirtying Aristotle's Hands? Aristotle's Analysis of 'Mixed Acts' in the *Nicomachean Ethics* III, 1." *Phronesis* 52: 270–300.

Sakezles, P. 2007. "Aristotle and Chrysippus on the Psychology of Human Action: Criteria for Responsibility." *British Journal for the History of Philosophy* 15: 225–252.

Sorabji, R. 1980. *Necessity, Cause, and Blame: Perspectives on Aristotle's Theory*. London: Duckworth.

The Problem of Freedom

Bobzien, S. 1998. "The Inadvertent Conception and Late Birth of the Free Will Problem." *Phronesis* 43: 133–175.

Chappell, T. 1994. *Aristotle and Augustine on Freedom*. New York: St. Martin's Press.

Donini, P. L. 2009 [1989]. *Aristotle and Determinism*. Louvain-la-Neuve: Peeters.

Dudley, J. 2004. *Aristotle's Concept of Chance. Contingency, Accidents, Freedom, and Necessity*. London: Ashgate.

Everson, S. 1990. "Aristotle's Compatibilism in the *Nicomachean Ethics*." *Revue de Philosophie Ancienne* 10: 81–99.

Frede, M. 2011. *A Free Will: Origins of the Notion in Ancient Thought*. Berkeley: University of California Press.

Hardie, W. F. R. 1968. "Aristotle and the Freewill Problem." *Philosophy* 43: 274–278.

Kahn, C. 1988. "Discovering the Will: From Aristotle to Augustine." 234–259 in J. M. Dillon and A. A. Long eds. *The Question of Eclecticism: Studies in Later Greek Philosophy*. Berkeley: University of California Press.

Natali, C. 2002. "Responsibility and Determinism in Aristotle's Ethics." 267–295 in M. Canto-Sperber and P. Pellegrin eds. *Le style de la pensée*. Paris: Les Belles Lettres.

Rapp, C. 1995. "Freiwilligkeit, Entscheidung, und Verantwortlichkeit (*EN* III 1–7)." 109–134 in O. Höffe ed. *Aristoteles: Die Nikomachische Ethik*. Berlin: Akademie Verlag.

Deliberation and Choice

Kuhn, H. 1960. "Der Begriff der Prohairesis in der *Nikomachischen Ethik*." 123–140 in D. Henrich ed. *Die Gegenwart der Griechen im neueren Denken: Festschrift für H. G. Gadamer zum 60. Geburstag*. Tübingen: J. C. B. Mohr.

McDowell, J. 1996. "Deliberation and Moral Deliberation in Aristotle's *Ethics*." 19–35 in Engstrom and J. Whiting eds. *Aristotle, Kant, and the Stoics*. Cambridge: Cambridge University Press.

Mele, A. R. 1981. "Choice and Virtue in the *Nicomachean Ethics*." *Journal of the History of Philosophy* 19: 405–424.

Natali, C. 1988. "Les fins et les moyens: un puzzle aristotélicien." *Revue de Philosophie ancienne* 6: 107–146.

Nielsen, K. 2011. "Deliberation as Inquiry: Aristotle's Alternative to the Presumption of Open Alternatives." *Philosophical Review* 120: 383–421.

Price, A. W. 2011. "Aristotle on the Ends of Deliberation." 135–158 in M. Pakaluk and G. Pearson eds. *Moral Psychology and Human Action in Aristotle*. Oxford: Oxford University Press.

Segvic, H. 2009. "Deliberation and Choice in Aristotle." 144–171 in her *From Protagoras to Aristotle: Essays in Ancient Moral Philosophy*. Princeton: Princeton University Press.

Sherman, N. 1985. "Character, Planning, and Choice." *Review of Metaphysics* 39: 83–116.

Tilley, J. 1994. "Virtue and Choice in Aristotle's Ethics." *Philosophia* 23–24: 173–177.

Tuozzo, T. M. 1991. "Aristotelian Deliberation Not of Ends." 193–212 in J. P. Anton and A. Preus eds. *Essays in Ancient Greek Philosophy IV: Aristotle's Ethics*. Albany: SUNY Press.

Wiggins, D. 1980 [1975–1976]. "Deliberation and Practical Reason." 221–240 in A. O. Rorty ed. *Essays on Aristotle's Ethics*. Berkeley: University of California Press.

Wish, Emotion, and Desire

Brinton, A. 1988. "Pathos and the Appeal to Emotion: An Aristotelian Analysis." *History of Philosophy Quarterly* 5: 207–219.

Cooper, J. 1999 [1996]. "An Aristotelian Theory of the Emotions." 406–423 in his *Reason and Emotion: Essays on Ancient Moral Psychology and Ethical Theory*. Princeton: Princeton University Press.

DeMoss, D. J. 1990. "Acquiring Ethical Ends." *Ancient Philosophy* 10: 63–80.

Dow, J. 2011. "Aristotle's Theory of the Emotions: Emotions as Pleasures and Pains." 47–74 in M. Pakaluk and G. Pearson eds. *Moral Psychology and Human Action in Aristotle.* Oxford: Oxford University Press.

Fortenbaugh, W. W. 2002 [1975]. *Aristotle on Emotions: A Contribution to Philosophical Psychology, Rhetoric, Poetics, Politics, and Ethics.* 2nd ed. with a new epilogue. London: Duckworth.

Hursthouse, R. 1984. "Acting and Feeling in Character: *Nicomachean Ethics* 3.i." *Phronesis* 29: 252–266.

Knuuttila, S. 2004. *Emotions in Ancient and Medieval Philosophy.* Oxford: Oxford University Press.

Konstan, D. 2006. *Emotions of the Greeks. Studies in Aristotle and Classical Literature.* Toronto: University of Toronto Press.

Kosman, L. A. 1980. "Being Properly Affected: Virtues and Feelings in Aristotle's *Ethics.*" 103–116 in A. O. Rorty ed. *Essays on Aristotle's Ethics.* Berkeley: University of California Press.

Lorenz, H. 2006. *The Brute Within: Appetitive Desire in Plato and Aristotle.* Oxford: Clarendon Press.

Mele, A. R. 1984. "Aristotle's Wish." *Journal of the History of Philosophy* 22: 139–156.

Moss, J. 2012. *Aristotle on the Apparent Good: Perception, Phantasia, Thought, and Desire.* Oxford: Oxford University Press.

Nussbaum, M. C. 1996. "Aristotle on Emotions and Rational Persuasion." 303–323 in A. O. Rorty ed. *Essays on Aristotle's Rhetoric.* Berkeley: University of California Press.

Pearson, G. 2011. "Non-Rational Desire and Aristotle's Moral Psychology." 144–169 in J. Miller ed. *Aristotle's Nicomachean Ethics: A Critical Guide.* Cambridge: Cambridge University Press.

2012. *Aristotle on Desire.* Cambridge: Cambridge University Press.

Rorty, A. O. 1984. "Aristotle on the Metaphysical Status of *Pathē.*" *Review of Metaphysics* 37: 521–546.

Sherman, N. 1993. "The Role of Emotions in Aristotelian Virtue." *Proceedings of the Boston Area Colloquium in Ancient Philosophy* 9: 1–33.

Striker, G. 1996. "Emotions in Context: Aristotle's Treatment of the Passions in the Rhetoric and His Moral Psychology." 286–302 in A. O. Rorty ed. *Essays on Aristotle's Rhetoric.* Berkeley: University of California Press.

Tuozzo, T. M. 1994. "Conceptualized and Unconceptualized Desire in Aristotle." *Journal of the History of Philosophy* 32: 525–549.

The Critique of Protagoras and Responsibility for One's Character States

Bondeson, W. 1979. "Aristotle on Responsibility for One's Character and the Possibility of Character Change." *Phronesis* 19: 59–65.

Brickhouse, T. C. 1991. "Roberts on Responsibility for Action and Character in the *Nicomachean Ethics.*" *Ancient Philosophy* 11: 137–148.

Chappell, T. 2005. "'The Good Man Is the Measure of All Things': Objectivity without World-Centredness in Aristotle's Moral Epistemology." 233–255 in C. Gill ed. *Virtue, Norms, and Objectivity: Issues in Ancient and Modern Ethics.* Oxford: Clarendon Press.

Destrée, P. 2011. "Aristotle on Responsibility for One's Character." 285–318 in M. Pakaluk and G. Pearson eds. *Moral Psychology and Human Action in Aristotle.* Oxford: Oxford University Press.

Di Muzio, G. 2008. "Aristotle's Alleged Moral Determinism in the *Nicomachean Ethics.*" *Journal of Philosophical Research* 33: 19–32.

Gottlieb, P. 1991. "Aristotle and Protagoras: The Good Human Being as the Measure of Goods." *Apeiron* 24: 25–46.

Ott, W. R. 2000. "A Troublesome Passage in Aristotle's *Nicomachean Ethics* iii.5." *Ancient Philosophy* 20: 99–108.

Roberts, J. 1989. "Aristotle on Responsibility for Action and Character." *Ancient Philosophy* 9: 23–36.

BOOKS III.6–V.11: INDIVIDUAL VIRTUES

Courage

Brady, M. E. 2005. "The Fearlessness of Courage." *Southern Journal of Philosophy* 43: 189–211.

Deslauriers, M. 2002. "*Andreia*, Divine and Sub-Human Virtue." 187–211 in I. Sluiter and R. Rosen eds. *Proceedings of the Penn-Leiden Colloquium on Ancient Values I.* Leiden: Brill.

Leighton, S. R. 1988. "Aristotle's Courageous Passions." *Phronesis* 33: 76–99.

Pears, D. 1978. "Aristotle's Analysis of Courage." *Midwest Studies in Philosophy* 3: 273–285.

1980. "Courage as a Mean." 171–188 in A. O. Rorty ed. *Essays on Aristotle's Ethics.* Berkeley: University of California Press.

Pearson, G. 2006. "Does the Fearless Phobic Really Fear the Squeak of Mice Too Much?" *Ancient Philosophy* 26: 81–91.

2009. "Aristotle on the Role of Confidence in Courage." *Ancient Philosophy* 29: 123–137.

Rogers, K. 1994. "Aristotle on the Motive of Courage." *Southern Journal of Philosophy* 32: 303–313.

Rorty, A. O. 1986. "The Two Faces of Courage." *Philosophy* 61: 151–171.

Sanford, J. 2010. "Are You Man Enough? Aristotle and Courage." *International Philosophical Quarterly* 50: 431–446.

Taylor, C. C. W. 2008. "Wisdom and Courage in the *Protagoras* and the *Nicomachean Ethics.*" 281–294 in his *Pleasure, Mind, and Soul: Selected Papers in Ancient Philosophy.* Oxford: Clarendon Press.

Ward, L. 2001. "Nobility and Necessity: The Problem of Courage in Aristotle's *Nicomachean Ethics.*" *American Political Science Review* 95: 71–83.

Temperance

Bogen, J., and J. Moravcsik. 1982. "Aristotle's Forbidden Sweets." *Journal of the History of Philosophy* 20: 111–127.

Curzer, H. J. 1997. "Aristotle's Account of the Virtue of Temperance in *Nicomachean Ethics* III.10–11." *Journal of the History of Philosophy* 35: 5–26.

MacIntyre, A. C. 1988. "*Sophrosunē*: How a Virtue Can Become Socially Disruptive." *Midwest Studies in Philosophy* 13: 1–11.

Madigan, A. 1986. "Dimensions of Voluntariness in *EN* III.12, 1119a21–33." *Ancient Philosophy* 6: 139–152.

Rupert, M. 2002. "Aristotle's Discussion of Temperance and Continence." *Dialogue* 45: 16–19.

Sisko, J. E. 2003. "Taste, Touch, and Temperance in *Nicomachean Ethics* 3.10." *Classical Quarterly* 53: 135–140.

Young, C. M. 1988. "Aristotle on Temperance." *Philosophical Review* 97: 521–542.

Liberality and Magnificence

Hadreas, P. 2002. "Aristotle on the Vices and Virtue of Wealth." *Journal of Business Ethics* 39: 361–376.

Hare, J. 1988. "*Eleutheriotes* in Aristotle's Ethics." *Ancient Philosophy* 8: 19–32.

Hunt, L. 1986. "Generosity and the Diversity of the Virtues." 216–227 in R. K. Kruschwitz and R. C. Roberts eds. *The Virtues: Contemporary Essays on Moral Character.* Belmont, CA: Wadsworth.

Pakaluk, M. 2002. "On an Alleged Contradiction in Aristotle's *Nicomachean Ethics.*" *Oxford Studies in Ancient Philosophy* 22: 201–219.

Swanson, J. A. 1994. "Aristotle on Liberality: Its Relation to Justice and Its Public and Private Practice." *Polity* 27: 3–23.

Ward, A. 2011. "Generosity and Inequality in Aristotle's *Ethics.*" *Polis* 28: 267–278.

Young, C. M. 1994. "Aristotle on Liberality." *Proceedings of the Boston Area Colloquium on Ancient Philosophy* 10: 313–334.

Magnanimity and Love of Honor

Bae, E. 2003. "An Ornament of the Virtues." *Ancient Philosophy* 23: 337–349.

Cooper, N. 1989. "Aristotle's Crowning Virtue." *Apeiron* 22: 191–205.

Cordner, C. 1994. "Aristotelian Virtue and Its Limitations." *Philosophy* 69: 291–316.

Crisp, R. 2006. "Aristotle on Greatness of Soul." 158–178 in R. Kraut ed. *The Blackwell Guide to Aristotle's Nicomachean Ethics.* Malden, MA: Blackwell.

Curzer, H. J. 1990. "A Great Philosopher's Not So Great Account of Great Virtue: Aristotle's Treatment of 'Greatness of Soul.'" *Canadian Journal of Philosophy* 20: 517–537.

 1991. "Aristotle's Much-Maligned *Megalopsuchos.*" *Australasian Journal of Philosophy* 69: 131–151.

Gauthier, R. A. 1951. *Magnanimité: L'idéal de la grandeur dans la philosophie païenne et dans la théologie chrétienne.* Paris: J. Vrin.

Hardie, W. F. R. 1978. "'Magnanimity' in Aristotle's Ethics." *Phronesis* 23: 63–79.

Held, D. 1993. "*Megalopsychia* in *Nicomachean Ethics* IV." *Ancient Philosophy* 13: 95–110.

Howland, J. 2002. "Aristotle's Great-Souled Man." *Review of Politics* 64: 27–56.

Pakaluk, M. 2004. "The Meaning of Aristotelian Magnanimity." *Oxford Studies in Ancient Philosophy* 26: 241–275.

Sarch, A. 2008. "What's Wrong with *Megalopsychia*?" *Philosophy* 83: 231–253.

Schütrumpf, E. 1989. "Magnanimity, *Megalopsuchia* and the System of Aristotle's *Nicomachean Ethics.*" *Archiv für Geschichte der Philosophie* 71: 10–22.

Sherman, N. 1988. "Common Sense and Uncommon Virtue." *Midwest Studies in Philosophy* 13: 97–114.

Somme, L. T. 1999. "La magnanimité chez Aristote." *Revue Thomiste* 99: 700–735.

2000. "La magnanimité chez Aristote (La Deuxième Partie)." *Revue Thomiste* 108: 62–78.

Stover, J., and R. Polansky. 2003. "Moral Virtue and *Megalopsychia*." *Ancient Philosophy* 23: 351–359.

Truthfulness

Gooch, P. W. 1987. "Socratic Irony and Aristotle's *Eiron*: Some Puzzles." *Phoenix* 41: 95–104.

Lane, M. 2006. "The Evolution of *Eironeia* in Classical Greek Texts: Why Socratic *Eironeia* Is Not Socratic Irony." *Oxford Studies in Ancient Philosophy* 31: 49–83.

Szabados, B. 1998. "Hypocrisy after Aristotle." *Dialogue* 37: 545–570.

Zembaty, J. S. 1993. "Aristotle on Lying." *Journal of the History of Philosophy* 31: 7–30.

Other Aristotelian Virtues

Broadie, S. 2003. "Aristotelian Piety." *Phronesis* 48: 54–70.

Burger, R. 1991. "Ethical Reflection and Righteous Indignation: *Nemesis* in the *Nicomachean Ethics*." 127–139 in J. P. Anton and A. Preus eds. *Essays in Ancient Greek Philosophy IV: Aristotle's Ethics*. Albany, NY: SUNY Press.

Coker, J. 1992. "On Being *Nemesētikos* as a Mean." *Journal of Philosophical Research* 17: 61–92.

Gottlieb, P. 1994. "Aristotle's Nameless Virtues." *Apeiron* 27: 1–15.

Gravelee, G. S. 2000. "Aristotle on Hope." *Journal of the History of Philosophy* 38: 461–477.

Leighton, S. 2002. "Aristotle's Account of Anger: Narcissism and Illusions of Self-Sufficiency." *Ratio* 15: 23–45.

Mayhew, R. 2007. "Aristotle on Prayer." *Rhizai* 4: 295–309.

Justice

OVERVIEWS OF JUSTICE

Collins, S. 2002. "Justice and the Dilemma of Moral Virtue in Aristotle's *Nicomachean Ethics*." 105–129 in A. Tessitore ed. *Aristotle and Modern Politics. The Persistence of Political Philosophy*. Notre Dame, IN: University of Notre Dame Press.

Curzer, H. J. 1995. "Aristotle's Account of the Virtue of Justice." *Apeiron* 28: 207–238.

Drefcinski, S. 2000. "Aristotle and the Characteristic Desire of Justice." *Apeiron* 33: 109–123.

Fritz, K. v. 1980. "Zur Interpretation des V. Buches von Aristoteles' *NE*." *Archiv für Geschichte der Philosophie* 62: 241–275.

Harrison, A. R. W. 1957. "Aristotle's *Nicomachean Ethics*, Book V and the Law of Athens." *Journal of Hellenic Studies* 77: 42–47.

Kraut, R. 2002. "Justice in the *Nicomachean Ethics*." 98–177 in *Aristotle: Political Philosophy*. Oxford: Oxford University Press.

2003. "Justice in Plato and Aristotle: Withdrawal versus Engagement," with reply by C. Rowe. 153–176 in R. Heinaman ed. *Plato and Aristotle's Ethics*. Burlington, VT: Ashgate.

Kussmaul, P. 2008. "Aristotle's Doctrine of Justice and the Law of Athens." *Dionysius* 26: 29–46.

Moraux, P. 1957. *A la recherche de l'Aristote perdu: Le Dialogue "Sur la Justice."* Louvain: Publications Universitaires de Louvain.

Pearson, G. 2006. "Aristotle on Acting Unjustly without Being Unjust." *Oxford Studies in Ancient Philosophy* 30: 211–233.

Williams, B. A. O. 1980. "Justice as a Virtue." 189–199 in A. O. Rorty ed. *Essays on Aristotle's Ethics*. Berkeley: University of California Press.

Young, C. 2006. "Aristotle's Justice." 179–197 in R. Kraut ed. *The Blackwell Guide to Aristotle's Nicomachean Ethics*. Malden, MA: Blackwell.

GENERAL VERSUS SPECIFIC JUSTICE

O'Connor, D. 1988. "Aristotelian Justice as a Personal Virtue." *Midwest Studies in Philosophy* 13: 417–427.

1991. "The Aetiology of Justice." 136–164 in C. Lord and D. O'Connor eds. *Essays on the Foundations of Aristotelian Political Science*. Berkeley: University of California Press.

Fossheim, H. 2011. "Justice in the *Nicomachean Ethics* Book V." 254–275 in J. Miller ed. *Aristotle's Nicomachean Ethics: A Critical Guide*. Cambridge: Cambridge University Press.

Ritchie, D. G. 1894. "Aristotle's Subdivisions of 'Particular Justice.'" *Classical Review* 8: 185–192.

Sherman, D. 1999. "Aristotle and the Problem of Particular Injustice." *Philosophical Forum* 30: 235–248.

DISTRIBUTIVE AND CORRECTIVE JUSTICE

Frank, J. 1988. "Democracy and Distribution: Aristotle on Just Desert." *Political Theory* 26: 784–802.

Harvey, F. D. 1965. "Two Kinds of Equality." *Classica et Mediaevalia* 26: 101–146.

Karasmanis, V. 1993. "The Mathematical Passage in *Nicomachean Ethics* 1131b5–15." *Ancient Philosophy* 13: 373–378.

Keyser, P. 1992. "A Proposed Diagram in Aristotle, *EN* V3, 1131a24–b20 for Distributive Justice in Proportion." *Apeiron* 25: 15–44.

Keyt, D. 1991 [1985]. "Aristotle's Theory of Distributive Justice." 238–278 in D. Keyt, and F. D. Miller eds. *A Companion to Aristotle's Politics*. D. Keyt and F. D. Miller eds. Oxford and Cambridge, MA: Basil Blackwell.

Mathie, W. 1987. "Political and Distributive Justice in the Political Science of Aristotle." *Review of Politics* 49: 59–84.

McKerlie, D. 2001. "Aristotle's Theory of Justice." *Southern Journal of Philosophy* 39: 119–142.

Neyers, J. W. 1998. "The Inconsistencies of Aristotle's Theory of Corrective Justice." *Canadian Journal of Law and Jurisprudence* 11: 311–328.

Rosen, F. 1975. "The Political Context of Aristotle's Categories of Justice." *Phronesis* 20: 228–240.

Springborg, P. 1984. "Aristotle and the Problem of Needs." *History of Political Thought* 5: 393–424.

Weinrib, E. J. 1992. "Corrective Justice." *Iowa Law Review* 77: 403–425.

RECIPROCITY AND EXCHANGE

Danzig, G. 2000. "The Political Character of Aristotelian Reciprocity." *Classical Philology* 95: 399–424.

Gordon, B. 1963. "Aristotle and the Development of Value Theory." *Quarterly Journal of Economics* 78: 115–128.

Judson, L. 1997. "Aristotle on Fair Exchange." *Oxford Studies in Ancient Philosophy* 13: 147–175.

McNeill, D. 1990. "Alternative Interpretations of Aristotle on Exchange and Reciprocity." *Public Affairs Quarterly* 4: 55–68.

Meikle, S. 1995. *Aristotle's Economic Thought*. New York: Oxford University Press.

Scaltsas, T. 1995. "Reciprocal Justice in Aristotle's *Nicomachean Ethics*." *Archiv für Geschichte der Philosophie* 77: 248–262.

NATURAL AND POLITICAL JUSTICE

Alexander of Aphrodisias. 1990 [1887]. "*hoti physei to dikaion*." 156–159 in *Questiones Ethicae, Commentaria in Aristotelem Graeca*. Supplementum Aristotelicum, vol. 2, pt. 1. I. Burns ed. Berlin: G. Reimer. Translated in *Ethical Problems*, by R. W. Sharples. Ithaca, NY: Cornell University Press.

Aubenque, P. 1980. "La Loi selon Aristote." *Archives de Philosophie du Droit* 25: 147–157.

1995. "The Twofold Natural Foundation of Justice According to Aristotle." 35–47 in R. Heinaman ed. *Aristotle and Moral Realism*. Boulder, CO: Westview Press.

Bodéüs, R. 1999. "The Natural Foundations of Right and Aristotelian Philosophy." 69–106 in R. C. Bartlett and S. D. Collins eds. *Action and Contemplation: Studies in the Moral and Political Thought of Aristotle*. Albany: SUNY Press.

Burns, T. 1998. "Aristotle and Natural Law." *History of Political Thought* 19: 142–166.

Corbett, R. 2009. "The Question of Natural Law in Aristotle." *History of Political Thought* 30: 229–250.

Destrée, P. 2000. "Aristote et la question du droit naturel (*Eth. Nic.*, V,10, 1134b18–1135a5)." *Phronesis* 45: 220–239.

Lockwood, T. 2006. "Ethical Justice and Political Justice." *Phronesis* 51: 29–48.

Miller, F. D. 1991 [1988–1989]. "Aristotle on Natural Law and Justice." 279–306 in D. Keyt and F. Miller eds. *A Companion to Aristotle's Politics*. Cambridge, MA: Blackwell.

Mulhern, J. J. 1972. "MIA MONON PANTACHOU KATA PHUSIN Ē ARISTĒ (*EN* 1135a)." *Phronesis* 17: 260–268.

Sharples, R. W. 2005. "An Aristotelian Commentator on the Naturalness of Justice." 279–293 in C. Gill ed. *Virtue, Norms, and Objectivity: Issues in Ancient and Modern Ethics*. Oxford: Clarendon Press.

Vega, J. 2010. "Aristotle's Concept of Law: Beyond Positivism and Natural Law." *Journal of Ancient Philosophy* 4: 1–31.

EQUITY (EPIEIKEIA)

Brunschwig, J. 1996. "Rule and Exception: On the Aristotelian Theory of Equity." 115–156 in M. Frede and G. Striker eds. *Rationality in Greek Thought*. Oxford: Oxford University Press.

Georgiadis, G. 1987. "Equitable and Equity in Aristotle." 150–172 in S. Panagiotou ed. *Justice, Law, and Method in Plato and Aristotle*. Edmonton, AL: Academic Printing and Publishing.

Hewitt, A. 2008. "Universal Justice and *Epieikeia* in Aristotle." *Polis* 25: 115–130.

Horn, C. 2006. "*Epieikeia*: The Competence of the Perfectly Just Person in Aristotle." 142–166 in B. Reis and S. Haffmanns eds. *The Virtuous Life in Greek Ethics*. Cambridge: Cambridge University Press.

Nussbaum, M. C. 1995. "Equity and Mercy." *Philosophy and Public Affairs* 22: 83–125.
Shiner, R. A. 1994 [1987]. "Aristotle's Theory of Equity." *Loyola of Los Angeles Law Review* 27: 1245–1264.

BOOK VI: INTELLECTUAL VIRTUES

Overviews of Aristotle's Intellectual Virtues

Chateau, J.-Y., ed. 1997. *La Vérité pratique, Ethique à Nicomaque Livre VI*. Paris: J. Vrin.
Gadamer, H. G. 1998. *Nikomachische Ethik VI*. Frankfurt am Main: Vittorio Klostermann.
Greenwood, L. H. G. 1909. *Aristotle: Nicomachean Ethics, Book Six*. Cambridge: Cambridge University Press.
Heidegger, M. 1997 [1924–1925]. *Plato's Sophist, Introductory Part*, 15–156. R. Rojcewicz and A. Schuwer trans. Bloomington: Indiana University Press.
Louden, R. B. 1997. "What Is Moral Authority? *Euboulia, Sunesis*, and *Gnomē* vs. *Phronēsis*." *Ancient Philosophy* 17: 103–118.
Monan, J. D. 1968. *Moral Knowledge and Its Method in Aristotle*. Oxford: Clarendon Press.
Natali, C. 2001. *The Wisdom of Aristotle*. G. Parks trans. Albany: SUNY Press.
Reeve, C. D. C. 2006. "Aristotle on the Virtues of Thought." 198–217 in R. Kraut ed. *The Blackwell Guide to Aristotle's Nicomachean Ethics*. Malden, MA: Blackwell.
    2013. *Aristotle on Practical Wisdom: Nicomachean Ethics VI*. Cambridge, MA: Harvard University Press.

The Relation of Desire and Practical Reason; Moral Virtue and Knowledge

Anscombe, G. E. M. 1977 [1965]. "Thought and Action in Aristotle." 72–78 in J. Barnes, M. Schofield, and R. Sorabji eds. *Articles on Aristotle*. Vol. 2. *Ethics and Politics*. London: Duckworth.
Broadie, S. 1987. "The Problem of Practical Intellect in Aristotle's *Ethics*." *Boston Area Colloquium on Ancient Philosophy* 3: 229–252.
Charles, D. 2009. "Aristotle on Desire and Action." 291–308 in D. Frede ed. *Body and Soul in Ancient Philosophy*. Berlin: De Gruyter.
    2011. "Desire in Action: Aristotle's Move." 75–93 in M. Pakaluk and G. Pearson eds. *Moral Psychology and Human Action in Aristotle*. Oxford: Oxford University Press.
Cooper, J. 1999 [1996]. "Reason, Moral Virtue, and Moral Value." 253–280 in his *Reason and Emotion: Essays on Ancient Moral Psychology and Ethical Theory*. Princeton: Princeton University Press.
Fortenbaugh, W. W. 1991 [1987]. "Aristotle's Distinction between Moral Virtue and Practical Wisdom." 97–106 in J. P. Anton and A. Preus eds. *Essays in Ancient Greek Philosophy IV: Aristotle's Ethics*. Albany: SUNY Press.
Irwin, T. H. 1975. "Aristotle on Reason, Desire and Virtue." *Journal of Philosophy* 72: 567–578.
Mele, A. R. 1984. "Aristotle on the Roles of Reason in Motivation and Action." *Archiv für Geschichte der Philosophie* 66: 124–147.
Miller, F. D. 1984. "Aristotle on Rationality in Action." *Review of Metaphysics* 37: 499–520.

Price, A. W. 2005. "Aristotelian Virtue and Practical Judgement." 257–278 in C. Gill ed. *Virtue, Norms, and Objectivity: Issues in Ancient and Modern Ethics.* Oxford: Clarendon Press.

Smith, A. D. 1996. "Character and Intellect in Aristotle's *Ethics*." *Phronesis* 41: 56–74.

Sorabji, R. 1980 [1973–1974]. "Aristotle on the Role of Intellect in Virtue." 201–220 in A. O. Rorty ed. *Essays on Aristotle's Ethics.* Berkeley: University of California Press.

Craft (Technē)

Angier, T. 2010. *Technē in Aristotle's Ethics: Crafting the Moral Life.* London: Continuum.

Baracchi, C. 2011. "Three Fragments on '*Techne*' in Aristotle's '*Nicomachean Ethics*': A Note on Exploration and Creativity." *Graduate Faculty Philosophy Journal* 32: 103–125.

Broadie, S. 1987. "Nature, Craft and *Phronēsis* in Aristotle." *Philosophical Topics* 15: 35–50.

Garrett, J. 1987. "Aristotle's Nontechnical Conception of *Technē*." *Modern Schoolman* 64: 283–294.

The Theoretical Virtues: Epistēmē, Nous, Sophia

Gigon, O. 1975. "*Phronēsis* und *Sophia* in der *Nicomachischen Ethik* des Aristoteles." 91–104 in. J. Mansfield and L. M. de Rijk eds. *Kephalaion: Studies in Greek Philosophy and Its Continuation.* Assen: Van Gorcum.

Nightingale, A. W. 2004. *Spectacles of Truth in Classical Greek Philosophy: Theoria in Its Cultural Context.* Cambridge: Cambridge University Press.

Salem, E. 2003. "Prudence and Wisdom in Aristotle's *Ethics*." *St. John's Review* 47: 25–50.

Wood, J. 2011. "Contemplating the Beautiful: The Practical Importance of Theoretical Excellence in Aristotle's *Ethics*." *Journal of the History of Philosophy* 49: 391–412.

Practical Wisdom (Phronēsis)

Abizadeh, A. 2002. "The Passions of the Wise: *Phronēsis*, Rhetoric, and Aristotle's Passionate Practical Deliberation." *Review of Metaphysics* 56: 267–296.

Annas, J. 1996. "Aristotle and Kant on Morality and Practical Reasoning." 237–258 in S. Engstrom and J. Whiting eds. *Kant and the Stoics: Rethinking Happiness and Duty.* Cambridge: Cambridge University Press.

Aubenque, P. 1963. *La Prudence chez Aristote.* Paris: Presses Universitaires de France. 1965. "La prudence aristotélicienne, porte-t-elle sur la fin ou sur les moyens?" *Revue des Études Grecques* 78: 40–51.

Barnes, J. J. Brunschwig, and M. Frede. 1990. "Le propre de la prudence." 79–96 in R. Brague and J. F. Courtine eds. *Herméneutique et ontologie. Mélanges en hommage à P. Aubenque.* Paris: Presses Universitaires de France.

Broadie, S. 1998. "Interpreting Aristotle's Directions." 291–306 in J. Gentzler ed. *Method in Ancient Philosophy.* Oxford: Clarendon Press.

Drefcinski, S. 1996. "Aristotle's Fallible *Phronimos*." *Ancient Philosophy* 16: 139–154.

Dunne, J. 1993. *Back to the Rough Ground: Phronēsis and "Technē" in Modern Philosophy and in Aristotle.* Notre Dame, IN: University of Notre Dame Press.

Fiasse, G. 2001. "Aristotle's *Phronimos*: A True Grasp of Ends as Well as Means." *Review of Metaphysics* 55: 323–338.

Hursthouse, R. 2006. "Practical Wisdom: A Mundane Account." *Proceedings of the Aristotelian Society* 106: 285–309.

Kirkland, S. 2007. "The Temporality of *Phronēsis* in the *Nicomachean Ethics*." *Ancient Philosophy* 27: 127–140.

Modrak, W. K. W. 1991. "Aristotle on Reason, Practical Reason, and Living Well." 179–192 in J. P. Anton and A. Preus eds. *Essays in Ancient Greek Philosophy IV: Aristotle's Ethics*. Albany: SUNY Press.

Reeve, C. D. C. 1992. *Practices of Reason: Aristotle's Nicomachean Ethics*. Oxford: Clarendon Press.

Rese, F. 2005. "*Praxis* and *Logos* in Aristotle: On the Meaning of Reason and Speech for Human Life and Action." *Epoche* 9: 359–377.

Taylor, C. C. W. 2008. "Aristotle on the Practical Intellect." 204–222 in his *Pleasure, Mind, and Soul: Selected Papers in Ancient Philosophy*. Oxford: Clarendon Press.

Wiggins, D. 1980 [1975–1976]. "Deliberation and Practical Reason." 221–240 in A. O. Rorty ed. *Essays on Aristotle's Ethics*. Berkeley: University of California Press.

Moral Perception: Particulars and Universals

Devereux, D. 1986. "Particular and Universal in Aristotle's Conception of Practical Knowledge." *Review of Metaphysics* 39: 483–504.

Fortenbaugh, W. W. 1964. "Aristotle's Conception of Moral Virtue and Its Perceptive Role." *Transactions of the American Philological Association* 95: 77–87.

Hankinson, R. J. 1990. "Perception and Maturation: Aristotle on the Moral Imagination." *Dialogue* 29: 41–63.

Irwin, T. H. 1978. "First Principles in Aristotle's Ethics." *Midwest Studies in Philosophy* 3: 252–272.

Louden, R. B. 1991. "Aristotle's Practical Particularism." 159–178 in J. P. Anton and A. Preus eds. *Essays in Ancient Greek Philosophy IV: Aristotle's Ethics*. Albany: SUNY Press.

Milliken, J. 2006. "Aristotle's Aesthetic Ethics." *Southern Journal of Philosophy* 44: 319–339.

Nussbaum, M. C. 1985. "The Discernment of Perception: An Aristotelian Conception of Private and Public Rationality." *Proceedings of the Boston Area Colloquium on Ancient Philosophy* 1: 151–201.

Price, A. W. 2005. "Was Aristotle a Particularist?" *Proceedings of the Boston Area Colloquium in Ancient Philosophy* 21: 191–212.

Shiner, R. A. 1979. "Ethical Perception in Aristotle." *Apeiron* 13: 79–85.

Walsh, M. 1999. "Role of Universal Knowledge in Aristotelian Moral Virtue." *Ancient Philosophy* 19: 73–88.

Woods, M. 1986. "Intuition and Perception in Aristotle's Ethics." *Oxford Studies in Ancient Philosophy* 4: 145–166.

The Nature of "Right Reason" (Orthos Logos)

Burnet, J. 1914. "On the Meaning of *Logos* in Aristotle's *Ethics*." *Classical Review* 28: 6–7.

Cook Wilson, J. 1913. "On the Meaning of *Logos* in Certain Passages in Aristotle's *Nicomachean Ethics*." *Classical Review* 27: 113–117.

Dryer, D. P. 1983. "Aristotle's Conception of '*Orthos Logos*.'" *Monist* 66: 106–119.

Glidden, D. K. 1995. "Moral Vision, *Orthos Logos*, and the Role of the *Phronimos*." *Apeiron* 28: 103–128.

Gómez-Lobo, A. 1995. "Aristotle's Right Reason." *Apeiron* 28: 15–34.

2001. "La recta razon en Aristoteles ¿Principio o proposicion particular?" *Convivium* 14: 48–65.

Rist, J. 1983. "An Early Dispute about Right Reason." *Monist* 66: 38–49.

The Unity of the Virtues

Coope, U. 2012. "Why Does Aristotle Think that Ethical Virtue Is Required for Practical Wisdom?" *Phronesis* 57: 142–163.

Cooper, J. 1998. "The Unity of Virtue." *Social Philosophy and Policy* 15: 233–274.

Deslauriers, M. 2002. "How to Distinguish Aristotle's Virtues." *Phronesis* 48: 101–126.

Dominick, Y. H. 2006. "Teaching Nature: Natural Virtue and Practical Wisdom in the *Nicomachean Ethics*." *Southwest Philosophy Review* 22: 103–111.

Drefcinski, S. 2006. "A Different Solution to an Alleged Contradiction in Aristotle's *Nicomachean Ethics*." *Oxford Studies in Ancient Philosophy* 30: 201–210.

Gardiner, S. 2001. "Aristotle's Basic and Non-Basic Virtues." *Oxford Studies in Ancient Philosophy* 20: 261–296.

Gottlieb, P. 1994. "Aristotle on Dividing the Soul and Uniting the Virtues." *Phronesis* 39: 275–290.

Halper, E. 1999. "The Unity of the Virtues in Aristotle." *Oxford Studies in Ancient Philosophy* 17: 115–146.

Irwin, T. H. 1988. "Disunity in the Aristotelian Virtues." *Oxford Studies in Ancient Philosophy* 7: 61–78.

Kraut, R. 1988. "Comments on 'Disunity in the Aristotelian Virtues.'" *Oxford Studies in Ancient Philosophy* 7: 79–86.

Lennox, J. G. 1999. "Aristotle on the Biological Roots of Human Virtue: The Natural History of Natural Virtue." 10–31 in J. Maienschein and M. Ruse eds. *Biology and the Foundation of Ethics*. Cambridge: Cambridge University Press.

Moss, J. 2011. "'Virtue Makes the Goal Right': Virtue and *Phronēsis* in Aristotle's Ethics." *Phronesis* 56: 204–261.

Müller, A. W. 2004. "Aristotle's Conception of Ethical and Natural Virtue." 18–53 in J. Szaif and M. Lutz-Bachmann eds. *Was ist das für den Menschen Gute? Menschliche Natur und Güterlehre*. Berlin: Walter de Gruyter.

Natali, C. 1984. "Virtù o scienza? Aspetti della Phronēsis nei *Topici* e nelle *Etiche* di Aristotele." *Phronesis* 29: 50–72.

2007. "Bonheur et unification des vertus chez Aristote." *Revista de Filosofia Antiga* 1: 1–27.

Pakaluk, M. 2002. "On an Alleged Contradiction in Aristotle's *Nicomachean Ethics*." *Oxford Studies in Ancient Philosophy* 22: 201–219.

Telfer, E. 1989–1990. "The Unity of Moral Virtue in Aristotle's *Nicomachean Ethics*." *Proceedings of the Aristotelian Society* 91: 35–48.

BOOK VII.1–10: AKRASIA

Book-Length Treatments

Cook Wilson, J. 1912. *On the Structure of Book Seven of the Nicomachean Ethics*. Oxford: Oxford University Press.

Dahl, N. 1984. *Practical Reason, Aristotle, and Weakness of the Will*. Minneapolis: University of Minnesota Press.

Destrée, P., and C. Bobonich eds. 2007. *Akrasia in Greek Philosophy: From Socrates to Plotinus*. Leiden: Brill.

Hoffmann, T. ed. 2008. *Weakness of Will from Plato to the Present*. Washington DC: Catholic University of America Press.

Natali, C. ed. 2009. *Aristotle's Nicomachean Ethics, Book VII: Symposium Aristotelicum*. Oxford: Oxford University Press.

Continence and Incontinence

Brickhouse, T. C. 2003. "Does Aristotle Have a Consistent Account of Vice?" *Review of Metaphysics* 57: 3–23.

Charles, D. 2011. "*Akrasia*: The Rest of the Story?" 187–209 in M. Pakaluk and G. Pearson eds. *Moral Psychology and Human Action in Aristotle*. Oxford: Oxford University Press.

Charlton, W. 1988. *Weakness of Will*. Oxford: Blackwell.

Davidson, D. 1969. "How Is Weakness of the Will Possible?" 93–113 in J. Feinberg ed. *Moral Concepts*. Oxford: Oxford University Press.

Drefcinski, S. 2000. "Can Continent People Have Practical Wisdom?" *Ancient Philosophy* 20: 109–118.

Francis, S. 2011. "'Under the Influence' – The Physiology and Therapeutics of *Akrasia* in Aristotle's Ethics." *Classical Quarterly* 61: 143–171.

Gosling, J. C. B. 1993. "Mad, Drunk, or Asleep? Aristotle's Akratic." *Phronesis* 38: 98–104.

Gould, C. S. 1994. "A Puzzle about the Possibility of Aristotelian *Enkrateia*." *Phronesis* 39: 174–186.

Grgic, F. 2002. "Aristotle on the Akratic's Knowledge." *Phronesis* 47: 336–358.

Henry, D. 2002. "Aristotle on Pleasure and the Worst Form of *Akrasia*." *Ethical Theory and Moral Practice* 5: 255–270.

Irwin, T. H. 2001. "Vice and Reason." *Journal of Ethics* 5: 73–97.

Kontos, P. 2009. "*Akolasia* As 'Radical' Ethical Vice: The Evidence of *NE* 1140b11–21." *Ancient Philosophy* 29: 337–347.

McDowell, J. 2009 [1996]. "Incontinence and Practical Wisdom in Aristotle." 59–76 in his *Engaged Intellect: Philosophical Essays*. Cambridge, MA: Harvard University Press.

McIntyre, A. 2006. "What Is Wrong with Weakness of Will?" *Journal of Philosophy* 103: 284–311.

Moss, J. 2009. "*Akrasia* and Perceptual Illusion." *Archiv für Geschichte der Philosophie* 91: 119–156.

Pickavé, M., and J. Whiting. 2008. "*Nicomachean Ethics* 7.3 on Akratic Ignorance." *Oxford Studies in Ancient Philosophy* 34: 323–372.

Price, A. W. 2006. "*Acrasia* and Self-Control." 234–254 in R. Kraut ed. *The Blackwell Guide to Aristotle's Nicomachean Ethics*. Malden, MA: Blackwell.

Purshouse, L. 2006. "Neoptolemus's Soul and the Taxonomy of Ethical Characters in Aristotle's *Nicomachean Ethics*." *British Journal for the History of Philosophy* 14: 205–223.

Robinson, R. 1977 [1954]. "Aristotle on *Akrasia*." 79–91 in J. Barnes, M. Schofield, and R. Sorabji eds. *Articles on Aristotle*. Vol. 2. *Ethics and Politics*. London: Duckworth.

Roochnik, D. 2007. "Aristotle's Account of the Vicious: A Forgivable Inconsistency." *History of Philosophy Quarterly* 24: 207–220.

Toner, C. 2003. "*Akrasia* Revisited: An Interpretation and Defense." *Southern Journal of Philosophy* 41: 283–306.

Wiggins, D. 1980 [1978–1979]. "Weakness of Will, Commensurability and the Objects of Deliberation and Desire." 241–266 in A. O. Rorty ed. *Essays on Aristotle's Ethics*. Berkeley: University of California Press.

The Practical Syllogism

Allan, D. J. 1955. "The Practical Syllogism." 325–340 in *Autour d'Aristote. Recueil d'Études de Philosophie Ancienne et Médiévale Offert à Monseigneur A. Mansion.* Louvain: Presses Universitaires de Louvain.

Bäck, A. 2009. "Mistakes of Reason: Practical Reasoning and the Fallacy of Accident." *Phronesis* 54: 101–135.

Corcilius, K. 2008. "Praktische Syllogismen bei Aristoteles." *Archiv für Geschichte der Philosophie* 90: 247–297.

Gottlieb, P. 2006. "The Practical Syllogism." 218–233 in R. Kraut ed. *The Blackwell Guide to Aristotle's Nicomachean Ethics*. Malden, MA: Blackwell.

Kenny, A. 1966. "The Practical Syllogism and Incontinence." *Phronesis* 11: 163–184.

McKerlie, D. 1991. "The Practical Syllogism and *Akrasia.*" *Canadian Journal of Philosophy* 21: 299–321.

Price, A. W. 2008. "The Practical Syllogism in Aristotle: A New Interpretation." *Logical Analysis and the History of Philosophy* 11: 151–162.

Welch, J. R. 1991. "Reconstructing Aristotle: The Practical Syllogism." *Philosophia* 21: 69–88.

BOOKS VII: 1–14/X.1–5: PLEASURE

Annas, J. 1980. "Aristotle on Pleasure and Goodness." 285–300 in A. O. Rorty ed. *Essays on Aristotle's Ethics*. Berkeley: University of California Press.

Bostock, D. 1988. "Pleasure and Activity in Aristotle's *Ethics.*" *Phronesis* 19: 251–272.

Festugière, A. J. 1936. *Le plaisir: (Eth. Nic. VII 11–14, X1–5).* Introduction, translation, and notes. Paris: J. Vrin.

Frede, D. 2006. "Pleasure and Pain in Aristotle's *Ethics.*" 255–275 in R. Kraut ed. *The Blackwell Guide to Aristotle's Nicomachean Ethics*. Malden, MA: Blackwell.

Gonzalez, F. J. 1991. "Aristotle on Pleasure and Perfection." *Phronesis* 36: 141–160.

Gosling, J. C. B. 1973–1974. "More Aristotelian Pleasures." *Proceedings of the Aristotelian Society* 74: 15–34.

Gosling, J. C. B., and C. C. W. Taylor. 1982. *The Greeks on Pleasure*. Oxford: Oxford University Press.

Gottlieb, P. 1993. "Aristotle's Measure Doctrine and Pleasure." *Archiv für Geschichte der Philosophie* 75: 31–46.

Hadreas, P. 1997. "Aristotle's Simile of Pleasure at *NE* 1174b33." *Ancient Philosophy* 17: 371–374.

2004. "The Functions of Pleasure in *Nicomachean Ethics* x 4–5." *Ancient Philosophy* 24: 155–167.

Heinaman, R. 1995. "Activity and Change in Aristotle." *Oxford Studies in Ancient Philosophy* 13: 187–216.

2011. "Pleasure as an Activity in the *Nicomachean Ethics.*" 7–45 in M. Pakaluk and G. Pearson eds. *Moral Psychology and Human Action in Aristotle*. Oxford: Oxford University Press.

Owen, G.E.L. 1977 [1971–1972]. "Aristotelian Pleasures." 92–103 in J. Barnes, M. Schofield, and R. Sorabji eds. *Articles on Aristotle*. Vol. 2. *Ethics and Politics*. London: Duckworth.

Ricken, F. 1976. *Der Lustbegriff in der Nikomachischen Ethik*. Göttingen: Vandenhoeck and Ruprecht.

Shields, C. 2011. "Perfecting Pleasures: The Metaphysics of Pleasure in *Nicomachean Ethics* X." 191–210 in J. Miller ed. *Aristotle's Nicomachean Ethics: A Critical Guide*. Cambridge: Cambridge University Press.

Strohl, M.S. 2012. "Pleasure as Perfection: *Nicomachean Ethics* 10.4–5." *Oxford Studies in Ancient Philosophy* 41: 257–287.

Taylor, C.C.W. 2003. "Pleasure: Aristotle's Response to Plato," with reply by S. Broadie. 1–27 in R. Heinaman ed. *Plato and Aristotle's Ethics*. Burlington, VT: Ashgate.

Van Riel, G. 2000. *Pleasure and the Good Life: Plato, Aristotle, and the Neoplatonists*. Leiden: Brill.

Warren, J. 2009. "Aristotle on Speusippus on Eudoxus on Pleasure." *Oxford Studies in Ancient Philosophy* 36: 249–282.

Webb, P. 1977. "The Relative Dating of the Accounts of Pleasure in Aristotle's Ethics." *Phronesis* 22: 235–262.

Weinman, M. 2007. *Pleasure in Aristotle's Ethics*. New York: Continuum.

Weiss, R. 1979. "Aristotle's Criticism of Eudoxan Hedonism." *Classical Philology* 74: 214–221.

Wielenberg, E. 2000. "Pleasure as a Sign of Moral Virtue in the *Nicomachean Ethics*." *Journal of Value Inquiry* 34: 439–449.

BOOKS VIII–IX: FRIENDSHIP (PHILIA)

General Overviews

Bégorre-Bret, C. 2001. *Ethique à Nicomaque, Livre VIII–IX: L'amitié*. Paris: Ellipses.

Fraisse, J.-C. 1974. *Philia: La notion d'amitié dans la philosophie antique*. Paris: J. Vrin.

Konstan, D. 1997. *Friendship in the Classical World*. Cambridge: Cambridge University Press.

    2001. *On Aristotle's Nicomachean Ethics 8 and 9*. (Aspasius, Anonymous, and Michael of Ephesus). Translation with notes. Ithaca, NY: Cornell University Press.

Nehamas, A. 2010. "Aristotelian *Philia*, Modern Friendship." *Oxford Studies in Ancient Philosophy* 39: 213–247.

Pakaluk, M. 1999. *Nicomachean Ethics Books VIII and IX*. Oxford: Clarendon Press.

Pangle, L.S. 2003. *Aristotle and the Philosophy of Friendship*. Cambridge: Cambridge University Press.

Price, A.W. 1997 [1989]. *Love and Friendship in Plato and Aristotle*. Oxford: Clarendon Press.

Schollmeier, P. 1994. *Other Selves: Aristotle on Personal and Political Friendship*. Albany: SUNY Press.

Stern-Gillet, S. 1995. *Aristotle's Philosophy of Friendship*. Albany: SUNY Press.

Whiting, J. 2006. "The Nicomachean Account of *Philia*." 276–304 in R. Kraut ed. *The Blackwell Guide to Aristotle's Nicomachean Ethics*. Malden, MA: Blackwell.

The Multiplicity of Friendships

Alpern, K. 1983. "Aristotle on the Friendship of Utility and Pleasure." *Journal of the History of Philosophy* 21: 303–316.

Cooper, J. M. 1999 [1977]. "Aristotle on the Forms of Friendship." 312–335 in his *Reason and Emotion: Essays on Ancient Moral Psychology and Ethical Theory.* Princeton: Princeton University Press.

1999 [1977]. "Friendship and the Good in Aristotle." 336–355 in his *Reason and Emotion: Essays on Ancient Moral Psychology and Ethical Theory.* Princeton: Princeton University Press.

Hadreas, P. 1995. "*Eunoia*: Aristotle on the Beginning of Friendship." *Ancient Philosophy* 15: 393–402.

Hursthouse, R. 2007. "Aristotle for Women Who Love Too Much." *Ethics* 117: 327–334.

Kosman, A. 2004. "Aristotle on the Desirability of Friends." *Ancient Philosophy* 24: 135–154.

Payne, A. 2000. "Character and the Forms of Friendship in Aristotle." *Apeiron* 33: 53–74.

Ricken, F. 2000. "Ist Freundschaft eine Tugend? Die Einheit des Freundschaftsbegriffs der *Nikomachischen Ethik*." *Theologie und Philosophie* 75: 481–492.

Rogers, K. 1994. "Aristotle on Loving Another for His Own Sake." *Phronesis* 39: 291–302.

Philia and Erōs

Burger, R. 2003. "Hunting Together or Philosophizing Together: Friendship and *Erōs* in Aristotle's *Nicomachean Ethics*." 37–60 in E. A. Velasquez ed. *Love and Friendship: Rethinking Politics and Affection in Modern Times.* Lanham, MD: Lexington Books.

Leontsini, E. 2013. "Sex and the City: Plato, Aristotle, and Zeno of Kition on *Erōs* and *Philia*." 129–141 in E. Sanders, C. Thumiger, C. Carey, and N. Lowe eds. *Erōs in Ancient Greece.* Oxford: Oxford University Press.

Price, A. W. 1997. "Aristotle on Erotic Love." 236–249 in his *Love and Friendship in Plato and Aristotle.* Oxford: Clarendon Press.

Sihvola, J. 2002. "Aristotle on Sex and Love." 200–221 in M. C. Nussbaum and J. Sihvola eds. *The Sleep of Reason: Erotic Experience and Sexual Ethics in Ancient Greece and Rome.* Chicago: University of Chicago Press.

Justice, Friendship, and Political Friendship

Annas, J. 1990. "Comments on J. Cooper." 243–249 in G. Patzig ed. *Aristoteles: Politik.* Göttingen: Vandenhoeck and Ruprecht.

Cooper, J. M. 1999 [1990]. "Political Animals and Civic Friendship." 356–377 in his *Reason and Emotion: Essays on Ancient Moral Psychology and Ethical Theory.* Princeton: Princeton University Press.

Irrera, E. 2005. "Between Advantage and Virtue: Aristotle's Theory of Political Friendship," *History of Political Thought* 26: 565–585.

Klonoski, R. 1996. "*Homonoia* in Aristotle's *Ethics* and *Politics*." *History of Political Thought* 17: 313–325.

Ricken, F. 1991. "Gemeinschaft als Grundwert der aristotelischen Ethik." *Theologie und Philosophie* 66: 530–546.

Schofield, M. 1999 [1998]. "Political Friendship and the Ideal of Reciprocity." 72–87 in his *Saving the City: Philosopher-Kings and other Classical Paradigms.* New York: Routledge.

Friendship and the Family

Belfiore, E. 2001. "Family Friendships in Aristotle's Ethics." *Ancient Philosophy* 21: 113–132.
Lockwood, T. 2003. "Justice in Aristotle's Household and City." *Polis* 20: 5–25.
2006. "The Best Regime of Aristotle's *Nicomachean Ethics*." *Ancient Philosophy* 26: 355–370.
Schollmeier, P. 2003. "Aristotle and Women." *Polis* 20: 26–46.

Friendship and Self-Love

Annas, J. 1988. "Self-Love in Aristotle." *Southern Journal of Philosophy* 27: 1–18.
Dziob, A. M. 1993. "Aristotelian Friendship: Self-Love and Moral Rivalry." *Review of Metaphysics* 46: 781–801.
Homiak, M. 1981. "Virtue and Self-Love in Aristotle's Ethics." *Canadian Journal of Philosophy* 1: 633–652.
McKerlie, D. 1991. "Friendship, Self-Love, and Concern for Others in Aristotle's Ethics." *Ancient Philosophy* 11: 85–101.
Pangle, L. S. 1999. "Friendship and Self-Love in Aristotle's *Nicomachean Ethics*." 171–202 in R. C. Bartlett and S. D. Collins eds. *Action and Contemplation: Studies in the Moral and Political Thought of Aristotle*. Albany: SUNY Press.
Politis, V. 1993. "The Primacy of Self-Love in the *Nicomachean Ethics*." *Oxford Studies in Ancient Philosophy* 11: 153–174.
Reiner, P. 1991. "Aristotle on Personality and Some Implications for Friendship." *Ancient Philosophy* 11: 67–84.
Simon, A. 2006. "Freundshaft und Selbstverständnis bei Aristoteles." *Rhizai* 3: 275–298.
Stern-Gillet, S. 2004. "Des deux concepts du 'soi' chez Aristote." 229–249 in E. Vegleris ed. *Cosmos et Psyché. Mélanges offerts à Jean Frère*. Hildesheim: Georg Olms Verlag.

Egoism and Altruism

Annas, J. 1977. "Plato and Aristotle on Friendship and Altruism." *Mind* 86: 532–554.
Gardiner, S. 2001. "Aristotle, Egoism, and the Virtuous Person's Point of View." 239–262 in D. Baltzly, D. Blyth, and H. Tarrant eds. *Power and Pleasure: Virtues and Vices*. Auckland: University of Auckland Bindery.
Gottlieb, P. 1996. "Aristotle's Ethical Egoism." *Pacific Philosophical Quarterly* 77: 1–18.
Kahn, C. 1981. "Aristotle and Altruism." *Mind* 90: 20–40.
Madigan, A. 1985. "*Eth. Nic.* 9.8: Beyond Egoism and Altruism?" *Modern Schoolman* 62: 1–20.
McKerlie, D. 1998. "Aristotle and Egoism." *Southern Journal of Philosophy* 36: 531–555.
O'Connor, D. 1990. "Two Ideals of Friendship." *History of Philosophy Quarterly* 7: 109–122.
Roberts, J. 1989. "Political Animals in the *Nicomachean Ethics*." *Phronesis* 34: 185–202.
Wielenberg, E. 2004. "Egoism and *Eudaimonia*-Maximization in the *NE*." *Oxford Studies in Ancient Philosophy* 26: 277–295.
Williams, B. A. O. 1973. "Egoism and Altruism." 250–265 in his *Problems of the Self*. Cambridge: Cambridge University Press.

Problems concerning the Need of Friendship

Adkins, A. W. H. 1963. "Friendship and Self-Sufficiency in Homer and Aristotle." *Classical Quarterly* 13: 30–45.

Biss, M. 2011. "Aristotle on Friendship and Self-Knowledge: The Friend beyond the Mirror." *History of Philosophy Quarterly* 28: 125–140.

Drum, P. 2003. "What Is the Value of Friendship as a Motivation for Morality for Aristotle?" *Journal of Value Inquiry* 37: 97–99.

Flakne, A. 2005. "Embodied and Embedded: Friendship and the Sunaisthetic Self." *Epoche* 10: 37–63.

Hitz, Z. 2011. "Aristotle on Self-Knowledge and Friendship." *Philosopher's Imprint* 11: 1–28.

Jacquette, D. 2001. "Aristotle on the Value of Friendship as a Motivation for Morality." *Journal of Value Inquiry* 35: 371–389.

Kraut, R. 1975. "The Importance of Love in Aristotle's *Ethics*." *Philosophy Research Archives* 1: 300–322.

Maher, D. 2012. "Contemplative Friendship in *Nicomachean Ethics*." *Review of Metaphysics* 65: 765–794.

Mansini, G. 1998. "Aristotle on Needing Friends." *American Catholic Philosophical Quarterly* 72: 405–417.

Millgram, E. 1987. "Aristotle on Making Other Selves." *Canadian Journal of Philosophy* 17: 361–376.

Sherman, N. 1987. "Aristotle on Friendship and the Shared Life." *Philosophy and Phenomenological Research* 47: 589–623.

Walker, M. 2010. "Contemplation and Self-Awareness in the *Nicomachean Ethics*." *Rhizai* 7: 221–238.

BOOK X 6–8: CONTEMPLATION, THE SUMMUM BONUM

Burger, R. 1990. "Wisdom, Philosophy and Happiness: On Book X of Aristotle's *Ethics*." *Proceedings of the Boston Area Colloquium on Ancient Philosophy* 6: 289–307.

Bush, S. 2008. "Divine and Human Happiness in the *Nicomachean Ethics*." *Philosophical Review* 117: 49–75.

Charles, D. 1999. "Aristotle on Well-Being and Intellectual Contemplation." *Proceedings of the Aristotelian Society*, Supplement 73: 205–223.

Cooper, J. M. 1999 [1987]. "Contemplation and Happiness: A Reconsideration." 212–236 in his *Reason and Emotion: Essays on Ancient Moral Psychology and Ethical Theory*. Princeton: Princeton University Press.

Dahl, N. O. 2011. "Contemplation and *Eudaimonia* in the *Nicomachean Ethics*." 66–91 in J. Miller ed. *Aristotle's Nicomachean Ethics: A Critical Guide*. Cambridge: Cambridge University Press.

Defourney, P. 1977 [1937]. "Contemplation in Aristotle's *Ethics*." 104–112 in J. Barnes, M. Schofield, and R. Sorabji eds. *Articles on Aristotle*. Vol. 2. *Ethics and Politics*. London: Duckworth.

Destrée, P., and M. Zingano eds. 2013. *Theoria: Studies on the Status and Meaning of Contemplation in Aristotle's Ethics*. Louvain-la-Neuve: Peeters.

Dudley, J. A. 1981. *Gott und Theōria bei Aristoteles. Die metaphysische Grundlage der Nikomachischen Ethik*. Bern: Peter Lang.

Eriksen, T. B. 1976. *Bios Theoretikos. Notes on Aristotle's Ethica Nicomachea X.6–8*. Oslo: Universitetsforlaget.

Kenny, A. 1992. *Aristotle on the Perfect Life*. Oxford: Oxford University Press.

Keyt, D. 1983. "Intellectualism in Aristotle." 364–387 in J. P. Anton and A. Preus eds. *Essays in Ancient Greek Philosophy*. Vol. 2. Albany: SUNY Press.

Long, A. A. 2011. "Aristotle on *Eudaimonia, Nous*, and Divinity." 92–114 in J. Miller ed. *Aristotle's Nicomachean Ethics: A Critical Guide*. Cambridge: Cambridge University Press.

Roochnik, D. 2008. "What Is *Theoria? Nicomachean Ethics*, Book 10.7–8." *Classical Philology* 104: 69–81.

Rorty, A. O. 1980 [1978]. "The Place of Contemplation in Aristotle's *Nicomachean Ethics*." 377–394 in A. O. Rorty ed. *Essays on Aristotle's Ethics*. Berkeley: University of California Press.

Scott, D. 1999. "Aristotle on Well-Being and Intellectual Contemplation: Primary and Secondary *Eudaimonia*." *Proceedings of the Aristotelian Society*, Supplement 73: 225–242.

White, M. J. 1980. "Aristotle's Concept of *Theōria* and the *Energeia/Kinēsis* Distinction." *Journal of the History of Philosophy* 18: 253–265.

Whiting, J. 1986. "Human Nature and Intellectualism in Aristotle." *Archiv für Geschichte der Philosophie* 68: 70–95.

The Relationship between the Politics and the Nicomachean Ethics

Adkins, A. W. H. 1991 [1984]. "The Connexion between Aristotle's *Ethics* and *Politics*." 75–93 in the D. Keyt and F. Miller eds. *Companion to Aristotle's Politics*. Cambridge, MA: Blackwell.

Aubenque, P. 1980. "Politique et éthique chez Aristote." *Ktema* 5: 211–221.

Betbeder, P. 1970. "Ethique et Politique selon Aristote." *Revue des Sciences Philosophique et Théologiques* 54: 453–488.

Bodéüs, R. 1993 [1982]. *The Political Dimensions of Aristotle's Ethics*. J. E. Garrett trans. Albany: SUNY Press.

Cashdollar, S. 1973. "Aristotle's Politics of Morals." *Journal of the History of Philosophy* 11: 145–160.

Flashar, H. 1971. "Ethik und Politik in der Philosophie des Aristoteles." *Gymnasium* 78: 278–293.

Hitz, Z. 2012. "Aristotle on Law and Moral Education." *Oxford Studies in Ancient Philosophy* 41: 263–306.

Newman, W. L. 1887. "Appendix A: On the Relation of the Teaching of the *Nicomachean Ethics* to That of the *Politics*." 385–400 in *The Politics of Aristotle*, vol. 2. Oxford: Clarendon Press.

Salkever, S. 2007. "Teaching the Questions: Aristotle's Philosophical Pedagogy in the *Nicomachean Ethics* and the *Politics*." *Review of Politics* 69: 192–214.

Schofield, M. 2006. "Aristotle's Political Ethics." 305–322 in R. Kraut ed. *The Blackwell Guide to Aristotle's Nicomachean Ethics*. Malden, MA: Blackwell.

Striker, G. 2006. "Aristotle's Ethics as Political Science." 127–141 in B. Reis and S. Haffmanns eds. *The Virtuous Life in Greek Ethics*. Cambridge: Cambridge University Press.

Vander Waerdt, P. A. 1985. "The Political Intentions of Aristotle's Moral Philosophy." *Ancient Philosophy* 5: 77–89.

1991. "The Plan and the Intention of Aristotle's Ethical and Political Writings." *Illinois Classical Studies* 16: 231–251.

Vergnières, S. 1995. *Ethique et politique chez Aristote*. Paris: Presses Universitaires de France.

HISTORICAL RECEPTION

Gauthier, R. A., and J. Y. Jolif. 1970. "L'exégèse de *l'Éthique à Nicomaque*: Essai d'histoire littéraire." 91–240 in *L'Ethique à Nicomaque*. Vol. 1, pt. 1. Edited and translated by R. A. Gauthier and J. Y. Jolif. Paris-Louvain, Belgium: Publications Universitaires.

Miller, J. ed. 2013. *The Reception of Aristotle's Ethics*. Cambridge: Cambridge University Press.

Hellenistic Reception

Annas, J. 1990. "The Hellenistic Version of Aristotle's Ethics." *Monist* 73: 80–96.

Irwin, T. 1990. "Virtue, Praise, and Success: Stoic Responses to Aristotle." *Monist* 73: 59–79.

2007. *The Development of Ethics: A Historical and Critical Study*. Vol. I. *From Socrates to the Reformation*. Oxford: Oxford University Press.

Long, A. A. 1968. "Aristotle's Legacy to Stoic Ethics." *Bulletin of the Institute of Classical Studies* 15: 72–85.

Moraux, P. 1973–2001. *Der Aristotelismus bei den Griechen: Von Andronikos bis Alexander von Aphrodisias*. 3 vols. Berlin: De Gruyter.

Russell, D. 2008. "Happiness and Agency in the Stoics and Aristotle." *Proceedings of the Boston Area Colloquium of Philosophy* 24: 83–112.

2010. "Virtue and Happiness in the Lyceum and Beyond." *Oxford Studies in Ancient Philosophy* 38: 143–185.

White, S. 2003. "Happiness in the Hellenistic Lyceum." 69–94 in L. J. Jost and R. Shiner eds. *Eudaimonia and Well-Being: Ancient and Modern Conceptions (Apeiron 35.4)*. Kelowna, BC: Academic Printing and Publishing.

Medieval Reception

Akasoy, A. A., and A. Fidora eds. 2005. *The Arabic Version of the Nicomachean Ethics*. With an introduction and translation by D. M. Dunlop. Leiden: Brill.

Arberry, A. J. 1955. "The *Nicomachean Ethics* in Arabic." *Bulletin of the School of African and Oriental Studies* 17: 1–9.

Bejczy, I. ed. 2008. *Virtue Ethics in the Middle Ages: Commentaries on Aristotle's Nicomachean Ethics, 1200–1500*. Leiden: Brill.

Di Blasi, F., J. P. Hochschild, and J. Langan eds. 2008. *Virtue's End: God in the Moral Philosophy of Aristotle and Aquinas*. South Bend, IN: St. Augustine's Press.

Doig, J. 2001. *Aquinas' Philosophical Commentary on the Ethics: An Historical Perspective*. Leiden: Kluwer.

Dunbabin, J. 1963. "The Two Commentaries of Albertus Magnus on the *Nicomachean Ethics*." *Recherches de Théologie ancienne et medieval* 30: 232–250.

Hoffmann, T., J. Müller, and M. Perkans eds. 2013. *Aquinas and the Nicomachean Ethics*. Cambridge: Cambridge University Press.

Jaffa, H. 1952. *Thomism and Aristotelianism*. Chicago: University of Chicago Press.

Nederman, C. J. 1997. *Medieval Aristotelianism and Its Limits: Classical Tradition in Moral and Political Philosophy, 12th–15th Centuries*. Brookfield, VT: Aldershot.

Renaissance and Early Modern Reception

Irwin, T. 2008. *The Development of Ethics: A Historical and Critical Study*. Vol. 2. *From Suarez to Rousseau*. Oxford: Oxford University Press.

Lines, D. 1999. "Commentary Literature on Aristotle's *Nicomachean Ethics* in Early Renaissance Italy: Preliminary Considerations." *Traditio* 54: 245–282.

2002. *Aristotle's Ethics in the Italian Renaissance (c. 1300–1600): The Universities and the Problem of Moral Education.* Leiden: Brill.

MacIntyre, A. 2006. "Rival Aristotles: Aristotle against Some Renaissance Aristotelians." 3–21 in his *Ethics and Politics: Selected Essays.* Cambridge: Cambridge University Press.

Schmitt, C. B. 1979. *Aristotle's Ethics in the Sixteenth Century: Some Preliminary Considerations.* Boppard: Harald Boldt Verlag.

1983. *Aristotle and the Renaissance.* Cambridge, MA: Harvard University Press.

Schneewind, J. B. 1990. "The Misfortunes of Virtue." *Ethics* 101: 42–63.

Modern Reception

Aubenque, P. 2002. "La place de *l'Éthique à Nicomaque* dans la discussion contemporaine sur l'éthique." 397–408 in G. Romeyer-Dherby and G. Aubry eds. *L'Excellence de la vie: sur L'Ethique à Nicomaque et L'Ethique à Eudème d'Aristote.* Paris: J. Vrin.

Berti, E. 1990. "La philosophie pratique d'Aristote et sa 'réhabilitation' récente." *Revue de Métaphysique et de Morale* 95: 249–266.

Broadie, S. 2006. "Aristotle and Contemporary Ethics." 342–361 in R. Kraut ed. *The Blackwell Guide to Aristotle's Nicomachean Ethics.* Malden, MA: Blackwell.

Habermas, J. 1973 [1971]. "Classical Doctrine of Politics in Relation to Social Philosophy." 41–81 in his *Theory and Practice.* J. Viertel trans. Boston: Beacon Press.

Hursthouse, R. 2007. "Aristotle Old and New." 428–439 in L. Hardwick and C. Stray eds. *A Companion to Classical Receptions.* Malden, MA: Blackwell.

MacIntyre, A. 2006. "Rival Aristotles: Aristotle against Some Modern Aristotelians." 22–41 in his *Ethics and Politics: Selected Essays.* Cambridge: Cambridge University Press.

Ricken, F. 1999. "Aristoteles und die moderne Tugendethik." *Theologie und Philosophie* 74: 391–404.

Simpson, P. 1992. "Contemporary Virtue Ethics and Aristotle." *Review of Metaphysics* 45: 503–524.

Aristotle and Eastern Philosophy

Cua, A. 2003. "The Ethical Significance of Shame: Insights of Aristotle and Xunzi." *Philosophy East and West* 53: 147–202.

MacIntyre, A. 1991. "Incommensurability, Truth, and the Conversation between Confucians and Aristotelians about the Virtues." 104–122 in E. Deutsch ed. *Culture and Modernity: East-West Philosophic Perspectives.* Honolulu: University of Hawaii Press.

Mullis, E. 2010. "Confucius and Aristotle on the Goods of Friendship." *Dao* 9: 391–405.

Sherman, T. 2006. "Being Natural, the Good Human Being, and the Goodness of Acting Naturally in the Laozi and the *Nicomachean Ethics*." *Dao* 5: 331–347.

Sim, M. 2007. *Remastering Morals with Aristotle and Confucius.* Cambridge: Cambridge University Press.

2010. "Rethinking Virtue Ethics and Social Justice with Aristotle and Confucius." *Asian Philosophy* 20: 195–213.

Yu, J. 2007. *The Ethics of Confucius and Aristotle: Mirrors of Virtue.* New York: Routledge.

Feminist Appropriations of Aristotle

Achtenberg, D. 1996. "Aristotelian Resources for Feminist Thinking." 95–117 in J. K. Ward ed. *Feminism and Ancient Philosophy.* New York: Routledge.

Curzer, H. J. 2007. "Aristotle: Founder of the Ethics of Care." *Journal of Value Inquiry* 41: 221–243.

Groenhout, R. 1998. "The Virtue of Care: Aristotelian Ethics and Contemporary Ethics of Care." 171–200 in C. Freeland ed. *Feminist Interpretations of Aristotle*. University Park: Penn State University Press.

Homiak, M. 1996. "Feminism and Aristotle's Rational Ideal." 118–140 in J. K. Ward ed. *Feminism and Ancient Philosophy*. New York: Routledge.

Modrak, D. 1994. "Aristotle: Women, Deliberation, and Nature." 207–222 in B. Bar On ed. *Engendering Origins*. Albany: SUNY Press.

Nussbaum, M. C. 1998. "Aristotle, Feminism, and Needs for Functioning." 248–259 in C. Freeland ed. *Feminist Interpretations of Aristotle*. University Park: Penn State University Press.

Index

Academy, 1, 385, 395, 398, 413
Achilles, 141, 146
Achtenberg, D., 234
Ackrill, J., 20, 34, 38, 92, 215, 352
action (*praxis*), 85–87, 187–188
   eupraxia, 187
   internally or externally good/bad, 102
   voluntariness, 86–87
activity
   in accordance with virtue, 7, 34, 38, 40,
     41, 61, 373
   activity (*energeia*) vs. motion (*kinēsis*),
     4, 301–303, 336–338
Adair, S., 112
Adams, R. M., 214
adultery, 328
Agathon, 366
agroikia (boorishness), 136
aim of the *NE* practical not
   theoretical, 363
Ajax, 141
Alcibiades, 141, 347
Alexander of Aphrodisias, 55, 385
Alexander the Great, 140
Allan, D. J., 185, 205, 222, 413, 419
ambidextrousness, 171
amusement as happy life
   arguments for and against, 358
Anacharsis, 358
Anaxagoras, 350, 361, 364, 366, 406, 407
Anaximander, 151
animality, 125
Annas, J., 38, 49, 208, 209, 314
Anscombe, E., 7
aporia (puzzle, perplexity), 36
Aquinas, T., 68, 153, 189, 194
Archilochus, 280

Arendt, H., 170
Aristippus, 395
aristocracy and polity, 274
aristocratic ideal, 140
Aristophanes, 148
Aristotelian definition, 323
Aristotle
   De Anima, 88, 124, 186, 187, 229, 250,
     321, 331
   De Interpretatione, 92
   De Motu Animalium, 190
   disappointment with, 199–200
   EE, received view on, 415
   Eudemian Ethics, 86, 87, 88, 90, 96,
     113, 145, 146, 181, 188, 194, 196, 200,
     204, 222, 226, 228, 229, 230, 235, 236,
     239, 410–424
   exoteric works, 183
   Generation and Corruption, 41
   Generation of Animals, 27
   Magna Moralia, 1, 29, 43, 199, 396
   Metaphysics, 3, 5, 21, 24, 101, 163, 170,
     189, 193, 195, 227, 291, 302, 321, 337,
     344, 414
   Meteorology, 27
   Organon, 194
   Parts of Animals, 27, 28, 41
   Physics, 86, 375
   Poetics, 173
   Politics, 5, 12, 42, 43, 49, 149, 151, 156,
     164, 171, 172, 188, 210, 229, 264, 269,
     272–277, 284, 322, 327, 351, 371–372,
     378, 379, 401, 416
   Posterior Analytics, 5, 141, 153, 183,
     188, 227, 231, 234, 245, 260
   Prior Analytics, 190, 192, 194
   Protrepticus, 1, 383–408

465

Lightning Source UK Ltd.
Milton Keynes UK
UKOW05f0343040615

252876UK00007B/215/P